Peru
a travel survival kit

Rob Rachowiecki

Peru – a travel survival kit

2nd edition

Published by
Lonely Planet Publications
Head Office: PO Box 617, Hawthorn, Vic 3122, Australia
Branches: 155 Filbert St, Suite 251, Oakland, CA 94607, USA
10 Barley Mow Passage, Chiswick, London W4 4PH, UK
71 bis rue du Cardinal Lemoine, 75005 Paris, France

Printed by
Colorcraft, Hong Kong

Photographs by
Rob Rachowiecki (RR)
Tony Wheeler (TW)
Front cover: Corpus Christi Procession of Saints, Peter M Miller, The Image Bank
Back cover: Machu Picchu (RR)

First Published
July 1987

This Edition
February 1991

Although the authors and publisher have tried to make the information as
accurate as possible, they accept no responsibility for any loss, injury or
inconvenience sustained by any person using this book.

National Library of Australia Cataloguing in Publication Data

Rachowiecki, Rob 1954-
Peru – a travel survival kit.

2nd ed.
Includes index.
ISBN 0 86442 095 1.

1. Peru – Description and travel – Guide-books.
I. Title.

918.504633

Rob Rachowlecki

Rob was born near London and became an avid traveller while still a teenager. He has visited countries as diverse as Greenland and Thailand. He spent several years in Latin America, travelling, mountaineering and teaching English, and he now works there part time as a leader for Wilderness Travel, an adventure tour company. His first book, with Hilary Bradt, was *Backpacking in Mexico & Central America* (Bradt Publications) and he has also authored *Climbing & Hiking in Ecuador* (Bradt Publications), and Lonely Planet's *Ecuador & the Galapagos Islands – a travel survival kit*. When not travelling, he lives in the US southwest where he writes, studies for a doctorate in biology, and helps his wife, Cathy, raise their daughters, two-year old Julia and baby Alison. His dream is to some day sail around the world.

From the Author

Many people in Peru, travellers and residents, Peruvians and gringos, helped me gather the information for this book. In Lima, the manager of the South American Explorers Club afforded me immeasurable help, information, friendship and a home away from home. Betsy Wagenhauser, Petra Schepens and Fernando Villafuerte were especially helpful. Sandra Ratto Risso and her staff at Chasquitur ably solved my many air travel problems. Carlos Milla Vidal and José Correa Castro shared with me both their friendship and their knowledge of the Cuzco area. The government-run tourism offices in the major cities were helpful with maps and information. I would also like to thank the Huarmey Tourist Authority.

Hilary Bradt, Marcy Clements, Paul Donahue, Barbara Fearis, Peter Frost, Max Gunther, Marcellino Morales, Val Pithkethly, Kath Renton, and Ricky Schiller shared information and/or travel experiences with me. Kath Renton was especially helpful with detailed information on the jungle.

I received many useful letters from readers/travellers who continue to provide me with great impetus for keeping these books up to date. From within the mess around my word processor I have managed to extract letters from Doug Brown (C), Gabrielle Brown (Aus), Adam P. Booth (UK), Virginia Clark (USA), David Doherty (Aus), John Edmund (UK), Gigi Gordon (USA), Eric Grabandt (Nl), William Hardiman (UK), Marjolyn Hazelwinkel (Nl), Helen Hindin (UK), Rosemary Hobin (USA), Rod House (Aus), Lee Kessler and Sally Andre (USA), Dr R. Kollinger (A), Robert Kuhlken (USA), Pamela Novak (Aus), Ros O'Sullivan (Ir), Reinhilde Pellinger (A), Mark Price (S), Brian Quinby (USA), Stanis Smith (C), Yoel Sniboleth (Isr), Lynn M. Taylor (UK), Bengisu Uamer (Tur), Joseph C. Williams (J), George Wright (USA). If I missed your name, I'm sorry; I should really buy a filing cabinet.

My biggest thanks go to my lovely wife, Cathy, who ably and cheerfully did the three jobs of working full time, child-raising, and running the house whilst I spent 2½ months in Peru updating the book. I couldn't have done it without you.

Dedication For Cathy, whom I met in Peru.

From the Publisher

This edition of Peru was edited by freelancers Allison White and Gillian Cumming. Miriam Cannell, working on her first LP publication, handled the in-house production and proofing. Sue Mitra also helped with proofing and provided editorial guidance. On the artistic side, Valerie Tellini took care of the maps and cover design, whilst Ann Jeffree was responsible for the layout and illustrations. Thanks to Stephen Alford for supplying extra illustrative references.

Thanks must also go to the travellers who have written to us with updates and anecdotes (apologies if we've misspelt your names):

Paul Beaver (USA), Irene Billeter (CH), Gabrielle Brown (Aus), Wayne Church (C), Virginia Clark (USA), Monica Cobb (C), Mike Coop (NZ), Maria Nelly Cuculiza (Per), Thomas Drusnitzer (C), John Edmund (UK), Caroline Ellis (USA), Eric Grabandt (Nl), Philip Grey (UK), Steven Hall (USA), S T Harders (Dk), William Hardiman (UK), Marjolyn Hazewinled (Nl), Helen Hindin (UK), Court Takanawa House B (J), Pedro Isztin (C), D Barnard & L Johnston (UK), Carmen Kay (USA), Lee Kessler (USA), Minna Kinnunen, Dr R Kollinger (A), Robert Kuhlken (USA), John Leonard, Mrs Letch (UK), Alberto Miori (Per), Pamela Novak (Aus), Carolyn Osiek (USA), Arto Ovaska (Per), Angela Owen (USA), Leah Rose (USA), Peruvian Safaris Josef & Maria Steenhout (B), Doug Stone, Lynn Taylor (UK), Antonio Tello (Per), Pocha Barreto Tosi (Per), William Ulfelder (USA), Ann Venegas (Per), Jeffrey Vogel (USA), James M Vreeland (Per), John Wecselman (Per), Joseph Wilken (Nl), Robert Wilkinson (USA), Kate & Spike Wilson (UK), George Wright (USA).

A - Austria, Aus - Australia, B - Belgium, C - Canada, CH - Switzerland, Dk - Denmark, Ir - Ireland, Isr - Israel, J - Japan, Nl - Netherlands, NZ - New Zealand, Per - Peru, S - Scotland, Tur - Turkey, UK - United Kingdom, USA - United States of America

Warning & Request

Things change: prices go up, schedules change, good places go bad and bad places go bankrupt - nothing stays the same. So if you find things better or worse, recently opened or long since closed, please write and tell us and help make the next edition better!

Your letters will be used to help update future editions and, where possible, important changes will also be included as a Stop Press section in reprints.

All information is greatly appreciated and the best letters will receive a free copy of the next edition, or any other Lonely Planet book of your choice.

Contents

CUZCO cont

THE CENTRAL HIGHLANDS 228

THE NORTH COAST..259

THE HUARAZ AREA..305

ACROSS THE NORTHERN HIGHLANDS...325

THE AMAZON BASIN 348

GLOSSARY 381

INDEX 381

Introduction

Peru is a wonderful country. Anyone from an archaeologist to a zoologist will be fascinated by Peru, and the discerning traveller cannot fail to be impressed by its cultural and geographical variety and the exciting travel possibilities this country has to offer.

Peru is frequently referred to as the 'land of the Incas', yet it could equally be called the 'land of the Moche' (or the Chavín or the Wari). It is true that the Incas formed the greatest empire on the continent and left mysterious cities such as Machu Picchu, the magnificent ruins of which can be visited today. Less well known, but equally true, is that the Incas were the last in a long series of Peruvian civilisations spanning several thousand years and that the ruins of many of these earlier civilisations can also be visited.

The Peruvian Andean mountains are arguably the most beautiful and accessible on the continent and the Cordillera Blanca has become world famous among trekkers, hikers and mountaineers. There are several other ranges in Peru which are less visited but no less magnificent. Many of the precipitous glacier-clad mountains have peaks of more than 6000 metres and the high valleys between are the haunts of a host of rarely seen animals.

Visitors may glimpse mammals such as the graceful vicuña or the inquisitive viscacha, and birds ranging from the tiny Andean hummingbird to the giant Andean condor. Soaring effortlessly on a wingspan that can exceed 3 metres and with a weight of more

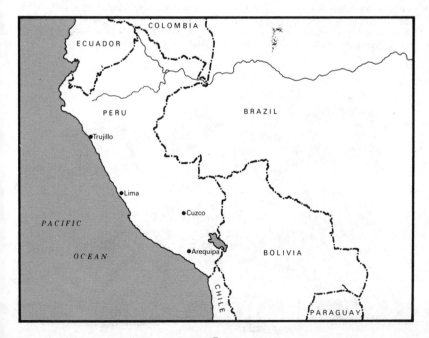

than 10 kg, the condor is the largest flying bird in the world.

But the Peruvian Andes is not just the scene of remote wilderness. It is also home to millions of highland Indians who still speak their ancient tongue of Quechua (or Aymara) and preserve much of their traditional way of life. Town and village markets are thronged with herds of produce-laden llamas led by Indians wearing the typical ponchos which provide effective protection against the climatic extremes of this environment. The larger cities also preserve the legacy of the Spanish conquistadors, and colonial churches and mansions covered with dazzling ornamentation can also be seen.

The traveller could easily spend weeks or months among the Peruvian highlands and yet would only be visiting a small portion of the country. More than half of Peru's area lies in the verdant Amazon Basin where air or river is often the only means of transportation. Exotic plants and animals amaze and intrigue the observant visitor. The dense tropical rainforest on the eastern edges of the Andes houses the greatest variety of birds on earth. Peru, although less than twice the size of Texas, is home to more than twice the number of bird species that are in the entire North American continent. It is a naturalist's paradise and, because it has been so little studied, a giant natural laboratory as well.

The Andes and the Amazon are but two of Peru's diverse geographical regions. The third is no less different or spectacular, for the entire coastal strip of Peru is desert. Lima, the capital, lies totally surrounded by bare rock and sand. Rivers from the Andes flow through this desert to the Pacific Ocean, creating small oases which have supported a variety of civilisations through the ages. To the north lie the ruins of Chan Chan, the greatest adobe (sun-dried brick) city in the world and capital of the Chimu Empire. To the south are the mysterious Nazca Lines – giant stylised animal shapes etched into the desert many hundreds of years before the Spanish conquest. The etchings, as big as football fields, are visible only from the air. How and why the Nazca Lines were made remains shrouded in mystery – just one of the many fascinating features to encounter on a journey to that most intriguing of all Andean countries, Peru!

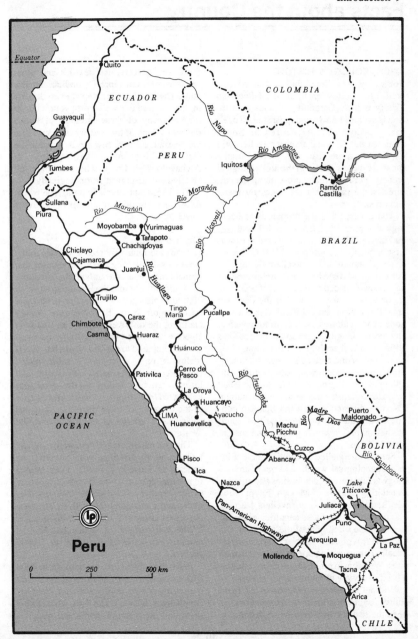

Facts about the Country

ARCHAEOLOGY & HISTORY

For many travellers, the first word that comes to mind when thinking of Peruvian history is Inca. Certainly, the Inca civilisation is the best known and most studied of all the pre-Columbian cultures of South America and the one that most travellers will experience more than any other. But the Incas are merely the tip of the archaeological iceberg. Peru had many pre-Columbian cultures, some preceding the Incas by many centuries.

The concept that the numerous archaeological sites of Peru date from different eras and hence belonged to distinct cultures was first seriously proposed by Mr E G Squier, an Englishman who travelled throughout Peru in the 1870s. Since then, archaeologists have slowly pieced together a chronological framework for the cultures of the Peruvian area. But it has been a difficult task because none of the cultures are known to have had any written language and so their record lies entirely in archaeological excavation. Furthermore, as one culture succeeded another, they tended to impose new values and attempted to eliminate the old, as happened when the Spanish conquered the Inca nation. The one difference with the Spanish conquest is that they did produce a written record of their exploits which gives some insight into the Incas.

Peru is unequalled in South America for its archaeological wealth and many archaeologists find Peru's ancient sites and cultures as exciting as those of Mexico, Egypt or the Mediterranean. For many travellers, learning about and visiting these centuries-old ruins is one of the highlights of their journey and even those with little interest in archaeology usually enjoy visiting one or two of the main sites. With this in mind, this section provides a brief overview of archaeology in Peru.

Without written records, one of the main sources of information for archaeologists has been the realistic and expressive decoration found on the ceramics, textiles and other artefacts of Peru's pre-Columbian inhabitants. These relics often depict everyday life in detail and so it is well worth your while to inspect many of these artefacts in Peru's museums. One of the best ways to visualise the overall cultural history is to visit the National Museum of Anthropology & Archaeology in Lima, where exhibits are labelled and displayed chronologically.

The sites and cultures in italic type which follow are described in greater detail in the travel sections.

The Stone Age

Humans are relatively recent arrivals in the New World. Not long ago it was thought that humankind spread throughout the Americas after migrating across the Bering Strait about 20,000 years ago. However, in 1986 there was a report in the British journal *Nature* claiming the discovery of human fossils in Brazil which dated back 32,000 years – still recent compared to the Old World but nevertheless a major discovery if substantiated (few archaeologists believe this date). All human remains found in the Americas belong to *Homo sapiens*; there is no evidence of the presence of more primitive hominids such as are known to belong to the Old World.

The first inhabitants of Peru were nomadic hunters and gatherers who roamed the country in loose-knit bands. They hunted fearsome animals which are long since extinct, such as giant sloths, sabre-toothed tigers and mastodons. They lived in caves, the oldest known of which is at Pikimachay in the Department of Ayacucho. Human remains here date from 14,000 to 20,000 years old.

From the earliest arrivals until about 4000 BC, cultural development mainly meant improving stone implements for hunting. People knew how to make fires, wore animal skins and made simple tools and weapons from stone and bone. As their prey became extinct they began hunting the animals we know today, such as deer, vicuña, guanaco and llamas. Hunting scenes were recorded in cave paintings at Lauricocha near Huánuco and Toquepala near Tacna.

Early Agriculture

About 4000 BC people began planting seeds and learning how to improve crops by simple horticultural methods such as weeding. The coastal strip then was wetter than today's desert and a number of small settlements were established, thus changing the status of the people from nomadic hunters and gatherers to settled agriculturalists and fishermen. Several of these settlements have been excavated, with the garbage mounds yielding the best information about life at that time. Although these places can be visited, there are no on-site museums or explanations; so looking at ancient garbage mounds is an activity with little to recommend it unless you're a professional archaeologist.

Some of the best known sites are Huaca Prieta in the Chicama Valley near Trujillo, Chilca and Asia, south of Lima. Chilca was inhabited about 4000 BC and the other two sites about 2000 BC. The inhabitants fished with nets or with bone hooks and collected seafood such as crabs and sea urchins. Various crops were cultivated, including cotton which appeared early (about 3000 BC) as well as chilli peppers, beans, squashes and, about 1400 BC, corn. The cotton was used to make clothing, mainly with the simple techniques of twining and later by weaving. The people lived in primitive one-room dwellings, lined with stone in Huaca Prieta, or they had branch or reed huts as in Asia. Ceramics and metalwork were still unknown although jewellery made of bone, shell, etc was used.

Roughly contemporary with these coastal settlements was the enigmatic site of Kotosh near Huánuco – one of the earliest ruins in highland Peru. Little is known about the people who lived here, but their buildings were the most developed for that period, and

pottery fragments found here predate by several hundred years those found in other parts of Peru.

Early Formative Period

This period extends from roughly 1250 BC to 850 BC and is known mainly from remains found in the Virú Valley and Guañape area, about 50 km south of Trujillo on the north coast. During this time, ceramics developed from rude undecorated pots to sculpted, incised and simply coloured pots of high quality. Weaving, fishing and horticulture also improved and simple funerary offerings have been found.

Chavín Horizon

This period is named after the site of Chavín de Huántar, 40 km east of Huaraz in the Department of Ancash. It is also known as the middle formative period and lasted from about 850 BC until 300 BC. It is termed a 'horizon' because its artistic and religious influences can be seen in several contemporary cultures, including the Cupisnique ceramics of the Lambayeque region (north of Trujillo) and the early pottery of Paracas Cavernas (south of Lima). Thus the Chavín influence was felt in a huge area covering most of the northern two-thirds of Peru's highlands and coast.

The salient feature of the Chavín influence is the repeated representation of a stylised jaguar, hence the Chavín is often termed a jaguar-worshipping cult. Most importantly, this period represents the greatest early development in weaving, pottery, agriculture, religion and architecture – in a word, culture. Many archaeologists see the Chavín Horizon as the most important cultural development of pre-Columbian Peru.

Late Formative Period

Around 300 BC the Chavín style suddenly and inexplicably disappeared and there was little unity in the cultures found in Peru during the next 500 years. Although none of these cultures were individually outstanding or widespread, several were locally important. The best known are the Salinar culture of the Chicama Valley area near Trujillo and the *Paracas Necropolis* south of Lima. Salinar ceramics show advanced firing techniques, whilst the textiles of the Paracas Necropolis are markedly improved and different from the earlier Paracas Cavernas; these textiles are considered the finest pre-Columbian textiles to have been produced anywhere in the Americas.

Regional Development

This period lasted from about 100 AD to 700 AD and, as its name suggests, was not marked by any single unifying horizon but by local development in several regions. Pottery, metalwork and weaving reached a pinnacle of technological development throughout Peru and hence this period is often referred to as either the Florescent or Classic.

Two distinct cultures of this period are particularly noted for their exceptional pottery – the *Moche* from the Trujillo area and the *Nazca* people from the south coast. These cultures recorded their ways of life in intricate detail on their ceramics and so provide archaeologists with an invaluable reference tool. Many of Peru's main museums have good collections of Nazca and Moche pottery. These two cultures also left some interesting sites which are worth visiting. The Moche built massive pyramids such as the *Temples of the Sun & Moon* near Trujillo and the Nazca made their enigmatic giant petroglyphs in the desert. These last are known as the *Nazca Lines* and are best appreciated from the air in one of the many overflights in small airplanes available in the town of Nazca.

Other cultures of importance during this period include the Lima culture with its main site at *Pachacamac*, 30 km south of Lima. There was also the Recuay culture, whose ceramics can be seen in the regional museum at *Huaraz*, and the *Cajamarca, Kuelap*, Gallinazo and Tiahuanaco cultures.

The Wari Empire

The ruin of the highland city of *Wari* (also Huari) is found about 25 km north of *Ayacucho*. Wari was the capital of the first expansionist empire known in the Andes. Unlike the earlier Chavín Horizon, expansion was not limited to the diffusion of artistic and religious influence. The Wari were vigorous military conquerors who built and maintained important outposts throughout much of Peru. These included *Pikillacta* near Cuzco, *Cajamarquilla* near Lima, *Wilcahuaín* near Huaraz, Wariwillka near Huancayo, Wiracochapampa near Huamachuco and Los Paredones near Cajamarca. The Wari culture was the first strongly militaristic and urban culture of Peru. Also, it was influenced by the Tiahuanaco religion from the Lake Titicaca region.

The Wari attempted to subdue the cultures they conquered by enforcing their own values and suppressing local oral traditions and regional self-expression. Thus from about 700 AD to 1100 AD, Wari influence is noted in the art, technology and architecture of most areas in Peru. More significantly, from an archaeologist's point of view, any local oral traditions which may have existed were forbidden by the conquerors and slowly forgotten. With no written language and no oral traditions, archaeologists must rely entirely on the examination of excavated artefacts to gain an idea of what life was like in the early Peruvian cultures. The Wari too, in their turn, were overthrown and their culture obliterated.

The Regional States

Because of their cultural dominance and oppression, it is not surprising that the Wari were generally not welcomed, despite their improvements in urban development and organisation. By about 1100 AD they had been overthrown, not by a new conquering force but by individual groups in their local areas. These separate regional states thrived for the next 400 years, the best known being the *Chimu* kingdom in the Trujillo area. Its capital was the huge adobe city of *Chan Chan* which is often referred to as the largest adobe city in the world. Chan Chan can easily be visited from Trujillo.

Roughly contemporary with the Chimu

was the Chachapoyas culture of the Utcubamba River basin in the Department of Amazonas. Its people built *Kuelap*, one of the most mysterious of the highland ruins, which is reasonably accessible to the traveller (half a day's walk from the nearest dirt road). Also contemporary with the Chimu were the Chancay people from the Chancay Valley just north of Lima. The best collection of Chancay artefacts is at the excellent Amano Museum in Lima. Further south was the Ica-Chincha culture whose artefacts can be seen in the Ica Regional Museum. There were also several small altiplano tribes who lived near Lake Titicaca and were frequently at war with one another. They left impressive, circular funerary towers dotting the bleak landscape – the best are to be seen at *Sillustani*. There were also the Chanka who lived in the Ayacucho-Apurímac area and, of course, there was the kingdom of Cuzco which was the predecessor of the greatest pre-Columbian empire on the continent.

The Inca Empire

The Inca Empire, for all its greatness, existed for barely a century. Prior to 1430, the Incas, whose emperor was believed to have descended from the sun, ruled over only the valley of *Cuzco*. The Cuzqueños were at war with the Chankas for some time and the hostilities culminated in the 1430s with a major victory for the Cuzqueños. This marked the beginning of a remarkably rapid military expansion. The Inca Empire, known as Tahuantinsuyo (the four corners), conquered and incorporated the cultures mentioned in the preceding section as well as most of the cultures in the area stretching from southern Colombia to central Chile. Like the Wari before them, the Incas imposed their way of life on to the peoples they conquered. Thus when the Spanish arrived, most of the Andean area had been thoroughly homogenised by Inca rule.

The Spanish Conquest

After Columbus' first landfall in 1492, the Spanish rapidly conquered the Caribbean islands and the Aztec and Mayan cultures of Mexico and Central America. By the 1520s, the conquistadors were ready to turn their attentions to the South American continent. In 1522 Pascual de Andagoya sailed as far as the San Juan River in Colombia. Two years later Francisco Pizarro headed south but was unable to reach even the San Juan. In November 1526, Pizarro again headed south, and by 1528 he had explored as far as the Santa River in Peru. He noted several coastal Inca settlements, became aware of the richness of the Inca Empire and returned to Spain to raise money and recruit men for the conquest. Pizarro's third expedition south left Panama in late 1530. He landed on the Ecuadorian coast and began to march overland towards Peru. Finally, in September 1532, Pizarro founded the first Spanish town in Peru – San Miguel de Piura. He then marched inland into the heart of the Inca Empire. In November 1532, he reached

"Do you eat gold?"
The Incas could not understand the Spaniards' greed for gold.

Cajamarca, captured the Inca emperor, Atahualpa, thus effectively putting an end to the Inca Empire.

Colonial Peru

The Inca capital of Cuzco was of little use to the Spaniards who were a seafaring people and needed a coastal capital to maintain communication with Spain. Accordingly, Pizarro founded Lima in 1535 and this became the capital of the Viceroyalty of Peru, as the colony was named.

The next 30 years were a period of turmoil, with the Incas still fighting against their conquerors and the conquistadors fighting among themselves for control of the rich colony. The conquistador Almagro was assassinated in 1538 and Pizarro suffered the same fate 3 years later. Manco Inca tried to regain control of the highlands and was almost successful in 1536, but by 1539 he had retreated to Vilcabamba in the jungle where he was killed in 1544. Succeeding Incas were less rebellious than Manco Inca; that is until 1572 and the rebellion of Tupac Amaru, in which this Inca was defeated and executed by the Spaniards.

The next 200 years were relatively peaceful. Lima became the main political, social and commercial centre of the Andean nations. Cuzco became a backwater, its main mark on the colonial period being the development of the Cuzqueño School of Art resulting from a unique blend of Spanish and highland Indian influences. Cuzqueño canvases can be admired now in Lima's museums, as can the many colonial churches which were built in Lima and the highlands during the 17th and 18th centuries.

The rulers of the colony were the Spanish-born viceroys appointed by the Spanish crown. Immigrants from Spain had the most prestigious positions whilst Spaniards born in the colony were generally less important. In this way the Spanish crown was able to better control its colonies. *Mestizos* or people of mixed Indian-Spanish stock came still further down the social scale. Lowest of all were the Indians themselves who were exploited and treated as serfs, at best, and often as expendable slaves. This led to an Indian uprising in 1780 under the self-styled Inca, Tupac Amaru II. The uprising was quelled and its leaders cruelly executed.

Independence

By the early 19th century, the inhabitants of Spain's Latin American colonies were dissatisfied with the lack of freedom and high taxation imposed upon them by Spain. Not only Peru, but the entire continent was ripe for revolt and independence.

For Peru the change came from two directions. José de San Martín liberated Argentina and Chile and in 1821 entered Lima. Meanwhile, Simón Bolívar had freed Venezuela and Colombia and in 1822 sent Field Marshall Sucre to defeat the Ecuadorian royalists at the battle of Pichincha. San Martín and Bolívar met privately in Guayaquil. What transpired still remains unknown, but as a result San Martín left Latin America to live in France and Bolívar and Sucre continued with the liberation of Peru. The two decisive battles of Peruvian independence were fought at Junín on 6 August 1824 and at Ayacucho on 9 December 1824. Despite a few royalists managing to hold out in the Real Felipe fortress near Lima until 22 January 1826, Peru was essentially an independent state.

As an independent state, Peru had a brief war with Spain in 1866, which Peru won, and a longer war with Chile from 1879 to 1883, which Peru lost. The latter was over the nitrate rich areas of the northern Atacama Desert and as a result of the war, Chile annexed a large portion of coastal southern Peru. The area around Tacna was returned in 1929.

Peru went to war with Ecuador over a border dispute in 1941. A treaty drawn up at Rio de Janeiro in 1942 gave Peru jurisdiction over what are now the northern sections of the departments of San Martín and Loreto, but Ecuador disputes this border and armed skirmishes occur between the two countries every few years.

The government has mostly been one of military dictatorships and coups with shorter periods of civilian rule. The most recent of these began in 1980 with the election of President Belaúnde Terry. He was replaced in the 1985 elections by Alán García Pérez. After 2 years of relative economic and political stability, the country began experiencing some of its worst economic and guerilla problems in years.

The main economic problems are inflation, which exceeded 2000% in 1989, and the foreign debt, which totals about US$20 billion. In 1985 the government placed severe restrictions on the amount Peru would pay on its foreign debt. This left the country isolated from the international banking community and the IMF. Peru was cut off from further sources of finance, with an annual interest bill equal to 27% of its annual export earnings.

The Maoist group *Sendero Luminoso* (shining path) has been waging a guerilla campaign against the central government for more than a decade, and the struggle has claimed over 18,000 lives. The group is now believed to be linked to drug cartels and is active mainly in the central part of the country. The presence of the Sendero means that travel is ill-advised in some areas, especially the central Andes. For details, see the 'Dangers & Annoyances' section in the Facts for the Visitor chapter.

The elections of June 1990 saw Alberto Fujimori, the 52-year-old son of Japanese immigrants, elected as president. He defeated the well-known novelist Mario Vargas Llosa, a right-winger who was advocating 'shock treatment' for Peru's ailing economy. Fujimori capitalised on fears that such treatment would mean more poverty and increased unemployment, and he was seen by many disillusioned voters as an alternative to the established parties and policies. His election policies were vague, but he favoured gradual reforms, government controls on prices, and a new currency pegged to the US dollar.

Fujimori took office on Peru's Independence Day, 28 July 1990, for a 5-year term.

Visiting Archaeological Sites

Visiting Peru without seeing the Inca ruins in the Cuzco area (especially Machu Picchu) is a bit like visiting Egypt without seeing the pyramids. If you're interested in more than just the Inca Empire, however, I recommend the following.

Trujillo is an excellent base for seeing Chan Chan (the huge adobe capital of the Chimu) as well as Moche pyramids and good museums. If you have any spare time in Huaraz, the 2500-year-old ruins of the Chavín are worth a day trip. The artefacts of Paracas are best seen in museums and the Nazca Lines can only be appreciated properly from the air. The funerary towers at Sillustani, near Lake Titicaca, are worth seeing if you have a spare day in Puno. Kuelap is great if you have the energy to go to such a remote area. Other sites, whilst worthwhile if you are particularly interested in archaeology or if you have plenty of time in Peru, don't offer as many rewards as the ones mentioned.

GEOGRAPHY

Peru covers 1,285,215 sq km and is the third largest country in South America. It is more than five times as large as the UK. It is bounded on the north by Ecuador and Colombia, to the east by Brazil and Bolivia, to the south by Chile and to the west by the Pacific Ocean. It lies entirely within the tropics with its northernmost point being only a few km below the equator and its southernmost point just over 18° south.

Geographically, Peru is divided into three main regions – a narrow coastal belt separated from the Amazon rainforest by a wide mountain range.

The narrow coastal strip is mainly desert and at the southern end it merges into the Atacama Desert, one of the driest places on earth. The extreme northern end, near Ecuador, is mangrove swamp. This coastal desert contains Peru's major cities and its best highway, the Pan-American, which runs the entire length of Peru and is asphalted for most of the way. The desert is irrigated in places by rivers running down the western slopes of the Andes; about 40 oases are formed in this way and are agricultural centres.

The Andes, the second greatest mountain chain in the world after the Himalaya, jut rapidly up from the coast. Heights of 6000 metres are reached just 100 km inland. It's a young range still in the process of being uplifted as the Nazca plate (under the

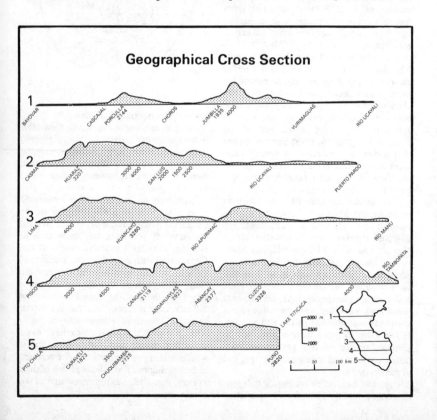

Geographical Cross Section

Pacific) slides under the South American plate. The Andes don't stop at the coast; 100 km offshore there is an ocean trench which is as deep as the Andes are high.

Huascarán, at 6768 metres above sea level, is Peru's highest mountain and the highest mountain anywhere in the tropical world. Most of Peru's Andes lie between 3000 and 4000 metres above sea level and support half the country's population. It is a rugged and difficult landscape with jagged ranges separated by extremely deep and vertiginous canyons. Although the roads are often in terrible condition, the traveller is rewarded by spectacular scenery.

The eastern slopes of the Andes are less precipitous, though no less rugged. They receive much more rainfall than the dry western slopes, so are clothed in a mantle of green cloud forest. As elevation is lost, the cloud forest becomes the rainforest of the Amazon Basin. This region has been penetrated by few roads and those which do exist go in for a short distance only. The traveller wishing to continue through the Amazon Basin to Colombia or Brazil must do so by river or air.

CLIMATE

Peru's climate can be divided into two seasons – wet and dry – though the weather varies greatly depending on the geographical region.

The desert coast is, as you'd expect it to be, arid. During summer (January to March) the sky is often clear and the weather tends to be hot and sticky. This is the time Peruvians go to the beach. During the rest of the year the grey coastal mist known as the *garúa* moves in and the sun is rarely seen. I find the weather on the coast rather depressing during most of the year. It doesn't feel like the tropics!

Moving inland, you soon rise above the coastal mist. Nazca, for example, is about 60 km inland and 600 metres above sea level – high enough to avoid the garúa, so it's hot and sunny for most of the year. Generally, the

western slopes of the Andes have weather like that of Nazca.

Entering the Andes proper, you begin experiencing the wet and dry seasons. If you're interested in trekking or hiking the Inca Trail to Machu Picchu, you'll probably want to go in the dry season which is from May to September. Although at that altitude it can be cold at night, with occasional freezing temperatures in Cuzco (3326 metres), the dry weather provides beautiful sunshine during the day. Because of this, the dry season in the Andes is known as summer and the warmer wet season is called winter. This leads to general confusion, for when it's summer on the coast it's winter in the highlands and vice versa. Confused? It gets even worse when you listen to a *Limeño* (inhabitant of Lima) arguing with a *serrano* (sierra or mountain dweller) about whether it's summer or winter. More important is whether it is the wet or dry season. The wet season in the mountains is from October to May but it usually doesn't get really wet until late January. Still, you can never tell for sure until you go!

Heading down the eastern slopes of the Andes it gets wetter. The driest months are the same as in the highlands, but the wet season tends to be more pronounced. The wettest months are from January until April, during which time roads on the eastern slopes of the Andes are often closed due to landslides or flooding. A similar weather pattern exists in the Amazon lowlands.

GOVERNMENT

Under present democratic rule, presidents hold office for 5 years and are permitted to run for the presidency every other election. Thus no president is allowed to govern for two consecutive terms. The president has a cabinet of 12 members. Voting is compulsory for all citizens aged between 18 and 60.

Peru is politically divided into 24 departments (states). The departments are further divided into provinces, of which there are 150, and the provinces subdivided into 1322 districts.

POPULATION & PEOPLE

Peru's population is over 20 million, almost half of which is concentrated in the narrow coastal desert. Lima alone has a population of almost six million and the second and third cities, Arequipa and Trujillo, also in the coastal region, have populations of about 750,000 each.

About half the population is found in the highlands – mostly rural Indians or mestizos who practice subsistence agriculture. There are few large cities in the highlands. The highlanders prefer to be called *campesinos* (country people or peasants) rather than Indians, which is considered insulting. Because of the very poor standard of living in the highlands, many campesinos have migrated to the coast but overpopulation problems in the cities mean their lot rarely improves.

More than 60% of Peru lies in the Amazon Basin east of the Andes. This region is slowly becoming colonised but as yet only 5% of the population lives there.

About half the population is Indian and a further third is mestizo. About 12% is White and 5% is Black. Most of the Blacks live on the coast and a few live in the Amazon region. There is a small Asian population and Chinese restaurants (*chifas*) are found throughout Peru.

RELIGION

In common with that of most Latin American countries, the religion is predominantly Roman Catholic. Some of the older towns have splendid colonial Catholic churches. Although churches of other faiths can be found, these form a small minority. The Indians, while outwardly Roman Catholic, tend to blend Catholicism with their traditional beliefs.

HOLIDAYS & FESTIVALS

Many of the main festivals favour the Roman Catholic liturgical calendar. These are often celebrated with great pageantry, especially in highland Indian villages where the Catholic feast day may well be linked with some traditional agricultural festival (such as spring or harvest) and be the excuse for a traditional Indian fiesta with much drinking, dancing, rituals and processions. Other holidays are of historical or political interest, such as National Independence on 28 and 29 July. On major holidays, banks, offices and other services are closed and transportation tends to be very crowded, so book ahead if possible.

The following list describes the major holidays, which may well be celebrated for several days around the actual date. Those marked by an asterisk * are official public holidays when banks, etc are closed; others are more local holidays.

1 January*
  New Year's Day
2 February
  Candlemas or the Virgin of Candelaria – especially in the highlands.
February-March
  Carnaval – usually held on the last few days before Lent, it's often celebrated with water fights, so be warned. It's a particularly popular feast in the highlands with the Carnaval de Abancay being one of the biggest.
March-April*
  Easter – Maundy Thursday afternoon and all of Good Friday are public holidays. Holy Week is celebrated with spectacular religious processions almost daily, with Ayacucho being recognised as having the best in Peru. Cuzco is also good for Easter processions.
1 May*
  Labour Day
June
  Corpus Christi – the 9th Thursday after Easter. The Cuzco processions are especially dramatic.
24 June
  Inti Raymi – also St John the Baptist. Inti Raymi celebrates the winter solstice and is the greatest of the Inca festivals. It's certainly the spectacle of the year in Cuzco and attracts many thousands of Peruvian and foreign visitors. Despite its commercialisation, it's still worth seeing the street dances and parades as well as the pageant held in Sacsayhuaman.
29 June*
  St Peter & St Paul
16 July
  Virgin of Carmen – mainly celebrated in the southern sierra, with Paucartambo and Pisac near Cuzco and Pucara near Lake Titicaca being especially important.

28 July*

> *Peru's Independence* – while celebrated throughout the country, in the southern sierra festivities can begin 3 days ahead with the feast of St James on 25 July.

30 August*

> *St Rose* – patron saint of Lima and of the Americas. Major processions in Lima.

8 October*

> *Battle of Angamos*

18 October

> *Lord of the Miracles* – celebrated with major religious processions in Lima; people wear purple.

1 November*

> *All Saint's Day* – an official public holiday.

2 November

> *All Soul's Day* – celebrated with gifts of food, drink and flowers taken to family graves; especially colourful in the sierra. The food and drink is consumed and the atmosphere is festive rather than sombre.

5 November

> *Puno Day* – spectacular costumes and street dancing in Puno.

8 December*

> *Feast of the Immaculate Conception*

25 December*

> *Christmas Day*

Local fiestas and festivals are held somewhere in Peru every week. Many are mentioned in the individual town descriptions.

LANGUAGE

For the traveller, Spanish is the main language. In the highlands, most Indians are bilingual, with Quechua being the preferred language in most areas except around Lake Titicaca where Aymara is spoken. For most Indians, Spanish is a second tongue and between one and two million are estimated not to speak Spanish at all. These people live in very remote areas and it is rare for the traveller to encounter Indians who speak no Spanish. Although English is understood in the best hotels, airline offices and tourist agencies, it is of little use elsewhere.

If you don't speak Spanish, take heart. It is an easy language to learn. Courses are available in Lima (see the Lima chapter) or you can study books, records and tapes while you are still at home and planning your trip.

These study aids are often available for free from many public libraries or you might consider taking an evening or college course. Once having learnt the basics, you'll be able to talk with people from all over Latin America because most of the countries use Spanish – apart from Brazil which is Portuguese-speaking.

Spanish is easy to learn for several reasons. Firstly, it uses Roman script. Secondly, with few exceptions, it is spoken as it is written and vice versa. Imagine trying to explain to someone learning English that there are seven different ways of pronouncing 'ough'. This isn't a problem in Spanish. Thirdly, many words are so similar to English that you can figure them out – *Instituto Geográfico Nacional* means the National Geographical Institute.

Even if you don't have time to take a Spanish course, at least bring a phrasebook and dictionary. Lonely Planet's *Quechua Phrasebook* and *Brazilian Phrasebook* are recommended, as is its forthcoming *Latin-American Spanish Phrasebook.* Don't dispense with the dictionary, because the phrasebook won't help you translate the local newspaper. My favourite dictionary is the paperback *University of Chicago Spanish-English, English-Spanish Dictionary.* It's inexpensive, small enough to travel with, yet has many more entries than most pocket dictionaries. It also contains words used in Latin America but not in Spain.

Although the Spanish alphabet looks like the English one, it is different. 'Ch' is considered a separate letter, so *champú* (which means shampoo) will be listed in a dictionary after all the words beginning with just 'c'. Similarly, 'll' is a separate letter, so a *llama* is listed after all the words beginning with a single 'l'. The letter 'ñ' is listed after the ordinary 'n'. Vowels with an accent are accented for stress and are not considered separate letters.

Pronunciation is generally more straightforward than it is in English. If you say a word the way it looks like it should be said, the chances are that it will be close enough to be understood. You will get better with practise of course. A few notable exceptions are 'll' which is always pronounced 'y' as in 'yacht', the 'j' which is always pronounced 'h' as in 'happy', and the 'h' which isn't pronounced at all. Thus the phrase *hojas en la calle* (leaves in the street) would be pronounced 'o-has en la ka-yea'. Finally, the letter 'ñ' is pronounced as the 'ny' sound in 'canyon'.

Grammar

Word order in Spanish is generally similar to English sentence construction with one notable exception. Adjectives follow the nouns they qualify instead of preceding them as they do in English. Thus 'the white house' becomes *la casa blanca*.

Articles, adjectives and demonstrative pronouns must agree with the noun in both gender and number. Nouns ending in *a* are generally feminine and the corresponding articles are *la* (singular) and *las* (plural). Those ending in *o* are usually masculine and require the articles *el* (singular) and *los* (plural).

There are, however, hundreds of exceptions to these guidelines which can only be memorised or deduced by the meaning of the word. Plurals are formed by adding *s* to words ending in a vowel and *es* to those ending in a consonant.

In addition to using all the familiar English tenses, Spanish also uses the imperfect tense and two subjunctive tenses (past and present). Tenses are formed either by adding a myriad of endings to the root verb or preceding the participle form by some variation of the verb *haber* (to have/to exist).

There are verb endings for first, second and third person singular and plural. Second person singular and plural are divided into formal and familiar modes. If that's not enough, there are three types of verbs – those ending in 'ar', 'er' and 'ir' – which are all conjugated differently. There are also a whole slough of stem-changing rules and irregularities which must be memorised.

Greetings & Civilities

good morning
  buenos días
good afternoon (or good evening)
  buenas tardes
yes
  sí
no
  no
hello
  hola
See you later.
  hasta luego
How are you?
  cómo estás? (familiar)
  cómo está? (formal)
please
  por favor
thank you
  gracias
It's a pleasure.
  con mucho gusto

Some Useful Phrases

Do you speak Spanish?
  habla usted castellano?
Where do you come from?
  de donde es usted?
What is your country?
  cual es su país?
Where are you staying?
  donde estás alojado?
What is your profession?
  cuál es su profesión?
What time do you have?
  qué hora tiene?
Don't you have smaller change?
  no tiene sencillo?
Do you understand? (casual)
  me entiende?
Where can I change money/travellers' cheques?
  donde se cambia monedas/cheques de viajeros?
Where is the ...?
  donde está el/la ...?
How much is this?
  a cómo?, cuanto cuesta esto?, cuanto vale esto?

too expensive
muy caro
cheaper
más barato
I'll take it.
lo llevo
What's the weather like?
que tiempo hace?
Buy from me!
comprame!
to the right
a la derecha
to the left
a la izquierda
Continue straight ahead.
siga derecho
I don't understand.
no entiendo
more or less
más o menos
when?
cuando?
how?
cómo?
How's that again?
cómo?
where?
donde?
What time does the next plane/bus/train leave for ...?
a qué hora sale el próximo avión/ómnibus/trén para ...?
where from?
de donde?
around there
para allá
around here
por aquí
It's hot/cold.
hace calor/frío

Some Useful Words
airport
aeropuerto
bank
banco
block
cuadra
bus station
terminal terrestre

cathedral, church
catedral, iglesia
city
ciudad
downhill
para abajo
exchange house
casa de cambio
friend
amigo/a
here
aquí
husband/wife
marido/esposa
Indian/peasant
campesino (never *indio*)
mother/father
madre/padre
people
la gente
police
policía
post office
correo
rain
lluvia
snow
nieve
there
allí
town square
plaza
train station
estación de ferrocarril
uphill
para arriba
wind
viento

Time
What time is it?
qué hora es? or *qué horas son?*
It is one o'clock.
es la una
It is two o'clock.
son las dos
midnight
medianoche
noon
mediodía

		Numbers	
in the afternoon		1	*uno/una*
de la tarde		2	*dos*
in the morning		3	*tres*
de la mañana		4	*cuatro*
at night		5	*cinco*
de la noche		6	*seis*
half past two		7	*siete*
dos y media		8	*ocho*
quarter past two		9	*nueve*
dos y cuarto		10	*diez*
two twenty-five		11	*once*
dos con veinticinco minutos		12	*doce*
twenty to two		13	*trece*
veinte para las dos		14	*catorce*
		15	*quince*
Sunday		16	*dieciseis*
domingo		17	*diecisiete*
Monday		18	*dieciocho*
lunes		19	*diecinueve*
Tuesday		20	*veinte*
martes		21	*veintiuno*
Wednesday		30	*treinta*
miércoles		40	*cuarenta*
Thursday		50	*cincuenta*
jueves		60	*sesenta*
Friday		70	*setenta*
viernes		80	*ochenta*
Saturday		90	*noventa*
sábado		100	*cien(to)*
		101	*ciento uno*
rainy season		200	*doscientos*
el invierno		201	*doscientos uno*
dry season		300	*trescientos*
el verano		400	*cuatrocientos*
		500	*quinientos*
		600	*seiscientos*
today		700	*setecientos*
hoy		800	*ochocientos*
tomorrow		900	*novecientos*
mañana		1000	*mil*
yesterday		100,000	*cien mil*
ayer		1,000,000	*un millón*

Facts for the Visitor

VISAS & DOCUMENTS

Many travellers who are entering Peru as tourists do not require visas. Notable exceptions are Australians, New Zealanders, Chileans, Venezuelans and citizens of most communist, African and Asian countries, except Japan. Travellers from those countries can normally obtain the required visas from the capital cities of neighbouring countries if they are travelling around South America. Alternatively, apply for one at a Peruvian embassy before you leave home.

Your passport should be valid for 6 months or more. A tourist card (a sheet of paper) is given to everyone on arrival in Peru. There is no charge for this card, but don't lose it as you will need it to extend your stay, for passport checks and to leave the country. If you lose it, another can be obtained at the immigration office in Lima and other major cities, or at the exit point from the country. It's best to get a new tourist card in a major city because the immigration officials hassle you if you try to exit without one and a bribe is sometimes necessary to obtain one when leaving the country.

On arrival you are normally asked how long you want to stay. If you're lucky and the duty officer is in a good mood, you may get the maximum of 90 days, but it depends on your nationality. I can usually get 90 days with my British passport but my American wife can only get 60. Don't ask me why. Some nationalities get even less. You are given an identical stamp in both your passport and tourist card which indicates how long you can stay. If you have a ticket out of the country you can usually get enough days to last until you leave, but make sure you show the duty officer your ticket as soon as you start dealing with him and before your passport is stamped, as they won't want to change it afterwards.

If you want to stay in Peru for longer than the 60 days (or whatever) you are given on arrival, it is not difficult to renew your tourist card. The only hassle is that this costs US$20. You are allowed two renewals to a maximum of 180 days in Peru. If you wish to stay longer than this, you must leave the country then return to begin the process over. It is relatively straightforward to leave the country overland to Ecuador, Chile or Bolivia. The easiest place for tourist card renewals is the migraciónes office in Lima where the process can take less than an hour. In other cities you may have to leave your passport overnight.

In addition to a passport and tourist card, you officially need a ticket out of the country. Evidence of sufficient funds for your stay is not normally required. It's rare to be asked for an exit ticket, unless you're one of those travellers that requires a visa in which case you may be asked to show it. If you buy an airline ticket for use as an exit ticket it can normally be refunded if you don't want to use it. Alternatively, buy an MCO (Miscellaneous Charges Order) from an airline belonging to IATA (International Air Transport Association). This can be used for any flight on an IATA airline or can be refunded if it hasn't expired. Airline departure desks outside Peru might not let you fly to Peru on a one-way ticket and may insist that you buy an onward ticket or an MCO before you can board the aircraft. (I saw this happen at the AeroPeru desk in Miami to a Japanese woman travelling on a Japanese passport but who was a resident of Peru.)

Bus tickets can be bought at land borders but these are usually expensive and are not transferable or refundable. If you don't have an exit ticket it's best not to worry, as you probably won't be asked to show one anyway.

Always carry your passport and tourist card when you are out of your hotel (or at least a photocopy of the passport pages with your photo and passport number) as there are occasional document checks on public transport and you can be arrested if you don't have identification. Another document which is useful for identification is a drivers' licence (as long as it has a photo) or any similar official looking document that has a recent photo of you. When travelling between towns, always carry your passport because there are passport controls at the entrance and exit points of most main towns, whether you arrive by bus, taxi, air, rail or boat. (While this was the case during the 1980s, in late 1989 I was asked to show my passport only once.)

Other Paperwork

International vaccination certificates are not required by law, but vaccinations are advisable. See the Health section.

Student cards are very useful. These save you money at most archaeological sites, museums, etc, (entrance fee discounts of 50% are common) and occasionally at youth hostels or even when buying airline tickets. It has to be a bona fide card because almost everyone knows what the card is supposed to look like and it's difficult to get away with anything that doesn't have your photograph and an official looking seal from the school or college. Expiry dates are checked too.

Working Holidays

Officially you need a work visa to work in Peru. You can, however, get a job teaching English in language schools, usually in Lima. Schools occasionally advertise for teachers in the newspapers, including the English language weekly, the *Lima Times*. They expect you to be a native English speaker and the pay is usually abysmal. Fermath Ingles at Tudela y Varela 215, Miraflores, pay just over US$1 an hour and that's above average. Another place is TRANSLEX on the Paseo de Republica in Miraflores. It pays a little more and has quite a high standard.

If, in addition to speaking English like a native, you actually have a bona fide teaching credential, so much the better. Various American and British schools will sometimes hire teachers of maths, biology and other subjects and often help you get a work visa if you want to stay. They also pay much better than the language schools. Members of the South American Explorers Club may find that their Lima office has contacts with schools which are looking for teachers.

MONEY

Until the end of 1985, the Peruvian currency was the *sol*, valued at S/17,300 to the US dollar. In 1986 a new currency was introduced by the simple (and, in Latin America, common) expedient of slashing the last three digits. The new currency was called the *inti*, and was worth I/17.30 to the US dollar when introduced. (Sol is the Spanish word for sun and inti means the same thing in Quechua, the Andean Indian dialect.)

By October 1990, the value of the US dollar had topped I/450,000 and it's only a matter of time before inflation causes the Peruvian Government to introduce yet another currency.

Bills of 500, 1000, 5000, 10,000, 50,000, 100,000, and 500,000 intis are circulating and larger bills are planned. Coins are not used at this time.

The Peruvian currency is frequently devalued. When I first visited Peru in early 1982, I received about 500 soles (half an inti) for the US dollar; in May 1990 the figure was I/37,000 then by July 1990, it had soared to 160,000 intis. All prices in this book are quoted in US dollars but, with the rampant inflation, these prices can be thought of as guides only, not gospel.

The easiest currency to exchange is the US dollar. Although hard currencies such as other dollars, pounds sterling, French and Swiss francs and German marks are exchangeable in the main cities, the US dollar is always preferable and sometimes the only currency you can change easily in the smaller towns. It is best to exchange in the main cities as much money as you think you'll need because exchange facilities may be worse or nonexistent elsewhere.

There are two rates of exchange. The 'official' exchange rate is lower than the 'financial' rate but that gap is slowly closing.

Obviously you'll want to exchange at the higher financial rate which is generally available for foreign exchange, but some banks will only give the official rate, so shop around. The financial rate is used for most foreign exchange transactions within Peru whilst the official rate is supposed to be used for international transactions, so if you pay for something with a foreign credit card, you'll be receiving the lower rate, to your disadvantage. Peruvian currency exchange rules can change at any time. The best source of information is a fellow traveller who has been there for a while.

Money can be changed in banks, *casas de cambio* (exchange houses) or with street changers. First class hotels and restaurants will also accept dollars. The best place to exchange varies and there are no hard and fast rules. In the early 1980s the Banco de la Nación was the best place to change money but by the mid-1980s the Banco de Crédito consistently gave the best rates.

During a period in 1987, all casas de cambio were closed by law. By late 1989,

however, the casas de cambio were giving the best rates of all. These also have the advantage of longer business hours. Street changers were giving a similar rate to the casas de cambio, but they are not worth the hassle except on the borders where they may be all that is available. If you do use street changers, count your money very carefully before handing over the dollars, as not all street changers are honest. Because the situation changes frequently, I have continued to mark both banks and casas de cambio on maps.

Banking hours are erratic. From January to March banks are open only from 8.30 to 11.30 am. During the rest of the year they are open longer – sometimes into the afternoon but don't count on it. Expect long lines and delays in banks and try to go early in the morning for the most efficient service. Casas de cambio are often open from 9 am to 6 pm, or later in tourist areas such as Cuzco, but tend to close at lunch for a couple of hours.

There is an advantage to carrying cash dollars. During the summer of 1985,

travellers' cheques were returning about 20% less than cash. Recently travellers' cheques were being changed in most places at a loss of about 5%. Because travellers' cheques are refundable in the event of theft or loss, it is worth carrying at least some of your money in this form, although a certain amount of cash is always useful. Most main brands of travellers' cheques are accepted but I definitely do not recommend Citibank cheques. This bank took more than a year to reimburse me for $200 in stolen cheques and had the gall to charge me about $20 for 'handling'. American Express are much easier to deal with.

The Banco de Crédito will sometimes change travellers' cheques into US dollars at a small commission (about 2%). This depends on the availability of cash dollars and so is more likely to occur in larger cities.

If you run out of money, it is a simple matter to have more sent to you, assuming that you have someone at home kind enough to send you money. A bank transfer is fastest by telex, although this will take at least 3 days. All you do is pick a Peruvian bank which will cooperate with your bank at home and telex your family, friend or bank manager to deposit the money in your name at the bank of your choice. Check with the bank to ensure that you can receive your money in the currency of your choice (US dollars). Only some banks will provide this service (at a small commission). Again, the Banco de Crédito is recommended. It is generally easier to receive dollar transfers in Ecuador, Chile, and Bolivia, so if you plan to travel to these countries, you might wait to have your money sent there.

If you change more money than necessary, you can buy back dollars at a slight loss when leaving the country. The loss depends on fluctuations of the dollar; it's usually a few per cent. Moneychangers work the main land borders whenever they are open, and the airport in Lima has a Banco de la Nación open during all international departures. Try not to end up with too much excess cash, as Peruvian currency is occasionally frozen, in which case the banks won't buy back intis.

This happens for a few days every couple of years.

COSTS

Costs in Peru are low, except in the main tourist towns (Lima and Cuzco) where they are higher though still moderate by Western standards. If you're on a very tight budget, you can get by on the classic bare bones budget of $5 per day, but that means staying in the most basic of hotels and travelling very slowly. Most budget travellers spend closer to an average of $10 per day mainly because of the large distances that have to be covered to properly visit Peru.

If you can afford to spend a little more, however, you'll probably enjoy yourself more too. The luxury of a simple room with a private hot shower and a table and chair to write letters home can be had for as little as $2 or $3 per person if you know where to go – this book will show you where. Saving time and energy by flying back from a remote destination which took you several days of land travel to reach is also recommended if you can afford to spend a bit more.

Travelling hard, eating well, staying in rooms with a private bath, taking an occasional flight, seeing a movie once in a while and drinking a couple of beers with dinner most nights may sound expensive, perhaps even decadent, to the 'purist' budget traveller. I did that for several months whilst researching this book and averaged $17 a day. Even if you demand the best available, in most parts of Peru it will cost much less than wherever home may be.

I sometimes meet travellers who spend most of their time worrying how to make every penny stretch further. It seems to me that they spend more time looking at their finances than looking at the places they're visiting. Of course, many travellers are on a grand tour of South America and want to make their money last, but you can get so burned out on squalid hotels and bad food that the grand tour becomes an endurance test. Travelling comfortably and enjoyably for 6 months can be more rewarding than a full year of strain and sacrifice.

Due to violent swings in the exchange rate, costs in both dollars and intis can change rapidly. Although dollar costs tend to stay comparatively stable, you can still experience a noticeable change in prices within a month. With annual inflation running at several hundred per cent (a recent report claims 2000%!) you may find that prices can triple (even in dollar terms) within a couple of months. By the same token, prices can fall equally rapidly. Bear this in mind when reading prices in these pages – they are a guideline only.

TIPPING

The cheapest restaurants do not include a tip in the bill. If you want to tip waiters, make sure you give it directly to them and don't leave it lying on the table. Tipping is not expected in very basic restaurants. In better restaurants, tip the waiter up to 15%. In many better restaurants a 10% service charge is included, but you can give the waiter an extra 5% if the service is good.

Taxi drivers are not tipped – bargain a fare beforehand and stick to it. Tip bell hops or porters about 50c per bag in the better establishments. If hiring a local guide, tip them about $3 per client for each full day's work if they are good, professional, multilingual guides – less if they aren't. If there's a group of you, tip about $1 per client per day. These are minimal recommendations; you can, of course, tip more.

TOURIST INFORMATION

The government tourist information agency, La Dirección General de Turismo, has offices in the major cities of Lima, Arequipa, Ayacucho, Cajamarca, Cuzco, Chiclayo, Huánuco, Huancayo, Huaraz, Ica, Iquitos, Piura, Pucallpa, Puno, Tacna, Tarma, Tarapoto, Trujillo and Tumbes. There's usually no-one who speaks English (with the notable exceptions of Lima and Cuzco), but staff are friendly and try to help. Maps are sometimes available.

GENERAL INFORMATION
Post

The Peruvian postal service is a lot cheaper than in more developed countries. Most of your letters will arrive safely but you can never be totally sure. For a few cents extra, you can send them *certificado* which is safe and gives you peace of mind. Although I haven't lost mail posting in this way, there isn't much you can do if it doesn't arrive.

Sending Mail Letters from Peru to the USA (as an example) can take from 1 to 3 weeks, depending where you mail from. Lima is by far the best place for the fastest service. Incoming mail, even to Lima, is usually slower. Ordinary mail from the USA to Cuzco can take up to a month.

The post office in each town is marked on the town maps. In some smaller towns it is often just part of a house or a corner of a municipal office. Lima has several post offices dotted around town. Opening hours

are very convenient. In many towns the post office is open from 9 am to 8 pm on weekdays, and a half day on Saturday or Sunday. In Lima the post office usually closes by 7 pm.

Mailing parcels is best done from Lima. Large parcels need to be checked by customs. You can mail parcels of up to 10 kg from the main post office in Lima. The *aduana* (customs) here is open from 9 am to 3 pm on weekdays. (Lunch is from noon to 1 pm.) At present no special forms are required – just show them the open parcel, then sew it up in a cloth sack. (Flour sacks obtainable from grocery stores work well.)

Parcels weighing more than 10 kg have to go from the special Aduana Correos, a huge concrete building on Calle Toma Valle (no number), a street which runs perpendicular to the airport entrance. Here you are shunted from desk to desk, getting various forms, filling out customs declarations, buying stamps, paying export taxes and so on. Then you have to sew everything into a cloth bag. It may be easier to send several 10 kg parcels from downtown rather than hassling with this.

Finally, small packages weighing less than 1 kg (2 kg to some destinations) can be sent in a drawstring bag (which is able to be opened) by the *paquetes pequeños* service which goes certified airmail. Regulations change from year to year. As long as you send everything by certified mail it is reasonably safe.

Receiving Mail There are several places where you can receive mail but most travellers use either the post office or American Express. Although some embassies will hold mail for you, others may refuse to do so and will return it to the sender. Ask before using your embassy. You can also have mail sent to you care of your hotel, but it's liable to get lost. The best place to receive mail is care of the South American Explorers Club, Casilla 3714, Lima 100 (for club members only). It will hold your mail for months, help you recover packages from customs if necessary

and return or forward mail according to your instructions if you leave the country.

If you have mail sent to the post office, remember that it is filed alphabetically, so if it's addressed to John Gillis Payson Esq, it could well be filed under G or E instead of the correct P. It should be addressed, for example, to John PAYSON, Lista de Correos, Correos Central, Lima, Peru. Ask your loved ones to clearly print your last name and avoid witticisms such as 'World Traveller Extraordinaire' appended to it. American Express also holds mail for clients. As an example, address mail: John PAYSON, c/o American Express, Lima Tours, Casilla 4340, Belén 1040, Lima. (Thanks to my father-in-law for allowing me to use his name.)

Telecommunications

ENTEL-Peru is the place to go for long distance national and international telephone, telex and telegram services, with the exception of Lima where the telephone company is La Compañía Peruana de Teléfonos.

ENTEL offices are marked on all street plans in this book. The bigger towns have telex and telegram services; the smaller towns have only the phone. Even the most remote villages can often communicate with a major city and so connect you into an international call. These cost about $7 for 3 minutes to the USA and about $10 to Europe. You must leave a deposit, which is often more than the call will cost. A receipt is issued and the difference is returned to you at the end. The system is slow but it works. Waiting time can sometimes be as short as 10 minutes, though it can also take an hour or more to get through. You may have to wait a further 15 minutes for your refund. Rates are cheaper on Sunday and in the evening after 9 pm.

ENTEL offices are usually open from 8 am to 10 pm but the Peruvian Telephone Company in Lima is open only until 9 pm. The best hotels can connect international calls to your room at almost any time. Collect or reverse-charge phone calls are possible to many countries which have reciprocal agreements with Peru – ask at the nearest ENTEL office. A (returnable) deposit is required for these calls.

Local calls (within the town you are in) are not as straightforward as putting a coin in a public telephone, as these are few in number, are limited to the major cities and don't operate on coins. Instead, you have to buy discs called *fiches RIN* which are available from street sellers, particularly newspaper vendors. Fiches RIN cost a few cents each. ENTEL offices usually have public phones available for local calls. If a public phone can't be found, you can often phone from a small store or restaurant and pay for the call.

Telephone directories are available at ENTEL offices and with private phones at stores and restaurants. The Yellow Pages are in Spanish.

A FAX service is now available in major Peruvian cities. It costs about $1.50 to send a page to the USA, and there is a minimal charge to receive a FAX.

Electricity

Peru uses 220 volts, 60 cycles AC, except Arequipa which is on 50 cycles.

Time

Peru is 5 hours behind Greenwich Mean Time. Although Peru is almost on the equator (from roughly 0° to 18°S) and the days are roughly of equal length year round, in the mid-1980s Peru introduced daylight-saving time to operate from December to March. When this occurred there was utter chaos in the airports with no-one knowing when the flights were taking off! Peru no longer uses daylight-saving time.

It is appropriate here to mention that punctuality is not one of the things that Latin America is famous for.

Weights & Measures

Peru uses the metric system exclusively, as I have throughout this book. A conversion table is at the back of the book.

Laundry

There are no self-service laundry machines in Peru. This means that you have to find someone to wash your clothes or else wash them yourself. Many hotels will have someone to do your laundry and this can cost very little in the cheaper places (under a dollar for a full change of clothes – much more in the expensive hotels). The main problem is that you might not see your clothes again for 2 or 3 days, particularly if it is raining and they can't be dried. There are laundromats (*lavanderías*) in the main cities but you still must leave the clothes for at least 24 hours. Most lavanderías only do dry-cleaning anyway.

If you wash clothes yourself, ask the hotel staff where to do this. Most of the cheaper hotels will show you a huge cement sink and scrubbing board which is much easier to use than a bathroom washbasin.

Often there is a well-like section full of clean water next to the scrubbing board. Don't dunk your clothes in this water to soak or rinse them as it is used as an emergency water supply in case of water failure. Use a bowl or bucket to scoop water out instead, or run water from a tap. Some towns, such as Chiclayo, suffer from water shortages and prohibit clothes washing in hotel rooms.

MEDIA
Newspapers & Magazines

Although it is a small country, there are literally dozens of newspapers available in Peru. Most towns of any size publish a local newspaper which is useful for finding out what's playing in the town cinemas and reading the local gossip, but has little national news and even less international news. The best newspapers are available in Lima, although many of these are sensationalist rags which luridly portray traffic accident victims on the front page whilst relegating world affairs to a few columns behind the sports section.

There are some good newspapers and one of the best is *El Comercio*, published in Lima. It comes in several sections and keeps up to date with cultural and artistic events in the capital as well as national and international news. A shorter version (missing the events sections) is available in other cities.

There is one English language tabloid called the *Lima Times* which is published weekly. Foreign newspapers and magazines are available at good bookshops and street stands.

The South American Explorers Club publishes a readable and recommended quarterly magazine, the *South American Explorer*, which has a host of articles about Peru and other parts of the continent.

Radio & Television

Peru has five major television channels plus cable, but the programming leaves a lot to be desired. Apart from interminable sports programmes, the choice is very bad Latin American soap operas or reruns of old and equally bad North American sit-coms. The evening news broadcasts are quite good, especially for local news. Occasionally a National Geographic special makes its way to the screen. These types of programmes are advertised for days ahead in the better newspapers.

If you carry a portable radio, there are plenty of stations with a better variety of programmes to choose from. Programmes are in Quechua and Spanish. The BBC World Service and the Voice of America can be picked up in Peru on short-wave radio.

HEALTH

It's true that most people travelling for any length of time in South America are likely to have an occasional mild stomach upset. It's also true that if you take the appropriate precautions before, during and after your trip, it's unlikely that you will become seriously ill. In a decade of travel in Latin America, I'm happy to report that I've picked up no major illnesses.

Vaccinations

Vaccinations are the most important of your predeparture health preparations. Although the Peruvian authorities do not, at present, require anyone to have an up-to-date international vaccination card to enter the country, you are strongly advised to read the following list and receive those appropriate for your trip. Pregnant women should consult their doctor before taking these vaccinations.

Yellow Fever This vaccination is very important if you are planning a trip to the eastern slopes of the Andes or the Amazon Basin, but is unnecessary if you intend to avoid the eastern lowlands. It lasts 10 years.

Typhoid Immunisation consists of two injections taken 4 weeks apart, which means some forethought is required. This vaccine makes some people feel unwell and its injection often leaves a sore arm, so try not to schedule the last shot for the day you're packing. A booster shot is recommended every 3 years, but this doesn't normally feel so bad. Capsules are also available.

Diphtheria-Tetanus Injections are administered to most people in developed countries whilst they are at school. Boosters are recommended every 10 years.

Polio Also generally administered at schools in developed countries, boosters are recommended every 10 years.

Cholera Vaccination is only necessary if an epidemic has been declared in Latin America. Protection only lasts 6 months.

Smallpox This was eradicated worldwide in 1978 and protection is no longer necessary.

Medical Treatment

If you take the precautions mentioned in the following sections you can look forward to a generally healthy trip. Should something go wrong, however, you can get good medical advice and treatment in the major cities. The best treatment is definitely in Lima and if you are seriously ill you should try to get there. Addresses of clinics and doctors are given in the sections on the main cities. Medical treatment is generally much cheaper than in more developed countries so it's usually worth going to the best available. Some doctors speak English.

Many prescription drugs are available in Peru, some of which are sold over the counter. If you need to buy any, make sure that they haven't expired and that they have been kept in a cool or refrigerated storage area.

Medical Kit

How large or small your first-aid kit should be depends on your knowledge of first-aid procedures, where and how far off the beaten track you are going, how long you will need the kit for and how many people will be sharing it. Here is a suggested checklist which should be amended as required:

Antiseptic cream
Aspirin or similar
Lomotil for diarrhoea
Antibiotics such as ampicillin and tetracycline
Throat lozenges
Ear and eye drops
Antacid tablets
Motion sickness medication
Alcohol swabs
Water purifier
Lip salve
Foot and groin powder
Thermometer in a case
Surgical tape, assorted sticky plasters (band-aids), gauze, bandages, butterfly closures
Scissors
First-aid booklet

A convenient way of carrying your first-aid kit so that it doesn't get crushed is in a small plastic container with a sealing lid, such as Tupperware.

Water Purification

If tap water is to be drunk or used to wash fruit and vegetables, purify it first. The most effective method is to boil it continuously for 20 minutes – which is no doubt inconvenient. Various water-purifying tablets are available but most of these aren't wholly effective – the hepatitis virus often survives. Also, they make the water taste strange and are not recommended for frequent and long-term use. The most effective method, and one that doesn't make the water taste as bad,

is to use iodine. You can use a few drops of prepared iodine solution but the problem is that it's difficult to know exactly how strong the solution is in the first place and how many drops to use. The following method is one that I learnt at the South American Explorers Club in Lima. It eliminates these problems and works very well.

Get hold of a small, 25 ml glass bottle and put 2 to 3 mm of iodine crystals in it. Don't use a plastic bottle as the iodine will make it brittle and cause it to crack. Both iodine crystals and suitable glass bottles can be obtained from pharmacies. When you need a purifying solution, fill the glass bottle with water and shake it well for about a minute and then let the crystals settle to the bottom. Only a minute amount of the crystals actually dissolve in the water, so you now have 25 ml of saturated (not concentrated) iodine solution which is always the same (saturated) strength. Carefully pour the saturated iodine solution into a litre of water and leave it for 15 minutes to produce clean drinking water. The advantage of this method is that only the iodine solution is used to purify your drinking water and the crystals are left at the bottom of the 25 ml bottle; they can be used and reused hundreds of times.

This is a safe and recommended method except for pregnant women and people with thyroid problems. Be sure to transfer only the saturated solution to your drinking water and not the actual crystals. Accidentally swallowing a whole iodine crystal will not do you any good at all.

Health Precautions

If you wear prescription glasses, make sure before leaving home that you have a spare pair and the prescription. The tropical sun is strong, so a prescription pair of sunglasses may be advisable. Also buy suntan lotion as the lotions available in Peru are not very effective. A minimum sunblocking factor of 15 is recommended.

Ensure that you have an adequate supply of the prescription medicines you use on a regular basis. If you haven't had a dental examination for a long time, do so to avoid risking a dental problem in Peru.

However fit and healthy you are, do take out medical insurance, preferably one with provisions for flying you home in the event of a medical emergency. Even if you don't get sick, you might be involved in an accident.

Heat & Sun The heat and humidity of the tropics make you sweat profusely and can also make you feel apathetic. It is important to maintain a high fluid intake and to ensure your food is well salted. If fluids and salts lost through perspiration are not replaced, heat exhaustion and cramps frequently result. The feeling of apathy that some people experience usually fades after a week or two.

If you're arriving in the tropics with a great desire to improve your tan, you've certainly come to the right place, but be very careful; the tropical sun will not only improve your tan, it will also burn you to a crisp. I know several travellers who have enjoyed themselves in the sun for an afternoon, then spent the next couple of days with severe sunburn. The power of the tropical sun cannot be overemphasised. Don't spoil your trip by trying to tan too quickly; use maximum protection suntan lotion (factor 15) applied frequently to all exposed skin. Peru doesn't sell strong suntan lotion, so bring it from home. Wearing a wide-brimmed sunhat is also a good idea.

Snake Bite This is extremely unlikely to occur, but should you be bitten, the snake may be nonvenomous. Expert opinions vary on the best treatment for snake bite.

To minimise your chances of being bitten, always wear boots, socks and long trousers when walking through undergrowth where snakes may be present. Don't put your hands into holes and crevices and be careful when collecting firewood.

Snake bites do not cause instantaneous death and antivenenes are usually available. Keep the victim calm and still, wrap the bitten limb tightly, as you would for a sprained ankle, then attach a splint to immobilise it. Seek medical help, if possible with the dead snake for identification. Don't attempt to catch the snake if there is even a remote possibility of being bitten again. Tourniquets and sucking out the poison are now comprehensively discredited.

Common Ailments
Hepatitis Hepatitis A is the more common form of this disease and is spread by contaminated food or water. The first symptoms are fever, chills, headache, fatigue, feelings of weakness and aches and pains. This is followed by loss of appetite, nausea, vomiting, abdominal pain, dark urine, light-coloured faeces and jaundiced skin; the whites of the eyes may also turn yellow. In some cases there may just be a feeling of being unwell or tired, accompanied by loss of appetite, aches and pains and the jaundiced effect. You should seek medical advice, but in general there is not much you can do apart from resting, drinking lots of fluid, eating lightly and avoiding fatty foods. People who have had hepatitis must forego alcohol for 6 months after the illness, as hepatitis attacks the liver and it needs that amount of time to recover.

Hepatitis B, which used to be called serum hepatitis, is spread through sexual contact or through skin penetration – it can be transmitted via dirty needles or blood transfusions, for instance. Avoid having your ears pierced, tattoos done or injections where you have doubts about the sanitary conditions. The symptoms and treatment of type B are much the same as for type A, but gamma globulin as a prophylactic is effective against type A only.

If you get hepatitis A, it's not the end of the world. If you're on a long trip, you don't have to give up and go home. Find a hotel that has a decent restaurant and get a room which isn't two flights of stairs and three hallways away from the nearest bathroom. Arrange with the hotel staff to bring you meals and drinks as you need them, and go to bed. Chances are that you'll be fit enough to travel again within a month.

Malaria This is another disease to think about before leaving. Malarial mosquitoes don't live above 2500 metres, so if you plan to stay in the highlands, don't worry about them. If you plan on visiting the jungle, purchase antimalarial pills in advance, as these have to be taken from 2 weeks before until 6 weeks after your visit. Dosage and frequency of pill taking varies from brand to brand, so check this carefully.

Chloroquine is recommended for short term protection. Long term use of Chloroquine can cause side effects and travellers planning a long trip into the Amazon Basin should discuss this risk against the value of protection with their doctor. However, chloroquine is quite safe for general use and it can be taken by pregnant women. Fansidar, once used as a chloroquine alternative, is now known to cause sometimes fatal side effects. Use of this drug should be only under medical supervision. Maloprim can have rare but serious side effects if the weekly dose is exceeded and some doctors recommend a check-up after 6-months continuous use. Doxycycline is another antimalarial for use where chloroquine resistance is reported; it causes hypersensitivity to sunlight, so sunburn can be a problem.

Thus people who spend a great deal of time in tropical lowlands may prefer not to take antimalarial pills on a semi permanent basis. In this case remember that malarial mosquitoes bite at night and you should wear long-sleeved shirts and long trousers from dusk until dawn, use frequent applications of an insect repellent and sleep under a mosquito net. Sleeping under a fan is also effective; mosquitoes don't like wind. The most effective ingredient in insect repellents is diethyl- metatoluamide, also known as 'Deet'. You should buy repellent with 90% or more of this ingredient; many brands, including those available in Peru, contain less than 15%, so buy it ahead of time. The rub-on lotions are most effective, while sprays are good for spraying clothes, especially at the neck, wrist, waist and ankle openings.

Diarrhoea The drastic change in diet experienced by travellers means that they are often susceptible to minor stomach ailments such as diarrhoea. After being in South America for a while, you tend to build up an immunity.

The main problem with diarrhoea is fluid loss leading to severe dehydration – you can actually dry out to the point of death if several days pass without adequate fluid replacement. So drink plenty of liquids. Caffeine is a diuretic, so the best drinks are weak tea, mineral water and caffeine-free soft drinks. Avoid milk. If you can, fast. By giving your body plenty of fluids and no food, you can often get rid of diarrhoea in about 24 to 36 hours. Rest as much as you can.

If necessary (before a flight or journey that can't be put off), stop the symptoms of diarrhoea by taking Lomotil or Imodium. These pills will not cure you, however, and it is likely that your diarrhoea will recur after the drug wears off. Rest, fast and drink plenty of fluids.

Dysentery If diarrhoea continues for several days and is accompanied by nausea, severe abdominal pain and fever, and if there is blood or mucus in your stool, it's likely that you have contracted dysentery. This serious illness is caused by contaminated food or water. Although many travellers suffer from an occasional bout of diarrhoea, dysentery is fortunately not very common. The two types are amoebic and bacillary. It is not always obvious which kind you have, so if you contract dysentery, seek medical advice.

Bacillary dysentery is characterised by a high fever and a rapid development of symptoms, including headache, vomiting and stomach pains. It generally does not last longer than a week, but is highly contagious.

Amoebic dysentery is more gradual in developing, has no fever or vomiting but is a more serious illness. It is not a self-limiting disease, but will persist until treated and can recur and cause long term damage.

A stool test is necessary to diagnose which kind of dysentery you have. In case of an emergency, tetracycline is the prescribed treatment for bacillary dysentery, metronidazole for amoebic dysentery.

With tetracycline, the recommended adult dosage is one 250 mg capsule four times a day. Children aged between 8 and 12 years should have half the adult dose; the dosage for younger children is a third the adult dose. It's important to remember that tetracycline should be given to young children only if it's absolutely necessary and only for a short period; pregnant women should not take it after the fourth month of pregnancy.

With metronidazole, the recommended adult dosage is one 750 mg to 800 mg capsule three times daily for 5 days. Children aged between 8 and 12 years should have half the adult dose; the dosage for younger children is a third the adult dose.

Altitude Sickness This occurs when you ascend to high altitude quickly – for example, flying from sea level into Cuzco (3326 metres). The best way to prevent altitude sickness is to spend a day or two travelling slowly to high altitudes, thus allowing your body time to adjust. Even if you don't do this, it is unlikely that you will suffer greatly in Cuzco because it is still relatively low. Problems generally begin from 3500 metres to 4500 metres, although acute mountain sickness has been fatal at altitudes of 3000 metres. A few people do become seriously ill, but most travellers experience no more than shortness of breath and headaches. If, however, you travel higher than Cuzco, you may well experience more severe symptoms, including vomiting, fatigue, insomnia, loss of appetite, a rapid pulse and irregular (Cheyne-Stokes) breathing during sleep.

The best plan upon arriving at high altitude is to take it easy for the first day and avoid smoking and alcohol. This will go a long way to helping you acclimatise. If you feel sick, the best treatment is rest, deep breathing, an adequate fluid intake and a mild pain killer such as Tylenol to alleviate headaches. If symptoms are very severe, the only effective cure is oxygen. The best way

to obtain this is to descend to a lower elevation – breathing oxygen from a cylinder provides only temporary relief, so you should descend. It's wise to always sleep at an altitude which is lower than the greatest height reached in a day.

The prescription drug Diamox has been shown to help with acclimatisation if taken the day before ascent and during the first few days at high altitude. There are some mild side effects, such as increased urination and tingling sensations in the extremities. If you are interested in trying Diamox, talk to your doctor.

Insect Problems Insect repellents go a long way in preventing bites (see Malaria section). When bitten, avoid scratching; unfortunately this is easier said than done. To alleviate itching, try Hydrocortisone cream, calamine lotion or soaking in baking soda. Scratching will quickly open bites and cause them to become infected. Skin infections are slow to heal in the tropical heat and all infected bites as well as cuts and grazes should be kept scrupulously clean, treated with antiseptic creams and covered with dressings on a daily basis.

Another insect problem is infestation by lice or crabs and scabies. Lice or crabs crawl around in your body hair and itch. To get rid of them, wash with a shampoo which contains benzene hexachloride, or shave the affected area. To avoid being reinfected, wash all your clothes and bedding in hot water mixed with shampoo. It's probably best to throw away your underwear if you had body lice or crabs. Lice thrive on body warmth; clothing which isn't worn will cause the beasties lurking within to die in about 72 hours.

Scabies are mites which burrow into your skin and cause it to become red and itchy. To kill scabies, wash yourself with a benzene benzoate solution, and wash your clothes too. Both benzene hexachloride and benzoate are obtainable from pharmacies in Peru.

Scorpions and spiders can give severely painful, but rarely fatal, stings or bites. A common way to be bitten is to put on your clothes and shoes in the morning without checking them first. Develop the habit of shaking out your clothing before putting it on, especially in the lowlands. Check your bedding before going to sleep. Don't walk barefoot and look where you place your hands when reaching to a shelf or branch.

Rabies Rabies is found in many countries and is caused by a bite or scratch from an infected animal. Dogs are a noted carrier. Any bite, scratch or even lick from a mammal should be cleaned immediately and thoroughly. Scrub with soap and running water, then clean with an alcohol solution. If there is any possibility that the animal is infected, medical help should be sought immediately. Even if the animal is not rabid, all bites should be treated seriously as they can become infected or can result in tetanus. A rabies vaccination is now available and should be considered if you are in a high-risk category – for example, if you intend to explore caves (bat bites could be dangerous) or work with animals.

DANGERS & ANNOYANCES

Peru has a reputation for thievery and, unfortunately, it is fully warranted. There's no denying that many travellers do get ripped off. On the other hand, by taking some basic precautions and exercising a reasonable amount of vigilance, you probably won't be robbed. What normally happens is that travellers are so involved in their new surroundings and experiences that they forget to stay alert and that's when something is stolen. It's good to know that armed theft is not as frequent as sneak theft and you should remember that crowded places are the haunts of pickpockets. This means badly lit bus and train stations or bustling markets.

Thieves look for easy targets. Tourists who carry a wallet or passport in a hip pocket are asking for trouble. Leave your wallet at home; it's an easy mark for a pickpocket. A small roll of bills loosely wadded under a handkerchief in your front pocket is as safe a way as any of carrying your daily spending money. The rest should be hidden. Always

use at least a closable inside pocket or preferably a body pouch, money belt or leg pouch to protect your money and passport.

You can carry the greater proportion of your money in the form of travellers' cheques. These can be refunded if lost or stolen, often within a few days. However, exchange rates for travellers' cheques can vary from 1% to 10% less than cash dollars, depending on the exchange regulations at the time you visit. Some airlines will also reissue your ticket if it is lost. You must give details such as where and when you got it, the ticket number and which flight was involved. Usually a reissuing fee (about $20) is charged, but that's much better than buying a new ticket.

Pickpockets are not the only problem. Snatch theft is also common so don't wear gold necklaces and expensive wristwatches or you're liable to have them snatched from your body. I've seen it happen to someone walking with me and by the time I realised that something had been stolen the thief was 20 metres away and jumping on to a friend's motorcycle. Snatch theft can also occur if you carry a camera loosely over your shoulder or place a bag on the ground for just a second.

Thieves often work in pairs or groups. Whilst your attention is being distracted, one thief is robbing you – whether it be a bunch of kids fighting in front of you, an old lady 'accidentally' bumping into you, someone dropping something in your path or spilling something on your clothes, the possibilities go on and on. The only thing you can do is to try, as much as possible, to avoid being in very tight crowds and to stay alert, especially when something out of the ordinary occurs.

To worry you further, there are the razor blade artists. No, they don't wave a blade in your face and demand 'Your money or your life!', as they're much too gutless for that kind of confrontation. They simply slit open your luggage with a razor blade when you're not looking. This includes a pack on your back or luggage in the rack of a bus or train, or even your trouser pocket. Many travellers carry their day packs on their chests to avoid having them slashed during day trips to markets, etc. When walking with my large pack, I move fast and avoid stopping which makes it difficult for anyone intent on cutting the bag. If I have to stop, at a street crossing for example, I tend to gently swing from side to side so I can feel if anyone is touching my pack and I look around a lot. I don't feel paranoid – walking fast and looking around on my way from bus station to hotel has become second nature to me, and I never place a bag on the ground unless I have my foot on it.

One of the best solutions to the rip-off problem is to travel with a friend and to watch one another. An extra pair of eyes makes a lot of difference. I often see shifty-looking types eyeing luggage at bus stations, but they notice if you are alert and are less likely to bother you. They'd much rather steal something from the tired and unalert traveller who has put their bag on a chair while buying a coffee, and who, 10 seconds later has their coffee, but no bag!

Definitely avoid any conversation with someone who offers you drugs. In fact, talking to any stranger on the street can hold risks. It has happened that travellers who have talked to strangers have been stopped soon after by 'plain clothes' police officers and accused of talking to a drug dealer. In such a situation, never get into a vehicle with the 'police', but insist on going to a bona fide police station on foot. Be wary of false or crooked police who prey on tourists.

It is a good idea to carry an emergency kit somewhere separate from all your other valuables. This kit could be sewn into a jacket (don't lose the jacket!) or even carried in your shoe. It should contain a photocopy of the important pages of your passport in case it's lost or stolen. On the back of the photocopy you should list important numbers such as all your travellers' cheque serial numbers, airline ticket numbers, credit card or bank account numbers, telephone numbers, etc. Also keep one high denomination bill with this emergency stash. You will probably never have to use it, but it's a good idea not to put all your eggs into one basket.

Definitely take out travellers' insurance, but don't get paranoid. Stay alert and you can spend months in Peru without anything being stolen.

Sendero Luminoso

This guerilla organisation controls and terrorises some of the remoter parts of Peru. Travel to and around most of Peru remains safe, as it has been for the 30 years the Sendero has been in existence. However, there is now evidence that the Sendero and the drug cartels are connected in their attempts to disrupt the stability of Peru and some of the drug growing regions of Peru are now dangerous to travel in.

The routes to avoid at this time are the overland bus trip from Lima to Pucallpa via Cerro de Pasco, Huánuco, and Tingo María; the Río Huallaga area north of Tingo María up to Tarapoto ; the central Andean area south of Huancayo, through Huancavelica, Ayacucho (where the Sendero movement had its foundations), to Abancay and down to Nazca; and the Cordillera Huayhuash area south of Huaraz. Although this sounds like a dismayingly long list, it actually covers a relatively small proportion of central Peru.

On a recent extensive trip to Peru I visited the entire coast; the south of the country (Cuzco, Lake Titicaca and Arequipa); Huaraz and the Cordillera Blanca; the jungle around Puerto Maldonado and Iquitos; and the highlands around Cajamarca. I had no problems with visiting these areas. You should check with the local tourist authorities for updates about the Sendero situation when you arrive. The Sendero's influence seems to ebb and flow. In the early 1980s the Ayacucho area was a definite no-go zone. During my 1986 visit I felt comfortable in all the danger regions mentioned earlier, including overland travel to Ayacucho. Now things are a bit more restrictive, but who knows for how long?

FILM & PHOTOGRAPHY

Definitely bring everything you'll need. Camera gear is very expensive in Peru and the choice of film is limited. Some good films are unavailable, such as Kodachrome slide film. Others are kept in hot storage cabinets and are sometimes sold outdated, so if you do buy film in Peru, check its expiry date.

Don't have film developed in Peru if you can help it, as processing is often shoddy. Likewise, carrying around exposed film for months is also asking for washed-out results. It is best to send film home as soon after it's exposed as possible. The mail service isn't totally reliable, so try to send film home with a friend.

I always buy either process-paid film or prepaid film mailers so I can place the exposed film in the mailer and not worry about the costs. The last thing you want on your return from a long trip is to worry about how you're going to find the money to develop a few dozen rolls of film.

Tropical shadows are very strong and come out almost black on photographs. Often a bright but hazy day gives better photographs than a very sunny one. Taking photographs in open shade or using fill-in flash will help. The best time for shooting is when the sun is low – the first and last 2 hours of the day. If you are heading into the Amazon lowlands you will need high-speed film, flash, a tripod or a combination of these to take photographs in the jungle. The amount of light penetrating the layers of vegetation is surprisingly low.

The Peruvian people are highly photogenic – from a charmingly grubby Indian child to the handsomely uniformed presidential guard – the possibilities for people pictures are endless. However, most people resent having a camera thrust in their faces and people in markets will often proudly turn their backs on pushy photographers. Ask for permission with a smile or a joke and if this is refused don't become offended. Some people believe that bad luck can be brought upon them by the 'evil eye' of the camera. Others are just fed up at seeing their pictures used in books, magazines and postcards and realising that somebody is making money at their expense. Sometimes a tip is asked for. This is especially true in the highly visited Cuzco area. Here, many locals will dress up in their traditional finery and pose against Andean backdrops. Some even bring their llamas into Cuzco's main square. These people consider themselves to be posing for a living and become angry if you try to take their picture without giving them a few cents. Be aware of people's feelings – it is not worth upsetting someone to get your photograph.

ACCOMMODATION

There is a lot of variety and no shortage of places to stay in Peru. These come under various names such as *pensión, residencial, hospedaje* and *hostal* as well as simply hotel, but there is no rule which tells you that one type is better or worse than the others. It is almost unheard of to arrive in a town and not be able to find somewhere to sleep, but during major fiestas or the high tourist season, accommodation can be tight. This is especially true around Christmas and New Year, and for several days around the Fiestas Patrias (Peru's Independence) on 28 July. Plan ahead for both accommodation and public transport at this time.

For this reason, as many hotels as possible are marked on the town maps. The fact that a hotel is marked on a map does not necessarily imply that it is recommended, particularly the cheapest and very basic accommodation described. See the Places to Stay sections for descriptions of the hotels. If you are going to a town specifically for a market or fiesta, try to arrive a day or so early if possible.

Sometimes it's a little difficult to find single rooms and you may get a room with two or even three beds. In most cases, though, you are charged for one bed and don't have to share, unless the hotel is full. Ensure in advance that you won't be asked to pay for all the beds or share with a stranger if you don't want to. This is no problem 90% of the time.

If you are travelling as a couple or in a group, don't assume that a room with two or three beds will be cheaper per person than a room with one bed. Sometimes it is and sometimes it isn't. If I give a price per person, a double or triple room will usually cost two or three times a single. If more than one price is given, this indicates that double and triples are cheaper per person than singles. Travellers on a tight budget should know that rooms with four or more beds are available in many cheap hotels and these work out cheaper per person if you're travelling in a group. I don't give these prices in my descriptions because of space considerations. Couples sharing one bed (*cama matrimonial*) are usually, though not always, charged a little less than a double room with people in separate beds. I have used US dollars when quoting prices because inflation would make figures in Peruvian currency obsolete.

Remember to look around a hotel if possible. The same prices are often charged for rooms of widely differing quality, even in the dollar-a-night cheapies. If you are shown into a horrible airless box with just a bed and a bare light bulb, you can ask to see a better room without giving offence simply by asking if they have a room with a window, or explaining that you have to write some letters home and is there a room with a table and chair. You'll often be amazed at the results. Never rent a room without looking at it first. In most hotels, even the cheapest, they'll be happy to let you see the room. If they aren't, then it usually means that the room is filthy. Also ask to see the bathroom and make sure that the toilet flushes and the water runs. If the shower looks and smells as if someone threw up in it, the staff obviously doesn't do a very good job of looking after the place. There's probably a better hotel at the same price a few blocks away.

Bathroom facilities are rarely what you may be used to at home. The cheapest hotels don't always have hot water. Even if they do, it might not work or might be turned on only at certain hours of the day. Ask about this if you're planning on a hot shower before going out to dinner – often there's only hot water in the morning. Another intriguing device you should know about is the electric shower. This consists of a cold water showerhead hooked up to an electric heating

element which is switched on when you want a hot (more likely tepid) shower. Don't touch anything metal whilst you're in the shower or you may discover what an electric shock feels like. The power is never high enough to actually throw you across the room, but it's unpleasant nevertheless. I managed to shock myself by simply picking up the soap which I had balanced on a horizontal water pipe (there wasn't a soap dish). Some hotels charge extra for hot showers and others simply don't have any showers at all. You can always use the public hot baths which are available in most towns.

As you have probably gathered by now, Peruvian plumbing leaves something to be desired. Flushing a toilet creates another hazard – overflow. Putting toilet paper into the bowl clogs up the system and so a waste receptacle is often provided for the paper. This may not seem particularly sanitary, but it is much better than clogged bowls and water on the floor. A well-run hotel, even if it is cheap, will ensure that the receptacle is emptied and the toilet cleaned every day.

Most hotels will provide a key to lock your room and theft is not very frequent. Nevertheless, carrying your own padlock is a good idea if you plan on staying in the cheapest hotels. Once in a while you'll find that a room doesn't look very secure – perhaps there's a window that doesn't close or the wall doesn't come to the ceiling and can be climbed over. In such cases it's worth looking for another room – assuming you're not in some tiny jungle town where there's nothing else. This is another good reason to look at a room before you rent it. You should never leave valuables lying around the room. It's too tempting for a maid who earns $2 a day.

Money and your passport should be in a secure body pouch while other valuables can usually be kept in the hotel strongbox. (Some cheaper hotels might not want to take this responsibility.) Alternatively, pack valuables out of sight at the bottom of a locked bag or closed pack. Don't become paranoid though. In several years of travelling in Peru, only once did I have something taken from my hotel room – and it was partly my fault. I left my camera on the bed instead of at the bottom of a closed pack and it was gone when I got back. I rarely hear of people who have been ripped off from their hotel rooms, particularly if they take basic precautions.

If you're really travelling off the beaten track, you may end up in a village that doesn't even have a basic pensión. You can usually find somewhere to sleep by asking around, but it might be just a roof over your head rather than a bed, so carry a sleeping bag or at least a blanket. The place to ask at first is probably a village store – the store owner usually knows everyone in the village and will know who is in the habit of renting rooms or floor space. If that fails, you may be offered floor space by the mayor (*alcalde*) or at the *policía* and allowed to sleep on the floor of the school house, the jail or the village community centre. This may turn out to be dangerous because the Sendero Luminoso guerillas tend to choose mayoral offices, police outposts, etc for their attacks. A tourist sleeping on the floor of a town hall in a small village was recently shot and killed by the Sendero – the exact story will never be known, but it is likely that the guerillas thought that the tourist had some political affiliations. It is recommended that travel to regions controlled by the Sendero be avoided (see Dangers & Annoyances section).

Bottom end hotels are the cheapest, but not necessarily the worst. Although these are usually quite basic, with just a bed and four walls, they can nevertheless be well looked after, very clean and good value for money. They are often good places to meet other travellers, both Peruvian and foreign. Prices in this section range from just under $1 to about $2 or $3 per person. Hotels are usually arranged in roughly ascending order of price.

Often I include some hotels for the sake of completeness, but a listing does not imply a recommendation – if a hotel has something more than a roof and a bed to recommend it, this is mentioned in the brief descriptions. Every town has hotels in the bottom end price range and in smaller towns that's all there is. Although you'll usually have to use communal bathrooms in the cheapest hotels, rooms with a private bathroom can sometimes be found for under $2 per person.

Youth hostels as we know them in other parts of the world are not common in Peru. The cheaper hotels make up for this deficiency. There are rarely camp sites in the towns; again, the constant availability of cheap hotels make town camp sites redundant for travellers on a budget.

Hotels in the middle price range usually cost from about $2.50 to $8 per person, and are also arranged in ascending order of price. They are not always better than the best hotels in the bottom group. However, you can find some very good bargains here. My wife and I stayed in some really pleasant places in this range. For example, a carpeted room with a beautiful mountain view, large and comfortable bed, writing desk and a clean private bathroom with heaps of hot water cost a princely $6 for the two of us. Even if you're travelling on a budget, there are always special occasions (your birthday?) when you can indulge in comparative luxury for a day or two.

Top end hotels are still very cheap by Western standards. This section is not always found in smaller cities. The government-run Hotel de Turistas is often the best place in many towns. Sometimes these can be pricey, but usually you'll find them within the middle price range. If you want reasonable comfort and would like to plan your trip before you leave Lima, you can stay in the Hotel de Turistas in most towns and make reservations for your entire itinerary at the ENTURPeru office (tel 721928, telex 20393) at Avenida Javier Prado Oeste 1358, San Isidro, Lima. The only drawback is the lack of flexibility in your itinerary.

Luxury hotels which cost from $25 to $50 per person are found only in a few of the major cities.

FOOD

If you're on a tight budget, food is undoubtedly the most important part of your trip expenses. You can stay in rock bottom hotels, travel 2nd class and never consider buying a souvenir, but you've got to eat well. This doesn't mean expensively, but it does mean that you want to avoid spending half your trip sitting on the toilet.

The worst culprits for causing illness are salads and unpeeled fruit. Stick to fruit which can be peeled such as bananas, oranges and pineapples. With unpeeled fruit or salads, wash the ingredients yourself in purified water. It can be a lot of fun getting a group together and heading out to the market to buy salad vegies and preparing a huge salad. You can often persuade someone in the hotel to lend you a suitable bowl, or you could buy a large plastic bowl quite inexpensively and sell or give it away later.

As long as you take heed of the salad warning, you'll find plenty of good things to eat at reasonable prices. You certainly don't have to eat at a fancy restaurant – its kitchen facilities may not be as clean as its white tablecloths. A good sign for any restaurant is whether the locals eat there – restaurants aren't empty if the food is delicious and healthy.

If you're on a tight budget you can eat from street and market stalls if the food looks hot and freshly cooked, though watch to see if your plate is going to be dunked in a bowl of cold greasy water and wiped with a filthy rag – it's worth carrying your own bowl and spoon.

Also worth remembering (if you're trying to stretch your money) is that chifas (Chinese restaurants) can offer good value. The key word here is *tallarines*, which are noodles. Most chifas will offer a tallarines dish with chopped chicken, beef, pork or shrimp for well under a dollar. Other dishes are also good but not quite as cheap. Many restaurants offer an inexpensive set meal of the day (especially at lunch time) which is usually soup and a second course. This is called simply *el menú*.

Some native fruits and vegetables

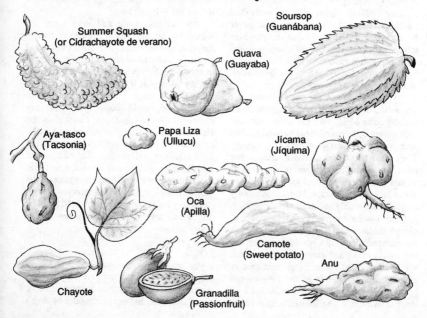

Summer Squash
(or Cidrachayote de verano)

Guava
(Guayaba)

Soursop
(Guanábana)

Aya-tasco
(Tacsonia)

Papa Liza
(Ullucu)

Jícama
(Jíquima)

Oca
(Apilla)

Camote
(Sweet potato)

Anu

Chayote

Granadilla
(Passionfruit)

Typical Peruvian dishes are tasty, varied and regional. This stands to reason – seafood is best on the coast whilst the Inca delicacy, roast guinea pig, can still be sampled in the highlands. A description of each region's dishes is given in the Places to Eat sections of the major cities. Spicy foods are often described by the term *a la criolla*. Here is a brief overview of some of Peru's most typical dishes:

Lomo Saltado – chopped steak fried with onions, tomatoes and potatoes, served with rice; a standard dish served everywhere, especially at long distance bus meal stops.

Cebiche de Corvina – white sea bass marinated in lemon, chilli and onions and served cold with a boiled potato or yam. It's delicious. If any one dish is to be singled out as most typical of Peru, it is this.

Cebiche de Camarones – the same thing made with shrimps. These dishes are appetisers rather than full meals.

Sopa a la Criolla – a lightly spiced noodle soup with beef, egg, milk and vegetables. It's hearty and filling.

Palta a la Jardinera – avocado stuffed with cold vegetable salad.

Palta a la Reyna – avocado stuffed with chicken salad. This is one of my favourite appetisers and it can make a light meal.

Most foodstuffs available at home are available in one form or another in Peru. The following basic glossary will help in translating Peruvian menus:

almuerzo	lunch
arroz	rice
azúcar	sugar
cabro, cabrito	goat
calamares	squid
camarones	shrimp
cangrejo	crab
carne	meat
cena	supper
cerdo, chancho	pork
cordero	mutton
choclo	corn on the cob
churrasco	steak
desayuno	breakfast
empanadas	meat/cheese pastries
ensalada	salad
estofado	stew
frutas	fruit
helado	ice cream
huevos fritos	eggs fried
huevos revueltos	eggs scrambled
langosta	lobster
lomo	beef
mantequilla	butter
mariscos	seafood
pan	bread
papas fritas	french fried potatoes
pescado	fish
pollo	chicken
postre	dessert
queso	cheese
sopa, chupe	soup
torta	cake
tortilla	omelet
trucha	trout
verduras	vegetables

DRINKS
Tea & Coffee

Tea (*té*) is served black with lemon and sugar. If you ask for tea with milk, British style, you'll get a cup of hot milk with a tea bag to dunk in it. Hot chocolate is also popular.

Coffee is available almost everywhere but is often disappointing. A favourite way of making coffee is to boil it for hours until only a thick syrup remains. This is then poured into cruets and diluted with milk or water. It doesn't taste that great and it looks very much like soy sauce, so always check before pouring it into your milk (or over your rice)! Instant coffee is also served. Espresso and cappuccino is sometimes available but only in the bigger towns. *Café con leche* is milk with coffee, and *café con agua* or *café negro* is black coffee.

Water

I don't recommend drinking tap water anywhere in Latin America. *Agua potable* means that the water comes from the tap but it's not necessarily healthy. Even if it comes from a chlorination or filtration plant, the plumbing is often old, cracked and full of crud. (Salads washed in this water aren't necessarily clean.) One possibility is to carry a water bottle and purify your own water (see the Health section). If you don't want to go through the hassle of constantly purifying water, bottled mineral water (agua mineral) is very cheap. Unfortunately, it's always of the fizzy variety – if you prefer the nonfizzy water you'll have difficulty finding it.

The advantage of buying a bottled drink in a store is that it is usually cheaper than in a restaurant; the disadvantage is that you have to drink it at the store because the bottle is usually worth more than the drink inside. (Canned drinks cost up to three times more than bottles.) You can pay a deposit, but you have to return it to the store you bought the bottle from; a different store won't pay for it. Many travellers pay a deposit on (effectively buy) a bottle of soft drink, beer or mineral water and then trade it in every time they want to buy a drink in a different place.

Soft Drinks

Many of the usual soft drinks are available, as are some local ones with such tongue twisting names as Socosani or the ubiquitous Inca Cola which is appropriately gold coloured and tastes like fizzy bubble gum. Soft drinks are collectively known as *gaseosas* and the local brands are very sweet. You can also buy Coca-Cola, Pepsi Cola, Fanta or orange crush (called *croosh*) and Sprite – the latter pronounced 'essprite'. Ask for your drink *helada* if you want it out of the refrigerator, *al clima* if you don't. Remember to say *sin hielo* (without ice) unless you really trust the water supply. Diet soft drinks have just become available in Lima, although the concept of Third World countries paying for a drink with no calories is a little absurd.

Fruit Juice

Juices (*jugos*) are available everywhere and are usually better than gaseosas to my taste, but cost more. Make sure you get jugo *puro*

and not con agua. The most common kinds are:

blackberry	*mora*
grapefruit	*toronja*
orange	*naranja*
passionfruit	*maracuya*
pawpaw	*papaya*
pineapple	*piña*
watermelon	*sandía*
local fruit (tasting like bitter orange)	*naranjilla*

Alcohol

Finally we come to those beverages which can loosely be labelled 'libations'. The selection of beers is limited to about a dozen types, but these are quite palatable and inexpensive. Beer comes in either large 660 ml or small 330 ml bottles. A large bottle costs as little as 60c in the cheaper bars but fancy restaurants often charge about $1 for a small bottle. Light lager-type beers and sweet dark beers are available.

On the coast there is Pilsen, which is made either in Callao or Trujillo. Experts claim that Pilsen Trujillo is better made than Pilsen Callao but they taste quite similar and are the strongest of the coastal beers. Slightly lighter and less strong is Crystal. Other light coastal beers are Garza Real and Dellmen, neither of which are remarkable. Dark beer is known as Malta or Cerveza Negra.

Two highland towns are known for their beer – Cuzco and Arequipa which make Cuzqueña and Arequipeña respectively. Both are available in lager and dark. Cuzqueña is Peru's best beer, according to many drinkers. Arequipeña tastes slightly sweet. In the jungle there is San Juan which is brewed in Pucallpa and advertises itself as 'the only beer brewed in the Amazon'. It's not a bad light beer. Imported beers are usually very expensive with the exception of the light Paceña from La Paz which is occasionally available.

Peru has a thriving wine industry and produces acceptable wines, though not as good as Chilean or Argentine varieties. The best wines are from the Tacama and Ocucaje wineries and begin at about $3 a bottle (more in restaurants). The usual selection of reds, whites and rosés is available – I'm afraid I'm not a connoisseur, so experts will have to experiment themselves.

Spirits are expensive if imported and not very good if made locally, though there are some notable exceptions. Rum is cheap and quite good; a white grape brandy called *pisco* (the national drink) is usually served as a pisco sour – a tasty cocktail made from pisco, egg white, lemon juice, sugar, syrup, crushed ice and bitters; *guinda* is a sweet cherry brandy and the local firewater, *aguardiente* or sugar cane alcohol, is an acquired taste and very cheap.

BOOKS & BOOKSHOPS

There are several good bookshops in Lima which sell books in English. The best place for guidebooks is the South American Explorers Club at Avenida Republica de Portugal 146. Other shops are listed in the Lima section.

Outside of Lima, the choice is more limited. Books in English are not so easily available, except in Cuzco and Arequipa, but most of the larger cities have magazines such as *Time* and *Newsweek*.

Before leaving home, you can mail order books and maps about Peru (and South America) from the South American Explorers Club's US office (tel (303) 320 0388), 1510 York St, Denver, CO 80206, USA. It has a free catalogue, a wide selection and a discount for club members. In Europe, maps and books can be obtained from Bradt Publications (tel 02407 3478), 41 Nortoft Rd, Chalfont St Peter, Bucks SL9 0LA, UK. It also has a catalogue.

Archaeology & History

One book stands out as the most readable account of the pre-Inca history of Peru. *The Ancient Civilisations of Peru* by J Alden Mason was published by Plata in 1975, although the 1st edition dates back to 1957 and is hence a little out of date. Despite this, I haven't seen a better book for the nonspecialist about pre-Inca Peru. More scholarly and up to date is *Peruvian Prehistory*, edited by Richard Keatinge (Cambridge University Press, 1988). It's a collection of essays reviewing Peruvian archaeology.

Two other books are recommended to the serious student of Peruvian archaeology. Both are scholarly works by professional archaeologists specialising in Peru and both have detailed references. *The Peoples & Cultures of Ancient Peru* by Luis G Lumbreras, translated by Betty J Meggers (Smithsonian Institution Press, Washington DC, 1974) and *Everyday Life of the Incas* by Ann Kendall (Batsford, London & Putnam's, New York, 1973).

A host of books deal with the Incas. Going back to the arrival of the Spanish conquistadors, the best book is undoubtedly John Hemming's excellent *The Conquest of the Incas* (Harcourt, Brace, Jovanovich, 1970), available as a Penguin paperback. I must confess to not being particularly interested in history (I came to South America originally to climb mountains and look at wildlife), but Hemming's lucid and well-written account kept me fascinated. If you read only one book on the Incas, make this it. Also there is Hemming's *Monuments of the Incas*, magnificently illustrated with Edward Ranney's B&W photographs of the major Inca ruins.

Another good choice is *The Royal Commentary of the Incas* written in the early 1600s by Garcilazo de la Vega. This historian was born in Cuzco in 1539 of an Inca princess and a Spanish soldier. His book is the most widely translated, easily available and readable of the contemporary accounts of Inca life.

Several books by Victor W von Hagen cover Inca history. Although a little outdated, they aren't bad. *Realm of the Incas* (New York, 1957) is a simple general account and *Highway of the Sun – A Search for the Royal Roads of the Incas* (1955, republished by Plata in 1975), is an account of a 1953 expedition to trace as many of the Inca's roads as possible. Another rather interesting account of archaeological exploration is Gene Savoy's *Antisuyo* (published as *Vilcabamba* in Britain) – but professional archaeologists claim that his work is sensationalist; makes a good read, though.

The mysterious topic of the Nazca Lines has generated several books, including Erich von Daniken's *Chariots of the Gods* in which he claims that the lines and other archaeological sites were built by or for prehistoric space travellers. More sober ideas come from María Reiche in *Mystery on the Desert* (Lima, 1949) and Tony Morrison's *Pathways to the Gods* (Michael Russell, UK, 1978). A theory that the Nazca people used hot-air balloons is described by Jim Woodman in *Nazca, the Flight of Condor 1* (Murray, 1980). *The Nazca Lines* by Johan Reinhard, (Editorial Los Pinos, Lima, 4th Ed 1988), presents a different perspective of the lines from a mountain worship point of view.

Natural History

There are no comprehensive guides to the flora and fauna of Peru. Bird-watchers are best served by various helpful books.

An Annotated Checklist of Peruvian Birds by Parker III, Parker and Plenge, (Buteo Books, 1982) is a checklist plus information on bird-watching in Peru.

For field guides try *The Birds of the Department of Lima, Peru* by Maria Koepcke, translated by Erma J Fiske (Harrowood Books, 2nd Ed 1983). The Department of Lima stretches for 350 km along the Peruvian desert coast and up into the Andes for 100 km, encompassing within this boundary a large area of Andean altiplano. Therefore, although the book covers only a relatively small area of Peru, it is very useful for bird-watching along most of the desert coast and the western and central parts of the Andean highlands.

For the eastern slopes of the Andes and the Amazonian lowlands the best book is the beautifully illustrated *A Guide to the Birds of Colombia* by S L Hilty & W L Brown, (Princeton University Press, 1986). Also useful is *A Guide to the Birds of Venezuela* by R M de Schauensee & W H Phelps Junior, (Princeton University Press, 1978). Both books are illustrated with comprehensive colour plates by Guy Tudor. Because Colombia has a land border with Peru, and Venezuela is only 600 km away from Peru, many of the rainforest species are the same.

Also useful is *South American Land Birds – A Photographic Aid to Identification* (Harrowood Books, 1982). This has colour photographs of about 40% of South America's birds, but there are no water birds. All of the continent's birds are described in *A Guide to the Birds of South America* by R M de Schauensee, (Livingston, Pennsylvania, 1970) but only some of the birds are illustrated. More detailed is *The Birds of South America* by R S Ridgely & G Tudor. This is a new multivolume book for the specialist and is expensive. The first volume, *The Oscine Passerines* (University of Texas Press, 1989), costs about $70 and covers in detail more than 700 species of the continent's song birds. Future volumes are planned.

Other books can be expected in the future. Barry Walker is working on a book on the birds of Machu Picchu National Park and some Danish ornithologists are working on a Peruvian birds guidebook.

Guidebooks on different aspects of Peruvian wildlife are not available. There are, however, several excellent books on South American natural history which contain some information on Peru. My favourite is Michael Andrews' *Flight of the Condor*, but Tony Morrison's *Land Above the Clouds* and

Andean goose

The Andes are also very good. *The Living Planet* by David Attenborough includes sections on the Amazon Basin and the Andes of Peru. There are also several books from National Geographic which are good.

Travel Guides

Apart from months of legwork, I used a great many books in compiling the information in this guidebook. Most of these are listed here. The books about Peru are often excellent but limited to either tourist highlights or to a specialised area. There are also some good books on South America in general which have chapters on Peru. These are mainly recommended for the traveller who wants one book for their grand tour of Latin America.

For the budget traveller, Lonely Planet's *South America on a Shoestring* (Hawthorn, 4th Ed 1990) is recommended for its many maps and money-saving information. It covers all the countries in South America, but not Central America.

A broader approach is available in *The South American Handbook*, published annually by Trade & Travel Publications, Bath, UK. It has been referred to as the South American Bible by some travellers, and it weighs about as much as one and is quite pricey. Its main drawbacks are some overdue updates and a lack of good city maps. It is suitable for everyone from budget travellers spending a year in Latin America to businesspeople on expense accounts visiting the major capitals, so there is a lot of extraneous information for most readers. Nevertheless, it is the best general book on the continent.

Another book which I enjoyed and thoroughly recommend is Lynn Meisch's *A Traveler's Guide to El Dorado & the Inca Empire* published by Penguin. Meisch is a weavings expert and has travelled professionally in Latin America to collect and document many of the traditional techniques. Her book is full of fascinating details on the crafts, cultures, markets, fiestas and archaeology of Colombia, Ecuador, Peru and Bolivia and has good background infor-

mation for the traveller. However, it doesn't set out to help with specific information on hotels, restaurants or transport.

A general guidebook is *The Real Guide to Peru* by Dilwyn Jenkins (Prentice Hall, 1989). Although its maps and hard travel information are not very detailed, it has some interesting background on Peru. Also noteworthy is *Peru – A Budget Travellers Guide* by John Forrest, Top Flat, 64 Belsize Park, London NW3 4EH. This slim (76-page) volume is updated more frequently than most guidebooks and though it's too small to be comprehensive, it provides recent information.

The Sierra Club's *Adventuring in the Andes* by Charles Frazier, 1985, also has some interesting background but lacks good maps and tries to cover too much in too few pages.

One of my favourite guidebooks covers only the Cuzco area but does that entertainingly and in some detail. *Exploring Cusco* by Peter Frost (Nuevas Imagenes, Lima, 4th Ed 1989) is highly recommended for anyone planning to spend any length of time in the Cuzco area – all the main sites are described. The book is available in Lima and Cuzco.

A detailed description of Lima, its history, museums and interesting sites is to be found in *The City of Kings – A Guide to Lima* by Carolyn Walton (Pacific Press, Lima, 1987). This book is recommended for anyone planning to explore Lima for more than a few days.

A Peruvian guide to the Huaraz area is *Callejón de Huaylas y Cordillera Blanca* by Felipe Díaz (Información Turística Kuntur, 2nd Ed 1989). This book is in Spanish (although an English edition is planned) and is a useful general guide with good background on archaeology, natural history, trekking and fiestas, among other subjects.

Various other guidebooks are available in Peru. The best is Reparaz's *Guide to Peru*, (Ediciones de Arte Rep, Lima, 5th Ed). Although it deals only with conventional tourism and limits itself to brief mentions of only a few major hotels, it does give detailed descriptions of many churches, historic buildings and museums, plus road descriptions for tourists travelling by private car. There are also various books in Spanish, again aimed at the tourist visiting the conventional sites.

Many of the other books available are of the coffee-table variety – fun to look through in the store and suitable as a souvenir or present rather than a traveller's guidebook.

There are also guides by Frommer, Waldo, Birnbaum, Fodor, etc which seem to cater to the 'today's Tuesday, so it must be Rio' crowd, and are fine if that's what you're looking for.

Hiking & Climbing

There are several books for hikers and climbers. A good all-round book is *Backpacking & Trekking in Peru & Bolivia* by Hilary Bradt (Bradt Publications, 5th Ed 1989). It has a wealth of fascinating background information as well as entertaining descriptions and maps of more than a dozen good backpacking trips in Peru and Bolivia. These include classic treks such as the Inca Trail to Machu Picchu and the Llanganuco/Santa Cruz loop in the Cordillera Blanca, as well as some little known hikes in less visited areas.

If you want information about backpacking in only the Blanca and Huayhuash ranges then the book to get (if you can find it) is Jim Bartle's *Trails of the Cordilleras Blanca & Huayhuash of Peru*. In 1989 this book was out of print but a new edition is planned for publication by Nuevas Imagenes, Lima, in the 1990s. It should be available from the South American Explorers Club (SAEC) in Lima and Denver and in the UK from Bradt Publications. This detailed book is full of maps and all the information you'll need for hiking in this most beautiful region. Jim Bartle is also an accomplished photographer and his postcards are available in Peru. He has written and illustrated a beautiful and inexpensive book of colour photographs, mainly of mountains, called *Parque Nacional Huascarán* which was published bilingually in 1985 in cooperation with the

Asociación Peruana para la Conservación de la Naturaleza.

Climbers will want to get *Yuraq Janka* by John F Ricker, published jointly in 1977 by the American Alpine Club and the Alpine Club of Canada. Although this book doesn't give detailed climbing routes, it has a wealth of background information and is the best book available for climbers wanting information about the Cordilleras Blanca and Rosko. Again, get this at the SAEC in Lima or mail order from Bradt Publications.

A new book which combines climbs and treks in the Cordilleras Blanca and Huayhuash is *The Peruvian Andes* by Ph Beaud, (Cordee, Leicester, UK & Cloudcap Press, Seattle, USA, 1988). This paperback is trilingual (French, English and Spanish) and hence lacks the detail of Bartle's trekking guide, but is very useful for climbing routes. It is expensive (about $24 in Peru for 280 pages).

Pure & Perpetual Snow by David Mazel, (FreeSolo Press, Colorado, 1987), is an account of an expedition to climb Ausangate and Alpamayo – not a guide, but presenting an idea of what climbing in Peru is like.

For travelling in the lowlands, Bradt Publications has two books called *South America: River Trips – Volumes I & II*. As their names suggest, they deal not with just Peru but with the whole continent. Volume I (1981) by George N Bradt covers a little more in Peru but lacks the excellently detailed and expert background information found in Volume II (1982) by Tanis and Martin Jordan.

Travel & Adventure

My favourite travel book about Peru is Ronald Wright's *Cut Stones & Crossroads: A Journey in the Two Worlds of Peru* (Viking Press, 1984), now available in Penguin paperback. It gives a good idea of what Peru and travelling around it are really like. Also excellent is *Journey Along the Spine of the Andes* by Christopher Portway, (Oxford Illustrated Press, 1984). This book describes the author's travels from Bolivia to Colombia and, again, is a realistic introduction to independent travel in the Andes.

Of the many good books about Amazon travel, the following two are recommended. As with the others, they don't deal with Peru alone but with the Amazon region as a whole. They are *The Rivers Amazon* by Alex Shoumatoff (Sierra Club Books, 1978) and *Passage Through El Dorado* by Jonathan Kandell (William Morrow, 1984).

The classic account of the 'discovery' of Machu Picchu in 1911 also makes a good read. Hiram Bingham's *Lost City of the Incas* has been printed several times by various publishers.

Fiction

Peru's most famous novelist is the internationally recognised Mario Vargas Llosa whose books have been translated into various languages including English. Among the best are *Aunt Julia & the Scriptwriter* and *The Green House*, both available in English translation from Avon Books.

Pablo Neruda, a Chilean poet, describes Machu Picchu as 'Mother of stone and sperm of condors' which is only one of the many powerful images he uses in his epic poem, *The Heights of Machu Picchu*. A 1966 translation by N Tarn is available from Farrar, Straus, & Giroux, New York.

MAPS

Bookshops have a limited selection of Peruvian maps. The best to choose from is the Instituto Geográfico Nacional at Avenida Aramburu 1190. Few city maps are published, and except for perhaps a detailed map of the whole of Lima, the city maps in this book are generally the best available. The SAEC has a good selection of hiking maps and a general country map.

THINGS TO BUY

Souvenirs are good, varied and cheap. Although going to villages and markets is fun, you won't necessarily save a great deal of money – similar items for sale in shops are often not much more expensive. In markets and smaller stores, bargaining is acceptable, indeed expected. In tourist stores in the major cities prices are sometimes fixed. Some of the best stores are quite expensive, but the quality of their products is often superior.

You can buy everything in Lima, be it a blow-pipe from the jungle or a woven poncho from the highlands. Although it is usually a little more expensive to buy handicrafts in Lima, the choice is varied, the quality is high and it's worth looking around some of Lima's gift shops and markets to get an idea of the items you'd like to buy. Then you might go to the areas which make the items you're interested in – but often the best pieces are in Lima.

Cuzco also has a great selection of craft shops but the quality is rarely as high as in Lima. Old and new weavings, ceramics, paintings, woollen clothing and jewellery are all found here. Cuzco has a good selection of the more traditional weavings.

The Puno/Juliaca area is good for knitted alpaca sweaters and knick-knacks made from the tortora reed which grows on Lake Titicaca. The Huancayo area is good for

carved gourds as well as for excellent weavings and clothing in the cooperative market. The Ayacucho area is famous for modern weavings and stylised ceramic churches. San Pedro de Cajas is known for its peculiar weavings which are made of rolls of yarn stuffed with wool (you'll recognise the style instantly when you see it). The Shipibo pottery sold in Yarinacocha near Pucallpa is the best of the jungle artefacts available. Superb reproductions of Moche and Mochica pottery are available in Trujillo. Shopping for these is described in more detail under the appropriate towns.

Crafts as souvenirs or gifts are relatively cheap by Western standards. A good rule of thumb is if you really like something very much, buy it (assuming you can afford it). You may not find exactly the same thing again and if you do find a better example, you can always give the first one away as a gift.

Souvenirs made from animal products are not normally allowed into most Western nations. Objects made from skins, feathers, turtle shells, etc should not be bought because their purchase contributes to the degradation of the wildlife in the rainforests.

WHAT TO BRING

As an inveterate traveller and guidebook writer, I've naturally read many guidebooks. I always find the What to Bring section depressing, as I'm always told to bring as little as possible. I look around at my huge backpack, my two beat-up duffel bags bursting at the seams, and I wonder sadly where I went wrong.

I enjoy camping and climbing, so I carry a tent, ice axe, heavy boots, etc. I'm an avid bird-watcher and I'd feel naked without my binoculars and field guides. And of course I want to photograph these mountains and birds which adds a camera, lenses, a tripod and other paraphernalia. In addition, I enjoy relaxing just as much as I enjoy mountain climbing and taking photographs of birds, so I always have at least two books to read in addition to all my indispensable guides and maps. Luckily, I'm not a music addict, so I'm able to live without a guitar, a portable tape player or a short-wave radio.

It appears that I'm not the only one afflicted with the kitchen sink disease. In Latin America alone, I've met an Australian surfer who travelled the length of the Pacific coast with his board, looking for the world's longest left-handed wave; a couple of Canadian skiers complete with those skinny boards; a Black man from Chicago who travelled with a pair of metre-high bongo drums; an Italian with a saxophone (a memorable night when those two got together); a Danish journalist with a portable typewriter; a French freak with a ghetto blaster and (by my count) 32 tapes; and an American woman with several hundred weavings which she planned to sell. All of these were budget travellers staying for at least 6 weeks and using public transport.

After confessing to the amount of stuff I travel with, I can't very well give the time honoured advice of 'travel as lightly as possible'. I suggest you bring anything that is important to you. If you're interested in photography you'll only curse every time you see a good shot (if only you'd brought your telephoto lens) and if you're a musician you won't enjoy the trip if you constantly worry about how out of practice you're getting.

There's no denying, however, that travelling light is much less of a hassle, so don't bring things you can do without. Travelling on buses and trains is bound to make you slightly grubby, so bring one change of dark clothes that don't show the dirt, rather than seven changes of nice clothes for a 6-week trip. Many people go overboard with changes of clothes, but one change to wash and the other to wear is the best idea. Bring clothes that wash and dry easily (jeans take forever to dry). Polypropylene clothing dries quickly – you can rinse out polypro underwear and it'll dry in 3 hours.

The highlands are often cold, so bring a windproof jacket and a warm layer to wear beneath, or plan on buying a thick sweater in Cuzco or one of the other Andean towns frequented by tourists. A down jacket

Top: Cathedral, Lima (TW)
Left: Guards outside the Presidential Palace, Lima (RR)
Right: Plaza Bolivar, Pueblo Libre, Lima (TW)

(bought at home) is well worth the investment if you get cold easily. A hat is indispensable; it'll keep you warm when it's cold, shade your eyes when it's sunny and keep your head dry when it rains. A great deal! A collapsible umbrella is great protection against sun and rain.

You can buy clothes of almost any size if you need them, but shoes are limited to size 43 Peruvian which is about 10½ North American. Suffice to say that I have US size 12 feet (don't laugh, they're not that big!) so I can't buy any footwear in Peru. (This is also true of most Latin countries, so bring a spare pair of shoes if you're planning a long trip.)

For light travelling, I often divide my trip into segments and take what I need for that segment and leave my other gear in storage. Most hotels will do this for you and if you're a member of the South American Explorers Club you can leave your gear in their Lima clubhouse for as long as you want. I go to Peru every year, so I have had a couple of bags of clothes and camping gear in storage more or less permanently for several years — that alone is worth the price of membership!

The following is a checklist of small, useful items that you will probably need:

Pocket torch (flashlight) with spare bulb and batteries
Travel alarm clock
Swiss Army style penknife
Sewing and repairs kit (dental floss makes excellent, strong, and colourless emergency thread)
A few metres of cord (also useful as a clothesline or for spare shoelaces)
Sunglasses
Plastic bags
Soap and dish, shampoo, toothbrush and paste, shaving gear, towel
Toilet paper (rarely found in cheaper hotels and restaurants)
Ear plugs for sleeping in noisy hotels or buses
Insect repellent
Suntan lotion
Address book
Notebook
Pens and pencils
Paperback book (easily exchanged with other travellers when you've finished)
Spanish-English dictionary
Small padlock
Large folding nylon bag to leave goods in storage
Water bottle
First-aid kit (see Health section)

Tampons are available in Peru, but only in the major cities and in regular sizes, so make sure you stock up with an adequate supply before visiting smaller towns and villages. If you use contraceptives, these are available in the major cities. The choice of contraceptives is limited, however, so if you use a preferred type you should bring it from home; they don't weigh much.

A sleeping bag is useful if you plan to travel on a budget (or for camping) because some of the cheaper hotels don't supply enough blankets and it can get cold at night. However, most hotels will give you another blanket if you ask, so a sleeping bag is useful but not indispensable if you plan to stay mainly in the major tourist areas.

You need something to carry everything around in. A backpack is recommended because it is less tiring than carrying baggage by hand and your hands are left free. On the other hand, it's often more difficult to get at things inside a pack and so some travellers prefer a duffel bag with a full-length zipper, or the traditional suitcase. Whichever you choose, ensure that it is a strong, well-made piece of luggage or you may find yourself wasting time replacing zippers, straps and buckles. If you bring a backpack, make it one with an internal frame. External frames snag on bus doors, luggage racks and airline baggage belts and are liable to be twisted, cracked or broken.

Getting There

There are four ways of getting to Peru: by air from anywhere in the world, by land from the neighbouring South American countries, by river boat up the Amazon from Brazil, and by sea.

AIR

Jorge Chávez International Airport in Lima is the main hub for flights to the Andean countries from Europe and North America and so it is easy to fly to Peru from those continents. There are also some international flights to Iquitos in Peru's Amazon region. Cuzco has international flights from Bolivia.

The ordinary tourist or economy class fare is not the most economical way to go. It is convenient, however, because it enables you to fly on the next plane out, rather than having to wait for 7 or 21 days as when you buy an advance purchase excursion (APEX) ticket. Also, an economy class ticket is valid for 12 months. If you want to economise further, there are several options.

Students with valid international student cards and those under 26 can get discounts with most airlines. Whatever age you are, if you purchase your ticket well in advance and stay a minimum length of time, you can buy an APEX ticket, which is usually about one-third cheaper than the full economy fare based on a round-trip purchase. Several restrictions normally apply. You must purchase your ticket at least 21 days (sometimes more) in advance and you must stay away a minimum period (this varies from 7 to 21 days) and return within 180 days (sometimes less, occasionally more). APEX tickets normally do not allow stopovers and there are extra charges if you change your dates of travel or destinations. Individual airlines have different restrictions and these change from time to time. A good travel agent can tell you about this. Stand-by fares are another possibility. Some airlines will let you travel at the last minute if they have available seats just before the flight. These stand-by tickets cost less than an economy fare but are not usually as cheap as APEX.

The cheapest way to go is via the so-called 'bucket shops', which are legally allowed to sell discounted tickets to help airlines and charter companies fill their flights. These tickets are usually the cheapest of all, particularly in the low seasons, but they often sell out fast and you may be limited to only a few available dates. While APEX, economy and student tickets are available direct from the airlines or from a travel agent, discount bucket-shop tickets are available only from the bucket shops themselves. Most of them are good and reputable companies, but once in a while a fly-by-night operator comes along and takes your money for a supercheap flight and gives you an invalid or unusable ticket, so check what you are buying carefully before handing over your money.

Bucket shops often advertise in newspapers and magazines; there is much competition and a variety of fares and schedules are available. Fares to South America have traditionally been relatively expensive, but bucket shops have recently been able to offer increasingly economical fares to that continent.

It is worth bearing in mind that round-trip fares are always much cheaper than two one-way tickets. They are also cheaper than an 'open jaws' fare, which enables you to fly into one city (say Lima) and leave via another (say Rio de Janeiro).

From North America

From Canada, there are flights with Canadian Pacific from Vancouver or Toronto to Lima.

From the USA, there are flights to Lima from Los Angeles, New York, and Miami. Generally speaking, the USA does not have such a strong bucket-shop tradition as Europe or Asia, so it's harder getting cheap flights from the USA to South America.

Sometimes the Sunday travel sections in the major newspapers (the *Los Angeles Times* on the west coast and the *New York Times* on the east coast) advertise cheap fares to South America, although these are sometimes no cheaper than APEX fares.

A travel agent which can find you the best deal to Peru (and anywhere else in the world) is Council Travel Services, a subsidiary of the Council on International Educational Exchange (CIEE). You can find their address and telephone numbers in the telephone directories of Berkeley, La Jolla, Long Beach, Los Angeles, San Diego and San Francisco (all in California), Amherst, Boston and Cambridge (in Massachusetts), New York City, Portland (Oregon), Providence (Rhode Island), Austin (Texas) and Seattle (Washington).

Typical APEX fares are US$480 from Miami, US$630 from New York and US$820 from Los Angeles. These fares are all round-trip fares and may include an internal flight from Lima to a city of your choice. People are often surprised that fares from Los Angeles in southern California are so much higher than from northerly New York. A glance at the world map soon shows why. New York at 74° west is almost due north of Miami at 80° and Lima at 77°. Thus planes can fly a shorter, faster and cheaper north-south route. Los Angeles, on the other hand, is 118° west and therefore much further away from Lima than New York.

It's always worth checking the Peruvian international airlines which are AeroPeru and Faucett; both fly from Miami and will often include a free round-trip domestic flight within Peru to the city of your choice if you fly from the USA with them. Both airlines sell 'Visit Peru' tickets which cost US$180 and allow unlimited in-country economy travel with their own airline. The tickets are valid for 30 days, allow only one stopover per city (except Lima), and must be purchased in the USA. If you wish to visit countries other than Peru, then consider AeroPeru's 'Visit South America' ticket which is valid for 45 days and limited to six South American destinations including Rio

de Janeiro and São Paolo (Brazil), Buenos Aires (Argentina), Santiago (Chile) and Guayaquil (Ecuador). Tickets must be bought in the USA and cost US$759 from Miami, US$999 from New York, and US$1054 from Los Angeles during the low season and US$150 more in the high season. ('High season' from North America usually means 1 July to 15 August and 15 December to 15 January, though season dates can vary between airlines.) AeroPeru has toll free numbers; throughout the USA and Canada: 1-800-255-7378 or 1-800-327-7080; in Los Angeles: 1-800-252-0458; in New York: 1-800-334-0556. Faucett, anywhere in the USA: 1-800-334-3356; in Florida 1-800-432-0468.

From Latin America
AeroPeru has offices in Buenos Aires, Argentina; La Paz, Bolivia; Rio de Janeiro and São Paolo, Brazil; Santiago, Chile; Bogotá, Colombia; Quito and Guayaquil, Ecuador; Caracas, Venezuela; Panama City, Panama; and Mexico City, Mexico. International passengers with AeroPeru can include a free round trip from Lima to a Peruvian city in the price of their international ticket. Flights from Latin American countries are usually subject to high tax and bucket-shop deals are not often available.

From Europe
Bucket shops generally provide the cheapest fares from Europe to South America. Fares from London are often cheaper than from other European cities; many Scandinavian budget travellers buy tickets from London bucket shops as cheap fares are difficult to find in their own countries.

In London competition is fierce. Bucket shops advertise in the classifieds of newspapers ranging from the *Times* to *Time Out*. I have heard consistently good reports about Journey Latin America (JLA) (tel 01 747 310816) Devonshire Rd, Chiswick, London W4 2HD, who specialise in cheap fares to the entire continent as well as arranging itineraries for both independent and escorted travel. They will make arrangements for you over the phone. Another reputable budget travel agency is Trailfinders (tel 01 938 3366) 42-48 Earl's Court Rd, London W8 6EJ. The useful travel newspaper *Trailfinder* is available from them for free. Typical round-trip fares from London are around UK£500.

From Australia

There is no real choice of routes between Australia and South America and there are certainly no bargain fares available. The most direct route is to fly from Australia to Tahiti with UTA or Qantas and connect from there with the weekly LAN-Chile flight to Santiago. From Chile you can then fly or travel overland to Peru.

Qantas has once-weekly Melbourne-Sydney-Tahiti flights. UTA fly once-weekly Sydney-Tahiti. Both connect with the LAN-Chile flight to Santiago with the option of a stopover on Easter Island.

Economy class fares from Sydney are A$2019 (one-way) and A$2572 (return); from Melbourne or Brisbane, economy class is A$2089 (one-way) and A$2695 (return). There are no APEX fares on flights from Australia to South America and no seasonal variations in fares. Also, the return economy fares are valid for 6 months from the date of departure. For more information contact the LAN-Chile office on the 10th floor, American Express Tower, 388 George St, Sydney 2000.

It is also possible to fly via New Zealand to Argentina with a combination of Air New Zealand and Aerolíneas Argentinas. The flight to Buenos Aires goes via the southern Argentinian city of Río Gallegos, which is a convenient point for travelling to Chile. A return excursion fare from the east coast of Australia to Buenos Aires will cost around A$2435.

The other alternative is to fly to the US west coast and fly from there or make your way overland to Peru. The return economy fare from Australia to Los Angeles or San Francisco ranges from A$1599 (low season), A$1749 (shoulder) to A$1849 (high season); one-way fare is A$1145. The low season is

from 1 February to 31 March and the high season from 16 June to 15 July, 16-30 September and 16 December to 15 January.

By shopping around you should be able to obtain a better deal, though not on the LAN-Chile flights. Check the ads in the travel sections of the Melbourne *Age* or the *Sydney Morning Herald*. Student Travel Australia (STA) has offices in all states and is a good place to look for cheap fares. In Melbourne, Sydney and Brisbane it is also worth trying the Flight Shops.

Because of the high cost of flying to the Americas, the other option is a round-the-world ticket. Some excellent deals are available, often for less than a return ticket to South America. They are usually valid for 6 months or a year with a number of stopovers, usually five, depending on the price of the ticket.

LAND

If you live in the Americas, it is possible to travel overland. However, if you start from North or Central America, the Pan-American Highway stops in Panama and begins again in Colombia, leaving a 200 km roadless section of jungle known as the Darien Gap. This takes about a week to cross on foot and by canoe in the dry season (January to mid-April) but is much heavier going in the wet season. Most overland travellers fly around the Darien Gap.

From South America it is straightforward to travel by public bus from the neighbouring countries of Ecuador, Chile and Bolivia.

Travellers bringing their own car will have to ship the vehicle to a South American port. On arrival, you should hire an agent to help you get the vehicle out of customs - doing it yourself is usually more time consuming and costly. Spare parts are expensive in South America; bring a vehicle which is common there, such as a Volkswagen or Toyota. Avoid fancy vehicles like Land Rovers or BMW's unless you carry a lot of spares. Theft is a great problem; fit extra locks everywhere and don't have easily removable lights, hubcaps or other external accessories. Buy a carnet if you plan on crossing international borders. Unleaded gasoline is hard to find. Never leave your vehicle unlocked and unattended.

RIVER

It is possible to travel by river boat all the way from the mouth of the Amazon at Belém in Brazil to Iquitos in Peru. Normally, travellers will need to break the journey up into several stages because very few boats do the entire trip.

The easiest way is to take one boat from Belém to Manaus in central Brazil and then a second boat from Manaus to Benjamin Constant on the Brazilian side of the Peruvian-Brazilian-Colombian border. At this point you can take local motor boats across the border to the small Peruvian port of Ramón Castilla. You can also reach Ramón Castilla by local motor boat from Leticia on the Colombian side of the tri-border. From Belém to Benjamin Constant will take about 2 weeks depending on the currents and which boat you are on. From Ramón Castilla on to Iquitos takes a further 2 or 3 days. The entire trip will cost roughly US$70 or less if travelling on the lower decks. Further information about river travel in Peru is found in the Getting Around and Amazon Basin chapters.

SEA

It is possible to arrive in Lima's port of Callao by both expensive ocean liners and cheaper freight vessels. Few people arrive by sea, however, because services are infrequent and are normally more expensive and less convenient than flying.

Getting Around

Peru is a big country and so you'll need several months to visit it all overland. If your time is limited, you'll have to choose the areas which are the most important to you. Public buses are frequent and reasonably comfortable on the major routes and are the normal form of transport for everybody. Less travelled routes are served by older and less comfortable vehicles. There are two railway systems which can make an interesting change from bus travel. Those in a hurry or desiring greater comfort or privacy can hire a car with a driver which is often not much more expensive than renting a self-drive car. Air services are widespread and particularly recommended for those short on time. In the jungle regions, travel by river boat or by air is normally the only choice.

Whichever form of transport you use, remember to have your passport on your person and not packed in your luggage or left in the hotel safe. You need to show your passport to board most planes. Buses may have to go through a transit police check upon entering and leaving major towns; in the past, passports had to be shown, but this rarely occurred on my last trip. Regulations change frequently so be prepared. If your passport is in order, these procedures are no more than cursory. If you're travelling anywhere near the borders you can expect more frequent passport controls.

AIR

Even the budget traveller should consider an occasional internal flight in Peru because they are inexpensive by Western standards. This is despite the two-tier fare system, reintroduced in August 1988, where foreigners pay more than residents. (While well-heeled tourists usually don't worry about the two-tier system, many budget travellers resent having to pay much higher fares because they are not residents. Information circulates in the budget hangouts about ways of travel-ling at the lower fare, so keep your ears open.)

One-way tickets are usually half the price of a round-trip ticket and so you can travel one-way overland and save time by returning by air.

If you are arriving in Lima (or Iquitos) with one of Peru's two international airlines, Faucett or AeroPeru, remember to ask about their internal flights before making your reservation. Usually they'll include a free trip from Lima to the city of your choice, but the ticket must be bought outside of Peru. They also sometimes offer 'Visit Peru' tickets for $180 which allow you unlimited air travel within Peru. Again, the ticket must be bought outside the country and you may have to decide upon an itinerary in advance. Faucett and AeroPeru only fly to and from countries in the Americas.

Once you have arrived in Peru, you'll find the same two airlines serving most of the major towns. Sample one-way fares for foreigners from Lima are $82 to Cuzco and $90 to Tumbes, including the 9% airport tax. There used to be a 7% student discount on air fares, but recently these have not been available. Both companies normally charge the same fare so use the one whose schedule most closely matches yours. Tickets can usually be signed over from one company to another if you want to change your schedule. This involves having the ticket 'released' by one airline before the other airline will accept it. In addition to Faucett and AeroPeru, you'll find several local airlines which tend to serve the smaller jungle towns with light aircraft. The military airline, known as Grupo 8, provide flights once a week to Cuzco and some jungle towns. These flights are cheaper than the regularly scheduled flights but difficult to get on. You have to go to the airport early in the morning of the flight and get on the waiting list. Sometimes, tickets are sold in advance but not always. Flights are always full and residents are

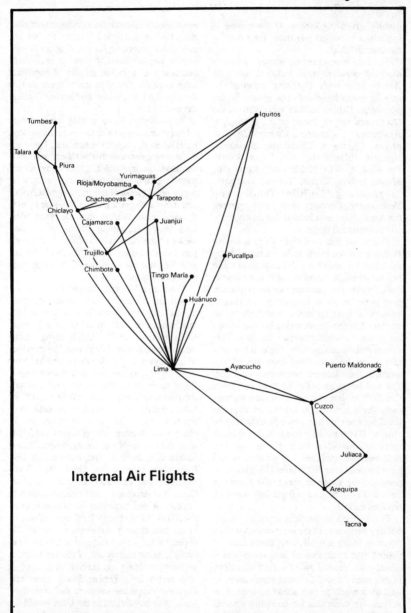

Internal Air Flights

Tumbes
Talara
Piura
Chiclayo
Rioja/Moyobamba
Chachapoyas
Cajamarca
Trujillo
Chimbote
Yurimaguas
Tarapoto
Juanjui
Iquitos
Pucallpa
Tingo María
Huánuco
Lima
Ayacucho
Puerto Maldonado
Cuzco
Juliaca
Arequipa
Tacna

usually given preference. If your time is limited, it is best to pay more for a regular commercial flight.

The following cities are served by scheduled air services with either Faucett or AeroPeru, or both. Note that some of the smaller towns have only one or two flights per week. Further details are given in the 'Air' sections of these cities: Arequipa, Ayacucho, Cajamarca, Cuzco, Chachapoyas, Chiclayo, Chimbote, Huánuco, Juanjui, Juliaca, Iquitos, Lima, Piura, Pucallpa, Puerto Maldonado, Rioja (for Moyobamba), Tacna, Talara, Tarapoto, Tingo María, Trujillo, Tumbes and Yurimaguas. Contrary to popular opinion, the Anta airport near Huaraz does not operate any commercial flights.

Flights are frequently late. Early morning flights are more likely to be on time but by the afternoon may have slid an hour or more behind schedule. AeroPeru offer more flights than Faucett and, perhaps as a consequence, tend to be late more frequently. If flying in or out of Cuzco, remember that there are no afternoon flights because weather conditions are often too windy later in the day. This means that the last morning flight, if it is very late, may be cancelled because of the weather, thus leaving passengers stranded. Try and book an early flight to and from Cuzco. You should show up at least an hour early for all domestic flights, as baggage handling and check-in procedures tend to be chaotic. It is not unknown for flights to leave up to an hour before their official departure time because predicted bad weather would have cancelled the flight later. (This has happened to me twice in about 100 flights in Peru and both times the flight left about 15 minutes early.)

Flights tend to be fully booked during holiday periods so make reservations well in advance. Make sure all reservations are confirmed and reconfirmed and reconfirmed again. As a general rule I would reconfirm flights both 72 and 24 hours in advance, as well as a week or two ahead of time. The airlines are notorious for bumping you off your flights if you don't reconfirm – I've even heard of people being bumped off after they had reconfirmed. Cuzco flights are especially notorious for booking problems. If it's impossible for you to reconfirm because you're in the middle of nowhere, have a reliable friend or travel agent do this for you. And don't show up for your flight at the last minute.

Some flights have seating assignments whilst others are on a first-come, first-seated basis when you board the airplane. There are no separate sections for smokers and nonsmokers on internal flights, nonsmokers have to suffer. Many flights have extraordinarily good views of the snowcapped Andes and it is worth getting a window seat even if the weather is bad, because the plane often rises above the clouds giving spectacular views of the mountains. When flying from Lima to Cuzco try and sit on the left-hand side for great views of the 6271-metre-high peak of Salcantay.

There is a 9% tax charged on domestic flights and a massive 31% on international tickets bought in Peru. So it is best to buy international tickets ahead of time in your home country or in neighbouring South American countries. If you want the freedom of not having to decide where or when you want to fly, remember that international flight taxes in neighbouring countries are substantially lower – 16% in Bolivia, 10% in Ecuador and only 2% in Chile. In addition to ticket taxes, a flat $15 departure tax is charged on all international flights and $7 on local flights out of Cuzco, Arequipa, Puerto Maldonado, Iquitos, and Juliaca and less from some other cities. Until 1988, local departure tax was only $2 and limited to Cuzco and Arequipa; other cities rapidly followed suit and departure taxes continue to rise. This is not strictly legal but nothing is being done about it. Residents pay about 20c departure tax – the local authorities are blatantly making money out of foreign tourists without providing any service for this.

A letter in a recent *South American Explorer* magazine suggests that travellers wishing to buy tickets to the USA would do best to buy them in Arica, Chile (where the tax is low) and fly with the special excursions offered by Lloyd Aereo Boliviano. (Note that all nonresidents flying into the USA require a visa.)

A maximum of 20 kg of checked luggage is allowed on internal flights (though you can frequently get away with more). Lost luggage is a depressingly frequent problem (although I must admit that it has yet to happen to me). Normally the luggage turns up on one of the next day's flights but be prepared – try and include valuables such as camera gear and essentials such as a warm coat (if heading to the highlands) or medication in your hand luggage. Always lock your checked luggage, make sure it is properly labelled and try to see that the correct destination tag is tied on by the check-in personnel.

If you fly with one of the small jungle airlines, the normal rule is to just show up at the airport in the morning and buy a seat on the next plane leaving for your destination. They leave as soon as they are full, which doesn't take long with a six-seater going to a popular destination. Less common destinations may be served only every few days. If you have a lot of luggage, you may be charged extra; 15 kg is about the maximum in a small airplane – if you're lucky – so travel light!

BUS
Long Distance

Without a doubt, buses are the most frequently used form of public transport in Peru. They go just about everywhere except for the deep jungle and Machu Picchu (which are accessible by train or foot only). This is hardly surprising when one considers that most Peruvians are too poor to be able to afford a car and can only afford to travel by bus. Bus fares are cheap because the cost of labour (booking office clerks, drivers and mechanics) is very low and because buses tend to run full and sell all their seats.

There are dozens (if not hundreds) of competing bus companies and they all have their own offices; there are no central bus terminals. In some towns, the different bus companies have their offices clustered around a few city blocks whilst in others the terminals are scattered all over town. I have tried to mark as many companies as possible on my city maps and the accompanying text will tell you which destinations are served by which companies.

It is always a good idea to buy your ticket in advance. This guarantees you a seat and also means that you can check out the schedules and prices of different companies without being encumbered by your luggage. There is sometimes a separate 'express' ticket window for people buying tickets for another day. Schedules and fares change frequently and vary from company to company; because of this I only give an approximate idea of how frequently buses leave and the average fares. Exact fares and schedules would be obsolete within a few months. Students with international student cards are officially allowed a 10% discount although some companies will not sell discounted tickets. At low travel periods, some companies try and sell more seats by offering discounted bus fares – watch for these if you are on a tight budget.

When you buy your ticket, try and avoid the seats at the back of the bus because the ride is nearly always bumpier. On some of the rougher mountain roads you can literally be thrown out of your seat in the back of the bus. Also try and avoid the seats over the wheel wells because you'll lose leg space. When you buy your ticket, always be sure to ask where the bus is leaving from because the ticket office and bus stop are sometimes on different streets.

When waiting in bus terminals, watch your luggage very carefully. Snatch theft is common and thieves work in pairs – one may distract you whilst the other grabs your bag. Razor blade artists abound, too. Whilst you're dozing off, leaning against your pack, somebody may try to slash through the pockets. Keep luggage where you can see it and stay alert. I hear depressingly frequent stories of theft in bus stations. I have been able to avoid losing my gear during many thousands of km of bus travel simply by staying alert. Thieves are looking for an easy rip off and won't bother you if you look on top of things. They will bother you, however, if you leave your pack leaning against the wall for 15 seconds when you're buying a bar of chocolate. Turn around with your chocolate and – no pack!

During the journey, your luggage will travel in the luggage compartment unless it is small enough to carry on board. This is normally reasonably safe. You are given a baggage tag in exchange for your bag which should be securely closed or locked if possible. I like to watch my pack getting loaded onto the bus and I usually exchange a few friendly words with the loader (who is often the driver's assistant) just to make sure that my bag is properly loaded and going to the right destination. During a long trip I get off and check my bag at stops and generally maintain a high profile. Of course, if you're on a night bus you'll want to sleep but I've not had any problem with anyone claiming my luggage in the middle of the night. Your hand luggage is a different matter. If you're asleep with a camera around your neck you may well wake up with a neatly razored strap and no camera at the end of it. I sleep with my carry-on bag (usually a day pack) strapped on to my person and with my arms around it.

Distances are large in Peru and you'll probably take some trips at night. The buses which travel the paved Pan-American Highway are reasonably comfortable and have reclining seats. The same kinds of buses are often used on the rougher roads into the mountains but they are generally less comfortable because the constant bumping and jarring has often broken the reclining mechanism on some of the seats. How good a seat you get is largely a matter of luck. On the more remote highways, the buses are often of the uncomfortable 'school bus' type. An irritating habit that bus companies have is to shift all the rows of seats forward so that they can get another row or two in the bus. This is fine if you're short or medium-sized, but can be a real pain if you're six-foot-one. The heating in buses doesn't always work

and it can literally get down to freezing inside the bus when travelling in the mountains at night, so bring a blanket, sleeping bag or warm clothes as hand luggage. Conversely, the air-conditioning rarely works and so it can get very hot and sweaty on some of the lowland trips, especially if the windows can't be opened.

Long-distance buses stop for at least three meals a day. The driver will announce how long the stop will be but it's usually worth asking again unless you're sure you heard right. 'Diez minutos' and 'treinta minutos' sound very much alike when the driver mumbles the words whilst stifling a yawn. And it's your responsibility to be on the bus when it leaves. Many companies have their own special rest areas and these are sometimes in the middle of the desert so you don't have any choice but to eat there. The food is generally inexpensive but not particularly appetising. I generally eat the lomo saltado (chopped beef fried with vegetables and served with rice) and find it's one of the standard, more edible dishes. Some travellers prefer to bring their own food.

These rest stops double as lavatory stops. Some of the better long-distance buses do have toilet cubicles aboard but don't rely on them. Sometimes they don't work and are locked, at other times they are used as an extra luggage compartment and, if they do work, somebody invariably vomits over the whole thing just before you go to use it. Rule number one of travel in Peru is to always carry your own roll of toilet paper because you will never find any in the toilets. Most rest stop areas have somewhere to buy essentials like toilet paper, toothpaste, chocolate and other snacks.

If you're travelling during long-holiday weekends or special fiestas, you may find that buses are booked up for several days in advance, so book as early as you can for these periods. Whenever you travel, be prepared for delays and don't plan on making important connections after a bus journey. Innumerable flat tyres, a landslide, or engine trouble can lengthen the 2-day journey from Lima to Cuzco to a 5-day odyssey. Such lengthy delays are not very common, but a delay of several hours can be expected quite frequently.

If you want to travel immediately, remember that you can often flag down a bus almost anywhere, even if it is a long distance one. Once, Cathy and I decided to go to Huaraz from Lima and as we were walking towards the Ormeño bus terminal, I saw a bus marked Huaraz standing at a traffic light. We quickly crossed the street, waving at the driver as we ran, and he let us onto the bus, thus saving us a walk to the terminal and a wait for the next bus. Of course, long-distance buses are less likely to stop if they are full or travelling at high speed.

A useful thing to carry on an overnight bus is a flashlight, because the driver nearly always shuts off the interior lights when the bus is underway. Being so close to the equator, it is dark for 12 hours and a flashlight enables you to read a book for a few hours before going to sleep. And when you do decide to sleep, ear plugs are a good idea.

In the mid-1980s, I travelled all over Peru by long-distance bus with no problems. By 1989, however, some routes had become dangerous because of guerrilla activity by the Sendero Luminoso. Trenches are dug across the road, buses are boarded, and passengers who are politicians, police or military are summarily executed. The other passengers are then allowed to continue after making a 'voluntary collaboration' of money or valuables. Although foreign travellers have not been singled out for any reason, you are advised not to travel on buses in areas controlled by the Sendero. This includes the overland bus route from Lima via Huánuco and Tingo María to Pucallpa; the bus route from Cuzco to Nazca via Abancay (the bus from Cuzco to Arequipa is no problem); and buses south of Huancayo to Huancavelica and Ayacucho and on to Abancay. The Huallaga valley north of Tingo María is dangerous because of intensive drug trafficking and the area around Tarapoto and Yurimaguas is becoming influenced by this.

The situation may have changed by the time you read this. The area around Ayacucho was definitely off limits in the early 1980s and yet was OK to travel in by the mid-1980s, for example. Things change. Ask at the tourist office, South American Explorers Club, travel agents, or other travellers what the current situation is in these and other areas.

Generally speaking, you are more likely to get hurt or killed in a car accident travelling at home than to be hurt or killed by the Sendero while travelling in Peru. But travel in the areas I mentioned above is not a good idea.

Local Bus

Local buses are usually slow and crowded, but very cheap. You can get around most towns for about 10c. Local buses often go out to a nearby village and this is a good way to see an area. Just stay on the bus to the end of the line, pay another 10c and head back again, usually sitting in the best seat on the bus. If you make friends with the driver, you may end up with an entertaining tour as he points out the local sights, in between collecting other passengers' fares.

When you want to get off a local bus, yell *Baja!*, which means 'Down!' Telling the driver to stop will make him think you're trying to be a back seat driver, and you will be ignored. He's only interested if you're getting off, or down from the bus. Another way of getting him to stop is to yell *Esquina!*, which means 'Corner!' He'll stop at the next one.

Truck

In remote areas, trucks often double as buses. Sometimes they are pick-up trucks with rudimentary wooden benches and at other times they are ordinary trucks; you just climb in the back, often with the cargo. I once had a ride on top of a truck carrying two bulls – for 12 hours my feet dangled just centimetres away from a pair of impressively large horns! If the weather is OK, you can get fabulous views as you travel in the refreshing wind (dress warmly). If the weather is bad you hunker down underneath a dark tarpaulin with the other passengers – unless the cargo happens to be two bulls in which case you stay on top and get soaked to the bone. It certainly isn't the height of luxury, but it may be the only way of getting to some areas, and if you're open-minded about the minor discomforts, you may find these rides among the most interesting in Peru.

Payment for these rides is usually determined by the driver and is a standard fare depending on the distance. You can ask other passengers how much they are paying; usually you'll find that because the trucks double as buses they charge almost as much.

TRAIN

There are two railway networks in Peru, which do not connect. Both go from the coast to the highlands and were major communication links between the *sierra* and the coast before the advent of roads and later air travel. Trains are less used today but nevertheless still play an important part in Peru's transport system.

There are two classes; 2nd class is very cheap and very crowded and uncomfortable while 1st class is about 25% more expensive, much more comfortable and still cheaper than a bus journey of comparable length. In addition, there are buffet and Pullman cars which require a surcharge. They are heated and give access to food service. There is also a more expensive tourist train from Cuzco to Machu Picchu. Generally, trains are slower than buses for a journey of equal length, but what you lose on speed you gain in the comfort of being able to stand up and stretch your legs.

In addition to the normal train (*tren*), there is a faster electric train called an *autovagon*. This is smaller and more expensive than the ordinary train and runs on only a few routes.

The central railroad runs from Lima to the mining town of La Oroya. Here it branches north and south. The northbound line goes to Cerro de Pasco but has been closed since the early 1980s. The southbound line goes to Huancayo and there are direct trains from Lima to Huancayo. The frequency of this service changes from year to year, though there is never more than one train a day. This trip takes a whole day and passes through the station of Galera, which is at 4781 metres above sea level and the highest standard-gauge train station in the world. In Huancayo you can change train stations and then continue to Huancavelica. The autovagon also runs the Huancayo-Huancavelica section.

The southern railroad runs from the coast at Mollendo through Arequipa to Lake Titicaca and Cuzco. With the decline of Mollendo's importance as a shipping port and the construction of the asphalted Pan-American Highway from Arequipa to Lima, the short Mollendo-Arequipa section is now closed. The Arequipa-Lake Titicaca-Cuzco section is, however, the longest and busiest section of Peru's railways. Trains from Arequipa to Puno, on the shores of Lake Titicaca, run every night. You can change at Juliaca, about 40 km before Puno, for daily trains to Cuzco (except on Sunday). The Arequipa-Juliaca (or Puno) service takes a whole night; the Puno-Cuzco service takes a whole day. In Cuzco there are two train stations; one for the service described above and the other for services to Machu Picchu. You cannot go directly from Arequipa or Lake Titicaca to Machu Picchu at this time; there are plans afoot to extend the track and make this possible in the future. There are several train and autovagon services from Cuzco to Machu Picchu every day.

The last segment of Peru's southern railway is found in the extreme south of the country. It is a border train which runs several times a day between Tacna in Peru and Arica in Chile.

The main drawback to travelling by train is thievery. The night train from Arequipa to Puno is especially notorious, particularly in the crowded and poorly-lit 2nd class carriages where a dozing traveller is almost certain to get robbed. Dark train stations are also the haunts of thieves, who often work in pairs or small groups. The answer to the problem is to travel by day and stay alert, to travel with a friend or group, and to travel 1st class. Above all, stay alert. The buffet and Pullman classes have a surcharge and are the safest carriages to ride in because only ticket holders are allowed aboard. Unfortunately, the train authorities are starting to exploit foreign tourists by charging ridiculously high surcharges for riding in buffet class. This is especially true of the Cuzco-Puno train where the foreign travellers' surcharge of $20 is three times more than the cost of the 1st class ticket!

For all services it is advisable to buy tickets in advance – the day before is usually best. This way you don't have to worry about looking after your luggage whilst lining up to buy a ticket at a crowded booking office window.

TAXI

There are many different kinds of taxis ranging from shared *colectivos* running a set route between two towns, to expensive *remisse* taxis parked in the stands outside a fancy hotel. Whatever kind of taxi you take, there are two things to remember: fares are invariably cheaper than in North America or Europe and you must always ask the fare in advance because there are no meters. It is quite acceptable to haggle over a taxi fare – drivers often double or triple the standard rate for an unsuspecting foreigner. Try and find out what the going rate is before taking a cab. About $1 is the fare for the cheapest and shortest run in Lima, a little less in other cities.

For short hops around a city, just flag down one of the many taxis which seem to be everywhere. They are recognisable by the small red taxi sticker in the windshield. The cars themselves can be of almost any model and colour – Volkswagen Beetles are among the most popular. The black remisse taxis outside the expensive hotels are usually the most convenient, comfortable and reliable, and some of their drivers speak English. They do a brisk trade in taking well-heeled tourists to the airport or Gold Museum. They are also the most expensive and have set rates which are often two or three times the rate of a taxi flagged down on the street.

Shared taxis or colectivos do set runs. One of the best known runs is along Avenida Arequipa between downtown Lima and the suburb of Miraflores – there is a set fare (about 15c) and the driver drives along with one hand out of the window holding up as many fingers as the number of seats available. You can flag them down on any corner and get off wherever you like. Other colectivo taxis work for *comités* and have a set run between major cities. These cost about twice as much as a bus fare and are about 25% faster than an express bus. Comités are shown on city maps and are worth investigating as an alternate form of long-distance transport. They will often pick you up from your hotel if this is prearranged.

Note that the term colectivo is also used to denote a bus, especially a minibus or van.

Finally, you can hire a taxi with a driver for several hours or even days. The cost varies depending on how far you expect to drive in a day and on how luxurious a vehicle you get. If you speak Spanish and make your own arrangements with a driver you could start around $30 to $40 per day, if you are driving on better roads and making occasional stops. On the other hand, a tourist agency could arrange a comfortable car with an English-speaking driver for about twice as much. Often, your hotel can help arrange a taxi for you. If you hire one for several days, make sure that you discuss eating and sleeping arrangements. Some drivers will charge enough to be able to make their own arrangements, whilst others will expect you to provide a room and three meals.

Tipping is not the norm, especially for short hops within the city. If you hire a driver for the day and he is particularly helpful or friendly, you may want to tip but this isn't considered obligatory.

BOAT

Although Peru has a long coastline, travel along the coast is almost entirely by road or air and there are no coastal passenger steamer services, although international cruise ships arrive in Callao once in a while.

In the highlands there are boat services on Lake Titicaca which, at just over 3800 metres, is the highest navigable lake in the world. Boats are usually small motorised vessels that take about 20 passengers from Puno to visit the various islands on the lake. There are departures every day and costs are low. There used to be a couple of larger steamships crossing the lake from Puno to Bolivia but this service no longer exists. Rumours indicate that steamship services may restart, but don't hold your breath. Instead there is a hydrofoil which is very expensive and can be booked through travel agents. It is much cheaper to take a bus from Puno to La Paz, Bolivia, which gives you the opportunity to 'cross' Lake Titicaca by a ferry over the narrow Strait of Tiquina.

It is in Peru's eastern lowlands that boat travel becomes of major importance. This is mainly of two types – small dugout canoes or larger cargo boats. The dugout canoes are usually powered by an outboard engine and act as a water taxi or bus on some of the smaller rivers. Sometimes they are powered by a strange arrangement which looks like an inboard motorcycle engine attached to a tiny propeller by a 3-metre-long propeller shaft. Called *peki-pekis*, these canoes are a slow and rather noisy method of transportation but are OK for short trips; they are especially common on Lake Yarinacocha near Pucallpa. As one gets further inland and the rivers widen, larger cargo boats are normally available.

Dugout Canoe

Dugout canoes often carry as many as 24 passengers and are the only way to get around many roadless areas. Hiring one yourself is very expensive. Taking one with other passengers is much cheaper but not as cheap as bus travel over a similar distance. This is because an outboard engine uses much more fuel per passenger/km than a bus engine.

Many of the boats used are literally dugouts, with maybe a splashboard added to the gunwales. They are long in shape but short on comfort. Seating is normally on hard, low, uncomfortable wooden benches accommodating two people each. Luggage is stashed forward under a tarpaulin, so carry hand baggage containing essentials for the journey.

If it is a long journey you will be miserable if you don't take the following advice, advice which is worth the cost of this book! *Bring* seat padding. A folded sweater or towel will make a world of difference to your trip. Pelting rain or glaring sun are major hazards and an umbrella is excellent defence against both. Bring sunblock lotion and wear long sleeves, long pants and a sunhat – I have seen people unable to walk because of second degree burns on their legs from a 6-hour exposure to the tropical sun. As the boat

Inca balsa raft

motors along, the breeze tends to keep insects away and it also tends to cool you down so you don't notice the burning effects of the sun. If the sun should disappear or the rain begin, you can get quite chilled, so bring a light jacket. Insect repellent is useful during stops along the river. A water bottle and food will complete your hand luggage. Remember to stash your spare clothes in plastic bags or they'll get soaked by rain or spray.

A final word about dugout canoes – they feel very unstable! Until you get used to the motion, you might worry about the whole thing just rolling over and tipping everybody into the piranha, electric eel or boa constrictor infested waters. Clenching the side of the canoe and wondering what madness possessed you to board the flimsy contraption in the first place doesn't seem to help. But dugouts feel much more unstable than they really are, so don't worry about a disaster; it almost never happens. I've ridden many dugouts without any problems, even in rapids. Nor have I met anyone who was actually dunked in.

River Boat

This is the classic way to travel down the Amazon – swinging in your hammock aboard a banana boat piloted by a grizzled old captain who knows the waters better than the back of his hand. You can travel from Pucallpa to the mouth of the Amazon in this way, although the number of boats doing the entire trip are few and far between. More likely you'll spend a few days getting to Iquitos where you'll board another, slightly larger boat and continue for a few more days to the border with Brazil and Colombia. From there, more boats can be found for the week-long passage to Manaus (Brazil) in the heart of the Amazon Basin.

Although cargo boats ply the Ucayali from Pucallpa to Iquitos, and the Marañon from Yurimaguas to Iquitos, they tend to leave only once or twice a week. The boats are small, but have two decks. The lower deck is normally for cargo and the upper for passengers and crew. Bring your own

hammock. Food is usually provided, but it is basic and not necessarily very hygienic; you may want to bring some of your own. To arrange a passage, ask around at the docks until you hear of a boat going where you want to go then find out who the captain is. It's usually worth asking around about the approximate cost, though often the captains will charge you the same as anybody else. Departure time often depends on a full cargo and *mañana* may go on for several days if the hold is only half full. Sometimes you can sleep on the boat whilst you are waiting for departure, if you want to save on hotel bills.

Boats to Iquitos are relatively infrequent and rather small, slow and uncomfortable. Beyond Iquitos, however, services are more frequent and comfortable. Things are generally more organised too; there are chalk boards at the docks with ship's names, destinations and departure times displayed reasonably clearly and accurately. You can look over a boat for your prospective destination and wait for a better vessel if you don't like what you see. Some boats even have cabins, though these tend to be rather grubby airless boxes and you have to supply your own bedding. I prefer to use a hammock. Food is usually included in the price of the passage, and may be marginally better on some of the bigger and better ships. If you like rice and beans – or rice and fish, or rice and tough meat, or rice and fried bananas – you'll be OK. If you don't like rice, you'll have a problem. Bottled soft drinks and beers are usually available – ask about this before the boat leaves because you definitely don't want to drink the water. Sanitary facilities are basic but adequate. A pump shower is usually aboard.

Occasionally, boats from Iquitos go all the way to the mouth of the Amazon, though this is very rare these days. However, the very fact that ocean-going vessels are capable of reaching Iquitos, indicates how vast this river is. Many people have misconceptions about sailing down the Amazon watching monkeys swinging in the tree tops, snakes gliding among the branches, and parrots and macaws flying across the river in front of you. In reality, most of the banks have been colonised and there is little wildlife there. Also, the boats often navigate the midstream, and the shoreline is seen only as a rather distant green line. In fact, some people find the monotonous diet and long days of sitting in their hammocks to be boring and they don't enjoy the trip.

I travelled this way from Iquitos all the way to Manaus and had a great time. I was already aware of and prepared for the lack of wildlife, and so I brought a couple of very thick books. Yet I found I barely had the time to read them, there was so much to do. Quarters were close on the passenger deck, and my elbows literally touched my neighbour's when I was in my hammock. Friendliness and an easy-going attitude are essential ingredients for a river trip. Most of the passengers are friendly and fun, and you can have a great time getting to know them. The views of the great river stretching all around were often very beautiful, particularly during the misty dawns and the searing sunsets.

On the first evening of a 7-day trip, I was sitting in the bow enjoying the cooling breeze and watching the sun go down. Soon, a small crowd of Peruvian and Brazilian passengers and crew gathered, and a rum bottle and guitar appeared. Within minutes, we had a first-rate party going with singing, dancing, hand clapping, and an incredible impromptu orchestra. One of the crew bent a metal rod into a rough triangle which he pounded rhythmically, someone else threw a handful of beans into a can and started shaking, a couple of pieces of polished wood were clapped together to interweave yet another rhythm, a mouth harp was produced, I blew bass notes across the top of my beer bottle and everyone had a great time. A couple of hours of rhythmic music as the sun went down became a standard part of the ship's routine and gave me some of my most unforgettable moments of South American travel.

Once or twice a day, the boat would pull into some tiny Amazonian port to load or off-load passengers and cargo. The arrival of a big boat was often the main event of the day in one of these small river villages, and the entire population might come down to the riverbank to swap gossip and watch the goings on. This, too, added to the interest of the trip.

For some people, boating down the Amazon is a monotonous and sweaty endurance test. For others it's a great experience – I hope my descriptions help you decide whether this is something you'd like to attempt or want to avoid.

CAR RENTAL

You can drive yourself, but this tends to be expensive. The cheapest car rental I found was from National Car Rental who have Volkswagen Beetles for $19 per day plus 18c per km and an optional $4 extra per day for insurance. The insurance covers accidents but not theft. This means that if you decided to rent a car for 3 days to go from Lima to Nazca and back (about a 6-hour drive without stops) you would have to pay about $150 plus petrol (which is just over $1 per gallon). If you rent by the week it's slightly cheaper – $220 per week plus insurance and petrol but your first 1000 km are free. Bear in mind that this is for a Volkswagen Beetle with an 'economical' company. Their Nissan Patrol 4WD Jeep costs $470 per week including 1000 free km. Budget, Avis and Hertz also have offices in Peru. Rental car agencies have offices at the major airports (Lima, Cuzco, Arequipa) and also downtown in the major cities.

If you decide that you want to drive yourself despite the expense, you need to be over 25 years old and must use a credit card charge as a deposit, although some agencies will accept $200 cash. A valid driver's licence from your home country is normally accepted. Bear in mind that the condition of the rental vehicles is often not very good, roads are badly potholed (even the paved Pan-American Highway) and drivers extremely aggressive. Road signs, where they exist, are often small and unclear. Petrol stations are few and far between. Vehicles such as jeeps are difficult to find and many companies are reluctant to rent ordinary cars for anything but short coastal runs. Theft is all too common and so you should not leave your vehicle parked in the street or you'll lose your hubcaps, windscreen wipers, or even your wheels. When stopping overnight, park the car in a guarded lot (the better hotels have them). As a general rule, I do not recommend self-drive car rental.

YOUR OWN CAR

You cannot drive your own car to Peru from North America because of the roadless rainforest of the Darien Gap between Panama and Colombia. Therefore you have to either ship your vehicle to South America or buy a car there. Both alternatives are expensive and fraught with problems – but it certainly is done, and once in a while you'll meet someone touring South America in their own VW bus. Read the warnings in the last paragraph of the Car Rental section. If that doesn't deter you, get a copy of a book about driving in Third World countries. A good one is *Overland & Beyond* by T & J Hewat, published by Lascelles of London. There are others.

HITCHHIKING

Hitching is not very practical in Peru for three reasons: there are few private cars,

public transport is relatively cheap, and trucks are used as public transport in remote areas, so trying to hitch a free ride on one is the same as trying to hitch a free ride on a bus. Many drivers of *any* vehicle will pick you up but will also expect payment. If the driver is stopping to drop off and pick up other passengers, ask them what the going rate is. If you are the only passenger, the driver may have picked you up just to talk with a foreigner, and he may wave aside your offer of payment. If you do decide to try hitching, make sure in advance of your ride that you and the driver agree on the subject of payment.

FOOT

Peru is certainly a good destination for adventurous treks in the Andes. Both the Inca Trail to Machu Picchu and the Cordillera Blanca have justly become world famous for hiking and backpacking. Several excellent guidebooks have been published specifically for foot travellers – see the the list in the Books & Bookshops section of the Facts for the Visitor chapter.

Walking around cities is generally safe, even at night, if you stick to the well-lit areas. Always be on the alert for pickpockets, though, and make inquiries before venturing into an area you don't know.

Lima

If, like me, you read the *Paddington Bear* books in your youth, Lima in 'darkest Peru' may conjure up images of an exotic city in the heart of a lush tropical jungle. Unfortunately, this is far from the reality. The city is a mainly modern and not particularly exotic one, sprawled untidily on the edge of the coastal desert. Despite its many urban problems, most visitors find Lima an interesting, if nerve racking, place to visit.

Lima is the capital of Peru. Because it was founded by Francisco Pizarro on 6 January 1535, the Catholic feast of Epiphany, or the Day of the Kings, its first name was the City of the Kings. Many of the old colonial buildings can still be seen here but, unfortunately, much of Lima's original colonial charm has been overwhelmed by a recent population explosion.

For almost 400 years, Lima remained a small city. Then, in the 1920s, unprecedented population growth began. This saw the urban population of 173,000 in 1919 more than triple in the next 20 years and, since 1940, there has been a further tenfold increase. Almost a third of Peru's 20 million inhabitants now live in Lima, making most of the city overcrowded, polluted and noisy. Much of the city's population growth can be attributed to the influx of very poor people from other areas of Peru, especially the highlands. They come searching for a better life with a job and, perhaps, opportunities for their children. Most end up living in the *pueblos jovenes*, or 'young towns'. These shanty towns, which surround the capital, lack electricity, water and adequate sanitation. Jobs are scarce; most work as *ambulantes* or street vendors selling anything from chocolates to clothes pins and earning barely enough for food. Their chances of improving their lot are very slim.

Lima's location in the centre of Peru's desert coastline gives it a climate and environment that can only be described as dismal. From April to December, the coastal fog, known as garua, blots out the sun and blankets the city's buildings in a fine grey mist. Unless they are repainted annually, the buildings soon take on a ghostly pallor from the incessant mist which coats the rooftops with a thin, concrete-like layer of hardened grey sludge. The situation is not much better during the few months of Lima's short summer – although the sun does come out, the smog makes walking the city streets a sticky and unpleasant activity. As the waste products of over 5 million Lima residents mostly end up in the Pacific, the beaches are overcrowded cesspools and the newspapers carry daily health warnings during summer.

Having read this far, you might well be wondering how to avoid Lima. However, if you're planning any kind of extensive travelling in Peru, you will find it virtually impossible to avoid the desert coastline and, in turn, Lima. Despite the city's drawbacks, having no choice is not the only reason to visit Lima. Its people are generally friendly and hospitable, there are plenty of opportunities for dining, nightlife and other entertainment and, perhaps most important of all, the great selection of museums includes some of the best in Peru. So it's worth trying to ignore the traffic jams and the crowds and getting to know something of the people and the culture of Peru.

Information

Tourist Information The Ministry of Industry & Tourism operates tourist offices in all major Peruvian cities. In Lima, their office (tel 323559) is at Jirón de la Unión 1066 (also known as Jirón Belén), about half a block from the Plaza de San Martín. Hours are 9 am to 6 pm, Monday to Friday, 9 am to 1 pm on Saturday, and some of the staff speak English. The office has a wealth of up-to-date information about transport, hotels and sightseeing throughout the more frequently visited parts of Peru. There is also a tourist information office at the airport. It's not as good but will help you find a hotel by phone.

A most useful source of general information is the *Peru Guide*. This free booklet, edited by Adriana von Hagen, is published monthly by Lima Tours, whose office is at Belén 1040, a few doors from the tourist office. The booklet can also be found at some of the better hotels, restaurants and tourist spots in Lima, as well as at the South American Explorers Club.

South American Explorers Club For many long-term travellers and expatriate residents, this club has become something of a legend. Since it was founded by Don Montague and Linda Rojas in 1977, the club has been involved in activities ranging from the 1980 clean up of the Inca Trail to the clean up of erroneous media reports about discoveries of 'lost' Peruvian cities in 1985. Primarily, however, it functions as an information centre for travellers, adventurers and scientific expeditions and the club's headquarters in Lima can provide excellent advice about travel anywhere in Latin America, with an emphasis on Peru.

The club has an extensive library of books, maps (some published by the club) and the trip reports of other travellers. A variety of the most useful books and maps are for sale and there are trail maps for the Inca Trail, the Mt Ausangate area, the Cordilleras Blanca and Huayhuash, as well as general maps of South America. You can also get useful current information on travel conditions, currency regulations, weather and so on.

The club is an entirely member-supported, nonprofit organisation. Annual membership costs $25 per person ($35 for a couple), which covers four issues of their excellent and informative *South American Explorer* magazine. (In the past, the magazine came out at irregular intervals but it is now published quarterly.) Members also receive full use of the clubhouse and its facilities. These include an information service and library, introductions to other travellers and notification of expedition opportunities, storage of excess luggage (anything from small valu-ables to a kayak), storage or forwarding of mail addressed to you at the club, a relaxing place to read, research or just have a cup of tea and a chat with the friendly staff, a book exchange, buying and selling of used equipment and discounts on the books, maps and gear sold at the club and other services. The storage facilities are particularly useful if you plan on returning to Peru – I leave climbing gear and other heavy stuff here from year to year. Nonmembers are welcome but are asked to limit their visits to the club to about half an hour and are not eligible for membership privileges. Paid-up members can stay all day – a welcome relief from the madhouse bustle of Lima. The club is highly recommended.

If you're in Lima, you can simply go to the clubhouse and sign up. Otherwise, mail your $25 (and any questions you have) direct to the club at Casilla 3714, Lima 100. The street address is Republica de Portugal 146, on the 13th block of Alfonso Ugarte in the Breña district of Lima, about a 10 or 15 minute walk from the Plaza San Martín. The club is open from 9.30 am to 5 pm on weekdays and has been known to open on Saturdays too. Phone 314480 for current hours.

The club's US office (tel (303) 320 0388) is at 1510 York St, Denver, CO 80206. The magazine is published here and if you're not sure whether or not you want to join, send them $4 for a sample copy of the *Explorer* and further information.

In 1989 the club's Quito office (tel 566076) at Toledo 1254 was opened. The postal address is Apartado 21-431, Eloy Alfaro, Quito, Ecuador. Travellers to Ecuador will find the same range of services here as is offered by the Lima office and access to these is included in the $25 annual membership fee.

Post The main post office is inside the city block on the north-west corner of the Plaza de Armas. Mail sent to you at Lista de Correos, Correos Central, Lima, should be collected here. The main office is open from 8 am to 6 pm Monday to Saturday and from

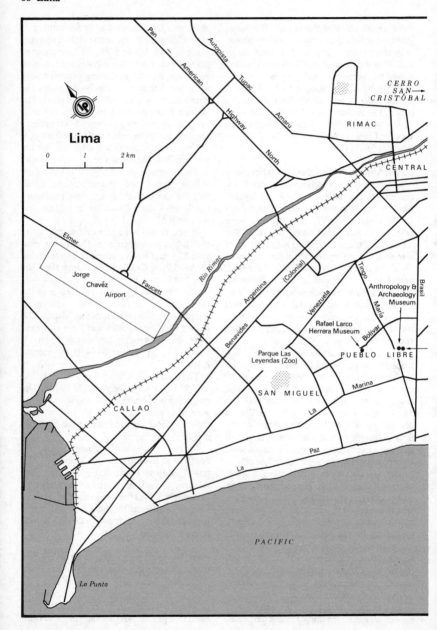

Lima

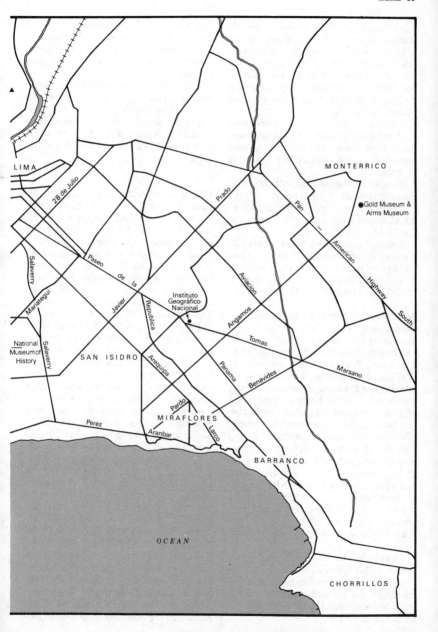

8 am to noon on Sunday morning. There are also branch post offices in various districts of Lima. The branch post office on Colmena (the popular name for Nicolas de Pierola west of the Plaza San Martín) is open until 8 pm Monday to Saturday. The post office at the airport is open from 8 am to 6 pm Monday to Saturday.

American Express clients can have mail held for them at Amex, c/o Lima Tours, Belén 1040, Lima. You can pick up mail between 9 am and noon and from 3 to 5 pm on weekdays.

Bring identification when collecting mail from either Amex or a post office.

Members of the South American Explorers Club can have mail held for them at Casilla 3714, Lima 100, Peru.

Sending parcels abroad is reasonably safe if you send them certificado. Lima is the best city to send parcels from. Further details of international parcel post are given in the Post section of the Facts for the Visitor chapter.

Telecommunications Long-distance and international telephone calls are made from the usually crowded and chaotic telephone office on Plaza San Martín, to the right of the Cine Metro. While most of Peru is served by ENTEL, Lima's telecommunications system is run by the Peruvian Telephone Company which keeps shorter hours and seems less efficient. They supposedly have direct dialling but it's usually out of order. You have to place your call through the receptionist, pay a big deposit at the cash register (bring extra money), wait an hour or more for your call to be announced over the loudspeakers, make your call, then wait up to half an hour for the balance of your deposit to be returned. It's not always that bad but it gets very crowded in the evenings. The office is open from about 9 am to 9 pm Monday to Saturday.

To make a local call, you'll need to buy tokens, called fiches RIN. They're sold by vendors on many street corners for a few cents each and are used instead of coins in the public telephone booths which are scattered around the city.

Telegrams and telexes can be sent from the office on the corner of Lampa and Emancipación in Lima. The 1st class hotels can connect you with the international operator and send telexes.

FAX services are available at many locations. One place providing a 24 hour service is on Avenida Bolivia by Alfonso Ugarte in Lima. The FAX number is (051) 1433-8031. It costs about $1.50 to send a page to the USA and a few cents to receive a page.

Money As you will have gathered from the Facts for the Visitor chapter, changing money in Peru can be a problem. Lima is the best place in the country to change money but, even there, it's by no means straightforward, especially if you're changing travellers' cheques. One of the few places in town which will exchange travellers' cheques for cash dollars for a small (about 2%) commission is the Banco de Crédito. The bank's main office is at Jirón Lampa 399 in Lima and is open from 8.30 to 11.30 am on weekdays throughout the year. In addition, it opens in the afternoon between 4 and 6 pm from April to December. As always, these hours are subject to change. Until recently, only the main office would change travellers' cheques, but the Miraflores (3rd block of Larco) and San Isidro offices have now started to do so. The Banco de Crédito has, in the past, changed travellers' cheques at rates almost as good as cash dollars, so ask.

Few of the other banks change money and, if they do, it is often at the unfavourable official rate. Casas de cambio, or exchange houses, usually give the good free rate for cash but pay several per cent lower for travellers' cheques. One traveller recently reported that MacDollar Cambio on Ocoña (behind the Hotel Bolívar) will change travellers' cheques to cash dollars. Casas de cambio are found near the Plaza San Martín, especially on Colmena going north-west, and on Larco in Miraflores. Their main advantage is that they are open for longer hours than the banks but shop around, particularly when exchanging a large amount of money.

Street changers often hang around the casas de cambio. The corner of Plaza San Martín and Ocoña is a favourite spot and, on some days, every person on the block seems to be buying or selling dollars. There is no real advantage to using street changers – their rates are never better than the best rates in banks or casas de cambio.

The Banco de la Nación at the airport sometimes changes money, but you can't rely on it. There are usually a couple of casas de cambio operating near the international arrivals exit. Exchange rates at the airport are generally 2% lower for cash and 10% lower for travellers' cheques than the best rates in town, although these are approximate figures and will fluctuate.

If you need to receive money from home, the Banco de Crédito is one of the best places to have it sent because it charges low service fees and allows you to have your money in US dollars, if they're available. Check with the main office for the telex number to which money can be sent. Other banks may charge high fees and/or pay you only in intis at the unfavourable official rate.

You can usually change excess intis back to dollars at a slight loss when you leave the country but, as this can be unreliable, try not to be left with a huge wad of intis when you leave. On one occasion I was told, on leaving Peru through Lima's International Airport, that the Peruvian Government had suspended trading on the inti and I couldn't change my excess intis back to dollars!

If you lose your travellers' cheques, I hope they're American Express. The American Express office is at Lima Tours (tel 276624), Belén 1040, and is open from 9.15 am to 4.45 pm weekdays. American Express is one of the easiest companies to deal with and refunds are usually available within 72 hours. Other travellers' cheques often take longer – (First National) Citibank took 1 year to process my claim for about $200 in stolen cheques, so I definitely cannot recommend using them. If you do, they're at Colmena 1070 in Lima, (tel 273930) – good luck. The

Bank of America (tel 717777) is at Augusto Tamayo 120, San Isidro. Visa (tel 275600) is represented at the central city branch of the Banco de Crédito in Lima. Mastercard (tel 441891) is at Miguel Seminario 320, San Isidro, Diners Club (tel 414272) at Canaval Moreyra 535, San Isidro and Thomas Cook (tel 278353) at Wagons-Lit, Ocoña 174, Lima. If you lose other travellers' cheques, go into any major bank and ask for assistance. They'll usually be able to tell you where to make a claim.

Note that during the Lima summer, from January to March, banks are open only in the mornings from 8.30 to 11.30 am. The government tried to introduce afternoon banking in 1986 but popular opinion didn't allow this to happen – everyone wants to go to the beach on hot summer afternoons. During the rest of the year, most banks are open in the afternoons but hours vary from bank to bank.

Visas Lima is one of the easiest places in Peru to have your tourist permit extended. Most European nationals receive a 90-day permit on arrival which can be extended for a further 90 days. A few nationalities (including US citizens) are given only 60-day permits but these can be renewed twice to give the same 180-day total. Those nationalities requiring tourist visas (Australians and New Zealanders are notable examples) can also renew for 60 days. Once your maximum of 180 days is up, you must leave the country. However, there is no law against crossing the border to a neighbouring country and returning the next day to start the process over again.

The Lima immigration office is on the 500 block of Paseo de la República and 28 de Julio. It opens at about 9 am on weekdays and it's best to go first thing in the morning if you want to get your extension the same day. Specially stamped paperwork used to be required but, as of 1986, this is no longer necessary. You will need your passport and the white immigration slip you received on entry (it's not a disaster if you lose it but the process becomes more time consuming and expensive). You also need a written request for an extension. This involves filling out a special form which costs about $1 and is available at the immigration office. These documents are presented with a fee of $20. The fee can be paid in intis but, as they use the highest rate, there is currently no saving in doing this. Sometimes (but rarely), you may be asked for a ticket out of the country, though you can get around this by showing enough money. The more affluent you look, the less hassle you'll have. Remember that regulations change frequently in Latin America and Lima is no exception!

A bus ticket from Lima to the Ecuadorian, Bolivian or Chilean border will cost you less than the $20 visa renewal fee so, if you're on a tight budget, you might want to spend your money travelling to a convenient border and re-entering the country instead.

A final word about student visas. You can get one if you're studying in Peru but, as they're usually more hassle than they're worth, many foreign students prefer to use tourist permits.

Foreign Embassies Travellers of most nationalities can enter the neighbouring countries of Ecuador and Chile simply by showing their passport and obtaining a tourist card at the border. Check details at the appropriate embassy.

To enter nearby Bolivia or Brazil, citizens of France, the USA, Australia, New Zealand and some other countries require visas; citizens of most western European countries do not.

Travel from Peru to all other South American countries is almost exclusively by air, though occasionally by ship. The principal countries with diplomatic representation in Lima are:

Argentina
  Pablo Bermudez 143, Jesus María (tel 729920, 245984), 8 am to 1 pm weekdays
Bolivia
  Los Castaños 235, San Isidro (tel 228231), 8.30 am to 1.30 pm weekdays

Brazil
  Comandante Espinar 181, Miraflores (tel 462635), 9 am to 1 pm weekdays
Chile
  Javier Prado Oeste 790, San Isidro (tel 407965), 8.45 am to 12.30 pm weekdays
Colombia
  Natalio Sanchez 125, 4th floor, Lima (tel 247949), 9 am to 12.30 pm weekdays
Ecuador
  Las Palmeras 356, San Isidro (tel 228138), 9 am to 1 pm weekdays
Venezuela
  Salaverry 3005, San Isidro (tel 415948), 9 am to noon weekdays

Most major English-speaking and European countries are represented in Peru. The main embassies are:

Austria
  Avenida Central 643, San Isidro (tel 428851), 10 am to noon weekdays
Belgium
  Angamos 380, Miraflores (tel 463335), 8.30 am to 3 pm weekdays
Canada
  Libertad 130, Miraflores (tel 444015), 8.30 to 11 am weekdays
Denmark
  Jirón Lampa 946, 2nd floor, Lima (tel 283620), 8 am to 2 pm weekdays
Finland
  Los Eucaliptos 291, San Isidro (tel 703750), 8.30 am to 4.30 pm weekdays
France
  Arequipa 3415, San Isidro (tel 704968), 9 am to noon weekdays
Germany
  Arequipa 4210, Miraflores (tel 459997), 9 am to noon weekdays
Ireland
  Carlos Povias Osores 410, San Isidro (tel 230808)
Israel
  Washington Building, 6th floor, 600 block of Arequipa, Lima (tel 321005), 10 am to 1 pm weekdays
Italy
  Gregorio Escobedo 298, Jesus María (tel 632727), 9 am to noon weekdays
Japan
  San Felipé 356, Jesus María (tel 630000), 9 am to 12.30 pm and 3.30 to 5.30 pm weekdays
The Netherlands
  Avenida Principal 190, San Borja (tel 751548), 9 am to noon weekdays

New Zealand
   Salaverry 3006, San Isidro (tel 621890), 8.30 am
   to 1.30 pm weekdays, till 4.30 pm 2 days a week
Norway
   Canaval Moreyra 585, San Isidro (tel 416377), 9
   am to noon weekdays
Spain
   Jorge Basadre 498, San Isidro (tel 705600), 9 am
   to 2 pm weekdays
Sweden
   Las Agatas 189, Balconcillo (tel 722425), 8.30
   am to 12.30 pm and 2 to 4.30 pm weekdays
Switzerland
   Salaverry 3240, San Isidro (tel 624090), 9 am to
   noon weekdays
UK
   Washington Building, 12th floor, 600 block of
   Arequipa, Lima (tel 283830), 10 am to 3 pm
   Monday to Thursday, 10 am to 1 pm Friday
USA
   Grimaldo del Solar 346, Miraflores (tel 443621),
   8.15 to 11 am weekdays except Wednesday; there
   is also the embassy office (tel 286000) on the
   1400 block of Garcilazo de la Vega and Avenida
   España, city centre

About 30 other nations are represented by consulates in Peru; you can find them in the phone book if you need them.

Bookshops The best selection of English-language guidebooks can be found at the South American Explorers Club. The ABC bookstores, the main branch of which is at Colmena 689, three blocks from the Plaza San Martín, have a good but expensive selection of English, German and French newspapers, magazines, coffee-table books, guidebooks, etc. Slightly cheaper and also good for books about Peru is the Librería AYZA on Jirón Unión. Bear in mind that most English-language books about Peru are much cheaper in Britain or the US than in Peru.

The capital's English-language weekly, the *Lima Times*, advertises a good selection of books about Peru. These can be obtained from the Lima Times offices at Carabaya 928, 3rd floor.

There is a good selection of paperback novels at the Librería El Pacífico, under the cinema of the same name in Miraflores. Used paperback novels in English can be bought or exchanged at the Book Exchange at Ocoña 211, two blocks from the Plaza San Martín. They have a good choice of 1000 page blockbuster novels to help while away interminable waits for late buses and planes. Their books are expensive, however. I recently saw a well-used copy of the first edition of this book for sale there at 50% above the original cover price! Members of the South American Explorers Club will find a free book exchange at the clubhouse.

Maps Again, the South American Explorers Club is a good place to begin looking for maps. The club has trail maps of the main hiking areas, road maps of Peru and detailed street and bus maps of Lima. If they don't have the maps you want, they'll know where you can get them.

For topographical maps, go to the Instituto Geográfico Nacional (IGN) (tel 451939) at Aramburu 1198, Surquillo. It's open from 8 am to 3 pm on weekdays; you need your passport to get in. The Servicio Aerofotográfico Nacional at Las Palmeras Air Force base in Chorrillos can sell you aerial photographs from 8.30 am to noon and 2 to 4 pm on weekdays. Some of these aerial photos are available from the IGN.

Lima is so huge that it is impossible, in a book such as this one, to do more than describe the main central city area. You are strongly advised to buy a street map of the city if you want to spend a few days looking around. The best is published by Lima 2000.

Many maps are sold by street vendors around the Plaza San Martín area. The quality varies widely and prices tend to be high, so try bargaining.

Laundry Many hotels can have your laundry done for you – the more expensive the hotel, the more expensive the laundry. Peru does not have self-serve coin-operated laundromats. Instead, you must leave your clothes with a lavandería, or laundry, and pick them up the following day, though same-day service can be arranged at extra cost.

Many lavanderías only do dry cleaning and others charge by the item rather than by the load. The lavandería I use is LavaQuick at Benavides 604 and La Paz in Miraflores. Here, you'll pay about $2 for a 4 kg load, washed, dried and folded. They offer 24 hour service, or same-day service if you pay a tip, and are open from 9 am to 6 pm Monday to Saturday, closing at 1 pm on Thursday. If you don't want to go to Miraflores, ask at your hotel for directions to the nearest lavandería.

Warning With literally millions of very poor and unemployed people, it is hardly surprising that Lima has a crime problem. Don't be overly worried – you are unlikely to be mugged or otherwise physically hurt but many travellers do have their belongings stolen. Please reread the Dangers & Annoyances section of the Facts for the Visitor chapter before arriving in Lima.

Occasionally, there are reports in the foreign press of bombings, blackouts and demonstrations in Lima. Whilst these undeniably occur, I've spent 5 years travelling in Peru and have come to the conclusion that Lima is as safe as any other major city. In February 1986, a 1 to 5 am curfew was imposed in Lima. This was lifted in 1989 but you should make inquiries about whether it is in effect when you arrive.

Medical Considered to be the best, but also the most expensive general clinic is the Clínica Anglo-American (tel 403570) on the 3rd block of Salazar, San Isidro. In San Borja, try the Clínica San Borja (tel 413141) at Avenida del Aire 333. In Lima, there's the Clínica Internacional (tel 288060) at Washington 1475. All of these clinics have 24 hour service and some English-speaking staff. Cheaper, and also good, is the Clínica Adventista (tel 459040) at Malecón Balta in Miraflores.

If you're bothered by intestinal problems, try Dr Alfredo Calderón at Carabaya 928, 3rd floor, Lima, an English-speaking doctor who has been recommended to me.

A highly recommended dentist is Dr Gerardo Aste (tel 417502), Antero Aspillaga 415, office 101, San Isidro. He speaks excellent English and did a very thorough and painless job of replacing a filling I broke in Peru. He is partnered by his son, who is also good.

If you have a spectacle prescription with you, you can have a spare pair of glasses made up very cheaply by one of Lima's numerous opticians. There are several along Cailloma in the city centre and around Schell and Larco in Miraflores. Having your eyes examined for a new prescription is also cheap but some ophthalmologists practising in Peru have archaic equipment and don't do a very good job. If you need a new prescription, ask at your embassy for a recommended ophthalmologist.

Tourist Police For emergencies ranging from robbery to rabies you can contact the tourist police for advice and assistance. They have been recommended to me by several people for their courtesy and helpfulness. English-speaking police are usually available and they can cut down on a lot of red tape if you need a police report to make an insurance claim or get a travellers' cheque refund. The policía de turismo (tel 237225, 246571) is at Salaverry 1156, Jesus María.

People wishing to visit foreign (English-speaking) prisoners (mainly in jail on drug charges) can contact the Foreign Prisoners' Fellowship (tel 457908), Church of the Good Shepherd, Avenida Santa Cruz 491, Lima, or write to Apartado 5152, Lima 18.

Spanish Courses Perhaps because Lima is not as attractive a city as, say, Quito in Ecuador, fewer people stay here to learn Spanish. Nevertheless, courses are offered. The Centro de Idiomas (tel 350601) at Avenida Manuel Olguin 215, Monterrico has relatively small (maximum six people) classes at three different levels, but they are expensive – about $8 to $10 per hour. You might also try Spanish for Foreigners, Wilson Cabanillas, at Jirón Cañete 214.

Employment Most job opportunities are for English teachers. Pay is usually very low and you're doing fairly well if you make $1 an hour. Native English speakers can try

Fermath Inglés, Tudela y Varela 215, Miraflores, or TRANSLEX on the Paseo de la República in Miraflores. Also try the Asociación Cultural Peruano/Britanico at Arequipa 3495.

If you actually have a teaching qualification, you might do better. The American school, the Colegio Roosevelt (tel 350590) in Monterrico, pays as much as $20 per day for substitute teachers. Bona fide teachers often hang out in Brenchley's Pub (see Places to Eat) so you might make further contacts there. American and British oil workers also drink there, though oil-related jobs are not easy to find unless you have some experience and qualifications.

Writers and photographers should pick up a copy of the *Lima Times*. You might be able to sell your work to this weekly newspaper – it won't make you rich but it will help pay the bills.

Tours The many travel agencies in Lima can sell you airline tickets, make your hotel reservations and provide you with tour services. For guided tours of Lima, (the city, the churches, the museums, Lima by night, the nearby archaeological sites such as Pachacamac, and so on), Vista Peru is one of the best, though their tours aren't particularly cheap, starting at $10 per person. Comfortable transport and English-speaking guides are provided. For reservations and information about Vista Peru, contact Lima Tours, Belén 1040.

There are also tourist departures to Cuzco and Machu Picchu. These excursions take 3 days and 2 nights and cost about $140 plus the air fare, but are not recommended unless you're in a great hurry. Other companies offer similar services and may be cheaper – Turicentro at José Pardo 497, Miraflores, for example, does the Cuzco-Machu Picchu trip for $90 plus the air fare. There are many travel and tour agencies in Lima along and near Colmena, north-west of the Plaza San Martín. Most of them are OK but Turismo Inkaico has sold invalid tickets and is not recommended. If you are buying tickets

from a travel agent, always check to see how much commission they're charging.

For adventure tourists, two companies have offices in Lima. Aventours (tel 441067) at Avenida La Paz 442, Miraflores specialises in river running and trekking in the Cuzco area. Explorandes at Bolognesi 159 in Miraflores also specialises in trekking and river-running adventures. These tours tend more towards the top end of the market; cheaper tours can be joined by travelling to the area in which you're interested and making contact there.

Various jungle lodges also have offices in Lima. The best lodge for seeing wildlife and the south-eastern Peruvian rainforest is the *Explorer's Inn* (tel 313047) run by Peruvian Safaris, Garcilazo de la Vega 1334, Lima, or write to PO Box 10088, Lima 1, Peru. More information on the Explorer's Inn is in the Puerto Maldonado section.

Things to See
The numerous museums, churches and colonial houses in Lima are enough to keep the sightseer occupied for several days. Most are described later in this section. Unfortunately, opening hours are subject to frequent change; check with the tourist office at Belén 1066 for up-to-date times. Entrance fees may also vary noticeably from those given here. Hours are often shortened drastically during the coastal summer season (January to March), with January one of the most difficult months to find places open all day. Mornings are generally the best time to go anywhere during summer.

Museums
Museo Nacional de Antropología y Arqueología This is one of the cheapest and best museums in Lima and should be high on the list of anyone at all interested in Peruvian archaeology. The well-organised collection traces the prehistory of Peru chronologically from the earliest archaeological sites to the arrival of the Spaniards. Chavín stone carvings, Nazca ceramics and Paracas weavings are all displayed here, along with collections

of the best artefacts from all major Peruvian cultures. The section on the Archaeology of Peru in the first chapter of this book is essentially based on a visit to this museum.

Entry to the museum costs 40c, plus another 40c if you want to use a camera, and English and Spanish-speaking guides are available for a tip. Hours are 10 am to 6 pm Tuesday to Sunday. The museum is at Plaza Bolívar, at the intersection of Avenida San Martín and Vivanco in Pueblo Libre. However, as there are plans to move it to a much larger site near Avenida La Marina in the Maranga district, you may want to check with the tourist office first.

Museo Nacional de la República Better known as the National Museum of History, this building once housed the revolutionary heroes San Martín (1821-22) and Bolívar (1823-26). The museum contains late colonial and early republican paintings, furnishings and independence artefacts and is mainly of interest to students of the Peruvian revolution. The building is next to the Anthropology & Archaeology Museum in Plaza Bolívar and is open the same hours. Entry costs 25c.

Museo de Oro del Peru The Gold Museum is actually two separate museums in the same private building, which is owned by the Mujica Gallo family. The incredibly rich gold museum itself is in a huge basement vault. The literally thousands of gold pieces range from ear plugs to ponchos embroidered with hundreds of solid gold plates. In addition, there are numerous other artefacts made of silver and precious stones and gems such as lapis lazuli, emeralds and pearls.

The Arms Museum, housed in the top half of the building, is reputed to be one of the world's best. Even if, like me, you have no interest in guns, you'll probably be fascinated by the thousands of ancient and bizarre firearms from all over the world which are displayed here. One of my favourite exhibits is a huge, ornately decorated blunderbuss. It's about 2 metres long, with a 5 cm bore and a flaring, trumpet-like muzzle, and dates from the 19th century. Although it looks more suitable for hunting elephants, it's labelled as a duck-hunting rifle!

The two museums are at Alonso de Molina 100, in the outlying suburb of Monterrico, east of central Lima. Hours are noon to 7 pm daily. The Gold Museum's private collection is high on the 'must see' list for many tourists visiting Peru on guided tours and admission is correspondingly high at $4 per person. This covers entry to both the Gold and Arms museums; separate tickets are not sold. Photography is prohibited but postcards and colour slides are for sale.

Museo Rafael Larco Herrera This private museum has one of the most incredible ceramics collections to be found anywhere – it is said to include about 55,000 pots. Many of the items were collected in the 1920s by a former vice-president of Peru. Entering the first rooms is like walking into a museum store – one is overwhelmed by shelf after shelf stacked to the high ceilings with thousands of ceramics grouped roughly into categories such as animals, people and medical practices.

Further into the museum, the best pieces are displayed in the uncluttered manner they deserve. As well as the ceramics you'll see mummies, a gold room, a small cactus garden, textiles made from feathers and a Paracas weaving which contains 398 threads to the linear inch – a world record. In a separate building is the famous collection of pre-Columbian erotic pots which illustrate, with remarkable explicitness, the sexual practices of several Peruvian cultures. All in all, this museum is highly recommended to everyone and certainly should not be missed by the ceramicist.

The museum is at Bolívar 1515 in Pueblo Libre (if you take a cab, make sure the driver does not confuse this museum with the nearby Museum of Anthropology & Archaeology). It is open from 9 am to 1 pm and 3 to 6 pm daily, except Sunday when it closes at 1 pm, and entry costs about $4. Photography is not allowed.

Museum of Art Housed in a very handsome building, Lima's art museum exhibits far more than art – its collection ranges from colonial furniture to pre-Columbian artefacts in addition to canvases spanning 400 years of Peruvian art. It's well worth a visit.

The museum is at Paseo de Colón 125, Lima and is open from 9 am to 6 pm Tuesday to Sunday. (Paseo de Colón is the popular name for 9 de Diciembre.) Admission is about $1 and photography is not allowed.

Amano Museum Those interested in Peruvian archaeology will want to make the effort to visit this museum. Its fine private ceramics collection is arranged chronologically to show the development of pottery through Peru's various pre-Columbian cultures. The museum specialises in the little-known Chancay culture, of which it has a remarkable collection of textiles.

Entry is free and in small groups (you have to form your own group), by appointment only. The tours are available on weekdays at 2, 3, 4 and 5 pm. Phone 412909 for an appointment. All groups are met at the door by a guide who will show you around in exactly 1 hour – it's best if you understand Spanish or have someone along to translate. You cannot wander around the museum at will but, by listening to the guide, you'll learn a good deal about the development of pottery in Peru and about the Chancay culture.

The museum is a little out of the way at Retiro 160, off the 11th block of Angamos in Miraflores, so give yourself plenty of time to get there – these people are extremely punctual, unlike many elsewhere in Peru.

Museo del Banco Central de Reserva This archaeological museum specialises in ceramics from the Vicus culture, as well as housing a small collection of other pre-Columbian artefacts and 19th and 20th century Peruvian art. In the heart of the city centre, it represents a welcome haven from the hustle and bustle of changing money or reconfirming airline tickets but is also worth visiting in its own right.

The museum, in the Central Reserve Bank at the corner of Ucayali and Lampa, is open from 10 am to 5 pm Tuesday to Saturday and 10 am to 1 pm on Sunday. Last time I was there, admission was only 3c.

National Museum This new museum, at Javier Prado Oeste 2466 in San Borja, has excellent models of Peru's major ruins as well as exhibits about Peruvian archaeology. The museum is open from 9 am to 7 pm, Tuesday to Friday and from 10 am to 7 pm Saturday and Sunday. Admission is $3.

Museum of the Inquisition The building housing this museum was used by the Spanish Inquisition from 1570 to 1820 and subsequently became the senate building. It is now a university library. Visitors can walk around the basement in which prisoners were tortured and there's a rather ghoulish waxwork exhibit of life-size unfortunates on the rack or having their feet roasted. In the library upstairs is a remarkable wooden ceiling.

The museum is at Junín 548, opposite the Plaza Bolívar in Lima (not the same as the plaza in Pueblo Libre), and is open from 9 am to 7.30 pm weekdays and 9 am to 4.30 pm on Saturday. Admission is free.

Museo de Ciencias de la Salud The Peruvian Health Sciences Museum has a unique collection of pre-Columbian artefacts ranging from mummies to pots. These indicate the extent of the medical knowledge of pre-Hispanic cultures, with exhibits showing how various injuries and diseases were diagnosed and cured. In another part of the museum, displays trace cultural developments in Peru from the Stone Age to the Inca civilisation. Medical instruments from the 18th and 19th centuries are also on show. This museum is of interest to everyone but should be particularly fascinating to health professionals. The exhibits are well labelled in both Spanish and English.

Apparently, the museum will arrange pre-Columbian banquets – meals consisting solely of the types of food available before

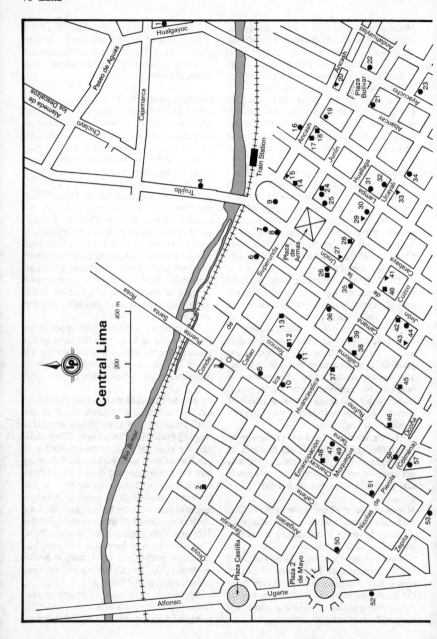

Central Lima

■ PLACES TO STAY

2 Hotel San Sebastian
12 Hotel Residencial Roma
13 Hotel Savoy
14 Hotel Comercio & Pacífico
17 Hotels Europa & San Francisco
18 Hostal España
24 Hostal Wiracocha
26 Pensión Unión
28 Hostal Damascus
37 Hotel Granada
38 Hotel Claridge
42 Hotel Richmond
45 Hotel La Casona
46 Hostal El Sol
48 Hotel Wilson & Youth Hostel Karina
56 Hotel Crillón
60 Gran Hotel Bolívar
63 Gran Hotel
64 Hostal San Martín
69 Hostal Belén
78 Lima Sheraton

▼ PLACES TO EAT

15 El Cordano Restaurant & Bar
20 Las Trece Monedas
27 Asociación Naturista Peruana
29 Cafe Adriatico
33 L'Eau Vive del Peru Restaurant
41 'No Name' Restaurant
43 Natur Vegetarian Restaurant
65 1900 Restaurant
75 Nakasone Restaurant

● OTHER

1 Bullring & Museum
3 Santuario de Santa Rosa de Lima &
  Museo Etnográfico de la Selva
4 Peña Hatuchay
5 Cine Imperio
6 Church of Santo Domingo
7 Post Office & Philatelic Museum
8 Francisco Pizarro Monument
9 Government Palace
10 Cine Central
11 Teatro Municipal
16 Church of San Francisco & Catacombs
19 Peña Machu Picchu
21 Museum of the Spanish Inquisition
22 Congress Building
23 General Market
24 Peruvian Health Sciences Museum
25 Cathedral
26 Cine Bijou
30 Museo del Banco Central de Reserva
31 Banco de Crédito
32 Palacio Torre Tagle
34 Church of San Pedro
35 AYZA Bookstore
36 Church of San Agustín
39 Teatro Segura
40 Church of La Merced
44 Cine Excelsior
47 Cine Tacna
49 Cine Lido
50 Cine Venecia
51 Cine Portofino
52 Museo de la Cultura Peruana
53 Cine Tauro
54 Turismo Chimbote (Bus)
55 Expreso Panamericano (Bus)
57 Post Office
58 Book Exchange
59 Cine Plaza
60 Faucett Airline
61 Cine Adan y Eva
62 International Telegrams
64 Parrilladas San Martín
66 Lima Tours & American Express
67 Tourist Information Office
68 AeroPeru
70 Cine Metro & International Telephone Office
71 Olano (Bus)
72 Cine República
73 Transportes Rodriguez (Bus)
74 South American Explorers Club
76 24 hour FAX location
77 Explorers Inn Office
79 Cine Conquistador
80 US Embassy
81 Museum of Italian Art
82 Peña Las Brisas del Lago Titicaca
83 Museum of Art
84 Circuito de Playas Beach (Bus)
85 Lima Immigration Office
86 Morales Moralitos (Bus)
87 Palace of Justice
88 TEPSA (Bus)
89 Antisuyo (Bus)
90 Bus to Chosica
91 Empresa Huaraz (Bus)
92 Ormeño (Bus)
93 Pisco (Bus)
94 Expreso Sudamericano (Bus)
95 Santa Catalina Convent
96 Buses to Pachacamac & Pucusana
97 Comité 12 to Huancayo
98 León de Huánuco (Bus)

Top: Library of Church of San Francisco, Lima (TW)
Left: Torre Tagle Palace, Lima (TW)
Right: Church of San Francisco, Lima (TW)

the arrival of the Spanish. You must have a group to arrange a banquet. Phone the museum (tel 270190) for full details. I've never tried this, so if you can get a group together, let us know how the food is.

The museum is just off the Plaza de Armas at Junín 270 and is open from 9 am to 5 pm daily except Sunday. Admission is $1.

Museo de la Cultura Peruana This small museum specialises in items more closely allied to popular art and handicrafts than to archaeology and history, including ceramics, carved gourds, recent art, traditional folk art and costumes from various periods and places.

The museum is at Alfonso Ugarte 650 and charges 10c admission plus an extra fee for photography. Hours are 10 am to 5 pm weekdays and 9.30 am to 5 pm on Saturday.

Museo de Historia Natural The Natural History Museum has only a modest collection of stuffed animals but, if you want to familiarise yourself with the fauna of Peru, it warrants a visit. Mammals, birds, reptiles, fish and insects are all represented.

The museum is at Arenales 1256 and is open from 8.30 am to 3.30 pm weekdays, 8.30 am to noon on Saturday and Sunday by previous arrangement. Admission is 15c.

Museo Etnográfico de la Selva This museum has a small but interesting collection of jungle artefacts obtained by Dominican missionaries in south-eastern Peru. Indian items such as clothes, headpieces, pottery, basketwork, jewellery and household items are displayed, together with numerous photographs showing the items in use.

The museum is in the grounds of the Santuario de Santa Rosa de Lima, on the 1st block of Avenida Tacna. Hours are 9.30 am to 1 pm and 3.30 to 7 pm daily and there is a 10c admission fee.

Museo de Arte Italiano Housed in a fairytale building in a park on the 2nd block of the Paseo de la República, the Museum of Italian Art is more attractive from the outside than it is inside. The exhibits are mostly reproductions and are badly labelled but, if you like Italian art, the museum is open from 9 am to 7 pm daily, except Monday, and admission costs about 30c.

Museo Numismatico del Banco Weise If you collect, study or have an interest in coins, this place is for you. The museum exhibits Peruvian coins, bills and medals from colonial days to the present. Admission is free and hours are 9 am to 1 pm weekdays. The Banco Weise is at Cuzco 245; the numismatic collection is on the 2nd floor.

Philatelic Museum Appropriately housed in the main post office, on the corner of the Plaza de Armas in Lima, the Philatelic Museum gives you the chance to examine, buy and trade Peruvian stamps. (The collection of Peruvian stamps is incomplete.) There is also a small exhibit of the Inca 'postal system'. The museum is open from 8 am to 1.30 pm and 2 to 4 pm weekdays, 8 am to 1.30 pm on Saturday and 8 am to noon on Sunday. Entry is free.

If you want to buy stamps for your collection, you'll find the museum shop open from 8 am to noon and 2 to 3 pm weekdays. Collectors and dealers meet at the museum on the last Sunday of each month to buy, sell and trade stamps.

Museo Taurino The Bullfight Museum is at the Plaza de Acho, Lima's bullring, at Hualgayoc 332 in the Rimac district. Even if you oppose bullfighting, you might want to visit the museum just to see the matadors' relics. These include a holed and bloodstained costume worn by a famous matador who was gored and killed in the Lima bullring some years ago. (Score one for the bulls!) Also worth seeing are some very good paintings and engravings of bullfighting scenes by various artists, notably Goya. Entry costs 20c and the museum is open on weekdays from 9 am to 1 pm and 3 to 6 pm.

Religious Buildings

Lima's many churches, monasteries and convents are a very welcome break from the city's noisy traffic and incessant crowds. Opening hours tend to be even more erratic than those of the museums – churches are often closed for restoration, religious services or because the caretaker is having an extended lunch – so you have to take your chances.

The Cathedral Completed in 1555, the original cathedral, on the south-east side of the Plaza de Armas, was soon deemed too small and another planned in its place. Work on the new cathedral began in 1564 and the building was still unfinished when it was consecrated in 1625. It was more or less complete by 1649 but was badly damaged in the 1687 earthquake and almost totally destroyed by another earthquake in 1746. The present reconstruction is based on the early plans.

The interior is stark compared to many Latin American churches. Of particular interest are the coffin and remains of Francisco Pizarro in the mosaic-covered chapel just to the right of the main door. For many years, there was debate over whether the remains were actually those of Pizarro. Recent investigations demonstrated that the remains previously on display were, in fact, those of an unknown conquistador. Since the transfer to the chapel of Pizarro's real remains, discovered in the crypt in the early 1980s, most authorities agree that the exhibit is now authentic. Also of interest is the well-carved choir and the small religious museum in the rear of the cathedral.

The cathedral's opening hours have changed regularly over the years. At last check, they were 10 am to 1 pm and 2 to 5 pm daily and admission was 30c, including entry to the religious museum. Photography was not allowed, though colour slides and postcards were on sale.

San Francisco This Franciscan church and monastery is famous for its catacombs. It is less well known for its remarkable library where you can see thousands of antique texts, some dating back to the time of the conquistadors.

The church is one of the best preserved of Lima's early colonial churches. Finished before the earthquake of 1687, which badly damaged most of Lima's churches, San Francisco withstood both this and the earthquake of 1746 better than the others. However, the 1970 earthquake caused considerable damage. Much of the church has been well restored in its original baroque style with Moorish (Arab) influence.

Tours are available with English or Spanish-speaking guides. Joining a tour is strongly recommended because it will enable you to see the catacombs, library, cloister and a very fine museum of religious art which are off limits to unguided visitors. The underground catacombs are the site of an estimated 70,000 burials and the faint-hearted may find the bone-filled crypts slightly unnerving.

The church is at the corner of Lampa and Ancash and is open daily from 10 am to 12.45 pm and 3 to 5.45 pm. The entry fee of $1.25 includes the guided tour. Spanish-speaking tours leave several times an hour and there are also tours led by English-speaking guides at least once an hour.

Convento de los Descalzos This infrequently visited convent and museum lies at the end of the Alameda de los Descalzos, an attractive if somewhat forgotten avenue in the Rimac district. (Though one of the poorer areas of Lima, Rimac is safe to visit.) The visitor can see old wine-making equipment in the 17th century kitchen, the refectory, the infirmary, typical cells of the Descalzos, or 'the barefooted' (a reference to the Franciscan friars), and some 300 colonial paintings of the Quito and Cuzco schools.

Entry to the convent and museum costs 30c and Spanish-speaking guides will show you around. A tour lasts about 40 minutes. The doors are open from 9.30 am to 1 pm and 3 to 6 pm daily except Tuesday.

Santuario de Santa Rosa de Lima Saint Rose, the first saint of the Western hemisphere, is particularly venerated in Lima, where she lived, and a peaceful garden and small church have been built roughly at the site of her birth. The sanctuary itself is a small adobe hut, built by Saint Rose in the early 1600s as a private room for prayer and meditation. Perhaps of greater interest is the Museo Etnográfico de la Selva in the same grounds. (Further information about opening hours and location is given in the Museums section.) Admission to the sanctuary is free.

Santo Domingo This is one of Lima's most historic churches because it was built on the land granted by Francisco Pizarro to the Dominican Friar Vicente Valverde in 1535. The friar accompanied Pizarro throughout the conquest and was instrumental in persuading him to execute Atahualpa after the Inca had been captured and ransomed in Cajamarca.

Construction of the church of Santo Domingo began in 1540 and was finished in 1599. Although the structure survived the earthquakes reasonably well, much of the interior was modernised late in the 18th century. The church contains the tombs of Saint Rose and the black Saint Martin de Porras (also of Lima), as well as an alabaster statue of Saint Rose which was presented to the church by Pope Clement in 1669. There is also fine tilework showing the life of Saint Dominic and pleasantly quiet cloisters in which you can walk and relax.

The church is on the first block of Camaná, across from the post office, and is open from 7 am to 1 pm and 4 to 8 pm daily. The monastery and tombs are open from 9.30 am to 12.30 pm and 3.30 to 5.30 pm Monday to Saturday and in the morning on Sunday and holy days. Admission is 30c.

La Merced Another historic church with a long and colourful history, La Merced was built on the site of the first mass celebrated in Lima in 1534, before Pizzaro's official founding of the city in 1535. The original building, a temporary affair, was soon replaced by a larger church. This, in turn, was torn down and construction of a third building began in 1628. The structure was seriously damaged by the 1687 earthquake but, once again, rebuilding was soon underway. Work started on a new facade after damage in the 1746 earthquake, and in 1773, the church suffered further damage when a fire destroyed all the paintings and vestments in the sacristy. Thus, most of today's church dates to the 1700s. An attempt was made to modernise the facade early this century, but in 1936, it was returned to its original appearance. Inside the church is an ornately carved chancel and an attractively decorated cloister.

As La Merced is on the busy pedestrian street of Jirón Unión at Miro Quesada, most visitors to Lima pass it several times. The church is open daily from 7 am to 12.30 pm and 4 to 8 pm and the cloister from 8 am to noon and 3 to 5.30 pm.

San Pedro Many experts consider this small baroque church to be one of the finest examples of early colonial architecture in Lima. It was consecrated by the Jesuits in 1638 and has changed little since. The interior, sumptuously decorated with gilded altars, Moorish-influenced carvings and an abundance of beautiful glazed tilework, is well worth seeing. The church is on the corner of Azangaro and Ucayali in the old centre. Opening hours are 7 am to 12.30 pm and 6 to 8 pm daily and admission is free.

San Agustín In contrast to San Pedro, the church of San Agustín has been altered much more than Lima's other early churches. The churrigueresque (an elaborately and intricately decorated Spanish style common in colonial Latin America) facade dates from the early 1700s and is the oldest part of the church to have remained intact. Much of the church was reconstructed at the end of the 19th century and again after the extensive damage of the 1970 earthquake. The church, on the corner of Ica and Camaná, can be visited daily from 8.30 am to noon and 3.30 to 5.30 pm.

Las Nazarenas This church was built in the 18th century and is not, in itself, of great interest. The site on which it is built, however, plays a part in one of the most passionate of Lima's traditional religious feasts.

The site used to be a shanty town inhabited mainly by liberated Black slaves. Early in the 17th century, an ex-slave painted one of the walls of the shanty town with an image of the crucifixion of Christ. Although the area was destroyed by an earthquake in 1655, the wall with the mural survived. This was considered a miracle and the church of the Nazarene was later built around the wall. On 18 October each year, a copy of the mural, known as the Lord of the Miracles, is carried around in a huge procession of many thousands of the faithful. The procession continues for 2 or 3 days, with the holy image being taken from church to church before being returned to Las Nazarenas.

The church is at the corner of Huancavelica and Tacna and can be visited from 7 to 11.30 am and 4.30 to 8 pm daily. Admission is free.

Other Sights

While the museums and religious buildings will undoubtedly take up most of the visitor's sightseeing time, Lima also has many plazas, buildings and other sites of interest.

Plaza de Armas The central and most important plaza in any Peruvian town is likely to be its Plaza de Armas and Lima is no exception. This large plaza, 140 sq metres, was once the heart of Lima but not one original building remains. The oldest surviving part, the impressive bronze fountain in the centre, was erected in 1650 and the oldest building on the plaza, the cathedral, was reconstructed after the 1746 earthquake.

The exquisitely balconied Archbishop's Palace to the left of the cathedral is a relatively modern building dating to 1924. The Government Palace on the north-east side of the plaza was built in the same period. Here, a handsomely uniformed presidential guard is on duty all day and the daily ceremonial changing of the guard takes place at 12.45 pm. The other buildings around the plaza are

Changing the guard, Presidential Palace

also modern: the municipalidad (town hall) built in 1945, the Unión Club and various stores and cafés.

On the corner of the plaza, opposite the cathedral, there is an impressive statue of Francisco Pizarro on horseback; (he was, in fact, a mediocre horseman). Apparently, the equestrian statue was once in the centre of the plaza but, as the clergy took a dim view of the fact that the horse's rear end faced the cathedral, the statue was moved to its present position.

Plaza San Martín Dating from the early 1900s, the Plaza San Martín is one of the major plazas in central Lima. The bronze equestrian statue of the liberator, General San Martín, was erected in 1921.

Jirón Unión Five blocks of this street join the Plaza de Armas and the Plaza San Martín. These five blocks are a pedestrian precinct and contain several good jewellery stores, bookshops and movie theatres as well as the Church of La Merced. Consequently, it is always very crowded with shoppers, sightseers, ambulantes and, inevitably, pickpockets. Few visitors to Lima miss this street and here it is essential to keep your valuables in an inside pocket or money belt.

Palacio Torre Tagle Built in 1735, this mansion is considered to be the best surviving colonial house in Lima. It now contains the offices of the Foreign Ministry, so entry on weekdays is either prohibited or restricted to the patio. On Saturday, you can enter the building between 9 am and 4 pm; a tip to the caretaker usually ensures access to the fine rooms and balconies upstairs. The house is at Ucayali 363.

Casa Aliaga This is one of Lima's most historic houses and is furnished completely in the colonial style. It is built on land given to Jerónimo de Aliaga by Pizarro in 1535 and has been occupied by the Aliaga family ever since. The house can be visited only with Vista Tours, who charge $10 for a half-day city tour which includes the Aliaga house.

Vista Tours (tel 276624) is a subsidiary of Lima Tours at Belén 1040 in Lima. The Aliaga house is at Jirón Unión 224.

Other Colonial Houses Other colonial houses are easier to visit though they are not as important as those already mentioned. The Casa Pilatos, now housing the National Culture Institute, is at Ancash 390 and is open from 8.30 am to 4.45 pm weekdays. The Casa de la Riva, run by the Entre Nous Society, is at Ica 426 and is open daily between 10 am and 5 pm. The Casa de Riva-Aguero houses the Catholic University library and a small folk-art collection. It's at Camaná 459 and is open from 5 to 8 pm weekdays. The Casa de Ricardo Palma is the home of the Peruvian author of that name and can be visited, for a small fee, from 10 am to 12.30 pm and 4 to 7 pm weekdays and from 10 am to noon on Saturday. The house is at Gral Suarez 189, Miraflores.

Zoo The zoo, in the Parque las Leyendas between Lima and Callao, is divided into three areas representing the three major geographical divisions of Peru: the coast, the sierra (or Andes) and the Amazon Basin. Peruvian animals make up most of the exhibits, though there are a few more typical zoo animals such as elephants. The zoo has recently been modernised and is open from 9 am to 5 pm daily except Monday. Admission is about 30c.

Viscacha

Archaeological Sites

There are two minor pre-Inca ruins in the Lima area. Both have on-site museums, entrance to which costs a few cents and which are open from 10 am to 5 pm daily except Monday. The Huaca Huallamarca is a restored Maranga temple dating from about 200 AD to 500 AD. It is at the corner of El Rosario and Nicolas de Riviera in San Isidro. The Huaca Juliana, a recently excavated pre-Inca temple, is one block off the 46th block of Arequipa in Miraflores and easy to get to.

Spectator Sport

Soccer, called *futbol*, is the national sport but is closely rivalled by volleyball, which is of a high standard. Peru's National Stadium, off the 7th, 8th and 9th blocks of the Paseo de la República, is the venue for the most important soccer matches and other events. The national team is quite good and qualified for the 1992 World Cup in Madrid.

Horse racing is also popular. Meetings are held most weekends and some weekday evenings at the Monterrico Racetrack, at the junction between the Pan-American Highway South and Avenida Javier Prado. I understand that, if you're reasonably well dressed and take your passport, you can use the members' stand.

Bullfighting and cockfighting both have a following in Lima. The bullfighting season is in late October and November and there is also a short season in March. Famous foreign matadors fight in the bullring at Acho in Rimac; bullfights are well advertised in the major newspapers and tickets are sold well in advance. Cockfighting occurs year round at the Coliseo de Gallos at Avenida Sandia 150, just off the Parque Universitario.

Miraflores

Miraflores is the Lima suburb visited most frequently by tourists. Until the 1940s, it was a beachfront community separated from the capital by countryside and haciendas. Lima's recent population boom has made this countryside the fashionably elegant residential district of San Isidro while Miraflores has become one of Lima's most important shopping, entertainment and residential areas.

Many of the capital's best restaurants and nightspots are found here and the pavement cafés are great places to see and be seen. As you'd expect, the prices and quality of everything ranging from sweaters to steaks will be higher in Miraflores than in other parts of the city. Miraflores is linked to Lima by the tree-lined Avenida Arequipa, along which run frequent colectivos and buses.

Market

There are several of these ranging from the incredibly crowded general market in central Lima to the leisurely and relaxed artists' market in Miraflores.

Lima's main market is at Ayacucho and Ucayali to the south-east of Avenida Abancay. The market officially occupies a whole city block but, as this area is not nearly large enough, the stalls and vendors congest the streets for several blocks around. You can buy almost anything here, but be prepared for extreme crowding and watch your valuables. Many people enjoy this eye-opening experience, despite the discomfort.

The streets behind the post office are the centre of a black market known as Polvos Azules, or 'blue powders' (for some unknown reason). It's as crowded as the main market, so watch your wallet just as closely. This is the place to find smuggled luxuries such as ghetto blasters and perfume, as well as a remarkable variety of other consumer goods.

Lima's main flower market, at the south end of the National Stadium (9th block of Paseo de la República), is a kaleidoscopic scene of beautiful flowers at bargain prices. The best selection is in the morning.

The Indian Artisans' Market is along the north side of Avenida de la Marina on the 600 to 1000 blocks. The selection of handicrafts here is fabulous but the quality and prices vary a good deal, so shop carefully. This is, perhaps, one of the less tourist-oriented handicraft markets but, obviously, any handicraft market relies on tourist consumption. Better quality at higher prices can be found at various handicraft stores in Lima and Miraflores (see the Things to Buy section).

The artists' market, which operates most afternoons and evenings on Parque Kennedy, in the heart of Miraflores, is a good place to see the work of local artists. This ranges from garish 'painting by number' monstrosities in oil to some good watercolours.

Places to Stay

Lima offers literally scores of hotels ranging from $1 per night cheapies to luxury hotels which could cost 100 times as much. It is impossible and unnecessary to list them all, but this selection should include something that suits you.

Generally speaking, hotels are more expensive in Lima than in other Peruvian cities. Most of the cheapest are in the central city area, with some well-known budget hotels to be found within a few blocks of the Plaza de Armas. At night, the city centre is not as safe as some of the more up-market neighbourhoods (such as Miraflores) and is also dirtier and noisier. However, there's no real problem as long as you don't parade around with a gold chain on your neck and a wallet peeking out of your hip pocket.

Mid-range and expensive hotels are all over Lima; there are some excellent luxury hotels both in the heart of the city and in Miraflores.

Whether you are staying in cheap or expensive accommodation, always ask about discounts if you plan to spend some time in Lima. Most places will offer cheaper weekly rates and may give you a discount for a stay of just a few days.

The one type of hotel you won't find in Lima is the government-run ENTURPeru Tourist Hotel. These exist in all major Peruvian cities except the capital, probably because the capital already has so many good hotels. Nevertheless, ENTURPeru's main reservation office is in Lima and, at this office, you can plan a complete Peru travel itinerary staying in good hotels. Over 40 cities have hotels which can be reserved at ENTURPeru. Reservations are free and room costs are no higher than they'd be if you went direct to the hotels in the cities you want to visit. ENTURPeru (tel 721928, 728227) is at Avenida Javier Prado Oeste 1358, Lima 27, in the San Isidro district. The telex number is 20393.

Places to Stay – bottom end

One of the cheapest of Lima's budget hotels is the basic *Hotel Europa* (tel 273351) at Ancash 376. This shabby old dive is safe and reasonably clean, so it's often full by mid-afternoon. Singles/doubles cost $1.20/2.20 and there are bigger rooms with up to six beds. The communal showers rarely have hot water. Around the corner at Azangaro 105 is the *Hostal España* (there's no sign on the street), a rambling old mansion full of plants, birds and paintings. Accommodation is basic, but clean, safe and friendly and costs about $2 per person. Nearby are the cheap but much grimier and less pleasant *Hotel Comercio* and *Hotel Pacífico* on the 1st block of Carabaya.

Perhaps the cheapest place in town is the *Hotel Richmond* at the intersection of Jirón de la Unión and Cuzco. It has a reasonably attractive old-fashioned lobby with marble stairs, but the rooms are grimy and the water erratic. I have also heard complaints about theft and a lack of safety here. The hotel charges about 60c per person, and about $1 per person in rooms with a private bath. Further along the same street at Unión 442, on the 3rd floor (go through the bookshop and café), is the clean, friendly *Pensión Unión*. It costs $1 per person and, sometimes, has hot water in the evenings. Despite recent fire damage, I understand it has reopened. The *Hostal Damascus* at Ucayali 199 is also very near to the centre and is fairly clean and friendly. A double room costs about $3 and a double with private bath is a little more expensive. Hot water is usually available.

Dormitory-style accommodation can be found at the *Asociación de Amistad Peruano/Europeo* on the 7th floor of Camaná 280. Baggage lockers are provided. Sleeping here is no cheaper than it is at the cheap hotels, but the association is a good source of information. The old *Gran Hotel* on Abancay 546 has spacious rooms but has seen better days. Accommodation in rooms with private bath costs $2 per person, a few cents less in a room with communal bath, and there is occasional hot water. The *Hostal Belén* at Belén 1049, opposite the tourist information office, has fairly reliable hot water and is reasonably clean. Rooms cost $2.50/3.50 for singles/doubles. The *Hostal Universo* at Azangaro 754 is quite close to several bus terminals and, although not very clean, it is safe. Rooms with private bath and hot water (sometimes) cost $2.50/4.

The *Youth Hostel Karina* at Chancay 617 is good value at $2.50 per person. Another low-budget possibility is the *Hotel Wilson* on the same block. Here, you'll pay $4.80 for a double room with bath. The *Hostal Wiracocha* at Junín 270 has been recommended, though it doesn't seem particularly special to me. Single/double rooms with bath and hot water are $4/5. Rooms without bath are about $1 cheaper, but the communal showers have cold water only. The *Hotel Claridge* at Cailloma 437 has clean, spacious rooms which used to cost over $10. However, recent reports indicate that doubles with bath are available for $5 – good value.

Two hotels on Ica have recently gained a lot of popularity among discriminating budget travellers. The *Hotel San Sebastian* at Ica 712 charges $3/5 for singles/doubles. It has many bathrooms with hot water, the rooms are clean and there is a helpful English-speaking landlady, left-luggage facilities and a rooftop terrace. Also popular is the *Hotel Residencial Roma* at Ica 326. It's clean, central and provides double rooms with bath and hot water for $8 and double rooms with shared bath for $6.

If you want to stay with a family, try the Rodriguez family (tel 236465) – they rent rooms at Colmena 730 for $3 per person.

Places to Stay – middle

The *Hotel La Casona*, in the city centre at Moquegua 289, has a very pleasant lobby with plants and flowers. The carpeted rooms are shabby but not too bad and the hot water is reliable. Singles/doubles with bath cost about $7/10, but discounts can be arranged if you're staying for a few days. The desk staff have been reported to be unfriendly and unhelpful.

A very attractive converted mansion with a view of the Pacific, the *Hostal Barranco* (tel 671753) is at Malecón Osma 104 in the Barranco suburb, just beyond Miraflores. Rooms vary from simple to very good with prices ranging from about $8 to $22 for a double, some with private bath. There is also a garden, pool and games room.

The *Youth Hostel* at Casimiro Ulloa 328 in Miraflores (tel 465488) charges about $5 per person, which is the cheapest accommodation you'll find in Miraflores. The hostel offers laundry facilities, travel information and a swimming pool. Other Miraflores hotels which charge about the same include the *Residencial Waldorf* on Pasaje Schell 121 (off the 3rd block of Avenida Schell) and the *Pension Jose Luis* at F Paula Ugarriza 727 (a private home with no sign). Both are recommended.

Miraflores has plenty of good mid-range hotels in which a clean single room with private bath will cost about $10 to $18. The following have been recommended for their service and for being pleasant. The *Residencial Inn* (tel 471704) at General Borgoño 280 charges $13 for a single room and breakfast. At the similarly priced *Hostal El Ejecutivo* at 28 de Julio 245, breakfast and a telephone in your room are included and *La Alameda* at Pardo 931 offers double rooms for $20, including breakfast. The *Hostal Residencial Aleman* at Arequipa 4707 charges $17/26 for singles/doubles, including an excellent breakfast, while the *Hostal Torreblanca* (of which I've heard mixed reports) at José Pardo 1543, offers singles/doubles for $18/25, again including breakfast. English is spoken at most of these places.

Also recommended is the *Hostal Miramar* at Malecón Cisneros 1244. Singles/doubles are $20/30, including breakfast, and some of the rooms have an ocean view.

Several similar, reasonably priced hotels are to be found in the city centre, all with private bathrooms and hot water. The family-run *Pensión Ibarra* at Tacna 359, Apt 162, 15th floor, has a good reputation. Double rooms cost $12 but discounts for longer stays can be arranged. The *Hostal El Sol* at Rufino Torrico 773 charges $10 per person. It's centrally located but reasonably quiet. The *Hotel Grand Castle* is opposite the Ormeño bus terminal at Zavala Loayza 218 and has been praised for its good service. Singles/doubles are $9/13. The clean *Hotel Eiffel* at Jirón Washington 949 offers double rooms with plenty of hot water for $15. Also good is the *Hostal Residencial Los Virreyes* at Cañete 826, near the Plaza 2 de Mayo. The $16/23 for singles/doubles includes breakfast. Again recommended, the pleasant, quiet *Hostal Granada* at Huancavelica 323 charges $18/24 for singles/doubles, including breakfast.

In the San Isidro residential district, midway between central Lima and Miraflores, are several quiet, mid-range hotels. These include the *Hostal Residencial Firenze* at S Tellería 203 and Chinchón which, at $10/12 for singles/doubles, is value for money. The *Hostal Residencial Collacocha* at Andrés Reyes 100 at the end of the Paseo Parodi charges $12/16.

Places to Stay – top end

In most Peruvian cities, many of the hotels in the medium price range are better than the top-end hotels. Lima is one of the few places where you can find luxury hotels, if you feel that you need them (and if you can afford it). It's worth asking about discounts at the more expensive hotels. All rates given in this section include taxes.

The street with the greatest selection of fancy city hotels is Colmena in the four blocks north-west of the Plaza San Martín. Cheapest is the *Hostal San Martín* (above the Parrilladas San Martín, right on the Plaza), where a double room with air-con, telephone, carpeting and a private bar costs $35. Next door, the new and modern *El Plaza* charges $37/45 for singles/doubles.

Across the street is the venerable *Gran Hotel Bolívar*. This is the oldest top-class hotel in town and a delightful place in which to wander. The hotel reputedly serves one of the better pisco sours in town and, if you can't afford a room, you can still luxuriate with a drink in the bar. A string quartet plays light classical pieces in the beautiful, domed, stained-glass rotunda during afternoon tea (pricey but charming). If you stay here, try to get rooms on the 2nd or 3rd floor – the upper floors seem less used and slightly musty. Rooms are $65/85. Similarly priced, but much more modern, the excellent *Hotel Crillón* at Colmena 589 has a Sky Room restaurant on the top floor (about the 21st) with stupendous views of Lima.

Other luxury hotels in the central city area include the *Lima Sheraton* at Paseo de la República 170, where you'll pay about $75 for a room, and the more modest *Gran Hotel Maury* at Ucayali 201, only one block from the Plaza de Armas and reputedly the hotel where the pisco sour was invented. Rooms here are $35/47.

On the way to Miraflores, in San Isidro, is the *Hotel Sans Souci* at Arequipa 2670. It looks pleasant and has been recommended, though I found the management distinctly unfriendly. Singles/doubles cost $25/30. A reasonably priced 1st class hotel in Miraflores is the *Hostal Ariosto* at La Paz 769. The guests often include famous people such as jazz musicians and writers, as well as a fair sprinkling of international business people and tourists. Rooms cost about $35/45 but discounted rates can be arranged for large groups and long stays. Also recommended in Miraflores is the similarly priced *Hotel Jose Antonio* at 28 de Julio 398.

Luxury hotels include the *El Pardo* at Pardo 420, with singles/doubles for $61/80, and the *Miraflores César* at La Paz and Diez Canseco which holds the dubious distinction of being the most expensive hotel in Miraflores (and, probably, in all of Peru) at $97/115 for singles/doubles.

Places to Eat

As with hotels, Lima has a vast selection of

restaurants of every price range and quality. However, there is one notable gap; there are no 24 hour restaurants and nothing seems to be open before 7.30 am except street vendors. So, if you want an early breakfast, you're out of luck (unless you're staying at one of the top hotels).

Note that taxes and service charges on meals can be exorbitant. Cheap restaurants might not charge extra, but check first if you're on a tight budget. The fancier restaurants can add about 28% to your bill in combined taxes and service charges. (The waiter then discreetly whispers 'This is the legal tax, señor – it doesn't include a tip'. Add up to 5% more.)

Places to Eat – budget Several cheaper restaurants will suit the budget traveller. The cheapest meals are the set menus served for lunch. These are called, simply, el menu, and cost well under $1 in the cheaper restaurants. There are two good and popular ones on the same block as the Hotel Europa. Try the unnamed chifa at Ancash 306 for large portions of tallarines (noodle dinners) for about 60c. A few doors away, the *Restaurant Machu Picchu* is also cheap and good.

My favourite restaurant in the area is *El Cordano*, a pink building at Ancash 202, opposite the train station. It's a little more expensive but has an interesting 1920s decor, excellent espresso coffee and a varied menu of typical Peruvian snacks and meals. It's also one of the few places in town which serves a good variety of different Peruvian beers as well as a choice of local wines and piscos. A bottle of the rough but drinkable house wine costs less than $1. It's a good place to meet people and is open from about 9.30 am to 9 pm.

Very clean and reasonably priced, the *Café Adriatico* at Ucayali 239 has inexpensive lunches and is also a good place for a light breakfast. There are a couple of cheap eateries near the Hotel Roma on the 300 block of Ica – the *Ciervo de Oro* is described by one enthusiast as 'the best cake shop in Peru', while the *Tic Tac Chifa* at Callao 184 near the Plaza de Armas is cheap and clean.

A good street for budget eating places is Quilca, between the Plaza San Martín and Avenida Garcilazo de la Vega, where you'll find about a dozen inexpensive restaurants. Another good cheap possibility, with private curtained booths, is the *Chifa Restaurant Nakasone* at Alfonso Ugarte 1360, convenient to the South American Explorers Club. There are plenty of other cheap restaurants all over Lima.

Places to Eat – middle A good lunch-time restaurant, the *Raimondi* at Miró Quesada 110 is popular with Lima's businessmen. There's no sign and the exterior gives no indication of the spacious comfort within. The food is good and, although you'll pay a little more here, it's not too expensive.

If you'd like to dine in elegant surroundings, there are several reasonably priced restaurants ($5 to $10 for a meal) housed in some of Lima's historic buildings. One of my favourites is the *L'Eau Vive* at Ucayali 370 where the food, prepared and served by a French order of nuns, features dishes from all over the world as well as some exotic cocktails. It's extremely quiet and prices are moderate. Hours are noon to 2.45 pm and 8.15 to 10.15 pm daily except Sunday. The nuns sing an 'Ave María' at 10 pm.

In the same price range, the *1900* at Belén 1030 has live folklórico music in the evenings. It's open from 10 am to 10 pm and the evening music starts at about 7.30 pm. For Peruvian food, try *Las Trece Monedas*. This restaurant, in a colonial mansion at Jirón Ancash 536, Lima, is open from noon to 4 pm and 7 to 11.30 pm daily but is closed on Sunday.

One of my favourite seafood restaurants in the middle price range is *Cebichería Don Beta* at José Gálvez 667 in Miraflores. (Don't be put off by the tiny exterior – it opens up inside.) This place is very popular among Peruvians for lunch but is quiet in the evenings.

Places to Eat – top end There are many top-class restaurants in the Lima area and prices, though high by Peruvian standards, are still very reasonable when compared to those in European or North American restaurants. If you want to spend $20 or $30 a head (including tax, tips and drinks) in a really luxurious place, the restaurants described in this section can all be recommended.

Three excellent restaurants in the little shopping mall between the 6th block of La Paz and the 4th block of Alcanfores in Miraflores – the *Carlin, El Suche* and the *El Condado* – all have good food, service and ambience, the Carlin being the best. (I have recently heard that the menu at El Suche has become somewhat limited.) At La Paz 635, *La Creperie* serves an exceptional array of crepes as well as other food. For a special meal with good seafood, I enjoy *La Rosa Nautica*. It's in a fabulous building at the end of a pier at Costa Verde in Miraflores. The ocean is floodlit and surfers sometimes surf through the pilings. To get there, take a taxi.

Limeños have recommended a newer, ocean-front restaurant which supposedly has better seafood. The name is *El Salto De Fraile*, or 'the priest's leap' – you can guess the story. It's at the Herradura beach in Chorrillos; again, take a taxi. In Barranco, *El Otro Sitio* at Sucre 317 has been recommended for its romantic location next to el Puente de Suspiros (the Bridge of Sighs), and for its good Peruvian food and live music in the evenings. It also offers an 'all you can eat' criollo buffet for about $10. *Los Condes de San Isidro* is in an attractive old house at Paz Soldan 290 in San Isidro. It's open for lunch from noon to 3 pm and for dinner from 7 to 11 pm. There are many other 1st class restaurants to try when you've exhausted these possibilities. Most are open for lunch and dinner and close between about 3 and 7 pm.

Vegetarian Food If you like vegetarian food, the *Asociación Naturista Peruana* at Ucayali 133 and the *Natur* at Moquegua 132, both in Lima, are very inexpensive and recommended, especially the friendly, family-run *Natur*. There are also two vegetarian restaurants in Miraflores which are slightly more expensive – the *Govinda* at

Schell 630, run by the Hare Krishnas and, a block away at Schell 598, the *Bircher Berner*. This restaurant gets my special award for the slowest service in Lima, but the food is good and there is a nice garden in which to sit while you wait for it.

Italian Food Lovers of Italian food will find several pizzerias on Olaya and Diagonal streets, by the Parque Kennedy in Miraflores. The *La Pizzería* is overpriced; other places are cheaper but none is outstanding. Some people say that the *Pizza Hut* at Espinar and 2 de Mayo in Miraflores has the best pizza. The *La Trattoria* at Bonilla 106, just off Larco by the Ovalo, is recommended for tasty, home-made pasta (which you can watch being made). There are also a number of quite reasonable pizzerias in Miraflores.

Cafés & Pubs Miraflores has many pavement cafés, one of the best known being the *Haiti*, on the traffic circle next to the El Pacífico cinema. The main attraction is its excellent location – good for watching the world go by while you have a coffee – but the food is, at best, mediocre. The *La Tiendecita Blanca*, on the other side of the traffic circle, is much better and has a superb pastry selection. Nearby, at Ricardo Palma 258, is *Vivaldis*, apparently one of the more 'in' places for young Mirafloreños. The *Liverpool*, on the same block, is a similar café but always seems to be less crowded and more expensive. Of the several pavement cafés along Larco, the *La Sueca* at Larco 759, has excellent pastries.

The Brenchley Arms is, as its name would suggest, a British pub. It's as genuine as you'll find in Peru and is run by Englishman Mike Ella and his Peruvian wife. (The couple bought the pub from the original owners, the Brenchleys, in mid-1990). The small but excellent dinner menu offers such delights as pork or lamb chops, liver and onions, hot pies and curries. Prices are reasonable, beer consumption is high – British beer is not imported into Peru but the local Pilsen and Crystal seem to do the trick – there is a dart board and you can read the British newspapers. This is the haunt of British and American expatriates who work for oil companies, schools or embassies and will be delighted to tell you about Peru's 'problems'. English is spoken, Spanish is not. The pub is at Atahualpa 174, a block from the El Pacífico cinema, and is open from 6 pm to closing time (which varies from 11 pm to...?). Meals are served from 7 to 9 pm 6 days a week – only snacks are available on Sunday, the cook's day off.

The Barranco district is a pleasant area for a stroll and has several good cafés. One of the best is Buen Gusto at Avenida Grau 323, a block away from the Barranco main plaza. The atmosphere is elegant and the service excellent, a great place for a light meal. Afterwards, you can walk over the Bridge of Sighs for a look at the Pacific Ocean.

Entertainment

The *El Comercio* newspaper lists cinemas, theatres, art galleries and music shows. If your Spanish is not up to this, the English weekly the *Lima Times* has an abbreviated listing of what's on. Generally speaking, the nightlife starts late and continues until 3 or 4 am, so it tends to be more popular at weekends. Cultural events, such as the theatre and the symphony, start earlier; films run from early afternoon.

Cinemas Seeing a film is one of the cheapest forms of entertainment and, with several dozen cinemas from which to choose, you can usually find something worth seeing. Foreign (non-Peruvian) films are usually screened with their original sound track and Spanish subtitles. Admission is typically well under $1. You can often see the latest Oscar nominees or Cannes winners along with the usual selection of horror, porn and kung fu. Some cinema clubs show better films – these are listed in the newspapers' cultural events section, separately from the ordinary cinema listings.

Theatre & Music The *Teatro Municipal*, at Ica 300 in the city centre, is the venue for symphony, opera, plays and ballet. The best seats are expensive and even cheap tickets cost several dollars. Another good venue is the *Teatro Segura* on the 200 block of Huancavelica. The *Teatro Arequipa*, on the 800 block of Avenida Arequipa, has revues in Spanish. For surprisingly good English-language plays, see the local theatre group *The Good Companions*, run by the British Council. It seems to do something new every month and advertises in the *Lima Times*. Phone them on 479760 for information.

Peruvian Music Live Peruvian music is performed at *peñas* where you can often sing along and dance. Drinks are served and, sometimes, food. There are two types of Peruvian music – *folklórico* and *criolla*. The first is more typical of the Andean highlands and is, therefore, less popular in Lima, while the second is more coastal. The peña with the best reputation among budget travellers, and deservedly so, is the *Hatuchay* at Trujillo 228 in Rimac. It's in a huge barn of a place just across the bridge, behind the presidential palace. The music is mainly folklórico and there is plenty of audience participation and dancing during the second half. Typical Peruvian snacks are served, as well as drinks. Peñas are generally fairly pricey, but this one is inexpensive at around $1.50 cover charge and there's no minimum consumption. Doors open at about 9 pm and music starts around 10 pm. Get there early or make advance reservations to ensure a good seat.

A well-recommended folklórico peña which is very popular with Limeños but little frequented by tourists is *Las Brisas del Lago Titicaca* at Wakulski 168, just off Brasil near the Plaza Bolognesi. It's open Thursday to Saturday from about 9.30 pm and the cover charge is $2. Another reasonably priced peña is the *Wifala* at Cailloma 633 in Lima where folklórico music is played. The *Peña Machu Picchu* at Azangaro 142 is a cheap, boozy, local place.

The *Karamanduka* at Benavides 621, Miraflores features criolla music and is much more expensive, catering to the richer Limeños. In Barranco, there is the *La Estación de Barranco* at Pedro de Osma 112 where a variety of folklórico and criolla music can be heard. Also in Barranco, next door to the *El Otro Sitio* restaurant at Sucre 315, the *El Buho Pub* offers criolla music. Although these places are a little cheaper than those in Miraflores, they are still fairly expensive. They have typically late-night Friday and Saturday hours, starting at about 10 pm.

Bars The best of the many good bars where you can have a drink and, sometimes, listen to music, are mainly in Miraflores. *The Brenchley Arms* pub at Atahualpa 174 is a good place to meet English-speaking locals – see the Places to Eat section for more information. The *Johann Sebastian Bar* at Schell 369 is quiet with classical music, expensive drinks and a pleasant ambience.

Two excellent but expensive bars in Miraflores feature live jazz most nights – the *Lions Club* at 338 Madrid, by the Plaza Bolognesi, and the newer and highly recommended *Satchmo's* at La Paz 538. Internationally famous musicians are sometimes featured and cover charges can be as high as $15, plus a minimum of two drinks.

Discos There are several American-style discotheques which tend to be dark and expensive. Although some have a members or couples-only policy, you can often get around this by showing your passport and telling the doorman you're a tourist. One of the better known (but by no means the best) is the *Arizona Colt*, below the El Pacífico cinema in Miraflores. It's a pick-up joint as much as anything else, but that's probably true of most discos. *La Miel*, across the street under the Indianapolis café at José Pardo 120, may be better. *Faces* at the Centro Comercial Camino Real, Level A 68/72, by the intersection of Camino Real and Choquehuanca in San Isidro, is a fairly new and popular dancing spot.

Other places to dance in the San Isidro area are the *Unicorn* at Paseo de la República 3030, *La Manzana* at Miguel Dasso 143, *Ebony Sicodelico* at Las Magnolias 841 and the *Las Rocas Club* at Rivera Navarrete 821.

I'm not a disco fan so I haven't been to any of these. I'll be happy to send a free copy of this book to whoever sends me the best discotheque information for the next edition.

Sport Swimming and surfing are popular during the summer months of January, February and March. However, the water is heavily polluted at all of Lima's beaches and newspapers warn of the serious health hazard posed by swimming and surfing.

Lima has several tennis and golf clubs and the 1st class hotels and tour agencies can help organise a game for you. Sudex Agency at Carabaya 933 can help with tennis and golf in Lima. Lima Tours at Belén 1040 has three buses a day to El Pueblo Inn, a country club 11 km east of Lima on the Central Highway. The bus costs $1 and admission to the country club is $1.50. Tennis, golf, riding, swimming and bowling are available.

You can go tenpin bowling and play pool at the Brunswick Bowl at Balta 135, Miraflores.

Things to Buy

Markets are not the best places to shop for souvenirs and handicrafts in Lima, with the possible exception of the Indian Artisans' Market described in the Market section. You'll find a better selection in shops and shopping arcades. The prices tend to be high but, as they vary, it pays to shop around. Two very similar-looking wall hangings, for example, may cost $30 and $40 in two different shops. Quality is usually good in the places mentioned in this section. Prices are fixed in some stores but you can bargain in others. If you're buying several items in a place, it's always worth asking for a discount. Remember: carry cash in a safe inside pocket or money belt when shopping.

Two of my favourite Lima shopping arcades are both on Belén, the smaller one at 1066 where the tourist information office is and the larger one at 1030 where the 1900 restaurant is. There are several other excellent shops on the same block – visit them all before making your choice. The wide variety of handicrafts from all over Peru include tightly woven rugs and wall hangings from Ayacucho; tapestries made from rolls of stuffed wool from San Pedro de Cajas; hangings, called *arpilleras*, showing scenes made of little cloth dolls; carved gourds from Huancayo; spears, blow pipes and pottery from the jungle; carved stone buildings from Ayacucho; carved and colourfully painted wooden boxes which open to reveal incredibly intricate scenes of Peruvian life, tooled leatherwork and the usual assortment of ponchos, sweaters and rugs.

Jewellery is also popular and reasonably priced and gold, silver and turquoise are common. There are several good jewellery stores along the pedestrian section of Jirón Unión. Cash dollars or travellers' cheques can be used in some of the better stores and exchange rates are often within 1% of the best rates in town. Don't use your credit card,

Chancay weaving design

though, because you'll end up paying about 25% more than with cash.

There are plenty of other handicraft stores in the city centre, especially along Colmena, but I like the places on Belén most of all. Miraflores also has some very nice shops and although they tend to be expensive, the quality and shopping atmosphere are as good as or better than you'll find anywhere. Highly exclusive jewellery and handicrafts stores are to be found in the very attractive El Suche arcade, off the 6th block of La Paz in Miraflores. The 5th block of La Paz is also good: La Gringa has an excellent selection and the El Alamo shopping arcade is recommended too. The fact that Peru's most expensive hotel, Césars, is on this block will give you an idea of what to expect.

Getting There & Away
Air The airport is divided into two sections. As you look at the building from the parking area, the national arrivals and departures section is to your right. To the left is the international section. If arriving on an international flight, especially during the day, look for a tourist information booth before going through immigration. They can advise you about current exchange rates and transport from the airport.

At immigration, request as many days as you need; otherwise, you'll get the standard 30 days. Keep the entry slip because you need to surrender it when leaving Peru. Avoid porters in the baggage claim area, unless you want to have your luggage trundled 20 metres outside the door and dumped into the most expensive taxi available. Going through customs, the far right lanes are usually the most hassle free for tourists. When several flights arrive at once, it can be a real zoo, so keep your wits and your luggage about you!

Facilities at the airport are not very good. The Banco de la Nación will not change travellers' cheques and, sometimes, won't even change cash dollars or excess intis back into dollars. Regulations change frequently. Casas de cambio will usually give you about 2% less than the best city rates for US cash dollars and 10% less for travellers' cheques, but it's worth bargaining with them for better rates. The cafeteria over the domestic flight lounges is open during the day, but not for early morning or evening flights. There is a very small coffee shop in the middle of the ground floor which is open most of the time, but it offers little more than coffee and stale, plastic-wrapped objects masquerading as sandwiches. A post office is open during the day and a long-distance telephone office is open until late at night. The 24 hour left-luggage room charges about $2 per piece per day. You will also find gift shops and a not particularly well-stocked duty-free area.

Domestic flights are almost exclusively with AeroPeru or Faucett. Their flight tickets are often interchangeable if they are endorsed from one airline to the other. The following cities are linked with Lima by flights of both airlines, unless otherwise indicated. Prices given are approximate one-way fares for nonresidents (residents are charged less). Schedules and prices change frequently but fares are likely to be lower, rather than higher, in the future.

Arequipa: 2 or 3 flights a day, $75
Ayacucho: 1 or 2 flights every morning, $41
Cajamarca: 2 AeroPeru flights a week, $59
Chachapoyas: 1 AeroPeru flight on Monday, $39
Chiclayo: 1 or 2 flights a day, $68
Chimbote: 2 Faucett flights a week, $29
Cuzco: 3 or 4 flights every morning, $82
Huánuco: 4 AeroPeru flights a week, $39
Iquitos: 2 to 4 flights a day, $73
Juanjui: 1 AeroPeru flight on Saturday, $61
Juliaca: 1 or 2 flights a day via Arequipa, $100
Piura: 2 flights a day, $82
Pucallpa: 2 flights a day, $50
Puerto Maldonado: 1 or 2 flights a day via Cuzco, $97
Rioja: 3 flights a week, $74
Tacna: 2 flights a day, $86
Talara: 1 or 2 flights a day, $86
Tarapoto: 2 flights a day, $57
Tingo María: 3 AeroPeru flights a week, $37
Trujillo: 2 or 3 flights a day, $50
Tumbes: 1 or 2 flights a day, $91
Yurimaguas: 3 flights a week, $77

Obtaining flight information, buying tickets and reconfirming flights is better done at an airline office or reputable travel agent than at the airport counters where things can be chaotic. However, if you want to leave for somewhere in a hurry, you can buy tickets at the airport on a space-available basis. Aero-Peru (tel 322995) and Faucett (tel 338180) both have offices in the Plaza San Martín, Lima. There is also an AeroPeru office (tel 478333) at Avenida José Pardo 601 and a Faucett office (tel 462031) at Avenida Diagonal 592, both in Miraflores. The Miraflores offices tend to deal only with international flights, while the Plaza San Martín offices do both national and international. Queues, especially for internal flights at AeroPeru, can be up to 2 hours long. To avoid a lengthy wait, only to be told that a flight is full or no longer operates, phone ahead or ask a travel agent or the international desk to make a computer reservation for you.

Aerocóndor (tel 329050, ext 117) has an office at the Hotel Sheraton for Nazca Lines overflights, but their flights are much cheaper if booked in Nazca. Grupo 8, the military airline, has an information desk in the domestic section of the airport. Most of their flights are into the jungle regions and are somewhat cheaper than those operated by the commercial airlines. The main drawbacks to flying with them are that departures are infrequent (about once a week) and you can only fly by getting to the airport early on the day of the flight and buying tickets on a space-available basis. Make sure you arrive as early as possible, get your name on the waiting list and be prepared for a long wait. Grupo 8 flies to Cuzco on Thursday morning – get your name on the list by 6 am and hope. (A recent report suggests that you can buy tickets 1 or 2 days in advance at the airport.)

About a score of international airlines have offices in Lima, especially along Colmena. Check the Yellow Pages under Transportes Aéreos for telephone numbers and call before you go – offices change addresses frequently.

If leaving on an international flight, first check in (at least 2 hours before departure is usually suggested, as many flights are overbooked). After you have obtained your boarding pass, go to the Banco de la Nación to pay the $15 international departure tax. Travellers' cheques are not accepted, only cash (intis or US dollars). Queues at the bank can be long and you might have to wait up to an hour. You can then go through the immigration desk (where your tax stamp, passport and entry slip are checked) and into the international departure lounge.

There is no departure tax when you leave Lima on a domestic flight. Again, overbooking is the norm, so be there at least an hour early. On all flights, domestic and international, it is essential that you reconfirm several times. Officially, you should reconfirm 24 to 72 hours in advance, but it's best to reconfirm upon arrival, then both 72 and 24 hours in advance and perhaps a couple of other times as well. Flights are changed or cancelled with depressing frequency, so it's worth phoning the airport or airline just before leaving for the airport.

If you're going to be travelling in a remote part of Peru, try to find a responsible travel agent or other person to reconfirm for you 72 hours before your flight. (Members of the South American Explorers Club can have the club reconfirm for them.) Passengers are often stranded for days because, having failed to reconfirm, they were bumped off their flight and found that all flights for several days were full. This is especially true during the busy months of July and August when tourists trying to get on flights, particularly to and from Cuzco, are literally driven to tears. *Reconfirm!*, then reconfirm again. Get to the airport at least an hour before the scheduled departure of your flight and, obnoxious as this may sound, push if you have to – it can get very crowded.

Bus Most travellers use the long-distance bus services to visit other Peruvian cities. The most important road in the country, the Pan-American Highway, runs north-west and south-east from Lima, roughly parallel to the coast and, at times, comes right down to the Pacific Ocean. It is paved for most of its length and comfortable, long-distance north and southbound buses leave Lima every few minutes; the drive to either the Ecuadorian border in the north or the Chilean border in the south takes approximately 24 hours. Other buses ply the much rougher roads inland into the Andes and even across the Andes and down into the eastern jungles.

Although buses play a major part in long-distance transportation, there is no central bus terminal. Instead, each bus company runs its own office and bus terminal. If the destination you want isn't mentioned in this section (and most of them are), ask the tourist office to help you.

Generally, you can buy tickets well in advance of your planned travel date and this is highly recommended, particularly if you want to travel on weekends or holidays. Lima's bus stations are notorious for thievery and it makes a lot of sense to find the station and buy your tickets unencumbered by luggage. Then, when it's time to leave, you can go to the terminal and climb onto the bus without having to watch your luggage while in a crowded line waiting to buy a ticket. Always ask if the bus leaves from the same place you bought the ticket as occasionally, the terminal is at a different location.

If you're on a budget, it pays to shop around. TEPSA is generally one of the fastest and most reliable of the bus companies but has fewer departures than some others and is the most expensive. Ormeño has many buses, frequent departures and fair service and is average in price. Morales Moralitos also has many departures and mid-range prices, but their service is often poor. Some of the cheaper companies, though providing a service that is slower and more subject to breakdowns, charge only half the price of a TEPSA fare. Special or promotional cheap fares are offered by various companies at various times. On the other hand, fares can increase for peak periods and holidays.

The biggest bus company in Lima, and the one I use if travelling overland along the coast or to Cuzco, is Ormeño at Carlos Zavala 145. There are various subsidiaries at the same address: Expreso Ancash, Expreso Continental, Expreso Chinchano and Transportes San Cristóbal. Between them they have frequent departures for Ica, Arequipa,

Tacna, Cuzco, Trujillo, Chiclayo, Tumbes, Huaraz, Caraz and various intermediate points. For the Huaraz area, you can also try Transportes Rodriguez at Roosevelt 354 or Empresa Huaraz at Leticia 655.

TEPSA, on Paseo de la República 129, has buses to Ica, Arequipa, Tacna, Trujillo, Chiclayo, Tumbes and Cajamarca. Olano, at Apurímac 543, services the northern coast, mountains and jungles with buses going to Trujillo, Chiclayo, Chachapoyas and Moyobamba. Empresa Transportes Chinchaysuyo at Grau 525 also has northbound buses for Casma, Trujillo, Piura and Tarapoto.

For the Huancayo area, try M Caceres at 28 de Julio 2195 (the same terminal as Nor-Oriente). For the Tarma/Chanchamayo area, there's the choice of Transportes Chanchamayo at Luna Pizarro 453 or Empresa Los Andes at 28 de Julio 2405.

Morales Moralitos is at Grau 141, with many subsidiary companies at the same address. Morales Moralitos goes to Nazca and Cuzco, Transportes CIVA goes to Huancabamba in the north, SOYUZ goes to Ica, ETUCSA goes to Huancayo and Ayacucho and Cruz del Sur goes to Arequipa, Puno and Cuzco. For Arequipa and Puno, you could also try Jacantaya at Colmena 1631.

Buses can be subject to long delays during the rainy season. This does not happen too often along the coast, where it rarely rains (although the violent floods of the 1983 El Niño year closed the Pan-American Highway in the northern part of Peru for several weeks), but it is an annual problem in the highlands and jungles. In the rainy season, especially between January and April, journey times can double or even triple because of landslides and bad road conditions.

Some companies offer more expensive 'through' international buses to Ecuador, Bolivia or Chile. These trips almost always involve a bus change at the border and, often, delays at these change points. It's cheaper to buy a ticket to the border town, then another ticket when you've crossed the border.

For approximate fares and journey times, see the section on the appropriate city.

Colectivo These are an alternative to buses for long-distance overland drives. The colectivo taxis cost almost twice as much as buses but, as they're generally about 20% faster, speed is their main advantage. After six or seven passengers and a driver have squeezed inside, they're not much more comfortable than the buses and departures are less frequent. If you want to pay for all the seats, you can get an *expreso* and, often, can leave right away.

Companies operating colectivo taxis are called comités. The main ones in Lima include Comité 11 at Leticia 587, which goes to Huaraz and Caraz. Comités 4 and 6, on the 600 block of Leticia, go to Ica. Comité 12 at Montevideo 736 goes to Huancayo and Ayacucho, Comité 13 at Cotabambas 347 goes to Trujillo and Cajamarca, Comité 14 at Leticia 604 goes to Huaraz and Comité 30 at Bolívar 1587 goes to Huancayo.

Train Peru has two railway systems. The train from Lima goes inland to Huancayo and does not connect with the train linking Arequipa, Lake Titicaca, Cuzco and Machu Picchu.

Lima's train station, Desamparados, is on Avenida Ancash, behind the Presidential Palace. Tickets to Huancayo cost about $3 in 1st class, $2.20 in 2nd, and can be bought the day before. First-class tickets sell out quickly. The train departs at 7.40 am, the trip takes about 10 hours and food is available. Schedules vary – the train may leave three times a week, daily or not at all. Check at the station. The journey, which reaches an altitude of 4780 metres, can be broken at Chosica (see Around Lima), at Matucana where there are a few basic hotels or at La Oroya, a cold, ugly mining town a little over halfway to Huancayo. Most people go all the way to Huancayo. If you wish, you can continue on from there to Huancavelica on another train. The railway north from La Oroya to Cerro de Pasco cannot be reached directly from Lima – you have to connect (and stay overnight) in La Oroya. The routes to Huancavelica and Cerro de Pasco are becoming unsafe because of Sendero guerilla activity.

Boat Lima's port is Callao, only 15 km from the city centre. Very few travellers arrive in Peru by ship and most of the vessels docking at Callao carry freight rather than passengers. The docks area is not particularly attractive and has a reputation for being somewhat dangerous for the unwary.

Getting Around

Airport Transport Lima's Jorge Chávez International Airport is in Callao, about 12 km from the city centre and 16 km from Miraflores. An ordinary taxi will take you from the city to the airport for about $3 (if you bargain) while a black remisse taxi of the kind found parked outside the main hotels will charge you two or three times as much.

Colectivo taxis can be found, from about 6 am to 6 pm, on the north side of the 700 block of Colmena, near Cailloma in the city centre. They take about six passengers for 50c each, with an extra charge for luggage, and leave when full. Airport buses cost about $2 per passenger and can be booked at Trans Hotel at Camaná 828 in Lima or Ricardo Palma 280 in Miraflores. Fares are higher if they pick you up from your hotel.

The cheapest way to get to the airport is on a city bus. Bus No 35, which runs along Alfonso Ugarte, passes the airport and costs a few cents. You can catch the airport bus from Plaza Dos de Mayo but, if you have a pile of luggage, this isn't recommended.

If you're looking for transport away from the airport, you'll find plenty of airport cabs charging anything from $10 to $17. You can halve these prices with some insistent bargaining. If you can carry your luggage about 200 metres, walk out of the main gate of the airport parking area and flag down a street taxi outside; you can get a ride for $3 or $4 if you bargain.

There is also an airport bus. It costs about $4 per passenger and will take you to your hotel. (The hotel booking agent in front of the international arrivals gate can help you make a telephone booking and get you onto the airport bus, but you may have to wait an hour before the bus leaves. Hotel bookings for the mid-range and top hotels can be made but not bookings in the very cheapest ones.) A less expensive bus leaves from in front of the national arrivals section, but recent increases in airport security may mean that buses are no longer allowed to park in front of the airport. Ask.

Bus Taking the local buses around Lima is something of a challenge. They're often slow and crowded, but they will get you to your destination very cheaply (fares are generally about 10c), along with the millions of Lima commuters who rely on the capital's bus service every day. Bus lines are identifiable by their destination cards, numbers and colour schemes.

The *Guía de Transportes de Lima Metropolitana*, published by Lima 2000, is now out of date and out of print. If it is ever updated and reprinted, it will show you where every bus line goes, tell you whether a route is serviced by a large omnibus or a small minibus and describe the bus's colour schemes and route numbers. At last count, there were over 180 bus lines listed in the old guide, so it's beyond the scope of this book to list them all. If you want to travel on the local buses, get more specific information from the tourist office.

A few colectivo lines operate cars or minibuses which simply drive up and down the same streets all day long. The most useful one travels along Avenida Arequipa and links Lima with Miraflores. These vehicles have no numbers or colour schemes and are identifiable by the driver waving his hand in the air – the number of fingers held up indicates the number of seats available. One of these lines operates buses along Avenidas Tacna, Garcilazo de la Vega and Arequipa. You can flag these buses down anywhere along their route and get off where you like for a fare of about 12c.

It takes a certain sense of adventure to use Lima's bus system but, if you can put up with the crush and bustle, it's a lot of fun. Don't forget to keep your money in a safe place – pickpockets haunt the crowded buses and theft is common.

Taxi If you can't face the crowded buses, you'll find that the taxis are generally reasonably priced and efficient. If there are three or four of you, they can be quite cheap. You'll pay less if you speak some Spanish and are prepared to bargain – taxis don't have meters so you have to agree on a price with the driver before you get in. As a rough guide, the cheapest ride will be under $1 and a trip from the city centre to Miraflores will be well under $2. Gringos are often, though not always, charged more.

Taxis can be identified by the red-and-white taxi sticker on the windshield. They can be any make or colour, Volkswagen Beetles being the most common. The black remisse taxis parked outside the best hotels and restaurants always charge two or three times more than other cabs.

There have been attempts to have meters introduced into taxis but there seems little likelihood that this will happen in the near future.

Car Rental The major car rental companies such as Hertz, Avis, Budget and National are all represented in Lima and have desks at the airport. National is usually the least expensive but, in general, car rental is not cheap. As there are plenty of hidden charges for mileage (per km), insurance and so on, make sure you read the rental agreement carefully before hiring a car. A deposit by credit card is usually required and renters normally need to be over 25. Your own driver's licence should be adequate for driving in Peru but beware of the bad roads and aggressive drivers. Also, make sure you park your car in a safe, guarded place at night and never leave any valuables locked in the empty car.

Leaving Lima

One traveller suggests that, if you're leaving Peru and have excess baggage that you don't want to take home with you (such as old but usable clothes, shoes, toiletries or medicines), you can donate it to Hermanas Ursulinas (the Ursuline Nuns) (tel 524370), Inclan 390, Miramar, Lima; English is spoken. This is behind the Fería del Pacífico, opposite Entrance No 4 of the exhibition grounds.

Around Lima

There are several nearby attractions which can be visited on day trips or weekend jaunts. Those excursions listed can all be done using public transport.

PACHACAMAC

These ruins are the closest major archaeological site to Lima and the most frequently visited. They are about 31 km south of the capital and are easily accessible by public transport.

Although Pachacamac was an important Inca site and a major city when the Spanish arrived, it predated the Incas by roughly 1000 years and had been a major ceremonial centre on the central coast long before the expansion of the Inca Empire. Most of the buildings are now little more than walls of piled rubble, except for the main temples which are huge pyramids. These have been excavated but, to the untrained eye, they look like huge mounds with rough steps cut into them. One of the most recent of the complexes, the Mamacuña, or 'House of the Chosen Women', was built by the Incas. It has been excavated and rebuilt, giving some idea of Inca construction. The complex is surrounded by a garden and, as the roof beams are home to innumerable swallows' nests, it is of interest to ornithologists as well as archaeologists.

The site is extensive and a thorough visit takes some hours. Near the entrance is a visitors' centre with a small museum and a cafeteria. From there, a dirt road leads around the site. Those with a vehicle can drive from complex to complex, leaving their car in various parking spots to visit each section. Those on foot can walk around the site. This takes about an hour at a leisurely pace but without stopping for long at any of the sections. Although the pyramids are badly preserved, their size is impressive. You can climb the stairs to the top of some of them and, on a clear day, they offer excellent views of the coast.

Vista operates guided tours to Pachacamac daily except Monday (information at Lima Tours, Belén 1040). Tours cost $15 per person, including round-trip transport, an English-speaking guide and a visit to the Archaeology & Anthropology Museum in Lima.

Those wishing to visit Pachacamac without a guided tour can do so by catching a minibus from the corner of Colmena and Andahuayalas, near the Santa Catalina convent, in Lima. The buses are line 120, light blue in colour with orange trim, and leave every 20 or 30 minutes, as soon as they have a load. The fare is about 25c. The journey takes roughly an hour – tell the driver to let you off near the *ruinas* or you'll end up at Pachacamac village, about 1 km beyond the entrance.

The ruins are open daily, except Monday, from 9 am to 5 pm. Entry costs about 30c and a bilingual booklet describing the ruins is available for $1. When you're ready to leave, flag down any bus outside the gate. Some of the passing buses are full, but you can usually get onto one within 30 minutes or so. Still, it's advisable not to leave it until the last minute.

THE CENTRAL HIGHWAY
The Central Highway heads directly east from Lima, following the Rimac River Valley into the foothills of the Andes. You'll find several places of interest along the first 80 km of the road east of Lima. Various confusing systems of highway markers and distances are used in different guidebooks but bus drivers usually know where you need to get off. The road continues to the mining town of La Oroya which is described in the Central Peru chapter.

Puruchuco
Puruchuco consists of a reconstructed pre-Inca chief's house. Although this is only a minor site, the small museum here is quite good and the drive out gives you a look at some of Lima's surroundings. Puruchuco is about 5 km from Lima along the Central Highway (using the highway distance markers) and 13 km from central Lima. It is in the suburb of Ate, just before the village of Vitarte, and is marked by a clear signpost on the highway. The site, several hundred metres along a road to the right, is open from 9 am to 5 pm Tuesday to Saturday. Admission is 30c. Information on how to get there is given later in this section.

Cajamarquilla
This large site dates to the Wari culture of 700 to 1100 AD and consists mainly of adobe mud walls, some sections of which are being restored. Admission is from 9 am to 5 pm Tuesday to Saturday and costs 30c. A road to the left at about Km 10 (18 km from central Lima) goes to the Cajamarquilla zinc refinery, almost 5 km from the highway. The ruins are about halfway along the refinery road and then to the right along a short, rough road. They aren't very clearly marked, though there are some signs, so ask.

Santa Clara
This village, at about Km 12 (20 km from central Lima) is the site of two well-known resorts, the *Granja Azul* and *El Pueblo*. The first is more of a restaurant with dancing on the weekends; the second resembles a country club and features a swimming pool, golf course, tennis courts and so on. Lima Tours runs several buses a day from Plaza San Martín to El Pueblo ($1 one way).

Chaclacayo
The village of Chaclacayo is at Km 27, about 660 metres above sea level – just high enough to rise above Lima's coastal garua, or sea mist. Normally, you can bask in sunshine here while about 6 million people in the capital below languish in the grey fog. A double cabin at one of the several vacation

hotels such as *Centro Vacacional Huampani* and *Centro Vacacional Los Cóndores* will cost about $30. There are pleasant dining, swimming and horse-riding facilities.

Chosica

The resort town of Chosica, 860 metres above sea level and almost 40 km along the Central Highway, was very popular with Limeños at the turn of the century. Today, its popularity has declined somewhat, though escapees from Lima's garua will still find it the most convenient place to take advantage of the numerous variously priced hotels in the sun.

Getting There & Away

Buses leave Lima frequently for Chosica and can be used to reach the other intermediate places mentioned earlier in this section. Most buses depart from near the intersection of the 15th block of Colmena and the 9th block of Ayacucho. The 200a green-and-red bus leaves from the 15th block of Colmena for Chosica, the 200b silver bus with red trim leaves from the 15th block of Colmena for Chosica, continuing to the village of Ricardo Palma a few km beyond, the 200c dark-green bus with white trim leaves for Chosica from the 15th block of Colmena and goes on to the fruit-growing area of Santa Eulalia, while the 201 cream-and-red bus leaves from the 15th block of Colmena for the village of San Fernando, passing through all points to Chaclacayo but not going to Chosica. The 202a bus leaves from the 8th block of Ayacucho for Santa Clara, the 202b green-and-blue bus leaves from the 12th block of Colmena (Parque Universitario) for Santa Clara and stops at the Granja Azul, the 202c bus leaves from the 8th block of Ayacucho for Jicamarca via Vitarte and Huachipa and takes you near Cajamarquilla, the 202d bus leaves from the 8th block of Ayacucho for Cajamarquilla refinery and the 204 bus goes from the 10th block of Ayacucho to Chosica. The fare to Chosica is about 50c.

The South Coast

The entire coastal lowlands of Peru are a desert interspersed with oases clustered around the rivers which flow down the western slopes of the Andes. Running through these desrt lowlands is the Pan-American Highway, which joins the Ecuadorian border in the north with the Chilean border in the south – a driving distance of about 2675 km. Most of this is paved and it is the best highway in the country. Lima lies roughly in the middle of the Peruvian coastline.

The south coast generally has more travellers than the north. This is because the Pan-American Highway south of Lima goes through many places of interest. Also, it is the route overland through Arequipa to those hugely popular destinations for the traveller in South America – Lake Titicaca and Cuzco.

The main points of interest for travellers along the south coast are: Pisco for the nearby wildlife, Ica for its museum and wine industry, Nazca for the famous Nazca Lines, the beautiful colonial city of Arequipa nestling under a perfect cone-shaped volcano, and Tacna for travellers heading to Chile. There are many other places worth visiting if you have the time.

PUCUSANA

This small fishing village, 68 km south of Lima, is a popular beach resort. From January to April it can get very crowded, especially at weekends, but for the rest of the year you can often have the place to yourself.

Beaches

There are four beaches. Pucusana and Las Ninfas beaches are small and on the town's seafront, so they tend to be the most crowded. La Isla, a beach on an island in front of the town, can be waded out to at very low tide. Boats frequently go there from the small harbour. The fare is just a few cents if there are several passengers or else you can hire boats by the hour for about $2 or $3, but you must bargain for the best rate. The most isolated beach is Naplo which lies almost a km away and is reached by walking through a tunnel.

There are good views from the cliffs around the town.

Places to Stay & Eat

There are four hotels, none of which are very fancy. The best is the new *Salón Blanco*. There is also an old *Salón Blanco* which is not so good. The *Hotel Bahía* is quite good and its restaurant is recommended. The cheapest is the *Hotel Delicias*. All of these can be found on or within a block of the seafront, as can several seafood restaurants. Hotel prices are between $1 and $2 per person, but are usually higher during the busy summer weekends which are best avoided.

Getting There & Away

Because Pucusana is about 8 km off the Pan-American Highway, the main companies running along the coast don't normally stop there. From Lima you must take the Pucusana colectivo 97 which frequently departs from the corner of Colmena and Andahuaylas near the Plaza Santa Catalina. The colectivos are red and blue with white trimming and charge about 75c for the trip which can take up to 2 hours.

CAÑETE

The full name of this small town, about 144 km south of Lima, is San Vicente de Cañete. Although the site predates the Incas, it is now of little interest except to river runners who sometimes take inflatable rafts or kayaks down the Río Cañete.

Places to Stay & Eat

The best hotel is *La Casona* on the Plaza de Armas. Singles/doubles with cold shower cost about $2/3 and it is often full. A couple of blocks away is the *Hotel Genova*, where basic but adequate singles/doubles cost $1.60/2.

There are several restaurants on the plaza, of which *Paris* is one of the best.

Getting There & Away
Expreso Chinchano, which is part of the Ormeño bus company in Lima, has buses every 1 or 2 hours for $1.50. The journey takes about 2½ hours from Lima. For journeys out of Cañete it is easiest to stand on the Pan-American Highway, about four blocks from the plaza, and wait for a passing bus.

CHINCHA
The small town of Chincha Alta is the next landmark, some 55 km beyond Cañete. The small Chincha Empire flourished in this area during the regional states period around the 13th century and was conquered by the Incas in the late 14th century. They retained importance within the Inca Empire and the Lord of Chincha was present at Cajamarca in 1532 when the Inca Atahualpa was captured by the Spaniards.

Now there is little to see and few travellers stop here unless they have a passionate interest in archaeology. The best of the surviving ruins are at Tambo de Mora on the coast, about 10 km west of Chincha, and at the nearby temple of La Centinela.

Places to Stay
The few simple hotels in town are the basic *Hostal Residencial San Francisco* at Callao 154 and the *Hotel Sotelo* at Benavides 260. Each charge about $1.50 per person. Better, but $1 per person more, is the *Hostal Residencial Majestic* on Diego del Almagro 114.

Just north of Chincha at the 197.5 km marker on the Pan-American Highway is the fancier *Hostal El Sausal* which costs about $8 per person.

PISCO
Pisco gives its name to the white grape brandy produced in this region and is the first town south of Lima frequently visited by travellers. It is a fairly important port of about 82,000 people and lies about 235 km south of the capital. Most visitors use Pisco as a base to see the wildlife of the nearby Ballestas Islands and Paracas Peninsula, but the area is also of considerable historical and archaeological interest.

The resort village of Paracas is about 15 km south of Pisco, but because accommodation is expensive and limited, most travellers stay in Pisco and make day trips to Paracas and the Ballestas Islands.

You can usually pay for tours with cash dollars. The Banco de Crédito will change cash dollars, but travellers' cheques are less easily negotiated.

The following sections refer to the Pisco-Paracas area as a whole.

History
Pisco is an oasis watered by the river of the same name, but the surrounding countryside is barren and sandy desert typical of Peru's coast. Until the start of this century, no-one suspected that the drifting dunes of this arid area had covered the site of a well-developed culture which predated the Incas by more than 1000 years. It was not until 1925 that the Peruvian archaeologist J C Tello discovered burial sites of the Paracas culture which existed in the area from about 1300 BC until 200 AD. These people are considered to have produced the finest textiles known in the pre-Columbian Americas.

Paracas Antiguo is the name given to the early centuries of the culture, about which little is known except that it was influenced by the Chavín Horizon. Most of our knowledge is about the later Paracas culture from about 500 BC to 200 AD. This is divided into two periods known as Paracas Cavernas and Paracas Necropolis, named after the two main burial sites discovered.

Cavernas is the earlier (500 BC to 300 BC) and is characterised by communal bottle-shaped tombs which were dug into the ground at the bottom of a vertical shaft which was often to a depth of 6 metres or more. Several dozen bodies of varying ages and both sexes – possibly family groups – were buried in some of these tombs. They were

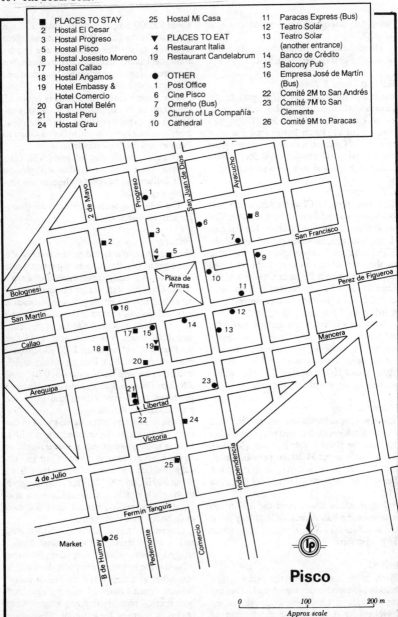

	PLACES TO STAY	25	Hostal Mi Casa	11	Paracas Express (Bus)
■				12	Teatro Solar
2	Hostal El Cesar	▼	PLACES TO EAT	13	Teatro Solar
3	Hostal Progreso	4	Restaurant Italia		(another entrance)
5	Hostal Pisco	19	Restaurant Candelabrum	14	Banco de Crédito
8	Hostal Josesito Moreno			15	Balcony Pub
17	Hostal Callao	●	OTHER	16	Empresa José de Martín
18	Hostal Angamos	1	Post Office		(Bus)
19	Hotel Embassy &	6	Cine Pisco	22	Comité 2M to San Andrés
	Hotel Comercio	7	Ormeño (Bus)	23	Comité 7M to San
20	Gran Hotel Belén	9	Church of La Compañía		Clemente
21	Hostal Peru	10	Cathedral	26	Comité 9M to Paracas
24	Hostal Grau				

Pisco

0   100   200 m

Approx scale

wrapped in relatively coarse cloth and accompanied by funereal offerings of bone and clay musical instruments, decorated gourds and well-made ceramics.

Paracas Necropolis (300 BC to 100 AD) is the site which yielded the treasure trove of exquisite textiles for which the Paracas culture is now known. This burial site is about 20 km south of Pisco and can still be seen, despite the coverage of drifting sands. It is near the J C Tello Museum on the north side of Cerro Colorado on the isthmus joining the Paracas Peninsula with the mainland.

The Necropolis consisted of a roughly rectangular walled enclosure in which more than 400 funerary bundles were found. Each consisted of an older mummified man (who was probably a nobleman or priest) wrapped in many layers of weavings. It is these textiles which are marvelled at by visitors now. They average about 1 metre by 2½ metres in size, although one measuring 4 metres by 26 metres has been found. This size is in itself remarkable because weavings wider than the span of the weaver's arms (a bit over a metre) are rarely found in Peru. The textiles consist of a wool or cotton background embroidered with multicoloured and exceptionally detailed small figures. These are repeated again and again until often the entire weaving is covered by a pattern of embroidered designs. Motifs connected with the nearby ocean, such as fish and seabirds, are popular, as are other zoomorphic and geometric designs. They have to be seen to be appreciated.

It is best to visit the Lima museums to view the Paracas mummies, textiles and other artefacts. The National Museum of Archaeology & Anthropology and the Rafael Larco Herrera Museum are particularly recommended. In the region, visit the J C Tello Museum in the Paracas Peninsula and the excellent Regional Museum in the departmental capital of Ica.

Our knowledge is vague about what happened in the area during the 1000 years after the Paracas culture disintegrated. A short distance to the south-east, the Nazca culture

Garments from the Paracas Necropolis

became important for several centuries after the disappearance of the Paracas culture. This in turn gave way to Wari influence from the mountains. After the sudden disappearance of the Wari Empire, the area became dominated by the Ica culture which was similar to and perhaps part of the Chincha Empire. They in turn were conquered by the Incas.

About this time a remarkable settlement was built by the expanding Incas, one of which is perhaps the best preserved early Inca site to be found in the desert lowlands today. This is Tambo Colorado, so called for the red-painted walls of some of the buildings. Hallmarks of Inca architecture such as trapezoidally shaped niches, windows and doorways are evident, although the buildings were made not from rock but from adobe bricks. It is about 50 km inland from Pisco and although not as spectacular as the Inca ruins in the Cuzco area, it is worth visiting by archaeology enthusiasts or travellers with the time.

Wildlife

The Paracas Peninsula and the nearby Ballestas Islands make up the most important wildlife sanctuary on the Peruvian coast. The area is particularly known for its bird and marine life. The birds nest on the offshore islands in such numbers that their nitrogen-rich droppings (guano) collect in quantities large enough to be commercially exploited for fertiliser. This practice dates from at least Inca times. Large sea lion colonies are also found on the islands.

The most common guano-producing birds are the Guanay cormorant, Peruvian booby and the Peruvian pelican. These are seen in colonies of several thousand birds. Less frequently seen, but of particular interest, are the Humboldt penguins on the Ballestas Islands and the Chilean flamingoes in the Bay of Paracas. The Andean condor occasionally descends to the coast and may be seen gliding majestically on the cliff thermals of the peninsula. The most useful guidebook to the coastal birds is *The Birds of the Department of Lima, Peru* by Maria Koepke. It is available from Harrowood Books, Newtown Square, Pennsylvania, USA, and sometimes from bookstores in Lima or at the Hotel Paracas.

Apart from the birds and sea lions, other seashore life is evident. The most obvious are the jellyfish, some reaching about 70 cm in diameter and with stinging tentacles trailing 1 metre or more behind them. One calm day when the sea was glassy smooth I was crossing the Bay of Paracas and saw a huge flotilla of jellyfish gently floating in the upper layers of the ocean. There must have been hundreds of them. Often they are washed up on to the shore where they will quickly dry out in the hot sun and form beautiful mandalic patterns on the sand. Sea hares, ghost crabs and seashells are also found by beachcombers strolling along the shore. Swimmers should be wary of jellyfish.

The Ballestas Islands

Except for the people collecting guano, it is prohibited to land on the islands, so the only way to visit the bird and sea lion colonies is to go on an organised boat tour. If you're the sort of person who shudders at the thought of an organised tour, take heart. These trips are fun, inexpensive and definitely worthwhile.

Various places in Pisco offer tours, but basically they are all the same. Everyone is put into one group irrespective of where they sign up (except those who take the more expensive Hotel Paracas tour). There are three agencies around the plaza which take it in turns to run trips.

The tours leave daily at about 7 am and cost about $4 per person. Usually they leave from the plaza or will pick you up from your hotel in a minibus. When everyone has been collected you will be driven to Paracas to board the rather ancient and slow boats for the excursion. There's no cabin so dress appropriately to protect against the wind and spray. The outward boat journey takes about 1½ hours and en route you will see the so-called Candelabra, which is a giant figure etched into the coastal hills rather like the

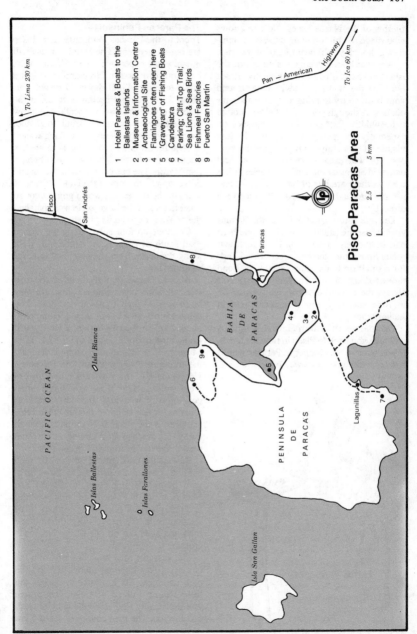

Pisco-Paracas Area

0   2.5   5 km

1 Hotel Paracas & Boats to the Ballestas Islands
2 Museum & Information Centre
3 Archaeological Site
4 Flamingoes often seen here
5 'Graveyard' of Fishing Boats
6 Candelabra
7 Parking; Cliff-Top Trail; Sea Lions & Sea Birds
8 Fishmeal Factories
9 Puerto San Martín

To Lima 230 km

Pan — American Highway

To Ica 60 km

Pisco

San Andrés

Paracas

PACIFIC OCEAN

Isla Blanca

BAHIA DE PARACAS

PENINSULA DE PARACAS

Islas Ballestas

Islas Farallones

Isla San Gallán

Lagunillas

figures of the Nazca Lines. No one knows who made the hill drawing or what it signifies, although you'll hear plenty of theories.

About an hour is spent cruising around the islands. You can't fail to see plenty of sea lions on the rocks and swimming around your boat, so try to bring a camera and binoculars. Although you can get close enough to the wildlife for a good look, some species, especially the penguins, are a little less visible. If you show some interest the boat operator will usually try to point out and name (in Spanish) some of the species. Wear a hat as there are lots of birds in the air and it's not unusual for someone to receive a direct hit!

On your return trip ask to see the flamingoes. These are usually found in the southern part of the bay and not on the direct boat route. Sometimes the boat operator will ask for a small tip to pay for the extra fuel and time needed to do this. The flamingoes aren't always there. The best times are supposedly in June and July, but I've seen them in January too.

On your return to the mainland, a minibus will take you back to Pisco in time for lunch. If you want to stay longer in Paracas, you'll have to make your own way back.

Flamingoes

The Paracas Peninsula

Tours to the Paracas Peninsula from Pisco are not so frequent. The Hotel Paracas will organise an expensive tour. Alternatively, hire your own taxi in Pisco and try to get a group together. A half-day taxi hire will cost about $25. Another option is to catch the colectivo into Paracas and walk, but allow yourself plenty of time. Bring food and, more importantly, plenty of drinking water.

Near the entrance to Paracas is an obelisk commemorating the landing of the liberator San Martín. The bus continues further in and will drop you in front of the Hotel Paracas if you ask the driver. It's worth going into the hotel to look at the large-scale wall map and the books for sale in its gift shop.

Continue on foot either along the tarmac road south of Paracas or, better still, walk along the beach from the hotel and look for seashore life.

About 3 km south of the hotel on the road is a park entry point where a small fee may be charged, though it's not always open. You can see it from the beach. A park complex is about 2 km beyond the entrance. Here you'll find an information centre and the J C Tello Museum. The information centre is free and the museum charges about 70c for entry. Unfortunately, the museum's best pieces were stolen a few years ago, but a small collection of weavings and other artefacts remains. A few hundred metres behind this complex is the Paracas Necropolis, though there's not much to see. Flamingoes are often seen in the bay in front of the complex.

Beyond the park complex the tarmac road continues around the peninsula, past a graveyard of old fishing boats, to Puerto San Martín, which is a smelly and uninteresting fishmeal plant and port on the northern tip of the peninsula. It's best to forget the tarmac road and head out on one of the dirt roads crossing the peninsula.

The first dirt road branches left from the tarmac, a few hundred metres beyond the park complex. Six km later it reaches the little fishing village of Lagunillas where you'll probably find someone to cook fresh fish for you. The road continues about 5 km more, roughly keeping parallel to the coast, then comes to a parking lot from where a footpath leads to a cliff-top lookout. Here there are grand views of the ocean with a sea lion colony on the rocks below and plenty of seabirds gliding by. Continue further in if you're adventurous.

You can also take a rough track to the Candelabra, although it's a long way. Shortly before Puerto San Martín a dirt road branches from the tarmac and heads for the site, about 7 km away. If you want to spend a lot of time exploring the Paracas Peninsula, obtain topographic map 28-K from the Instituto Geográfico Nacional in Lima.

Tambo Colorado
The easiest way to visit this early Inca coastal site is to hire a taxi in Pisco for half a day, which will cost about $25. Otherwise you can take the Oropesa bus which leaves Pisco for Huancayo every morning at 10 am. The road goes through the middle of the site, so you can't miss it. Once you get to the site, ask the locals about when to expect a return bus from the mountains – there's usually a couple every afternoon. An on-site caretaker will answer your questions and collect a few cents.

Places to Stay – bottom end
Due to the nearby fishing industry, Pisco is occasionally full of fishing folk, hotels are booked out and prices rise. This is unpredictable because in order to avoid overfishing, short seasons are periodically declared. These last a few days every few months and are the times to avoid – but no one knows for sure when an open season will be declared.

There are several basic hotels (cold water only) which charge about $1 per person per night. These include, in roughly descending order of attraction, the *Hostal Angamos*, *Progreso*, *Peru*, *Callao*, *Grau* and *Mi Casa*. The first two aren't bad. A little more expensive is the *Hostal Josesito Moreno* at $1.50 per person. It has cold water and is grimy, but it's close to the Ormeño bus terminal.

The *Hostal Pisco* used to be a popular cheap hotel. I paid $1 to stay there in mid-1983, but by 1986 singles/doubles cost $4/6 or $8/12 with private bath. This was overpriced. Now it charges about $2 per person, which seems reasonable. (This indicates how difficult it is to keep prices straight in travel survival kits!)

The *Hotel Embassy* is clean and good. It charges about $3.50 for a double room with a private bath and tepid water. There is a bar on the roof if you want somewhere to go in the evenings. Next door is the *Hotel Comercio* which isn't great – singles/doubles with a private bath and cold water cost $2/3 and the place could do with a clean.

Not as old as the Comercio is the *Hostal El Cesar*. It's good and charges $1.50 per person without a private bath and $3.50 for a double room with a private bath and hot water.

Places to Stay – middle
The *Gran Hotel Belén* is the best in Pisco. Singles/doubles with a communal bath cost $3.50/5 and $4.50/7.50 with a private bath and hot water. (There has been criticism of the hot water supply.)

Places to Stay – top end
Paracas, 15 km south of Pisco, is a resort town full of private seaside villas which are empty for most of the year. There are two hotels. The *Hotel Paracas* on the bay is the best with an excellent, though expensive, dining room and a garden complete with swimming pool and games. Singles/doubles cost about $22/30. The hotel organises trips to the Ballestas Islands which cost about twice as much as the trips from Pisco – the only advantage is its better and faster boats. The hotel is open to nonresidents and has a small gift shop where books about the area can be bought. It also has large-scale wall maps to study.

The other hotel is the medium priced *El Mirador* which is in sand dunes at the entrance to town. It didn't seem to be doing a great deal of business when I was last there but I've heard it's quite good.

Places to Eat & Drink

For early risers heading for the Ballestas Islands, the *Restaurant Italia* next to the Hostal Pisco serves a small and slightly pricey breakfast. You can sometimes find cheaper cafés open early on the Plaza de Armas. (The Italia remains popular throughout the day.) There aren't any really good restaurants.

For main meals, try the *Restaurant Candelabrum* next to the Hotel Embassy. It is friendly and serves a good variety of food at slightly higher prices than most places in town. Generally reports are good, although a couple of readers have been disappointed.

There are several restaurants on the Plaza de Armas of which the *As de Oro* has received frequent recommendations, but I found the service mediocre and the menu limited, although reasonably priced. There's a chifa next door.

There are some simple pavement cafés on the west side of the plaza and plenty of cheap places within a block of the plaza – none of which are outstanding.

The *Balcony Pub* on the corner of the plaza is popular with young locals (teens and early 20s) and does indeed have a balcony with views of the plaza. Only drinks are served.

If you want to eat freshly caught seafood, go to the fishing village of San Andrés which is about 3 or 4 km south of Pisco. There are several cheap restaurants lining the shore and although it's not fancy, the food is good.

Getting There & Away

Bear in mind that Pisco is about 5 km west of the Pan-American Highway and many coastal buses travelling between Lima and Ica or Nazca don't stop there. There are direct buses to Pisco from both Lima and Ica. If you're not on a direct bus make sure you ask if the bus goes into Pisco or you may be left at the turn-off with 5 km to walk or hitch.

The Ormeño bus company has a terminal a block away from the Plaza de Armas. Buses leave for Lima ($2, 4 hours) and Ica (40c, 1 hour) roughly every hour. Ormeño also has

four buses a day to Nazca ($2, 3½ hours) and three buses to Arequipa ($8, 16 hours). A couple of buses a day go up to Ayacucho ($7) and tickets can be bought for Cuzco, but a change of bus is involved. The bus ride to Ayacucho or Cuzco via Abancay is not recommended at this time because of guerilla activity.

Other long distance bus companies include Paracas Express (three buses daily to Lima) and Empresa José de Martín (six buses daily to Lima).

To get to Paracas it's best to first go to Pisco and then catch a local bus, although Paracas Express will go on to Paracas from Lima if there's enough demand.

Getting Around

There are two local buses. Comité 9M to Paracas leaves from the market about every half hour and costs 25c. Comité 2M to San Andrés leaves every few minutes for 10c. Buses usually leave when they're full, so if you go to San Andrés and then try and continue to Paracas you may wait a long time. It's often better to return to Pisco and take the Paracas bus from the market.

ICA

Ica is a pleasant colonial town of about 150,000 people. It was founded by Jerónimo Luis de Cabrera in 1563 and is the capital of the Department of Ica. It lies about 305 km south of Lima and 80 km from Pisco. The Pan-American Highway heads inland from Pisco, rising gently to 420 metres above sea level at Ica. Because of this, the town is high enough to rise above the coastal garua (sea mist) and the climate is dry and sunny. The desert surrounding Ica is noted for its huge sand dunes.

Many visitors stop here. Ica is irrigated by the river of the same name and the oasis is famous for its grapes. There is a thriving wine and pisco-producing industry and the distilleries and wineries can be visited. There are attractive colonial churches, an excellent museum and several annual fiestas.

Information

Tourist Information This is at Cajamarca 179 and is open from 7.30 am until 3 pm from Monday to Friday. Recent reports indicate that the FOPTUR tourist office (tel 235247) is now at Avenida Grau 250.

Money Street moneychangers hang about on the corner of the plaza by the AeroIca office. They prefer cash dollars but travellers' cheques may be negotiable. Also try the Banco de Crédito which sometimes changes money. The Hotel de Turistas changes money at the unfavourable 'official' rate. Ica is not reliable for moneychanging so do this in Lima or Arequipa if you can.

Warning I have received reports of theft in Ica. It's a quiet-looking town but stay alert, nevertheless.

Wineries

Wineries and distilleries are known as *bodegas* and can be visited year round, but the best time is from late February until early April during the grape harvest. At other times there's not much to see.

The best of Peru's wine comes from the Tacama and Ocucaje wineries. Unfortunately, these are among the most difficult to visit because they are fairly isolated. The Vista Alegre winery makes reasonable wine and is the easiest of the large commercial wineries to visit. Some smaller family run wineries can also be visited.

To get to the Vista Alegre winery, walk across the Grau bridge and take the second left turn-off. It's about a 3-km walk and all the locals know it. Alternatively, the No 8 or No 13 city buses go near there and pass the main plaza. The entrance to the winery is a large yellow-brick arch. It's open from 9 am until 5 pm on weekdays, but it's best to go in the morning. About 8 km further on is the Tacama winery, but no buses go there so you'll have to hire a taxi or walk. The Ocucaje winery is about 36 km south of Ica and a short distance off the Pan-American Highway. Again, you need to hire a taxi to get there although it might be possible to take

a bus bound for Nazca and get off at the Ocucaje turn-off.

The easiest of the small local bodegas to visit are in the suburbs of Guadalupe, about 3 km before Ica on the road from Lima. City buses frequently depart for here from opposite the Hostal Europa in Ica. In Guadalupe you'll find the Bodegas Peña, Lovera and El Carmel within a block or two of the plaza. There are many stalls selling huge bottles of various kinds of piscos and wines. Also recommended is the Bodega Mejía, which is 17 km south of Ica and reached by a bus which leaves from the market about every hour. The bus sign says San Juan Olivo.

If you just want to buy some local wine or pisco without going to the source, a good place to go is the east side of the Plaza de Armas which has several liquor shops.

Museums

While Ica's two museums are both interesting, one must be visited. Don't miss the Regional Museum in the south-western suburbs; it's about 1½ km from the centre and can be reached by taking a No 17 bus from the Plaza de Armas. It's also a pleasant walk. The museum is open from 8 am to 6 pm daily except Sunday when it closes at noon. Entry to the museum costs 65c with an extra 35c camera fee. It is one of the best small regional museums in Peru. It's very informative and well laid out and because it's fairly small you don't feel overwhelmed and can learn a great deal. Interesting maps and paintings can be bought as souvenirs.

There are excellent collections of artefacts from the Paracas, Nazca and Inca cultures and some superb examples of Paracas weavings as well as textiles made from feathers. There are beautiful Nazca ceramics, well-preserved mummies, trepanned skulls and trophy heads, *quipus* (the knotted strings used by the Incas as mnemonic devices) and many other objects. Perhaps the weirdest exhibit is a rehydrated mummy hand. This centuries-old dried out hand was placed in a rehydrating saline solution so that it could be examined microscopically and checked for diseases that the owner of the hand may have had.

The second Ica museum is the Cabrera Stone Museum on the Plaza de Armas. There's no sign but you'll find it at Bolívar 170. It's one of the strangest museums you'll ever see and consists of a collection of 11,000 carved stones and boulders depicting pre-Columbian surgical techniques and day-to-day living. The owner, Dr Javier Cabreras (who is descended from the city founder) claims that these stones are hundreds of years old, but most authorities don't believe him. You can see some of the stones in the museum entrance, but for a proper look at them and a guided tour you must shell out $5! The museum is open from 9 am to 1 pm and from 4 to 8 pm.

Churches

The rather bare church of San Francisco has some fine stained-glass windows. The church of La Merced was rebuilt in 1874 and contains finely carved wooden altars. The cathedral contains the tomb of a local priest, Padre Guatemala, to whom miracles have been attributed. The church of El Señor de Luren boasts an image of the Lord which is venerated by pilgrims biannually.

Nazca Lines

It's much cheaper to fly over the lines from Nazca but if you're in a hurry you can do it from Ica for about $70 per person. A minimum of three is required. There's an AeroIca office at Ica.

Fiestas

Ica has more than its share of fiestas. The most famous is the wine harvest festival held every March. It's called the Festival Internacional de Vendimia or the Vintage Festival. There are processions and beauty contests, cockfights and horse shows, arts and crafts fairs, music and dancing, and of course the pisco and wine flow freely.

In October the religious pilgrimage of the Lord of Lurén culminates in a traditional all-night procession on the third Monday of the month. This festival is repeated in March

and sometimes coincides with Holy Week celebrations.

The Carnival of Yunza takes place in February. Participants dress in beautiful costumes and there is public dancing. One dance involves circling a tree until it is pulled down. There is also the water-throwing typical of any Latin American carnival.

The founding of the city on 17 June 1563 is celebrated every June during Ica week. The more important Ica Tourist Festival is held in the latter half of September.

Places to Stay – bottom end

The prices listed are average costs. All hotels raise their prices substantially during the festivals, especially the March harvest festival when hotels are often fully booked.

Of the super cheapies the *Hostal Europa* is quite good at $1 per person. The rooms are basic but the beds are clean and there's a washbasin in each room. Three similarly priced hotels which are conveniently together are the *Hostal Royal, Diaz* and *Ica*. The Ica is supposed to be the best and has an annexe a few blocks away if the main hotel is full. They're all just basic cold water cheapies and quite a few budget travellers stay at them.

Around the corner is the basic *Hostal Progreso*. Other hotels which cost about $1 per person include the *Hostal Amazonas*, which is clean and has rooms with private baths (cold water) but no singles, and the less attractive *Hostal Grau* which has some rooms with a private cold-water bath but again no singles. The friendly *Hostal Sol de Oro* charges $3 for double rooms with private baths and hot water. The few single rooms cost almost as much.

If all of these are full and you're on a tight budget, try the *Hostal San Martín, Titos, Libertad* or the *Hotel Lima*, but these are very basic.

For the slightly more affluent budget traveller there's the clean *Hostal Olimpia* which charges $1.30 per person. It only has communal showers with cold water, though there is a cheap restaurant. The *Hostal La Viña* costs $1.70 per person for rooms with a

Top: Desert Coast (RR)
Bottom: Sea Lions, Ballestas Islands (RR)

Top: Peruvian Boobies, Ballestas Islands (RR)
Left: Mummies, Cemetery of Chauchilla, Nazca (RR)
Right: Cathedral, Plaza de Armas, Tacna (RR)

private bath and cold water. The *Hotel Jacaranda* charges about the same or a few cents more for a room with a private bath and there is hot water.

The *Hotel Confort* has clean, simple rooms with the kind of tepid electric shower which may give you a shock if you're not careful. Singles/doubles cost $2/3. Similarly priced is the ever-popular *Hotel Colón*, which is a rambling and noisy old building on the Plaza de Armas. It has cheaper rooms with communal showers. It certainly has some character, though check the water as there are occasional failures. It also has an inexpensive restaurant. The *Hotel Presidente* looks quite good at $2.30 per person for rooms with a private bath, hot water and a sauna next door.

Places to Stay – middle
The clean *Hotel Las Brisas* is recommended for those who want inexpensive comfort – good beds and hot showers for $3 per person. Also good is the *Hotel Siesta* and the *Hostal Silmar* where singles/doubles cost $5/7 if it's not harvest festival. Both hotels have the expected clean rooms and private baths with hot water. The *Hotel Sol de Ica* is new, clean and good value. Singles/doubles cost $6/8 with a private hot shower.

If you're looking for peace and quiet, try the *Hostal San Isidro* away from the town centre near the Regional Museum. It charges $2.70 per person, but not all the rooms have private showers or hot water.

Some way out of town is the *Hostal Medanos* (tel 231666) at the 300 km marker on the Pan-American Highway. It has a swimming pool and costs $6 per double.

Places to Stay – top end
There are no really good hotels in the town centre, though the government-run *Hotel de Turistas* comes fairly close. About 2 km from the Plaza de Armas, it's a very modern building. Singles/doubles cost $13/18, which includes a continental breakfast.

Out on the Pan-American are two more good hotels. The *Hostal El Carmelo* (tel 232191) at the 301 km marker has

singles/doubles at $8/11 while the luxurious *Hotel Las Dunas* (tel 231031) at the 300 km marker has singles/doubles at $50/60 (most expensive at weekends). All of these hotels have swimming pools and restaurant facilities, and the Las Dunas offers tennis, golf, horse riding and Nazca Lines overflights, at a price.

Places to Eat
If you're staying in one of the better hotels you'll find the food is good, if not expensive. Cheaper restaurants are to be found in the town centre, but none are first class.

The best place used to be the *Pizzería Venezia* which had decent coffee, served late breakfasts and a lot more than just pizzas. It recently changed management and is now called *Restaurant El Espía* – I don't know how good it is. The *Restaurant San Isidro* on the way to the Regional Museum is good for meat dishes. There are several chifas and other inexpensive restaurants on Calle Lima, the *Chifa Hong Kong* being a good one. For economy, the *Hotel Colón* restaurant has been recommended and there are several other cheap restaurants along Calle Grau heading east from the Plaza de Armas.

Getting There & Away
Ica is a main bus destination on the Pan-American Highway and is easy to get to from Lima, Nazca and Arequipa.

Bus Most of the bus companies are clustered around a little park at the west end of Salaverry, so it's easy to wander around comparing prices and schedules. Several companies run frequent buses up and down the Pan-American and charge approximately the same, with the exception of TEPSA which charges about 25% more and is said to be the most efficient, although it has less frequent departures.

Northbound to Lima costs about $3 and takes about 5 hours. Pick from hourly departures with Ormeño, eight daily buses with Señor de Luren, four daily with Cruz del Sur, hourly slow (and slightly cheaper) buses with SOYUZ, amongst others. To go further

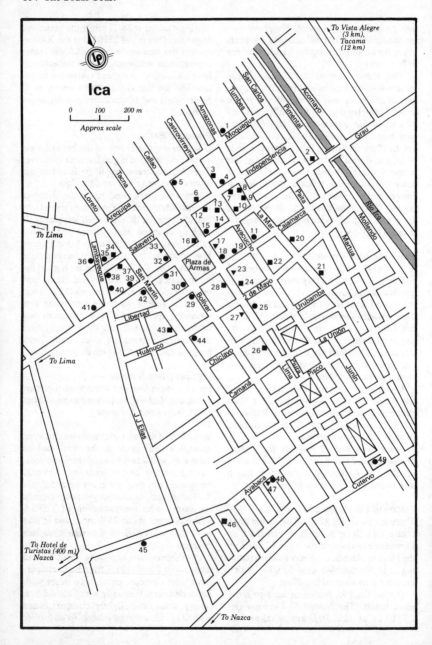

Ica

0   100   200 m
Approx scale

To Vista Alegre
(3 km),
Tacama
(12 km)

Castrovirreyna
Amazonas
Tumbes
San Carlos
Moquegua
Acomayo
Pimentel
Grau

Callao
Independencia

Tacna
Paita
Río Ica

Arequipa
La Mar
Calamarca

Loreto
Avecicho
Mollendo

To Lima
Salaverry

Lembayeque
San Martín

Plaza de
Armas
Bolivar
2 de Mayo
Urubamba
Mocarua

Libertad
La Unión

Huánuco

Chiclayo
Lima
Pisco

Camaná
Paita

To Lima

J J Elías

Junín

Ayabaca
Cutervo

To Hotel de
Turistas (400 m)
Nazca

To Nazca

■ **PLACES TO STAY**

2	Hostal San Martín
3	Hotel Las Brisas
6	Hostal Royal, Hostal Diaz & Hostal Ica
7	Hostal Europa
8	Hostal Amazonas & Hotel Presidente
9	Hostal Titos
10	Hostal Silmar
12	Hotel Siesta
13	Hostal Progreso
14	Hostal Grau
16	Hotel Colón
20	Hotel Confort
21	Hostal Sol de Oro
22	Hostal Libertad
24	Hotel Sol de Ica
26	Hostal Olimpia
28	Hotel Lima
34	Hostal Ica Anexo
37	Hotel Jacaranda
43	Hostal La Viña
46	Hostal San Isidro

▼ **PLACES TO EAT**

17	Wine & Pisco shops
23	Restaurant Espía
27	Chifa Hong Kong

33	Restaurant Mogambo
47	Restaurant San Isidro

● **OTHER**

1	Market Area
4	Bus to Guadalupe
5	Post Office
11	Colectivos to Nazca
15	Banco de Crédito
18	Colectivos to Lima
19	Tourist Office
25	Cine Ica
29	La Merced Church
30	Cabrera Stones Museum
31	Cine Dux
32	AeroIca
35	Roggero (Bus)
36	Emp Grimaldi (Bus)
38	Ormeño (Bus)
39	TEPSA (Bus)
40	Cruz del Sur, Cóndor de Aymares, Sur Andino, Soyuz, Morales (Buses)
41	Transportes Señor de Luren (Bus)
42	San Francisco Church
44	ENTEL
45	Regional Museum
48	La Palma Market
49	Church of Señor de Luren

Using a quipu

north of Lima, change in Lima. For Pisco (40c, 1 hour) there are more morning buses than afternoon buses. Make sure your bus goes into Pisco and not just to the turn-off from the Pan-American Highway.

Southbound to Nazca costs $1.50 and takes about 3 hours. Most companies go there once or twice a day.

Buses to Arequipa cost $6 and take about 15 hours, though most travellers stop at Nazca. Ormeño has four departures daily and Cruz del Sur has two buses every night. One of the latter continues to Tacna on the Chilean border.

If you're heading to the highlands you can get to Cuzco (via Arequipa) with Ormeño for $11. Departures are every 2 days. Several other companies will get you to Cuzco but expect to change buses in Arequipa. Make sure you're on a direct bus if you don't want to stay overnight somewhere.

Colectivo If you're in a hurry to get to Lima or Nazca take a colectivo taxi. These leave from the Plaza de Armas as soon as they have a car load. Fares are $5 to Lima (3½ hours) and $2 to Nazca (2 hours).

HUACACHINA

This is a tiny resort village nestled in huge sand dunes about 5 km west of Ica. There's a small lagoon which Peruvians swim in because it's supposed to have curative properties, though it looks murky and uninviting. The surroundings are pretty – graceful palm trees, colourful flowers, attractive buildings in pastel shades and the backdrop of giant sand dunes. It's a pleasant side trip from Ica and a very quiet place to rest.

Places to Stay & Eat

There are two hotels and both are around the lagoon. To the right of the bus stop is the attractive pink *Hotel Mossone*. There's no sign. Singles/doubles cost $6/10 with a bath. A little further around the lagoon is the blue *Gran Hotel Salvatierra* which charges about $3 per person in simple but clean rooms with cold water showers.

The hotels will prepare your meals (ask in advance) or you can eat simply at the *Bar-Recreo Curasi* which is a block away from the lagoon and serves cheap, typically Peruvian meals. There are also food vendors by the lagoon or you could bring a picnic lunch.

Getting There & Away

The red bus marked Huacachina leaves two or three times an hour from the church of Señor de Luren in Ica, heads along Calle Lima, past the Plaza de Armas and out to the village. This takes about 15 minutes and costs 10c.

NAZCA

From Ica, the Pan-American Highway heads roughly south-east, passing through the small oasis of Palpa, famous for its orange groves, then rises slowly to Nazca at 598 metres above sea level, about 450 km south of Lima. Although only a small town of about 30,000 people, it is frequently visited by travellers interested in the Nazca culture and the world famous Nazca Lines.

History

Like the Paracas culture to the north, the ancient Nazca culture was lost in the drifting desert sands and forgotten until this century. In 1901, the Peruvian archaeologist Max Uhle was the first to excavate Nazca sites and to realise that he was dealing with a separate culture from other coastal peoples. Before his discovery, only five Nazca ceramics were known in museums and no one knew how to classify them. After 1901, thousands of ceramics were found. Most were discovered by *huaqueros* or 'grave robbers' who plundered burial sites and sold their finds to interested individuals or museums. Despite the amateurish and destructive excavations of the huaqueros, archaeologists have been able to construct a fairly accurate picture of the Nazca culture.

The Nazca culture appeared as a result of the disintegration of the Paracas culture around 200 AD. It is divided into three periods: early (200 AD to 500 AD), late (500 AD to 700 AD) and terminal (700 AD to 800 AD). These periods coincide with the types of ceramics studied by archaeologists. Ceramics, because they are preserved so much better than items made of cloth or wood, and because they are often decorated with representations of everyday life, are the most important tool for unravelling Peru's ancient past. The designs on the Nazca ceramics show us their plants and animals, their fetishes and divinities, their musical instruments and household items and the people themselves.

The early Nazca ceramics were very colourful and showed a greater variety of naturalistic designs. Pots with double necks joined by a stirrup handle have often been found, as well as shallow cups and plates. In the late period, the decoration was more stylised. (The decorations were, in all cases, much more stylised than the vigorously natural styles of the contemporary Moche culture of the northern coast.) The designs painted on the ceramics of the terminal

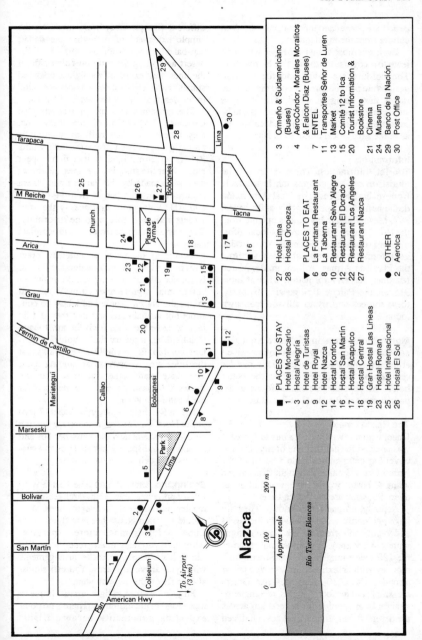

Nazca

Approx scale
0   100   200 m

Río Tierras Blancas

■ PLACES TO STAY
1   Hotel Montecarlo
3   Hostal Alegría
5   Hotel de Turistas
9   Hotel Royal
12 Hotel Nazca
14 Hostal Konfort
16 Hostal San Martín
17 Hostal Acapulco
18 Hostal Central
19 Gran Hostal Las Líneas
23 Hostal Roman
25 Hotel Internacional
26 Hostal El Sol
27 Hotel Lima
28 Hostal Oropeza

▼ PLACES TO EAT
6   La Fontana Restaurant
8   La Taberna
10 Restaurant Selva Alegre
12 Restaurant El Dorado
22 Restaurant Los Angeles
27 Restaurant Nazca

OTHER
2   Aeroica
3   Ormeño & Sudamericano
    (Buses)
4   AeroCóndor, Morales Moralitos
    & Falcon Díaz (Buses)
7   ENTEL
11 Transportes Señor de Luren
13 Market
15 Comité 12 to Ica
20 Tourist Information &
    Bookstore
21 Cinema
24 Museum
29 Banco de la Nación
30 Post Office

period are poorer and influenced by the Wari culture from the highlands.

Even the most casual observer will soon learn to recognise the distinctive Nazca style. The colours are vivid and the stylised designs are painted directly on to the ceramic rather than being moulded. The effect is strong and attractive. Nazca ceramics can be seen in the museums of Lima and Ica, as well as in the small local museum in Nazca.

Information

Tourist Information There is no official tourist office, but information is available from several sources. The local Asociación de Guías plans to open an office at Bolognesi 397. Meanwhile, many guides operate from the Hotel Nazca which provides local information as do many of the hotels. You can also get information at a bookshop a block from the Plaza de Armas. A local guide, Marco Martinez, has an information office at Lima 315 on the Parque Bolognesi. Obviously, these sources will try to sell you their own tours!

Money Moneychanging in Nazca is not very easy, though you can use cash dollars (albeit at the unfavourable official rate) to pay for services on the airlines and in the better hotels. Moneychangers can be found in the park in front of the Hotel de Turistas.

The Nazca Lines

Once, whilst travelling on a bus to Nazca, I was amazed to find that one of my (gringo) travelling companions hadn't heard of the Nazca Lines. I naively thought that anyone going to Nazca would have heard all about them. So, what are the Nazca Lines?

Actually, no-one really knows. They are huge geometric designs drawn in the desert and visible only from the air. Some designs represent a variety of giant animals such as the 180-metre-long lizard, a 90-metre-high monkey with an extravagantly curled tail or a condor with a 130-metre wingspan. Others are simple but perfect triangles, rectangles or straight lines running for several km across the desert. All in all, there are several dozen

different figures. They were made by the simple expedient of removing the darker sun-baked stones from the surface of the desert and piling them up on either side of the lines, thus exposing the lighter coloured stones below. The best known lines are found in the desert about 20 km north of Nazca.

The questions remain; who constructed the lines and why? How did they know what they were doing when the lines can only be properly appreciated from the air? Maria Reiche, a German mathematician, has spent most of her life studying the lines and thinks they were made by the Paracas and Nazca cultures during the period from 900 BC to 600 AD, with some additions by the Wari settlers from the highlands in the 7th century. She considers the lines to be an astronomical calendar.

This is by no means accepted by other writers. Tony Morrison considers the lines to be ritual walkways linking *huacas* or sites of ceremonial significance. Jim Woodman thinks the Nazca people knew how to construct hot-air balloons and that they did, in fact, observe the lines from the air. Johann Reinhard has a theory that involves mountain worship. Erich von Daniken thinks that the lines are extraterrestrial landing sites. There are many other theories. (See the Books & Bookshops section in the Facts for the Visitor chapter.)

Maria Reiche gives evening talks (7 pm) at the Hotel de Turistas if there are enough people. As she is now well into her 80s and sometimes indisposed, her sister or an assistant usually deliver her talk instead.

Seeing the Nazca Lines The best way to fully appreciate this giant archaeological mystery is to take a flight over the lines. Most people fly from Nazca because flying from Lima or Ica is much more expensive. Although you can make reservations in Lima, it's cheaper to make arrangements when you arrive in Nazca. You can almost always fly on the day you want.

Flights are taken in light aircraft (three to nine seats) in the mornings. There's no point expecting punctuality because flights

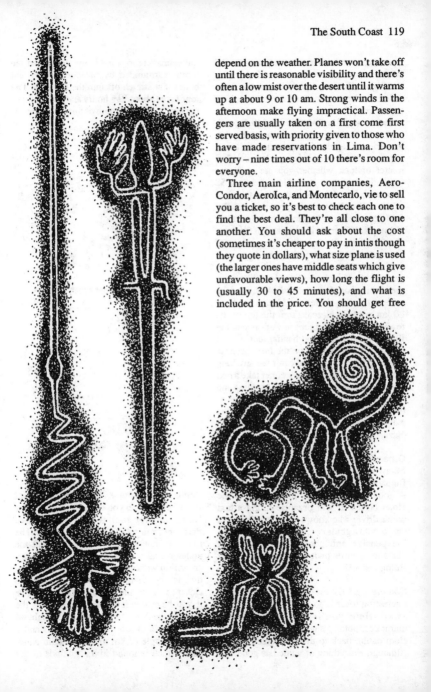

depend on the weather. Planes won't take off until there is reasonable visibility and there's often a low mist over the desert until it warms up at about 9 or 10 am. Strong winds in the afternoon make flying impractical. Passengers are usually taken on a first come first served basis, with priority given to those who have made reservations in Lima. Don't worry – nine times out of 10 there's room for everyone.

Three main airline companies, Aero-Condor, AeroIca, and Montecarlo, vie to sell you a ticket, so it's best to check each one to find the best deal. They're all close to one another. You should ask about the cost (sometimes it's cheaper to pay in intis though they quote in dollars), what size plane is used (the larger ones have middle seats which give unfavourable views), how long the flight is (usually 30 to 45 minutes), and what is included in the price. You should get free transportation to and from the airport and sometimes a light breakfast is included after the flight. (Eat very lightly before the flight unless you're used to small airplanes making tight turns.)

Fares vary from about $20 to $40 depending on the exchange rate, passenger demand, government regulations and other variables. Each week the fares seem to alter, so it's a matter of luck whether you are in Nazca when the fares are low. Also, there's a $2 airport tax which is not included in the price of the ticket. The airlines' prices are usually fairly competitive. Montecarlo, the smallest airline, is affiliated with the hotel of the same name and usually includes a free night of accommodation with each flight.

If you can't or don't want to fly, you can get an idea of what the lines look like from the observation tower (*mirador*), built on the side of the Pan-American Highway about 20 km north of Nazca. From the top of the tower you get an oblique view of three of the figures (lizard, tree and hands), but it's not very good. Don't walk on the lines because it damages them and you can't see anything anyway. To get to the tower either take a taxi or catch a northbound bus in the morning and hitchhike back. Don't leave it too late as there's little traffic. You can also take the Nazca Lines mirador tour from the Hotel Nazca for $4.

Other Excursions

Many people come to Nazca, take an overflight, and go on, but there's a lot more to see. A good place to go for information is the Hotel Nazca. It will organise hiring a taxi with a driver who knows the ruins. The hotel works with a guide cooperative which is both inexpensive and good. The cooperative plans to open its own information office at Bolognesi 397.

Cemetery of Chauchilla One of the most interesting tours is to this cemetery, 30 km away. Here you'll see bones, skulls, mummies, pottery shards and fragments of cloth dating back to the late Nazca period. Although everything of value has gone, it's

quite amazing to stand in the desert and see tombs surrounded by bleached skulls and bones that stretch off into the distance. The tour takes about 2½ hours and costs $5 per person, with a minimum of three passengers.

Pre-Incan method of beautifying skulls

Paredones Ruins & Cantallo Aqueduct For $5 per person you can extend the Nazca Lines mirador tour to take in the Inca Paredones ruins and Cantallo aqueduct. The ruins are not very well preserved but the underground aqueducts, built by the Incas, are still in working order and provide irrigation to the nearby fields. These sites are closer to Nazca and within walking distance if you have several hours spare. Cross the river on the Arica Bridge and go straight on for a couple of km to the Paredones and a further couple of km to the Cantallo aqueduct, which is found in the grounds of the

Hacienda Cantallo. I haven't done this walk, so check locally first.

Cahuachi West of the lines is Cahuachi, the most important known Nazca centre. A 3-hour tour costs $5. There are several pyramids and a site called El Estaquería which consists of rows of logs half buried vertically in the ground – their function is a mystery. The site is being excavated and it may be closed to visitors.

Some of the destinations already mentioned can be combined, but there must be a minimum of three people on a tour. One or two people are OK so long as three are paid for.

Sacaco A 6-hour tour costing $10 each for four people goes 113 km to Sacaco to look for fossils, though I don't know anyone who has done it.

Vicuña Sanctuary An all-day trip to this sanctuary at Pampas Galeras, high in the mountains 90 km east of Nazca, will cost $10 each for four people. Other tours can be arranged if you know where you want to go.

Museum On the plaza is the small town museum which is open daily from 9 am to 7 pm and costs 15c to visit.

Places to Stay – bottom end
The most popular hotel for budget travellers is the friendly *Hotel Nazca* run by the Fernandez family who organise the excursions listed. Basic but clean singles/doubles cost $1.20/2 and there is usually hot water in the communal showers. The family plan to open a restaurant.

A good, new place, in competition with the Nazca for the budget traveller's dollar, is the *Hostal Alegría*, next to the Ormeño and Sudamericano bus terminals. They also have tour information. Other hotels in this price range include the family-run *Hostal El Sol* which has a cafeteria for breakfasts, and the *Hotel Lima*, which also has a restaurant and singles/doubles with private bath for

$2.20/3.30, as well as cheaper rooms with communal showers.

If these sound too expensive there are plenty of cold water cheapies. (In Nazca's heat the lack of hot water is no real hardship.) The *Hostal Konfort* has reasonable singles/doubles for $1.10/2 and the *Hostal San Martín* is similar. Other cold-water cheapies which look less attractive are, in roughly descending order of attraction, the *Acapulco, Oropeza, Royal, Central* and *Roman*.

Places to Stay – middle
The *Hotel Internacional* looks quite good. Singles/doubles with a private bath cost $3/5 and bigger rooms with patios cost an extra $1.50. It also has a secure car park. The *Hotel Montecarlo* has a swimming pool, bar and cafeteria. Singles/doubles cost $4/7, or for about $2 extra you can stay in a bungalow. The cheaper rooms have problems with hot water. If you fly over the Nazca Lines with them they'll give you a free night at the hotel (the cheaper rooms) so if you plan on doing this check in early and spend the afternoon luxuriating around the pool.

A new and comfortable hotel on the plaza is the *Gran Hostal Las Lineas* where singes/doubles cost $5/7 in carpeted rooms with private hot showers.

Places to Stay – top end
The best hotel in Nazca is the government-run *Hotel de Turistas* where singles/doubles cost $20/26, which includes a continental breakfast and use of the swimming pool. There are cheaper rates for Peruvian residents. At about the same price is the lovely converted hacienda *Hotel de la Borda*, which has pretty gardens, a pool and serves knock-out pisco sours in its bar. It's a few km out of town by the airport, so take a taxi.

Places to Eat
The best hotels serve good food, but are expensive. Cheaper meals can be found all over Nazca; there seems to be a restaurant on every block. Two places popular with travellers are *La Fontana* and *La Taberna*,

opposite each other on Calle Lima. The latter sometimes has live music on Saturday nights. The *Restaurant Selva Alegre* is a cheap place for good chicken and the *Restaurant Los Angeles* has a set lunch for 60c. The *Cebichería El Tiburón* is a typical coastal fish restaurant. There are plenty of other cheap restaurants where locals go but many seem to close down or change hands every couple of years.

Entertainment
The Hotel de Turistas will allow travellers to use its pool for about $1.25 (no charge if you are a guest).

Nazca has a cinema and sometimes there is music in the restaurants on weekends.

Getting There & Away
Nazca is a major destination for buses on the Pan-American Highway and is easy to get to from Lima, Ica or Arequipa. Ormeño has the most frequent departures, with several buses a day to Lima ($3.50, 8 hours) as well as intermediate points. It also has two or three buses a day to Arequipa ($5, 10 hours) and Tacna ($6, 14 hours).

Buses to Cuzco with Ormeño leave every 2 days and cost $11 for the 30 to 40-hour trip. It used to go via Abancay but now goes via the safer Arequipa route. Several other companies are along the main street and have similar destinations and prices.

Comité 12 has fast colectivo taxis to Ica leaving when they are full (usually at least hourly during the day) from in front of the Restaurant Sheylita, ($1.50, 2 hours).

CHALA
The first town of any importance on the Pan-American Highway south-east of Nazca is the fishing village of Chala about 170 km away. In Inca times, fresh fish were sent by runners from here to Cuzco – an amazing effort. Chala's main attractions are fresh seafood and the opportunity to break the long journey to Arequipa, but most travellers just tough it out and keep going. Maybe that's a good reason to stop, as you won't see too many tourists.

Places to Stay
The best place is the government-run *Hotel de Turistas* at Calle Comercio 601 at the south end of the beach. The verandah faces the ocean but the bedrooms don't. Opposite is the *Hostal Otero*. Neither are very expensive. I've heard of a cheaper place on the beach.

CAMANÁ
From Chala, the Pan-American Highway runs close to the coast until it reaches Camaná, about 220 km away. The views of the ocean are often very good as the highway torturously clings to sand dunes dropping down to the sea.

Camaná is 175 km from Arequipa and the road is paved, so it's a popular summer beach resort with Arequipeños. The beaches are good but are 5 km from the centre, so you must take the local bus to La Punta to visit them. At La Punta there are private holiday bungalows but no tourist facilities.

Places to Stay
The reasonably priced government-run *Hotel de Turistas* at Calle Lima 138 has a garden. The *Hostal Central* and *Velarde* on Calle 28 de Julio are both cheaper.

MOLLENDO
The Pan-American Highway leaves the coast at Camaná and heads inland for 135 km to the junction of Repartición. Here, a major branch road heads east into the Andes for 42 km to Arequipa. The Pan-American turns south towards the coast and, after a further 15 km, divides again. The south-eastern branch goes on towards the Chilean border while the south-western road heads to Mollendo.

This small port of 15,000 people is about 110 km south-west of Arequipa and is a popular beach resort for Arequipeños during the January to March summer season but is very quiet for the rest of the year. Mollendo is normally reached by road from Arequipa after travelling through interesting desert with delicate brown, pink and grey colours, particularly attractive in the oblique light of

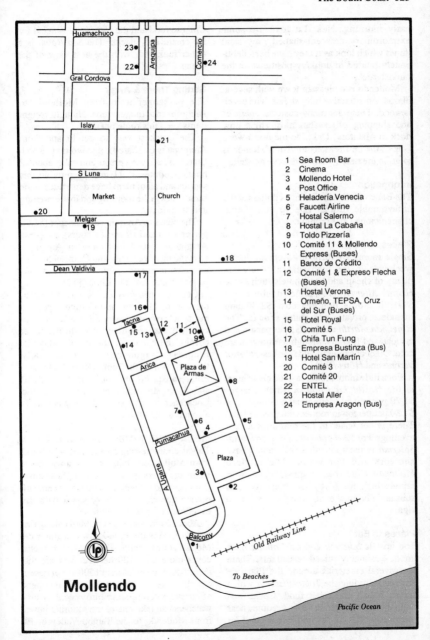

1 Sea Room Bar
2 Cinema
3 Mollendo Hotel
4 Post Office
5 Heladería Venecia
6 Faucett Airline
7 Hostal Salermo
8 Hostal La Cabaña
9 Toldo Pizzería
10 Comité 11 & Mollendo Express (Buses)
11 Banco de Crédito
12 Comité 1 & Expreso Flecha (Buses)
13 Hostal Verona
14 Ormeño, TEPSA, Cruz del Sur (Buses)
15 Hotel Royal
16 Comité 5
17 Chifa Tun Fung
18 Empresa Bustinza (Bus)
19 Hotel San Martín
20 Comité 3
21 Comité 20
22 ENTEL
23 Hostal Aller
24 Empresa Aragon (Bus)

Mollendo

early morning. Near La Joya are some extraordinary crescent-shaped grey sand dunes which look as if they have been deliberately poured in unlikely positions on the pinkish rock.

Mollendo is a pleasant town with several plazas and attractive hilly streets. The beach is good. There are many customs agencies and shipping offices but most ships now dock in Matarani, 15 km to the north-west. One of the best reasons to visit Mollendo is to go to the nearby nature reserve at Mejía.

Information

The Banco de Crédito changes dollars at the unfavourable official rate so you should change money at Arequipa.

Places to Stay

Single rooms are difficult to obtain during weekends in the high season. There are plenty of cheap and basic hotels such as the *Hostal Aller* where singles/doubles cost $1/1.70. Some doubles cost $2.30 and include a private cold water shower. The *Hotel San Martín* charges $1 per person and is clean and friendly, though its showers are cold. Other cheapies include the basic *Hostal Verona* and *Hotel Royal*.

For a little more money, a good clean hotel is the *Hostal La Cabaña* which charges $1.20 per person (communal bathrooms) or $1.80 per person in rooms with private bath. There is hot water in the mornings and/or evenings. For $2 per person, the clean *Hostal Salermo* is recommended. All rooms have showers and hot water. The modern *Mollendo Hotel* has singles/doubles with private bath for $5/8, but drops its rates substantially in the off season; there's no sign.

Places to Eat

The hostals *Salermo* and *La Cabaña* have good, reasonably priced restaurants. There are several cafeterias around the Plaza de Armas, including the *Toldo Pizzería* which serves Italian and other food. Cheap restaurants are found along Calle Arequipa near the market. The *Chifa Tun Fung* is good for Chinese food and the *Heladería Venecia* for ice cream and snacks. The *Sea Room* is a rather funky bar with the best view of the ocean.

Getting There & Away

The passenger train from Mollendo to Arequipa no longer runs, though freight trains keep this route open.

The quickest way to get to and from Arequipa is by shared colectivo taxis which charge $2.30 per person and take about 2 hours. Comités 1, 11 and 20 provide this service and all of them have departures at the same times in the morning and in the evening and at midday.

The buses to Arequipa are cheaper ($1.70 per person) and slower (3 hours). Empresa Aragon has six buses daily to Arequipa, Ormeño has three daily and Cruz del Sur has one afternoon bus daily. TEPSA runs four buses a week direct to Lima ($12).

Comité 5 has frequent colectivo taxis to the Port of Matarani and Comité 3 goes to the beach resort of Mejía for 30c. Neither company has an office, so go to the street corner indicated on the map and wait. Empresa Aragon has five buses daily through Mejía to the Tambo River Valley and Empresa Bustinza has buses at 7 am, 12.30 and 6 pm through Mejía, La Curva and Cocachacra to El Fiscal (70c, 1½ hours). It also has a daily bus to Tacna.

MEJÍA & THE TAMBO RIVER VALLEY

This is an interesting area and easily visited from Mollendo. Mejía is a summer beach resort for Arequipeños and is a ghost town from April to December. There are plenty of private homes, a couple of snack bars, an excellent beach, but no hotels.

About 6 km south-east of Mejía along the coastal road is the little-known Lagunas de Mejía Nature Reserve. These coastal lagoons cover more than 100 hectares and are the largest permanent lakes in 1500 km of desert coastline, hence they attract great numbers of coastal and migratory bird species. Birdwatchers can take one of the morning buses from Mollendo to the Tambo Valley or El

Fiscal and get off at the reserve. There's no sign, but you can see the lagoons from the road. Buses return every afternoon.

The road continues along the Tambo River Valley which is an important irrigation project with rice and sugarcane plantations. The road joins the Pan-American Highway at El Fiscal from where buses return to Mollendo at 5 and 10 am and 4 pm. El Fiscal has a petrol (gas) station and an overpriced fly-blown restaurant. It's the only place in about 100 km of desert road. You can wait here to flag down buses to Arequipa or Moquegua.

MOQUEGUA

Moquegua is a dry and dusty town with some interesting buildings. Many of these, even the cathedral, are roofed with sugarcane stalks covered with dried mud – a type of wattle and daub construction. Although the town is built on the Moquegua River, it is one of the driest towns in Peru and feels almost as if it should be in the middle of the Sahara. No wonder, as the Peruvian coastal desert reaches its driest point here and merges into the Atacama Desert of northern Chile, the driest in the world. The river does manage to provide enough moisture for some agriculture (mainly grapes and avocados), but a couple of km from the river you would never believe that agriculture is possible.

Moquegua has a population of about 10,000 and is the capital of the small department of the same name. It is 1412 metres above sea level and 220 km south-east of Arequipa. At the north-eastern end of town is a small hill which can be easily climbed for an excellent view of Moquegua (and the mud roofs) as well as the arid mountains surrounding it. The pleasant and shady Plaza de Armas, with a wrought iron fountain and topiary hedges, is a welcome relief from the desert. There really isn't much to do, but I found it ... different.

Places to Stay

There are about eight hotels, most of them quite basic with cold water in the shared

bathrooms. The *Hostals Cornejo, Torata* and *Comercio* are quite good and clean and charge about $1.30 per person. Slightly cheaper are the *Hospedaje El Ovalo, Hostal Central* and *Alojamiento Moderno*.

The *Hostal Los Limoneros* has a pleasant garden and simple, clean singles/doubles with private bath for $3/5.30, or a little less with shared bath. There's only cold water. The *Hotel de Turistas* has hot water but is about 3 km from the town centre. Singles/doubles with bath cost about $6/10.

Places to Eat

The cheapest places are, as usual, around the market, but there are better restaurants on Avenida Moquegua, north-east of the plaza. My favourite restaurant is *A Todo Vapor*, which means 'full steam ahead!' It's clean and good value.

Getting There & Away

The easiest way to get to Moquegua is by bus from either Arequipa or Tacna. The bus offices are around the market. Buses to Lima (about $10, 19 to 23 hours) leave three times daily with Ormeño, twice daily with Cruz del Sur and Angelitos Negros and once a day with TEPSA (more expensive). These buses make intermediate stops at Camaná, Chala, Nazca and Ica.

Buses to Arequipa ($1.70, 3½ hours) leave with Cruz del Sur eight times daily and five times daily with Angelitos Negros or Ormeño.

Buses to Tacna ($1, 2 hours) depart eight times daily with Ormeño, four times daily with Cruz del Sur and twice daily with Angelitos Negros. The latter also has two or three buses daily to Ilo ($1, 2 hours).

Transportes Lacustre and San Martín have buses several times a week over a little-used rough road and a 4600-metre-high pass (Abra Choquijarani) to Puno ($5, 11 hours). Transportes Moquegua has five buses a day to the mining town of Cuajones (no hotels but interesting desert and mountain scenery – a day trip).

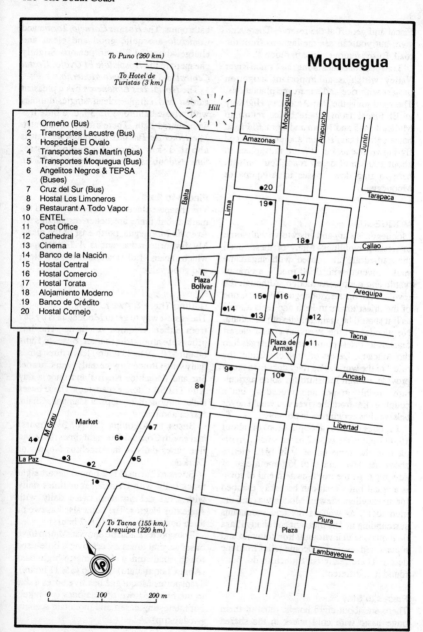

To Puno (260 km)

To Hotel de
Turistas (3 km)

Moquegua

Hill

Amazonas

Moquegua

Ayacucho

Junín

1 Ormeño (Bus)
2 Transportes Lacustre (Bus)
3 Hospedaje El Ovalo
4 Transportes San Martín (Bus)
5 Transportes Moquegua (Bus)
6 Angelitos Negros & TEPSA
   (Buses)
7 Cruz del Sur (Bus)
8 Hostal Los Limoneros
9 Restaurant A Todo Vapor
10 ENTEL
11 Post Office
12 Cathedral
13 Cinema
14 Banco de la Nación
15 Hostal Central
16 Hostal Comercio
17 Hostal Torata
18 Alojamiento Moderno
19 Banco de Crédito
20 Hostal Cornejo

Balta

Lima

●20

●19

Tarapaca

Callao

●18

Plaza
Bolívar

●17

Arequipa

●15 ●16

●14

●13

●12

Tacna

Plaza de
Armas

●11

●9

●10

Ancash

●8

Libertad

Market

M Grau

●7

●6

●4

La Paz

●3

●2

●5

●1

To Tacna (155 km),
Arequipa (220 km)

Piura

Plaza

Lambayeque

0   100   200 m

ILO

This is the departmental port, about 95 km south of Moquegua. It's mainly used to ship out copper from the mine at Toquepala in the Department of Tacna further south, but some wine and avocados are exported from Moquegua too. The government-run *Hotel de Turistas* has singles/doubles with a private bath for $10/14. There are few cheap hotels.

TACNA

At 18° south of the equator and 1293 km south-east of Lima, Tacna is the most southerly major town in Peru. It is the capital of its department, has a population of about 46,000 and lies 560 metres above sea level. Tacna is only 36 km from the Chilean border and has strong historical ties with that country. It became part of Chile in 1880 during the War of the Pacific and remained in Chilean hands until 1929 when its people voted to return to Peru. Tacna has some of the best schools and hospitals in Peru, though whether this is because of the Chilean influence is a matter of opinion.

Tacna is a clean and pleasant city but a little more expensive than the rest of Peru. The main reason to go there is to cross the land border which is well served by road and rail. (Remember that this international tourist traffic attracts thieves, so be careful.) The most interesting thing to see in Tacna is the railway museum. Most people find that a day is more than enough to stay in Tacna.

Information

Tourist Information The new tourist office is run by FOPTUR (tel 715352) at San Martín 405 at the end of the Plaza de Armas. It's open Monday to Friday from 9 am to 3 pm. The old office (tel 713501) is about 2 km east of the town centre at Avenida Bolognesi 2088 (there's no number on the building and it may no longer operate).

Money Street moneychangers give the best rates for cash and can be found in front of the Transportes Peru Internacional bus station and also on Avenida Bolognesi. Banks are not quite as good, but may be the only place to change travellers' cheques. The best for this is the Banco de Crédito. Beware of casas de cambio which often give the official rate – 20% lower than the street rate.

When crossing the border it doesn't make much difference if you change your Peruvian intis to dollars before changing them to Chilean pesos or going direct from intis to pesos. If you have a large amount of intis left you gain about 2% if you change them to dollars in Peru before crossing the border. You get a better rate buying pesos in Chile than in Peru. As can be expected, the situation changes from month to month so try and talk to travellers coming the other way to check that there haven't been any major changes.

Consulates Both Bolivia and Chile are represented by consulates in Tacna and it's worth checking with them if you're crossing the border to ensure that there hasn't been some recent change in regulations.

Entering Chile is generally straightforward for most travellers who simply receive a tourist card at the border. This is normally valid for 90 days and is free for most Europeans, Canadians, US citizens, Australians, New Zealanders and most other nationalities. Visas ($5.25) are available for one entry only and are required for French nationals and citizens of communist or African countries. The Chilean Consulate is close to the train station and is open from 8 am to 12.30 pm, Monday to Friday.

Few travellers enter Bolivia from Tacna without stopping at Puno, but it is possible to do so via a little-used road to Juli on the south shore of Lake Titicaca. For this reason there is a Bolivian consul in Tacna but he doesn't get much business. One year I went to the consulate just to check on opening times and was almost dragged in by a very excited man who grabbed my passport and peered at it, all the while telling me there was 'No problema, no problema'. He scurried around his huge desk and agitatedly dug through a drawer overflowing with impressive looking rubber stamps and ink pads. He carefully selected an immaculate page in my passport and covered it with five different stamps, all the while continuing his chattering litany, 'No problema, no problema'. The stamps were carefully numbered, dated and signed with a flourish. Finally, wielding a large wooden stamp, he delivered the coup de grace – an imprint reading GRATIS to show the world that he, at least, would not consider accepting a bribe. With a benign

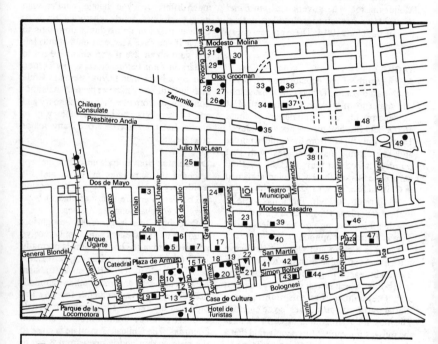

smile my passport was returned to me complete with Tourist Visa No 027-85 – the 27th visa he had issued that year. It was December. I hadn't the heart to tell him that I wasn't going to Bolivia.

The consulate is open from 9 to 11.30 am and from 4 to 5 pm, Monday to Friday. For details on documents required for entry to Bolivia, see the Puno section.

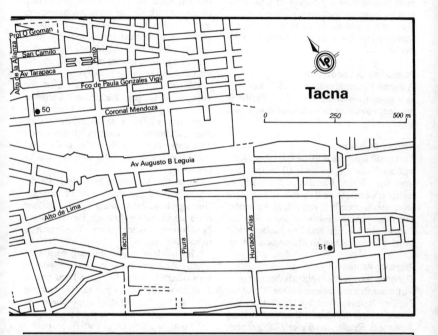

18	El Viejo Almacén Restaurant	17	Banco de Crédito
21	Pizzería Pino	19	Bolivian Consulate
22	Café Genova	20	Faucett & National Rent-a-Car
41	Chifa Say Wa	26	Cruz del Sur (Bus: 2 offices)
46	El Paraíso Vegetarian Restaurant	27	Ormeño (Bus)
		31	Cruz del Sur (Bus: 2 offices)
		32	SurPeruano (Bus)
●	OTHER	33	Angelitos Negros (Bus)
		35	Buses to Boca del Río
1	Entrance to Train Station	36	Sudamericano, Roggero &
2	Museo Ferroviario		Berrios (Buses)
5	Banco de la Nación	38	TEPSA (Bus)
8	Expreso Tacna (Bus)	40	ENTEL
10	Cine San Martín	49	Taxis to Arica
11	AeroPeru	50	Trans Peru (to Arica) (Bus)
14	Post Office & Telegrams	51	Tourist Office (old location)
15	FOPTUR Tourist Office		

National Railway Museum

The Museo Ferroviario is at the train station and is open from 8 am to 3 pm, Monday to Friday. Admission was 3c last time I was there! It's a 'must' for railway enthusiasts and even if you're not crazy about trains there is an interesting display of turn of the century engines and other rolling stock. It also has a philatelic section displaying stamps with railway themes from all over the world.

Parque de la Locomotora

A British locomotive built in 1859 and used as a troop train in the War of the Pacific is the centrepiece of this pleasant downtown park.

History Museum

This small museum is in the Casa de Cultura and is officially open from 10 to noon and from 4 to 8 pm, Monday to Saturday. In reality it's often closed, though you can find someone to open it if you ask at the office. The main exhibit deals with the War of the Pacific which is explained by paintings and maps. There are a few archaeological pieces.

Plaza de Armas

The main feature of the plaza is the huge arch – a monument to the heroes of the War of the Pacific. It is flanked by larger than life bronze statues of Admiral Grau and Colonel Bolognesi. Nearby, the 6-metre-high bronze fountain was designed by the French engineer, Eiffel. The fountain supposedly represents the four seasons. Eiffel also designed the cathedral which is noted for its clean lines, fine stained-glass windows and onyx high altar. The plaza is a popular meeting place for Tacneños in the evenings and has a patriotic flag-raising ceremony every Sunday morning.

Around Tacna

Pocollay is a suburb 5 km from Tacna and can be reached by walking east on Avenida Bolognesi or taking a bus along that street. It is popular with Tacneños for its restaurants which are especially busy on Sundays.

Dishes served include patasca a la tacneña, which is a thick spicy vegetable and meat soup; picante de guatita or hot peppered tripe (better than it sounds!); cazuela de ave or a thick chicken and vegetable soup; choclo con queso or hot corn on the cob with cheese; chicharrones de chancho or deep-fried chunks of pork, usually served with popcorn; asado de chancho or roast pork; cordero a la parilla or barbecued lamb; and that most typical of Peruvian highland dishes, cuy chactado or fried guinea pig, usually spicier than that served in the mountains.

Continuing north-east of Tacna are the villages of Calana, Pachía and Calientes which are 15, 17 and 24 km from Tacna respectively. The area is known for its pleasant climate and countryside (by desert standards). In Pachía there's a good typical restaurant, the *Bochio*, and Calientes has its hot springs.

Tacna's main seaside resort is Boca del Río, about 55 km south-west of the city. Buses go from Tacna along a good road, but there are no hotels although Tacneños have built summer homes there. The beach is reportedly good.

The modern copper-mining centre of Toquepala is near a cave in which rock paintings dating to 8000 BC have been found. They clearly illustrate a guanaco hunt among other things. It's not easy to get there and there's no hotel, although the people at the mine may be able to help with floor space.

Places to Stay – bottom end

Hotels in Tacna sometimes suffer from water shortages and the cheapest hotels had no water when I was last there. Maybe this has changed, but the following hotels are dry: hostals *Imperio* and *Nevado* charging about 60c per person and hostals *San Pedro, Tauro* and *Paris* charging about 80c per person.

The *San Cristóbal Hotel* managed to keep its water running and charged only 60c per person. Close to the train station is the basic but clean *Hostal 2 de Mayo* where singles/doubles cost $1/1.60. It sometimes manages to produce hot water in the communal showers.

Other basic cold water cheapies include the *Hostal Pacífico* for $1.05 per person, the *Hostal Lider* for $1.20 per person, the *Hostal Cuzco* and *Hostal Don Abel* which have singles/doubles at $1.20/1.80 and the *Hostal Junín* where singles/doubles cost $1.30/2.

A basic clean hotel that has been recommended by travellers is the *Hotel Las Vegas* which charges $1.30 per person and has a good and inexpensive restaurant. The *Hostal La Alameda* and *Hotel Don Quijote* charge $1.30 per person or $1.60 if you prefer a private bath. Similarly priced is the unfriendly *Hotel Alcazar*. There's also an hotel without a sign by the Ormeño bus depot which charges $2.30 for a double room with a cold shower. There are no singles and it's often full.

Places to Stay – middle

The *Hotel Copacabana* is clean and good and has singles/doubles with a private cold-water bath for $2/2.70. Also good and clean is the *Hostal Inclan* where singles/doubles with bath and hot water in the evenings cost $2/3. The *Hostal Premier* costs a few cents more but only has cold water. The *Hostal Hogar* is simple, friendly and clean and sometimes has hot water. Singles/doubles cost $2.30/3 or $3/4 with a private bath. The new looking *Hostal El Inca* is also good. Singles/doubles with private bath and hot water cost $2.70/4.30. The clean *Hotel Lima* looks nice. Its singles/doubles cost $4.50/5.50 and its baths are, at best, tepid. It has a good, reasonably priced restaurant.

Clean and reasonably comfortable are the *Hotel Emperador* and *Hotel Central*, where singles/doubles with hot showers cost $3.70/6. The Central has room telephones and the *Plaza Hotel* is the best of the mid-priced hotels. Its singles/doubles cost $4.70/8.

Places to Stay – top end

There are two good hotels and both have restaurant and bar facilities. The government-run *Hotel de Turistas* has singles/doubles for $11/14 which includes a continental breakfast. It has a small swimming pool. The modern *Hotel Camino Real* has a discotheque and its singles/doubles cost $8.30/12.

Places to Eat

One of the best and most popular restaurants in town is the Italian style *El Viejo Almacén*. It charges between $2 and $3 for a meal and has good steaks, pasta, ice cream, espresso coffee, cheap local wine and desserts. Nearby are the cheaper *Pizzería Pino* and the *Café Genova* which have pavement tables and good coffee.

If you don't want Italian food, try the *Restaurant Sur Peruano* at Ayacucho 80. It's inexpensive and popular with the locals, especially at lunch time, and is open from 7 am to 3 pm and from 6.30 to 9 pm, Monday to Saturday. Wash down some of their local food with a 500 ml pitcher of the rough and hearty vino de chacra (field wine) which costs only 50c.

Good Chinese food is to be had at the *Chifa Say Wa*. There is a vegetarian restaurant, the *El Paraíso*, which I haven't tried. For chicken, try *El Pollo Pechugon* where half a grilled chicken and French fries will cost you about $1.30. The *Helados Piamonte* on Bolognesi, a block from the Hotel de Turistas, is recommended for ice cream. The restaurants at the *Lima* and *Las Vegas* hotels are quite good and not expensive.

Getting There & Away

Tacna is the end point for some of the buses southbound from Lima, although there are more frequent buses from Arequipa. There is an air service from Lima and Arequipa. It is easy to get here from Arica in Chile.

Air There are daily flights from Tacna to Arequipa, which continue to Lima with either AeroPeru or Faucett, both of which have offices in downtown Tacna. All flights currently leave in the early afternoon and you must stay overnight in Arequipa if you wish to make connections to Cuzco or Juliaca. Approximate fares to Arequipa are $30 and to Lima $86. The airport is 5 km south of town.

Domestic flights are subject to a 9% tax if the ticket is bought in Peru. AeroPeru and Faucett have offices in Arica, Chile, where the tax is 2%.

If you fly from Lima to Tacna, cross to Arica by land, then fly from Arica to Santiago – you'll save about $100 over the international Lima-Santiago fare bought in Peru.

Bus Several companies run buses to Lima, a journey taking 21 to 26 hours. The cheapest is Sudamericano which charges $9.50 on its nightly service. Cruz del Sur also has a nightly bus and charges $11.50 but sometimes give special fares of about $10 in the low season. Ormeño also has four services daily for $11.50. Other companies to look at are SurPeruano, Angelitos Negros and Roggero. TEPSA are the most reliable but the most expensive with two daily departures for $15.50 and a presidential nonstop service every Saturday for $21. These companies will sell you tickets to Camana, Chala, Nazca or Ica.

Buses to Arequipa take 6 to 7 hours and cost about $2.70. Ormeño, Angelitos Negros and Cruz del Sur each have five departures daily. These companies all have buses to Moquegua ($1.30, 2½ hours).

Cruz del Sur has the only direct bus to Cuzco, leaving daily at 6.30 am ($11.50, 24 hours). SurPeruano sells tickets for Puno ($8) but the trip entails a full day stopover in Arequipa (leave Tacna 9.30 pm, arrive Arequipa 4 am, leave Arequipa 4 pm and arrive Puno 5 am). Empresa Berrios has a bus ($1.70, 3 hours) to Toquepala.

Buses to the coastal resort of Boca del Río leave when full from where Avenida Leguia turns into Zarumilla. Fares are 70c for the 1-hour journey.

The international buses to Arica (Chile) leave hourly all day from Transportes Peru. The trip costs $1.30 and the bus stops at the border – it often takes a long time to cross if there are many passengers. There are a couple of other companies nearby but Transportes Peru has the most comfortable service.

Colectivo Shared taxis to Arica (five passengers) cost $2.30 per person and are the most efficient way of getting to Chile. They stop at the border and the driver helps you through. There are several companies which leave as soon as a car is full, so ask around to find out which car is going next. Make sure you tell the driver you have a passport because locals with *salvo conductos* (passes) have different and faster border formalities.

Expreso Tacna have a daily taxi to Arequipa at about noon which costs $6 per passenger.

Train Trains go from Tacna to Arica and back several times a day and this is the cheapest way to cross the border. Turn of the century locomotives can be seen in the Tacna train station while you wait for the train. There are two departures in the early morning and two more at about early and mid-afternoon. Tickets cost 80c and the trip takes 1½ hours. Your passport is stamped at the train station, there is no stop at the actual border and you receive your entry stamp when you arrive. There are four daily return trains from Arica, so you can make a day trip of it. There are no moneychangers at the station.

Getting Around
Airport Transport There is no airport bus, so you must either take a taxi ($1.50) or walk about 5 km. You can go directly from the airport to Arica by taxi. This is convenient but expensive – about $20.

GOING TO CHILE
Border crossing formalities are relatively straightforward in both directions. Taxis are the quickest way of crossing whilst trains are the cheapest. The border closes at 10 pm. Chile is an hour ahead of Peru (2 hours if daylight saving time is in effect). A casa de cambio in Arica is at 18 de Septiembre 330, where you can change both intis and dollars into pesos. You used to gain about 2% by changing your excess intis into dollars in

Peru before arriving, but ask other travellers for the latest details.

From Arica you can continue south into Chile by air or bus or north-east into Bolivia by air or one of the two trains a month. There are plenty of hotels and restaurants; Arica is quite a lively place. For information about travel in Chile, go to the Chilean tourist office (tel 32101) which is above the post office at Avenida Prat 305, or consult Lonely Planet's *Chile & Easter Island – a travel survival kit.*

Arequipa

At 2325 metres above sea level in the mountainous desert of the western Andes, Arequipa is a city of the highlands rather than one of the coastal lowlands. It is, however, better connected with the coastal transportation network than it is with the highlands and is therefore often included with the south coast in many guidebooks.

The Pan-American leaves the coast at Camaná and heads east into the Andes. At Repartición, 135 km beyond Camaná, the Pan-American swings south but a major highway continues climbing eastwards for a further 40 km to Arequipa, capital of its department and the main city of southern Peru. Arequipeños claim that with a population of about 800,000 the city is Peru's second largest, but it vies with Trujillo for this honour.

It certainly is a beautiful city surrounded by spectacular mountains. The most famous of these is the volcano El Misti which is 5822 metres high and has a beautiful conical peak, topped by snow. It rises majestically behind Arequipa's cathedral and is clearly visible from the Plaza de Armas. To the left of El Misti is the higher and more ragged Chachani (6075 metres) and to the right is the lower peak of Picchu Picchu.

Many of the city's buildings date to colonial times and are often built from a very light-coloured volcanic rock called *sillar*. The buildings dazzle in the sun which shines almost every day and hence Arequipa has earned the nickname, 'the white city'.

History

Arequipa has a long history. There is archaeological evidence of pre-Inca settlement by Aymara Indians from the Lake Titicaca area. Some scholars consider that the Aymaras named the city – *ari* means 'peak' and *quipa* means 'lying behind' in Aymara – hence Arequipa is 'the place lying behind the peak' (probably referring to the conical peak of Misti). Other people claim that it is a Quechua name. An often heard legend says that the 4th Inca, Mayta Capac, was travelling through the valley and was enchanted by it. He ordered his retinue to stop, saying, '*Ari, quipay*' which translates to 'Yes, stay'.

The Spaniards refounded the city on 15 August 1540 and the date is remembered with a week-long fair in Arequipa. The fireworks show in the Plaza de Armas on 14 August is particularly spectacular.

Unfortunately, the city is built in an area highly prone to earthquakes and none of the original buildings remain. Arequipa was totally destroyed in the earthquakes and volcanic eruptions of 1600. Further major earthquakes occurred in 1687, 1868 and more recently, in 1958 and 1960. For this reason, many of the city's buildings are built low to withstand earthquakes. Despite these disasters, several 17th and 18th century buildings survive and are frequently visited. Without doubt, the most interesting of these is the Santa Catalina monastery.

Information

Tourist Information The tourist office (tel 213101) is on the Plaza de Armas at Portal Municipal 112 and is open from 8 am to 3 pm, Monday to Friday. It didn't give out general information when I was last there, so make your questions specific.

The local newspaper *El Pueblo* lists cinemas but is not much use otherwise.

Money Rates are pretty close to what they are in Lima. The moneychangers in the street outside the Banco de Crédito have been giving as good a rate as anywhere, so give them a try.

Bookshops The ABC bookstore at Santa Catalina 217 has a selection of English novels, magazines and books about Peru. There is a map store on Mercaderes, half a block from the plaza. You can buy topographic maps of the mountains for mountaineering.

Tours Various tourist agencies advertise city tours but it's easy enough to visit the most interesting places yourself as they're all within walking distance.

Churches

Visiting hours for churches in Arequipa are erratic. They vary every time I visit the city. The tourist office usually knows when specific churches are open to visitors, but even it can't keep up with the changes. Those churches whose hours are not listed here are normally open from 7 to 9 am and from 6 to 8 pm.

Convent of Santa Catalina This place wins my 'most fascinating colonial religious building in Peru' award, so even if you've overdosed on churches, you should try and see this convent. Actually, it's not just a religious building, but is also a good-sized complex, almost a city within a city. It was built in 1580 and enlarged in the 17th century. The convent is surrounded by imposing high walls and the 450 nuns who lived within led a completely secluded life and never ventured outside the convent. Accordingly, the place was shrouded in mystery for almost 400 years until it was finally opened to the public in 1970.

Now, the few remaining nuns continue to live a cloistered life, but are only in the northern corner of the complex. The rest is open to the public, who are free to wander around. It's like stepping back in time to a forgotten world of narrow twisting streets and tiny plazas, beautiful courtyards and simple living quarters.

Santa Catalina has been completely and excellently restored and the delicate pastel colours of the buildings are attractively contrasted with bright flowers, period furnishings and religious art. It is a paradise for photographers who often spend all day here as the moving sun makes subtle changes in the lighting. It's a wonderful place to just relax and wind down, write your journal and perhaps reflect upon your trip.

There are two ways of visiting Santa Catalina. One is to wander around slowly, discovering the intricate architecture of the complex; the other is to get slightly lost then find your way again, revisiting the areas you enjoyed the best. This is the way I recommend as being the most fun. Alternatively, you can hire a guide. Ask for a guide when you buy your entrance ticket and you'll be given the next available one. It helps if you speak Spanish. Guide services are free but a tip is appreciated. Entrance costs $1.50 and it's open from 9 am to 4 pm daily. There is a small cafeteria which sells delicious home-made snacks cooked by the nuns.

The Cathedral The imposing cathedral stands on the Plaza de Armas. The original structure, dating from 1656, was destroyed by fire in 1844. The second building was toppled by the earthquake of 1868 and so most of what you see has been rebuilt since then. The outside is impressive but the inside is surprisingly bare. As with many of Arequipa's churches, the interior emphasises an airy spaciousness and luminosity and the high vaults are much less cluttered than churches in other parts of Peru.

La Compañía Just off the south-eastern corner of the Plaza de Armas, this church is one of the oldest in Arequipa and noted for its ornate main facade which bears the inscription, Año 1698, although the side porch dates from 1654. This Jesuit church was so solidly built that it withstood the earthquakes that toppled the cathedral and other buildings. Inside, many of the original murals were covered with plaster and white paint by 19th century restorers, but the polychrome cupola of the San Ignacio chapel survived and is worth visiting. Opening times vary from year to year. Recently the church was open from 8 am to noon and from 3 to 8 pm and cost 10c to visit.

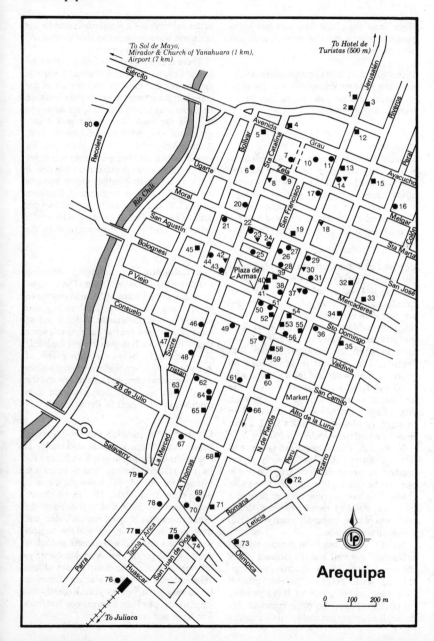

Arequipa

0   100   200 m

San Francisco This church was originally built in the 16th century and has been damaged by earthquakes. It still stands and visitors can see a large crack in the cupola – testimony to the power of the quakes. There is an impressive silver altar but the rest of the church has a relatively simple interior (by Peruvian standards).

La Recoleta A short walk from the city centre is the monastery of La Recoleta, built on the west side of the Chili River in 1648 by the Franciscans and now completely rebuilt. This is the most interesting place to visit in Arequipa after Santa Catalina. The Franciscans were among the most active of the Catholic missionaries and study and education played a large part in their activities. I was fascinated by their huge library of more than 20,000 books, many of which are centuries old. They have several *incunables* or books dating from before 1550, and their oldest volume dates from 1494. There is also a museum of Amazonian exhibits collected by the missionaries. These include a large collection of stuffed birds and animals, as well as objects made by the Indians. There is also an extensive collection of preconquest artefacts and religious art of the Cuzqueño school. You can visit the cloisters and monks' cells.

The monastery is open from 9 am to 1 pm and from 3 to 5 pm, Monday to Friday, and on Saturday morning. Admission is 70c. A Spanish-speaking guide is available (tip expected). Make sure that you don't miss the library, especially if you're a bibliophile.

Other Churches If you're particularly interested in colonial churches then you could also visit the churches of San Agustín, Santo Domingo, Santa Teresa and La Merced.

Museums

For a city of its size, Arequipa doesn't have a good selection of museums. One of the best is in the monastery of La Recoleta. The Municipal Museum has a few paintings, historical documents, photographs, maps and other paraphernalia pertaining to the city's history. It is open from 9 am to 1 pm and from 3 pm to 6 pm, Monday to Friday. Admission is a few cents. There is an archaeological collection at the University of San Agustín on Avenida Ayacucho about a km east of the centre. It's open from 9 am to 3 pm, Monday to Friday. A donation is expected.

Inca war weapons

Colonial Houses

Many beautiful colonial houses, now being used as art galleries, banks or offices, can be visited. One of the best is Casa Ricketts, built in 1738. It was first a seminary, then the archbishop's palace, then a school, before passing into the hands of one of Arequipa's upper crust families and finally being sold to the Banco Central. It now houses a small art gallery and museum, as well as bank offices. Entry is free and it's open from 8 am to noon and from 3 to 6 pm, Monday to Friday. Also worth seeing are the Casa de Moral, now owned by the Banco Industrial, and the Goyaneche Palace.

Yanahuara

This suburb is within walking distance of the town centre and makes a good excursion. Go west on Avenida Grau over the bridge and continue on Avenida Ejército for about six or seven blocks. Turn right on Avenida Lima and walk five blocks to a small plaza where you'll find the church of Yanahuara which dates from 1750. There's a mirador (viewing platform) at the end of the plaza from where there are excellent views of Arequipa and El Misti.

Head back along Avenida Jerusalén (in Yanahuara), which is the next street parallel to Avenida Lima, and just before reaching Avenida Ejército you'll see the well-known Picantería Sol de Mayo where you can stop for an excellent lunch of typical Arequipeño food. The round trip should take about 1½ hours, starting from the town centre, but if you get tired there's the green Yanahuara No 152 city bus which leaves Arequipa along Puente Grau and returns from Yanahuara Plaza to the city every few minutes.

Cayma

A little way beyond Yanahuara is Cayma, another suburb with an often visited church. To get there continue along Avenida Ejército about three blocks beyond Avenida Jerusalén and then turn right on Avenida Cayma and climb up this road for about a km. The church of San Miguel Arcángel is open from 9 am to 4 pm and the church warden will take you up the small tower for a tip, where you'll have excellent views, particularly in the afternoon. Buses marked Cayma go there from Arequipa along Avenida Grau.

Tingo

Tingo is another of the frequently visited suburbs of Arequipa, 5 km south of the city. There's a small lake, swimming pools and typical restaurants which are popular with Arequipeños on Sundays, but it's pretty quiet during the rest of the week. Catch a No 15 Tiabaya bus from the corner of Avenidas Palacio Viejo and La Merced.

Places to Stay – bottom end

The *Gran Hotel* is among the cheapest at 65c per person, but it's dirty and only has cold water. The *Pensión Tacna* at 90c and the *Hostal San Juan* at $1 per person are a little better, but they're next to the bus offices and therefore noisy. The *Hostal Sucre* at Sucre 407 is a cold water cheapie that has been recommended as clean and friendly. It costs about $1 per person.

The *Hotel Tradicional* is basic, but secure and friendly, and charges $1 per person. The *Hostal Mercaderes* is in this price range. The *Hostal Mirador* charges about the same (but beware of overcharging) and only has cold water in the shared bathrooms. A few rooms (not singles) have great views over the Plaza de Armas. The *Hotel San Francisco* has hot water in the morning and charges $1 per person. Nearby is the cheap and basic *Hostal Comercio*.

One of the best of the really cheap and basic hotels is the clean *Hotel Crillon Serrano* which has very friendly staff and warm water in the morning. Singles/doubles cost $1/1.80 and rooms with a private bath cost 20c more.

The reasonably clean and friendly *Hostal Royal* has hot water and singles/doubles cost $1.90/2.30. The *Hostal Virrey* also has hot water and singles/doubles with private bath cost $1.70/2.30. The *Hostal Wilson* charges $1.50 per person and has some rooms with private baths.

One of the most popular hotels for budget travellers is the well-known *Residencial Guzman* where singles/doubles cost $2.25/3.50. The rooms are small and a bit run down, but the people are friendly and helpful (especially with train information and

tickets) and there's a nice courtyard where early breakfasts are served. There are some cheaper dormitory-style rooms, but the lines to the hot showers can get a bit long when the place is full.

The *Hostal Nuñoz* at Jerusalén 528 (no sign) is good, secure and friendly and charges $4 for a double room with a bath and $1.70 per person in rooms with communal baths and hot water. On the plaza is the *Hospedaje Cuzco* which has hot water, but no rooms have plaza views. The cheap balcony restaurant does have views. Similarly priced is the basic *Hostal V Lira* which has hot water. The *Hostal Americano* is basic but clean and friendly and has hot water. Also, there are beautiful red geraniums in the passageways. Singles/doubles cost $1.70/2.70. Next door is the similarly priced *Hostal Ejercicios* which is clean but only has cold water. *Jorgé's Hotel* charges the same, but also has singles/doubles with private bath for $2.30/4.30. It is central and provides both hot water and tourist information. The *Hotel Florida* charges about the same and is reasonable. Similarly priced is the *Hotel Metro* on Alto de la Luna next to the San Camilo vegetable market. It's clean and has hot water.

The new but basic *Hostal Grace* near the train station has singles/doubles for $2/3.50 in rooms with communal showers. The *Hostal Florentina* has singles/doubles with hot-water communal showers for $2/3; rooms with private bathrooms cost $1 more. In this price range try the good and friendly *Hostal Extra* which has a garden, rooms with private showers and hot water and is close to the Ormeño bus station. It's a bargain and is often full. Also friendly is the *Hostal Excelsior* which has hot water and a few rooms with private showers. Fairly close to the train station is the *Hostal Parra* which has hot water in the morning and is clean. Closer to downtown is the *Hotel Imperio* which has hot showers and a few doubles with private bathrooms.

The *Hostal Santa Catalina* near the convent is popular with German-speaking travellers. Singles/doubles with a shared bath cost $2/3. It's reported to be clean and friendly, but with an erratic hot water supply. *Hostal Europa* and *Hostal Paris* are next to each other and close to the train station but are fairly basic and have hot water in the morning only. They charge $2 per person in rooms with a private bath and a little less in rooms with shared showers. The *Hostal La Merced* has large clean singles/doubles with private baths and hot water for $2.70/4.30. The *Hostal Premier* is similarly priced and has some slightly cheaper rooms without private baths, but the communal showers don't look too clean.

Places to Stay – middle

My favourite hotel in Arequipa is the charming and very respectable *La Casa de Mi Abuela* (tel 223194) at Jerusalén 606. Singles/doubles with a private shower and hot water cost $4/6. There's an attractive garden full of singing birds, and tables and chairs are provided to eat breakfast there. Breakfast in bed is available and is not expensive. Each room has a radio and a stock of beer and soft drinks which you pay for when you leave. Also, there are some bungalows. It's clean and well run and very secure – you must ring a bell to get in. A little cheaper is the nearby *Residencial Rivero* which is clean and friendly.

Several good hotels have singles/doubles at $5.50/8. They are all rather similar, fairly modern, clean and comfortable places, and all rooms have a private bath and hot water. They include the *Hotel Crismar*, the *Hotel Viza* which has carpeted rooms with telephones and is a bit run down though not bad, and the *Hotel Jerusalén* which has a restaurant and provides the luxury of a sit-down bathtub in some rooms – good if you're fed up with showers. One traveller recommends the *Hotel Conquistador* (singles/doubles cost $6/9) as the best value hotel in Peru.

Places to Stay – top end

The *Hotel Maison Plaza* is on the Plaza de Armas and singles/doubles cost $9/12 with a bath, but only two rooms have plaza views. Also on the plaza is the very modern *Hostal*

El Portal where singles/doubles cost $16/22, plus a 50% surcharge if you have a plaza view. This is probably the best run and most comfortable hotel in town and even boasts a roof-top swimming pool.

Slightly cheaper is the government-run *Hotel de Turistas* which is in an attractive building surrounded by gardens in the Selva Alegre suburb, about 1½ km north of the town centre. The modern *Hotel Presidente* is similarly priced.

Places to Eat

Most restaurants in Arequipa close by about 9 pm, which is earlier than restaurants in Peru's other big cities.

There are many restaurants around the Plaza de Armas, particularly on the Santa Catalina side. The *Balcony Restaurant* in the Hospedaje Cuzco is great for views; the food is OK and cheap. Below the balcony are a few more cheap to middle-priced restaurants. There are plenty of cheap chicken places; you can get half a grilled chicken for about $1 in several places along San Juan de Dios.

For coffee drinkers, two cafés on the first block of San Francisco have good espresso, cappuccino and snacks. The best coffee, and also the most expensive, is at *Monzas*.

For local food my favourite place is the *Sol de Mayo* which is at Jerusalén 207 in the Yanahuara district. (See the Yanahuara section.) It is open only for lunch and serves good and reasonably priced Peruvian food. Try rocoto relleno (hot peppers stuffed with meat, rice and vegetables), cuy chactado (seared guinea pig), ocopa (potatoes with a spicy hot sauce and fried cheese), chupe de camarones (shrimp soup), chancho al horno (suckling pig), anticucho (shish kebab of beef or beef hearts), cebiche (marinated seafood), and wash it down with chicha (fermented maize beer). A luncheon visit to the Sol de Mayo should be combined with a visit to the Mirador de Yanahuara. A taxi from downtown should be under $1.

One of the better (and pricier) restaurants downtown is *Le Paris* which has a a variety of good food. Another recommended and worthwhile restaurant is the *Bonanza* which serves a good variety of reasonably priced dishes and is popular with Arequipeños. Carnivores should try the *Illari* steakhouse; meals start at about $2 and the restaurant has a pleasant ambience with folk music on some evenings.

Vegetarians might want to try the *Govinda* which is good, very cheap and run by the Hare Krishnas. Also recommended for vegetarian meals is the *La Vie Claire* in the passage behind the cathedral. (Both restaurants have been praised and occasionally criticised by travellers.) In this passage you'll also find the good *La Chimenea* which serves a variety of food, the *Helados Lamborghini* which is good for ice cream, and the *1900 Pub Pizzería* which has good pizzas. Good Italian food is available at *Pizzería San Antonio*. If you want Chinese food, the *Chifa Ha Wa Yan* is good.

Entertainment

Things are generally pretty quiet mid-week, with the exception of the *El Sillar* nightspot. An irritating habit of some places is to advertise a nightly peña when in fact there's rarely anything going on except from Thursday to Saturday nights.

The El Sillar at Santo Domingo 118 (at the back of the courtyard) has a nightly peña at 7.30 pm. The cover charge is about $1.50 and the show has been recommended.

Romie's Peña by the San Francisco church has long been popular. It's a very lively but tiny bar, so get there before the doors are closed. This can be a fine art, as at 9 pm it may be empty, but by 10 pm it will be full to overflowing. The music is usually good, but eat first because it only serves drinks.

The *Illari* steakhouse also has good live folk music once or twice a week, and a good atmosphere. There are other places which you'll see advertised, but don't believe everything you read.

There are several discotheques, one being the *Carnaby Discotheque* which is open mid-week, though don't expect crowds! There's also the usual selection of cinemas, some of which show English-language movies with Spanish subtitles.

Getting There & Away

Air There are three or four direct flights to Lima, two to Tacna, one or two to Cuzco and one to Juliaca every day. Both AeroPeru and Faucett have offices on the Plaza de Armas and their fares are usually the same. One-way to Lima costs about $75; less to the other cities.

All non-Peruvian passengers must pay a $6 departure tax at the airport.

Bus Most bus and colectivo offices are on San Juan de Dios, mainly around the 600 block (between Alto de la Luna and Salaverry).

Lima is between 17 and 21 hours away and TEPSA has the fastest service on its daily nonstop *presidential* bus which is the most expensive at about $12. The regular service, with stops, takes 3 or 4 hours longer and costs about $9. Ormeño has eight daily buses to Lima and SurPeruano has two daily buses which are often the cheapest and slowest. Expreso Victoria has four departures daily but is usually more expensive. Also try Cruz del Sur which has three daily buses, Angelitos Negros with one, and others. Recently, Angelitos Negros was reported to have the cheapest fare to Lima.

For intermediate points, most buses stop in Nazca ($5) as well as Camaná, Chala and Ica, but remember that Pisco is about 5 km off the Pan-American Highway and not all buses go there. Change in Ica if necessary. For north of Lima, change in Lima.

If you're going inland to Lake Titicaca, try Transportes Jacantay. It has two afternoon buses daily to Juliaca (12 hours) and one to Puno ($5, 13 hours). SurPeruano also goes to Puno. Cruz del Sur has the only direct service to Cuzco ($9, about 21 hours) which goes via Imata. It's a wild and rough route, with departures at 4 and 6 pm daily. Bear in mind that Cruz del Sur has four or five offices scattered along San Juan de Dios, so find out where the bus leaves from. (Most travellers heading to these places prefer the train.)

Transportes Aragon has five departures daily for the coast at Mollendo. Many of its buses go on to Mejía. Cruz del Sur has afternoon departures to Mollendo and there are others. For Ilo, there are buses with Cruz del Sur and Angelitos Negros.

If you're heading for Moquegua or Tacna (for Chile), Angelitos Negros has five daily departures for Moquegua ($1.60, 3½ hours) and seven departures for Tacna ($2, 6 hours). Other companies which do this route are Ormeño (five daily to Tacna) and Cruz del Sur (five to Tacna and eight to Moquegua).

For sightseeing in the Department of Arequipa, try Empresa Nieto which has daily dawn departures for Chivay ($1.60, 5 hours). Its bus goes on to Yanque, Achoma and Maca on the upper Colca Canyon. Transportes Palma also has daily early morning buses to Chivay which continue on to Cabanaconde ($3.20, 10 hours). Cruz del Sur and Delgado bus companies are also reported to have buses to the Colca Canyon. Empresa Jacantay has a 6.30 am departure for Cabanaconde via Huambo. (A round trip to the Colca Canyon via Sihuas, Huambo, Cabanaconde and Chivay can therefore be done using public transport). The Jacantay bus leaves a couple of streets away from its office, so get precise directions when you buy the ticket.

For buses to Corire ($2, 3 hours) to visit the Toro de Muerte petroglyphs, go with Transportes San Antonio which has three daily buses. Cruz del Sur has occasional buses on through Corire to Aplao and Cotahuasi, where there is a basic hotel.

Colectivo These shared taxis take five passengers and cost 1½ to two times more than a bus. They are faster, but not necessarily more comfortable. Usually they'll pick you up from your hotel.

Comité 4 goes to Lima daily at 2 pm ($14, 17 hours). Comité 3 has a daily service at 10 am to Puno ($9, 9 hours), but ensure you've made it perfectly clear that you're going to Puno because many passengers go only as far as Juliaca and the driver may be reluctant to continue the 44 km to Puno with only one passenger. Comités 1 and 20 have three or four cars a day to Mollendo ($2.30, 2 hours) and Comités 2 and 15 have two departures daily to Majes ($3) and Chuquibamba ($5.50, 5 hours) to visit the Majes Canyon irrigation project and Corire.

Train The Arequipa-Juliaca route is bleak, but the views of the altiplano are interesting and you may see flamingoes, vicuñas, alpacas and llamas. Unfortunately, daylight trains do not run, so you can't see much! The journey to Juliaca (and Puno) is much more comfortable by train than by bus.

The night train leaves Arequipa at 9 pm each evening and arrives at Juliaca at 6 am the following day. This train continues to Puno, an hour away, or you can connect with the day train to Cuzco which leaves Juliaca at 9 am. Thus it is possible to buy a through ticket to Cuzco from Arequipa, which arrives at 6 pm.

An extremely large number of people have their bags slashed or stolen or their pockets picked on the night train, particularly in the overcrowded and badly lit 2nd class and, to a lesser extent, in 1st class. There are also a large number of thieves mingling with the crowds, waiting for the night train in the bustling Arequipa train station. Watch your baggage carefully and constantly. You are safest buying the buffet or Pullman class tickets in addition to your 1st class ticket.

The buffet car has food available but this isn't included in the price of your ticket. The Pullman car has comfortable reclining seats for sleeping. Both these carriages are heated (it gets very cold on the altiplano at night and most of the journey is at altitudes of more than 4000 metres). Attendants keep the doors locked and allow only ticket holders into the carriages and also keep an eye on luggage. Oxygen is available if you begin to suffer from altitude sickness.

If you buy a Pullman ticket to Cuzco you may have to change carriages in Juliaca in the morning as the Pullman car doesn't normally continue to Cuzco. You'll continue in 1st or buffet class.

Fares from Arequipa change frequently. During the past 5 years you could pay anywhere between $2 and $7 for a 1st class ticket to Juliaca, with fares in 2nd class at about 25% lower. There is a flat surcharge of $2.50 for buffet and $3 for Pullman class (on top of the 1st class fare). Fares to Cuzco are about twice as much, but the Pullman surcharge to Cuzco can be as much as $20. The price of a ticket depends on fluctuating exchange rates and various regulations, so see for yourself what the going rate is when you get there.

It's best to buy tickets in advance rather than trying to do so whilst guarding your luggage in the predeparture crowds. Ticket office opening hours change constantly and there are usually very long lines, which can mean you'll be waiting for several hours. You can buy tickets from various travel agencies such as Continental Tours and Conresa Tours on the 400 block of Jerusalén. Each charge about a 25% commission but provide a transfer from your hotel to the station. Shop around for the best deal. If the Pullman surcharge to Cuzco is too expensive, consider taking 1st class for the Juliaca-Cuzco section which is done in daylight when it is easier to guard your luggage.

I've occasionally heard talk of starting a comfortable sleeper service on the night train, using quaint old-fashioned sleeper coaches. It sounds nice, but I doubt that anything will come of these ideas.

Getting Around
Airport Transport There are no airport buses, although the No 3 bus to Zevallo and Aeropuerto goes along Grau and Ejército and passes within 1 km of the airport – ask the driver where to get off. A taxi from downtown costs about $1.50.

Around Arequipa

Several long-distance excursions can be made from Arequipa. The most popular is the tour of the Colca Canyon. Others include climbing the volcano El Misti and other mountains, visiting the Majes Canyon and the petroglyphs at El Toro Muerto and hiking in the Valley of the Volcanoes.

Although many of these places can be visited by public transport, this is often inconvenient. So, taking a tour is sometimes worth the extra money unless, of course, you have the time and prefer the adventure of taking infrequent ramshackle buses to remote areas. The main advantage of taking a tour is that you can stop at the most interesting points for sightseeing and photography, whilst on public transport the bus just keeps going.

If you decide to go on a guided tour you'll have many options as there are dozens of tour companies operating out of Arequipa. Some of these aren't very good, so make sure you discuss exactly what to expect before parting

Petroglyphs at El Toro Muerto

with your money. Guides should be able to produce a Tourist Guide card.

The greatest variety of excursions are offered by Anthony Holley. He is an Englishman and long time resident of Arequipa who knows the area extremely well and personally conducts all his groups using 4WD Land Rovers. He charges about $20 per person per day (sometimes more for very long trips) and requires a minimum of six people. He'll take you anywhere you want to go and is a great source of useful information. When not on tour he parks his blue Land Rover in front of the Santa Catalina monastery every morning and uses his vehicle as a mobile office. At other times he can be contacted at home (tel 224452) or you can call his wife, Señora Maureen (tel 212525), between 8 am and 3.30 pm on weekdays. Otherwise write to Casilla 77, Arequipa, Peru.

Holley's Unusual Excursions will take you everywhere except the Colca Canyon, as this tour is offered by several other tour operators. Most of these operators will lump their clients together in one group. Conresa tours at Jerusalén 409 often provides the vehicle and the lowest price – about $12 for the day trip with a full bus. Unfortunately, the minibuses used don't have adequate leg room for tall people, unless you're lucky enough to get one of the front seats. Guides don't always speak English.

Continental and Catalina tours also run tours to the Colca Canyon, though Catalina has been criticised for offering large and comfortable buses for the tour and then piling passengers into slow and overcrowded minibuses. Many companies also advertise other trips but these rarely go due to lack of interest. The most expensive and comfortable tours are offered by Lima Tours.

If you can form a group, consider hiring a taxi. Comité 3 will charge about $60 for a car and driver for an all-day trip to the Colca Canyon, or $80 for a 2-day trip. Five passengers can be accommodated. The main advantage is speed and the ability to stop the vehicle wherever you want for photos or rests. Several of the other comités will also provide this service.

Finally, you can drive yourself. National Car Rental will rent a VW Beetle for $19 per day and 19c per km, or a small Toyota Jeep for $26 per day and 26c per km. Larger vehicles are available and these sometimes have special tariffs or weekly rates. The minimum age is 25 and the minimum deposit is $200 or a credit card. Read the rental agreement with great care as the insurance clauses are often inadequate and an accident or theft may leave you paying hundreds of dollars more than you expected.

COLCA CANYON

Controversy rages about whether or not this is the world's deepest canyon. The sections which you can see from the road on a standard guided tour are certainly very impressive but are not the deepest parts of the canyon. To see the deepest sections you have to make an overnight trip and hike in. Some measurements of the depth of the canyon are taken only from the north rim which is higher than the south, so decide for yourself! Anyway, it certainly warrants a visit if you have the time.

Most guided tours leave Arequipa (2325 metres) well before dawn and climb northwards through desert scenery and over the pass separating Chachani and El Misti. The road continues through the nature reserve of Pampas de Cañihuas (about 3850 metres) where vicuñas and sometimes guanacos are sighted. Later in the trip domesticated alpacas and llamas are frequently seen, so it is possible to see all four members of the South American cameloid family in a day. This is not normally easy to do.

After 2 to 3 hours a breakfast stop is made at Viscachani (4150 metres). The road continues through bleak altiplano over the high point of about 4800 metres from where the snowcaps of Ampato (6288 metres) are seen. Then the road drops spectacularly to Chivay which is about 160 km from Arequipa.

The thermal hot springs of Chivay are normally visited (bring swimming gear and towel) and the tour bus continues west following the south bank of the upper Colca Canyon. The landscape is remarkable for its

Top: Church of San Agustin, Arequipa (TW)
Left: Santa Catalina Convent, Arequipa (RR)
Right: Santa Catalina Convent, Arequipa (RR)

Top: Plaza de Armas, Cathedral & Volcán Misti, Arequipa (RR)
Left: Cloister of La Compañía, Arequipa (TW)
Right: Church of Yanahuara, Arequipa (TW)

Inca and pre-Inca terracing which goes on for many km and is the most extensive I've seen in Peru. The journey is worthwhile to see the terracing alone. Along the route are several villages whose inhabitants are involved in agriculture and continue using the terraces today. At Yanque an attractive church which dates from the early 1700s is often visited.

About 20 km beyond Chivay, and about 4 km before Achoma, is the *Colca Tourist Lodge* where lunch is taken either on the way in or out. Soon after leaving the lodge the bus often stops for the driver to point out a small carved boulder which is supposed to represent a pre-Columbian map of the terracing. The end point of the tour is at the lookout known as Cruz del Cóndor, about 60 km beyond Chivay and an hour before you get to the village of Cabanaconde. As the name suggests, Andean condors are sometimes seen here; early morning or late afternoon are the best times for this. From the lookout the view is impressive with the river flowing 1200 metres below. Mt Mismi, on the other side of the canyon, is about 3200 metres above the canyon and some guides will tell you that the depth measurement should be taken from Mismi's summit. In fact, deeper sections can be seen if you go further in but this requires leg work from Cabanaconde.

Most tours go back the way they came and the return trip takes from 10 to 12 hours. It is possible to continue through Cabanaconde and Huambo to the Pan-American Highway at Sihuas. The road is in very bad condition and is not shown on all maps.

Alpaca

Guanaco (Huanacu)

Llama

Vicuña

The Lamoid family in Peru

Places to Stay

Chivay, at an altitude of about 3700 metres, is the capital of the Province of Caylloma and has a couple of cheap and basic pensións. One is the *Hotel Moderno* on the Plaza de Armas. A cab driver in Arequipa told me that there is a newly opened *Hotel Turistico de Colca* which charges $2.50 per person and has hot water in the communal baths. When in Chivay, don't neglect to visit the hot springs which are 5 km to the north-east of the village by road. Here there is a clean swimming pool and changing rooms, a basic cafeteria and an admission fee of 5c.

The government-run *Colca Tourist Lodge*, near Achoma about 20 km beyond Chivay, is the most comfortable place to stay in the Colca River Valley. Although it is some distance from the canyon itself, it is a good centre for walking and inspecting the pre-Columbian terracing. Singles/doubles with a bath and hot water cost $8/12. Meals are available. The place is often empty but if you want to make a reservation call ENTURPeru (tel 721928) in Lima or try at one of the better travel agencies in Arequipa.

Cabanaconde has one basic pensión which charges 75c a night. Ask here for directions to walk to the canyon; it takes about 6 hours one way so be prepared to camp.

Getting There & Away

If you don't want a guided tour, see the Arequipa section for details on bus companies which have daily dawn departures to Chivay. Some continue from Chivay past the tourist lodge (where you can get off) and on to Cabanaconde. The section of road between Cabanaconde and Huambo veers away from the canyon. It is also the roughest part of the road and there is little transport. Jacantay bus company in Arequipa does the trip to Cabanaconde through Huambo, and this may be the best way to go, though I've never tried it.

The advantage of going with a tour is that the bus will stop at good locations for photography, etc, whilst public buses don't. Also, there have been a few reports of small groups of tourists being robbed, therefore it is safer to go with a larger group.

RIVER RUNNING

An excellent guide to the Colca Canyon appears in *Kayak Through Peru* by the Polish Canoandes Expedition, 1981. It can be obtained in bookshops in Lima, but it's not easy to find. The Colca Canyon is a dangerous and difficult river and not to be undertaken lightly. A few commercial outfitters do expensive rafting trips through portions of the river in August.

You can also do easy float trips on the Majes River. Aretour on the plaza in Arequipa will organise 2-day trips from Arequipa to Majes for $48 per person. This includes round-trip transport, a night at the Majes Hostal, meals and a river float trip. The San Antonio bus company and Comités 2 and 15 also go to Majes.

EL MISTI

This 5822-metre-high volcano is technically one of the easiest ascents of any mountain of this size in the world. Nevertheless it is hard work and you normally need an ice axe. It is recommended that you talk to Señor Carlos Zarate at Tristan 224. He is an expert on climbing El Misti and other mountains and can provide up-to-date information, rent out equipment and put you in contact with a guide. I've also heard that the Mountaineering Club at Romana 206 in south-eastern Arequipa can help with information, guides and transportation.

To get to the mountain by public transport, take a bus to Chiguata. Buses leave at about 6 am and 1 pm from Avenida Sepulveda in the Miraflores district and take about an hour to reach Chiguata for a fare of 25c. From Chiguata to the base camp takes about 8 hours or more along rough trails. It's a hard uphill slog and there's little if any water en route. From the base to the summit and back takes a further 8 hours and there's no water. The downhill hike from the base camp to Chiguata takes 3 hours or less.

If you hire a vehicle you can get much higher up the mountain than by public transport and it saves you having to hassle with your luggage on a crowded public bus. Anthony Holley is used to dropping climbers off at the highest and most convenient place (above the Aguada Blanca dam at 4000 metres), but the service is expensive. I've heard that Turandes at Calle Mercaderes 130 also provide this service, but I don't know how reliable they are.

If you're a beginner climber, remember that people have died in these mountains and it's not as easy a climb as it looks. The main problems are the lack of water, the altitude and extreme weather conditions. Carry plenty of drinking water and cold weather gear and be aware of the main symptoms of altitude sickness. If in doubt, go back down.

Maps of the area can be obtained from the Instituto Geográfico Nacional and the South American Explorers Club in Lima. Also try the San Francisco bookstore on Mercaderes and the climbing club and guides in Arequipa.

TORO MUERTO

This is a magnificent and unusual archaeological site in the high desert. It consists of hundreds of carved boulders spread over about 2 sq km of desert. Archaeologists are uncertain of the cultural origins of this site but it is thought that it was made by the Wari culture about 1200 years ago.

To reach the site by public transport, take a San Antonio bus to Corire ($1.40, 4 hours) and then walk for about 1½ hours. In Corire there is one basic hotel, the *Hostal Willy*, which charges about $1 per night and can provide information on reaching the site. It can get very hot and dry, so bring plenty of extra water.

The Toro Muerto petroglyphs can also be visited more conveniently but expensively on full-day tours from Arequipa. Anthony Holley does the round trip, along with stops at other sites of interest, for $20 per person.

VALLEY OF THE VOLCANOES

This unusual valley is covered with scores of small and medium-sized volcanic cones and craters – a veritable moonscape. The 65-km long valley surrounds the village of Andagua near the snowcapped mountain of Coropuna which, at 6305 metres, is the highest peak in southern Peru. It is a weird and remote area which is seldom visited by travellers. Perhaps that's a good reason to go.

To get there, take a Cruz del Sur bus from Arequipa through Corire on to Andagua. It only runs three times a week, out on Sunday, Wednesday and Friday, and back on Monday, Thursday and Saturday. There is a basic hotel in Andagua. Topographical maps of the area are available at the usual places.

The Lake Titicaca Area

Generations of school children have been taught that Lake Titicaca, at 3820 metres above sea level, is the highest navigable lake in the world and this alone seems to make it a tourist attraction. In fact, there are many navigable lakes at altitudes of over 4000 metres, such as Lake Junín in Peru's central Andes, but Lake Titicaca is widely believed to be the world's highest simply because it has frequent passenger boats and is better known than other higher lakes. If you like trivia, amaze your friends with the fact that Lake Titicaca, at over 170 km in length, is also the largest lake in South America and the largest lake in the world above 2000 metres. At this altitude, the air is unusually clear and the deep blue of the lake is especially inviting. Because various interesting boat trips on the lake can be taken from Puno, Peru's major port on Lake Titicaca, many travellers stay overnight in Puno en route to either Cuzco or Bolivia.

There are many other reasons to spend more time in the area, not the least of which is the incredibly luminescent quality of the sunlight on the altiplano. Horizons seem limitless and the earthy tones of the scenery are as deep as the lake itself. These colours are reflected in the nut-brown faces of the people of the altiplano, as well as in their colonial churches and archaeological monuments, several of which are well worth visiting. The Department of Puno is also famous for its folk dances which are the wildest and most colourful in the Peruvian highlands. And, if this isn't enough, there are fascinating Andean animals to be seen – huge herds of domesticated alpaca and llama and sparkling highland lakes full of water birds such as the giant Andean coot and various species of rosy-coloured flamingo.

JULIACA

With a population of about 100,000, Juliaca is the largest town in the Department of Puno and has the department's only commercial airport. It is also an important railway junction with connections to Arequipa, Puno and Cuzco. At an elevation of 3822 metres, Juliaca is the first altiplano town many overland travellers visit en route from the coast to Cuzco or Lake Titicaca. Unfortunately, it is of comparatively little interest and most people prefer to go on to Puno where there are better hotels and a view of Lake Titicaca.

If you arrive from the coast, especially by air, remember to take it easy for 1 or 2 days – see Altitude Sickness in the Health section of the Facts for the Visitor chapter.

The main reasons to stay here relate to making train or plane connections, taking the rarely travelled northern route into Bolivia or visiting the Monday market. There is also a daily market along the railway tracks at which you can buy almost anything. The selection of woollen goods (both sheep and alpaca) is good and prices are very competitive with those in Puno and Cuzco.

Information

Juliaca's Clínica Adventista de Juliaca is the best hospital in the Department of Puno. The town's moneychanging facilities are limited – for cash dollars try the casa de cambio or the *ferretería* (hardware store) shown on the Juliaca map. Otherwise, go to Puno. There is an ENTEL for long distance and international phone calls.

Places to Stay – bottom end

You'll find several cheap, basic, cold-water places by the train station. The *Hotel Don Pedro*, at 65c/$1.10 for singles/doubles, and the slightly more expensive *Hostal Loreto* have little to recommend them beyond their low prices and proximity to the train station. Other basic cheapies are the *Hotel del Sur, Juliaca* and *Ferrocarril*, all charging around 75c per person. The *Hostal San Antonio* has been recommended as the best of the super-cheapies but it isn't up to much either.

More expensive, though more agreeable

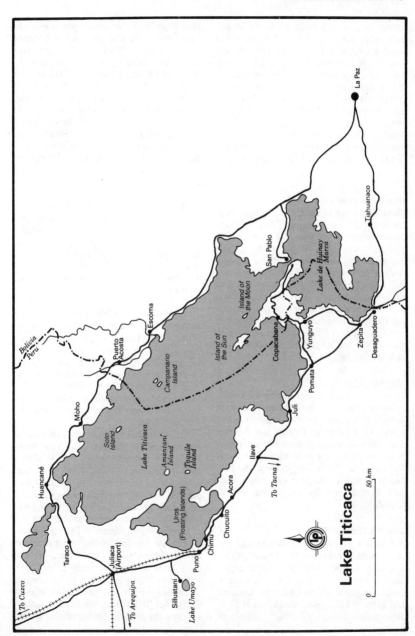

Lake Titicaca

is the clean and friendly *Hotel Yasur*, my recommendation for a budget hotel. It has singles/doubles with bath for $2.20/3.50 and rooms with communal bath for $1.50/2.50. Hot water is available morning and evening but, unfortunately, it is unreliable. As the Yasur fills up fast, get there as early as you can. Also worth trying is the *Hostal Sakury* which charges $1.40 per person in single rooms with shared bath and $2/3 in rooms with private bath. The hostal claims to have hot water but, again, this is unreliable.

Places to Stay – middle

The clean, comfortable *Hostal Peru*, close to the train station, charges $2.70/4.70 for rooms with shared bath, $3.70/5.70 with private bath, and has hot water in the evening. The newer *Hotel Royal* charges $4/6.50 for singles/doubles with private bath and hot water and $2 per person in rooms with communal bath. If you're looking for a higher level of comfort, try the government-run *Hotel de Turistas* on the outskirts of town (take a taxi). It costs about twice as much as the Hotel Royal but the price includes continental breakfast.

Places to Eat

Juliaca's town centre seems to have a simple restaurant on every block – they're nothing to write home about but you certainly won't starve. Good choices include the *Pollería Riko Riko*, which sometimes has live music at the weekends, the restaurant at the *Hotel Royal*, seemingly the best in town, the *Restaurant del Altiplano*, a cheap, interesting-looking place on the railway plaza, and the *Café Dorado*.

Getting There & Away

Air Juliaca airport serves both Juliaca and Puno, with AeroPeru and/or Faucett flights to Cuzco, Arequipa and Lima. Both airlines have offices in town (see the Juliaca map). Fares are about $40 to Cuzco or Arequipa and $100 to Lima, plus an additional $7 in airport taxes. There are no flights to Bolivia.

Bus There are buses to most points in southern Peru. The cheapest long-distance services are offered by Transportes Jacantaya, who operate daily buses to Arequipa (5 pm, 10 hours, $4.70) and Lima (26 hours, $13). Cruz del Sur charges a few cents more and also has a 5 pm bus to Lima, as well as three buses a day to Cuzco (11 hours, $5.20) and three buses a day to Arequipa. SurPeruano has a late-afternoon bus to Arequipa with connections to Lima and Tacna. These companies also operate buses to Puno but the colectivo service is much more convenient.

Colectivo These shared taxis frequently ply the 44 km route between Juliaca and Puno and provide a good service. The Comité 1 vehicles cost just under $1 per passenger and take about 45 minutes to travel the good road to Puno. They leave from the railway plaza as soon as they are full – two or three times an hour.

Train Juliaca is the busiest railway crossroad in Peru. The single train station serves Puno to the south, Cuzco to the north-west and Arequipa to the south-west. Although you can get off at intermediate points, these are of little interest to most travellers. If you want to take the train on to Machu Picchu, you have to change stations in Cuzco – there is no direct service between Juliaca and Machu Picchu.

Tickets in 2nd class are often sold out in advance and, in 1st class (which has numbered and reserved seats), this is almost always the case, so think ahead. The ticket windows are open from 7 to 10 am, 4 to 7 pm and 8 to 10 pm daily, except Sunday when they're open from 7 to 10 am and 4 to 6 pm. Ticket queues are invariably long.

Fares change frequently. During the past 5 years, 1st class fares to Cuzco, for example, have varied between about $2 and $8; 2nd class fares are approximately 25% lower. Fares vary wildly according to fluctuations in exchange rates and government regulations; you'll have to check the current situation for yourself. On top of the 1st class

■	PLACES TO STAY	▼	PLACES TO EAT
5	Hotel Yasur	6	Pollería Riko Riko
7	Hotel Juliaca	13	Café Dorado
8	Hotel Ferrocarril	26	Restaurant del Altiplano
9	Hostal San Antonio		
16	Hotel del Sur	●	OTHER
18	Hostal Sakury	1	Post Office
19	Hotel Royal	2	Cruz del Sur (Bus)
23	Hotel Don Pedro	3	Transportes Jacantaya
24	Hostal Peru		(Bus)
25	Hostal Loreto	4	Transportes 3 de Mayo
		10	ENTEL-Peru

11	Empresa Victoria del Sur
12	Cinema
14	SurPeruano (Bus)
15	Money Exchange
17	Money Exchange
	(in Ferretería)
19	AeroPeru
20	Comité 3 to Arequipa
21	Aquarius Discotheque
22	Faucett Airline
27	Comité 1 to Puno
28	Train Station

Juliaca

0   100   200 m

fare, travellers to Arequipa pay an extra charge of $2.50 in buffet class and $3 in Pullman class. Travelling to Cuzco, the surcharge was $20 for foreign travellers and about $3 for residents. It is OK to travel 1st class on the day trip to Cuzco, particularly if you travel in a group, but watch your luggage like a hawk. If you can afford it, Pullman class is safer.

Trains leave for Puno at about 7 am and for Cuzco at about 8.30 am. There is no Sunday service to these towns. Night trains to Arequipa leave at about 8.45 pm every night. Times are approximate because the trains don't originate in Juliaca and may or may not reach Juliaca on time.

Passengers arriving on the overnight train from Arequipa and continuing on to Cuzco normally have a couple of hours between trains to wander around. Many salespeople at the station sell alpaca sweaters and ponchos so, if you prefer, you can do your shopping through the carriage window. Bargain hard – prices tend to drop just before the train leaves.

Beware of thieves. Read the warnings in the Arequipa Train section and watch your belongings with an eagle eye.

Getting Around

Airport Transport At the time of writing, there was no airport bus. Bargain for a taxi and expect to pay about $1.50 to $2.

THE NORTHERN ROUTE INTO BOLIVIA

Decrepit 3 de Mayo buses full of Andean Indians travel from Juliaca to Huancané several times a day. The 3-hour journey costs about 75c. The company has no office; just show up and pay on the bus. Occasionally, buses continue to Moho, on the route to Bolivia, or to Rasapata. Huancané has a simple hotel near the Plaza de Armas. I am told that there's a basic pensión in Moho but I've never been there.

Most days, there is a bus from Huancané to Moho, a trip that takes a day on foot. A truck runs from Moho to Bolivia once a week, usually on Saturday. The nearest Bolivian town is Puerto Acosta, a day's walk from Moho. In Puerto Acosta you'll find a Bolivian immigration office, a couple of basic hotels and bus connections with La Paz. This little-travelled, adventurous route into Bolivia is recommended only for experienced off-the-beaten-track travellers who have little concern for time or comfort. I'd like to hear from anyone who takes this route.

The nearest Bolivian consul is in Puno. See the Puno section for more information about entering Bolivia.

PUNO

Puno was founded on 4 November 1668 near the site of a now-defunct silver mine called Laykakota. However, apart from the cathedral, there are few colonial buildings to see. The town itself is drab and not very interesting but it does offer a good selection of hotels and there is plenty to see in the environs.

For many travellers, Puno (at 3830 metres) is the highest place in which they'll spend any time. The weather at this altitude can be extreme. It's very cold at night, particularly during the winter months of June, July and August when temperatures can drop well below freezing. If you're cold, buy a thick alpaca sweater from the market – they're cheap. The rainy season is October to May. During the wettest months (December to April), flooding and landslides sometimes close the roads but the train usually keeps running. Because the sun is very strong at this altitude, sunburn is a common problem; remember to wear a wide-brimmed hat and use a sunblock lotion.

Information

Tourist Information The tourist office (tel 351449, 353804) has moved at least four times in the last few years. The most recent address is Arequipa 314.

Post & Telecommunications Puno has a post office and an ENTEL for international phone calls. Both are open 7 days a week.

Money Although Bolivian pesos can be exchanged in Puno, travellers to and from Bolivia are advised to buy or sell Bolivian pesos at the border.

You will find the Banco de la Nación on the Plaza de Armas and other banks nearby on Calle Lima. Moneychangers hang out in front of the banks and give better rates. Casas de cambio operate intermittently – there were none open when I was last in Puno but several existed a couple of years earlier.

Some hotels may change money, particularly for guests; try the Hostal Monterrey or the Hotel Arequipa, among others.

Bolivian Consul The consul's office, on the top floor of a building at the back of the small courtyard at Arequipa 136, is not easy to find, though there is a small sign. The office is open from 8.30 am to 12.30 pm and 2.30 to 4.30 pm Monday to Friday.

Citizens of Canada, Israel and Western European countries (except France) don't require visas or tourist cards and can enter Bolivia with just a passport. Everyone else needs a tourist card or, in the case of nationals of communist countries, a visa. The tourist card, which is free, is valid for 30 days and can be obtained from the consul in Puno within 24 hours of application. It can be renewed in Bolivia. If you plan to enter Bolivia, it's worth checking with the consul to see whether the situation has changed.

Cathedral

The cathedral, on the Plaza de Armas, was completed in 1757. The interior is more spartan than you'd expect after seeing the well-sculpted lower part of the main facade, though there is a silver-plated main altar.

Museum

Just off the plaza is the town's main museum, a private collection bequeathed to the city on the owner's death. Known as the Museo Carlos Dreyer, it is open from 9 am to 7 pm weekdays and charges about 50c admission.

Opening hours change frequently and it's best to go in the morning.

Views

There are two good viewing spots. The best is Huajsapata Park, a little hill about a 10-minute walk south-west of town. It is topped by a larger-than-life white statue of the 1st Inca, Manco Capac, looking out over Lake Titicaca, the legendary site of his birth. The view of the town and the lake is excellent but, unfortunately, the park is badly maintained and frequently used as a latrine, so watch where you step.

There are also good views from the balcony near the arch on Calle Independencia. The arch, Arco Deustua, was built in honour of the Peruvians who died in the battles of Junín and Ayacucho during the fight for independence.

Market

The market is always interesting, especially in the morning when the salespeople are setting up their stalls. It's full of Indian ladies behind piles of potatoes or peanuts and is also a good place to buy woollen clothes.

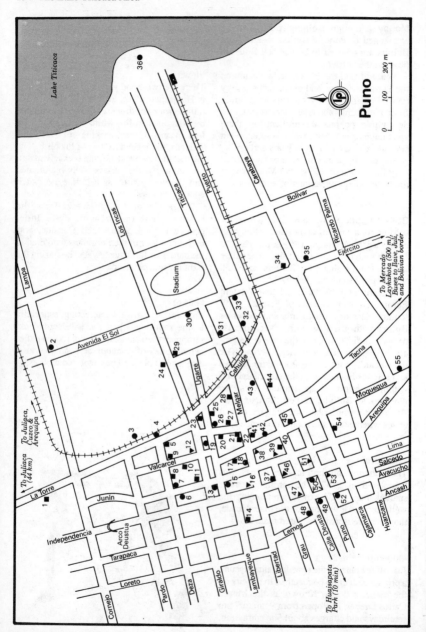

Puno

■ PLACES TO STAY		45	Hostal Rosario	13	Parque Pino
		54	Hotel Tumi		(or San Juan)
1	Hostal Don Miguel			15	FOPTUR Tourist
5	Hotel Ferrocarril	▼	PLACES TO EAT		Information
8	Hotel Centenario			18	Turismo Titicaca
9	Hostal Los Uros	12	Las Rocas Restaurant	19	Market
10	Hostal Italia	16	Restaurant	20	Colectur
11	Hotel Arequipa		Ambassador	21	Comité 3
14	Hotel Sillustani	37	La Hostería Pizzería	26	Transturin (Bus)
16	Hostal Colonial	38	Delta Café, Club 31,	30	Jacantaya & Cruz
17	Hostal Extra		Restaurant		del Sur (Bus)
20	Hostal Lima		Sillustani & Inter-	31	SurPeruano (Bus)
21	Hostal Colón		nacional	32	Empresa San Martín
22	Hostal Taurino	39	Kimano Bar		(Bus)
23	Hostal San Carlos	46	Café Chimu	33	La Perla del Altiplano
24	Hotel Embajador	47	Bar Restaurant		(Bus)
25	Hostal Europa		Los Olivos	35	Public Hot Showers
27	Hostals Venecia,	51	Samana Bar	36	Port (Boats to Uros
	Central &	53	Restaurant Ito		& Taquile)
	Panamericana			42	Post Office
28	Hostal Florida	●	OTHER	43	Hot Showers
29	Hotel Los Incas				(Gymnasium)
34	Hostal Real	2	Buses to Juliaca	48	Museo Carlos
37	Hostal Monterrey	3	Train Station		Dreyer
40	Hostal Nesther	4	Comité 1 (to Juliaca)	49	Cathedral
41	Hostal Roma & Hotel	6	Bolivian Consul	50	Plaza de Armas
	Internacional	7	Twin Cinemas	52	Tranextur
44	Hostal Posada Real		(Cine Puno)	55	ENTEL

Fiestas & Folklore

The Department of Puno is noted for its wealth of traditional dances – up to 100 different varieties. Some dances are rarely seen by tourists while others are performed in the streets during the various annual fiestas. Many have specific significance and, if you make friends with the locals, they'll explain this to you. Although the dances often occur during processions celebrating Catholic feast days, they usually have their roots in completely different, preconquest celebrations. These are often tied in with the agricultural calendar and may celebrate such events as planting or harvesting. Even if you have difficulty understanding the meaning of the dances, you'll be fascinated by the extremely rich, ornate and imaginative costumes which are often worth more than an entire household's ordinary clothes. Included in this show of colour and design are grotesque masks, dazzling sequinned uniforms and animal outfits, to mention a few.

The elaborately outfitted dancers are accompanied by musicians playing a host of traditional instruments. Most of the brass and string instruments have obvious Spanish influences but many of the percussion and wind instruments have changed little since Inca times. These include *tinyas* (hand drums or tambourines) and *wankaras* (larger drums) as well as a host of different shakers, rattles and bells. Inca wind instruments include the very typical and well-known panpipes. These come in a variety of lengths and tones ranging from tiny, high-pitched instruments to huge base panpipes almost as tall as the musician. The pipes, often made from bamboo, are known as *antaras, sikus* or *zampoñas*, depending on their size and range. *Flautas* (flutes) are also seen at most fiestas. The most common are simple bamboo penny whistles called *quenas*, while others are large blocks that look as though they've been hollowed out of a plank of wood. The most esoteric of these flutes is the *piruru* which is carved from the wing bone of an Andean condor.

Seeing a street fiesta with dancing can be planned or it can be a matter of luck. Some celebrations are held in one town and not in another; at other times, such as carnival, there are fiestas everywhere. Ask at the tourist office about any fiestas in the surrounding area.

Apart from the major Peruvian fiestas listed in the Facts about the Country chapter, the following is a selection of fiestas that are particularly important in the Lake Titicaca region. Candlemas is one of the most spectacular.

6 January
    Epiphany
2 February
    Candlemas (or Virgen de la Candelaria)
7-8 March
    Saint John
2-4 May
    Alacitas (Puno miniature handicrafts fair)
    Holy Cross (Huancané, Taquile, Puno)
25 July
    Saint James (Taquile)
24 September
    Our Lady of Mercy
1-7 November
    Puno week

This list is not exhaustive – there are other fiestas. Most are celebrated for several days before and after the actual day.

Places to Stay

Many of Puno's cheaper hotels have only cold showers and, at this altitude, most people find them more unpleasant than invigorating. If you want to economise, you can stay in a cheap hotel and use the public hot showers. The best, on Avenida El Sol, charges about 25c for a 30-minute hot shower and is open between 7 am and 7 pm daily, except holidays. You can also try the gymnasium on Calle Deusta; it is open from 7 am to 3 pm Tuesday to Sunday.

Places to Stay – bottom end

The better hotels fill up quickly when the evening trains arrive, so try to find a room as soon as possible. The prices given may rise during fiestas and sometimes in the evening, though hotels are supposed to display the

prices of their rooms on a board. Many hotels in Puno have triple and quadruple rooms which work out quite cheaply if you are travelling with friends.

There are plenty of cheap, basic hotels near the corner of Libertad and Tacna, most of which are none too clean and have only cold showers. Even if they claim to have hot water, it doesn't always work. One of the best of the supercheapies is the *Hostal Taurino* at 50/90c for singles/doubles (cold showers in communal bathrooms). Other similarly priced dives are the *Hostal Venecia* and *Central* and the *Hotel Centenario*. The *Hostal Rosario* and *Roma* cost a few cents more without offering anything better. The *Hostal Colonial*, at 75c per person, isn't too bad and sometimes has hot water. The *Hostal Extra*, which costs about the same, usually has hot water in the evening and also has a reasonably attractive courtyard – unusual in Puno hotels. The *Hostal Colón* is similar but dirtier and its security has been questioned.

For a little more money you can have hot water but, because of water shortages, it is often available only at certain hours of the day, usually in the evening. If you like a hot shower in the morning, your choice is more limited. The *Hostal San Carlos* has hot water in the evening and offers reasonable singles/doubles for 90c/$1.50. The *Hostal Europa* has similarly priced rooms as well as singles/doubles with private bath for $1.50/2.25. This hotel has built up a reputation among budget travellers as *the* place to stay in Puno and is often full. It's clean, with left-luggage facilities and hot water in the evening.

Another good hotel in this price range is the quiet *Hostal Los Uros*. It has a cafeteria, which is open for early breakfasts, and hot water in the evening. There are only a few single rooms but plenty of triples and even quads, which work out very cheaply if you're travelling in a group. In fact, most of Puno's hotels have plenty of large, shared rooms; the *Hotel Los Incas* has mostly triples and quads for about $1 per person and sometimes has hot water in the communal showers.

Several quite reasonable hotels offer clean singles/doubles with private bath for around $2/3.25. The *Hostal Nesther* has hot water from 7 to 9.30 am, the clean, central *Hostal Lima* offers hot water both morning and evening (though the water was barely luke-warm when I took a morning shower there) and the popular and helpful *Hostal Monterrey* has hot water in the evening. The Monterrey also has singles/doubles with shared bath for $1/1.50. The *Hotel Arequipa* is similar and, like the Monterrey, will often change cash dollars, though there have been recent reports of baggage theft from rooms at the Arequipa. At around the same price, the *Hostal Posada Real* has received good reports.

Places to Stay – middle

The cheapest place in this category is the *Hotel Tumi* at $3/5 for singles/doubles with bath, but the rooms are not much better than the best hotels in the budget price range. The *Hotel Internacional* charges $4.50/7 for rooms with bath but complaints have been made about the service.

Most hotels in this category have fixed prices, often in US dollars, but you can always try bargaining. For example, the *Hotel Embajador* halved its official rates ($9/14) for some travellers I met. The comfortable rooms have bath with round-the-clock hot water.

At the *Hotel Ferrocarril*, across from the train station, you can stay in clean singles/doubles for $8/11. Each room has central heating and a bath with one of those shocking electrical showers that you have to use with care – make sure it's working properly before taking the room. There is also a cold-water annexe with cheaper rooms. The hotel restaurant is reasonably priced and features folk music every evening at 7.30 pm. Some travellers reported receiving a free, welcome pisco sour when they stayed there.

Also in this price range is the good, clean *Hostal Italia* where those who suffer from the cold will be provided with a room heater. Make sure your hot shower works because a few of the cheaper rooms on the ground floor have no hot water. You can bargain at the

Italia. Similar in price are the *Hostal Real* and *Don Miguel*.

Places to Stay – top end

The best place in Puno itself is the *Hotel Sillustani* where carpeted singles/doubles with bath and all-day hot water cost $12/16. The hotel has a reasonable restaurant and breakfast is usually included in the price of the room.

The expensive government-run *Hotel Isla Esteves* is attractively located on an island in the western part of Lake Titicaca. The island is connected with Puno by a 5 km road over a causeway but, as there are no buses, access is a pain. Taxis charge $1.50 for the trip. Many of the rooms look directly out over the lake and the exceptionally beautiful views are the hotel's main attraction. The restaurant is no more than mediocre. Prices are about $25/40 for singles/doubles, including continental breakfast.

Places to Eat

Several restaurants near the corners of Moquegua and Libertad provide a good choice. The *Delta Café* is cheap and recommended for an early (from about 7.30 am) breakfast. The *Restaurant Sillustani* and the *Internacional* are among the town's best, and may have music in the evenings, though both have received mixed reviews from travellers. *Club 31* is cheap and uncrowded, while *Las Rocas Restaurant* has good food and reasonable prices.

There are several other cheap restaurants along Lima – the *Restaurant Ambassador* is good. *La Hostería Pizzería*, near the Hotel Monterrey, serves mediocre pizzas, the *Café Chimu* has been recommended for breakfast and pastries, the *Kimano Bar* and the *Bar Restaurant Los Olivos* are fairly popular with locals and the *Restaurant Ito*, on the corner of the plaza, has been recommended, though its opening hours are erratic. The *Hotel Ferrocarril* has a medium-priced Italian restaurant where you can hear folk music at around 7.30 pm every evening.

Entertainment

The cinema has two separate theatres, each showing a different film. English-language movies with Spanish subtitles are sometimes screened.

For nightly folk music, try the *Hotel Ferrocarril* peña at 7.30 pm. All other places are pretty much a question of luck, though the weekend is the best time to come across a good musical evening. The *Restaurant Sillustani* and the *Internacional* sometimes have music, particularly at weekends, and you might hear of other restaurants with a show.

My favourite bar is the *Samana*. Its fireplace, thatched roof and wooden benches provide a pleasant atmosphere and there is live music most weekends for a cover charge of about 40c (no minimum). It is occasionally closed. A bar on the same block as the Hotel Monterrey advertises folk music but looks like a macho sort of place – there were no women when I visited.

Getting There & Away

Air The nearest airport is in Juliaca, about 44 km away. The AeroPeru and Faucett offices are also in Juliaca but several travel agents in Puno will sell you tickets. See the Juliaca section for further information about flights.

Bus The roads are in bad shape and most people choose to travel in greater comfort on the train. For those who prefer to use the bus, the following services are available.

If you're heading for Cuzco, try Cruz del Sur or Jacantaya whose offices are conveniently located next to one another. Between them, they operate four or five buses to Cuzco, most of which are overnight. Fares for the 11-hour trip are about $5. These companies also offer services to several other major cities, including Arequipa (13 hours, $5) and Lima (32 hours, $12). Sur-Peruano has a service to Arequipa (about $5) and La Perla del Altiplano buses to Tacna leave on Monday and Friday at 5.30 pm. There are three Empresa San Martín buses a week to Tacna ($5, 15 hours), leaving at

3 pm. There are also other companies offering bus services.

Buses to towns on the south side of the lake and the Bolivian border depart from the Avenida El Ejército side of the Laykakota market.

For buses to Juliaca, go to the corner of Lampa and El Sol. Buses leave frequently, cost about 25c and take about 1½ hours.

Colectivo The main colectivo service, Comité 1, charges about 80c per person for the 45-minute trip to Juliaca. The cars leave frequently (as soon as they are full) from in front of the train station.

Comités 2 and 3 have a shared taxi service to Arequipa every morning (about $9, 9 hours).

Train For the first few km out of Puno, the railway line follows the shores of Lake Titicaca and the views are good. There is a junction at Juliaca; from here, the train continues to Cuzco or branches south to Arequipa. The Cuzco train leaves daily, except Sunday, at 7.25 am, while the night train for Arequipa leaves at 7.45 pm each evening. Be alert for thieves in the dimly lit station, especially early in the morning and in the evening, and be particularly careful on the night train. (See the warnings in the Arequipa Train section.)

At one time, the ticket office was open from 6.30 to 8 am, 9.30 to 11.30 am, 2 to 5 pm and 7 to 8.30 pm on weekdays and from 6.30 to 8 am, 2 to 4 pm and 7 to 8.30 pm on Sunday, but these hours change frequently.

Fares have varied tremendously over the last few years. A 1st class ticket to Cuzco, for example, has cost from about $2 to $8, depending on regulations and exchange fluctuations. Fares to Arequipa are similar and 2nd class is about 25% lower. There is usually a surcharge of about $3 for Pullman class train travellers to Arequipa. When I last travelled between Puno and Cuzco, however, 1st class fares were about $2.60 and buffet class cost a whopping $20 extra. The railway company (ENAFER) does not provide any kind of service for the extra

money – the guards merely lock the door so you won't get robbed and then proceed to fleece you themselves.

You should buy your ticket the night before. Sometimes, however, the numbered 1st class seats are sold out, especially on the Cuzco train. The problem is that the ticket office is reluctant to sell tickets earlier than the night before and tour companies often buy up blocks of tickets for their tours. I have received reports of travellers queueing for hours (lines are always long) and then being told that no seat is available. You may have to check the tour agencies for spare tickets – they often have them – but you'll pay a blatant commission of about 25%. It's a real racket, but there's not a great deal you can do about it.

Around Puno

There are four main excursions to take from Puno. Two are lake trips – one to the floating islands of Los Uros and the other to the Island of Taquile. The other two are land trips; one visits the archaeological site of Sillustani and the other, a drive along the southern shores of the lake, takes in various small towns which are famous for their colonial churches and their fiestas.

All these excursions can be done cheaply on public transport. Tour companies will arrange guided trips, but these are more expensive and not necessarily worth the extra money. I went on a guided tour of the archaeological site of Sillustani because there is little literature about the site and I wanted to learn as much about it as I could. I was with a small group of non-Spanish-speaking travellers, who were also particularly interested in Sillustani and, like me, wanted an informative visit. I arranged the excursion with Rey Tours of Puno. They charged us $10 each and promised a private vehicle to pick us up from the hotel and an English-speaking guide to explain the ruins. The old bus that did arrive was almost an hour late and stopped to pick up two more small groups along the way, as well as a few friends of the driver. We were charged an extra fee for admission to the site and, to top it all, the guide knew very little more about the ruins than we did and spoke no English – I ended up translating for him.

Of course, anyone who has spent any time travelling in Latin America knows that these things happen and that you have to expect and accept them. However, when you're paying for it, this is more difficult. If you do take a guided tour, you might want to sign a written agreement or defer payment until the trip is underway.

SILLUSTANI

The Inca Empire was known as Tahuantinsuyo, or 'The Land of Four Quarters'. The southern quarter was called Collasuyo after the Colla tribe which, along with the rival Lupaca tribe, dominated the Lake Titicaca area and later became part of the Inca Empire.

Little is known about the Colla people. They were a warlike tribe who spoke Aymara, not Quechua, and they had unusual burial customs for their nobility. Their dead were buried in funerary towers called *chullpas*, which can be seen in various places in the Puno area. The most impressive of these are the chullpas of Sillustani, the tallest of which reaches a height of about 12 metres; there are several others almost as tall. Standing on a small hilltop in the Lake Umayo peninsula, these towers look very impressive against the bleak landscape. They are either round or square and house the remains of Colla nobility, who were buried in family groups complete with food and belongings for their journey into the next world. The only opening into the towers was a small hole facing east, just large enough for a person to crawl through. After a burial, the entrance was sealed. Nowadays, nothing remains of the burials. The chullpas, however, are well preserved and worth seeing, both for their architecture and for their impressive location.

The outside walls of the towers are made from massive coursed blocks. These are rem-iniscent of Inca stonework but were not built by the Incas; archaeologists consider this architecture more complicated than that of the Incas. Some of the chullpas of Sillustani are unfinished. Carved but unplaced blocks and a ramp used to raise them to the correct height are among the points of interest at the site. A few of the blocks are decorated – the carving most often noticed by visitors is that of a lizard.

Sillustani is surrounded by Lake Umayo. This interesting Andean lake is home to a variety of plants and water birds and ornithologists should particularly watch for the giant Andean coot, the white-tufted and silvery grebes, the puna ibis, the Andean goose, the black-crowned night-heron, the speckled and puna teals, the yellow-billed pintail, the Andean lapwing, the Andean gull (strange to see a 'sea' gull so far from the ocean) and, if you're lucky, one of the three species of flamingo found in the Andean highlands.

Getting There & Away

A daily Tranextur bus leaves from the Plaza de Armas in Puno at 3.30 pm for the Sillustani site, which is about 30 km north-west of Puno. Tickets cost $2 and can be bought at various travel agencies in Puno. The round trip takes about 3½ hours and allows you about 1½ hours at the ruins. This schedule is convenient because the afternoon light is the best for photography, though the site can be pretty crowded in the afternoon. Admission to the ruins costs a further $2 (much less for residents), plus 20c entry to the small on-site museum. Dress warmly and bring sun protection.

If you prefer more time at the site, you could hire a taxi for $10 to $15. If you can get a group together, this isn't much more expensive than the Tranextur bus.

Camping by the lake is reportedly possible but no facilities are provided.

THE FLOATING ISLANDS

The floating islands of the Uros people are the Puno area's major tourist attraction and, as a result, have become somewhat overcommercialised. Despite this, the excursion remains popular because there is nothing quite like it anywhere else.

The Uros people used to speak their own language but nowadays speak Aymara. Inter-marriage with Aymara-speaking Indians has seen the demise of the pure-blooded Uros and none exist today. Always a small tribe, they began their unusual floating existence centuries ago in an effort to isolate themselves from the Collas and the Incas. Today, about 300 people live on the islands but the attractions of shore life are slowly eroding even this small number.

The lives of the Uros are totally interwoven with the *tortora* reeds which grow abundantly in the shallows of Lake Titicaca. These reeds are harvested and used to make everything from the islands themselves to little model boats for sale to tourists. The islands are constructed from many layers of reeds. The reeds rot away from the bottom and are replaced at the top, so the ground is soft and springy and you must be careful not to put your foot through a rotted-out section. The biggest of the islands contains several buildings, including a school. The building walls are still made of tortora but some of the roofs are now tin.

From tightly bundled reeds, the Uros build canoe-shaped boats for transport and fishing. A well-constructed boat can carry a whole family for about 6 months before beginning to rot. You can usually persuade one of the Uros to give you a ride on a boat, but be prepared to pay and give a tip for taking photographs.

Plenty of women will try to sell you their handicrafts such as models made from tortora and embroidered wall hangings. Many visitors find it annoying to be constantly pestered to buy souvenirs, give presents to the children and hand out money every time a camera is lifted. Begging and selling is more common here than in any other part of Peru that I've visited so, if you find this difficult to deal with, go elsewhere. If you prefer, you can give food instead of money – the islanders particularly like fresh fruit. I went with a sack of oranges and became a hit with the kids.

Getting There & Away

Getting to the Floating Islands is easy; just go down to the docks and hang around – within minutes, you'll be asked to take a trip to the islands. You can hire an expensive private boat or go with the next group. Boats generally leave every 30 minutes or so from 7 am until early afternoon. The standard trip, visiting the main island and perhaps one other, takes about 4 hours. Boats leave as soon as they have 15 or 20 passengers and charge a fixed price – usually around $2.50

per person. All the boats are small, rather decrepit motorboats with no life jackets, though I've never heard of an accident.

Many tour agencies in Puno will sell you tickets for an Uros trip but they usually use the same boats as independent travellers and charge more. Unless you insist on a private tour and are prepared to pay more for it, going down to the docks and buying your own ticket is the best idea.

En route, you may well see the Uros paddling around in their reed boats, fishing or gathering tortora reeds. Various species of bird live on and around the lake (see the Sillustani section). Even though the Uros and their floating islands are rather sad, the ride on the lake can be beautiful in good weather.

TAQUILE ISLAND

This is a real island, not a floating one, and it is less frequently visited than Uros. The long trip is best done with an overnight stay, though day trips from Puno are possible.

Taquile is the most fascinating of islands. The men wear tightly woven woollen caps and always seem to be walking around the island knitting them. The headwear looks like a floppy nightcap and can only be described as cute. The women weave the elegant-looking waistcoats which the men wear with their knitted caps, rough-spun white shirts and thick, calf-length black pants, giving them a very raffish air. The women, in their many-layered skirts and delicately embroidered blouses, also look very handsome. These garments, which are among the best made traditional clothes that I've come across in Peru, can be bought in the island's cooperative store.

The people of Taquile speak Quechua, rather than the Aymara of most Titicaca Indians, and maintain a strong sense of group identity. They rarely marry non-Taquile people and their lives are untrammelled by such modernities as roads and electricity. There are no vehicles, not even bicycles, on the island and, more surprisingly, there are no dogs.

Although Taquile is very peaceful, the islanders are by no means content to let the world pass them by. When enterprising individuals from Puno began bringing tourists to visit the island, the islanders fought the invasion. It wasn't the tourists they objected to, it was the Puno entrepreneurs. Now the passenger boats to Taquile are owned and operated by the islanders themselves. This control enables them to keep tourism at what they consider to be reasonable levels. This may be the key to maintaining a respectful, cooperative relationship between locals and tourists – something sadly lacking on the floating islands of the Uros.

Unfortunately, I did receive one report of thieving and begging, so the place obviously isn't perfect. Perhaps tourism is beginning to have negative effects. Try to minimise the impact of your visit.

The island's scenery is beautiful. The soil is a deep, earthy, red colour which, in the strong highland sunlight, contrasts magnificently with the intense blue of the lake. The backdrop of Bolivia's snowcapped Cordillera Real on the far side of the lake completes a splendid picture. The island is 6 to 7 km long with several hills, which have Inca terracing on the sides and small ruins on top. Visitors are free to wander around exploring these ruins and enjoying the peaceful scenery.

St James Day (25 July) is a big feast day on Taquile. Dancing, music and general carousing go on for several days until the beginning of August, when the Indians traditionally make offerings to mother earth, Paccha Mama. New Year's Day is also festive and rowdy.

Places to Stay & Eat

Some people elect to stay overnight on Taquile. A steep stairway, from which there are lovely views, leads from the dock to the centre of the island. The climb takes about 20 minutes, more if you're not acclimatised, and it is strongly recommended that you don't do it immediately after arriving from the coast – climbing stairs at 4000 metres is a painful, breathless and potentially dangerous experience if you're not used to it. In the centre, a group of the inhabitants will greet you and, if you wish, will arrange accommodation. Individuals and small groups are assigned to island families who will put you up in their rustic houses – there are no hotels as such. There is a standard charge of about 70c per person and gifts of fresh food are appreciated. Beds are basic and facilities minimal. You will be given some blankets but bring a sleeping bag as it gets very cold at night. Bathing means doing what the locals do – washing in cold water from a bucket and using the fields as a latrine. If you like a little comfort, overnighting in Taquile is not for you.

If you do decide to stay the night, remember to bring a flashlight as there is no lighting. It's also a good idea to get the lie of the land while it's still light – some friends of mine became completely lost on the island in the dark, couldn't find the house where they were staying and ended up having to rough it for the night.

The few simple restaurants in the centre of the island sell whatever is available: fresh lake trout if you're lucky, boiled potatoes if you're not. You can usually buy bottled drinks but they have been known to run out. Boiled tea is usually safe to drink, though it's worth bringing a water bottle and purifying tablets if you have them. Also bring extra food unless you're prepared to take pot luck on what's available in the restaurants. Make sure you have small bills because change is limited and there's nowhere to change dollars. Bring extra money too – many travellers are unable to resist the high quality of the unique woven and knitted clothes sold in the island's cooperative store.

Although conditions are primitive by Western standards, visiting Taquile is a wonderful experience and some travellers stay for several days. The people are friendly and the life style is peaceful and relaxed. I stayed here once at the time of a full moon and watched the sunset and moonrise from a small Inca ruin atop one of the island's hills. It was windless and still and, as the mirror-like lake darkened slowly, I felt that Taquile was its own little world, completely detached from the rest of the earth. When the moon came up over the 7000-metre snowcaps of the Cordillera Real, it seemed twice as bright and much larger than normal in the crystalline air over the lake. An unforgettable evening.

Getting There & Away

A boat for Taquile leaves the Puno dock every day (twice a day if there's enough demand). Departure time is usually about 8 or 9 am; you can either go down to the dock the day before to check the departure time or show up by 7.30 am and see what's available. The 24-km trip takes 4 hours (including a brief stop at the Uros Islands) and costs $4. You then get about 2 hours on the island and the return trip leaves at 2.30 pm, arriving in Puno around nightfall. Remember to bring adequate sun protection – the intensity of the tropical sun bouncing off the lake at almost 4000 metres can cause severe sunburn.

Tour agencies also offer this trip but it's cheaper and just as easy to go down to the docks and get your own ticket.

AMANTANÍ ISLAND

This island is similar to and a few km north of Taquile. Because it is further away from Puno, Amantaní is visited less often and has fewer facilities than Taquile. Basic food and accommodation are available but tend to be limited. You can get board and lodging for about $2 per day or eat in one of the few 'restaurants'. Boats to Amantaní leave the Puno dock between 7.30 and 8.30 am most mornings – ask around for the next departure – and round-trip fares are about $4. Several boats and islanders have been recommended, but transport depends on what's in town and where you stay depends on the islanders – they have a quota system that gives everybody a fair chance to make some money.

From Puno, it is possible to make a round trip via the Uros Islands and Amantaní to Taquile and back to Puno. It is more difficult to do the trip in reverse because fewer boats go from Taquile to Amantaní. Most boats to Amantaní stop at the Uros Islands and you stay overnight on Amantaní. There is a boat from Amantaní to Taquile most days for a fare of $1. If you plan on doing this trip, ask for one-way boat tickets (otherwise, you'll usually be sold the round-trip ticket to Amantaní and Taquile as a matter of course).

THE ISLANDS OF THE SUN & MOON

The most famous island on Lake Titicaca is the Island of the Sun, legendary birthplace of Manco Capac, the 1st Inca. Both the Island of the Sun and the Island of the Moon have Inca ruins. They are in the Bolivian portion of the lake and you should visit them from the Bolivian port of Copacabana, about 11 km beyond the border town of Yunguyo.

THE SOUTH SHORE TOWNS

An interesting bus excursion can be made to the towns of Chimu, Chucuito, Ilave, Juli, Pomata and Zepita on the southern shores of Lake Titicaca. If you start early enough, you can visit all of them in a day and be back in Puno for the night. Alternatively, you can stay in one of the south shore towns or continue on to Bolivia.

Getting There & Away

If you're interested in visiting any of the towns along the south shore of Lake Titicaca, go to the Avenida El Ejército side of Puno's Mercado Laykakota. Cheap, very slow buses, slightly dearer, faster minibuses and even more expensive colectivo taxis leave from here for the south shore towns and the Bolivian border. Buses to the nearer towns, such as Ilave, are more frequent but, if you're patient, you should be able to leave for the town of your choice within an hour. Minibus fares to the border are under $2 and proportionately less to closer towns.

Chimu

The road east of Puno closely follows the margins of the lake. After about 8 km, you reach the village of Chimu – hikers might find this a pleasant lakeshore walk. Chimu is famous for its tortora-reed industry and its inhabitants have close ties with the Uros. Bundles of reeds can be seen piled up to dry and there are always several reed boats in various stages of construction. Although this is an interesting sight, I found the villagers not particularly friendly to sightseers (though a correspondent tells me that their initial reserve can be overcome).

Chucuito

The village of Chucuito, about 18 km east of Puno, was of some importance as a major Lupaca centre and a precolonial stone sundial can be seen in the main plaza. Chucuito has two attractive colonial churches – Santo Domingo, with its small museum, and La Asunción. Opening hours are erratic. There is a trout hatchery east of the town .

Places to Stay The expensive *Tambo Titikaka Motel* on the outskirts of Chucuito charges about $12 per person. Its main attraction is the superb view of the lake.

Ilave

Near Chucuito, the road turns south-east away from the lake (though the waters can usually be seen in the distance) and soon reaches Platería, a village once famous for its silverware. About 40 km from Puno, the road passes through the straggly community of Molleko. This area is noted for the great number of mortarless stone walls that snake eerily across the bleak altiplano.

Ilave is 56 km from Puno. It doesn't have the interesting colonial architecture of the other towns but its position at the crossroads gives it some importance. Ilave also has a Sunday market. A daily bus travels the little-used road to Tacna. Unfortunately, the bus leaves at 4 pm and travellers miss much of the scenery. The journey takes about 14 hours and costs $5.50.

Juli

The road returns to the lake near the bay of Juli, where flamingoes are sometimes seen. Juli is 80 km from Puno and famous for its four colonial churches. They are all in a greater or lesser state of disrepair but are slowly being restored as funds become available. The oldest, San Juan Bautista, dates from the late 1500s and contains richly framed colonial paintings depicting the lives of St John the Baptist and St Teresa. This church is now a museum with erratic opening hours – try visiting in the morning.

The Church of La Asunción, finished in 1620, offers excellent vistas of Lake Titicaca from its large courtyard. Its belfry was struck by lightning and shows extensive damage. The Church of Santa Cruz has lost half of its roof. The Church of San Pedro, on the main plaza, is in the best condition. It is interesting to see the churches in their unrestored state and get some idea of what the magnificent colonial churches of such popular tourist centres as Cuzco would look like had they not been carefully and extensively restored.

An infrequent and irregular service to Bolivia operates from Juli's small port. In addition to a boat, there is a hydrofoil which leaves most days and costs about $100 per passenger. Further information can be obtained in Puno or from La Paz travel agencies.

Market day in Juli is Thursday.

Places to Stay Juli has two hotels. The *Hotel Los Tréboles*, on the main square, costs about 50c a night and is pretty grungy. The *Hotel Turistas* is better. It's about 20 minutes out of town, by the lake, and charges about $4 per person.

Pomata
Beyond Juli, the road returns to the lake shore again and continues to Pomata, 106 km from Puno. As you arrive in Pomata you'll see the Dominican church, dramatically located on top of a small hill. It was founded in 1700 and is known for its many baroque carvings and for its windows, made of the translucent stone, alabaster. Work on its restoration may have finished. As with the other churches in the region, you can never tell exactly when it will be open.

Just out of Pomata, the road forks. The main road continues south-east through Zepita (where there is another colonial church) to the Bolivian border town of Desaguadero, while a side road, leading to the other border crossing at Yunguyo, hugs the shore of Lake Titicaca.

Places to Stay I am told that Pomata's one cheap hotel, the *Hotel Puma Uta*, is OK.

GOING TO BOLIVIA
For many travellers, Puno and Lake Titicaca are stepping stones to Bolivia, which borders the lake to the south. (For more information about Bolivian entrance formalities, see the Bolivian Consul information in the Puno section.)

Lake Titicaca
The steamer service from Puno to the Bolivian port of Guaqui was discontinued several years ago. There is sporadic talk of restarting this service – check with a travel agent to find out if the steamer is sailing again. The voyage used to take about 11 hours and cost $27.50.

The available boats and hydrofoils from Puno to La Paz are much more expensive than a bus ride. The Transturin service, which costs about $80, includes a catamaran cruise-ship crossing of the southern portion of Lake Titicaca and a visit to the Island of the Sun. Part of the journey is done by bus. Transturin has an office in Puno (tel 352771) at Tacna 149 as well as a La Paz office at Camacho 1321. Crillon Tours, at Camacho 1223 in La Paz, runs a guided hydrofoil service across the southern part of the lake, also visiting the Island of the Sun and using buses for part of the trip from Puno to La Paz. Fares are reportedly about $160 (though Crillon Tours did not confirm this).

Overland

There are two overland routes to Bolivia: via Yunguyo or via Desaguadero. Each has its advantages and both will be described.

The Yunguyo route is the more attractive and has the added interest of the boat crossing at the Strait of Tiquina. It is a little longer and more complicated than the Desaguadero route and so, in the past, some travellers preferred to go via Desaguadero. Extensive flooding in early 1986 temporarily closed the Desaguadero route and it remains a slow trip because of road damage.

Via Yunguyo Buses leave from the Laykakota market in Puno for the border town of Yunguyo (3 hours, $1.50). Cruz del Sur also services this route. Yunguyo has a couple of basic hotels but, as there is little of interest in Yunguyo, most people go on to Bolivia. You will find moneychangers in the main plaza and on the street by the border, which is about 2 km away. Change just enough to get you to La Paz and count your money carefully. The border is open from 8 am to 6 pm and, as you'll need to visit several huts, ask the officials where to go next.

Bolivian immigration formalities take place in Copacabana, 11 km beyond Yunguyo. Available transport ranges from trucks to buses and is more frequent on Sunday, which is market day in Yunguyo. On weekdays, you may have to wait 1 or 2 hours. Copacabana is a much more pleasant place than Yunguyo and has several hotels so, if you want to break your journey, do so here.

Remember that Bolivian time is 1 hour ahead of Peruvian time.

There are about three buses a day from Copacabana to La Paz. The trip takes approximately 5 hours, including a boat crossing of the Strait of Tiquina. You have to register with the Bolivian navy to cross – a simple formality but don't miss your bus!

If you leave Puno early in the morning, you can reach La Paz in a single day. For an extra couple of dollars, a Puno to La Paz ticket with a company such as Colectur is the most convenient option. They will drive you to Yunguyo, stop at the money exchange, show you exactly where to go for exit and entrance formalities and drive you to Copacabana, where you are met by a Bolivian bus for the trip to La Paz. Although this costs about $6, being guided through the border formalities and provided with a through service is attractive to some travellers.

In La Paz, you can find agents for the through service to Puno in the Residencial Rosario at Illampu 704, and nearby at Colectur at Ilampu 626. Different international exchange rates make the La Paz to Puno trip more expensive than the same journey in the other direction.

Transturin offers an expensive (about $80) twice-weekly tour. You travel in a comfortable coach to Juli and Pomata to visit the churches, cross the border in Yunguyo, have lunch in Copacabana, take a 3½-hour boat trip to the Island of the Sun and continue by bus to La Paz, accompanied by a guide throughout.

Via Desaguadero Buses leave Puno's Laykakota market every 1 or 2 hours for Desaguadero ($1.80, 3 hours), where there are two basic hotels. The *Hotel Montes* charges about 70c per person but is not recommended. A little better is the *Hotel Bolívar*, right next to the border on the Bolivian side, for $1.50 per person. The town's best restaurant is in this hotel.

The border is open from 8 am to noon and 2 to 5 pm daily, though you can cross back and forth easily enough outside these hours if, for example, you want to eat at the Bolívar. You will find moneychangers at the border and a casa de cambio around the corner. When I crossed this border some years ago, there were several different offices to visit; now, there appears to be one on each side of the border. Always ask the officials where you should go next. The border officials here have been repeatedly criticised for corruption so keep your wits about you.

Before the 1986 floods, several buses a day ran from Desaguadero to La Paz, passing the ruins of Tiahuanaco. You can break your journey here. Travellers arriving from La Paz will find minibuses running back to Puno until midafternoon.

Companies in Puno will sometimes offer through bus trips to La Paz via Desaguadero but, when I was last in Puno, this service had been suspended because of road damage.

BOLIVIA TO PERU

There is rarely any hassle at either border and you can get 90 days without difficulty. This is good if your tourist card has almost expired – just go to La Paz for an evening and come back to Peru the next day. See the Visas & Documents section in the Facts for the Visitor chapter for more information.

The Cuzco Area

This chapter covers the Department of Cuzco which includes the city of Cuzco, many smaller towns and villages, nearby archaeological sites and the Inca Trail to Machu Picchu. The most direct road link from here to the coast goes via Abancay, the capital of the Department of Apurimac, then on through the southern part of the Department of Ayacucho to join the Pan-American Highway near Nazca. Unfortunately, guerilla attacks have recently made this road dangerous. At this time, overland travellers to Cuzco are advised to take a bus from Arequipa or a train from Puno, both of which are safe. However, this situation may change, so ask locally.

Although the Department of Cuzco lies in exceptionally beautiful Andean surroundings, its beauty is not the area's main attraction for tourists. Almost every visitor to Peru comes to Cuzco, the heart of the once-mighty Inca Empire, to see the most fascinating and accessible archaeological ruins on the continent.

CUZCO

Cuzco is the hub of the South American travel network and, in this respect, is reminiscent of Kathmandu in Nepal. Both cities attract thousands of travellers who come not just to visit a unique destination but also to experience an age-old culture that is very different to their 20th century Western way of life.

Cuzco is the archaeological capital of the Americas and the continent's oldest continuously inhabited city. Massive Inca-built stone walls line most of Cuzco's central streets and form the foundations of colonial and modern buildings. The streets are often stepped and narrow and thronged with Quechua-speaking descendants of the Incas.

Cuzco is the capital of its department. Population figures vary between 140,000 and 400,000 – the lower estimates are prob-ably more accurate. The city is 3326 metres above sea level and, during your first few days, you should take care not to overexert yourself, particularly if you've flown in from Lima at sea level.

History

Cuzco is a city steeped in history, tradition and legend. Indeed, it is often difficult to know where fact ends and myth begins. When Columbus arrived in the Americas, Cuzco was the thriving, powerful capital of the Inca Empire. According to legend, the city was founded in the 12th century by the 1st Inca, Manco Capac, the son of the sun. During his travels, Manco Capac plunged a golden rod into the ground until it disappeared. This point was cuzco, or 'the earth's navel' in the Quechua language, and it was here that he founded the city that was to become the centre of the Western hemisphere's greatest empire.

Parts of this legend are undoubtedly based on fact – the Inca Empire did have its origins around the 12th century, Cuzco did become its capital and Manco Capac was one of the earliest Inca leaders – but the archaeological record shows that the area was occupied by other cultures for several centuries before the rise of the Incas. Very little is known about these pre-Incas except that some of them were involved in the Wari expansion of the 8th and 9th centuries.

The Incas had no written language and their history was entirely oral, passed down through the generations. The empire's main expansion occurred in the 100 years or so prior to the arrival of the conquistadors. As the oral records of that important period are relatively accurate, our knowledge of Cuzco's history dates back to about the middle of the 15th century. Led by Francisco Pizarro, the Spanish reached Cuzco in 1533 and, from that point on, written records (the so-called chronicles) were kept. These included accounts of Inca history as related by the Incas to the Spanish chroniclers. The most famous of these accounts was written by Garcilaso de la Vega. He was born in Peru in 1539, the son of an Inca princess and a Spanish conquistador, and lived in the Cuzco area until the age of 21. He then moved to Spain where he died in 1616. Although neither his writings nor those of the other chroniclers can be considered entirely accurate, they do give a good overview of Inca history.

The reigns of the seven Incas who succeeded Manco Capac spanned a period from around the 12th century to the early 15th century. The small tribe they governed was one of several groups living in the Andean highlands during the 13th and 14th centuries. These Incas left few signs of their existence, though the remains of some of their palaces can still be seen in Cuzco. In chronological order, they were:

1. Manco Capac – The Palace of Colcampata is traditionally attributed to Manco Capac, the 1st Inca, but some sources claim that it was built by Huascar shortly before the arrival of the Spaniards. The massive retaining walls with 11 niches can be seen next to the Church of San Cristóbal, on a hill on Cuzco's north-western outskirts. The walls, at least to my untrained eye, seem too well made to be attributable to the 1st Inca, but the story persists.
2. Sinchi Roca – Some of the walls of his palace, the Palace of Cora Cora, can be seen in the courtyards of houses to the right of Calle Suecia as you walk uphill from the Plaza de Armas.
3. Lloque Yupanqui
4. Mayta Capac
5. Capac Yupanqui
6. Inca Roca – The huge blocks of this Inca's palace now form the foundations of the Museum of Religious Art and include the famous 12-sided stone of Hatunrumiyoc.
7. Yahuar Huacac
8. Viracocha Inca – His palace was demolished to make way for the present cathedral on the Plaza de Armas.

The 9th Inca, Pachacutec, began the empire's great expansion. Until his time, the Incas had dominated only a small area close to Cuzco, frequently skirmishing with, but not conquering, various other highland tribes. One such tribe, the expansionist Chancas, occupied a region about 150 km east of Cuzco and, by 1438, was on the verge of conquering Cuzco. Viracocha Inca and his eldest son, Urcon, believed that their small empire was lost but Viracocha Inca's third son refused to give up the fight. With the help of some of the older generals he rallied the Inca army and, in a desperate final battle, managed to rout the Chancas. According to legend, the unexpected victory was won because the boulders on the battlefield turned into warriors and fought on the side of the Inca.

The victorious younger son changed his name to Pachacutec and proclaimed himself the new Inca over his father and elder brother. Buoyed by his victory over the Chancas, he began the first wave of the expansion which was to eventually create the Inca Empire. During the next 25 years, he conquered most of the central Andes between the two great lakes of Titicaca and Junín.

As a mighty military figure, historians have frequently compared Pachacutec to the likes of Alexander the Great and Genghis Khan. He was also a great urban developer. Pachacutec devised the city's famous puma shape and diverted the Sapphi and Tullumayo rivers into channels which crossed the city, keeping it clean and providing it with water. He built agricultural terraces and many buildings, including the famous Coricancha temple and his palace on what is now the western corner of the Plaza de Armas. Parts of the walls are visible to diners at the Roma Restaurant.

There was, of course, no Plaza de Armas before the arrival of the Spanish. In its place was an even greater square divided by the Sapphi Canal. The area covered by today's Plaza de Armas was known as Aucaypata and, on the other side of the Sapphi, the area now called the Plaza Regocijo was known as the Cusipata. Together, they formed a huge

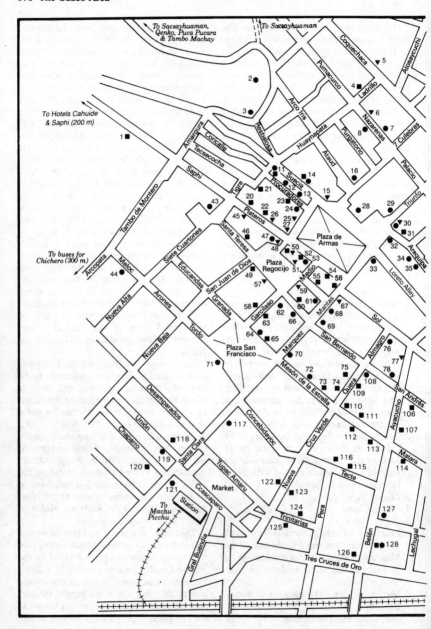

To Sacsayhuaman, Qenko, Puca Pucara & Tambo Machay

To Sacsayhuaman

To Hotels Cahuide & Saphi (200 m)

To buses for Chichero (300 m)

To Machu Picchu

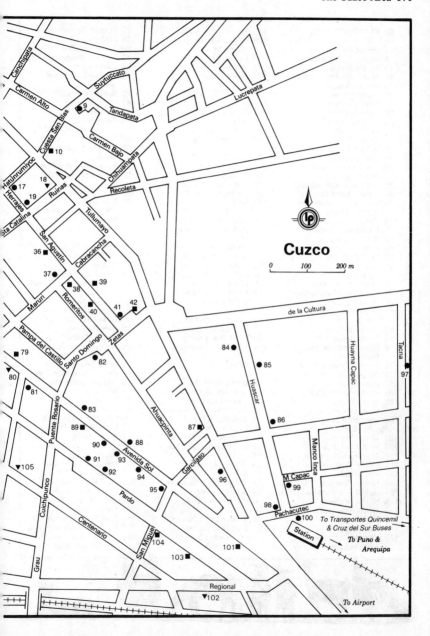

Cuzco

0   100   200 m

■ PLACES TO STAY

1 Hostal Familiar
4 Hostal El Archaeologo
10 Hostal San Blas
11 Hostal del Procurador
14 Hostal Suecia
20 Hostal Caceres
21 Hostal Bolívar
22 Hotel America
23 Cuzco Amazonic
Lodge (Booking
Office)
31 Hotel Conquistador
36 Hostal Royal
38 Hotel Internacional
San Augustín
39 Hotel Panamericano
40 Hotel Libertador
42 Residencial Torres &
Hostal Limaqpampa
46 Picoaga Hotel
48 Espaderos Hostal
49 Hotel Royal Inca
50 Hostal Samari
52 Hostal Chaski
54 Hotel Virrey
55 Hotel Espinar
56 Hostal Wiracocha
58 Hotel Los Marqueses
60 Hotel Cusco
63 Hotels Garcilaso I,
II & III
65 Hostal El Solar
73 Hostal Mesón
74 Gran Hostal Machu
Picchu
75 Hostal Colonial Palace
79 Hotel El Dorado
87 Hostal Bambu
89 Hostal Alhambra 2
101 Hotel Savoy
103 Hostal Raymi
104 Leonard's Lodging
106 Hotel El Sol
107 Tambo Hotel
109 Hostal del Inca
110 Gran Hostal Chavín
111 Hostal Qorikancha
112 Hostal Inti
113 Hostal Colonial
114 Hostal Los Portales
115 Hostal Aragon
116 Hostal Monarca
118 Hotel Peru
120 Hotel Imperio
122 Hostals Comercio &
San Pedro

123 Hostal La Posada
124 Hostal Trinitarias &
Hostal Milan
125 Hostal San Martín
126 Hostal Tambo Real
128 Hotel Belén

▼ PLACES TO EAT

5 Quinta Eulalia
6 Picantería La Chola
15 Café El Ayllu
18 El Fogon de las
Mestizas
25 Chef Victor & Res-
taurant Pizzaiola
26 Pollería Haway
27 Restaurant Roma
30 Restaurant Tumi
45 Restaurant Jadanes,
Café Haylliy & Others
48 Govinda Vegetarian
Restaurant & Café
Varayoc
50 Restaurant El Mesón
de los Espaderos
51 Café Wiphala
57 El Truco Restaurant/
Nightclub
59 La Mamma Pizzería
& Other Italian
Restaurants
67 Trattoria Adriano
77 Restaurant Victor
80 Chifa Hong Kong
105 Ajha Wasi Restaurant

● OTHER

2 Colcampata Ruins
3 San Cristobal Church
7 Nazarenas Church
8 Archaeological Museum
9 San Blas Church
11 Explorandes
12 Expediciones Mayuc
13 Ormeño Ticket Office
14 Laundry
16 Regional History
Museum
17 Religious Art Museum
19 Bilboquet Bar
24 Adventure Centre
28 Cathedral
29 Church of El Triunfo
30 FOPTUR Tourist
Information &
Tourist Police

32 El Muki Discotheque
33 La Compañía Church
34 Santa Catalina Convent
35 Santa Catalina Museum
37 Cine Cuzco
41 Musical Instrument
Shop
43 Santa Teresa Church
44 Cine Ollanta
47 Kamikaze Bar
53 Peña Hatuchay &
Cross Keys Pub
61 Lloyd Aero Boliviano
62 Garcilaso Colonial
House
64 Explorers' Inn Office
66 Manu National Park
Office
68 La Merced Church
69 English Books
70 Marqués de Valleum-
broso Colonial House
71 San Francisco Church
72 Cine Colón
76 Banco de la Nación
78 Centro Comercial
Cuzco
81 Telephones, ENTEL
82 Santo Domingo Church
& Coricancha
83 Faucett Airline
84 Ormeño Bus & Local
Buses to Urubamba
85 Cine Azul
86 Urcos Minibus
88 Manu Nature Tours
90 AeroPeru
91 Milla Turismo
92 Peruvian Andean Treks
93 Cuzco Centre of
Native Art
94 Immigration Office
95 Post Office
96 Empresa Hidalgo (Bus)
97 Local Bus to Pisac
98 Empresa Oriental (Bus)
99 Transportes Oropesa
(Bus)
100 Puno\Arequipa Train
Station
102 La Peña de Don Luis
108 Inca Craft Market
117 Santa Clara Church
119 Cine Unión
121 San Pedro Church
127 Morales Moralitos (Bus)
128 Transportes Señor de
los Animas (Bus)

Battle dress   Ceremonial dress   Judicial dress

Uniforms of the Inca emperor

central plaza which was the focus of the city's social life.

Pachacutec was fortunate to have a son, Tupac Yupanqui, who was every bit as great a leader as his father. During the 1460s, Tupac Yupanqui helped his father subdue a great area to the north, which included the northern Peruvian and southern Ecuadorian Andes of today as well as the northern Peruvian coast. After he took over as ruler in 1471, becoming the 10th Inca, the empire continued to expand dramatically. By the time of Tupac Inca's death around 1493, the Inca Empire extended from Quito in Ecuador to south of Santiago in Chile.

Huayna Capac, the 11th Inca, was the last to rule over a united empire. When he assumed power after the death of his father, the empire was by far the greatest ever known in the Western hemisphere and there was little left to conquer. Nevertheless, Huayna Capac marched (he would, in fact, have been carried in a litter) to the northernmost limits of his empire, in the region today marked by the Ecuadorian-Colombian border. Here, using Quito as his base of operations, the Inca fought a long series of inconclusive campaigns against the tribes of Pasto and Popayán. He also sired a son, Atahualpa, who was born of a Quitan mother.

By this time, Europeans had discovered the New World and various epidemics, including smallpox and the common cold, swept down from Central America and the Caribbean. Huayna Capac died in such an epidemic around 1525. Shortly before his death he divided his empire, giving the northern part around Quito to Atahualpa and the southern Cuzco area to another son, Huascar.

Both sons were well suited to the responsible position of ruling an empire, so well suited that neither wished to share power and a civil war ensued. Huascar was the more popular contender because, having lived in Cuzco for most of his life, he had the people's support. Atahualpa, on the other hand, had lived in outposts of the empire and had few followers around Cuzco. He did, however, have the backing of the army which had been fighting the northern campaigns. In 1532, after several years of warfare, Atahualpa's battle-hardened troops won the major battle of the civil war and captured Huascar outside Cuzco. Atahualpa, the new Inca, retired to Cajamarca to rest.

Meanwhile, Francisco Pizarro landed in northern Ecuador and marched south in the wake of Atahualpa's conquests. Although Atahualpa was undoubtedly aware of the Spanish presence, he was too busy fighting the civil war to worry about a small band of foreigners. By the autumn of 1532, however, Pizarro was in northern Peru, Atahualpa had defeated Huascar and a fateful meeting was arranged between the Inca and Pizarro.

The meeting, which took place in Cajamarca on 16 November 1532, was to change the course of South American history. The Inca was ambushed by a few dozen armed conquistadors, who succeeded in capturing Atahualpa, killing thousands of unarmed Indians and routing tens of thousands more. The conquest of the Incas had begun.

The conquest succeeded for two main reasons. Firstly, Pizarro realised that the emotion of the recent civil war still ran high and decided to turn this to his advantage. Accordingly, after holding Atahualpa prisoner and then murdering him, he marched into Cuzco and was accepted by the people because their loyalties lay more with the defeated Huascar than with Atahualpa.

The second reason was the superior Spanish weaponry. Mounted on horseback, protected by armour and swinging steel swords, the Spanish cavalry was virtually unstoppable. The Spaniards hacked dozens of unprotected Indian warriors to death during a battle. The Indians responded with their customary weapons – clubs, spears, slingshots and arrows – but these were rarely lethal against the mounted, armour-plated conquistadors. Furthermore, in the early battles, the Indians were terrified of the Spaniards' horses and primitive firearms, neither of which had been seen in the Andes before.

It took Pizarro almost a year to reach Cuzco after capturing Atahualpa. In an attempt to regain his freedom, the Inca offered a ransom of a roomful of gold and two rooms of silver. This was to be brought from Cuzco. To speed up the process, Pizarro sent three soldiers to Cuzco early in 1533 to strip Coricancha, or the 'Gold Courtyard', of its rich ornamentation. Pizarro himself entered Cuzco on 8 November 1533 after winning a series of battles on the road from Cajamarca. By this time, Atahualpa had been killed and Pizarro appointed Manco, a half-brother of Huascar, as a puppet Inca. For almost 3 years, the empire remained relatively peaceful under the rule of Manco Inca and Pizarro.

In 1536, Manco Inca realised that the Spaniards were there to stay and decided to try and drive them from his empire. He fled the Spanish and raised a huge army, estimated at well over 100,000. He laid siege to the Spaniards in Cuzco and almost succeeded in defeating them. Only a desperate, last-ditch breakout from Cuzco and a violent battle at Sacsayhuaman saved the Spanish from complete annihilation. Manco Inca retreated to Ollantaytambo and then into the jungle at Vilcabamba.

The Inca Empire was Andean, so situating its capital in the heart of the Andes at Cuzco made a lot of sense. The Spaniards, however, were a seafaring people and needed to maintain links with Spain. Therefore, in 1535, Pizarro founded his capital at Lima on the coast. Although Cuzco remained very important during the first postconquest years, its importance declined once it had been captured, looted and settled. By the end of the 16th century, Cuzco was a quiet colonial town. All the gold and silver was gone and many of the Inca buildings had been pulled down to make room for churches and colonial houses. Despite this, enough Inca foundations remain to make a walk around the heart of Cuzco a veritable journey back in time.

Few events of historical significance have occurred in Cuzco since the Spanish conquest, apart from two major earthquakes and one important Indian uprising. The earthquakes, in 1650 and 1950, brought colonial and modern buildings tumbling down, yet most of the Inca walls were completely unaffected. The only Indian revolt which came at all close to succeeding was led by Tupac Amaru II in 1780 but he, too, was defeated by the Spaniards. The battles of Peruvian Independence in the 1820s achieved what the Inca armies had failed to do, but it was the Hispanic descendants of the conquistadors who wrested power from Spain and life in Cuzco after independence continued much as before.

The discovery of Machu Picchu in 1911 affected Cuzco more than any event since the arrival of the Spanish. With the development of international tourism in the second half of this century, Cuzco has changed from a provincial backwater to Peru's foremost tourist centre. Until the 1930s, its main link with the outside world was the railway line to Lake Titicaca and Arequipa. Now, the modern international airport allows daily flights to Lima and other destinations and roads link Cuzco with the coast. Going to Peru and missing Cuzco is as unthinkable as visiting Egypt and skipping the pyramids.

Information

Tourist Information The official Ministry of Tourism on Calle Tecsecocha doesn't normally deal with tourist inquiries. The tourist office (tel 237364) is on the north-eastern corner of the Plaza de Armas at Portal Belén 115, under the tourist police office. Hours are 8.30 am to 12.30 pm Monday to Saturday and 2.30 to 5.30 pm Monday to Friday.

There's usually an English-speaking staff member who can give you up-to-date details of train schedules, opening hours, festivals and so on. The office has left-luggage facilities and sells entrance tickets to the various sites around Cuzco. It is also helpful with budget travel information to Machu Picchu.

There is also a tourist office at the airport which is sometimes open in the mornings.

Post The post office is open from 8 am to 7 pm Monday to Saturday. On Sunday and holidays, it's open from 8 am to noon. The post office will hold mail addressed to you c/o Lista de Correos, Correos Central, Cuzco, Peru for up to 3 months. For some strange reason letters were, until recently, divided into male and female sections!

Telecommunications ENTEL on Avenida Sol has both national and international telephone and telex services and is open from 7 am to 10.30 pm. Expect to wait up to an hour for international calls. There are also three international courier services on Avenida Sol: Jet Courier at 346, Masterpost at 604 and World Courier at 615.

Money Over the last couple of years, I have found that casas de cambio give consistently better service than banks, with better exchange rates and less fuss. There are several on the Plaza de Armas and along

BVENGOBIERNO
ATOPA AMAROLE
TAN LA CAVESE ELCVZCO

The execution of Tupac Amaru I in Cuzco
(Waman Puma)

Avenida Sol. They are usually in or next to souvenir stores or travel agents and so tend to remain open as long as the store is open – often till after dark and on Sunday. It's worth shopping around, particularly if you change a large amount, as exchange rates can vary. Many hotels will accept dollars but their exchange rates are not usually as favourable as those offered by the casas de cambio. Street moneychangers can be found outside the banks and casas de cambio, especially at the Plaza de Armas end of Avenida Sol. Their rates may be marginally better than you'll get at the casas de cambio, but bargain hard and count your intis carefully before handing over your dollars. The Banco de la Nación used to be the only place you could change money and, as the casas de cambio do close down occasionally, particularly during times of major financial flux, the bank is sometimes still your only option.

American Express Travellers' cheques can be changed with some of the casas de cambio and street changers. The American Express agent doesn't sell or exchange travellers' cheques nor refund lost or stolen travellers' cheques – these services are only available in Lima. The agent used to be at Lima Tours, Avenida Sol 567, next to Faucett Airline. However, a recent report indicates that the Banco de Crédito on Avenida Sol is now the American Express agent.

Visas If your tourist card is about to expire, you can renew it for $20 at the migraciónes office on Avenida Sol, next to the post office. Hours are 8.30 am to 4 pm Monday to Friday and 8.30 am to 1 pm on Saturday. You may only be given a 30-day extension so, if you have the time, consider going to Bolivia for a day – you'll get 60 or 90 days on your return and save the $20 renewal charge.

Tourist Police The tourist police office, above the tourist information office on the Plaza de Armas, is open 24 hours a day. Some English is spoken and the police are trained to deal with problems pertaining to tourists. If you have something stolen,

they'll help with the official police reports needed for insurance claims and will also tell you how to place a radio announcement offering a reward for the return of your property, particularly if it has little commercial value (such as your exposed camera film, journal or documents).

Visitor Ticket It is difficult and expensive to buy individual entrance tickets to the major sites in and around Cuzco. Instead, you have to buy the so-called Visitor Ticket. This costs $10, gives access to 14 different sites and can be purchased from the tourist office or at one of the sites. Tickets bought at the tourist office are valid for 10 days, while those from travel agencies are valid for 5 days.

Ten dollars represents good value if you want to visit most of the sites but, if you only want to see a couple of them, the ticket is expensive. Within Cuzco, it's valid for the cathedral, Santo Domingo and Coricancha, San Blas, Santa Catalina, the Historical Museum and the Religious Art Museum. It also covers Sacsayhuaman, Qenko, Puca Pucara, Tambo Machay, Pisac, Chinchero, Ollantaytambo and Pikillacta, all outside Cuzco. The biggest drawback to the Visitor Ticket is that each site can only be visited once. Other museums, churches and colonial buildings in and around Cuzco can be visited free or for a modest individual admission charge.

For $5, you can get partial tickets to visit some sites. One ticket will get you into the cathedral, the Religious Art Museum and San Blas, while another is valid for Coricancha, Santa Catalina and the Historical Museum. If you want to visit both the cathedral and Coricancha, this option will end up costing as much as the Visitor Ticket.

Student Cards Although many of the admission fees at the ruins and other sites are quite high, you can often get a discount of up to 50% if you present a current international student card with photograph. Wherever you go, ask about reductions for students.

Top: Boat to Amantaní on Lake Titicaca (RR)
Left: Reed boat at Uros Islands, Lake Titicaca (TW)
Right: Puno boat dock, Lake Titicaca (RR)

Top: Fiesta, Department of Puno (RR)
Bottom: Sillustani chullpas, near Puno (TW)

Books & Bookshops The best source of general information about Cuzco and the surrounding area, including maps of the Inca Trail, Machu Picchu and all the other sites, is the highly recommended book *Exploring Cuzco* by Peter Frost. It is available from bookstores in Cuzco and at the South American Explorers Club in Lima.

Also excellent are two books by John Hemming, *The Conquest of the Incas* and his large coffee-table book *Monuments of the Incas*, the latter illustrated with Edward Ranney's superb B&W photographs.

Three or four bookstores around the Plaza de Armas sell English-language guidebooks and books about Peru. There is also a store at Mantas 191 (just off the plaza) which sells new and used paperbacks.

Medical The best clinic is at the regional hospital on the Avenida de la Cultura.

Spanish Courses The EXCEL language centre, on Marquez by the Plaza San Francisco, is cheap and has been recommended.

Employment The EXCEL language centre has hired English teachers for about $1 per hour, but you'll need to commit yourself for several weeks. You may find other places if you ask around.

Laundry Cuzco has good laundry facilities. Several hotels on or near the Plaza de Armas will wash, dry and fold your clothes in half a day for $1 per kg. As you walk around the plaza area, you'll see the obvious signs. The lavandería at Calle Suecia 328 might not be the cheapest but it has been around for years and is unlikely to close down. There are also laundry services on Procuradores and Plateros.

Photography The best light for photography occurs in the early morning and late afternoon when the sun is low. The shadows in the middle of the day tend to come out very black in photographs.

Some locals dress in traditional finery and lead their llamas past the most photogenic spots. This is not a coincidence; they expect a tip for posing and see themselves as working models, not beggars. The standard tip for a quick shot seems to be about 10c. Some tourists object to paying for these photographs, in which case they shouldn't take them. On the other hand, if you make friends with your potential model, they will help you get shots that are worth paying for.

If you want natural-looking, unposed shots, please be sensitive and discreet. Some travellers seem more concerned with taking a good photograph than with their subject's feelings. Not everyone takes kindly to being constantly photographed doing such mundane things as selling vegetables, breast feeding their children or loading their llama.

A wide selection of film is available in Cuzco but it's very expensive.

Fiestas The area celebrates many festivals and holidays. Apart from the national holidays, the following dates mark crowded, lively occasions which are especially important in Cuzco:

Easter Monday
> The procession of the Lord of the Earthquakes dates from the earthquake of 1650 (see the statue in the cathedral).

2-3 May
> A hilltop Crucifix Vigil is held on all hillsides with crosses atop them.

Corpus Christi
> This moveable feast usually occurs on a Thursday in early June (after Trinity Sunday) with fantastic religious processions and celebrations in the cathedral.

24 June
> Cuzco's most important festival is *Inti Raymi*, or the 'festival of the sun'. It attracts tourists from all over the world and the entire city seems to celebrate in the streets. The festival culminates in a re-enactment of the Inca festival at Sacsayhuaman.

24 December
> This date marks the *Santuranticuy*, or 'Christmas Eve', shopping festival.

Folk dancer in Cuzco

Other festivals are important in particular villages and towns outside Cuzco and these are mentioned in the appropriate sections.

Warning Visitors to the Cuzco area should be careful of the altitude and the thieves and it's worth rereading the Altitude Sickness and Dangers & Annoyances sections of the Facts for the Visitor chapter.

Also, don't buy drugs. Dealers and police often work together and Procuradores is only one of several areas in which you can make a drug deal and get busted, all within a couple of minutes.

Things to See

There are four things to remember when sightseeing: firstly, buy your Cuzco Visitor Ticket; secondly, carry a student card if you have one; thirdly, don't get so excited by what you're seeing that you forget about your pockets and your camera – thieves congregate in the same places as sightseers; and fourthly, opening hours are erratic and can change for any reason from feast days to the caretaker wanting a beer with his friends.

The 1986 earthquake was not severe enough to cause large loss of life but did do substantial damage to many of Cuzco's buildings. Most of those hit hardest were on streets running south-east to north-west. For some reason, the seismic waves caused much less damage to buildings on streets on a south-west to north-east axis. Several buildings lost entire upper floors and many lost roofs. Some are being supported by temporary pilings during restoration. Most buildings mentioned in this chapter have now reopened. The most famous of the badly damaged buildings are the churches of Santo Domingo (over the Inca temple of Coricancha) and La Compañía (on the Plaza de Armas), which were closed to the public in 1986. At the time of writing, Santo Domingo and Coricancha were open and La Compañía closed, though it may be open by the time you read this. Several buildings, including the cathedral, are open but surrounded by scaffolding and under repair.

Plaza de Armas

In Inca times the plaza, called Huacaypata, was twice as large as it is today. It was the heart of Inca Cuzco and remains the heart of the modern city. Two flags often fly here – the red-and-white Peruvian flag and the rainbow-coloured flag of Tahuantinsuyo (representing the four quarters of the Inca Empire). Colonial arcades surround the plaza. On the north-eastern side is the cathedral, fronted by a large flight of stairs and flanked by the churches of Jesus María and El Triunfo, and on the south-eastern side is the very ornate church of La Compañía. Some Inca walls remain, notably those of the palace of Pachacutec which were found in the Roma restaurant on the plaza's western corner. The quiet pedestrian alleyway of Loreto, both sides of which have Inca walls, is a pleasant means of access to the plaza.

Churches

Cuzco's numerous colonial churches are better preserved and much more ornate than those in other cities. Their maintenance directly correlates with the importance of the tourist industry in Cuzco. As there are literally scores of churches, only the most important are described in this section. Hours tend to vary. A good time to visit is in the early morning, when the churches are open for services. Officially, they are closed to tourists at this time but, if you go in quietly as one of the congregation, you can see the church as it should be seen – a place of worship, not just a tourist site.

Religious festivals are a superb time to see the churches. One year, I visited the cathedral at Corpus Christi time. The church had been completely cleared of pews and, in their place stood huge pedestals supporting larger-than-life statues of various saints in rich vestments. Each saint was being venerated by candlelight and thousands of candles illuminated the ornate church interior. The place was thronged with people, including several bands of musicians who wandered around in the smoky atmosphere playing mournful Andean tunes in honour of the saints. As with many highland feast days, it was a fascinating combination of ancient and colourful pagan festivities, sombre and prayerful Catholic ritual and modern Latin American mayhem.

Remember, though, that churches are places of worship and act accordingly, especially if you visit during a service. Photography, particularly flash photography, is normally not allowed – the intensity of repeated flashes seriously damages the pigment of the centuries-old art work inside.

The Cathedral Started in 1559 and taking almost 100 years to build, the cathedral is Cuzco's main church and also one of the city's greatest repositories of colonial art. Many of the hundreds of canvases are from the Cuzco school of painting. This style combines the art of 16th and 17th century Europe with the imagination of Andean Indian artists who had only a few Spanish canvases as a guide to what was considered artistically acceptable.

The cathedral has been combined with two other churches. To the left, as you face it, is the Church of Jesus María dating from 1733. The Church of El Triunfo, to the right, is normally used as the entrance to the three-church complex. El Triunfo is the oldest church in Cuzco and dates from 1536. The cathedral proper is to your left.

Right in front of the entrance is a vault containing the remains of the famous Inca historian, Garcilaso de la Vega. Born in Cuzco in 1539, Garcilaso de la Vega left Peru in 1560 for Spain, where he died in 1616. His remains were returned to Cuzco a few years ago by the King and Queen of Spain.

As you go into the main part of the cathedral, turn right. In the far corner is the entrance to the sacristy, where you can sometimes see wood carvers doing restoration work amid the smell of fresh cedar. The sacristy is covered with paintings of Cuzco's bishops, starting with Vicente de Valverde, the bloodthirsty friar who accompanied Pizarro during the conquest. Look for Manuel de Mollinedo, Bishop of Cuzco from 1673 to 1699 and one of the most influential supporters of the Cuzco school of art. The crucifixion at the back of the sacristy is attributed to the Flemish painter Van Dyck, though some local guides claim it to be the work of the 17th century Spaniard Alonso Cano. A similar painting hangs in the Religious Art Museum.

In the corner of the cathedral, next to the sacristy, is a huge painting of the Last Supper by Marcos Zapata. This fine example of the Cuzco school – a European style of painting with Indian influence – depicts a supper consisting of the Inca delicacy cuy, or roast guinea pig!

The original wooden altar is at the very back of the cathedral, behind the present silver altar which stands some 10 metres from the rear wall. Directly opposite the silver altar is the magnificently carved choir. It dates from the 17th century and is one of the finest in Peru.

On the far left outside wall of the main altar, you'll find a large painting of the great earthquake of 1650. The city of those days, as shown in the painting, is recognisable as Cuzco even today. The inhabitants are parading around the plaza with a crucifix, praying for an end to the earthquake. Miraculously, the earthquake stopped (don't they all?) and the city was saved. This crucifix, called El Señor de los Temblores, or 'The Lord of the Earthquakes', can be seen in the alcove to the right of the door leading back into El Triunfo. The image has been blackened by the countless votive candles which have been lit beneath it and the candles are now kept well away from the statue to prevent further smoke damage. The statue is paraded around on Easter Monday.

There are many splendid side chapels, some containing the elaborate silver trolleys used to cart the religious statues around during processions and others with intricate altars.

The cathedral is open to tourists from 10 am to noon and 3 to 6 pm. Entrance is with the Cuzco Visitor Ticket through the side chapel of El Triunfo. The huge main doors are open for worship between 6 and 10 am – there is no admission charge during these hours, but tourism is officially prohibited.

Discreet, respectful visits normally do not cause a problem.

La Compañía This church on the Plaza de Armas is often lit up at night and can be seen from the train as you come in from Machu Picchu after dark – a splendid sight. Its foundations contain stones from the palace of Huayna Capac, the last Inca to rule an undivided, unconquered empire.

The church was built by the Jesuits, hence its name: the Church of the Company of Jesus. Work commenced in 1571. The church was destroyed by the 1650 earthquake but reconstruction began almost immediately. The Jesuits planned to make this the most magnificent of Cuzco's churches. However, the Bishop of Cuzco complained that its splendour should not rival that of the cathedral and, finally, Pope Paul III was called upon to arbitrate. His decision was in favour of the cathedral but, by the time final word reached Cuzco, La Compañía was almost complete. It has an incredible baroque facade and is one of the most ornate churches in Cuzco.

The interior has the usual array of fine paintings and richly carved altars. Two large canvases near the main door show early marriages in Cuzco and are noteworthy for their wealth of period detail.

Before the 1986 earthquake, La Compañía was open to tourists from 11 am to noon and 5 to 6.30 pm. Admission was free. After the earthquake, however, the church was temporarily closed.

La Merced La Merced is considered to be Cuzco's third most important colonial church. It was destroyed in the 1650 earthquake and rebuilt; the present structure, consisting of two sections, dates from 1654.

The church itself is open for worship from 7 to 9 am and 5 to 7.30 pm. To the left of the church, at the back of a small courtyard, is the entrance to the monastery and museum. It is open from 8.30 am to noon and 2.30 to 5.30 pm daily, except Sunday. Entry costs about 50c.

The Order of La Merced was founded in Barcelona in 1218 by San Pedro Nolasco. Paintings based on his life hang around the walls of the beautiful colonial cloister. The church on the far side of the cloister contains the tombs of two of the most famous conquistadors, Diego de Almagro and Gonzalo Pizarro. Also on the far side of the cloister is a small religious museum which houses vestments said to have belonged to the conquistador/friar Vicente de Valverde. The museum's most famous exhibit is a priceless, solid-gold monstrance about a metre in height and covered with hundreds of jewels.

San Francisco This church and monastery, dating from the 16th and 17th centuries, is more austere than many of Cuzco's other churches but does have a large collection of colonial religious paintings and a well-carved, cedar-wood choir. One of the paintings measures 9 by 12 metres, supposedly the largest painting in South America, and shows the family tree of St Francis of Assisi, founder of the order. His life is celebrated in the paintings hung around the colonial cloister.

Also of interest are the two crypts, which are not totally underground. Inside are plenty of human bones, some of which have been carefully arranged into phrases designed to remind visitors of the transitory nature of life.

The monastery is open from 9 am to noon and 3 to 5 pm daily, except Sunday. Entry costs about 30c and, for a tip, a Spanish-speaking guide is available. San Francisco is not visited as often as other major churches, so you can often have the place to yourself.

Santa Clara This 16th century church, part of a strict convent, is difficult to visit. Seeing it became a minor challenge and I finally found that you can usually get in for mass if you go around 6 or 7 am. It is worth making the effort because this is one of the more bizarre churches in Cuzco, indeed, in all Peru.

Mirrors cover almost the entire interior; I've heard that the early clergy used them to entice the local Indians into church for worship. The nuns provide the choir during mass, sitting at the very back of the church and separated from the priest and the rest of the congregation by an ominous-looking grille of heavy metal bars stretching from wall to wall and floor to ceiling.

San Blas This simple adobe church is comparatively small, but its exquisitely carved pulpit has been called the finest example of colonial wood carving in the Americas. Legend claims that its creator was an Indian who miraculously recovered from a deadly disease and subsequently dedicated his life to carving this pulpit for the church. Supposedly, his skull is nestled in the top-most part of the carving. In reality, no-one is certain of the identity of either the skull or the wood carver.

San Blas is open from 10 am to noon Monday to Saturday and 3 to 6 pm daily. Entry is with the Cuzco Visitor Ticket.

Santa Catalina This convent, reputedly a beautiful building, was closed for restoration in the early 1980s but has recently reopened. There is also a colonial and religious art museum here. Hours are 9 am to noon and 3 to 6 pm daily, closed on Friday. Entry is with the Cuzco Visitor Ticket.

Santa Teresa Santa Teresa is a closed convent and difficult to visit. Its church is said to be one of the most beautiful in Cuzco.

Santo Domingo The Church of Santo Domingo is famous as the site of Coricancha, Cuzco's major Inca temple. The church has twice been destroyed by earthquakes, first in 1650 and again in 1950. It was also damaged in the 1986 earthquake, but recent reports indicate that it has reopened following closure for repairs. Photographs in the entrance show the extent of the 1950 damage – compare the state of the colonial building with that of the Inca walls, which sustained minimal damage in these earthquakes. Also in the entrance is a doorway carved in the Arab style – a reminder of the centuries of Moorish domination in Spain. Remains of

the Inca temple are inside the cloister. Colonial paintings around the outside of the courtyard depict the life of Saint Dominic. The paintings contain several representations of dogs holding torches in their jaws. These are God's dogs, or 'dominicanus' in Latin, hence the name of this religious order.

Admission to both the cloister and the Inca ruins is by the Cuzco Visitor Ticket. Opening hours are 9 am to noon and 2 to 5 pm.

Inca Ruins in Cuzco
Most Inca ruins are outside the city and will be described separately. The main ruin within Cuzco is Coricancha. Other ruins have been converted into colonial or modern buildings but their walls remain visible.

Coricancha This Inca ruin forms the base of the colonial Church of Santo Domingo. Once the Inca Empire's richest temple, all that remains of Coricancha is the stonework; the precious stones and metals were looted by the conquistadors.

In Inca times Coricancha, Quechua for 'Golden Courtyard', was literally covered with gold. The temple walls were lined with some 700 solid gold sheets, each weighing about 2 kg. There were life-size gold and silver replicas of corn which were ceremonially 'planted' in agricultural rituals. Also reported were solid-gold treasures such as altars, llamas and babies, as well as a replica of the sun which was lost. Within months of the arrival of the first conquistadors, this incredible wealth had all been melted down.

Various religious rites took place in the temple. The mummified bodies of several previous Incas were kept here, brought out into the sunlight each day and offered food and drink, which was then ritually burnt. Coricancha was also an observatory from which priests monitored major celestial activities.

Most of this is left to the imagination of the modern visitor, but much of the stonework does remain and ranks with the finest Inca architecture in Peru. The most famous part of Coricancha, a curved, perfectly fitted wall 6 metres in height, can be seen from outside the site. This wall has withstood the violent earthquakes which destroyed most of Cuzco's colonial buildings.

Once inside the site, the visitor enters a courtyard. The octagonal font in the middle was once covered with 55 kg of solid gold. Inca side chambers lie to either side of the courtyard. The largest, to the right, were said to be temples to the moon and stars and so, perhaps, were appropriately covered with sheets of solid silver. However, the conquistadors looted the temple riches so fast and so thoroughly that records are hazy. The walls are perfectly tapered upwards and, with their niches and doorways, are excellent examples of Inca trapezoidal architecture. The fitting of the individual blocks is so precise that, in some places, you can't tell where one block ends and the next begins as you glide your finger over them.

Opposite these chambers, on the other side of the courtyard, are smaller temples dedicated to thunder and the rainbow. Three holes have been carved through the walls of this section to the street outside. Their purpose is not known but various theories have been advanced. Perhaps they were drains, either for the sacrificial *chicha* drink or for blood or, more mundanely, for rainwater. Alternatively, they may have been speaking tubes connecting the inner temple with the outside. Another noteworthy feature of this side of the complex is the floor in front of the chambers. It dates from Inca times and is carefully cobbled with pebbles.

The buildings described cover only two sides of the square. There was a larger chamber on each of the other two sides but only small segments of their foundations remain.

After the conquest, Coricancha was given to Juan Pizarro. He was not able to enjoy it for long because he died in the battle at Sacsayhuaman in 1536. In his will, he bequeathed Coricancha to the Dominicans and it has remained in their possession ever since. Today's site is a rather bizarre combination of Inca and colonial architecture, topped with a modern protective roof of glass and metal. Visiting hours are 9 am to noon and 2 to 5 pm.

Other Inca Walls in Cuzco The other Inca buildings in Cuzco are not visitor sites in themselves but can still be admired, most of them from outside.

Walking south-east away from the Plaza de Armas along the narrow alley of Loreto, you have Inca walls on both sides. The wall on the right-hand side belongs to Amarucancha, or the 'Courtyard of the Serpents'. Perhaps its name derives from the pair of snakes carved on the lintel of the doorway near the end of the enclosure. Amarucancha was the site of the palace of the 11th Inca, Huayna Capac. The Church of La Compañía was built here after the conquest and there is now a school behind the church. On the other side of Loreto is the longest-surviving Inca wall in Cuzco. It's also one of the best. The wall belonged to the Acllahuasi, or the 'House of the Chosen Women'. After the conquest, the building became part of the closed convent of Santa Catalina and so went from housing the Virgins of the Sun to housing the pious Catholic nuns.

Heading north-east away from the Plaza de Armas along Calle Triunfo, you soon come to the street of Hatunrumiyoc, named after the well-known 12-sided stone. The stone is on the right, about halfway along the second city block, and can usually be recognised by the small knot of Indians selling souvenirs next to it. This excellently fitted stone belongs to a wall of the palace of the 6th Inca, Inca Roca. It is technically brilliant but by no means an unusual example of polygonal masonry. In Machu Picchu, there are stones with more than 30 angles (though these are corner stones and are therefore counted in three dimensions) and a block with 44 angles in one plane has been found at Torontoy, a minor ruin roughly halfway between Machu Picchu and Ollantaytambo.

There is a great difference between the wall of Hatunrumiyoc and that of the Acllahuasi. The first is made of polygonal stone blocks in no regular pattern, while the second is made from carefully shaped rectangular blocks which are 'coursed', or layered, in the manner of modern-day bricks. Both styles are common in Inca architecture. In general, the polygonal masonry was thought to be stronger and was therefore used for retaining walls in terraces. The coursed masonry, which was considered more aesthetically appealing, was used for the walls of Inca temples and palaces.

Museums & Colonial Buildings

Many museums are in colonial houses, the interiors of which are often as interesting as the exhibits.

Archaeological Museum The Archaeological Museum was moved to a colonial mansion after its former site was damaged in the 1986 earthquake. This mansion, the Casa Cabrera, was the home of the founder of Cordoba in Argentina and now houses the offices of the Banco de los Andes. Although many of the pieces exhibited at the museum's former site are now in storage, the remainder are well worth seeing. Admission is presently only 15c, but may increase, and opening hours are 8 am to noon and 3 to 6 pm Monday to Friday. In the same building is a small art museum with a changing collection, entry to which is free.

Regional History Museum The museum building rests on Inca foundations and is also known as the admiral's house after the first owner, Admiral Francisco Aldrete Maldonado. It was badly damaged in the 1650 earthquake and rebuilt by Pedro Peralta de los Rios, the Count of Laguna, whose crest is above the porch. Further damage, which occurred during the 1950 earthquake, has now been fully repaired, restoring the building to its position among Cuzco's finest colonial houses.

The architecture has several interesting features, including a massive stairway guarded by sculptures of mythical creatures and a corner window column which looks like a statue of a bearded man but, from outside, appears to be a naked woman. The facade is plateresque, an elaborately ornamented 16th century Spanish style suggestive of silver plate. The building's restored interior is filled with colonial furniture and paintings arranged in chronological order.

Entry is with the Cuzco Visitor Ticket and the museum is open from 9 am to noon daily, except Sunday, and 3 to 6 pm Monday to Friday.

Religious Art Museum This building, originally the palace of the Inca Roca and then used as the foundation for the residence of the Marquis of Buenavista, later became the archbishop's palace and is still often referred to by that name. The church donated the mansion to house a religious art collection. Many of the paintings are notable for the accuracy of their period detail, particularly a series showing Cuzco's 17th century Corpus Christi processions. The interior is also known for its colonial tilework.

The museum is open from 9.30 am to noon and 3 to 6 pm daily, except Sunday when it is only open in the afternoon. Entry is with the Cuzco Visitor Ticket.

The Prison

You can visit the local men's prison on Thursday and Sunday between 9 am and noon. The prison, or *cárcel*, is en route to the airport and well known to taxi drivers. On entry, you have to leave your passport and state your purpose ('Christian goodwill work' is a good answer). The prisoners appreciate fruit, meat and cooking oil and sell various handicrafts at excellent prices.

Tours

Tour agencies fall roughly into two groups; those that provide standard tours of Cuzco and the various other ruins in the area and those that offer trekking, climbing or river-running adventure tours.

The standard tours include a half-day city tour, a half-day tour of the nearby ruins (Sacsayhuaman, Qenko, Puca Pucara and Tambo Machay), a half-day tour of the Sunday markets at either Pisac or Chinchero, a full-day trip to the Sacred Valley (Pisac and Ollantaytambo and, perhaps, Chinchero) and a full-day visit to Machu Picchu. There are many tour companies and most of them are pretty good. If you decide to take a tour, ask questions before you pay. Is there an English-speaking guide? Will there be many tourists who don't speak English, requiring the guide to repeat everything in two or three languages? How big will the group be? What kind of transport is used?

Costs vary, so it's worth shopping around. The cheaper tours are liable to be crowded, multilingual affairs while the more expensive ones can be tailored to the needs of the individual. Kantu Tours and Pisac Tours, both on the Plaza de Armas, run quite good, fairly cheap tours.

Milla Turismo, at Avenida Pardo 675, is run by the extremely knowledgeable Carlos Milla. He speaks excellent English and will provide you with a private vehicle and driver, as well as a guide if required. This is more expensive than a standard tour but can be quite reasonable if you form a small group. Carlos can tailor an itinerary to suit you and will provide guides to little-known ruins in the Cuzco area. Some of his guides are interested in the spiritual and mystical features of Inca culture and will take you to ruins with a view to explaining this aspect of Inca life.

Various expensive Lima-based agencies have offices in Cuzco. They cater mainly to private groups and include Exprinter and Dasatour in the Hotel Cusco, Receptor and Universal Tours at the Hotel Savoy and Lima Tours at Avenida Sol 567. Turismo Inkaico has been criticised by travellers for unreliability.

Many agencies run adventure trips. One of the most popular, rafting down the Urubamba for 1 or 2 days, costs about $20 a day. The Inca Trail is also a popular adventure. You can hire porters, cooks and guides or just rent some equipment and carry it yourself. Tents, sleeping bags, backpacks, stoves – everything you might need for hiking – can be hired in Cuzco, usually for around $1 to $2 per item per day. On the whole, I've found that the better agencies don't just provide equipment, preferring to organise their tours and arrange porters and guides. However, if you only want to hire equipment, there are several cheaper agencies on Procuradores and around the Plaza de Armas.

Expediciones Mayuc at Calle Procuradores 354 offers trekking and river-running adventure tours. Run by Chando Gonzales, this agency is not the cheapest but does provide excellent services for rafting the Urubamba, Tambopata and Colca rivers and also covers all trekking routes in the area. Another excellent general adventure agency is Explorandes (tel 469889, 450532), at Procuradores 372 and in Lima at Bolognesi 159, Miraflores. It is the oldest established and among the most expensive. Aventours (tel 237307), at Pardo 545, is run by Ricky Schiller who provided me with excellent trekking and river-running services. Their Lima office (tel 441067) is at La Paz 442, Miraflores. Andean Adventures at Portal de Panes 137, on the plaza, is competitively priced. This agency is run by Aurelio Aguirre and Raul Medina and has been recommended several times. Also recommended is Snow Tours at Procuradores 347 (run by a Finn and his Peruvian wife), and Río Andes at Procuradores 372 (run by Georgie Fletcher).

If mountaineering interests you, contact Peruvian Andean Treks, on Avenida Pardo, which has some of the best guides and equipment for climbing the local snowpeaks.

Those who want to visit the jungle should contact Manu Nature Tours at Avenida Sol 627-B, 4th floor, or Manu Expeditions at Procuradores 372. (See the Manu National Park section later in this chapter for more details.) If you're planning a trip to lodges in the Puerto Maldonado area, reservations for the Explorers Inn can be arranged at Peruvian Safaris (tel 235342) on the Plaza San Francisco 122, 2nd floor, and for the Cuzco Amazonico Lodge at their office on Procuradores. (Additional information is provided in the Puerto Maldonado section of the Amazon Basin chapter.)

At the corner of Procuradores, on the Plaza de Armas, you'll find the Adventure Centre. This is run by Explorandes, Rio Andes and Manu Expeditions and can provide you with information about a variety of different trips.

Details of the cheapest agencies have not been included because, while some good trips are available through them, they change names and owners quite often and are less stable than the more expensive outfitters. Your best bet is to ask other budget travellers for reports on the cheaper agencies, then check them out yourself.

Also remember that, if you have a little extra time, you can visit all the places mentioned using the very cheap public transport system. Details of this option are given later in this chapter.

Places to Stay

The most visited city in Peru, Cuzco has about 100 hotels of all types. It gets rather crowded here during the dry season (June to August), which coincides with the North American and European summer holidays. At this time, accommodation can be a little tight, especially during the 10 days before Inti Raymi (the major annual summer solstice festival) on 24 June, and around 28 July when the national Fiestas Patrias is held. The best hotels are often fully booked for Inti Raymi and accommodation prices usually rise substantially during these periods. Nevertheless, you will always be able to find somewhere to stay. For the rest of the year, many hotels are almost empty and, in this buyer's market, it is well worth bargaining for better rates.

Many travellers want to spend time visiting nearby villages or hiking the Inca Trail and most hotels in Cuzco will store excess luggage so that you don't have to lug it around with you. Always securely lock and clearly label all pieces of luggage. It's unlikely that anyone will razor blade your pack open inside a hotel, but light fingers may, occasionally, dip into unlocked luggage. Don't leave any valuables in long-term storage and ask for a receipt.

I have stayed in about 10 hotels in Cuzco, ranging from the 1st class to basic places charging about $1.50 per night. Whatever the price, I usually found the plumbing inadequate – even the best hotels occasionally have hot water problems, most of which are eventually resolved. You may also find that hot showers are available only at specified times of day or at haphazard intervals.

Places to Stay – bottom end

One of the cheapest places in town, the basic *Hostal Bolívar*, is often described as a classic gringo dive and is occasionally checked by the police for drugs or passport violators. Accommodation costs well under $1 per person, depending on the season, exchange rates and so on. The *Hotel Imperio* is right next to the Machu Picchu train station. It has hot water and charges $1 per person, $1.50 in rooms with private shower. It is friendly, has reliable left-luggage facilities and has been recommended by several budget travellers.

Also cheap (about $1 per person) are the basic *Hostal Royal* and the even more basic *Residencial Torres*. There are several other simple hotels charging around $1/1.70 for singles/doubles, all with hot water. They include the *Hostal San Martín, San Pedro* and *La Posada*, all near the Machu Picchu train station; the clean *Hostal Bambu*, which is close to the Puno train station, and the *Hostal Colonial*. Another option for budget travellers is the *Santo Domingo Convent* at Ahuacpinta 600, in the grounds of Colegio Martín de Porres. It's cheap, safe, friendly and has hot water, but you have to provide your own sleeping bag and there's an 11 pm curfew.

One of the best cheap hotels is the *Hostal Familiar* where accommodation in a basic room costs $1.75 per person (more around fiesta times). It is clean and friendly, has a pleasant courtyard and provides hot showers and safe luggage storage. A few of the more expensive rooms have private showers. The *Hotel Espaderos*, just off the plaza, is similarly priced. It has hot water and has been recommended as good value. The rambling *Hostal Caceres* on Plateros is creaky but clean. It costs $1.50 per person and has hot water, though there aren't many bathrooms. Travellers disagree about the safety of the hotel's left-luggage facilities – leave your luggage locked and ask for a receipt. The similarly priced *Hostal Antarki*, near the Santa Teresa Church, has been described by one traveller as 'marvellous, friendly and cheap'.

In the $1.50 to $2 per person price range, try the *Hotel Peru*. It's popular with Peruvians and convenient to the Machu Picchu train station but has an erratic hot water supply. The *Hostal del Procurador* has hot water and comfortable beds but its left-luggage facility has been criticised. The basic *Hostal Samari* and the *Hostal Monarca* are OK; the *Hostal Panamericano* and the *Hostal Limaqpampa* are not so good.

At $2.50 per person, the *Hostal El Archaeologo* is popular with backpackers but has no single rooms. It is clean and has a pleasant garden, hot water and kitchen facilities. Similarly priced and also good is the *Gran Hostal Machu Picchu*, a colonial-style building around a courtyard. It offers hot water and, for $4 per person, some rooms with private bath.

Other hotels charging about $2.50/4 for singles/doubles include the *Hostal Suecia* and the *Hostal Huaynapata*, both of which

are small, friendly, safe and recommended by travellers, the clean and secure *Hostal San Blas* and the popular but not particularly special *Hostal América*. You could also try the clean *Hostal Meson* or, nearby, the *Hostal Koricancha*, which has been renovated since the 1986 earthquake. In the same area is the *Gran Hostal Chavín*; it has hot water in the patio during the day. The reasonably clean *Hostal Trinitarias* also has hot water and offers some rooms with private showers (rooms with communal showers are cheaper) and a luggage-storage service. A few doors away, the *Hostal Milan* is similar but has somewhat erratic hot water. The *Hotel Corona Real* is friendly and convenient to the Puno train station but, again, the hot water is unpredictable. The *Hostal Belén* has rooms with private bath and hot water for $2 per person, but it's shabby and run down.

Places to Stay – middle

The *Hotels Saphi* and *Cahuide* have become one hotel offering simple, comfortable singles/doubles with private bath and hot water for $3/5 (you can bargain for lower rates in the off season). It's a huge, rambling building with a rooftop garden, left-luggage facilities and a breakfast cafeteria. The similarly priced *Hostal El Solar* on the Plaza San Francisco has hot water and is comfortable. At around the same price, you can stay on the Plaza de Armas at the *Hostal Chaski*, but none of the rooms has a plaza view. The clean *Hostal Los Portales* has an erratic water supply – ask for hot water an hour before taking a shower. Singles/doubles with communal bath cost $3/4, $4/6 with private bath. The hostal also has several rooms with four beds.

Singles/doubles with bath cost $4/6 at the *Hostal Tambo Real*. The hostal is clean and friendly but only has hot water from 6 pm to 10 am. The *Hostal Aragon* charges about the same in the low season, but the prices double during the high season.

The clean, quiet *Hostal Raymi* offers comfortable singles/doubles with carpets, private bath and hot water for about $5.50/8, but beware of the tendency to overcharge tourists. It has a small garden and is convenient to the Puno train station. Closer to the city centre, the *Hotel El Sol* and the *Hostal del Inca* are both good; the Inca will lower its rates in the low season.

At the *Hotel Garcilaso II* (not to be confused with the more expensive *Garcilaso I* up the street), singles/doubles with bath and hot water are $6/10. The *Garcilaso III* is a bit cheaper. The *Hotel los Marqueses* has a wonderful colonial ambience and charges $7/12 for attractively furnished singles/doubles around a beautiful courtyard. It's excellent value but often full. Similarly priced are the *Hotel Mantas*, next to the Church of La Merced, and the *Hostal Loreto* at the Plaza de Armas end of the Loreto alley. Both are recommended. Many of the rooms at the Loreto have genuine Inca walls – worth it if you can get in but the place is often full. Also recommended in this price range is the small, helpful *Leonard's Lodgings* at Avenida Pardo 820. The *Hotel Virrey* is right on the Plaza de Armas and has two rooms with plaza views. Singles/doubles cost $10/15 but the service is reportedly poor.

Places to Stay – top end

The *Hostal Wiracocha* is on the corner of the Plaza de Armas but has no rooms with plaza views. The restaurant is reasonable though, with excellent espresso coffee. Rooms are about $15/20 for singles/doubles but prices rise for Inti Raymi. The pleasant and friendly *Hostal Inti* has heated, carpeted, comfortable singles/doubles with a telephone for $14/22, including breakfast. For around the same price, you can stay at the *Tambo Hotel*, the colonial-style *Hostal Colonial Palace* (lower prices can easily be arranged and the hotel has been recommended) or the *Hotel Conquistador* (on the corner of the Plaza de Armas). All are good. The *Hotel Espinar* is friendly, centrally located and charges $23/35, as does the modern *Hotel Garcilaso I*. Bargain in all these hotels during the low season.

Getting into the luxury class, the renovated *Hotel Internacional San Agustín* ($35/50 for singles/doubles) is good. The handful of 1st class hotels in Cuzco all charge around $40/60 for singles/doubles. Despite the high cost, or perhaps because of it, many of these hotels are booked out by tour groups during the high season so, if you want luxury, book ahead through a travel agent. Cuzco's luxury hotels include the *Hotel Libertador*, which is the most expensive and considered to be the best, the new *Hotel Royal Inca*, where no two rooms are alike, the *Alhambra 2* , the modern *Picoaga Hotel*, and the *Hotel Savoy* (which, despite its five-star rating, is the poorest of Cuzco's 1st class hotels). The *Hotel Cusco* is old but good – I've had reports that you can halve the price here by bargaining. There is also the *Hotel El Dorado* with its interesting lobby and excellent, though expensive, restaurant featuring musicians.

Places to Eat

As you'd expect in a city with such a cosmopolitan range of visitors, Cuzco has a great variety of restaurants catering to every taste and budget. With literally hundreds of eateries from which to choose, I have limited this section mainly to places I have tried personally. They can be very popular, especially during the busy season, so make a reservation or be prepared to wait for a table, particularly at the better restaurants.

Breakfast & Snacks One of the best choices for breakfast and a popular meeting place throughout the day is the simple and reasonably priced *El Ayllu* café next to the cathedral. They always play classical music and offer a great selection of juices, coffee, tea, yoghurt, cakes, sandwiches and other snacks. Two other restaurants on the plaza, the *Hotel Wiracocha* restaurant and *Chef Victor*, have very strong espresso coffee for coffee addicts. Chef Victor also serves huge, reasonably priced meals all day. Other cafés which are good for breakfasts, snacks and meeting people are the *Piccolo Bar* near Chef Victor, the *Café Wiphala* on Plaza Regocijo and the *Café Varayoc* around the corner from the Wiphala, the last two being particularly popular and recommended.

Local Food Several very inexpensive restaurants serve tasty, authentic Peruvian food. They often have outside patios and are usually open only for lunch or afternoon snacks. Monday seems to be the day off for many. People with very finicky stomachs might question the hygiene but, if you stick to cooked food, you're unlikely to get sick.

If you want something really Andean, try roast guinea pig, or cuy, an Inca delicacy. Often, this has to be ordered a day in advance. Other typical local dishes include anticucho de corazon (a shish kebab made from beef hearts), rocoto relleno (spicy bell peppers stuffed with ground beef and vegetables), adobo (a spicy pork stew), chicharrónes (deep-fried chunks of pork ribs, called chancho, or of chicken, called gallina), lechón (suckling pig), choclo con queso (corn on the cob with cheese), tamales (boiled corn dumplings filled with cheese or meat and wrapped in a banana leaf), cancha (toasted corn) and various locros (hearty soups and stews). The meal is often washed down with chicha, which is either a fruit drink or a fermented, mildly alcoholic corn beer.

The local restaurants which serve these Andean specialities are often called *picanterías*, literally 'spicy places', or *quintas*, literally 'country houses' but here referring to inns in the nearby suburbs. Often, they have a *sapo*. This is a popular picantería game, rather like darts in an English pub or pool in an American bar. The sapo, a metal toad, is mounted on a table and players toss a metal disc as close to it as possible. Top points are scored when the disc is thrown into the toad's mouth. Men will sometimes spend the whole afternoon drinking beer or chicha and competing at this old test of skill.

One of the best quintas and the closest to the central city area is the *Quinta Eulalia* which has a colourful courtyard. It's only open for lunch (as are most quintas) and there is no sign – go to Choquechaca 384. Further afield, try the *Quinta Zárate* on Calle Tortera Paccha, on the eastern outskirts of town (it has a nice garden), or the *El Mirador* on the

longer eastern approach road towards Sacsayhuaman, both with good views of the city. Neither is easy to find so take a taxi there and walk back. Peter Frost recommends the *Quinta El Carmen* in San Jerónimo, a small town about 5 km from Cuzco.

Picanterías within walking distance of the centre include *La Peña de Don Luis, Ajha Wasi* and *El Fogon de las Mestizas*, all highly popular with Peruvians and best visited at lunch time. The *Picantería La Chola* is said to be the most typical of Cuzco's restaurants, resembling a Cuzqueña *chichería*, or Andean chicha tavern. It has been rather watered down to cater to tourist tastes and I don't think it's that good – the best chicherías are unsigned holes-in-the-wall and should be visited with Peruvian friends.

International Food Most places mentioned in this section serve Peruvian food as well as international dishes. There are several Italian restaurants. My favourite, and that of many travellers judging by the lines during the high season, is the medium-priced *Trattoria Adriano*. It often has delicious dessert cake as well as great pasta dishes. *La Mamma Pizzería* is quite good but not especially cheap. There are two other Italian/international restaurants next door to La Mamma – they look good, though I haven't tried them.

The Bilboquet serves French crêpes in a bar atmosphere and has a happy hour from 6.30 to 7.30 pm. According to an Aussie female correspondent, it also offers 'cute waiters'.

If you're economising, try the Hare Krishna *Govinda* vegetarian restaurant. The food is good, cheap and wholesome and their bread lasts for several days if you want to take some on a trek.

Cuzco's Chinese restaurants are also fairly cheap; the *Chifa Hong Kong* on Avenida Sol is one of the best.

Peruvian Food Several clean restaurants on the Plaza de Armas serve a wide variety of good, reasonably priced Peruvian and international food. *Chef Victor* lacks ambience but makes up for it with huge servings. (There are two Chef Victors, one on the plaza and the other on Ayacucho. They are similar, though I think the one on Ayacucho is a little better.)

Also on the plaza, the *Restaurant Pizzaiola* is a bit more expensive but serves big, tasty portions. The *Restaurant Roma* and *El Paititi* both have genuine Inca walls. El Paititi was part of the House of the Chosen Women and now offers slightly pricey food in a white-tablecloth environment. The Roma was part of the Inca Pachacutec's palace, which became the house of Francisco Pizarro after the Spanish conquest. It was one of Cuzco's first good restaurants and, despite its eclipse by slightly better places, remains a good and reasonably priced choice (though the pizza has been criticised as 'poor and outlandish'). Local musicians often play here in the evenings, for which there may be a small cover charge.

Tucked away behind the cathedral and almost forgotten in the corner of the plaza, the rather undistinguished-looking *El Tumi Restaurant* is moderately priced and good value. At the opposite corner of the plaza (the entrance is just off the plaza) is a place for dedicated carnivores, *El Mesón de los Espaderos*, which serves steaks, steaks or steaks. Get there early and sit in the attractively carved balcony overlooking the Plaza de Armas.

Close to the plaza, along the first block of Calle Plateros, there is a whole string of inexpensive restaurants whose names and owners tend to change every few years. Most have been recommended by one traveller or another, though I occasionally hear gripes from someone. They include the *Café Haylliy* for good snacks, the *El Tronquito* and *Los Candiles* for tasty, cheap, set meals, the Japanese-run *Café Shantam* which serves vegetarian food, *Pollería Haway* for chicken, *La Red* for seafood and several others.

Gringo Alley This nickname is given to Procuradores, or 'tax-collector's' street, the alley leaving the Plaza de Armas on the north-west side. It has a good selection of cheap bars, pizzerías, restaurants and cafés, which are popular with backpackers and good places to meet people. Names and owners seem to change periodically, though the *Chez Maggy* pizzería has been there for years. It's a good street to explore if you're on a budget.

Places to Eat – top end Some of the top hotels have excellent restaurants where prices are high and often charged in dollars rather than intis. The food is somewhat bland and popular with tourists who have particularly delicate stomachs or want to minimise health risks. Local musicians often play. The best hotel restaurants are at the *El Dorado* and the more expensive *Libertador*.

The fanciest restaurant not attached to a hotel is *El Truco*, which has a nightly dinner and show (from 8.30 to 10.30 pm) and is quite good value. Make reservations in the high season because it's popular with tour groups. The food (Peruvian and international) is good, as is the show. There is a $1 cover charge for the music plus a table charge (you have to sit at a table) of about $1. The cheapest plates are also about $1, so even budget travellers can afford an occasional look at the smoother end of Cuzco's night life.

Entertainment
The *Roma* and *El Truco* restaurants have live entertainment with dinner every night. Several other restaurants offer live music in the evening – they have signs in their windows. If you'd rather listen to music in a slightly looser (and cheaper) bar environment, you'll find several places.

One of my favourite night spots is the *Peña Hatuchay*, a dive on the Plaza de Armas across the square from the cathedral – you can hear the lively music coming from an upstairs window on the corner of the little street of Media. The entrance at Portal de Confiturías 233 (up a small, dark stairway in the middle of the block) is not very obvious, so ask. The Hatuchay is to the left, at the back of the building. It's very popular with both locals and travellers, the main attraction being the nonstop, live, folklórico music played by several different bands during the evening. It's the longest running of Cuzco's cheaper night spots – many others change names, locations or owners every 1 or 2 years but the Hatuchay has been providing a good night out for at least 8 years to my knowledge. Only small glasses of beer or pisco with lemon are served here, so you come for the local music, the dancing and the raucous atmosphere. It gets very crowded indeed and the toilet facilities are not for the sensitive – arrive with an empty bladder!

There are two other night spots in the same building. The *Do-Re-Mi*, just to the left of the stairs, is a criolla peña, more popular with locals than with foreigners. The music has a coastal influence and the singer keeps up a constant stream of terrible jokes and satirical comments – OK if you understand Spanish. One of the main attractions used to be a very flamboyant, tall, skinny black guy with huge hands who played the *caja*, a box that the musician sits on and drums with his hands. He would arrive around midnight wearing a pink suit and a wild grin and had a great scatty voice to match his appearance. The Do-Re-Mi was great fun in 1984-5 but seemed to go downhill thereafter. When I last stopped by it was almost empty, except for a few professional musicians practising. Who knows what's happening there now – go and see for yourself. These places open about 9 pm but don't get going until after 10 pm and, on a busy night, may stay open until 2 or 3 am.

Also in the Hatuchay building is the *Cross Keys Pub*, easily identifiable from the Plaza de Armas by the huge metal keys hanging outside. Inside is a dart board and a pub-like ambience. The pub is run by a British ornithologist, Barry Walker, and his Peruvian wife and the staff speak English. It's not as cheap as some other places but it does have a happy hour from 6 to 7 pm and is a great place to meet people. The Cross Keys is only open in the evening.

Other nightspots on the Plaza de Armas include an upstairs club/bar which you enter through a guarded grille gate near the Piccolo Bar, about halfway along the block. This club has gone through four name and owner changes in the last few years, its most recent incarnation being the *Banana Bar*. It's quite a good members-only dance bar and most travellers can get in by showing a passport or, often, just their face. The club has an attractive balcony looking out over the plaza.

Also well recommended is the *Kamikaze*, up the stairs at the north-western corner of the Plaza Regocijo, a block from the Plaza de Armas. It has a '60s feel and lively taped music and, occasionally, features live performers such as guitarists singing Chilean protest songs, traditional Bolivian highland groups, jazz musicians, local bands and classical guitarists among others. A 60c cover charge applies.

I haven't tried the new bar on the Plaza Regocijo, next door to El Truco, but I'm told it's good. Another reader recommendation is *Valentinos* at the corner of Loreto and Maruri. It plays lively, taped salsa music until 4 am and is popular with Peruvians.

Several places offer disco dancing. Apart from the Banana Bar, there is the fairly expensive *El Muki*, just off the plaza in front of the Hotel Conquistador. It's dark, with plenty of alcoves, and has a couples-only rule at the door (though they usually don't count when a mixed group goes in). *Las Quenas*, in the Hotel Savoy basement, is popular with Peruvians.

Things to Buy

The best place to see local artisans making and selling their handicrafts is around the Plaza San Blas and the streets leading to it from the Plaza de Armas. The San Blas area has a reputation as Cuzco's artisan quarter and is worth visiting not only to buy and to watch them at work but also to see the interior of some of the buildings. Prices and quality vary greatly, so shop around. The very best pieces may cost 10 times more than what, superficially, appear to be the same items in a store on the Plaza de Armas, but the difference in quality is significant. Bargaining is expected, except in a few of the more expensive stores where prices are fixed.

Going to the general market to buy crafts is not a good idea – neither the prices nor the quality are any better than elsewhere and thieves abound. The main Cuzco market is a colourful affair in front of the Machu Picchu train station. Don't bring much money or a camera because the thieves are extremely professional and persistent. If you like to shop in a market atmosphere, there's a crafts market on the corner of Quera and San Bernardo and another behind the Faucett Airline office on Avenida Sol. A nightly crafts market is also held under the arches around the Plaza de Armas. You will often be approached on the street by people trying to sell you all kinds of crafts. This can become a little wearisome when you're not in a buying mood – the only thing to do is say 'No, gracias' as firmly as possible and show absolutely no interest; the slightest spark of curiosity will inevitably result in 5 minutes of pestering.

Some of the best places (though not the cheapest) include Taller Olave, to the left of Plaza San Blas, for exceptionally fine and expensive reproductions of colonial sculptures and precolonial ceramics, Santiago Rojas at Suytuccato 751, for Paucartambo fiesta masks, Taller Mérida at Carmen Alto 133, for earthenware statues of Indians, and Josefina Olivera at Santa Clara 501, by the Machu Picchu train station, for old ponchos and weavings. There are many stores along Hatunrumiyoc and Cuesta San Blas which sell almost anything.

Getting There & Away

Air Cuzco's airport claims international status because of the twice-weekly flights to La Paz, Bolivia. All departures and arrivals are in the morning because winds often make landing and takeoff difficult in the afternoon. Airport departure tax is $15 for international flights and $7 for internal flights. Expensive!

Flights to Bolivia cost about $120 but you may be able to save a few dollars by paying with intis at the official rate. Departures are with Lloyd Aereo Boliviano (LAB) on Wednesday and Saturday. The LAB office is one block off the Plaza de Armas. Tickets bought in La Paz are cheaper because Bolivian tax on international tickets is about half the 31% charged in Peru.

There are two or three direct flights a day to Lima ($82) and at least one a day to Arequipa ($40) and Puerto Maldonado ($36) with Faucett and AeroPeru airlines. There are usually daily flights to Ayacucho and several a week to Juliaca. Same-day connections to Tacna via Arequipa and to most northern cities via Lima can be organised, but allow several hours connecting time as flights from Cuzco are frequently very late. Contrary to popular opinion, no direct flights operate between Cuzco and Iquitos; you have to fly to Lima and connect from there.

LAB, AeroPeru and Faucett all have offices in central Cuzco and don't normally sell tickets at the airport counters. The military airline, Grupo 8, sells tickets at the airport for its flights (usually on Thursday) to Lima and Puerto Maldonado. These flights don't always go, are usually full and normally cannot be booked in advance (though there's no harm in trying). Although fares are somewhat cheaper than those of the commercial airlines, Grupo 8 flights are difficult for tourists to get on. Go to the airport before 6 am on the day of the flight packed and ready to go, get your name on the waiting list and hope. Grupo 8 also fly via Puerto Maldonado to Iberia or Iñapari for the Brazilian border.

Flights tend to be overbooked, especially during the busy season, so confirm your flight when you arrive in Cuzco, then reconfirm 72 hours in advance and again 24 hours before departure. If you buy your ticket from a reputable travel agent in Cuzco, they'll reconfirm for you. Having ensured that your flight has been properly and frequently reconfirmed, check in at least 1 hour before departure time. Check-in procedures at Cuzco airport are often chaotic and even people with confirmed seats and boarding passes have, occasionally, been denied boarding because of overbooking errors.

(Don't get overly paranoid; this doesn't happen all the time.) During the rainy season, flights can be postponed for 24 hours because of bad weather.

When flying from Cuzco to Lima, check in as early as possible to get a seat on the right-hand side of the plane for the best views of Salcantay's 627-metre peak. Some pilots like to fly quite close to the mountain and the views are stupendous. (Sit on the left from Lima to Cuzco.) Occasionally, a different route is taken over Machu Picchu, but not often.

A taxi from the airport to the centre of Cuzco costs a little over $1; the local bus costs a few cents.

Bus – Cuzco area Cuzco has no central bus terminal. For buses to Pisac, go to Avenida Tacna, about 1½ km east of the town centre, where a line of minibuses waits to leave at frequent intervals throughout the day. Buses to Urubamba leave from the Ormeño office on Avenida Huascar, about 1 km east of the centre. (Urubamba buses are not run by the Ormeño company.) These buses change their departure points every 1 or 2 years, so check with the tourist office or other travellers before hiking out there with your gear. Fares are under $1 and it takes about 1½ hours to reach Urubamba, a little less to Pisac. The Pisac buses will drop you off at the Inca site of Tambo Machay. You can walk back from there to Cuzco and visit the other nearby ruins en route. To get to Ollantaytambo, change at Urubamba.

Tourist buses leave at 2 pm daily from the Plaza de Armas, at the corner by the tourist office, and go to Sacsayhuaman, Qenko and Tambo Machay. The round trip takes about 4 hours and costs $2, including a Spanish-speaking guide. Tourist buses to Pisac and Ollantaytambo leave at 8 am and cost about $5, also with a local guide. Ask at the tourist office for more details.

For Chinchero, there is a service from Avenida Arcopata. Frequent trucks and minibuses leave on Sunday morning for the market. On other days of the week, go as early as possible and be prepared to wait;

services are infrequent and erratic. The fare is about 30c. Trucks for Limatambo, Mollepata and on to Abancay and other destinations leave from here most mornings but, as is usual with truck services, there is no set time. Ask around for departure information.

On the road south-east of Cuzco, frequent minibuses from Avenida Huascar go to Oropesa and Urcos. Take these buses to visit the ruins of Tipon, Pikillacta and Rumicolca. Empresa Oriental, at the south end of Avenida Huascar, has buses going through these towns and on to Sicuani ($1.50, 4 hours) several times a day.

Bus – long distance If you want to visit the jungle, try Transportes Quincemil which runs several trucks a week to Puerto Maldonado. No buses make this wildly spectacular but difficult journey. The road is in bad shape and the trip from Cuzco takes 2 to 3 days in the dry season (a week or more in the wet) by truck at a cost of about $10. You could also get the truck at Urcos. The journey can be broken at Ocongate or Quincemil where there are basic hotels. Trucks to Ocongate leave in the early morning from in front of the Church of Santo Domingo and take half a day. As I've never gone beyond Ocongate, except by air from Cuzco to Puerto Maldonado, I'd like to hear from anyone who has done this trip.

Cruz del Sur, next to the Transportes Quincemil office, provides bus services to the south of the country, with three buses a day to Sicuani ($1.60) and a bus every evening to Juliaca ($4.80, 11 hours) and Puno ($5.25, 12 hours). Most people prefer the much more comfortable day train. Cruz del Sur also has a nightly service to Arequipa via Imata (22 hours, $8); it's a rough journey on a little-travelled road. The service continues to Lima (42 hours, $14). Expect delays in the rainy season.

A cheaper and only slightly quicker route to Lima goes via Abancay (8 hours), Puquio and Nazca (33 hours). This used to be the most frequently travelled bus route between Cuzco and the capital. However, at the time of writing, serious problems with the

Sendero Luminoso guerillas made the trip dangerous and only Morales Moralitos and Transportes Señor de los Animas were offering it. It is definitely not recommended. Ormeño buses used to go via Abancay but now travel via Arequipa. If services on the Abancay route resume, it will be an indication that travel is becoming safer again. Ormeño tickets are available at their Procuradores office and the buses leave from the station on Avenida Huascar. Ormeño has two departures a week to Lima.

Empresa Hidalgo operates two or three buses a week along the rough but spectacular inland Andean route to Ayacucho. Many travellers consider this the most impressive (and difficult) route between Cuzco and the coast. Again, problems with guerilla attacks make it an inadvisable risk.

All the journey times given are average and apply in good conditions. In the wettest months of the rainy season, especially January to April, long delays are possible.

Train Cuzco has two train stations, one near the end of Avenida Sol serving Puno and Arequipa and another next to the main city market serving Machu Picchu and Quillabamba. It has therefore been impossible to travel directly from Arequipa or Puno to Machu Picchu; you must change lines at Cuzco. To make matters worse, the two stations are not within easy walking distance of each other. However, there are plans afoot to link the Machu Picchu railway line with the line for Puno and Arequipa which may make the Machu Picchu station obsolete, though this is unlikely to happen in the near future.

The train for Puno leaves at 8 am daily, except Sunday, and takes about 10 hours. It passes through Juliaca at about 5 pm, allowing you to connect with the nightly train from Juliaca to Arequipa which leaves at about 8.45 pm.

First class tickets for the Puno train are often sold out so, if possible, buy a ticket the day before. The ticket office is open for ticket sales on the day train from about 6.30 am Monday to Saturday. For advance sales, try

9.30 to 11 am and 3 to 5 pm Monday to Saturday and 8 to 10 am on Sunday. The hours at the ticket office tend to be erratic and change frequently. If you have problems getting a ticket, try booking through a travel agent. They may charge a fee; shop around for the best deal.

Fares have varied wildly for several years now, depending on currency fluctuations and railway regulations. During the 1980s, 1st class fares to Puno ranged from about $2 to $9. When I took this train to Puno in 1989, it cost $2.60 in 1st class; in 1986, it was $7.20. Fares to Juliaca are a few cents cheaper than those to Puno and fares to Arequipa are almost twice as much. Second class fares are about 25% lower. While 1st class is currently quite cheap, buffet or Pullman class tickets cost nonresidents an exorbitant $20 on top of the 1st class fare (residents only pay a surcharge of about $5). Nonresidents get no better service in buffet or Pullman class than in 1st class and the only difference is that the carriage is locked and only ticket holders allowed to board, thus minimising the risk of robbery. (For further details of the classes, see the Arequipa chapter.) As on all Peruvian trains, be careful of thieves. Because this is a day train and you can stay awake, it's reasonably easy in 1st class to look after your luggage and avoid being robbed, particularly if you travel with friends, but watch your belongings carefully.

The Machu Picchu train departs several times a day and is the most frequently used train in Peru. This, combined with the station's location near the crowded central market, makes it a prime target for thieves. In recent years, Peruvian police have increased patrols around the station and on the trains, greatly reducing the risk of rip-offs but, because it's so crowded, you still have to be very vigilant.

There is a bewildering variety of trains. Some go only as far as Machu Picchu while others continue to Quillabamba at the end of the line. Some are express and others are local, stopping everywhere. The electric autovagon is generally smaller, faster and more expensive than other trains. Some of these services are designated for tourists only and are better guarded and much more expensive, with reserved seating. Schedules change frequently and the following information can therefore be used only as a rough guide – before travelling, check at the station, the tourist information office or a reliable local travel agent to determine current services. Often, an extra train runs during the height of the tourist season (June to August). Also, of course, trains are often late, with the exception of the tourist autovagon which is on time surprisingly often.

There is no other way to get to Machu Picchu by public transport. There are no roads and the helicopter service of the 1970s was stopped because the vibration of the choppers was damaging the ruins. Even if you choose to walk in along the Inca Trail, you must take a train to Km 88, the starting point of the trek. Everyone travelling to and from Machu Picchu uses the train (except hikers coming in from Mollepata or Chilca – see Hilary Bradt's *Backpacking & Trekking in Peru & Bolivia*, 5th Ed).

Apart from Cuzco, the following stations are of interest to travellers; they are listed in order away from Cuzco.

Ollantaytambo station can be reached by road. This enables travellers to visit the Sacred Valley ruins by bus and then continue from Ollantaytambo to Machu Picchu without returning to Cuzco. All trains stop here. The tourist train's schedule to and from Machu Picchu requires passengers to travel between Cuzco and Ollantaytambo by railway company bus.

The halt at Km 88 is where hikers leave the train to begin the Inca Trail. Only the local train stops here.

The next important station is at Aguas Calientes but is misleadingly called Machu Picchu station. It is served by all trains except the tourist train and is the place to go if you want to spend the night near the ruins without staying at the very expensive Machu Picchu Hotel.

The closest train station to the Machu Picchu ruins themselves, Puentes Ruinas, is

2 km beyond the Machu Picchu station at Aguas Calientes. All trains stop here, except the Quillabamba autovagon which will also do so if you ask in advance. As the tourist train doesn't go beyond Puentes Ruinas, you must travel on the local train or the Quillabamba autovagon if you plan to continue beyond this point.

Santa Teresa station is 18 km beyond Puentes Ruinas. There is a tenuous road link with Cuzco (about 15 hours by truck) and a basic hotel. It is also the end of the Mollepata to Santa Teresa trek (see *Backpacking & Trekking in Peru & Bolivia* 5th Ed by Hilary Bradt).

The jungle-edge town of Quillabamba is the end of the line. A new train station being built in Urubamba may be operational sometime in the 1990s.

The local train is the cheapest and stops everywhere. As it is also the one with the worst reputation for robbery, you are better off travelling 1st class. The train leaves Cuzco daily, except Sunday, at 5.30 am and 2 pm and takes about 4 hours to reach Machu Picchu and 7 hours to Quillabamba. First class fares are $1.90 to Machu Picchu and $3 to Quillabamba. Second class is about 20% cheaper.

The autovagon (tourist train) to Quillabamba leaves daily at 1.30 pm and takes 3 hours to Aguas Calientes, 5½ hours to Quillabamba. The fare is about $3.90 to Machu Picchu and $6 to Quillabamba. Vendors are not allowed aboard and the autovagon doesn't stop at many stations, so bring some food.

The autovagon stops at Ollantaytambo and Puentes Ruinas (for the Machu Picchu ruins). Normally, only round-trip tickets are sold. The idea is that you leave in the morning, spend 2 or 3 hours at the ruins and return in the afternoon – a tiring day with inadequate time at the ruins. Nevertheless, this is the way many, perhaps most, people visit Machu Picchu. It is difficult, but not impossible, to buy tourist-train tickets to travel on separate days – it's best to use a travel agent if you plan to do this.

During the high season, tourist trains leave

Cuzco at 6.30 and 10 am. Passengers on the 10 am departure are taken to Ollantaytambo by railway bus and continue from there by train. Passengers on the early train leave Puentes Ruinas (the Machu Picchu ruins station) at 2.30 pm and are taken to Ollantaytambo, where they transfer to railway buses for Cuzco. Passengers on the 10 am train leave Puentes Ruinas at 5.30 pm and return directly to Cuzco. This is a new system used during the high season; during the low season, passengers may be limited to one departure a day and do the entire trip by train. Occasionally, three trains run if there is enough demand.

The trip takes about 3 hours each way and costs about $45, plus the fare for the 20-minute bus ride from the station to the ruins and admission to the site. Travel agents sell the trip for about $62, including the bus from the Puentes Ruinas station to the ruins and entrance to the ruins, more if they provide lunch, a guide or a transfer between your hotel and the train station.

When this comparatively expensive system was introduced recently, the railway company ENAFER prohibited nonresidents from using the cheap local train. They simply refused to sell local train tickets to nonresidents, trying to force everyone to use the fast, comfortable and reliable, but extremely expensive, tourist train. As this is far beyond the budget of many travellers, ways around the system were soon devised. You could get a Peruvian friend to buy a ticket, or you could buy a local train ticket to Quillabamba (no tourist trains go there), get off wherever you want and discard the excess section. The tourist information office suggested that budget travellers take a local bus to Ollantaytambo where there's no problem buying local train tickets. Check with other travellers or the tourist office for the latest details – things change every year.

The Cuzco train station has two entrances with separate ticket windows. The right-hand entrance serves the tourist trains; the left-hand entrance is for the local train and the Quillabamba autovagon. The ticket offices are usually open from about 6 am but

close for 1 or 2 hours several times during the day. Opening hours change frequently, so check. The station entrance for the Quillabamba autovagon is to the side of the building; ask when you buy your ticket.

Around Cuzco

THE NEARBY RUINS

This term refers to the four ruins closest to Cuzco: Sacsayhuaman, Qenko, Puca Pucara and Tambo Machay. They are often visited in a day, even less if you're on a guided trip, and entry is with the Cuzco Visitor Ticket. The cheapest and most convenient way to visit the ruins is to take a Sacred Valley bus to Pisac and get off at Tambo Machay, the ruin furthest from Cuzco and, at 3700 metres, the highest. From there, you can walk the 8 km back to Cuzco, visiting all four ruins along the way. Colourfully dressed locals often wait near the sites with their llama herds, hoping to be photographed. Tipping is expected (about 10c is usual) and photographers trying for a free shot will get an unfriendly reception. Travellers wanting a more in-depth description of these and other ruins, as well as details of hikes in the area, are directed to Peter Frost's excellent book *Exploring Cuzco*.

Tambo Machay

This small ruin, about 300 metres from the main road, consists of a beautifully wrought ceremonial stone bath and is therefore popularly called El Baño del Inca. Puca Pucara, the next ruin, can be seen from the small signalling tower opposite. There is usually a guard at Tambo Machay who will punch your Cuzco Visitor Ticket for this site and also for Puca Pucara.

Puca Pucara

As you return from Tambo Machay, you'll see this small site on the other side of the main road. In some lights, the rock looks very red and the name literally means 'red fort'. It is the least interesting and least visited of the four ruins.

Qenko

The name of this small but fascinating ruin is variously written qenqo, qenco, q'enqo or qenko and means 'zigzag'. Qenko consists of a large limestone rock completely covered with carvings, including the zigzagging channels which give the site its name. These are thought to have been used for the ritual sacrifice of chicha or, perhaps, blood. Tunnels are carved below the boulder and there's a mysterious-looking cave with altars carved into the rock, so bring a light. Qenko is about 4 km before Cuzco, on the left-hand side of the road as you descend from Tambo Machay.

Sacsayhuaman

This huge ruin is the most impressive in the immediate Cuzco area. The name means 'satisfied falcon' but most local guides cannot resist telling visitors that the long Quechua name is most easily remembered by the mnemonic 'sexy woman'.

The most interesting way to reach the site is to climb the steep street of Resbalosa, turn right at the top, go past the Church of San Cristóbal and continue until you come to a hairpin bend in the road. Here, you'll find the old Inca road between Cuzco and Sacsayhuaman. Follow it to the top; the ruins are to the left. The climb is short but steep

and takes almost an hour from Cuzco, so make sure you're acclimatised before attempting it. (An acclimatised athlete wrote to me complaining that the walk took barely 20 minutes!) The old road is also a good descent route when returning from visits to the other nearby ruins. The site is open from dawn till dusk and the guards are very active in demanding to see your Cuzco Visitor Ticket. Arriving at dawn will give you the site to yourself – tour groups begin arriving in midmorning.

Although Sacsayhuaman seems huge, what today's visitor sees is only about 20% of the original structure. Soon after the conquest, the Spaniards tore down many walls and used the blocks to build their own houses in Cuzco. They left the largest and most impressive of the original rocks, one of which weighs over 300 tons. Most of them form part of the main battlements.

The Incas envisioned Cuzco in the shape of a puma with Sacsayhuaman as the head. The site is essentially three different areas, the most obvious being the three-tiered zigzag walls of the main fortifications. The 22 zigzags form the teeth of the puma and are also a very effective defensive mechanism – an attacker must expose a flank when attacking any wall. Opposite is the hill called Rodadero with its retaining walls, curiously polished rocks and a finely carved series of stone benches known as the throne of the Inca. Between the zigzag ramparts and Rodadero Hill lies a large, flat parade ground which is used for the colourful tourist spectacle of Inti Raymi, held every 24 June. The site is being actively excavated following the recent discovery of seven mummies behind the Rodadero Hill.

The magnificent zigzag walls remain the site's major attraction even though much of this fortification has been destroyed. Three towers once stood above these walls. Only the foundations remain but the 22-metre diameter of the largest, Muyuc Marca, gives an indication of how big they must have been. Muyuc Marca, with its perfectly fitted stone conduits, was used as a huge water tank for the garrison. Other buildings within the ramparts provided food and shelter for an estimated 5000 warriors. Most of these structures were torn down by the Spaniards and by later inhabitants of Cuzco and the resulting lack of evidence makes a precise description of Sacsayhuaman's function difficult. Most authorities agree, however, that the site had important religious as well as military significance.

The fort was the site of one of the most bitter battles of the Spanish conquest. About 2½ years after Pizarro's entry into Cuzco, the rebellious Manco Inca recaptured the lightly guarded Sacsayhuaman and used it as a base to lay siege to the conquistadors in Cuzco. Manco was very nearly successful in defeating the Spaniards and only a desperate last-ditch attack by 50 Spanish cavalry led by Juan Pizarro finally succeeded in retaking Sacsayhuaman and putting an end to the rebellion. Although Manco Inca survived and retreated to the fortress of Ollantaytambo, most of his forces were killed. The thousands of dead littering the site attracted swarms of carrion-eating Andean condors, hence the inclusion of eight condors in Cuzco's coat of arms.

THE SACRED VALLEY

The beautiful Vilcanota/Urubamba river valley is about 15 km north of Cuzco as the condor flies. The climate is pleasant because of the elevation (600 metres lower than Cuzco) and there is much to do – visit Inca ruins, bargain in Indian markets, stroll through Andean villages or take an exciting river-running trip down the Sacred Valley.

The most important points of interest in the valley are the ruins at Pisac and Ollantaytambo, both of which require the Cuzco Visitor Ticket for admission. Other lesser sites can also be visited. Accommodation is available in the towns of Pisac, Calca, Yucay, Urubamba and Ollantaytambo. Various tour companies in Cuzco visit the Pisac and Ollantaytambo sites on half and full-day guided bus tours of the Sacred Valley but, if you have a few days, taking local buses and staying in the valley itself is more rewarding.

River Running

One of the Sacred Valley's most pleasant activities is running the river in an inflatable rubber raft. Several companies, including Mayuc, Explorandes, Aventours, RioAndes and Andean Adventures, do this almost every day. For about $25 per person, they will pick you up from your hotel in Cuzco, drive you to the village of Huambutio where the run begins, provide you with an experienced river guide, life jacket, paddles and lunch and, at the end of the day, take you into Pisac. (Cheaper trips which don't include lunch or the Pisac visit are also available.) All your luggage can be safely left aboard their vehicle while you're on the river. The rapids are exciting (you'll get wet) but not dangerous and the views are splendid. More ambitious river-running trips can also be arranged on the Urubamba River near Ollantaytambo, as well as trips of several days on the Tambopata, Colca and Manu rivers.

PISAC

Pisac is 32 km from Cuzco by paved road and the most convenient starting point for a visit to the Sacred Valley. There are two Pisacs, one is the colonial and modern village lying beside the river and the other an Inca fortress on a mountain spur about 600 metres above.

For most of the week, colonial Pisac is a quiet, Andean village and there's little to do except sit and relax in the plaza or visit the bakery for some bread fresh from the old-fashioned clay oven. The village comes alive on Sunday, however, when the famous weekly market takes place. This attracts traditionally dressed locals from miles around and garishly dressed tourists from all over the world. Despite being a big tourist attraction, this bustling, colourful market retains at least some of its traditional air. Selling and bartering of produce goes on alongside stalls full of weavings and sweaters for the tourists. Many of the stall holders come from Cuzco and, even after hard bargaining, prices in Pisac are not much lower than those in Cuzco. The main square is thronged with

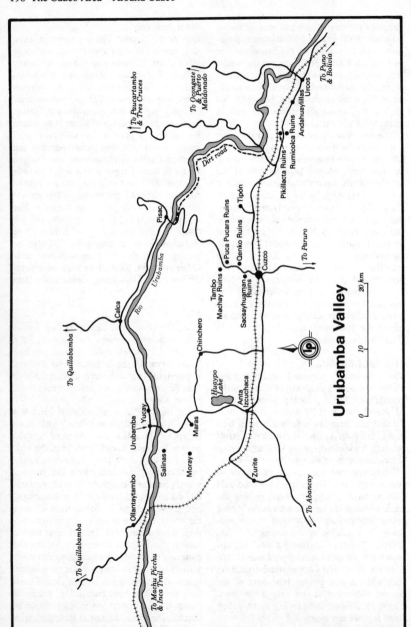

Urubamba Valley

To Paucartambo
& Tres Cruces

To Ocongate
& Puerto
Maldonado

To Puno
& Bolivia

Urcos

Andahuayllillas

Rumicolca Ruins

Pikillacta Ruins

Dirt road

Tipón

Puca Pucara Ruins

Qenko Ruins

Pisac

Río Urubamba

Cuzco

To Paruro

Tambo Machay Ruins

Sacsayhuaman Ruins

Calca

Chinchero

To Quillabamba

Huaypo Lake

Anta Izcuchaca

Yucay

Urubamba

Maras

Salinas

Moray

Zurite

To Abancay

Ollantaytambo

To Quillabamba

To Machu Picchu
& Inca Trail

20 km

10

0

people and becomes even more crowded after the mass (said in Quechua), when the congregation leaves the church in a colourful procession, led by the mayor holding his silver staff of office. Things start winding down about lunch time and, by evening, the village returns to its normal somnolent state.

There is a smaller market on Thursday and a few stall holders sell souvenirs every day during the high season, but it's pretty quiet compared to Sunday.

The Inca ruins above the village are among my favourites, partly because the walk there is so spectacular and partly because the site is less visited than others on the tourist circuit and so, except on Sunday, you don't see too many people. The ruins are reached either by a new, 10-km paved road up the Chongo Valley or by a shorter but steep footpath from the plaza. There is little traffic along the road but it is sometimes possible to hire a pick-up truck in Pisac to drive you to the ruins. The footpath to the site leaves town from the left-hand side of the church. There are many crisscrossing trails but, as long as you generally head towards the terracing, you'll get to the ruins without much difficulty. Allow roughly 1½ hours for the spectacular climb.

The ruins are on a hilltop with a gorge on either side. The western gorge (to the left of the hill as you climb up on the footpath) is the Kitamayo Gorge; to the right, or east, is the Chongo Gorge where the road ascends. Pisac is particularly well known for its agricultural terracing which sweeps around the south and east flanks of the mountain in vast, graceful curves, almost unbroken by steps which would promote erosion, take up valuable cultivation space, require greater maintenance and make walking and working along the terraces more difficult. Instead, the different levels of terracing are joined by diagonal flights of stairs made of flagstones set into the terrace walls.

Above the terraces are some cliff-hanging footpaths, well defended by massive stone doorways, steep stairs and, at one point, a tunnel carved out of the rock. Walking along these paths is exciting – the views are won-

derful and a pair of caracara hawks often accompanies you. This highly defensible site guards not only the Urubamba Valley below but also a pass into the jungle to the northeast. Pisac's main religious centre, near the top of the terraces, features extremely well-built rooms and temples. Some new excavations are under way at the back (north end) of the ruins; you can see a series of ceremonial baths being reconstructed. As you look across the Kitamayo Gorge from the back of the ruins, you'll see hundreds of holes honeycombing the cliff wall. These are Inca tombs which, unfortunately, were robbed before being examined by archaeologists. The site is large and warrants several hours or a whole day of your time. People occasionally camp near the ruins but there is no water. If you decide to spend the night, please don't break the law by lighting fires; use a stove for cooking or bring cold food. A recent fire ruined a large portion of the vegetation above the terraces. Fires also

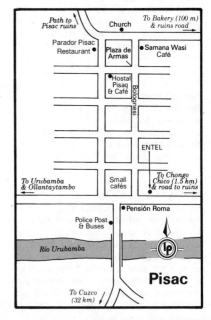

Pisac

advertise your presence. Friends camping near the ruins recently were robbed while sleeping, so keep a low profile.

Information

There is an ENTEL telephone near the bridge into town. Calle Bolognesi has several interesting-looking handicraft stores where you can see crafts being made.

Places to Stay

Pisac is a small village and accommodation is limited, especially before market day, so get there early or take a day trip from Cuzco. The most expensive place is the *Hostal Pisaq* on the square, where singles/doubles cost about $4/6. It's reasonably clean and friendly and provides communal hot showers and basic meals. Cheaper but dirtier, the *Pensión Roma* by the bridge has a few doubles for $1.50. Some families rent rooms in their houses; ask around. The *Chongo Chico* is in an old farmhouse 1½ km from town. It has beautifully carved furniture and used to be the best place to stay but its reputation has gone downhill since the recent death of its owner.

Places to Eat

The *Samana Wasi* is the best of Pisac's several very basic cafés and the *Hostal Pisaq* café isn't too bad. ENTURPeru runs the *Parador Pisac* restaurant, but I haven't tried it. The others have little to recommend them.

Getting There & Away

For a fare of about 30c, you can catch one of the minibuses which leave frequently from the stop on Avenida Tacna in Cuzco, some continuing along the Urubamba Valley to Urubamba. This is the cheapest way to travel but also the most crowded. Many agencies in Cuzco operate more expensive tourist buses, especially on market day, or you can hire a cab for about $10. When returning to Cuzco or continuing down the Urubamba Valley, wait for a bus by the bridge.

CALCA

About 18 km beyond Pisac, Calca is the most important town in the valley but of little interest to the traveller. There are some small and unspectacular ruins in the vicinity and a couple of very basic hotels, the best of which is the *Hostal Pitusiray*, but most people don't stay.

YUCAY

The pretty little village of Yucay is approximately 18 km beyond Calca. It has the valley's fanciest hotel, the *Alhambra 3*, which charges about $45 for a double room in a beautiful old hacienda. There is also an interesting little private museum. The outdoor restaurant next door, *El Bohio*, is usually open for lunch.

URUBAMBA

Urubamba is about 4 km beyond Yucay, at the junction of the valley road with the Chinchero road. The town is pleasant, though not exceptional, and a convenient base from which to explore the Sacred Valley. About 6 km further down the valley is the village of Tarabamba. You can cross the river here by footbridge and continue along a footpath, climbing roughly southwards up a valley for a further 3 km to the salt pans of Salinas. These have been used for salt extraction since Inca times. The local salt-extracting cooperative charges about 25c for entry to this little-visited and incredible site.

Also interesting are the experimental agricultural terraces of Moray. This site is more difficult to reach. First, you have to climb or get a ride up the steep road from Urubamba, across the river and as far as the Church of Tiobamba. From here, take a track on the right for 3 km to the village of Maras, then follow the trail a further 7 km to Moray. It is sometimes possible to visit Maras by car, depending on the condition of the road. The only facilities in Maras are very basic stores, so you should be self-sufficient.

Pottery

Pablo Seminario, a local potter, has a workshop on the road leading from the petrol station on the main valley road into the town centre. Walk about eight blocks and you'll find El Retamal on the left. Pablo does beautiful reproductions of pre-Hispanic pottery, as well as his own original work which is different to anything else you'll see in Cuzco. He speaks English and is happy to explain his art to visitors. Pieces are for sale here, but nowhere else.

Places to Stay & Eat

There are a couple of very basic cheap hotels in the town centre. The best is the friendly *Hotel Urubamba*, a couple of blocks from the central plaza and about 10 minutes from the main road, for less than $1 per person. You'll find simple restaurants on the plaza and along the road leading from the petrol station on the main valley road into the town centre.

For a little luxury, try the government-run *Centro Vacacional Urubamba* which has a very cold swimming pool, an adequate restaurant and comfortable, if impersonal, singles/doubles with clean hot showers for about $6/10.

Best of the hotels is the very friendly and pleasant *Hostal Naranjachayoc* where comfortable singles/doubles with heaters and hot water cost about $35/45. (Substantial discounts can be obtained during the low season.) There is an attractive garden, good home-made food in the restaurant and a roaring wood fire in the bar. Both these hotels are on the main valley road, the Naranjachayoc on the Yucay side of town and the Centro Vacacional on the Ollantaytambo side.

Also worth trying, especially for lunch, is the *Quinta Los Geranios* restaurant on the main valley road near the petrol station.

Getting There & Away

Minibuses leave Cuzco several times a day from the bus stop on Avenida Tacna.

In the mid to late 1980s, a railway construction project was busily under way, apparently extending the Machu Picchu railway line to Urubamba, but things seem to have ground fo a halt. Who knows when the project might be finished.

Buses back to Cuzco or on to Ollantaytambo stop at the only petrol station on the main road.

OLLANTAYTAMBO

This is the end of the road as far as the Sacred Valley is concerned – only rail and foot traffic goes beyond. Like Pisac, Ollantaytambo is a major Inca site at which you use the Cuzco Visitor Ticket. You can also buy a single-entry ticket to Ollantaytambo for $2 at the ruins. The site, a massive fortress, is one of the few places where the Spanish lost a major battle during the conquest. Below the ruins is the village of Ollantaytambo, built on traditional Inca foundations and the best surviving example of Inca city planning. The village was divided into blocks called *canchas*, each cancha with just one entrance leading into a courtyard. Individual houses were entered from this courtyard, not directly from the street.

The huge, steep terraces guarding the Inca fortress are spectacular and bring gasps of admiration from visitors arriving in the square below. Ollantaytambo is the fortress to which Manco Inca retreated after his defeat at Sacsayhuaman. In 1536, Hernando Pizarro led a force of 70 cavalry here, supported by large numbers of native and Spanish foot soldiers, in an attempt to capture the Inca. The steep terracing was highly defensible and Pizarro's men found themselves continuously showered with arrows, spears, stones and boulders. They were unable to climb the terraces and were further hampered when the Inca, in a brilliant move, flooded the plain below the fortress through previously prepared channels. The Spaniards' horses had difficulty manoeuvring in the water and Pizarro decided to beat a hasty retreat. This almost became a rout when the conquistadors were followed down the valley by thousands of the victorious Inca's soldiers.

Manco Inca's victory was short lived; soon afterwards, the Spanish forces in Cuzco were relieved by the return of a large Chilean expedition and Ollantaytambo was again attacked, this time with a cavalry force over four times the size of that used in the first attack. Manco Inca retreated to his jungle stronghold in Vilcabamba and Ollantaytambo became part of the Spanish Empire.

It is probable that the Incas themselves saw Ollantaytambo as a temple rather than as a fortress but the Spanish called it a fortress and it has usually been referred to as such ever since. The temple area is at the top of the terracing. Some extremely well-built walls were under construction at the time of the conquest and have never been completed. The stone used for these buildings was quarried from the mountainside 6 km away, high above the opposite bank of the Urubamba River. Transporting the stone blocks from the quarry to the site was a stupendous feat and involved the effort of thousands of Indian workers.

Places to Stay & Eat

The cheapest accommodation costs about $1 per person in basic, cold-water places such as the *Hostal Miranda*, the unnamed hostal next door and a couple of triple rooms above the *Café Alcazar*, which is also a reasonable place to eat. The *Parador Turistico*, in a pleasant old building, is better; it has the best restaurant in town and has hot water (sometimes). Dormitory-style accommodation costs about $3 per person, including a continental breakfast. There used to be 10 rooms; now there are two rooms with four and eight beds respectively. You'll find a few basic cafés on the plaza.

On the outskirts of town, near the train station and about 1 km from the centre, the

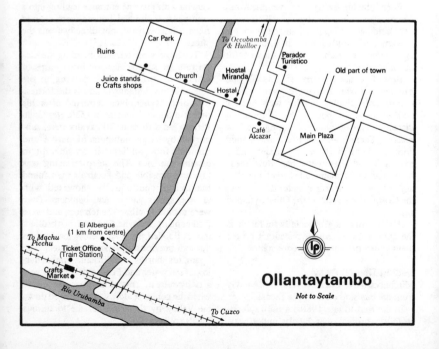

Ollantaytambo

Not to Scale

North American-run *El Albergue* is a very clean, pleasant but rustic hostal. Washing facilities are limited to cold-water buckets and the sauna. The folks who run the place have been there for many years and know the area inside out. They charge $5 per person in singles, doubles and triples but are limited to 18 guests. Continental breakfast and use of the sauna cost about $1 each. During the June to September season, El Albergue is often full with trekking groups and it may be closed at other times, so don't rely on staying here. You can contact the hostal through Luzma Tours (tel 233350) on Cuzco's Plaza de Armas.

Getting There & Away

You can get to Ollantaytambo from Cuzco by either bus or train but you must use the train if you want to go on to Machu Picchu.

Bus Minibuses leave from Urubamba's petrol station several times a day, but services tend to peter out in midafternoon. Buses from Cuzco are infrequent; most people change in Urubamba.

Train Ollantaytambo is an important station and all trains between Cuzco and Puentes Ruinas (for the Machu Picchu ruins) or Quillabamba stop at Ollantaytambo 1½ to 2 hours after leaving Cuzco. Schedules change frequently and you should check at the Ollantaytambo station for exact details. Read the information on trains in the Cuzco chapter to find out which are running and remember that the local train is often extremely overcrowded by the time it reaches Ollantaytambo, making standing the rule rather than the exception in 2nd class. First class is better. The tourist autovagon charges the same expensive fare from Ollantaytambo to Machu Picchu as it does from Cuzco; the local train is much cheaper.

CHINCHERO

Access to Chinchero requires a Cuzco Visitor Ticket. The site combines Inca ruins with an Andean Indian village, a colonial country church, wonderful mountain views and a colourful Sunday market.

The Inca ruins, consisting mainly of terracing, are not as spectacular as those at Pisac but are interesting nevertheless. If you walk away from the village through the terraces on the right-hand side of the valley, you'll find various rocks which have been carved into seats and staircases.

On the opposite side of the valley, a clear trail climbs upwards before heading north and down to the Urubamba River valley about 4 hours away. At the river, the trail turns left (downstream) and continues to a bridge at Huayllabamba where you can cross the river. From here, the Sacred Valley road will take you to Calca (turn right, about 13 km) or Urubamba (turn left, about 9 km). You can flag down a bus until midafternoon.

The main village square features a massive Inca wall with 10 huge, trapezoidal niches. Local women sell chicha along this wall during the market on Sunday. The colonial church just above the main square is built on Inca foundations. The church is in regular use but lack of funds has prevented restoration and it's interesting to compare its interior to those of the highly restored churches of Cuzco.

The Sunday market is marginally less touristy than the Pisac market and the local produce market is important to inhabitants of surrounding villages. Prices in the craft section are similar to those in Pisac or Cuzco but it's good to see the local people still dressed in traditional garb. This is not done just for the tourists – if you come midweek when there is no market and few tourists, you'll still see the women dressed in traditional clothing.

Places to Stay & Eat

There is a small, cheap hotel but it's not always open. The tourist office in Cuzco may have current information. There is no restaurant; the hotel may provide meals and a village store sells very basic supplies. Camping is possible below the terracing.

Getting There & Away

Trucks leave Cuzco from Calle Arcopata early every morning and, on Sunday morning, minibuses leave fairly frequently for the market. This service is slowly expanding to include one or two minibuses on weekdays.

THE INCA TRAIL

This is the best known and most popular hike on the continent and is walked by thousands of people every year. Many of these adventurers are not prepared for the trip, though every guidebook to South America at least describes the trail and most provide a map. If walking to Machu Picchu is a lifelong ambition, go ahead and enjoy yourself – it certainly is an exceptional hike. If you are an experienced backpacker looking for solitude or remote mountain villages, then I suggest hiking any one of the many other available trails.

If you decide that the Inca Trail is not to be missed, please don't defecate in the ruins, leave garbage anywhere, damage the stonework by building fires against the walls (it blackens and, worse still, cracks the rocks) or pick the orchids and other plants in this national park. I'm sure that 99% of readers would never consider doing any of these things but there always seems to be one person in 100 who will thoughtlessly cause more damage than the other 99. The South American Explorers Club organised an Inca Trail clean-up in 1980 and collected about 400 kg of unburnable garbage. Other clean-up campaigns since then have recorded similar figures. Please remove your empty cans and other rubbish and bury your faeces away from the trail and water sources.

Many adventure travel companies in the USA offer Inca Trail treks. This is the most expensive way to go but all the logistics and equipment are organised in advance. I have led treks for Wilderness Travel (tel 1-800-247-6700) for many years and recommend them. If you'd like to go on an organised trek which includes an Inca Trail clean-up campaign, contact The Earth Preservation Fund, affiliated with Journeys (1-800-345-4453).

If you arrive without a previously organised trek, there are several options. You can hike with what you can carry on your back or you can hire porters, guides and cooks from an adventure travel agency in Cuzco. Many budget travellers hire just one porter to carry a pack and this is inexpensive. You should carry a stove (wood is scarce), a sleeping pad and warm bag, and a tent or other protection against the rain. All this equipment can be rented inexpensively in Cuzco. Also bring insect repellent, sunblock lotion, water purification tablets or iodine and basic first-aid supplies. I know of people who have hiked the Inca Trail with a sheet of plastic and a bag of peanuts. Fine. They can go hungry and freeze if they want to but such behaviour is irresponsible and foolish. The trek takes 3 full days, temperatures can drop below freezing at night and it rains even in the dry season. There is nowhere to buy food. The ruins are roofless and provide no shelter. Caves marked on some maps are usually wet, dirty overhangs. Although the total distance is only 33 km, there are three high passes to be crossed, one of which reaches a height of 4200 metres. The trail is often steep, so don't be lulled into a false sense of security by the relatively short distance. Hike prepared.

You can obtain detailed maps and information from the South American Explorers Club in Lima as well as from trekking agencies and the tourist office in Cuzco. Many maps do not include the new section of trail joining Phuyupatamarca with Huiñay Huayna. Most maps, with the notable exception of the one available from the South American Explorers Club, do not have contours marked on them. The trail is fairly obvious for most of the way and it's difficult to get lost, especially if you carry a compass. The map in this book is perfectly adequate. There have been occasional reports of robberies on the trail and you are advised not to travel alone. The dry season from June to September is the most popular time and the most crowded. For the rest of the year the trail is fairly empty but also very wet – the mud can be 30 cm deep for long stretches.

I hope this practical information puts the

trail into perspective. Most of the other things you have read about it are also true. The views of snowcapped mountains and high cloud forest can be stupendous, weather permitting, and walking from one beautiful ruin to the next is a mystical and unforgettable experience. Enjoy the hike but be careful not to spoil it for the people coming after you.

Getting There & Away

Most people take the train from Cuzco to Km 88. The tourist train and autovagon don't stop here so you have to take the local train. It has a well-deserved reputation for thievery – watch your pack like a hawk and be particularly aware of thieves working in groups, some distracting your attention while others snatch your camera, slash your pack or pick your pockets.

Ask where to get off because, although everyone knows the stop, it is very small and badly marked. At Km 88, you cross the river; there is now a footbridge as well as the curious ski lift-type contraption which used to be the only way across. As you cross the river, you have to either buy a trail permit or present one obtained from the Ministerio de Cultura in Cuzco. It's easier to buy it at the trail head (but check with the Cuzco tourist office for the latest of the ever-changing regulations). The $14 fee includes entry to Machu Picchu (itself about $10). You're ready to begin the walk.

After crossing the river at Ollantaytambo, you can walk along the south bank of the Urubamba River. Although I have never done this, reports indicate that it adds a pleasant 20 km to the trip and that the trail is easy and well marked until you run into the Inca Trail at Llactapata, about 1 km up from Km 88.

You are not allowed to bring backpacks into Machu Picchu (if arriving on the Inca Trail, carry them through the edge of the ruins and leave them with the guard at the entrance). Doing the hike in reverse (from Machu Picchu to Km 88) is officially not permitted.

The Hike

It is interesting to note that various translations of Quechua names are possible and that those most frequently given are not necessarily the best or most accurate. Anthropologist Cristina Kessler-Noble has provided some interesting variations.

After crossing the Urubamba River (2200 metres) and taking care of trail fees and registration formalities, you can either turn right (west) to see the little-visited site of Q'ente, or 'hummingbird', 1 km away, or turn left and begin the Inca Trail as it climbs gently through a eucalyptus grove for about 1 km. You will see the minor ruin of Llactapata, or 'town on hillside', to your right and soon cross the Río Cusichaca, or 'joyful bridge', on a footbridge before heading south along the east bank of the river. Although there are camping possibilities just before Llactapata, most people elect to keep going to the village of Huayllabamba, or 'grassy plain', on the first day. It's about 7 km along the river to the village, climbing gently all the way and recrossing the river after about 4 km. Look over your shoulder for views of the snowcapped Veronica, 5750 metres above sea level.

Huayllabamba, at an elevation of about 2750 metres, is a tiny village 5 or 10 minutes above the fork of the Llullucha (a Quechuan word for a type of herb) and Cusichaca rivers. You cross the Llullucha River on a log bridge. It is possible to camp in the plaza in front of the school but beware of thieves slitting your tent at night. If you want to get away from the crowds, continue south along the Cusichaca to the ruins of Paucarcancha about 3 km away. You can camp here, though if you do so, you'll need to carry water up from the river.

The Inca Trail itself climbs steeply up along the south bank of the Llullucha River. After a walk of about 30 minutes, the river forks. Continue up the left fork for about 500 metres, then cross the river on a log bridge. There are several flat campsites on both sides of the bridge. The area is known as 'three white stones', but I've never worked out which boulders are referred to. This site is

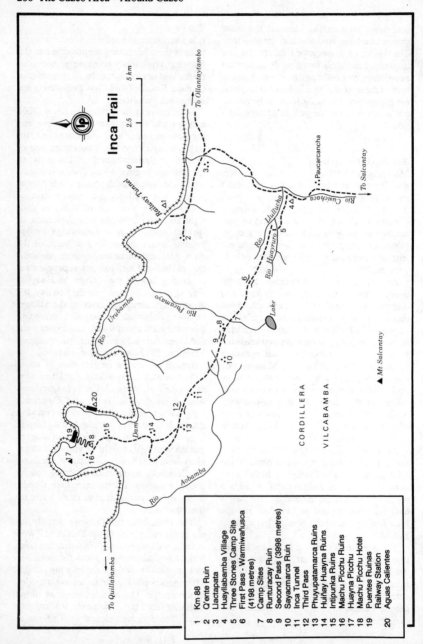

Inca Trail

5 km

2.5

0

To Ollantaytambo

To Salcantay

To Quillabamba

Río Urubamba

Railway Tunnel

Río Pacamayo

Río Huayruro

Río Llullucha

Río Cusichaca

Río Aobamba

Paucarcancha

Lake

CORDILLERA VILCABAMBA

▲ Mt Salcantay

1 Km 88
2 Q'ente Ruin
3 Llactapata
4 Huayllabamba Village
5 Three Stones Camp Site
6 First Pass – Warmiwañusca
   (4198 metres)
7 Camp Sites
8 Runturacay Ruin
9 Second Pass (3998 metres)
10 Sayacmarca Ruin
11 Inca Tunnel
12 Third Pass
13 Phuyupatamarca Ruins
14 Huiñay Huayna Ruins
15 Intipunka Ruins
16 Machu Picchu Ruins
17 Huayna Picchu
18 Machu Picchu Hotel
19 Puentes Ruinas
20 Railway Station
    Aguas Calientes

usually the first camp for most people who start from Km 88 in the morning.

Further on, the trail turns right beyond the log bridge and sweeps back to the Llullucha. It is a very long, steep climb to the Warmiwañusca, or 'dead woman's', Pass. At 4198 metres above sea level, this pass is the highest point of the trek and it's best to rest for the night at the three stones campsite to further acclimatise before making the ascent. The trail passes through cloud forest for about 1½ hours before emerging on the high, bare mountain. At some points the trail and stream bed become one, so be prepared for wet feet. Generally, the trail climbs steeply but there are a couple of small, flat areas in the forest where you could camp and a flat area above the forest where water is available and camping possible, though it is very cold at night. From here, follow the left-hand side of the valley for the 3 hour climb to the pass. It takes longer than you'd expect because the altitude slows you down.

From Warmiwañusca, you can see the Pacamayo, or 'sunrise', River far below and the ruin of Runturacay halfway up the hill, above the river. The trail descends to the river where there are good campsites. The downward climb is long, taking over an hour, and a strain on the knees. At an altitude of about 3600 metres, the trail crosses the river below a small waterfall – don't venture too far into the vegetation below. Climb to the right towards Runturacay, or 'egg hut', an oval-shaped ruin with superb views about an hour's walk above the river. You can also camp here and, about 10 minutes away from the ruins, to your left as you look out into the valley, there is a trickle of water. Previous campers have left this ruin in an unsavoury condition.

Above Runturacay, the trail climbs to a false summit before continuing past two small lakes to the top of the second pass at 3998 metres, about 1½ hours above Runturacay. There are good views of the snowcapped Cordillera Vilcabamba. The clear trail descends past another lake to the ruin of Sayacmarca, or 'dominant town', which is visible from the trail 1 km before

you reach it. The site, a tightly constructed town on a small mountain spur, is the most impressive of those seen along the trail so far and offers superb views. A long, steep staircase to the left of the trail leads to the site. The trail itself continues downwards and crosses the headwaters of the Río Aobamba, or 'wavy plain', 3600 metres above sea level. There is enough room here for a small campsite.

As the trail goes through some beautiful cloud forest on the gentle climb to the third pass, you'll find a causeway across a swampy, dried-out lake and, further on, a tunnel, both Inca constructions. The highest point of the pass, at almost 3700 metres, is not very obvious. There are great views of the Urubamba Valley from here. You soon reach the beautiful ruin of Phuyupatamarca, or 'town above the clouds', about 3650 metres above sea level and approximately 3 hours beyond Sayacmarca.

Phuyupatamarca has been well restored and contains a beautiful series of ceremonial baths with water running through them (purify it before drinking). A ridge above the baths offers camping sites with spectacular views. There are sometimes camp guards here.

From Phuyupatamarca, the newly opened (1985) section of the Inca Trail is much shorter than the old route which traverses the mountain. The new section makes a dizzying dive into the cloud forest below, following an incredibly well-engineered flight of hundreds of Inca steps. This route is by far the more interesting of the two but is not marked on many maps. It rejoins the old trail near the electric power pylons built down the hill to the dam on the Urubamba River. Follow the pylons down to a white hotel which provides youth hostel-type facilities for about $2 per bed, much less if you sleep on the floor. Hot showers, meals and bottled drinks are available and camping is possible nearby. A 500-metre trail behind the hotel leads to the beautiful Inca site of Huiñay Huayna which cannot be seen from the hotel.

Huiñay Huayna is normally translated as 'forever young' but a much more attractive translation was recently explained to me. As Huiñay is the Quechua infinitive for 'to plant the earth', a more accurate translation may be 'to plant the earth, young', perhaps a reference to the young, springtime earth of planting time. From planting comes growing; thus one has 'growing young', as opposed to 'growing old', and hence the popular catch-all translation 'forever young'.

Whatever it means, this exquisite little place warrants the short side trip and 1 or 2 hours of exploration. Climb down to the lowest part of the town where it tapers off into a tiny and very exposed ledge overlooking the Urubamba River far below. This ruin is about a 3-hour descent from Phuyupatamarca. The very difficult climb down to the Urubamba River below is prohibited. The land is owned by the electric company and there are no trails.

From Huiñay Huayna, the trail contours around through the cliff-hanging cloud forest and is very thin in places, so watch your step. It takes about 2½ hours to reach Intipunku, or 'sun gate', the penultimate site on the trail and the last point on the Inca Trail where you're allowed to camp. There's no water but there is room for a couple of tents. You'll get your first view of Machu Picchu from here.

The descent from Intipunku to Machu Picchu takes 30 minutes. Backpacks are not allowed into the ruins and, immediately upon arrival, park guards ask you to check your pack at the lower entrance gate and have your trail permit stamped. It is rather a brusque return to rules and regulations when all you want to do is quietly explore the ruins. The pass is only valid for the day it is stamped, so try to arrive in the morning. Sometimes, you can persuade the guards to stamp it for the next day.

After you've explored the ruins, you can stay at the expensive hotel near the site or camp on the road below the site (see the Machu Picchu section). Alternatively, you can take the 6-km road (buses are available) down from the ruins to the railway line and go to the village of Aguas Calientes 2 km up the railway tracks. Here, there are cheap, basic hotels, restaurants and hot springs (see Aguas Calientes). You can also take the afternoon train and be in Cuzco, Ollantaytambo or Quillabamba by evening.

MACHU PICCHU
This is undoubtedly the best known and most spectacular archaeological site on the continent. During the busy, dry-season months of June to September, up to 1000 people a day come to visit the Lost City of the Incas, as Machu Picchu is popularly known. Despite this huge tourist influx, the site manages to retain its air of grandeur and mystery and is considered a must for all visitors to Peru.

History
Machu Picchu is both the best and the least known of the Inca ruins. It is not mentioned in any of the chronicles of the Spanish conquistadors and archaeologists today can do no more than speculate on its function. Although Machu Picchu was known to a handful of Quechua peasants who farmed the area, the outside world was unaware of its existence until the American historian Hiram Bingham stumbled on it almost by accident on 24 July 1911. Bingham's search was for the lost city of Vilcabamba, the last stronghold of the Incas and, at Machu Picchu, he thought he had found it. We now know that the remote and inaccessible ruins at Espiritu Pampa, much deeper in the jungle, are the remains of Vilcabamba, while Machu Picchu is a mysterious site, never revealed to the conquering Spaniards and virtually forgotten until some 80 years ago.

The site discovered in 1911 was very different to the one we see today. All the buildings were thickly overgrown with vegetation and Bingham's team had to be content with roughly mapping the site. Bingham returned in 1912 and 1915 to carry out the difficult task of clearing the thick forest from the ruins and also discovered some of the ruins on the Inca Trail. Peruvian archaeologist Luis E Valcárcel undertook

Top: Llamas in front of the Cathedral, Plaza de Armas, Cuzco (TW)
Left: Blind musician, the Inca street of Hatunrumiyoc, Cuzco (TW)
Right: La Compañía floodlit at night, Cuzco (TW)

Left: Quechua women & children, Cachin, Cordillera Urubamba (RR)
Right: View from Intihuatana, Machu Picchu (RR)
Bottom: Hikers on the Inca Trail to Machu Picchu (RR)

further studies and clearing in 1934, as did a Peruvian-American expedition under Paul Fejos in 1940-41. Despite these and more recent studies, knowledge of Machu Picchu remains sketchy. Over 50 burial sites were discovered containing over 100 skeletal remains, about 80% female. An early theory that it was a city of chosen women who catered to the Incas' needs has lost support and it is now thought that Machu Picchu was already an uninhabited, forgotten city at the time of the conquest. This would explain why it wasn't mentioned to the Spaniards. It is obvious from the exceptionally high quality of the stonework and the abundance of ornamental rather than practical sites that Machu Picchu must once have been an important ceremonial centre.

There have been two recent reports of new finds in the area. The first, in the early 1980s, was of some burial sites on Huayna Picchu mountain. The other, in late 1986, involved the exciting discovery of a city about twice the size of Machu Picchu and 5 km north of it, according to a Peruvian government spokesman. Local and US archaeologists have named the city Maranpampa (or Mandorpampa). Neither of the new sites is easily accessible to the general public, though there are plans to open Maranpampa to tourists.

Admission

The site is open daily from 7.30 am to 5 pm, so watching dawn or dusk in Machu Picchu is difficult unless you arrive via the Inca Trail and camp at Intipunku. Because the site is surrounded by high mountains, you can see sunrise and sunset over the ruins during visiting hours, though it's already broad daylight when the sun comes up over the surrounding mountains. The changes in colour and light early and late in the day are very beautiful.

Machu Picchu is Peru's showpiece site and entrance fees are correspondingly high. Foreigners pay about $10 for a single day's visit and there's no longer any student discount. The site is exceptionally difficult to enter other than through the gate and the

guards (who wear hard hats) are very vigilant, so resign yourself to paying. If you want to visit the ruins for 2 days, the second day costs only $6.

Many visitors buy a Machu Picchu combined-ticket book from one of the tourist agencies in Cuzco. This includes round-trip tickets for the tourist train (autovagon), the bus to and from the ruins, admission to the ruins and lunch at the Machu Picchu Hotel. Make sure your ticket contains all these sections and shop around. The combined ticket costs at least $60, often more, depending on the agency. Most agencies will also provide an English-speaking guide. This ticket doesn't enable you to cut corners by, for example, travelling on the cheaper local train or bringing a sandwich lunch but, if you want to go 1st class all the way, consider the combined-ticket book to save the hassle of buying the individual tickets. The main drawback is that the combined ticket is valid for just 1 day and you only get to spend 2 or 3 hours in the ruins before it's time to start returning to the train station. A cheaper version of the combined ticket is sometimes available from the train station in Cuzco and includes train, bus and entrance fees, but no lunch or guides.

You are not allowed to bring large packs or food into the ruins and packs have to be checked at the gate. You can visit all parts of the ruins but don't walk on any of the walls as this will loosen the stonework as well as prompt an angry cacophony of whistle blowing from the guards. As the guards check the ruins carefully at closing time and blow their whistles loudly, trying to spend the night is also difficult.

You can buy a so-called Boleto Nocturno for $10; this will get you into the ruins at night and is particularly popular around full moon. Buy the ticket from the entrance booth during the day – tickets are not sold at night. The gates are locked behind you when you go in at night and you have to call for the guard when you're ready to leave. The last time I did this, the guard fell asleep and I had to yell and whistle for about 20 minutes before he finally woke up!

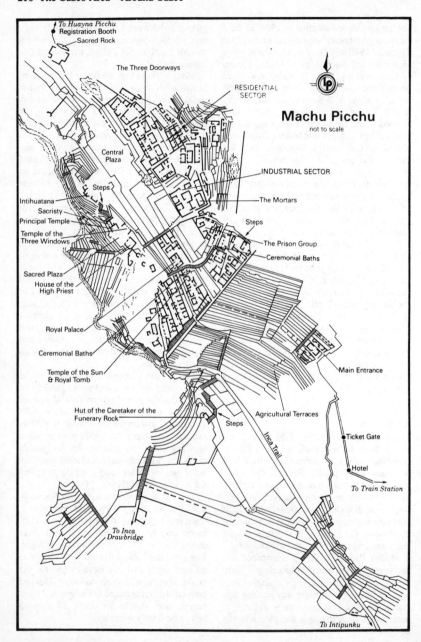

To Huayna Picchu
Registration Booth
Sacred Rock

The Three Doorways

RESIDENTIAL
SECTOR

Machu Picchu

not to scale

Central
Plaza

INDUSTRIAL SECTOR

Steps

Intihuatana
Sacristy
Principal Temple
Temple of the
Three Windows

The Mortars

Steps

The Prison Group

Ceremonial Baths

Sacred Plaza
House of the
High Priest

Royal Palace

Ceremonial Baths

Temple of the Sun
& Royal Tomb

Main Entrance

Hut of the Caretaker of the
Funerary Rock

Steps

Agricultural Terraces

Ticket Gate

Hotel

To Train Station

Inca Trail

To Inca
Drawbridge

To Intipunku

Post

The post office booth at the Puentes Ruinas train station is usually open for the afternoon train departure. All postcards are franked with a special Machu Picchu souvenir postmark.

Museum

A small museum a few hundred metres behind the train station shows photos of Hiram Bingham and gives a little information about the ruins. If you're pressed for time, go straight to the ruins.

Inside the Ruins

Unless you arrive on the Inca Trail, you'll officially enter the ruins through a guarded ticket gate on the south side of Machu Picchu. About 100 metres of footpath bring you to the maze-like entrance of Machu Picchu proper where the ruins lie stretched out before you, roughly divided into two areas separated by a series of plazas. The area to the left of the plazas contains most of the more interesting sites. Immediately beyond the entrance are agricultural terraces above and below.

Beyond these terraces, a long staircase climbs up to your left to a hut on the southeast spur. This vantage point affords the most complete overview of the site for that classic photograph. The hut, known as the 'Hut of the Caretaker of the Funerary Rock', is one of the few buildings which has been restored with a thatched roof, making it a good shelter in case of rain. The Inca Trail enters the city just below this hut. The carved rock behind the hut may have been used to mummify the nobility and explains the hut's name.

If you continue straight into the ruins instead of climbing the stairs to the hut, you soon come to a beautiful series of 16 connected ceremonial baths that cascade across the ruins accompanied by a flight of stairs. Just above and to the left of the baths is Machu Picchu's only round building, the Temple of the Sun. This curved, tapering tower is said to contain Machu Picchu's finest stonework. Inside is an altar and a curiously drilled trapezoidal window which

looks out on the site. This window is popularly named the 'Serpent Window' but it's unlikely that snakes lived in the holes around it. Probably, the holes were used to suspend a ceremonial gold sun disk. At the time of writing, the Temple of the Sun is temporarily cordoned off while archaeologists excavate a newly discovered room in the temple floor.

Below the towering temple, an almost hidden natural rock cave has been carefully carved with a step-like altar and sacred niches by the Inca's stonemasons. The mummies discovered at this site give it the name of the Royal Tomb.

Climbing the stairs above the ceremonial baths, you reach a flat area of jumbled rocks, once used as a quarry. Turn right at the top of the stairs and walk across the quarry on a short path leading to the four-sided Sacred Plaza. The far side contains a small lookout platform with a curved wall and a beautiful view of the snowcapped Cordillera Vilcabamba in the far distance. Below, you can see the Urubamba River and the modern buildings of a hydroelectric project. The remaining three sides of the Sacred Plaza are flanked by important buildings. The Temple of the Three Windows commands an impressive view of the plaza below through the huge, trapezoidal windows which give the building its name. With this temple behind you, the Principal Temple is to your right. Its name derives from the massive solidity and perfection of its construction. The damage to the rear right corner of the temple is the result of the ground settling below this corner rather than any inherent weakness in the masonry itself. Opposite the Principal Temple is the House of the High Priest, though archaeologists cannot say with certainty who, if anyone, lived in this building.

Behind and connected to the Principal Temple lies a famous small building called the Sacristy. It has many well-carved niches, perhaps used for the storage of ceremonial objects, as well as a carved stone bench. The Sacristy is especially known for the two rocks flanking its entrance; each is said to contain 32 angles but I come up with a different number whenever I count them!

A staircase behind the Sacristy climbs a small hill to the major shrine in Machu Picchu, the Intihuatana. This Quechua word loosely translates as the 'hitching post of the sun' and refers to the carved rock pillar, often mistakenly called a sun dial, which stands at the top of the Intihuatana hill. This rock was not used in telling the time of day but, rather, the time of year. The Inca's astronomers were able to predict the solstices using the angles of the pillar; thus the Inca, who was the son of the sun, was able to claim control over the return of the lengthening summer days. Exactly how the pillar was used for these astronomical purposes remains unclear but its elegant simplicity is remarked upon by many modern observers. It is recorded that there were several of these Intihuatanas in various important Inca sites but all, with the known exception of this one, were smashed by the Spaniards in an attempt to wipe out what they considered to be the blasphemy of sun worship.

At the back of the Intihuatana is another staircase. It descends to the Central Plaza which separates the important sites of the Intihuatana, Sacred Plaza and Temple of the Sun from the more mundane areas opposite. At the lower end of this area opposite is the Prison Group, a labyrinthine complex of cells, niches and passageways both under and above ground. The centrepiece of the group is a carving of the head of a condor, the natural rocks behind it resembling the bird's outstretched wings. Behind the condor is a well-like hole and, at the bottom of this, the door to a tiny underground cell which can only be entered by bending double.

Above the Prison Group is the largest section of the ruins, the Industrial & Residential Sectors. These buildings are less well constructed and had more mundane purposes than those across the plaza.

Walks near Machu Picchu

Five fairly short walks can be taken starting from and returning to the ruins, the most famous of which is the climb up the steep mountain of Huayna Picchu at the back of the ruins. Huayna Picchu is normally trans-

lated as 'young peak' but it is interesting to note that picchu, with the correct glottal pronunciation, refers to the wad in the cheek of a coca-chewing, Quechua-speaking mountain dweller – the wad looks like a little peak in the cheek.

At first glance, it would appear that Huayna Picchu is a difficult climb but there is a well-maintained trail so, although the ascent is steep, it's not technically difficult. You begin by walking to the very end of the Main Plaza and turning right between two open-fronted buildings. Just beyond is a registration booth where you have to sign in; it's only open until about 1 pm. The 1-hour climb takes you through a short section of Inca tunnel. The view from the top is spectacular but, if you lack either time or energy, I think the view from the Hut of the Caretaker of the Funerary Rock is equally good.

The second walk begins with a climb part of the way up Huayna Picchu. About 10 minutes from the lowest point of the trail, a thin path marked Peligro – Prohibido El Paso, which means 'Danger – Entrance Prohibited', branches off to your left. It is, in fact, possible to continue down the rear of Huayna Picchu along a recently cleared but still rather difficult trail to the small Temple of the Moon. Lack of proper trail maintenance means that you do this section at your own risk, though it may have been completely cleared by the time you read this. The descent takes over 30 minutes and the ascent back to the main Huayna Picchu trail rather longer. The spectacular trail drops and climbs steeply as it hugs the sides of Huayna Picchu before plunging into the cloud forest for a while. Suddenly, you reach a cleared area where the small, very well-made ruins are found. Unfortunately, they are covered in graffiti.

A much less steep and very scenic walk from the Hut of the Caretaker of the Funerary Rock takes you past the top of the terraces and out along a narrow, cliff-clinging trail to the Inca drawbridge. The trail is marked; there is also a registration booth at which you're supposed to register before 3 pm but its opening hours are erratic. The 20-minute walk gives you a good look at the vegetation of the high cloud forest and a different view of Machu Picchu. The drawbridge itself is less interesting than the walk to reach it. You are not allowed to walk right up to it and have to be content with viewing it from behind a barrier about 100 metres away. Someone crossed both the barrier and the bridge a few years ago and fell to their death.

The Inca Trail ends just below the Hut of the Caretaker of the Funerary Rock and heads back to the notch in the horizon called Intipunku, or the 'gate of the sun'. Looking at the hill behind you as you enter the ruins, you can see both the trail and Intipunku. This hill, called Machu Picchu, or 'old peak',

gives the site its name. It takes about 45 minutes to reach Intipunku and, if you can spare about 5 hours for the round trip, it's possible to continue as far as Wiñay Wayna (see the Inca Trail).

The fifth walk, an ascent of the hill of Machu Picchu, is the most difficult and rarely done. Take the Inca Trail for a few minutes and look for a trail to your right passing through a gap in the walls of the terraces. It's not very obvious and there's no sign. If you find the trail, it will be very overgrown but you can force your way through the thick vegetation to the top of the peak. Allow well over an hour for the climb and be prepared for disappointment unless the trail has recently been cleared.

Places to Stay & Eat

The government-run *Hotel de Turistas* is the only place to stay at Machu Picchu itself. Singles/doubles/triples cost $45/55/65, including continental breakfast but, despite the expense, it's often full. If you want to stay here, make a reservation through a travel agency in Lima or Cuzco or at the ENTUR-Peru office (tel 721928) in Lima. You can sometimes get a room on the day you arrive, especially during the low season, but don't rely on it. The best thing about this hotel is the never-ending supply of hot water in the showers in every room. The hotel has no telephone (except to call the reception desk) and there is only emergency radio communication with Cuzco.

If you want to stay overnight to allow yourself a full day at the ruins, there are two cheap choices. The best is to stay at Aguas Calientes (see the next section), 2 km towards Cuzco on the train tracks from the Puentes Ruinas station. Alternatively, you can camp at the campsite by the river about 200 metres from the station. Floodlights discourage theft. Washrooms with cold showers are available or you can wash in the river. The cost is $2 per tent irrespective of the number staying in the tent. This still leaves the problem of looking after your gear while visiting the ruins. There are backpack-

Descending from Huayna Picchu

storage facilities at the ruins entrance but you have to lug your gear up the hill first.

The only place to eat at the ruins is in the hotel. The hotel restaurant serves expensive breakfast and supper and a cafeteria on the patio offers expensive self-service lunches. During the busy season, lunch queues can be very long. There is also a souvenir shop/snack bar where you can buy bottled drinks for about the same price as in the cafeteria. Bring a packed lunch and water bottle if you want to economise. It's illegal to bring food into the ruins because many tourists litter the site. Don't leave any rubbish whatsoever.

Cheap snacks and drinks can be purchased at the train station in the afternoon.

Getting There & Away

Most visitors take the autovagon from Cuzco, arriving at the Puentes Ruinas train station about 3½ hours later. The train journey begins with a climb out of Cuzco. Because it is too steep for normal railroad curves, this is accomplished in four back-and-forth zigzags. The tracks then drop gently through mainly agricultural countryside to the important station of Ollantaytambo where all trains stop. From here, you can see Mount Veronica (5750 metres) to your right and the Urubamba River gorge to your left. The train descends down the narrow gorge with superb views of the very difficult white water of the lower Urubamba. (The Cuzco to Ollantaytambo section can be done one-way by railway company bus.)

At Puentes Ruinas station, you are about 2000 metres above sea level and roughly 700 metres below the ruins of Machu Picchu. A fleet of buses waits to take you up to the ruins on a 6 km road (the Hiram Bingham Highway, opened in 1948) which zigzags thrillingly up the mountainside. One-way bus tickets cost about $3 and can be obtained at the train station ticket office, across the platform facing the left-hand side of the train as you come in. (People with combined tickets have the return bus ticket to the ruins included.) There are about 12 buses but, on

a busy day, you may have to wait up to an hour if you miss the first wave of buses, so it's worth hustling a bit as you get off the train.

Unfortunately, Machu Picchu is so geared to the arrival of the tourist train that it is sometimes difficult to get a bus to the ruins at other times. Usually, a bus meets the local train but, if you walk the 2 km from Aguas Calientes, you may find no bus or a driver who wants to wait an hour until all 22 seats are filled. If there's a group of you, it's possible to buy all 22 tickets. Otherwise, you'll have to walk. (Many budget travellers prefer this to paying $3 for a 20-minute bus ride.) Rather than climb 6 km by road, the shorter and steeper footpath is a better hike. Cross the bridge behind the train station and turn right. The path, marked by arrows, crosses the road at several points on the ascent but the drivers will not normally stop for passengers at intermediate points. It's a 1½ hour climb from the station but the descent takes only a leisurely 40 minutes.

The tourist trains leave for the return trip in the afternoon. Departure times vary according to the season – there may be one train at 3.30 pm, two trains at 2 and 5 pm or some other schedule. The buses start descending from the ruins about 2 hours before departure time and, during the high season, bus lines can get very long. Buying tickets for the tourist train can be a bit of a problem as the seats are often fully booked by passengers on day trips from Cuzco.

If you have time, the most economical way to travel is on the local train (1st class) or the Quillabamba autovagon to Aguas Calientes. Spend the night there, a full day at Machu Picchu ruins and another night at Aguas Calientes, then return on the local train or autovagon. This avoids the tourist train completely and maximises your time at the ruins.

The ruins are most heavily visited between about 11 am and 2.30 pm. As many tours combine visits of Machu Picchu with the Sunday markets at either Pisac or Chinchero, Sunday is fairly quiet but Friday, Saturday and Monday are busy. June to

August are the busiest months. Try to plan your visit early or late in the day, especially during the dry season (the whole day is best) and you'll have several hours of peace and quiet. An early, wet, midweek morning in the rainy season will virtually guarantee you the ruins to yourself.

For the Budget Traveller

The Machu Picchu section contains a bewildering amount of information; this is a summary of pertinent details. As the $10 entry fee cannot be avoided, it's worth spending a whole day at the ruins. The tourist train is very expensive, so use the cheap local train to Aguas Calientes from Ollantaytambo if you can't get tickets in Cuzco. From the budget hotels and restaurants in Aguas Calientes, you can walk (uphill) to the ruins in about 2 hours and return in about 1½ hours.

AGUAS CALIENTES

This tiny village is the closest to Machu Picchu and is therefore a frequent destination for travellers wanting to do more than just visit Machu Picchu on the standard 1-day train trip from Cuzco. The scenery here is pretty and it's a good place to meet other travellers and relax in the countryside.

Hot Springs

Trekkers completing the Inca Trail may want to soak away their aches and pains in the natural thermal springs from which the village of Aguas Calientes derives its name. To get there, follow the path past the youth hostel for about 10 minutes. The hot springs are open from 5 am to 8 pm and entry costs 30c. Often, there's no gatekeeper early in the morning.

The government has tried to improve the hot springs by building shallow concrete pools, changing cubicles (without doors) and a cafeteria (which is usually closed). They seem to have forgotten to build a toilet (you can guess what people use instead) but there is a shower pipe surrounded by discarded shampoo and soap wrappers. It's rather disappointing but definitely has the potential to

improve. Check it out, if only for the pretty walk.

Places to Stay

The cheap *Hostal Los Caminantes*, next to the railway line, is a dark, rambling, rather dirty building. Accommodation costs 65c per person in three, four and five-bed rooms and $1.10/1.60 in singles/doubles. The dank showers have only cold water. The *Hostal Qoñi*, better known as *Gringo Bill's* because of its American owner, is a better choice at about $2 per person. However, the owner is no longer there and may have sold the place. There is also the new *Hotel Machu Picchu* near the train station which is cheap and clean. The government-run youth hostel *Albergue Juvenil* charges $2.25 per person in rooms which usually contain four very narrow bunk beds. There is sometimes hot water in the communal bathrooms and meals are available. It's clean but rather spartan and cheerless and considered a white elephant by many – it has about 200 beds but is usually 75% empty.

Cheap accommodation used to be available in some of the houses and restaurants by the railway line but these have pretty much shut down since the youth hostel opened. Occasionally, Aguas Calientes gets invaded by a huge group of Peruvian students and these other places can provide accommodation in such emergencies.

Places to Eat

Most of the restaurants are clustered along the railway tracks and are not particularly good. Some have been criticised for undercooked food or unhygienic conditions and travellers get sick here more often than elsewhere. The tap water is not safe to drink. Two restaurants I have found to be reasonably clean are the *Aiko* and *El Refugio*, both serving good meals for under $1. The *Samaná* and *El Mirador* restaurants have also been recommended and there are several others you can experiment with.

There's not much to do in the evening except hang out in one of the restaurants and talk to other travellers over a beer. There is a discotheque/ciné-theatre/nightclub called *El Clave del Sol* on the right-hand side of the path on the way to the hot springs, which opens occasionally. It's run by a Frenchman who likes to show obscure French films without subtitles.

Getting There & Away

To Machu Picchu Aguas Calientes, the nearest village to the ruins, is still a walk of about 8 km from Machu Picchu, though you can take public transport. From Aguas Calientes, head roughly west along the railway line. There is no road or proper footpath, but with so few trains, most people just walk the 2 km along the track to the ruins station, beating the crowds to the ruins. There are a couple of tunnels so you might want to take a torch. A road between Aguas Calientes and the ruins station is being built and may be finished by the time you read this. There may also be a bus service running on it.

The station beyond Aguas Calientes, Puente Ruinas, is the station for the ruins. A steep 6-km road climbs the 600 metres from the Urubamba River valley floor to the ruins. If you're on foot, you don't have to follow the road – the signposted footpath is shorter, steeper and very narrow. You emerge breathless at the top about 1½ hours later. A seat on one of the fleet of 22-seater buses which runs from the station to the ruins costs about $3. Normally, buses leave when full, which means every few minutes after the tourist train arrives and rather infrequently at other times. There is also an early morning bus which takes site employees up to work. Most people walk – it's cool first thing in the morning and gives you a good look at the high mountain cloud forest. Orchids often bloom along the path, especially in the rainy months.

To Cuzco & Quillabamba For some reason, the Aguas Calientes train station is known as Machu Picchu and, as the road does not reach Aguas Calientes (nor Machu Picchu), you have to use the train. The ticket office is on the north side of the railway tracks. Usually, only the local train stops here and many people prefer to walk 2 km to Puentes Ruinas for a better selection of faster trains to Cuzco. The local trains for Cuzco stop at Aguas Calientes at around 8.30 am and 5 pm, take 4 to 5 hours and cost about $2. The trains to

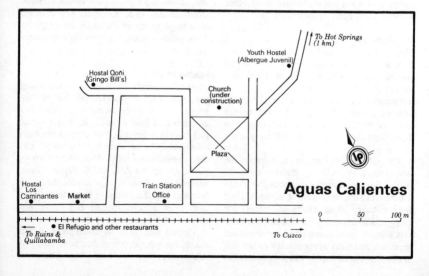

Quillabamba pass through at about 9.30 am and 6 pm, take 3 hours and cost about $1.

There is also a local autovagon which passes through at 7.15 am on the way to Cuzco (3¼ hours, $4) and at 4.30 pm on the way to Quillabamba (2 hours, $2).

SANTA TERESA

From this village, about 20 km beyond Aguas Calientes on the way to Quillabamba, it is possible to find trucks to Cuzco. The rough journey takes about 15 hours during the dry season and is very difficult during the rainy months of November to April. Santa Teresa is also the termination point for a 4-day trek from the village of Mollepata, through the Cordillera Vilcabamba and passing Salcantay. (See Hilary Bradt's book *Backpacking & Trekking in Peru & Bolivia*.) The basic hotel here charges $1.50 per person and a local lady serves decent meals; ask. The local trains between Cuzco and Quillabamba stop in this off-the-beaten-track place, described by one correspondent as 'magical and fun'.

SOUTH-EAST OF CUZCO

The railway and the road to Puno and Lake Titicaca head south-east from Cuzco. En route are several sites of interest which can be visited from Cuzco in a day.

Tipón

This little-known Inca site consists of some excellent terracing at the head of a small valley and is noted for its fine irrigation system. To get there, take the Transportes Oropesa bus from Cuzco and ask to be set down at the Tipón turn-off, 23 km beyond Cuzco and a few km before Oropesa. A steep dirt road from the turn-off climbs the 4 km to the ruins.

Pikillacta & Rumicolca

Pikillacta is the only major pre-Inca ruin in the Cuzco area and can be reached on an Urcos minibus from Cuzco. Pikillacta means 'the place of the flea' and was built around 1100 AD by the Wari culture. Entry is with the Cuzco Visitor Ticket. The site is just past

a lake on the left-hand side of the road, about 32 km beyond Cuzco. It is a large city of crumbling, two-storey buildings, all with entrances strategically located on the upper floor. A defensive wall surrounds the city. The stonework here is much cruder than that of the Incas.

Across the road from Pikillacta and about 1 km away is the huge Inca gate of Rumicolca, built on Wari foundations. The cruder Wari stonework contrasts with the Inca blocks.

The area's swampy lakes are also interesting. You can see Indians making roof tiles from the mud which surrounds the lakes.

Andahuaylillas

Andahuaylillas is about 40 km beyond Cuzco and 7 km before Urcos. This pretty Andean village is famous for its beautifully decorated church, comparable to the best in Cuzco, and attractive colonial houses. The church hours are erratic but you can usually find a caretaker to open it for you (a tip is expected). You can reach Andahuaylillas on the Urcos minibus.

FROM CUZCO TO THE JUNGLE

There are three overland routes from Cuzco to the jungle. One is via the railway to Quillabamba (described in the section on Quillabamba). The other two are poor dirt roads on which it's best to travel in the dry months (June to September); they can be very muddy and slow in the wet months, especially January to April. One road heads to Paucartambo, Tres Cruces, Shintuyo and towards Manu National Park and the other goes through Ocongate and Quince Mil to Puerto Maldonado.

Paucartambo

The small village of Paucartambo lies on the eastern slopes of the Andes about 115 km from Cuzco along a very narrow, though well-maintained dirt road. There are fine views of the Andes and the high Amazon Basin beyond. Travel on the one-way dirt road is from Cuzco to Paucartambo on Monday, Wednesday and Friday and return on Tuesday, Thursday and Saturday. Trucks for Paucartambo leave Cuzco early in the morning from near the Urcos bus stop. The journey takes about 5 hours.

Paucartambo is particularly famous for its very authentic and colourful celebration of the Fiesta de la Virgen del Carmen, held annually on and around 16 July with traditional street dancing, processions and wonderful costumes. Relatively few tourists have seen this fiesta simply because it's been difficult to reach and because, once you're there, you either have to camp, find a room in one of two extremely basic small hotels or hope a local will give you floor space. Tourist agencies in Cuzco, realising the potential of this fiesta as a tourist attraction, are beginning to run buses specifically for the fiesta. If you go this way, you will probably be able to sleep on the bus.

Tres Cruces

About 45 km beyond Paucartambo is the famous jungle view at Tres Cruces. The sight of the mountains finally dropping away into the Amazon Basin is exceptionally beautiful and made all the more exciting by the sunrise phenomenon which occurs around the time of the winter solstice on 21 June. For some reason, the sunrise here tends to be optically distorted, causing double images, halos and unusual colours, particularly during May, June and July. (Other months are cloudy.) At this time of year, various adventure tour agencies advertise sunrise-watching trips to Tres Cruces. You can also take the thrice-weekly truck service to Paucartambo and ask around for a truck going on to Tres Cruces – Señor Cáceres in Paucartambo will reportedly arrange sunrise-watching trips. Some Inca ruins are within walking distance of Paucartambo – ask for directions in the village.

Manu National Park

This 180-hectare rainforest park is the biggest in Peru and one of the best places in South America to see a wide variety of wild-life. Some Indian groups continue to live here as they have for generations and UNESCO declared the area a Biosphere Reserve in 1977 and a World Natural Heritage Site in 1987. One reason the park is so successful in preserving such a large tract of virgin jungle is that it is remote and relatively inaccessible. In addition, it has not been exploited by rubber tappers, loggers or hunters, so wildlife is less wary and disturbed than in much of Peru's rainforest. There are park guards and conservation efforts are underway – the Asociación de Conservación para la Selva Sur (ACSS) (tel 236200), Avenida Sol 627-B, Office 305, Cuzco, accepts donations, raises funds by selling its jaguar poster (available in Cuzco), supports research and provides information. It is supported by Wildlife Conservation International of the New York Zoological Society.

Visiting the national park on your own requires a great deal of time, self-sufficiency, money and an ability to travel in difficult conditions. It is easier and more worthwhile to go with an organised group. As it costs about the same to hire a dugout canoe for a week for one person as it does for six, group travel makes sense. If you want to set up a trip in advance, contact an adventure travel company in the USA, such as Wilderness Travel (1-800-247-6700), 801 Allston Way, Berkeley CA 94710, USA. Various agencies in Cuzco also organise trips to the park. The best time to go is during the dry season from June to October; the park may be inaccessible or closed during the rainy months. Agencies will take care of all permits, transport, accommodation, food, guides and other arrangements. Most visits to the park are for at least 7 days.

Two Cuzco tour operators have been recommended: Manu Nature Tours (tel 234793) at Avenida Sol 627-B, Office 401, Cuzco, directed by Boris Gómez, and Expediciones Manu at Procuradores 372, Cuzco, directed by Hugo Pepper and Mario Ortiz. Manu Nature Tours flies into the park in light aircraft and operates a small lodge by a lake in the park itself. There are trails nearby and scientists often base their research at the lodge. Bilingual naturalist/ecologist guides are provided. The tours cost roughly $150 per person per day, but substantially cheaper tours can be arranged if you're prepared to spend time driving and boating into the park instead of flying, if you want to camp rather than stay in the lodge, or if you would prefer a Spanish-speaking boatman to a bilingual naturalist guide. (The guide is recommended for a better appreciation of the rainforest.) Talk to Boris Gómez for more information on the various alternatives and prices.

Expediciones Manu is cheaper, but reliable, and uses bus and canoe to enter the park. Their guides are not necessarily bilingual ecologists and you'll still end up paying around $70 per person per day.

Several general adventure tour companies such as Mayuc in Cuzco arrange trips to Manu, sometimes acting as brokers for one of the two agencies already mentioned in this section. I've heard of tours being offered for as little as $50 per person per day and posters advertising Manu departures are often seen around Cuzco during the dry season. Shop around and don't automatically assume that the cheapest deal is the best one.

If you want to form your own expedition, I suggest you read *South America: River Trips*, Vol 1 by G Bradt and Vol 2 by T & M Jordan, both published by Bradt Publications and both containing sections on Manu, though the information is now somewhat outdated. The South American Explorers Club in Lima can help members obtain up-to-date information.

The park is divided into the Reserve Zone and the Park Zone but there is no real difference between the rainforest in the two areas. Visitors are only permitted to enter the Reserve Zone. Scientists can enter both zones. Officially, you need a permit from the national park office at Calle Heladeros 157, Office 34, Cuzco. They can give you current information and issue a permit to visit the park, though permits are not given automatically. I have heard that solo travellers may find it difficult to get a permit and that it's better to go in a recognised group.

Once you have your permit, obtain all your supplies in Cuzco as camping gear is not available in the park and fruit is the only food that can be bought.

The first stage of the journey involves taking a cargo truck from Cuzco via Paucartambo and Pilcopata to Shintuyo. Trucks along the one-way road leave on Monday, Wednesday, Friday and Sunday from Avenida Pachacutec, near the Transportes Quincemil office, or from the nearby Calle Huarorupata (the extension of Calle Manco Capac). The trip can take up to 2 days in the dry season and is often broken at Pilcopata. The fare is about $3. Breakdowns, flat tyres, extreme overcrowding and delays are frequent and, during the rainy season (and even in the dry), vehicles slide off the road. It is safer, more comfortable and more reliable to take the costlier tourist buses offered by the Cuzco tour operators mentioned earlier. Alternatively, a group of you could hire a private truck but expect to pay about $400. Truck drivers Raoul Pilaris and Armundo Carasco have been recommended.

About 40 km before Shintuyo is the village of Atalaya. There are two lodges near here, both on the Río Alto Madre de Dios and both charging about $20 per night. The *Amazonia Lodge* is in an old hacienda in the foothills of the Andes and there are trails nearby. The *Quinta Erika* is run by a German woman who has lived in the jungle for nearly 40 years.

The village of Salvación, about 10 km closer to Shintuyo, has a park office and a couple of basic hotels. Ask around here for boats into the park – the park personnel may know of any trips planned for the near future and, if you're lucky, you might be able to join them.

Shintuyo is closer to the park but has fewer hotel facilities. You can arrange to camp at the mission station by talking to the priest. I have heard reports of some adventurers who claim they had a small balsa raft built here for about $10 – the priest can introduce you to a reliable carpenter. I've not been to Shintuyo myself but a friend who knows the area well and has some river-running experience tells me that the Río Alto Madre de Dios is a mean river and you'd kill yourself going down it on a balsa raft.

Most people hire a boat in Shintuyo, usually for a week; otherwise, you get dropped off at the park entrance and left to camp in one place. It's much better to have a boat available to get you around the park. Expect to pay about $350 for a week, plus about $100 for petrol. You might have to wait several days for a boat to become available unless you've made advance arrangements through the operators in Cuzco; they'll rent you a boat and boatman even if you don't take a full tour.

The boat journey down the Río Alto Madre de Dios to its junction with the Manu River takes a day. The airstrip at this river junction, known as Boca Manu, is often the starting point for commercial trips into the park, eliminating the time-consuming truck and boat approach. There are no regular air services and a light plane must be chartered from Cuzco or, possibly, Puerto Maldonado.

If you turn right (south-east) at Boca Manu and continue down the fairly busy Madre de Dios past gold-panning areas to Puerto Maldonado, you won't see much wildlife. This takes 2 to 3 days and may cost as little as $10 if you can find a boat heading that way.

The virgin jungle of the park lies up the Manu River north-west of Boca Manu. At the Romero guard post, about an hour from Boca Manu, you pay a park entrance fee of $10 per person. Near here are a few trails. A further 6 hours upstream is Cocha Salvador, one of the largest and most beautiful lakes in the park, where there are camping and hiking possibilities. Other areas further into the park also have trails and camping. If you're patient, wildlife can be seen in most areas. This is not wide-open habitat like the African plains. The thick vegetation will obscure many animals and a skilled guide is very useful in helping you to see them.

However you do it, an expedition to Manu Park will not be cheap and, unless you go on a guided tour, the park is not easy to reach. It is, however, the best place in Peru to see jungle habitat and wildlife. Allow at least 1 week for the trip.

If you want cheaper or shorter alternatives, one of the lodges in the Puerto Maldonado area is the best choice. The Tambopata Wildlife Reserve is a good place to go.

The Road to Puerto Maldonado

This road is almost 500 km long and takes about 2½ days to travel in the dry season. Trucks leave daily from Transportes Quince Mil in Cuzco. Fares to Puerto Maldonado are about $10; the cheapest places are in the back and the more expensive ones are in the cab with the driver. Most tourists travel on the daily flight from Cuzco to Puerto Maldonado, but the difficult, tiring trip by road is a good chance to see the beautiful scenery of the Andes' eastern slopes.

The road follows the south-eastern route to Puno until it reaches Urcos, where the dirt road to Puerto Maldonado begins. About 125 km and 7 hours from Cuzco, you come to the highland town of Ocongate which has a couple of basic hotels. About an hour's drive beyond Ocongate is the village of Tinqui (you can sleep in the school). It is the starting point for a 1-week hike encircling Ausangate, the highest mountain in southern Peru at 6384 metres. (See Hilary Bradt's *Backpacking & Trekking in Peru & Bolivia*.)

Now, the road begins to drop steadily. The next town of any size is Quince Mil, 240 km from Cuzco and the halfway point. The area is a gold-mining centre and the hotel here is often full. You are now less than 1000 metres above sea level, still in the Department of Cuzco.

The road drops a further 100 km into the jungle before reaching the flatlands, where it levels out for the last 140 km into Puerto Maldonado. (See also the Amazon Basin chapter.)

QUILLABAMBA

Quillabamba lies on the Urubamba River at the end of the railway line from Cuzco and Machu Picchu. At only 950 metres above sea level, it is hot and humid and can properly be called a jungle town, the only one in Peru reached by train. Because it is so accessible and close to Cuzco, it is a worthwhile destination for travellers wanting a glimpse of the high jungle. The town itself is quiet and pleasant, if not particularly interesting, and can be used as a base for trips deeper into the jungle.

Places to Stay

There are over a dozen hotels from which to choose, all cheap and some quite good. The *Hostal Comercio* charges 50c or 60c per person, depending on whether you have a (rather dank) private bathroom. Similarly priced are the basic *Hostal Progreso* (no singles), *Hostal San Antonio* (dormitory accommodation), *Hostal San Martín* (dirty), *Hostal Thomas*, *Hostal Urusayhua* and *Alojamiento Dos de Mayo*, all with cold-water communal bathrooms only. The *Hostal Convención* charges $1/1.30 for singles/doubles. It has a courtyard and some rooms overlooking the Plaza de Armas.

Clean, cheap and recommended, the *Hostal Alto Urubamba* charges $1.10/1.80 for singles/doubles with shared bath, $1.40/2.25 with private bath. The pleasant *Hostal Cuzco* is also clean but has an erratic water supply. Rooms with private bath cost $1.70/2.30 – only cold water is available but Quillabamba is hot enough to manage quite well without hot showers.

The *Hostal Quillabamba* is recommended for its clean rooms and rooftop restaurant. The *Hostal Lira* is also good, though its ground-floor restaurant is less attractive. Both hotels have hot water and charge about $2/3 for singles/doubles with private bath.

The newest and best hotel in town is the *Hostal Don Carlos*, where singles/doubles with private bath and hot water cost $3/4.

Places to Eat

The rooftop restaurant at the *Hostal Quillabamba* has good views and offers adequate meals for about $1, but the service is slow. The *Hostal Lira* has a reasonable restaurant and the clean *El Rancho Restaurant* serves good grilled chicken. Several *heladerías*, or ice-cream parlours, on the Plaza de Armas serve light refreshments.

Getting There & Away

Bus & Truck Trucks for Cuzco leave from Avenida Lima or the market on an irregular basis. Ask around. The journey takes roughly 15 hours and costs about $2. This rough route, high over the spectacular pass of Abra de Malaga, is a favourite road for ornithologists, who see many different species of birds as the ecological zones change from subtropical to subglacial.

Pick-up trucks (there is also one bus) leave every morning from the market for the village of Kiteni, further into the jungle. The 6-hour trip costs $2.

A correspondent suggests asking around the plaza for trucks to Huancalle (a long, bumpy ride). At Vilcabamba, a 3-hour walk from Huancalle (a road is planned), ask for directions or hire a guide for the 3 to 5-day hike to the ruins of Espiritu Pampa, where there are three or four families. (More details are found in Frost's *Exploring Cuzco*.)

Train Two parallel bridges link the train station with the town. The pedestrian bridge leads to a steep flight of stairs which takes you to the bottom of town. If you don't feel like climbing 172 steps, take a colectivo truck or shared taxi from the station to the market place for about 25c.

The ticket office at the train station is open from 4.30 to 5.40 am, noon to 2.15 pm and 8.30 to 10.15 pm daily, except Sunday when it's only open at night. You can buy train tickets a day in advance but autovagon tickets are sold only on the morning of departure, though you can buy tickets on Saturday for the Sunday autovagon. Get your autovagon tickets as early as possible because, despite assurances that it's never sold out, it sometimes is, especially at weekends.

The autovagon leaves at 5.15 am and takes about 2 hours to Aguas Calientes (for Machu Picchu) and 5¼ hours to Cuzco. Fares are $2

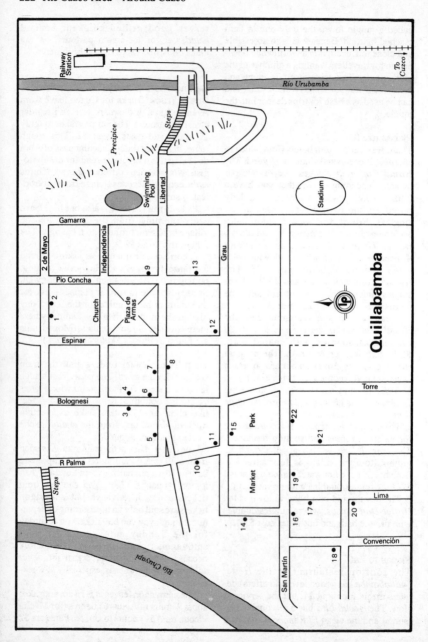

1	Hostal Alojamiento Dos de Mayo
2	Hostal Alto Urubamba
3	ENTEL
4	Cinema
5	Hostal Comercio
6	El Rancho Restaurant
7	Hostal Don Carlos
8	Banco de Crédito
9	Hostal Convención
10	Hostal Thomas
11	Trucks & Buses to Kiteni
12	Banco de Los Andes
13	Hostal San Antonio
14	Hostal Quillabamba
15	Taxis
16	Hostal San Martín
17	Hostal Urusayhua
18	Hostal Lira
19	Hostal Progreso
20	Trucks to Cuzco
21	Hostal Cuzco
22	Town Hall (Municipalidad)

and $6 respectively. This is an express train which does not stop at Puentes Ruinas, the closest station to Machu Picchu. Vendors are not allowed on board and all that is available is warm coke, so bring your own food.

The local trains leave at 5.30 am and 2 pm, stop at all stations and take about 3 hours to Machu Picchu ($1) and 7½ hours to Cuzco ($3). Second class is very crowded but tickets are about 20% cheaper.

KITENI & BEYOND

Kiteni is the end of the road as far as this section of the jungle is concerned. This small jungle town has one cheap, basic hotel.

It is possible to continue by river but, as food and accommodation are often nonexistent, you're advised to be self-sufficient. The first major landmark is the Pongo de Manique, a steep-walled canyon on the Urubamba River. There is a basic hotel in the area. The canyon is dangerous and, in the rainy season (from November to May), the water is too high for boats to go through it. Boats as far as the pongo can occasionally be found, on inquiry, in Kiteni. The 2-day round trip costs about $20. Expect to camp.

During the dry season, a few boats continue through the pongo – the river after the canyon is relatively calm, though there are still some rapids. There are few settlements until you reach the oil town of Sapahua, 2 to 4 days beyond the pongo. (One reader paid $35 for a boat to Sapahua in 1987, but the dollar was very strong against the inti that year. Expect to pay more if you can find a boat.) There is basic food and accommodation here and the American and British oil workers are often interested in a new face. From Sapahua, there are flights to Satipo with SASA and some flights to Lima for the oil workers. These are not cheap.

Sometimes, it is possible to continue down the Urubamba to the village of Atalaya 2 or 3 days away. A member of the South American Explorer's Club says that the trip to Atalaya is difficult on public transport because there are few boats between the pongo and Sapahua. Instead, you could build (or have someone else build) a balsa raft after passing the Pongo de Manique (which is too dangerous to raft). En route are the communities of San Iratio (the last place before the pongo), Timpia (where you can have a raft built), Choquorian, Camisea, Liringeti, Miaria, Sapahua, Boteo Pose, Sepal, Puerto Ira and Atalaya. Basic food and accommodation can be obtained from friendly locals in these villages. In return, they often prefer useful gifts to money – flashlights and batteries, fish hooks and lines or basic medicines are good. In Atalaya, there are three simple hotels and an airstrip with SASA air connections to Satipo. Boats can be found to continue down the river, now the Ucayali, as far as Pucallpa (about 1 week, $10), though this is currently not a safe destination. The route from Kiteni onwards is obviously little travelled and adventurous, especially beyond the Pongo de Manique, but it is possible for experienced and self-sufficient travellers.

CUZCO TO THE COAST BY ROAD

Until recently, most buses between Cuzco and Lima went via Limatambo, Abancay, Chalhuanca, Puquio, Pampas Galeras and Nazca, a route frequently taken by budget travellers who didn't want to fly and who wanted to see some of the spectacular scenery as the road drops from the Andes to the desert coast. Unfortunately, Sendero Luminoso guerilla activity has made the route dangerous and few bus companies go this way at present, most going via Arequipa instead. When the major companies (such as Ormeño and Cruz del Sur) start using this route again, it will be a good indication that the region is returning to normal. Meanwhile, the trip between Abancay and Puquio is definitely not recommended. (It's OK to go as far as Mollepata, but ask locally for updates.) Information in this section is based on the edition of this book prepared in 1987 when the route was safe.

LIMATAMBO

The infrequently visited little village of Limatambo is 80 km west of Cuzco by road. Most people do no more than pass through Limatambo on the bus, which is a shame because it's worth a visit.

The village is named after the small, well-made Inca ruin of Rimactambo, or 'speaker's inn'. The site, better known as Tarahuasi after the hacienda in whose grounds it is located, is about 2 km from Limatambo on the road towards Cuzco and easy to find. It is better constructed than many other *tambos* because it was probably used as a ceremonial centre as well as a resting place for the Inca *chasquis* or 'runners' who carried messages from one part of the empire to another. For those interested in ruins, the exceptional polygonal retaining wall with its 12 man-sized niches is, in itself, worth the trip.

There is a basic and inexpensive hostal in Limatambo, as well as a swimming pool which is popular with the locals. The village is in pretty, mountainous countryside at the upper end of the valley of a headwater tributary of the Apurimac River and is a retreat for Cuzco citizens wanting a weekend away from the city.

You can get to Limatambo from Cuzco on the bus to Abancay or on the truck to Mollepata.

MOLLEPATA

The old village of Mollepata is a few km off the main Cuzco to Abancay road and a couple of hours beyond Limatambo. It is the starting point for a trek to Santa Teresa, beyond Machu Picchu, and a longer alternate start to the Inca Trail. Directions for both hikes are given in Hilary Bradt's *Backpacking & Trekking in Peru & Bolivia*. You can also hire an *arriero*, or muleteer, in Santa Teresa for the trek – they know the trails. Allow about 5 days to Santa Teresa and 4 days to Huayllabamba on the Inca Trail. Mules are not allowed on the Inca Trail so, after Huayllabamba, you'll have to carry your own gear or hire porters (you can do this at Huayllabamba).

Getting to Mollepata is straightforward if not particularly comfortable. Trucks leave Cuzco from the end of Calle Arcopata early every morning, usually about 7 am. The dusty but scenic drive takes 5 hours. Although you can buy basic supplies in Mollepata, it's best to bring everything from Cuzco. There is no hotel; you can camp if you ask around but don't leave belongings unattended. If you plan to carry your own gear and dispense with mule drivers and guides, there's no need to stay.

ABANCAY

This sleepy rural town is the capital of the Andean Department of Apurimac, one of the least-explored departments in the Peruvian Andes. It is an 8-hour drive west of Cuzco and 2377 metres above sea level. Despite its status as a departmental capital and the main town between Cuzco and the coast, Abancay has no scheduled air service and the place has a forlorn, forgotten air. Some travellers use it as a resting place on the long, tiring bus journey between Cuzco and the coast or Cuzco and Ayacucho, but since 1989, the town is rarely visited because of guerilla problems.

Things to See

Abancay is not totally devoid of interest. Its particularly colourful carnival, held in the week before Lent, is a chance to see Andean

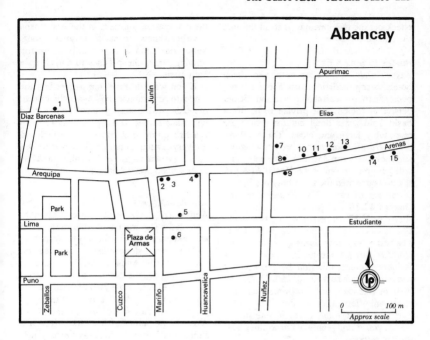

1   Hotel de Turistas
2   Post Office
3   Cine Nilo
4   Market
5   Municipalidad & Cine Municipal
6   Cathedral
7   Hostal Abancay
8   Minibuses to Cuzco
9   Señor de Huanca (Bus)
10 Hotel Gran
11 Morales (Bus)
12 Hostal & Restaurant El Misti
13 Hidalgo (Bus)
14 Ormeño (Bus)
15 Hostal Luramen

festival celebrations uncluttered by the trappings of international tourism and includes a nationally acclaimed folk-dancing competition. Hotels tend to fill early, so get there a couple of days before the carnival gets

underway. Another festival is held on 3 November, Abancay Day.

Those with an interest in Inca ruins may want to visit the Hacienda of Saihuite, 45 km from Abancay on the main road towards Cuzco, near the turn-off to Huanipaca and Cachora. Here, you'll find several large, carved boulders, the Stones of Saihuite. These intricately decorated stones are similar to the more commonly visited carved rock at Qenko, near Cuzco, but are considered more elaborate.

During the dry season (June to October), walkers and climbers may want to take advantage of the best weather to head for the sometimes snowcapped peak of Ampoy, about 10 km north-north-west of the town and approximately 5000 metres high. For the rest of the year the weather tends to be wet, especially during the first 4 months of the year.

Travellers passing through town can

check out the two cinemas or stroll through the plazas.

Places to Stay & Eat

At the *Hotel Gran*, the best of the very cheap hotels, accommodation costs about 50c per person in rooms with shared bath and 75c per person in rooms with private bath. It's a basic, cold-water hotel but the rooms are reasonably large and clean. The similarly priced *Hostal Abancay* has broken windows and looks very run down. A few cents more will get you a room at the *Hostal El Misti*. It's no better then the Gran but does have a restaurant of sorts. The *Hostal Luramen* charges $1.30 per person in rooms with shared bath, $2 per person with private bath. The place is clean and hot water is available. The best hotel in town is the government-run *Hotel de Turistas*, located in a pleasant, old-fashioned country mansion. Singles/doubles with shared bath cost $3.50/5.50, $5.75/7.50 with private bath and hot water, and the restaurant offers meals for about $3.

If you don't want to eat in one of the hotels, you'll find plenty of cheap cafés near the bus stations.

Getting There & Away

At the time of writing, transport was limited because of terrorism but, when the region is again safe to travel in, the following information will be useful.

The easiest town to reach is, not surprisingly, Cuzco. There are several minibuses every day. These are cramped, but faster than ordinary buses, and leave from the corner of Nuñez and Arenas. The 6-hour trip costs about $5.25. You could also try these minibuses for a trip to Saihuite.

The bus companies have cheaper departures to Cuzco and Lima (via Nazca) every 2 days. It is one of the inexplicable lunacies of Peruvian bus travel that all buses to the coast leave within hours of one another and you can be stuck for 2 days before the next buses leave. Most companies marked on the map on Calle Arenas serve Cuzco ($4, 8 hours), Nazca ($13, 26 hours) and Lima ($15, 34 hours). Times given are average for

the dry season; journeys in the wet season have been known to take three times as long. Señor de Huanca is the only company running large, cheap buses to Cuzco on a daily basis.

If you want to travel north-west into the Andes to Andahuaylas and Ayacucho instead of heading to the coast, you will be rewarded with magnificent wild scenery. However, it is a difficult route and transport is rough and not very regular. Señor de Huanca provides buses to Andahuaylas and Hidalgo has a bus to Ayacucho every 2 days or so.

ANDAHUAYLAS

Andahuaylas, the second most important town in the Department of Apurimac, is 135 km west of Abancay on the way to Ayacucho. As I have never stopped there, I can't tell you much about it. Andahuaylas does have an airport but, despite rumours to the contrary, there have been no scheduled flights for some years. The town's best hotel is the government-run *Hotel de Turistas* on Avenida Lozano Carrillo. Its prices are similar to those at the Abancay tourist hotel. There are also some cheaper options. This is a very quiet little town and a good place to break your journey if your schedule is relaxed and you're fed up with being bounced around on the atrociously surfaced mountain roads. Andahuaylas' main attraction, the beautiful mountain lake of Pacucha, is 10 km from town and accessible by car.

CHALHUANCA

Chalhuanca has a basic hotel and a restaurant which is often used as a meal stop on the Cuzco to Nazca run. It is 120 km south-west of Abancay.

PUQUIO

This village, 189 km beyond Chalhuanca, also has a basic hotel and restaurant. For the last 50 km before Puquio, the road traverses an incredibly wild-looking area of desolate, lake-studded countryside that is worth staying awake for.

PAMPAS GALERAS

About 65 km beyond Puquio and 90 km before Nazca, the road passes through the vicuña sanctuary of Pampas Galeras. Here, you'll see herds of vicuña from the bus and, if you're self-sufficient, you can get off and camp. Most people visit Pampas Galeras Reserve from Nazca.

The Central Highlands

The central Peruvian Andes is one of the least visited and most neglected areas of Peru. The harsh mountain terrain has made ground communications especially difficult and the region also suffers from a lack of air services. Huancayo, for example, is both the capital of the Department of Junín and Peru's fifth largest city with a population of some 350,000 yet, like two of the area's other departmental capitals (Huancavelica and Cerro de Pasco), it lacks a commercial airport. The departmental capital of Ayacucho, founded in 1540, received its first permanent public telephone link with the outside world in 1964, at a time when there were still only a few dozen vehicles servicing the city. The people of the central Andes are mainly rural, involved in subsistence agriculture and among the poorest in Peru.

It was in this environment of isolation and poverty that the Sendero Luminoso, or 'Shining Path', Peru's major terrorist organisation, emerged in the 1960s and grew in the 1970s. The violent activities of the Sendero escalated dramatically in the 1980s and headlines all over the world proclaimed Peru's internal unrest. Following reports of atrocities and mass murders in the central Peruvian highlands, committed not only by the terrorists but also by government troops during incompetent attempts to subdue the insurgents, tourism declined from the high levels of the late '70s. During 1983 and 1984, the departments of Ayacucho, Huancavelica and Apurímac were almost completely deserted by tourists and Peruvian authorities strongly discouraged travellers from visiting them.

By 1985, however, things had quietened down considerably and tourism once again returned to these areas, albeit very slowly. I spent several weeks travelling here then and found little external evidence of the Sendero. Unfortunately, this situation did not last and, in the late 1980s, much of the area was again under Sendero control. Places covered in the first section of this chapter, up to and including Huancayo, are still OK to visit; travel to the rest, including Huancavelica, Ayacucho, Cerro de Pasco, Huánuco, Tingo María and associated smaller towns, is not safe at this time, especially overland. Nevertheless, these sections remain in this edition in the hope that safe travel to the region will again become possible. Ask locally before attempting to visit the towns in this chapter. I found that the tourist information office in Lima could give an accurate idea of whether or not the region was considered safe for travellers.

When I visited here in the mid-1980s, I found delightful, friendly colonial towns which were among the least spoilt in the entire Andean chain. The travel itself was exciting too, not only because of the magnificent mountain views but also because it involved a certain amount of effort. The region still has more communications problems than most other areas of Peru and traversing the bad roads is a minor challenge.

Inca pot showing bound prisoner

The Central Highlands is certainly the area of Peru that has received the most negative publicity because of recent terrorist activities. The extensive area north of Huancavelica and Ayacucho is not as prone to terrorist-related problems and is also remote and infrequently visited. This includes the Department of Junín with its interesting handicrafts, as seen at Huancayo's weekly Sunday market. Many of the nearby villages are worth visiting to see the handicrafts being made. North of Huancayo are many little-known but worthwhile attractions: the fabulous Franciscan monastery of Ocopa, the private astronomical observatory in Tarma, the bird life of the Lake of Junín and magnificent scenery everywhere. If you want to travel to a lesser-known part of Peru, read on.

LA OROYA

The highland industrial town of La Oroya, population 35,000, proudly calls itself 'the metallurgical capital of Peru'. Unless you're interested in metallurgy – which, in La Oroya, translates into the huge, state-run, CENTROMIN smelter and refinery with its attendant slag heaps – you'll not want to linger in this cold, unattractive place. However, because La Oroya is a major junction, most travellers to central Peru's interior at least pass through the town.

La Oroya is over 3700 metres above sea level; the railway line which links La Oroya with Lima 187 km away passes through the station of La Galera. At 4781 metres above sea level, La Galera is the world's highest station on a standard-gauge track. On the trip from Lima, oxygen is available in 1st class, and if you're not yet acclimatised, you may be glad to know it's there – even sitting quietly in your seat is a breathless experience. During the second half of the trip, the scenery is stark and bare, awesome rather than pretty, and the snow often comes to below 5000 metres. You'll sometimes see llama and alpaca, but unfortunately, La Oroya's several mining operations tarnish the landscape's natural splendour.

As you can imagine, the huge vertical change in such a relatively short length of track makes this stretch of railway line one of the most exciting in the world for train enthusiasts (not to mention ordinary travellers). The *South American Handbook* claims that, along its whole length, the railway traverses 66 tunnels, 59 bridges and 22 zigzags. I lost count but the figures seem about right. (For fares and schedules, see the Lima section.)

From La Oroya, the railway continues north beyond Cerro de Pasco to Goyllarisquizga mine and south to Huancayo, where you can connect with the train to Huancavelica. The connection for the northern section to Cerro de Pasco leaves before the arrival of the train from Lima. Most travellers from Lima take the train direct to Huancayo in a day.

La Oroya is also linked with Lima by road. From La Oroya, roads lead in all directions: north to Cerro de Pasco and Huánuco (and then down into the northern jungle), east to Tarma (and down into the central jungle), south to Huancayo, Huancavelica and Ayacucho (and on to Cuzco), and west to Lima. All these central highland towns are described in this chapter.

Information

For obvious reasons, La Oroya is a place to travel through, not to. It is possible to reach several other central highland towns from Lima in a day and, therefore, few travellers stop here. If you should be stranded, you'll find a few basic hotels and restaurants near the train station. The *Hostal San Martín*, 2 or 3 km out of the town centre towards Lima, is said to be marginally better than the places by the station. Buses leave from near the train station.

TARMA

This small town on the eastern slopes of the Andes, 60 km east of La Oroya, is known locally as 'the pearl of the Andes'. Tarma is 3050 metres above sea level and about the same size as La Oroya, but it's a much more pleasant town and offers better places to stay.

Tarma has a long history. It is named after

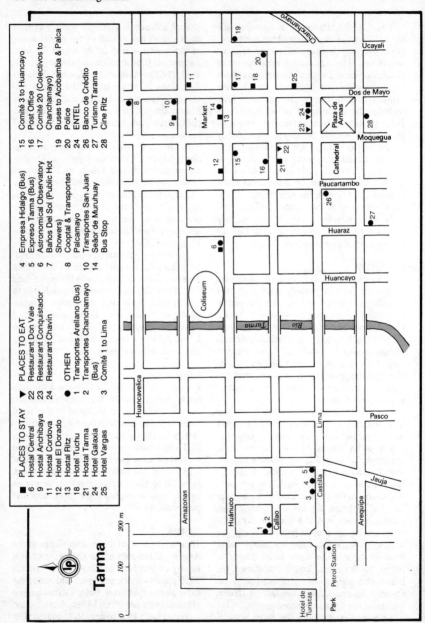

Tarma

PLACES TO STAY	
■ 6	Hostal Central
9	Hostal Anchibaya
11	Hostal Cordova
12	Hotel El Dorado
13	Hostal Ritz
18	Hotel Tuchu
21	Hostal Tarma
24	Hotel Galaxia
25	Hotel Vargas

PLACES TO EAT	
▼ 22	Restaurant Don Vale
23	Restaurant Conquistador
24	Restaurant Chavín

OTHER	
● 1	Transportes Arellano (Bus)
2	Transportes Chanchamayo (Bus)
3	Comité 1 to Lima
4	Empresa Hidalgo (Bus)
5	Expreso Tarma (Bus)
6	Astronomical Observatory
7	Restaurant Chavín
7	Baños Del Sol (Public Hot Showers)
8	Cooptal & Transportes Palcamayo
10	Transportes San Juan
14	Señor de Muruhuay Bus Stop
15	Comité 3 to Huancayo
16	Post Office
17	Comité 20 (Colectivos to Chanchamayo)
19	Buses to Acobamba & Palca
20	Police
24	ENTEL
26	Banco de Crédito
27	Turismo Tarama
28	Cine Ritz

the Tarama people, who lived in this area before the arrival of the Incas. The overgrown Inca and pre-Inca ruins to be found in the hills and mountains surrounding the town are not well known and there's plenty of scope for adventurers to discover ruins on the nearby peaks. The town seen today was founded by the Spanish soon after the conquest (the exact date is uncertain – I've read 1534, 1538 and 1545). Nothing remains of the early colonial era but there are a number of attractive 19th and early 20th century houses with white walls and red-tiled roofs.

Information

The FOPTUR tourist office (tel 2945) is at Dos de Mayo 775.

The Turismo Tarama travel agency (tel 2286) doubles as an information centre and can provide local guides. The agency has produced a very useful and informative booklet, *Folleto Turistico de la Provincia de Tarma* by Rafael Cárdenas Santa María, which costs about $1. Turismo Tarama is at Huaraz 537 and is open from 8.30 am to 12.30 pm and 2.30 to 5.30 pm daily, except Sunday. Señor Cárdenas is often there to answer questions.

Things to See

The big attraction of the year is undoubtedly Easter. Many processions are held during Holy Week, including several candle-lit ones after dark. They culminate on the morning of Easter Sunday with a marvellous procession to the cathedral along a beautiful route which is entirely carpeted with flower petals.

The annual Fiesta of El Señor de Los Milagros, or 'the Lord of the Miracles', takes place in late October; 18, 28 and 29 October are the principal feast days. (No, I don't know why there's a 10-day gap.) This is another good opportunity to see processions marching over beautiful flower-petal carpets.

Other fiestas include Tarma Week near the end of July and San Sebastián on 20 January.

Also worth visiting is the small Astronomical Observatory run by the owner of the Hostal Central. Tarma is high in the mountains and the clear nights of June, July and August provide some good opportunities for stargazing. The owner was away when I visited Tarma, so I didn't get a chance to use the observatory – I'd welcome any first-hand reports.

The cathedral is modern (built in 1965) and is of interest because it contains the remains of Peruvian president, Manuel A Odría. He was born in Tarma and organised construction of the cathedral during his presidency. The clock in the clock tower dates from 1862.

Several nearby excursions are described at the end of the Tarma section. These include visits to the religious shrine of Señor de Muruhuay (9 km from Tarma), the cave of Guagapo (33 km), and the weaving village of San Pedro de Cajas (50 km).

Places to Stay – bottom end

At 75c/$1.40 for singles/doubles, the basic *Hostal Ritz* on the market is one of the cheapest places, though the outside rooms are noisy. The communal showers have cold water. The nearby *Hostal Anchibaya* is similar, while the dingy-looking *Hostal Tarma* charges 90c per person. The *Hostal Cordova* doesn't look much better; it charges $1.20/1.75 for singles/doubles, plus an extra 20c for rooms with private bath. If you're staying in a cold-water cheapie, you can use the hot public showers at *Baños del Sol*, half a block from the market.

The old but adequate *Hostal Central* is interesting because the owner has an astronomical observatory in the hotel. Singles/doubles cost $1.30/1.90, plus about 25c per person extra for rooms with private bath. Hot water is available occasionally.

Among the better cheap hotels is the *Hotel Tuchu*, which charges $2/3.10 for singles/doubles with private bath and hot water in the morning. The *Hotel Vargas* has spacious rooms and some hard beds if you're fed up with soft and sagging mattresses. Rooms with private bath and hot water in the morning cost $2.20/4. The similarly priced *Hotel El Dorado* has the same facilities and has been recommended by some travellers.

The best of the cheaper hotels is the clean *Hotel Galaxia* on the Plaza de Armas. Unfortunately, as it has only 16 rooms, it's often full. Singles/doubles are $3.25/5.25 and all rooms have private bath and hot water in the morning.

Places to Stay – middle

The town's best accommodation is the government-run *Hotel de Turistas*; you can make a reservation at ENTURPeru in Lima (tel 721928). Set in pleasant gardens at the west end of town, the hotel charges $5/8 for singles/doubles with communal bath, $9.50/13.50 with private bath. Prices include continental breakfast.

Places to Eat

Plenty of cheap restaurants line Avenida Lima (which becomes Avenida Castilla in the west end of town). The *Restaurant Chavín* on the Plaza de Armas is good and the nearby *Conquistador* is acceptable and cheap. The best restaurant in town is the *Don Vale*. It's only open at meal times (11.30 am to 2.30 pm and 7 to 10.30 pm) and offers reasonable meals for about $1.

Getting There & Away

There are two areas of town from which transport leaves frequently: near the market and the western end of Avenida Castilla.

Along Avenida Castilla, Expreso Tarma buses leave hourly for La Oroya for $1.10. Three Comité 1 cars a day go to Lima; the trip costs $6 and takes 6 hours. Empresa Hidalgo has a slower and cheaper overnight bus to Lima and two buses a day to Huancayo ($1.40, 3 hours), while Transportes Arellano operates a daily night bus to Lima ($4). Transportes Chanchamayo runs a cheap but slow overnight truck to the lowland towns of La Merced and San Ramón (collectively known as Chanchamayo).

Transportes Chanchamayo buses from Lima to Chanchamayo pass through the market soon after dawn but are often already full. (Transportes Chanchamayo's Lima office is in the rough La Victoria area at Luna Pizarro 453, so take a taxi to and from the terminal.) The colectivo taxis of Comité 20 are the most convenient way to get to Chanchamayo. They leave from the market when they're full and charge $2.30 per passenger for the precipitous 2-hour descent to La Merced at about 600 metres. It's worth doing the trip just for the views. (In 1986, this road was closed for repair every day except Sunday and travellers could only leave Tarma for Chanchamayo before 6.30 am or after 5 pm. Repairs should be completed by the early 1990s but make local inquiries to find out whether the road is fully open.)

Getting Around

Several companies operate local bus services from near the market. Most of these go to Acobamba (to visit the shrine of El Señor de Muruhuay) and some continue to Palcamayo (to visit the famous Guagapo caves). Transport to San Pedro de Cajas is irregular and cannot be relied upon – ask around. The companies marked at 8, 14 and 19 on the Tarma map are local bus companies.

ACOBAMBA

The village of Acobamba, 9 km from Tarma, is famous for the religious sanctuary of El Señor de Muruhuay, visible on a small hill about 1½ km away.

The sanctuary is built around an image of Christ painted onto the rock. Historians claim that it was painted by a royalist officer after losing the Battle of Junín (a major battle of independence fought on 6 August 1824). Despite this, legends relating to the painting's miraculous appearance persist. The first building erected around the image was a roughly thatched hut. It was replaced in 1835 by a small chapel. The present sanctuary (the third) was inaugurated on 30 April 1972. It is a very modern building with an electronically controlled bell tower and is decorated with huge weavings from San Pedro de Cajas.

The colourful feast of El Señor de Muruhuay, held throughout May, has been celebrated annually since 1835. Apart from the religious services and processions, there are ample opportunities to sample local produce and to see people dressed in traditional clothes. Stalls sell chicha (corn beer) and cuy (roast guinea pig) but be wary unless your stomach is used to local food. There are dances, fireworks, very few gringos and no hotels – most visitors stay in nearby Tarma.

PALCAMAYO

This attractive village is 28 km from Tarma and serviced by several colectivos a day. From Palcamayo, you can visit the Gruta de Guagapo, a huge limestone cave in the hills about 4 km away. The Guagapo Cave has been the subject of various expeditions from all over the world. It is one of Peru's largest and best known caves and is officially protected as a National Speleological Area. Several other less well-known caves in the area would also be of interest to speleologists (those who study caves).

A full descent into the Guagapo Cave requires caving equipment and experience. It is well over 1 km long and contains waterfalls, squeezes and underwater sections, so although it is possible to enter the cave for a short distance, you soon need to wade. A local guide, Señor Modesto Castro, has explored the cave on numerous occasions and can provide you with ropes, lanterns, and so on. He lives in one of the two houses below the mouth of the cave and has a collection of photographs and newspaper clippings describing the exploration of the cave.

To get to the cave, ask in Palcamayo. You'll be shown a dirt road winding off into the hills – it's a pleasant 4-km walk. The cave has a large opening in the side of the mountain to the right of the road and Señor Castro's house is on the left-hand side of the road. Bottled drinks are available and prospective expeditions could camp.

The Palcamayo area is also known for the many little-explored Inca and pre-Inca ruins in the surrounding hills. Although they are not very interesting to the casual tourist, an adventurer equipped with camping gear could spend days wandering the hilltops looking for ruins.

SAN PEDRO DE CAJAS

The village of San Pedro de Cajas, high in the Andes at an altitude of 4040 metres, is known throughout Peru for the excellence of its unique tapestries, which are often exported. Made of stuffed rolls of wool (difficult to visualise until you actually see some), the tapestries can be bought from the weavers for less than you'd pay in Lima. However, as the village is not oriented to tourists, facilities are very limited and you'll need some elementary Spanish.

A bed at the basic hotel will cost under $1. Not surprisingly, there are no hot showers, but the people are friendly. You can eat at the basic restaurant or arrange simple meals at the hotel. Some weavings are available here; ask around if you want to see more. The village has no moneychanging facilities, so change as much money as you'll need before you get there.

Market day is every second Wednesday. It is a locally important livestock and produce market, not a craft market.

Getting There & Away

Catching a bus from Tarma to Palcamayo is easy enough but buses continuing on to San Pedro are infrequent. You can walk or hope to hitch a ride along the 16-km dirt road from Palcamayo to San Pedro, past the Guagapo Cave. The road climbs most of the way to San Pedro, which is about 800 metres higher than Palcamayo.

If you want to travel all the way to San Pedro by bus, ask around the north side of the Tarma market early in the morning. A bus also leaves from the La Oroya train station at about 2 pm and there are daily buses from Junín.

JAUJA

The main road to Huancayo heads south-east from La Oroya along the Central Andes, passing several towns of importance along the way. The first of these is the historic town of Jauja which lies on a junction about 80 km south-east of La Oroya, 60 km south of Tarma and 40 km north of Huancayo.

Before the time of the Incas, this area was the home of an important Huanca Indian community and Huanca ruins can be seen on the skyline of the hill about 3 km south-east of Jauja. With many other little-known ruins, the area is ideal for adventurous walking. Jauja was Pizarro's first capital in Peru, though this honour was short lived. Some finely carved wooden altars in the main church are all that remains of the early colonial days.

About 4 km from Jauja is Laguna de Paca, a small, pleasant resort offering a hostal, a few rowing boats and fishing.

There is a colourful weekly market on Wednesday mornings.

Places to Stay & Eat

Most visitors to Jauja stay in Huancayo and travel to Jauja on one of the frequent buses linking the two towns. If you do choose to stay in Jauja, try the basic *Hotel Ganso de Oro* in front of the train station. Singles/doubles cost about $1.25/2 and hot water is sometimes available. This hotel tends to fill up by early afternoon. The *Hotel Santa Rosa*, on the corner of the main plaza by the church, is similarly priced but has no hot water. The best accommodation is offered by the government-run *Albergue de Paca*, by the lake of that name. Rooms here cost about $5/8, including continental breakfast; reservations can be made in Lima at ENTURPeru (tel 721928).

Jauja has several cheap, basic restaurants, the best of which are the ones in the *Ganso de Oro* and *Paca* hotels.

Getting There & Away

The train from Lima to Huancayo stops at Jauja. (See the Lima and Huancayo sections for further train information.)

ETURSA minibuses leave for Jauja from Amazonas 789 in Huancayo as soon as they are full – about twice an hour. They charge about 80c for the hour-long drive and are the most convenient way of getting to Jauja.

CONCEPCIÓN

South of Jauja, the road branches to follow both the west and east sides of the Mantara River valley to Huancayo. Travelling along the east side, you come to Concepción, a small village about halfway between Jauja and Huancayo. Although the village itself is of no more than passing interest, the nearby Convent of Santa Rosa de Ocopa is well worth a visit.

Set in a pleasant garden, this beautiful building was built by the Franciscans in the early 1700s as a training centre for their missionaries heading down into the jungle regions. During the years of missionary work, the friars built up an impressive collection which is on display in the convent museum. Exhibits include stuffed jungle wildlife, Indian artefacts, photographs of early missionary work, old maps, a fantastic library of some 20,000 volumes (many centuries old), a large collection of colonial religious art, mainly of the Cuzqueño school, and many other objects of interest.

The convent is open daily, except Tuesday, from 9 am to noon and 3 to 5 pm and entry is 60c (30c for students). Frequent colectivo taxis leave from the Concepción Plaza de Armas for Ocopa, about 5 km away.

Places to Stay & Eat

The best of the few basic hotels is the pleasant *Hotel Real* on the main plaza. It charges about $1 per person and has hot water in the morning. The *Hotel El Paisanito*, about a half block from the plaza, is cheaper and even more basic.

There are a couple of simple restaurants which tend to close soon after dark.

Getting There & Away

The easiest way to get to Concepción is to take one of the frequent colectivo taxis from Huancayo. These leave from the corner of Calixto and Ancash, behind the civic centre, and charge about 60c per passenger. A cheaper alternative is one of the buses which leave frequently from the corner of Calixto and Mantaro.

HUANCAYO

Huancayo is a modern city with a population of about 360,000. It lies on the flat Mantaro River valley, which is one of the most fertile in the Central Andes and supports a large rural population. At an altitude of 3260 metres and about 300 km from Lima, Huancayo is the capital of the central Andean Department of Junín. As the major commercial centre for the area, it is of great importance as a market town for people living in the many nearby villages. However, despite its size and departmental status, Huancayo is still relatively undeveloped.

The town itself is not particularly interesting but its weekly Sunday market, where both crafts and produce from the Mantaro River valley are sold, is famous among locals and travellers. In addition, Huancayo is a good base from which to visit the many interesting villages of the Mantaro Valley.

Information

Tourist Information The government-run Dirección de Turismo, in the civic centre on Calle Real, is open from 7 am to 2.15 pm Monday to Friday. The office is a great source of information about sightseeing in the Mantaro Valley, things to do and how to get around on public transport. The enthusiastic young woman to whom I spoke bemoaned the fact that Huancayo always seemed to be forgotten in the tourist scheme of things and then provided me with a huge list of places in the Mantaro Valley that I should see. To visit everything would take a couple of weeks, so I'll try to outline the best places in this section. Definitely visit this tourist bureau if you want to spend some time in the area and especially if you speak Spanish.

Money There are several casas de cambio on Avenida Real, between the civic centre and the Plaza de Armas, and these are usually the best places to change cash. You may find travellers' cheques difficult to change in casas de cambio but the banks marked on the Huancayo map (especially the Banco de Crédito) will often change them, albeit at a loss of up to 10%. Of course, the situation varies from year to year (and from month to month) and you may find that changing travellers' cheques is no problem.

Guests of most major hotels should be able to exchange US dollars (cash and travellers' cheques) at their hotel.

Warning Huancayo has gained quite a reputation for theft; the bus and train stations and the Sunday market are said to be crawling with thieves. I had no problem (admittedly, I'm used to this kind of situation) but many travellers have complained about bag snatching, luggage slashing and pickpocketing.

Things to See

Head north-east on Avenida Giraldez for a good view of the city. About 2 km from the town centre is Cerrito de la Libertad where, apart from the city view, there are snack bars and a playground. Two km further on, (there is a sign pointing to the right and an obvious path), you come to the eroded geological formations known as Torre Torre.

In the city itself, the cathedral and the Church of La Inmaculada are both modern and not particularly noteworthy. La Merced, on the first block of Avenida Real, is the most interesting church; although there isn't much to see, this is where the Peruvian Constitution was approved in 1839.

Places to Stay – bottom end

Many cheap hotels are to be found in the area between the Plaza de Armas and the train station to Lima. There are also a couple of cheap hotels in front of the train station to Huancavelica, but the central ones are better. The *Hotel Residencial Huancayo* charges $2 for a double room and has hot water in the communal showers all day. It is popular with travellers. Also popular, and deservedly so, is the small and simple *Hostal Dani*, where rooms are $1.40 per person. The English-speaking landlady is friendly and helpful and there is all-day hot water. The *Hostal Santo Domingo*, a couple of blocks from the Sunday craft market, is one of the cheapest

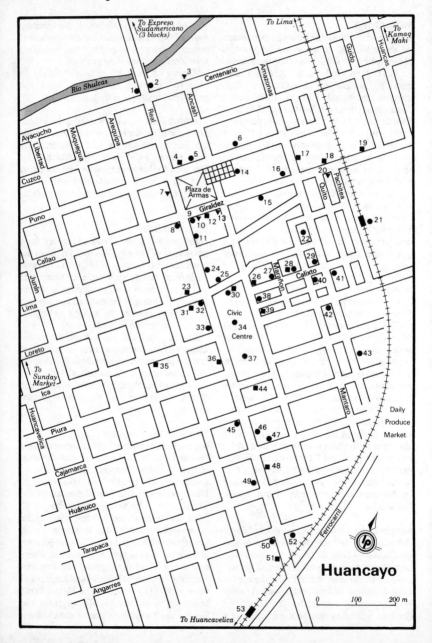

Huancayo

■ PLACES TO STAY

4	Hostal Palermo
10	Hotel Kiya
12	Hotel Santa Felicita
17	Residencial Baldeon
18	Hotel Residencial Huancayo
19	Hostal Dani
23	Hotel Centro
26	Hotel Prince
28	Hotel Pierola
30	Hotel El Inca
31	Hostal Roma
35	Hostal Santo Domingo
36	Hotel El Real & Hotel Torre Torre
39	Hotel de Turistas
44	Hotel El Dorado
48	Hotel Presidente
51	Percy's Hotel

▼ PLACES TO EAT

3	Flamingo Grill
7	Chifa Porvenir
10	Chifa Imperial
13	Restaurant Olimpico & Café Giraldez
20	Lalo's

● OTHER

1	Church of La Merced
2	Banco de la Nación
5	Cine Central
6	ETUCSA Bus & Duchas Tina
8	Banco de los Andes
9	Banco de Crédito
11	Casa de Cambio
14	Cathedral
15	Comités 3 & 30 to Tarma & Lima
16	Comité 1 to Tarma
21	Central Train Station to Lima
22	Plaza Amazonas (Buses to Chupaca & Pilcomayo)
24	Casa de Cambio
25	Empresa Hidalgo (Bus)
27	Arzapalo (Bus)
28	Expreso Huaytapallana Bus
29	Etursa Minibus to Jauja
30	Comité 22 to Lima
32	Comité 12 to Lima
33	ENTEL
34	Post Office
37	Municipalidad
38	Taxis to Concepción
40	Buses to San Jeronimo & Concepción
41	Buses to La Oroya
42	Church of La Inmaculada & Buses to Hualhuas & Cochas
43	Market
45	Banco de Crédito
46	Cines Real & Andino
47	M Caceres Bus to Lima
49	Alarcon Bus to Satipo
50	Transportes Ayacucho (Bus)
52	Molina Bus to Ayacucho
53	Train Station to Huancavelica

hotels in town. It's reasonably good, charges about $1 per person and sometimes has hot water.

Other cheap hotels include the *Hotel Prince*, which has basic singles/doubles with bath for $1.80/2.80 and some rooms with shared showers for about 50c less. Hot water is available early in the morning and in the evening. (Note that some of the rooms do not have windows.) The *Hotel Torre Torre*, near the civic centre, is basic but reasonably clean and has rather dark rooms with private hot showers for $2.20/3. There are also cheaper rooms with shared showers. Next door is the even simpler *Hotel El Real* at $1 per person.

The big *Hotel El Inca*, right opposite the Hidalgo bus station on Loreto, has doubles with bath and cold shower for $2.20. There

is hot water in the communal showers. It's adequate if you arrive late at night and can't be bothered looking further. A couple of blocks from the Plaza de Armas is the *Hotel Centro*. It has only cold water and doesn't seem very good; doubles cost $2. The *Residencial Baldeon* at $1.40 per person is better. It has hot water and sells good home-made pies.

Other cheapies include the *Hostal Palermo* on the Plaza de Armas and the *Hotel Pierola* and the *Hostal Roma*, neither of which look very good. At the overpriced *Percy's Hotel* near the Huancavelica train station, rooms with bath but no hot water cost $3 per person.

Slightly up-market, the modern *Hotel El Dorado* has clean, carpeted rooms with bath for $2.50 per person but a somewhat erratic hot-water supply. It's a block from the civic centre and has huge signs all over the 5th floor.

If you stay in a hotel with no hot water, have a hot shower at *Duchas Tina*, behind the cathedral. The public hot showers there are open all day.

Places to Stay – middle

Two clean, mid-range hotels on the Plaza de Armas, the *Santa Felicita* and the *Kiya*, charge $4.50/5.50 for singles/doubles with bath, hot water, soap and towel. Rooms also have telephones.

The centrally located *Hotel de Turistas* is a pleasant-looking old building with some wooden balconies. Singles/doubles with bath and hot water cost $7/10, including continental breakfast, and there are some cheaper rooms with shared bath. The hotel also offers a pleasant restaurant and bar. The more modern *Hotel Presidente* is similarly priced.

Places to Eat

Visitors should try the local speciality, Papa a la Huancaina, which consists of a boiled potato topped with a tasty white sauce of cheese, milk, hot pepper and butter. The whole concoction is served with an olive and eaten as a cold potato salad. Despite the hot pepper, it's not too spicy – in fact, I find that it has a distinctly peanut-like flavour.

There are several good restaurants on or near the Plaza de Armas. The best is the *Restaurant Olimpico* which has good meals for about $1, efficient service and a huge open kitchen allowing you to watch your food being prepared. The *Chifa Imperio* (in the Hotel Kiya) is also good for Chinese food and the *Café Giraldez* has been suggested for its fried chicken. If you're on a tight budget, try the *Chifa Porvenir* – it looks rather divey but serves reasonable meals for 50c. *Lalo's* is cheap and popular but the service can only be described as chaotic.

Entertainment

Huancayo offers little in the way of nightlife. You could try one of the three cinemas marked on the Huancayo map. The *Flamingo Grill* at Ancash and Ayacucho has some kind of peña late on Friday and Saturday nights – I've never been there. In the interests of researching this book, I did go to *El Molino Discotheque* at the north-west end of Calle Huancas, by the river. It's the usual basic dancing place (mainly disco records) with a dark bar. Despite the couples-only rule, the woman friend who accompanied me was hassled unmercifully. I don't like discos

much and just wanted to sit at the bar and talk to Andrea about local handicrafts – the local machos figured that if I didn't want to dance with my friend, one of them could take my place. (I offer this vignette as an illustration of what going out in Peru may involve.) The Flamingo is OK if you do like to disco or want to meet some local drinking/dancing companions. Other nightspots offering dancing are to be found at El Tambo, an area 1 or 2 km north-west of the city centre and a block or two to the right of Avenida Real. Taxi drivers know it.

Things to Buy

There are two main markets in Huancayo; the daily produce market and the Sunday craft market. The very colourful daily produce market is held along the railway tracks and in a nearby covered area (see the Huancayo map). At the meat section in the Mercado Modelo (as the indoor market is known), you can buy various Andean delicacies including fresh and dried frogs, guinea pigs, rabbits and chickens. Although it's a daily market, the most important day is Sunday which coincides with the weekly craft market.

The Sunday craft market occupies five or six blocks along Calle Huancavelica to the north-west of Ica. A good variety of weavings, sweaters and other textile goods, embroidered items, ceramics and wood carvings is sold here, as well as the carved gourds in which the area specialises. These are made in the nearby villages of Cochas Grande and Chico. The noncraft items range from cassette tapes to frilly underwear. You must bargain hard here to get the best prices; gourds are reputedly the best buy. This is definitely the place to watch your pockets, your wallet and your camera.

Kamaq Maki, which is Quechua for 'Creative Hand', is an excellent craft cooperative with a good selection of high-quality goods from the departments of Junín and Huancavelica. Kamaq Maki is a cooperative of several hundred local craftspeople who preserve traditional techniques and designs in their work. (They consider themselves to be farmers first and craftspeople second which, in itself, is a traditional arrangement.) The quality of goods is high and prices tend to be fixed. Kamaq Maki is open from 8 am to noon and 2 to 6 pm on weekdays and from 10 am to noon and 3 to 5 pm on weekends and holidays. Their store (which is almost a craft museum) is at Brasilia 200. (It's off the Huancayo map; continue north-east along Calle Huancas three blocks beyond Centenario to San Carlos and turn right for a couple of long blocks. Brasilia is on your left.) Anyone even remotely interested in crafts should definitely visit the cooperative. They'll be happy to ship goods home for you.

Getting There & Away

As the Huancavelica area has become subject to Sendero activity recently, ask locally before travelling there.

There is no airport, so many travellers take the train from Lima. This spectacular ride is occasionally suspended. Bus or car is marginally quicker than the train.

Bus If you're on a tight budget, it's worth checking around the various bus companies as one or two may be offering special fares. For example, the last time I took the bus to Lima, I went with Empresa Hidalgo. They had two morning buses and three night buses and charged $3 for the 9 to 11-hour trip. In comparison, ETUCSA had more frequent departures but charged $3.50 per passenger, Expreso Sudamericano were charging $4 and Empresa Los Andes charged $4.50, all for the same trip.

Empresa Hidalgo operates twice-daily buses to Tarma (2 hours, $1.40) and to Huancavelica (4 hours, $1.80).

Arzapalo has two or three buses (usually overnight) to Cerro de Pasco (8 hours, $2.70).

When I was last in Huancayo, ETUCSA was the only company running a regular service to Ayacucho (14 to 18 hours, $4.50, very cold and bumpy), with a bus every other day. The road to Ayacucho is notoriously bad, so schedules and the companies controlling them change particularly frequently on this route. Direct services from Huancayo to Cuzco are not normally available and travellers to Cuzco should take a bus to Ayacucho and try there. The Huancayo-Ayacucho-Cuzco trip passes through spectacular scenery, but as the area is under Sendero control, buses are stopped by the guerillas fairly often. Passengers are sometimes shot for their political affiliations and the survivors asked for money and valuables. For obvious reasons, this route is definitely not recommended at this time.

ETUCSA also has daily departures for La Merced and the jungle town of Satipo. Alarcon runs three buses a week to Satipo on the very rugged and beautiful direct road. I've never done this trip and would like to hear from anyone who does.

Local buses to most of the nearby villages leave from the street intersections shown on the Huancayo map. The companies rarely have offices or fixed schedules. You just show up and wait until a bus is ready to leave. Ask other people waiting with you for more details. The tourist office is a good source of local bus information.

If you're in a hurry to get somewhere, consider taking one of the colectivo taxis. They are about twice as expensive but 25% faster than the buses and each company usually has several departures a day. Comités 12, 22 and 30 go to Lima; Comités 1 and 30 go to Tarma.

Train Huancayo's two train stations are in different parts of town and are not linked by train (though the tracks do connect). The central station serves Lima. The journey takes about 10 hours (though the train is often late) and costs about $3 in 1st class, $2.20 in 2nd class. First class tickets usually sell out the day before. Schedules change frequently but there is usually a departure at 7 am every Monday, Wednesday and Friday. This spectacular journey is described in the Lima and La Oroya sections.

The Huancavelica train station is at the south-eastern end of town. Train is the best mode of transport to Huancavelica because the road is not very good. There are two types

of trains: the faster autovagon and the slower tren. The autovagon takes 3½ hours, costs $2 and leaves at 7 am and 1.30 pm daily, except Sunday. Try to buy your ticket before you travel as this service is very popular and the train is often full. The tren takes about 5 hours, leaves at 7.30 am daily, except Sunday, and costs $1.50 in 1st class, $1.20 in 2nd class. Ticket selling hours are a bit erratic – the ticket window usually opens about 6 am and closes after the morning trains leave. It reopens at about 12.30 pm for the afternoon autovagon and may open again in the evening.

Getting Around

Adventure Tours A local man, Luis 'Lucho' Hurtado, speaks good English and knows the surrounding area well. He can guide you on adventurous treks down the eastern slopes of the Andes and into the high jungle on foot, horseback or public transport. It isn't luxurious but it's a good chance to experience something of the 'real' rural Peru. Lucho's father has a ranch in the middle of nowhere at which you can stay and meet all kinds of local people. I met Lucho briefly at the South American Explorers Club and he impressed me as being honest and knowledgeable. I have heard repeated recommendations of his trips. If you are unable to get a group together, you may be able to join up with another group. The trips usually last from 3 to 8 days and cost about $20 to $30 per person per day, including simple food. Accommodation is rustic and trips may involve some camping. If you're interested in a guide for some off-the-beaten-track travel, look for Lucho at Calle Huancas 209 (tel 2223950) – he advertises in the *Hostal Dani*. His postal address is Apartado 510, Huancayo.

Apart from trips, Lucho and his wife Beverly give Spanish lessons, Peruvian cooking classes and information on local crafts and music.

Around Huancayo – Mantaro Valley

Two main road systems link Huancayo with the villages of the Mantaro Valley and are

Top: Inti Raymi Festival, Sacsayhuaman (RR)
Left: Chinchero Market (RR)
Right: A deformed & trepanned skull from Inca times (RR)

Left: Quechua women & children, near Cochayoc, Cordillera Urubamba (RR)
Right: Cuzco from Sacsayhuaman Hill (RR)
Bottom: Market scene, Pisac (RR)

known simply as the left and right of the river. With Huancayo lying in the southern part of the valley, left translates into west and right into east. It is best to confine your sightseeing on any given day to one side or the other because there are few bridges.

Perhaps the most interesting excursion is on the east side of the valley where you can visit the twin villages of Cochas Grande and Cochas Chico, about 11 km from Huancayo. These villages are the major production centres for the incised gourds which have made the area famous. Oddly enough, the gourds are grown mainly on the coast and imported into the highlands from the Chiclayo and Ica areas. Once they reach the highlands they are dried and scorched, then decorated using woodworking tools. The gourds are available at the Huancayo Sunday craft market but, if you speak Spanish and can hit it off with the locals, you can see them being made and buy them at Cochas.

Other villages of interest for their handicrafts include San Agustín de Cajas, Hualhuas and San Jerónimo de Tuman. Cajas is known for the manufacture of broadbrimmed wool hats, though this industry seems to be dying. Hualhuas is a centre for the manufacture of wool products – ponchos, weavings, sweaters and other items. San Jerónimo is known for its filigree silverwork and also has a 17th century church with fine wooden altars. While the villages can easily be visited from Huancayo, most buying and selling is done in Huancayo and the villages have few facilities for shopping or anything else. The key here is the ability to speak Spanish and make friends with the locals.

Continuing north of these east-side villages, you soon come to Concepción (see before Huancayo). From here, it is possible to visit the fascinating Convent of Ocopa.

HUANCAVELICA

Huancavelica, 147 km south of Huancayo, is the capital of the department of the same name. This area is high and remote; most of the department lies above 3500 metres and has a cold climate, though it can get T-shirt-hot during the sunny days of the dry season – May to October. The rest of the year tends to be wet, and during the rainiest months between February and April, the roads are sometimes in such bad shape that Huancavelica can be virtually cut off from the rest of Peru.

This historic city is nearly 3700 metres above sea level and has a population of only 20,000. Before the arrival of Europeans, Huancavelica was a strategic Inca centre, and shortly after the conquest, the Spanish discovered its mineral wealth. By 1564, the Spaniards were sending Indian slaves to Huancavelica to work in the mercury and silver mines. The present town was founded in 1571 under the name of Villa Rica de Oropesa and retains a very pleasant colonial atmosphere. It's a small but attractive town visited by few tourists even at the best of times. Unfortunately, however, Huancavelica is not a recommended destination at present because of Sendero activity.

This area, along with the Department of Ayacucho, remains one of the most sensitive to terrorist problems. It seemed quiet when I was there in mid-1986 and the locals seemed to think that there was little to worry about. By the late 1980s, however, the area was again off the tourist map. Ask in the Lima or Huancayo tourist office about the stability of the situation before embarking on a trip to this charming and remote highland town.

Information

Tourist Information There used to be a tourist office on the 2nd floor of Manuel Segura 122 (no sign) but I don't know if it's functioning at this time.

Police I had to register at the PIP office (see the Huancavelica map) on arrival. This was a quick, straightforward formality – they just wanted to see my passport and write down my name and number. Later, during my first evening in Huancavelica, I was visited in my hotel room by three plain-clothes policemen. I showed the proper amount of indignation and they soon left. It seemed just as well that I had already registered with the PIP. Ask about current regulations when you arrive.

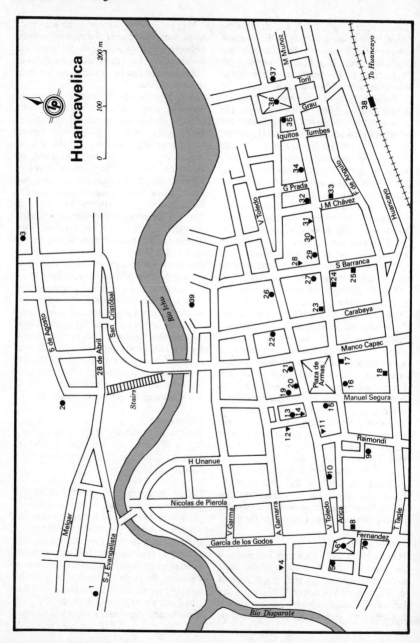

Huancavelica

Money Your best bet is to change money in Huancayo as there are no casas de cambio in Huancavelica and the banks cannot be relied upon to even change cash, let alone travellers' cheques. The Banco de Crédito is your best chance, but don't rely on it.

If you're staying at the Hotel de Turistas, you can pay your bill in dollars but at a loss.

Things to See
Churches There are eight churches of note. Santa Ana, now in a bad state of disrepair, was founded in the 16th century and was followed in the 17th century by the cathedral, Santo Domingo, San Francisco, San Cristóbal and La Ascension. San Sebastián came even later but appears to be in a worse state of repair than most of the others, while San Francisco is famous for its 11 intricately worked altars. The cathedral has been restored and contains what has been called the best colonial altar in Peru. It is certainly a magnificent church. Santo Domingo is currently under restoration.

Post Office The post office on the Plaza de Armas is worth a look because of the tumbledown old colonial building in which it is housed.

Hot Springs The San Cristóbal hot springs (marked on the Huancavelica map) are fed into a large, slightly murky swimming pool in which you can relax for about 5c. For 10c you can have a shower. There is a bar and café and it's reasonably pleasant. You can hire a towel, soap and a bathing suit if you've forgotten yours (though their selection of bathing wear is limited and unlovely). The springs are open from 6 am to 4.30 pm daily.

Market Market day is Sunday and, although there are smaller daily markets, Sunday is the best day to see the locals in traditional dress (see the next town, Lircay). The main market area is by the river and there is a smaller market off the main street, M Muñoz.

Places to Stay

Most hotels are very cheap and have only cold water, but with the natural hot baths in town, this is not a great hardship.

The cheapest place is the *Hostal San Francisco* followed by the very simple, reasonably clean *Hostal Peru*, where you can stay for just 50c per person, or 75c for a couple sharing a bed. A little more expensive but not any better looking is the *Savoy* at 70/90c for singles/doubles and the *Santo Domingo* for 75c per person. The best of the supercheapies is the *Hotel Tahuantinsuyo* which has some well-lit singles/doubles with table and chair for 90c/$1.50 (add 30c for rooms with bath). Their advertised hot water was, at last report, broken down and may remain so for years.

If you want hot water, try the *Hostal Mercurio*. It costs about $1.40 per person but prices jump to around $3 if you want a private bath. This place is clean but the rows of rooms painted institutional green look somewhat grim.

The best in town is, of course, the government-run *Hotel de Turistas* on the Plaza de Armas. It's nice enough and charges about $9/13 for singles/doubles with bath, about 30% less with shared bath. Prices include a continental breakfast and hot water is available.

Places to Eat

There are no particularly good restaurants in Huancavelica. The restaurant at the *Hotel de Turistas* is the most expensive and no more than mediocre. Elsewhere in town you can eat for $1 or less. There are several chicken places along M Muñoz between the two main plazas, the best of which is *Litós Pollería*. You'll find other cheap restaurants along the same street; the *Chifa Imperio* and *El Dorado* are probably the best of these, though they're nothing to get excited about. *La Japonesita*, just off M Muñoz, is not a sushi place but does serve excellent trout. This is fished from the large nearby Andean lake of Chochococha which, at 4600 metres above sea level, must be one of the highest commercial fish sources in the world.

Another street worth trying is V Toledo. Here you'll find the *Restaurant Joy*, which has reasonable lunches, and the recommended *Ganso de Oro*. Just around the corner from the Joy is the *Recreo La Cantuta*. It's a good place to enjoy an outdoor beer and meet the locals over a game of sapo. (This old Peruvian game of skill is played by throwing brass disks at an open-mouthed brass toad mounted in the middle of a table, trying to get your disk into the toad's mouth.)

There are plenty of other cheap, basic places to eat. Most close early and some only serve lunches.

Getting There & Away

Despite being the capital of its department, Huancavelica has no commercial airport and you have to travel overland. The train from Huancayo is more comfortable than the buses from anywhere else.

Bus Almost all major bus departures are from Avenida M Muñoz. The bus trip to Huancayo takes 4 to 5 hours and costs almost $2; there are two buses a day with Empresa Hidalgo and two a day with Huascar. At about $6.50, the cheapest bus to Lima is run by Empresa Transportes Huascar, but they only have Saturday and Monday departures at present. Expreso Huancavelica buses cost $1 more but have a daily 5 pm departure for the journey of some 15 hours via Huancayo and La Oroya, terminating in Lima's fairly seamy La Victoria district. Empresa Hidalgo will sell you tickets to Lima but you have to change buses at Huancayo. Oropesa, which has an office on the same street, used to run buses to Lima but appeared to be temporarily closed when I was last in town.

There are no direct services to Ayacucho – to get there, go back to Huancayo and catch the daily Huascar bus to Lircay.

Train There are three trains to Huancayo every day, except Sunday when there is no service. The autovagon leaves at 7 am and 1 pm, takes almost 4 hours and costs about $2. The ordinary train leaves at 7.30 am and takes about 6 hours. Tickets cost $1.50 in 1st class, $1.20 in 2nd. As autovagon and 1st class tickets sell out very fast, you should try to buy tickets a day in advance. Recently, ticket office hours were 10 to 11 am and 4 to 5 pm, but 'helpless' gringos can sometimes coax the station master into selling tickets outside these hours.

LIRCAY

The small colonial town of Lircay is almost 80 km south-east of Huancavelica. Its main claim to fame is as the centre for the department's traditional clothing, which can be seen at Huancavelica's Sunday market. The predominant colour is black, but the men wear rainbow-coloured pompoms on their hats and at their waists (supposedly love tokens from women) and the women wear multicoloured shawls over their otherwise sombre clothing. The town has a couple of basic hotels.

IZCUCHACA

Izcuchaca, the main village between Huancayo and Huancavelica, has a basic hotel, a pottery centre, hot springs and archaeological ruins, which are accessible only on foot. There is also an historic bridge which, legend has it, was built by the Incas and defended bitterly by Huascar against the advance of Atahualpa's troops during the civil war which was raging in the Inca Empire when the Spaniards arrived.

AYACUCHO

Founded by the Spanish in 1540, Ayacucho is a small city lying 2731 metres above sea level. It has a population of 31,000 and is the capital of its department. Despite its remoteness and small size, Ayacucho is arguably Peru's most fascinating Andean town after Cuzco and is well worth a visit.

Five hundred years before the Inca Empire, the Wari Empire dominated the Peruvian highlands. The Wari's ruined capital, 22 km north-east of Ayacucho, is easily reached along the paved road which now links it with Ayacucho. Ayacucho played a major part in the battles for independence and a huge nearby monument marks the site

of the important Battle of Ayacucho, fought in 1824.

As mentioned at the beginning of this chapter, the central Andes is one of Peru's most forgotten areas. Ayacucho is no exception to this. Its first road link with the Peruvian coast was not finished until 1924, and as late as 1960, there were only two buses and a few dozen vehicles in the city. Departmental statistics show that in 1981, there were still only 44 km of paved roads in the department, only 7% of the population had running water in their houses and only 14% had electricity. Thus, Ayacucho has retained its colonial atmosphere more than most Peruvian cities and many of the old colonial buildings have been preserved.

It is in this remote environment that the Sendero Luminoso (Shining Path) guerilla movement was born, beginning in 1962 as the Huamanga Command of the Frente de Liberación Nacional (FLN). In 1965, the Huamanga Command broke with the national FLN organisation and, in the late 1960s, flirted with communism. In the 1970s, when the Sendero was a little-known local organisation headquartered at Ayacucho's University of Huamanga, non-violent political discussion and dissent within the confines of the campus were its main activities.

The violence with which the world press has frequently identified the Sendero began in the early 1980s and peaked in 1982. The strong military measures taken in 1983, in an attempt to control the organisation, were frequently criticised because of the killing of civilians. The spread of the Sendero was halted for a few years in the mid-1980s but, by the late 1980s, strong Sendero presence was felt not only in Ayacucho but through much of the central Peruvian Andes. The Sendero's objectives appear to be the overthrow of Peru's present democratic system, the destruction of all bourgeois elements in the country and the return of land to the peasant farmers. The violence employed in the pursuit of these aims has meant that the Sendero has relatively little popular support in Peru.

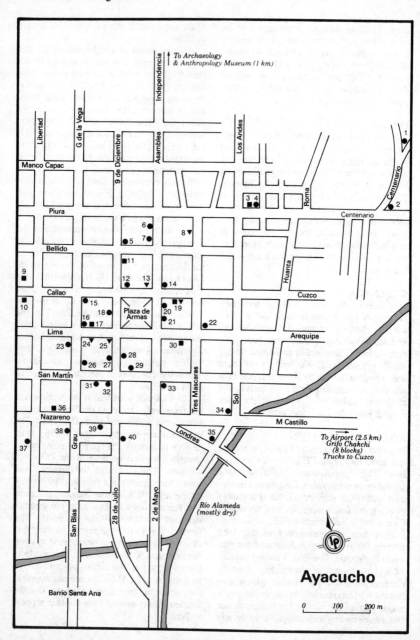

To Archaeology
& Anthropology Museum (1 km)

Independencia

Libertad

G de la Vega

9 de Diciembre

Asamblea

Los Andes

Centenario

Roma

Manco Capac

Piura

■ 3 ● 4

Centenario

● 6
● 5 ● 7   ▼ 8

Bellido

■ 11

● 9

● 12 ● 13
      ▼   ● 14

Huanta

Cuzco

Callao

■ 10

● 15
   ● 18
■ 16 ■ 17

Plaza de
Armas

■ ▼ 19
● 20
● 21

● 22

Arequipa

Lima

● 23

▼ 24 ▼ 25
● 26 ● 27

■ 30

● 28
   ● 29

San Martín

● 31
      ● 32

● 33

Tres Mascaras

Sol

● 34

M Castillo

■ 36

Nazareno

● 38 ● 39

● 40

● 37

Grau

28 de Julio

2 de Mayo

Londres

● 35

To Airport (2.5 km)
Grifo Chakchi
(8 blocks)
Trucks to Cuzco

San Blas

Río Alameda
(mostly dry)

Barrio Santa Ana

Ayacucho

0   100   200 m

■ PLACES TO STAY

3	Hostal Magdalena
9	Hostal Sixtina
10	Hostal Samary
11	Hotel de Turistas
17	Hotel Santa Rosa
19	La Colmena Hotel
30	Hostal Central
36	Hotel Santiago & Hotel La Crillonesa

▼ PLACES TO EAT

8	Marisquería El Ancla
13	Los Portales Café
19	Alamo Restaurant
24	Restaurant La Fortaleza
25	El Baccara Restaurant

● OTHER

1	Buses to Huari, Quinua & Huanta
2	Statue
4	ETUCSA (Bus)
5	Santo Domingo Church
6	Post Office & ENTEL
7	Cinema
12	Morochuco Tours & AeroPeru
14	San Agustín Church
15	San Francisco de Paula Church
16	Faucett Airline
18	Prefectura
20	Cinema
21	Cathedral, University, Consejo Municipal & FOPTUR
22	Empresa Transportes Huamanguina (Bus)
23	Transportes Molina (Bus)
26	Empresa Transportes Ayacucho (Bus)
27	La Compañía Church
28	Banco de la Nación
29	Ayacucho Tours
31	Hidalgo (Bus)
32	Banco de Crédito
33	La Merced Church
34	Transportes Cangallo (Bus)
35	Empresa Transportes Fajardo Etmufa (Bus)
37	Ormeño (Bus)
38	Santa Clara Church
39	Market
40	San Francisco de Asis Church

It is worth noting that tourists and travellers have not been the direct target of Sendero attacks, though they can occasionally become involved by being in the wrong place at the wrong time and a few travellers have been killed. At the time of writing, the Ayacucho area is not recommended to travellers. Make inquiries in Lima to see whether the situation has improved.

Information

Tourist Information The FOPTUR tourist office (tel 912997) is at Portal Municipal 46, on the plaza, and is open from 7.30 am to 3.45 pm Monday to Friday. The office is a good source of information and leaflets.

Ayacucho Tours and Morochuco Tours used to organise local sightseeing tours and provide information. With the recent lack of visitors, they haven't been of much use but they may be worth checking if tourism picks up again.

Money Make every effort to arrive with as much money as you'll need as the banks may not change cash dollars or may do so at a low rate. The two tour companies mentioned above may accept cash dollars for their services, again at a poor rate, and the Hotel de Turistas will let you pay your bill in cash dollars. Straightforward exchange is not easy.

Things to See

Within the city there are many churches, colonial buildings and museums to visit. As opening times have been disrupted, you should ask at the tourist office for current hours. Opening hours during Holy Week tend to be much longer.

Archaeology & Anthropology Museum

To get there, walk north from the Plaza de Armas along Asamblea, which soon turns into Independencia. The museum is in the Centro Cultural Simón Bolívar, a little over a km from the town centre on your right – you can't miss it.

I was told that the museum is normally open from 8.30 am to 6 pm daily, except Sunday, but the sign on the door gives 8 am to noon as the opening hours, so you'd be advised to try in the morning. Entry is less than 10c. Huari ceramics make up most of the small exhibit.

Churches The 17th century cathedral on the Plaza de Armas has a religious art museum which was closed when I was last in Ayacucho. Other colonial churches from the 16th, 17th and 18th centuries are marked on the Ayacucho map. Opening hours are erratic but they're well worth visiting if you can figure out when you can get in.

Colonial Houses Most of the old mansions are now mainly political offices and can often be visited upon presentation of your passport. The offices of the Department of Ayacucho (the Prefectura) on the Plaza de Armas are a good example. The armed guard will let you in with your passport between 8 am and noon on weekdays. The mansion was constructed between 1740 and 1755 and sold to the state in 1937. On the ground floor is a pretty courtyard and the visitor can see the cell of the local heroine of independence, María Parado de Bellido. Go upstairs to see some excellent tilework.

Also worth a look is the Salon de Actas in the Consejo Municipal, next to the cathedral, with its excellent view of the plaza. The tourist office can suggest others.

Fiestas
Ayacucho's Holy Week celebration, held the week before Easter, has long been considered Peru's finest religious festival and it attracts visitors from all over the country. Rooms in the better hotels are booked well in advance and even the cheapest places are often full.

Each year, the tourist bureau prints a free brochure describing the Holy Week events with street maps showing the main processions. Visitors are advised to get this detailed information. The celebrations begin on the Friday before Palm Sunday and continue for 10 days until Easter Sunday. Each day is marked with solemn yet colourful processions and religious rites which reach a fever pitch of Catholic faith and tradition. The Friday before Palm Sunday is marked by a procession in honour of La Virgen de los Dolores, or 'Our Lady of Sorrows', during which it is customary to inflict 'sorrows' on bystanders by firing pebbles out of slingshots. Gringos have been recent targets, so be warned.

In addition to the religious services, Ayacucho's Holy Week celebrations include numerous secular activities – art shows, folk-dancing competitions and demonstrations, local music concerts and street events, sporting events (especially equestrian ones), agricultural fairs and the preparation of typical meals.

Places to Stay
Because of the lack of tourists, hotels tend to have plenty of rooms available and are cheaper than in other parts of Peru.

Clay church handicraft from Ayacucho

Places to Stay – bottom end

One of the cheapest is the basic *Hostal Magdalena*, next to the ETUCSA bus terminal. It charges about 60c per person and sometimes has hot water. The clean and pleasant *Hostal Samary* is better and has hot water in the morning. Singles/doubles with bath cost $1.30/2 and there are also cheaper rooms with shared bath. Another reasonable cheap hotel is the *Hotel La Crillonesa*. Hot water is available in the morning and single rooms are about $1.

The best cheap hotels in town are the *La Colmena* and the *Santa Rosa*. They charge about $1.40/2.10 for clean rooms with bath and hot water at least once, usually twice a day. Both hotels have pleasant courtyards.

Other cheap hotels to try are the *Hostal Central*, *Hostal Sixtina* and *Hotel Santiago*, none of which seems particularly good or bad.

Places to Stay – middle

The government-run *Hotel de Turistas* is the best in town. Reservations can be made at ENTURPeru in Lima (tel 721928). Singles/doubles with bath and hot water cost $7/10, including continental breakfast. Rooms with shared bath are available for $5/6.50.

Places to Eat

The *Alamo Restaurant* starts serving breakfast at 7 am, offering pancakes and yoghurt as well as the usual eggs and sandwiches. It is open all day and serves good cheap food. Beer is not sold but this restaurant is recommended to budget travellers.

Marginally more expensive, but still cheap (there are no fancy or expensive restaurants in Ayacucho), the *Restaurant La Fortaleza* is also good and does serve beer. *Los Portales* café, on the Plaza de Armas, is another good place with a sawdust-on-floor ambience. If you're in the mood for seafood, try the *Marisquería El Ancla*, which makes a reasonable cebiche and sometimes has music on Friday night.

Getting There & Away

Ayacucho is most easily reached by air. If you travel by road, be prepared for long delays during the rainy season (the worst months are February to April), especially if you're coming from the Cuzco direction, though the road between Huancayo and Ayacucho is also very bad. Both routes are spectacular. The following information was written before the current bout of Sendero problems.

The best road to Ayacucho is the one from Lima via Pisco. Ormeño claims 18 hours for this trip but it's closer to 22 or 24 hours, even more during the wet months. The route follows the south coast almost as far as Pisco and then turns inland to Castrovirreyna, a small mountain town 12 to 14 hours from Lima. Castrovirreyna has several basic restaurants and buses usually stop here for meals. The road climbs to Castrovirreyna in an incredible series of hairpin bends, hugging the mountain side and often wide enough for only one vehicle, which makes the journey a little more exciting.

Beyond Castrovirreyna, the road reaches an altitude of about 4800 metres as it passes several blue, green and turquoise Andean lakes. The road flirts with the snow line for over an hour with dramatic views of high Andean scenery and snowcaps. Finally, the road begins its descent towards Ayacucho and the countryside becomes greener as forests of the dwarf polyepsis trees appear. Those who suffer from *soroche* (altitude sickness) in the high passes are relieved by the arrival in Ayacucho, a mere 2731 metres above sea level.

Air Both AeroPeru and Faucett have offices in central Ayacucho and have daily flights to Lima or Cuzco for $41. The airport is about 3 km from the town centre so you could walk. Alternatively, catch a taxi for about $1.50 or one of the irregular buses from the Plaza de Armas.

Bus Ormeño buses to Lima cost about $7.50 and leave most days of the week. The Hidalgo service is cheaper at about $6.50, with departures most days. Hidalgo also has two buses a week to Cuzco. These are always full and seats for the 30-hour, $8 trip have to be booked in advance. Buses to the intermediate town of Andahuaylas run three times a week.

Transportes Molina has old buses which depart every afternoon for Huancayo and cost $3.50. They also have three buses a week to Andahuaylas.

Empresa Transportes Ayacucho runs three buses a week to Huancayo, three to Andahuaylas and two to Lima. ETUCSA has a daily bus to Huancayo for $3.50.

Note that these companies change their routes and services rather frequently.

The cheapest way to get to Cuzco is to wait at the Grifo (petrol station) Chakchi for a truck and ride in the back with the locals. This is slow and uncomfortable but the views are great and you will experience the Andes from a very different perspective. Trucks leave most days.

Getting Around
Pick-up trucks and occasional buses will take you to many local villages, including Quinua, and to the Huari ruins, departing from beyond the statue at the east end of Avenida Centenario.

There are four local city buses, one of which goes from the Plaza de Armas to the airport.

Trucks to Cangallo leave from the Puente Nuevo area which is the bridge on Londres over the Río Alameda. Departures are normally in the morning. Empresa Transportes Fajardo Etmufa and Transportes Cangallo, both near the Puente Nuevo, have a bus or truck to Cangallo which will continue on to Vilcashuamán if there is enough demand. Empresa Transportes Huamanguina also services this route at irregular intervals. The half-day trip costs a little over $1.

AROUND AYACUCHO
Three places are often visited from Ayacucho. A trip to the village and battlefield of Quinua is normally combined with a visit to the Huari ruins. The Inca ruins of

Vilcashuamán can also be visited. The rough road from Ayacucho to the jungle settlements of San Francisco and Luisiana on the Apurimac River is considered dangerous because of terrorist activity.

Huari Ruins & Quinua
Pick-up trucks leave for Quinua from the end of Avenida Centenario in Ayacucho about once an hour. The fare for the 1-hour ride is 30c. The 37-km road climbs about 550 metres to Quinua, 3300 metres above sea level – an attractive route. After about 20 km, you will pass the extensive ruins of Huari sprawling for several km along the roadside. The small site museum is usually closed – there are more Huari artefacts to be seen in the Ayacucho museum. The five main sectors of the ruins are marked by road signs; the upper sites are in rather bizarre forests of Opuntia cacti. As the ruins have not been restored, however, there is not much for the untrained eye to see and interested travellers may want to try and find a guide from Morochuco or Ayacucho Tours. Don't leave it too late to look for onward or return transport because pick-ups can get hopelessly full in the afternoon.

Huari is built on a hill, and as the road from Ayacucho climbs through it, there are reasonable views from the pick-up truck. The road climbs beyond Huari until it reaches the pretty village of Quinua. The pick-up truck usually stops at a plaza. Steps from the left-hand side of the plaza, as you arrive from Ayacucho, lead up to the village church. The church is on an old-fashioned cobblestone plaza and a small museum nearby displays various relics from the major independence battle which was fought in this area. The museum is open from 8 am to 1 pm daily, except Mondays, and costs about 5c to visit.

To reach the battlefield, turn left behind the church and head out of the village along Jirón Sucre which, after a walk of about 10 minutes, rejoins the main road. As you walk, notice the red-tiled roofs which are elaborately decorated with ceramic model churches. Quinua is famous as a handicraft centre and these model churches are especially typical of the area.

The white obelisk which is intermittently visible for several km as you approach Quinua now lies a few minutes walk in front of you. The impressive monument is 40 metres high and features carvings commemorating the Battle of Ayacucho, fought here on 9 December 1824. The walk up from Quinua and the views are pleasant.

There is no accommodation in Quinua and only very basic food supplies. There is a small market on Sunday.

Vilcashuamán

Vilcashuamán, or 'sacred falcon', was considered the geographical centre of the Inca Empire. It was here that the Inca road between Cuzco and the coast crossed the road running the length of the Andes. Little remains of the city's earlier magnificence; Vilcashuamán has fallen prey to looters and many of its blocks have been used to build more modern buildings. The once magnificent Temple of the Sun now has a parish church on top of it. The only structure still in a reasonable state of repair is a five-tiered pyramid, called an *usnu*, topped by a huge double throne carved from stone and used by the Inca.

Vilcashuamán is near the village of Cangallo, about 120 km south of Ayacucho. Daily trucks and occasional buses travel to Cangallo, where basic accommodation is available. Morochuco and Ayacucho Tours can provide a guided service.

NORTH FROM LA OROYA

So far, this chapter has described travel east or south from the central Andean crossroads town of La Oroya. If you decide to go north instead, you will pass through the highland towns of Junín, Cerro de Pasco, Huánuco and Tingo María, ending up in the important jungle town of Pucallpa. It is this section of Peru's Central Andes which is described in this part of the chapter. However, the route is not recommended at this time because of frequent Sendero activities.

JUNÍN

The village of Junín is about 55 km due north of La Oroya. I have never heard or read of a hotel here but there must be some kind of basic accommodation available. An important independence battle was fought at the nearby Pampa of Junín (where there is a monument).

About 10 km beyond the village is the interesting Lago de Junín. This lake is about 30 km long and 14 km wide and is Peru's largest lake after Titicaca. At more than 4000 metres above sea level, it is the highest lake of its size in either the Americas or the Western world. Lago de Junín is known for its bird life, some authorities claiming that 1 million birds live on the lake or its shores at any one time. It is a little-visited area and an excellent destination for anyone interested in seeing a good variety of the water and shore birds of the high Andes.

CERRO DE PASCO

Cerro de Pasco is 4333 metres above sea level and has a population of about 30,000. It is Peru's highest major town, the capital of its department and a miserable place. The altitude makes the town bitterly cold at night and its main reason for existence is mining. Cerro de Pasco is about 40 km north of Lago de Junín and, although it has the closest hotels to the lake, accommodation is poor.

Places to Stay

When I was there, I could find no hotels with hot water. The town's four or five hotels were all basic, cold and unattractive. On the other hand, they provide a bed and a roof over your head, which has to count for something.

The best is supposedly the *Gran Hotel Cerro de Pasco*, in the suburbs, but it is overpriced and the hot shower rarely works. In the town centre, the *Hotel El Viajero* and the *Hotel Santa Rosa*, both by the Plaza de Armas, are as good as any.

HUÁNUCO

Huánuco is 105 km north of Cerro de Pasco and almost 2500 metres lower, providing welcome relief for soroche sufferers. The

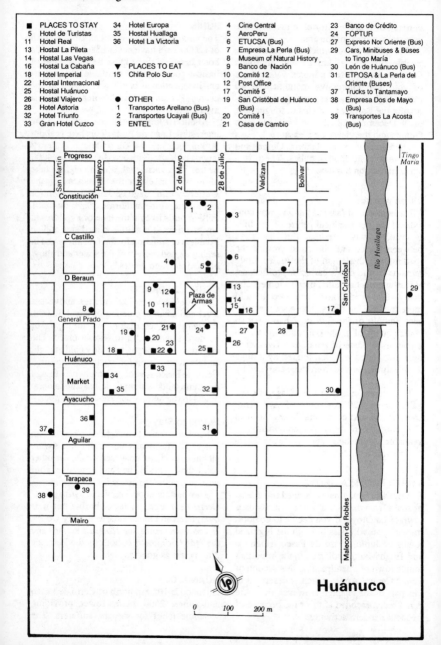

■	PLACES TO STAY	34	Hotel Europa		4	Cine Central	23	Banco de Crédito
5	Hotel de Turistas	35	Hostal Huallaga		5	AeroPeru	24	FOPTUR
11	Hotel Real	36	Hotel La Victoria		6	ETUCSA (Bus)	27	Expreso Nor Oriente (Bus)
13	Hostal La Pileta				7	Empresa La Perla (Bus)	29	Cars, Minibuses & Buses
14	Hostal Las Vegas	▼	PLACES TO EAT		8	Museum of Natural History		to Tingo María
16	Hostal La Cabaña	15	Chifa Polo Sur		9	Banco de Nación	30	León de Huánuco (Bus)
18	Hotel Imperial				10	Comité 12	31	ETPOSA & La Perla del
22	Hostal Internacional				12	Post Office		Oriente (Buses)
25	Hostal Huánuco	●	OTHER		17	Comité 5	37	Trucks to Tantamayo
26	Hostal Viajero	1	Transportes Arellano (Bus)		19	San Cristóbal de Huánuco	38	Empresa Dos de Mayo
28	Hotel Astoria	2	Transportes Ucayali (Bus)		20	Comité 1		(Bus)
32	Hotel Triunfo	3	ENTEL		21	Casa de Cambio	39	Transportes La Acosta
33	Gran Hotel Cuzco							(Bus)

Huánuco

0   100   200 m

elevation is only 1894 metres above sea level. Huánuco is on the upper reaches of the Río Huallaga, the major tributary of the Río Marañon before it becomes the Amazon. Huánuco is also the capital of its department and the site of one of Peru's oldest Andean archaeological sites, the Temple of Kotosh (also known as the Temple of the Crossed Hands). The town has an interesting natural history museum and a pleasant Plaza de Armas.

Information

Tourist Information The FOPTUR tourist office (tel 2124) is on the Plaza de Armas at General Prado 714. Huánuco Tours at General Prado 691 may also be able to help.

Money Huánuco has branches of the Banco de la Nación and Banco de Crédito and there is a casa de cambio on the corner of the Plaza de Armas. Between them, you should be able to get money changed, but don't expect very good rates.

Museum of Natural History

This museum is a surprise – one would not expect a museum of this calibre in a town of Huánuco's size. It is small but well organised and the exhibits are labelled. The museum director, Señor Nestor Armas Wenzel, is dedicated and enthusiastic and delights in showing visitors around. He particularly likes to talk to foreign visitors and has flags and 'Welcome' in many languages decorating the entrance lobby. Admission is about 40c. The museum is open from 9 am to noon and 3 to 6 pm weekdays and 10 am to 1 pm on Sunday.

Kotosh vessel

The Temple of Kotosh

This archaeological site is also known as the Temple of the Crossed Hands because of the life-size moulding, made of mud, of a pair of crossed forearms which was discovered in the ruins by an archaeological team in the early 1960s. The Crossed Hands can now be seen in the Museum of Archaeology & Anthropology in Lima. The moulding is dated to between 4000 and 5000 years old and no others are known to exist.

Little is known about Kotosh, one of the most ancient of Andean cultures. The temple site is overgrown and difficult to reach, though it lies only 5 km from Huánuco, and unless you are very interested in Kotosh, there is little to see. Most people are better off seeing the Crossed Hands in the Lima museum. If you really want to visit the ruins, head south on Jirón San Martín until you come to a lake, then head west out of town on the road to La Unión. There is a stream to cross and the footbridge has been down for some time. The tourist information office can give you more precise information – I haven't been to the ruin.

Places to Stay

This is the most pleasant town between Lima and Pucallpa and, although Huánuco's hotels are generally not very good, they tend to fill quickly. You can usually find a bed but the choice can be very limited by late afternoon, so start looking as early as possible. (With the current inadvisability of travel from Lima to Pucallpa, this is probably no longer true.)

Places to Stay – bottom end

The cheapest place in town is the *Hostal La Cabaña* for $1/1.60 singles/doubles. It has received fairly good reports but I found it very basic with a broken water supply. Perhaps it will have been fixed by the time you get there.

For $1.30/2.30, you can choose from the *Hotel Astoria, Triunfo, Huallaga* and *Viajero*. The first is probably the cleanest of an unprepossessing bunch.

The *Hostal La Victoria* is basic and

charges $1.70/2.70 for singles/doubles. The similarly priced *Hotel Europa* is also very basic but does have a lot of rooms, which means that you may be able to get a bed there later in the day. Also in this price range are the better *Hostal Internacional* and *Hotel Imperial*, both of which offer rooms with bath at a slightly higher price.

Places to Stay – middle

At $3/4.50 for singles/doubles with bath and, if you're lucky, hot water, try the *Hostal La Pileta* or the *Hostal Las Vegas*. The *Gran Hotel Cuzco* isn't bad and has hot water for at least part of the day and a cafeteria. It's popular with Peruvian businessmen. Singles/doubles with bath are $4/6. For a few cents more, the secure *Hostal Huánuco* has a good hot-water supply and is often full. There are some slightly cheaper rooms with shared bath.

The old fashioned government-run *Hotel de Turistas* on the Plaza de Armas looks pleasant but its hot-water supply has been criticised. Perhaps that's why rooms are a relatively low $6/9 for singles/doubles with bath and continental breakfast. The town's best, the *Hotel Real* on the Plaza de Armas, is almost twice as expensive but not much better than the Turistas.

Places to Eat

I looked hard but couldn't find anywhere remarkable to eat. The *Chifa Polo Sur* and *El Café*, both on the plaza, seemed to be among the best.

Getting There & Away

Huánuco is on the main Lima to Pucallpa highway between the jungle and the coast so transport is plentiful. There is also an airport. The overland trip is now dangerous because of Sendero activity and the following bus information is based on the situation before the present problems. Flying is safer.

Air AeroPerú has flights to Lima for $39. Schedules change frequently and the number of flights can vary from one to four a week. The airport is 8 km from town.

Bus & Colectivo With about half a dozen different bus companies competing on the route to Lima, you'd expect a wide choice of departure times. There isn't. In one of the typically tiresome quirks of travel in Peru, you have to take a night bus or not travel at all. The best service is with León de Huánuco, which runs three buses a night to Lima (10 hours, $6.50). Other companies operating night buses to Lima are San Cristóbal de Huánuco, Expreso Nor Oriente, Empresa La Perla, La Perla del Oriente and Transportes Arellano in rough descending order of reliability.

Pucallpa is also a 10-hour, $6.50 trip. León de Huánuco has a 4 pm departure which arrives at the depressing time of 2 am – you might be allowed to sleep on the bus until dawn. ETPOSA/La Perla del Oriente (they share an office) have a noon departure, though trying to find a hotel in Pucallpa at 10 pm is not much better.

You could avoid the problem of late-night arrivals in Pucallpa by travelling to Tingo María and spending the night there, though not many buses leave Tingo María for Pucallpa during the day either. There are services to Tingo María throughout the day; Comité 1 has shared taxi colectivos during the morning and Comité 5 colectivos run all day ($3.50, 2½ hours). If you walk to the general transport stop beyond the Río Huallaga bridge (10 minutes from the town centre), you'll find shared taxis, cheaper minibuses, and cheaper and slower Empresa La Marginal buses, all heading to Tingo.

Comité 1 has shared cars for Cerro de Pasco in the morning ($3.50, 2½ hours). There are also Comité 12 cars to Cerro de Pasco and, usually, one car each morning continues on to La Oroya (4 to 5 hours, $6). Sometimes, cars go all the way to Lima, particularly if a group takes up all the seats.

Transportes Ucayali has three overnight buses to Cerro de Pasco ($1.50) which continue on to La Oroya ($2.80) and Huancayo (9 hours, $3.50). They also run a day bus. ETUCSA has a night bus to Huancayo.

To visit the remote towns of La Unión, Tantamayo and other villages, head for Jirón

San Martín, a couple of blocks south of the market. Here you'll find a daily morning Empresa Dos de Mayo bus to La Unión (7 hours, $3.30). Transportes La Acosta also services this route. For Tantamayo (12 hours to cover 150 km!), *mixtos* (half truck and half bus) leave every morning from the corner of San Martín and Aguilar. This is a good place to look for transport to other remote villages in the area.

LA UNION

This town is roughly halfway between Huánuco and Huaraz. It is feasible to travel this way to the Cordillera Blanca. La Unión has a couple of basic hotels and transport is available from here on to Chiquían, near the Cordillera Huayhuash. From Chiquían (where there are basic hotels), you can continue on to Huaraz and the Cordillera Blanca. This is a little-travelled and, by all accounts, spectacular route.

About 2 to 3 hours walk from La Unión are the Inca ruins of Huánuco Viejo.

TANTAMAYO

The small, remote village of Tantamayo is in the mountains north of Huánuco. The hotel can provide information for visiting the several ruins which are within a few hours walk. Guides can be hired.

TINGO MARÍA

The 118-km road north from Huánuco climbs over a 3000-metre pass before dropping steadily to Tingo María, which lies in the lush, tropical slopes of the eastern Andes at an altitude of 649 metres. The town is on the edge of the Amazon Basin and is hot and humid most of the time. Tingo María could thus be described as a jungle town, yet it is surrounded by steep Andean foothills. Whether Tingo María should be included in the Central Highlands or the Amazon Basin chapter is typical of the somewhat arbitrary decisions a guidebook writer must make.

Tingo María is a thriving market town. Among its main products are coca (for cocaine) and to a lesser extent, marijuana, so the town is rather unsavoury and not particu-larly friendly to tourists. It also has a bad reputation for theft. It is definitely not a good place to buy drugs. I saw few foreign visitors here; most people go on to the jungle at Pucallpa.

Recent reports indicate that drug-growing activity in the area has escalated and that the growers and the Sendero have formed some kind of alliance. At the time of writing, the overland route to and from Tingo María was dangerous and definitely not recommended. Most of this section is based on the previous edition, researched when the situation was safe.

Money The Librería Victoria doubles as an exchange house and will change dollars at a rate about 10% lower than in Lima. The banks, if they exchange at all, tend to give even poorer rates. Better exchange rates are in Pucallpa.

Things to See

The university has a botanical garden which, though rather run down and overgrown, has labels on some of the plants allowing you to learn something about them. The garden is often locked but the gate keeper who lives in the shack behind the gate will open it up for you if you whistle and yell.

The university, which is about 3 km out of town, is supposed to have a small zoo but I couldn't find anyone who knew about it.

Comité 13 colectivos run every 30 minutes or so out to the Cuevas de Lechuza (owl caves) for 50c. The caves are about 8 km away and you'll be charged a $3 'national park fee'. There are no facilities, however, apart from an urchin manning a few planks nailed together into a toll booth – there are no guides, no information and no lights. The caves are supposed to contain nocturnal parakeets – personally, I went only as far as the toll booth.

Places to Stay

Although there seem to be a lot of hotels, they are generally of a low standard. Hotels are often full so you should look for a room as soon as you arrive. I ended up staying in

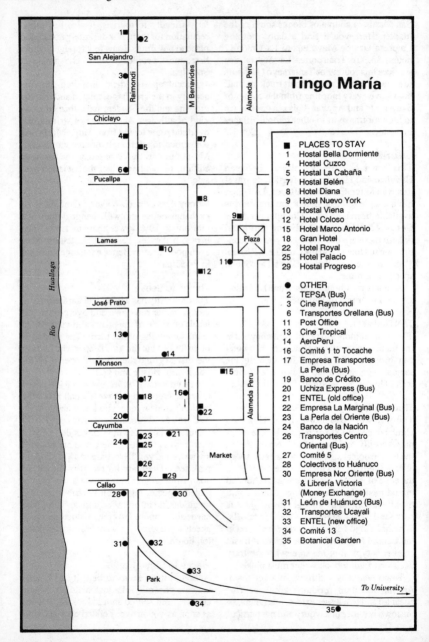

Tingo María

	PLACES TO STAY
1	Hostal Bella Dormiente
4	Hostal Cuzco
5	Hostal La Cabaña
7	Hostal Belén
8	Hotel Diana
9	Hotel Nuevo York
10	Hostal Viena
12	Hotel Coloso
15	Hotel Marco Antonio
18	Gran Hotel
22	Hotel Royal
25	Hotel Palacio
29	Hostal Progreso
	OTHER
2	TEPSA (Bus)
3	Cine Raymondi
6	Transportes Orellana (Bus)
11	Post Office
13	Cine Tropical
14	AeroPeru
16	Comité 1 to Tocache
17	Empresa Transportes La Perla (Bus)
19	Banco de Crédito
20	Uchiza Express (Bus)
21	ENTEL (old office)
22	Empresa La Marginal (Bus)
23	La Perla del Oriente (Bus)
24	Banco de la Nación
26	Transportes Centro Oriental (Bus)
27	Comité 5
28	Colectivos to Huánuco
30	Empresa Nor Oriente (Bus) & Librería Victoria (Money Exchange)
31	León de Huánuco (Bus)
32	Transportes Ucayali
33	ENTEL (new office)
34	Comité 13
35	Botanical Garden

one of the 'better' hotels (the Nuevo York) because it was the first of the half dozen I tried to have a room available. The management told me that the room wasn't ready and I would have to wait half an hour for the maid to finish cleaning it. I asked for the key so that I could go up and drop off my pack. When I reached my room, I found all the doors and windows open and a very harassed-looking maid attempting to clean the badly scuffed linoleum-tiled floor of what appeared to be bird dung. Upon inquiry, I learned that the previous occupants were a couple of machos in town for a cockfighting competition who were travelling with their prize cocks. The birds had evidently shared the bedroom. My opinion of cockfighting and its aficionados, never very high, took a turn for the worse. Perhaps I should be thankful that the men weren't bullfighters.

Places to Stay – bottom end
The cheapest hotels charge $1.30/2.30 for basic singles/doubles with shared cold-water bath. None of these places has much to recommend them. The better ones are the *Hostal La Cabaña*, *Hostal Cuzco* and *Hotel Palacio*. Not so good are the *Hostal Bella Dormiente*, *Hostal Belén* and *Hostal Progreso*.

Two fairly good cheap hotels are the *Hotel Marco Antonio* and the *Hostal Viena*, both offering singles/doubles with communal bath for $1.70/2.70 as well as better rooms with private bath ($2.30/3.30 at the Viena and about 50c more at the Marco Antonio). The *Gran Hotel* is also in this price range but is not as good. The grim-looking *Hotel Coloso* is reasonably clean and has rooms with private bath for $2.30 per person.

Places to Stay – middle
Three hotels charge roughly $3/5 for singles/doubles with private bath. The cheapest and oldest of the three, the *Hotel Royal*, doesn't look too bad. Modern and reasonably clean (if the cockfighters aren't in town) are the *Hotel Nuevo York* and *Hotel Diana* – the Diana is the best in the town centre.

The government-run *Hotel de Turistas* is the best place to stay but it's a couple of km out of town and you'll need a taxi to get there. Prices are about $7/10 for singles/doubles with private bath. Continental breakfast is included.

Places to Eat
Raimondi is the best street for restaurants, though none is particularly noteworthy or memorable. Guests at the *Hotel de Turistas* will find the best food in the hotel.

Getting There & Away
Air AeroPeru has an office in town and the airport is about 2 km away. AeroPeru can sometimes be persuaded to give you a ride in their pick-up truck, but don't rely on it. A taxi will cost about $1.50. There are flights to and from Lima ($37) about three times a week, but no flights to other major cities at this time.

If you go to the airport and ask around, you can find light aircraft flying as far as Juanjui. From there, buses or other light aircraft can take you to Tarapoto. (For more information about light aeroplane flights, see the Tarapoto and Tocache sections.) There are flights on most days.

Bus Tingo María is a major bus stop on the route between Lima and Pucallpa and travel along that road was easy before the current Sendero problems. You can also get there, with difficulty, along the Huallaga Valley road from Tarapoto. This road is in terrible shape, especially from Juanjui to Tocache. Leaving Tingo María is harder because the Lima to Pucallpa buses tend to come through both late and full and few people get off in Tingo. Try to leave in the morning to allow time for problems. Unfortunately, most bus departures are in the evening.

León de Huánuco operates the most buses on the Pucallpa to Lima run, with three night buses to Lima (about 18 hours, $8.50) and one night bus to Pucallpa (about 8 hours, $5.30). Other bus companies servicing this route include Transportes Ucayali and La

Perla del Oriente; although their buses are not very good, they do schedule day departures. The following companies currently have only night departures but schedule changes are frequent: TEPSA, Transportes Orellana, Nor Oriente, Transportes Centro Oriental and Empresa Transportes La Perla in rough descending order of reliability (though transport out of Tingo María is often unreliable with all companies).

If you're going only as far as Huánuco, colectivos and shared Comité 5 cars leave frequently from the corner of Raimondi and Callao. The cars are faster and more expensive (about 2½ hours for $3.50). The minibuses cost about $1 less and take an hour more. The long-distance buses are even slower and cheaper.

Those heading north along the Huallaga River valley to Tarapoto can try León de Huánuco (which runs a couple of buses a week), a car from Comité 1 or one of the small Empresa La Marginal buses which leave several times a day for Tocache. From Tocache, you can continue by light plane (it's not too expensive – see Tocache in the Across the Northern Highlands chapter). Uchiza Express also operates buses to Tocache. Occasionally, these companies have buses beyond Tocache.

The North Coast

The scenery of the Peruvian coast north of Lima is similar to that of the south coast; both areas are part of the great South American coastal desert. On the coastal drive north from Lima you pass huge, rolling sand dunes, dizzying cliffs, oases of farmland, busy fishing villages, relaxing beach resorts and archaeological sites dating back thousands of years, as well as some of Peru's largest and most historic cities.

Few travellers are able to fully appreciate this area of Peru. Most are so wrapped up in visiting the world-famous Inca ruins and Lake Titicaca to the south that the northern part of the country is largely ignored. Those who do travel north tend to head either straight to the Ecuadorian border, 24 hours away, or along the coast for 4 hours then inland to the Callejón de Huaylas and the beautiful mountains of the Cordillera Blanca. Slowly travelling the north coast, however, allows greater involvement with the local people and often gets you away from the gringo 'scene'.

Chancay pot

ANCÓN

The first town north of Lima is Ancón, a big luxury resort about 40 km from the capital. This is the seaside resort of Lima's upper class, with clubs, fancy restaurants and private summer homes. It's not really geared to tourists and the few hotels are expensive.

En route from Lima to Ancón on the Pan-American Highway, you'll see something of the opposite end of Peru's social scale – the pueblos jovenes, or 'young towns'. These shanty towns often have no running water, electricity or other facilities. They are built by peasants migrating to Lima from the highlands in search of jobs and a higher standard of living.

CHANCAY

Beyond Ancón are the spectacular Pacasmayo sand dunes. There are two roads – one snakes along a narrow ledge at the bottom of the dunes and the other goes over the top. Both offer superb views of the dunes, which stretch on for some 20 km to the small village of Chancay. The Chancay subculture existed in this area from about 1100 AD to 1400 AD. The black-on-white ceramic style for which this coastal culture is noted is best seen at the excellent Amano Museum in Lima. Chancay itself is a small fishing village of some 10,000 inhabitants and has little to see, though there is a simple, friendly hotel.

THE CHURÍN ROAD

About 20 km north of Chancay, a turn-off to the right leads to the small mountain towns of Sayán, Churín and Oyón. This road follows the Río Huaura valley and an Expreso Huaral bus from Lima travels this road daily. About 5 km from the turn-off, you come to the reserve of Loma de Lachay. This curious hill seems to gain most of its moisture from the coastal mists, creating a unique microenvironment of dwarf forest with small animals and birds. There are no facilities at this reserve.

Between Sayán and Churín, the road climbs through strange rock formations and tropical scrub vegetation. Churín, 190 km from Lima, is a minor resort known for its good hot springs. There are a couple of cheap hotels on Avenida Larco Herrera, the main street, the best of which is the *Hostal Internacional Churín*. There is also the cheaper *Alojamiento Jardín*. Several inexpensive restaurants serve local food such as trout and cuy (guinea pig).

Beyond Churín, the road continues through the village of Oyón and on to the southern parts of the Cordillera Raura, a remote, snowcapped mountain range.

HUACHO

The small town of Huacho (population 40,000) is over 140 km north of Lima at the mouth of the Río Huaura. Buses from Huacho go up the valley. Across the river is the village of Huaura, where San Martín proclaimed Peru's independence. There are two or three basic hotels in Huacho.

BARRANCA & PARAMONGA

About 190 km north of Lima you reach Barranca. Though small, Barranca is the biggest town in the area and has the best facilities. Most buses along the coast stop here on their way to Supe, Pativilca, Paramonga and the turn-off for Huaraz and the Cordillera Blanca, all of which lie within a few km of Barranca. Everything happens on the main street, which is also the Pan-American Highway, but there's little to see here.

At the small fishing port of Supe, a few km south of Barranca, there are a couple of basic hotels. The archaeological site of Aspero is nearby. Although Aspero is one of the oldest sites in Peru, it has little to offer the untrained eye.

The village of Pativilca is a few km north of Barranca. It has one very basic hotel and a few simple restaurants, but most people stay at Barranca. Just north of Pativilca, the road to Huaraz and the Cordillera Blanca

branches off to the right. This spectacular road climbs through cactus-laden cliff faces and is worth travelling in daylight. Many people see no more of the north coast than the Pan-American Highway between Lima and the mountain turn-off at Pativilca.

Three or 4 km beyond the Huaraz turn-off is the archaeological site of Paramonga. This huge adobe temple is attributed to the Chimu civilisation, which was the ruling power on the north coast before being conquered by the Incas in the mid-1400s. The massive temple, surrounded by seven defensive walls, is clearly visible on the right-hand side of the Pan-American Highway and is worth a visit. Entry is about 20c and the small on-site museum is open from 8 am to 5 pm. Local buses travelling between Barranca and Paramonga will drop you off near the entrance.

A few years ago, I got to know Barranca better than I'd bargained for. I was in a great hurry to get from Ecuador to Lima, so I took direct long-distance buses from Quito to the border and from the border to Lima. When I reached Peru, I heard a rumour about a general strike, but as the buses were running in Tumbes, I bought my ticket to Lima. By the time I reached the outskirts of Barranca I had been travelling virtually nonstop for 40 hours and was beginning to breathe more easily – after all, it was only another 4 hours to Lima. Then the general strike began. Logs were pulled across the highway and rather menacing-looking groups of workers stood at these barricades, turning back all vehicles, even taxis and private cars. For 2 full days, a 2-km line of vehicles waited in the tropical sun outside Barranca. I understand that transport was paralysed throughout the country during this period. Meanwhile, the passengers slept on the bus and walked into town to eat. The protest was over an increase in the price of milk. This is a good example of the perils of planning too tight a schedule when travelling in Peru!

Places to Stay & Eat

There are a couple of movie theatres in Barranca and plenty of cheap restaurants, the best of which is the *Chifa Lung Fung* on the main street (but beware of the overcharging of gringos for 'servicio especial' – check your bill). You'll find several hotels along the main street. The best of these is the *Hotel Chavín* which charges about $6 for a clean double room with bath. Of the cheaper places, the *Pacífico* is quite good.

HUARMEY

North of Paramonga, the Pan-American Highway enters a particularly deserted stretch and soon crosses the line dividing the departments of Lima and Ancash. The government-run *Hotel de Turistas* at Huarmey, 290 km north of Lima is the best hotel on the 420-km stretch of road between Lima and Chimbote. A double room with bath costs about $10. Reservations can be made at ENTURPeru in Lima (tel 721928).

There's nothing to do in Huarmey except spend the night in the hotel, though if you have your own transport, you'll find some excellent deserted beaches nearby.

CASMA & SECHÍN

The small town of Casma is 370 km north of Lima. The archaeological site of Sechín is about 5 km away and easily reached from Casma. Casma was once an important colonial port which was sacked by various pirates during the 1600s, but its importance has declined greatly and the town was largely

destroyed by the earthquake of 31 May 1970. There's not much to do in either the port (11 km from the town) or the town itself and most people only come here to visit the Sechín ruins or to travel to Huaraz via the Punta Callán road, a route offering excellent panoramic views of the Cordillera Blanca.

Sechín

This site is one of the oldest in Peru (1500 BC) and among the more important and well-preserved of the coastal ruins. First excavated by the renowned Peruvian archaeologist J C Tello in 1937, it has suffered some damage from grave robbers and natural disasters. This site is 5 km south-east of Casma and easily reached on foot or by taxi; there are good road signs. To get there, head south of Casma on the Pan-American Highway for 3 km, then turn left and follow the paved road to Huara for a further 2 km to the site. If you're descending from Huara, you can visit the ruins en route to Casma if you don't have too much gear.

The site at Sechín, part of which was thought to have been buried by a landslide, is still being excavated and only some of the area is open to visitors. This consists of three outside walls of the main temple which are completely covered with bas-relief carvings of warriors and of captives being eviscerated. The gruesomely realistic carvings are up to 4 metres high. Which warlike peoples

Sechín ruins

were involved in building this temple remains a mystery and is one of the site's main points of interest. Inside the main temple are earlier mud structures which are in the process of being excavated – you can't go in but there is a model in the small, modern, on-site museum.

There are several other early sites in the Sechín area, most of which are still unexcavated because of a lack of funds. From the museum you can see Sechín Alto in the distance – a large, flat-topped hill. The fortress of Chanquillo consists of several towers surrounded by concentric walls. It can be visited but is best appreciated from the air. Aerial photographs are on display at the museum. If you wish to explore more than just Sechín, the museum attendant can give directions and there is a detailed area map in the museum.

The Sechín ruins and museum are open daily from 9 am to 5 pm and cost 50c to visit. There is a small shady garden and picnic area – bring your own food. The entry ticket also allows you to visit the Mochica ruins of Pañamarca, 10 km inland from the Pan-American Highway on the road to Nepeña (the turn-off is about halfway between Casma and Chimbote). The Pañamarca ruins are badly weather damaged.

Places to Stay

Casma has three hotels, the best of which is the pleasant *Hostal El Farol*. It's set in a garden and has a simple cafeteria and bar and helpful, friendly staff. There's a useful map in the lobby if you plan to explore some of the ruins in the area. The hotel is just off the main road, between the bus stop area and the Plaza de Armas and a couple of blocks from each – there's a sign on the main road. Singles/doubles with communal shower are $1.70/3 or $2.30/4.30 with private shower. There's only cold water, but Casma is so warm that this is no great hardship.

If you want to save a few cents, try the basic, unattractive *Hostal Central* on the Plaza de Armas. The clean *Hotel Sanchez*, a block from the plaza, has rooms at similar prices to those at El Farol.

Places to Eat

My wife and I stayed at *El Farol* a few years ago and wanted to have breakfast. We were the only customers in the hotel's cafeteria but were told that breakfast would be no problem. We asked what they had (you soon learn to ask *Que hay?* before choosing in small restaurants). The assistant strode purposefully to the refrigerator and swung the door open and we all peered hopefully inside. We couldn't help but laugh at the half full bottle of Pepsi and the small, sadly wrinkled papaya. The assistant, slightly crestfallen, soon recovered and offered to go out and buy some eggs and bread. We returned 30 minutes later to a good breakfast, complete with papaya juice.

There are no particularly good restaurants in Casma. One of the best is the inexpensive *Chifa Tio Sam* next to the Hotel Sanchez, near the plaza. Several cheap and basic places are near the main bus stops if you're waiting for a bus.

Getting There & Away

Many companies run buses north and south along the Pan-American Highway but, because Casma is so small, most don't have offices. If you're heading for Trujillo or Lima, you can flag down a bus as it comes through and hope for a seat. Empresa Turismo Chimbote, with an office on the main street, has five buses a day to Lima but only two or three seats are available from the Casma office – the rest are sold in Chimbote. It's best to book for your departure as soon as you arrive. Chinchaysuyo also has an office on the main street and a couple of daily buses to both Lima and Trujillo – you have a better chance of getting a seat but the buses are old. TEPSA has an office but it's not always open. Trips to Lima average $4 and 6 hours; buses to Trujillo are about $2 and 3 hours.

There are also frequent colectivos to Chimbote, 50 km to the north, from where there are better facilities. These take 1¼ hours and charge $1.

Several small companies run buses to Huaraz along a dirt road over the Cordillera

Negra. The route begins with good views of the desert foothills of the western Andes and climbs up the fertile Casma Valley, finally emerging over the Punta Callán Pass. The pass is 30 km from Huaraz and, from its altitude of 4224 metres, you will have one of the best overall panoramic views of the Cordillera Blanca. It's worth doing the journey during the day with Empresa Moreno (7 hours, $3). Empresa Chinchaysuyo has only night buses (though you might just catch the dawn from Punta Callán). Empresa Huaraz has three buses a week. If these are all full, try Empresa Soledad (though their offices were closed last time I was there).

All the bus offices and stops are within a few blocks of one another, clustered together on the main road at the junction where the Pan-American Highway arrives in Casma from Lima. You won't have any trouble finding the buses – it's a small town.

CHIMBOTE

This is the first major town along the north coast; it is 420 km north of Lima. Chimbote is Peru's largest fishing port and millions of tons of fish were landed here in the 1960s. Since then, the industry has declined because of overfishing. Despite this and despite the 1970 earthquake (which destroyed much of the city), the population has continued to grow dramatically and is now close to 200,000 – about the same as Cuzco's. The comparison stops there, however. The town's several large fishmeal factories give the town a pervasive and distinctive odour. There are also some steel mills. The beaches are dirty but good for watching bird life.

Unless you're interested in the fishing or steel industries, there's not much to do in Chimbote, but the town can be used as a base for excursions into the Santa River valley, where there are some little-explored archaeological ruins. It's also a good place to stay overnight if you're heading for Huaraz by the spectacular Cañon del Pato route.

Information

The tourist office at Bolognesi 465 can provide information about touring a local steel mill if you're interested. Also ask them about visiting the ruins of the Santa Valley.

Santa Valley

The Santa River flows into the ocean at Santa, about 20 km north of Chimbote. The river valley is a little-explored area and poorly serviced by public transport – a few buses go up this road en route to Huaraz. Aerial reconnaissance has revealed dozens of pre-Inca sites (read Gene Savoy's *Antisuyo*), including a Great Wall about 50 km long.

Adventurous travellers could explore the valley on foot – you don't need too much gear because it doesn't rain or get cold. A blanket and sleeping pad will suffice. Climbing the hills on either side of the valley will bring you to ruins which are very rarely visited. A possible place from which to start is Tanguche. It is the first place inland from Santa and is marked on most maps. Parts of the Great Wall can be seen nearby and many more ruins lie further inland in the hills edging the Santa Valley.

Carry your own food and plenty of water bottles – the Santa River runs all year round but you should purify the water before drinking. This trip is only for self-sufficient travellers with experience in travelling rough and an interest in exploring the desert.

Places to Stay

Chimbote offers a good selection of hotels. For those on a tight budget, the very basic *Hostal Huascarán* and *Oriental* charge less than $1 per person. As in many of the cheaper hotels, the water supply is erratic. The *Hostal Augusto* has rooms with private cold showers for just over $1 per person. Similarly priced are the *Hotel Venus, Felice* and *María Isabel*. Try the *Hostal El Santa* for rooms with bath at about $2 per person, though I've had mixed reviews about its cleanliness.

Slightly upmarket, the *Hotel Riviera* and *San Felipe* charge about $3.50/5.50 for clean singles/doubles with bath and hot water. The more expensive *Hotel Presidente* is also quite good.

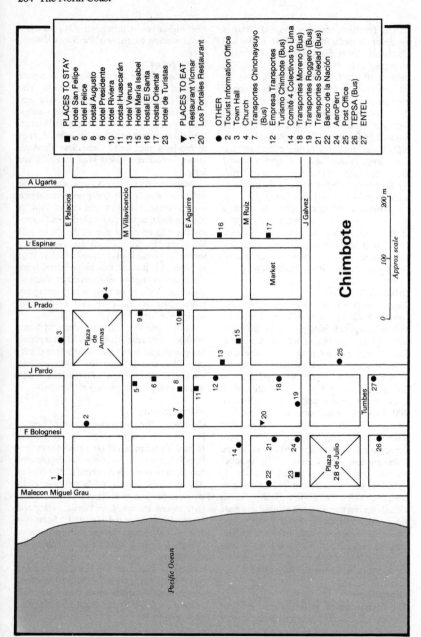

PLACES TO STAY
5 Hotel San Felipe
6 Hotel Felice
8 Hostal Augusto
9 Hotel Presidente
10 Hotel Riviera
11 Hostal Huascarán
13 Hotel Venus
15 Hotel María Isabel
16 Hostal El Santa
17 Hostal Oriental
23 Hotel de Turistas

PLACES TO EAT
1 Restaurant Vicmar
20 Los Portales Restaurant

OTHER
2 Tourist Information Office
3 Town Hall
4 Church
7 Transportes Chinchaysuyo (Bus)
12 Empresa Transportes
14 Turismo Chimbote (Bus)
    Comité 4 Colectivos to Lima
18 Transportes Moreno (Bus)
19 Transportes Roggero (Bus)
21 Transportes Soledad (Bus)
22 Banco de la Nación
24 AeroPeru
25 Post Office
26 TEPSA (Bus)
27 ENTEL

Chimbote

Approx scale
0   100   200 m

Pacific Ocean

The best in town is the government-run *Hotel de Turistas*. Rooms with bath cost $10/14, including continental breakfast, and there are also some cheaper rooms with communal bath. Reservations can be made at ENTURPeru in Lima (tel 721928).

Places to Eat

There are no fancy restaurants in central Chimbote. The best place is the café in the *Hotel de Turistas*. *Los Portales* is good and inexpensive and the *San Remo*, near the Pardo/Villavicencio corner of the plaza, serves seafood. You could also try the *Restaurant Vicmar* near the waterfront.

Getting There & Away

Air Twice a week, flights between Lima and Trujillo stop at the nearby airport. Schedules change frequently, and at times, no flights are available. There is an AeroPeru office in the city centre. Fares to Lima are about $30.

Bus & Colectivo The most frequent service to Lima ($4, 7 hours) is with Empresa Transportes Turismo Chimbote; there are buses every 1 or 2 hours. Comité 4 colectivos to Lima are a couple of hours faster but almost twice as expensive.

Going north along the coast to Trujillo, Chiclayo and Piura, as well as to Lima, are TEPSA (the most expensive), Transportes Roggero and Transportes Chinchaysuyo buses. Chinchaysuyo also has buses to Cajamarca.

Transportes Moreno and Transportes Soledad operate services to Huaraz. Most buses go via Casma, but some travel via the Santa River valley through Huallanca and the wild Cañon del Pato to Caraz and Huaraz. This route is the most spectacular approach to Huaraz from the coast. When I was last in Chimbote, only night buses went via the Cañon del Pato but I understand that Transportes Moreno now schedules day departures – check. The Moreno terminal has a bad reputation for pickpockets (as, indeed, does much of the town).

TRUJILLO

The coastal city of Trujillo, with 750,000 inhabitants, vies with Arequipa for the status of Peru's second largest city. It is the capital of the strangely H-shaped Department of La Libertad and its only important city. Trujillo is about 560 km (9 hours) north of Lima and warrants a visit of several days. Founded in 1536 by Pizarro, it is an attractive colonial city and retains much of its colonial flavour.

Nearby is the ancient Chimu capital of Chan Chan, which was conquered by the Incas, and several other Chimu sites. Also in the area are the immense Moche Pyramids of the Sun and Moon which date back about 1500 years. If all this culture wears you out, you can relax at one of the pleasant beaches around Trujillo.

Information

Tourist Information The tourist office (tel 246941) on the Plaza de Armas at Pizarro 402 is run by the tourist police who can be distinguished by their smart white uniforms. They are the most friendly and helpful policemen that I've met in a decade of travel in Latin America. I recommend them highly. They patrol the major archaeological sites with the specific aim of aiding and protecting visitors. The office is open daily from 8 am to 7.30 pm.

There is also a government-run tourist office (tel 241936) at Independencia 628.

Money Changing money in Trujillo is a distinct pleasure because some of the banks are housed in colonial buildings. One of my favourites is the Banco Nor Peru in the Casa de la Emancipación. It gives good rates for both cash and travellers' cheques. You can also change money at the more modern Banco de Crédito or with one of the casas de cambio on the main street of Gamarra. If you check a few places, you should be able to find exchange rates comparable to those in Lima. This is the best place on the north coast to change money.

Recently, you could get better rates with street moneychangers than in the banks or

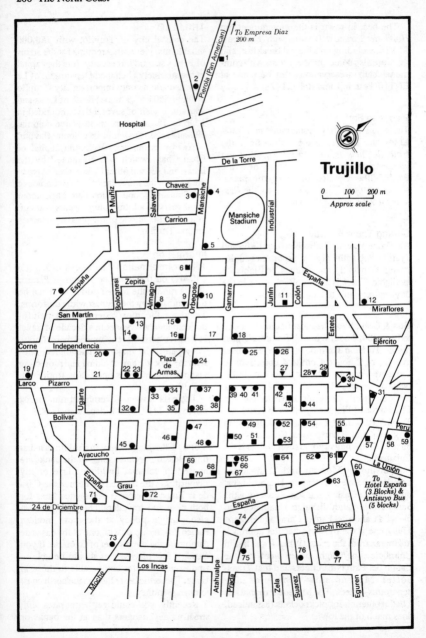

To Empresa Díaz
200 m

Pierola (Pan American)

Hospital

De la Torre

Trujillo

0   100   200 m
Approx scale

Chavez

P Muñiz

Salaverry

Mansiche

Carrion

Mansiche
Stadium

España

Industrial

España

Miraflores

Zepita

Bolognesi

Almagro

Orbegoso

Gamarra

Junín

Colón

San Martín

Corne

Independencia

Estete

Ejército

Pizarro

Ugarte

Plaza
de
Armas

Bolívar

Ayacucho

Peru

La Unión

To
Hotel España
(3 Blocks) &
Antisuyo Bus
(5 blocks)

Grau

España

24 de Diciembre

Sinchi Roca

Los Incas

Mochi

Atahualpa

Prada

Zela

Suarez

Eguren

■ PLACES TO STAY

1	Hotel Primavera
6	Hotel Oscar
11	Hotel San Martín
16	Hotel de Turistas
42	Hotel Americano
43	Hostal Colón
46	Hostal Residencial Los Escudos
50	Hotel Continental & Hostal Acapulco
51	Hostal Vogi
55	Hostal Recreo
56	Hotel Paris
57	Hostal Las Vegas
61	Hostal Peru
64	Hostals Central & Lima
66	Hotel Turismo
68	Hotel Opt Gar
70	Hotel San José

▼ PLACES TO EAT

9	ABC Chicken Restaurant
27	Marco's Café & Café Romano
28	Pizarro & Recreo Restaurants
40	El Mesón de Cervantes
66	Chifa Oriental & Chifa Ak Chan
67	Restaurant Oasis & Restaurant 24 Horas

● OTHER

2	Cassinelli Museum
3	Compañía de Transportes Piura (Bus)
4	Bus Stop for Chiclayo
5	Buses to Chan Chan, Huanchaco & Arco Iris
7	Dancin' Discotheque
8	Banco de la Nación & Migraciónes Office
10	Cine Primavera
12	EMTRAFESA
13	University Zoology Museum
14	La Compañí Church
15	Comité 14
17	Santo Domingo Art Gallery

18	San Francisco Church
19	Local Bus to Buenos Aires Beach
20	Post Office
21	Santo Domingo Church
22	Archaeology Museum
23	Las Tinajas Bar
24	Cathedral
25	Casa de los Léones
26	Santa Clara Church
29	TEPSA Ticket Office
30	Plazuela El Recreo
31	Panamericana (Bus)
32	AeroPeru
33	Tourist Office & Tourist Police
34	Casa Urquiaga
35	Cine Ideal
36	Casona Orbegoso & Republican Museum
37	Faucett Airline
38	Banco de Crédito
39	Casa de la Emancipación & Banco Nor Peru
41	Palacio Iturregui
42	Cine Peru
44	Empresa Antisuyo (Bus)
45	Ruined Church of Belén
47	San Agustín Church
48	Market
49	ENTEL
52	Chinchaysuyo Bus (See also Ref. 75)
53	Expreso Norpacifico (Bus)
54	Carmelite Church & Art Museum
58	Expreso Sudamericano (Bus)
59	Cine Trujillo
60	Bull Ring
62	Comité 12
63	Old City Wall
65	Teatro Ayacucho
69	Cine Star
71	Local Buses to Casa Grande
72	TEPSA Bus Station
73	TEPSA & Norpacifico (Buses)
74	Cine Chimu
75	Chinchaysuyo Bus (See also Ref. 52)
76	Local Bus to Pyramids of the Sun & Moon
77	Market

casas de cambio. Shop around. Money-changers are found around the Plaza de Armas and near the banks at the intersection of Pizarro and Gamarra.

Visas You can renew your visa or tourist card at the migraciónes office at Almagro 225, 3rd floor, next to the Banco de la Nación. I've heard that it's a long process.

Medical The best place for general medical services is the Anglo-American Hospital opposite the Cassinelli Museum. They don't charge very much.

Colonial Buildings

The colonial mansions and churches are most attractive and worth visiting. Unfortunately, they don't seem to have very regular opening hours and the listed times may change without notice. There are also some excellent museums.

The single feature which makes Trujillo's colonial centre especially distinctive is the beautiful wrought-iron grillework fronting almost every colonial building in the city. This, combined with the buildings' pastel shades, results in a typical Trujillano ambience not found in Peru's other colonial cities.

Plaza de Armas

The very spacious and attractive main square has an impressive central statue of the heroes of Peruvian independence. The plaza is fronted by the cathedral which was begun in 1647, destroyed in 1759 and rebuilt soon afterwards. The cathedral has a famous basilica and is often open in the evenings around 6 pm.

There are several elegant colonial mansions around the plaza. One is now the Hotel de Turistas and contains a small museum of Moche ceramics. Another, the Casa Urquiaga, stands next to the tourist office and now belongs to the Banco Central de la Reserva del Peru. It has a small ceramics museum and can be visited during banking hours for free.

The tourist police at the corner of the plaza will be happy to give you a detailed description and history of the central statue and surrounding buildings, but you should speak Spanish.

On Sundays at 9 am there is a flag-raising ceremony on the Plaza de Armas complete with a parade, *caballos de paso* or 'pacing horses' and *marinera* dances.

Churches

Apart from the cathedral, the colonial churches of Santo Domingo, San Francisco, La Compañía, San Agustín and Santa Clara are worth a look, though getting inside is largely a matter of luck. They are close to one another and it's easy to stroll from one to the next. San Agustín, with its finely gilded high altar, dates from 1558 and is usually open. You certainly won't get into the Church of Belén – the 1970 earthquake left it completely in ruins. Nevertheless, it is instructive to see what an unrestored church looks like.

Art Galleries

Several of the colonial buildings contain art galleries with changing shows. Admission is normally free or a nominal few cents. The Santo Domingo Art Gallery, is open from 9.30 am to 1 pm and 4 to 8.30 pm daily.

The Casa de los Léones (also known as the Ganoza Chopitea Residence) has changing exhibitions; it's open from 10 am to 1 pm and 4 to 9 pm daily. The collections can often be very good, depending on your taste, and make a change from the interminable religious and colonial art that is the stock of most museums – good modern Peruvian art is sometimes shown as well as some rather arcane pieces that you may never have a chance to see elsewhere.

The cathedral has a museum of religious and colonial art, which is open from 9 am to 1 pm and 4 to 7 pm from Tuesday to Saturday, and on Sunday mornings. There are similar opening hours at the Carmelite Museum in the Monastery of El Carmen. It specialises in colonial and religious art.

The Casona Orbegoso, on the 5th block of Calle Orbegoso, is a beautiful 18th century mansion with a collection of art of that period.

Palacio Iturregui

This early 19th century mansion is unmistakable and impossible to ignore – it's painted an overpowering shade of blue. Its main claim to fame is that General Iturregui lived here when he proclaimed Trujillo's independence from Spain in 1820. Trujillo was one of the first cities in Peru to declare its independence. The mansion is now used by the swanky Club Central, which will allow you to visit between 11 am and noon on weekdays.

Cassinelli Museum

This archaeological museum is on the western outskirts of town, in the basement of a petrol station. It's open from 8 to 11.30 am and 3 to 5.30 pm on weekdays and admission is about $1.

When I visited this museum, I found the petrol station without difficulty and spotted several pots and other pieces through the windows. I went inside and asked to see the collection and was told to wait a few minutes. I looked at the haphazardly displayed pots in the garage office and wondered if this was it. After all, what could I expect in an oily garage? After a few minutes, however, I was led through a locked door, down a narrow flight of stairs and through a second locked door – this one heavily armoured. On entering the basement, I was astonished to see hundreds of ceramics carefully displayed on shelves which filled the room. The curator showed me dozens of his favourite pieces, letting me hold and examine several as he explained where they came from and what they represented.

Among the most interesting were the whistling pots, which produced clear notes when they were blown. I was especially intrigued by a pair of pots representing a male and a female bird – they appeared to be tinamous. Superficially, they were very similar, but when they were blown, each produced a completely different note. These notes corresponded to the distinctive calls of the male and female birds.

The exhibits were fascinating and well set out and I was the only visitor. I was very pleased to be able to handle a few of the pots myself. The whistling pots were superb. The rather bizarre location of the museum added to its uniqueness. All in all, this was among the best museum experiences I have had in Peru and I give this place a whole-hearted recommendation.

Señor Cassinelli has also put together a collection of his best pots and exhibits them (under glass) in the front rooms of the Hotel de Turistas. Viewing them is free.

Archaeology Museum

The university-run Archaeology Museum at Pizarro 349 is open from 7 am to 2 pm Monday to Friday. It has an interesting collection of art and pottery and a reproduction of the murals found in the Moche Pyramid of the Moon. Entry costs about 50c.

Zoology Museum

The Zoology Museum is also run by the university and has similar hours to the Archaeology Museum. The stuffed animals in the collection are mainly Peruvian.

Beaches

The beach at the Trujillo suburb of Buenos Aires is easily reached by black-and-white local buses which pass the stop on Larco and España several times an hour. You can swim at the beach, though the water tends to be rough, and there are several seafood restaurants on the waterfront. Go in a group so that someone (several people) can watch your possessions while you're in the water. It's safe enough in front of the restaurants, but walking along the beach away from the Buenos Aires area is dangerous. The track from Buenos Aires to Chan Chan is especially notorious for muggings. The tourist office map of the area calls this track a *via de evitamiento*, or 'route to be avoided'.

There is a much better beach in the village of Huanchaco, 11 km to the north (see the Huanchaco section).

Caballos de Paso

Breeding, training and watching the caballos de paso (pacing horses) is a favourite Peruvian activity. The idea is to breed and train horses which pace more elegantly than others. Trujillo and Lima are both centres of this upper-class pastime. Trujilleños will tell you that the activity originated in the Department of La Libertad.

Fiestas

Trujillo's major festival is called El Festival Internacional de la Primavera, or 'the International Spring Festival', held annually for about 40 years. Its attractions include international beauty contests, parades, national dancing competitions (including the marinera), caballos de paso displays, sports and various other cultural activities. It all happens in the last week in September and better hotels are fully booked well in advance.

The last week in January is also busy with the national marinera contest. The marinera is a typically coastal Peruvian dance which involves much waving of handkerchiefs. Students of folk dance should not miss this one.

Places to Stay – bottom end

It is perhaps because Trujillo is so far away from the more heavily visited areas of Peru that its hotels are cheaper than those in most other major cities. The cheapest, while nothing to write home about, offer double rooms for $1 and even the more expensive hotels are cheap in comparison with those in Cuzco or Arequipa.

One of the cheapest is the very basic *Hostal Peru* at 60c/$1 for singles/doubles. The *Hotel Paris* opposite charges 70c/$1. For some strange reason, the *Hostal Lima* has become popular with gringos; stay here if you want to meet other budget travellers, though it's noisy and looks like a jail. Singles/doubles are 80c/$1. The *Hostal Central* next door is similarly priced and the *Hostal Colón* is also in this price range. None of these hotels have private showers or hot water and their standards of cleanliness are not very high. For around the same price, try the reasonably clean *Hotel San José*. The *Hotel España*, close to the Antisuyo bus station, is basic but clean and costs a little more.

The best budget hotel, for my money at least, is the *Hotel Americano*. It is housed in a rambling old mansion which is rather dingy but has character. The rooms are really basic but are kept fairly clean and some have baths with cold water. Singles/doubles with bath cost $1.60/2.50, a little less with communal bath. (One traveller wrote and complained that my recommendation was 'run down'. At this price, what did he expect? I stayed here

again in 1989 and it's just the same – old, dingy, full of character, reasonably clean and cheap.)

Places to Stay – middle

The *Hostal Las Vegas* looks clean but is otherwise unremarkable and charges $2.70/4.70 for singles/doubles with bath. The *Hotel San Martín* has over 100 rooms and so is almost never full. It's characterless but reasonably clean and there's hot water in the private showers. Singles/doubles with bath cost $3/5. The *Hotel Turismo* is also clean. Rooms with telephone, bath and slightly erratic hot water cost $3.30/4.70. The clean, modern *Hostal Vogi*, at $3.30/5.30 with bath and hot water, is also good. Two other mid-range hotels which I haven't tried are the *Hotel Oscar* and the *Hostal Recreo*.

The *Hotel Continental* has clean, carpeted singles/doubles with telephone, music, bath and hot water for $5/7. The similarly priced *Hostal Acapulco* next door rates itself a three-star hotel but looks neither as good nor as clean as its neighbour – its main attraction is the Turkish bath on the premises. Also in this price range is the pleasant *Hostal Residencial Los Escudos*. It's locked and secure (ring the bell to be let in), has a garden and serves continental breakfast. The clean, well-run *Hotel Opt Gar* has a good restaurant and singles/doubles at $5/7.50. At about the same price, the clean *Hostería El Sol* has been recommended. It's at Calle Los Brillantes 224, about 2 km north-west of the centre (a taxi costs under $1).

Places to Stay – top end

The government-run *Hotel de Turistas* is good – make reservations at ENTURPeru (tel 721928) in Lima. Singles/doubles with bath and continental breakfast cost $13/18 and there are also a few cheaper rooms with shared bath. The hotel is in a beautiful building right on the Plaza de Armas and has an excellent ceramic museum on the premises. Stay here if you have a few extra dollars.

Slightly cheaper is the clean and modern *Hotel Primavera* a little way from the centre.

The most expensive hotel in town is the modern *Hotel El Golf*. It has a swimming pool and other facilities, but as it is well away from the centre, you'll have to take a taxi. Stay here if you're with a convention.

Places to Eat

There are plenty of restaurants near the market, and for the impecunious, the food stalls in the market itself are among the cheapest places to eat in Trujillo. Restaurant prices are also very reasonable. A block from the market are several Chinese restaurants; the *Chifa Oriental* and *Chifa Ak Chan* are recommended. The nearby *Restaurant 24 Horas* is inexpensive and always open. The *Restaurant Oasis* next door is good for fritadas and other local food. Across the street, the restaurant in the *Hotel Opt Gar* serves some of the best international food in town.

My favourite restaurants are both on the 700 block of Pizarro. The *Café Romano* has strong espresso coffee and *Marco's Café* serves delicious home-made cakes and pies as well as ice cream. Both cafés offer a variety of good food. If you're economising, ask for the set lunch or dinner at well under $1.

A good choice for a cheap set lunch in pleasant surroundings is *El Mesón de Cervantes*. It has an outside courtyard with shaded tables. The *Pizarro* and *Recreo* restaurants look less elegant but are good value for money. If you like fried chicken, the *ABC* chicken restaurant has large portions.

There used to be three or four vegetarian restaurants in the area around the 700 block of Bolívar. They were all closed recently and I couldn't find any others open. Ask around if you're a vegetarian – there must be a vegetarian restaurant somewhere.

Entertainment

One of Trujillo's many cinemas is often the best choice for an evening out. The place to go in the evening is a bar called *Las Tinajas*, on the corner of the plaza, which is full of young Peruvians. It has a balcony with a plaza view and folklórico groups occasion-ally play late in the evening. A discotheque named simply *Dancin'* is another place to try.

I have received reports that single women tend to receive a lot of attention from males in Trujillo bars. This can reach exasperating, even harassing levels.

Getting There & Away

Trujillo is Peru's major north-coast city and is serviced by scores of buses making the 24-hour run along the Pan-American Highway between Lima and the Ecuadorian border (and intermediate coastal points). There are also daily flights to and from Lima and other cities.

Air Both Faucett and AeroPeru have offices in Trujillo. Between them, they operate two or three flights a day to Lima. One-way fares are about $50, less for residents. AeroPeru also has daily flights to Chiclayo, two flights a week to Cajamarca, two flights a week to Tarapoto, one flight a week to Juanjui and one flight a week to Iquitos via Yurimaguas. There are no flights from Trujillo to Piura or Tumbes at this time. Schedules vary so often that there is little point in giving the days on which flights operate.

Bus & Colectivo Most major companies operate up and down the coast along the Pan-American Highway. A few go inland. Prices and schedules vary widely from company to company and from month to month. There is no set pattern and the details given below are only intended as a rough guide. Bear in mind that buses to Lima tend to leave at night, so if you want to travel by day, book in advance. Most buses leave Trujillo full and advance booking is recommended for any departure.

TEPSA buses are usually the most expensive. The TEPSA ticket office is on Estete, well away from the two bus depots. You can buy tickets at both office and depot, but make sure you know which place the bus is leaving from. The two TEPSA terminals are marked on the Trujillo map; the one on Almagro is very crowded and is the point of departure for buses originating in Trujillo. The terminal on Moche is small and less crowded and is the place to catch buses passing through Trujillo. Try this depot if the other buses are full. Several other companies (including Norpacifico and Transportes Roggero) have offices on Moche for buses passing through. Chinchaysuyo has two depots, but most buses leave from Prada (this is a slightly rough location, so take a taxi and watch your belongings). Empresa Antisuyo also has two depots – the one further from town is used for more departures. (See the Trujillo map for locations.)

If you're heading north, the first major stop is Chiclayo. This journey costs $2 and takes up to 4 hours by bus. The locals stand on Avenida Mansiche outside the stadium and catch the next bus heading north. All northbound buses with empty seats will stop here. If you'd rather not bother about watching your luggage while you wait on the side of the road, the most frequent Chiclayo service is with EMTRAFESA (12 buses a day).

Several bus companies provide services to Piura ($4, 9 hours) and/or Tumbes ($9, 16 hours). TEPSA and Expreso Sudamericano both run night buses to Tumbes and Transportes Roggero has an afternoon bus to Tumbes. Transportes Roggero and CIA de Transportes Piura each operate a night bus to Piura, and Chinchaysuyo has both a day and a night bus to Piura.

The trip to Lima takes 9 hours and, when I did it in late 1985, it cost about $6. I did the same journey 6 weeks later and it cost just under $5. In 1989, the trip was $2.70. So, if you think you've noticed dozens of price 'errors' in this book, you might begin to understand why! The most comfortable service to Lima is with TEPSA but they only have three night buses. If you prefer to travel during the day, Chinchaysuyo has several departures a day for Lima. Other companies with buses to Lima usually have only one service a day (usually overnight). They include Expreso Norpacifico, Expreso Sudamericano, Transportes Roggero and Peru Express. Many will sell tickets to intermediate points between Trujillo and Lima.

There are various bus services inland. Chinchaysuyo has a direct bus to Huaraz ($6, 10 hours) but most departures are at night. If you want to travel by day, leave from Chimbote instead. You may be able to get a ticket from Trujillo and change in Chimbote, thus avoiding a night there.

Connections from Chiclayo to Cajamarca are better than those from Trujillo, so if you plan to visit both cities, you may want to consider going to Chiclayo first. Empresa Diaz buses run from Trujillo to Cajamarca. The terminal is on the north Pan-American Highway, about 1 km north-east of the town centre. The journey to Cajamarca takes about 8 hours and costs $3. If you can't find a direct bus, you could take any bus to Chiclayo and get off at the Cajamarca turn-off (about 15 km past Pacasmayo) to wait for a Cajamarca-bound bus. It's a hot place to wait but there are a couple of basic cafés for cold drinks. If you leave Trujillo fairly early in the morning, you should be able to connect with a bus from Chiclayo. Finally, if bussing seems too much of a hassle, book a shared taxi seat with Comité 12, leaving at 12.30 pm daily ($6.50, 5½ hours).

If you want to head east from Trujillo to Otuzco, Santiago de Chuco, Huamachuco and Cajabamba (this is the much rougher and longer old route to Cajamarca), the best regular service is with Antisuyo. Unfortunately, this attractive route is driven only at night, but perhaps the schedule will change.

Chinchaysuyo used to run two buses a week on the long northern route into the jungle via Chiclayo, Bagua Grande and Moyobamba to Tarapoto, but the service was recently stopped, partly due to rough road conditions and partly due to problems with drug traffickers and the Sendero in the Moyobamba to Tarapoto area. If this route opens up again, the exceedingly long, rough and tiring journey takes 24 hours when the going is good (which it usually isn't). It's a spectacular route though, and well worth travelling.

Top: Inca trail porters in traditional clothes (RR)
Left: Descending steps on the Inca trail (RR)
Right: The train for Machu Picchu pauses in Ollantaytambo (TW)

Top: Inca trail hikers viewing Sayacmarca (RR)
Bottom: Don Victor Delgado loads mule team, Cordillera Vilcabamba (RR)

Getting Around
Airport Transport The airport, about 10 km north-west of Trujillo, can be reached cheaply on the bus to Huanchaco, though you'll have to walk the last km or so. Ask the driver where the airport turn-off is. A taxi to or from the city centre costs $2 to $3.

ARCHAEOLOGICAL SITES AROUND TRUJILLO
The Moche and Chimu cultures left the greatest mark on the Trujillo area, but are by no means the only ones. In the March 1973 *National Geographic* article, Drs M E Moseley & C J Mackey claimed knowledge of over 2000 sites in the Moche River valley, which enters the ocean near Trujillo. Many of these sites are small and well-nigh forgotten, but others include the largest pre-Columbian city in America (Chan Chan) as well as pyramids which required in excess of an incredible 100 million adobe bricks to construct.

Five major archaeological sites can be easily reached from Trujillo by local bus or taxi. Two of these sites are Moche, dating

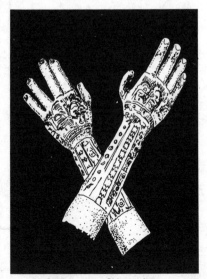

Golden arms – Chimu culture

from about 500 AD. The other three, from the Chimu culture, date from about 1200 AD to 1300 AD.

Warning
I have heard several reports of single travellers, especially women, being mugged, robbed or raped while visiting the more remote archaeological sites. You are advised to stay on main footpaths at all times, not to visit the ruins late in the day and to go with a friend or hire a guide to accompany you.

Guides
One guide has been recommended to me several times. Pedro Puerta, who has an office at Km 560 on the north Pan-American Highway, just past the Templo Arco Iris, speaks English and is enthusiastic and knowledgeable about all the ruins in the area. He can be contacted through the Hotel de Turistas and charges about $3 per hour, plus taxi/bus fares. He will take a small group of you and will arrange tours to wherever you want to go.

Another guide who has been recommended by several travellers is Clara Bravo (tel 243347). She can be found at Huayna Capac 542 in Trujillo.

Various travel agents in Trujillo provide guide services. Trujillo Tours at Gamarra 440-448 is one of the best.

Archaeology & History
One of the earliest groups in Peru to be studied are the Huaca Prieta people, who lived at the site of that name around 3500 BC to 2300 BC. These hunter/gatherers also began to develop simple agriculture. They grew cotton and varieties of bean and pepper but corn, now a staple, was unheard of. Finds of simple fishing nets and hooks indicate that the Huaca Prieta people primarily ate seafood. They lived in single-room shacks half buried in the ground and most of what is known about them has been deduced from their middens, or garbage piles. Hence we know that they were a preceramic people, didn't use jewellery and had developed netting and weaving. At their most artistic,

they decorated dried gourds with simply carved patterns; similarly decorated gourds are produced today as a Peruvian handicraft. Hot stones may have been dropped into these gourds to cook food.

Huaca Prieta is one of the most intensively studied early Peruvian sites but, for the non-archaeologist, it's more interesting to read about than to visit. After all, it's simply a prehistoric pile of garbage. If you want to go, it's about 30 km north of Trujillo on the south side of the Chicama Valley, by the coast. Colectivos go from Avenida España to Cartavio; from there, it's a walk of about 7 km.

After the decline of the Huaca Prieta site, a developmental era began. Weaving improved, agriculture developed with the advent of corn and, particularly importantly, the making of ceramics began and simple funerary offerings were made. Burial sites in the Chicama and Virú valleys gave archaeologists an insight into this development, but

no specific site is particularly important to the traveller. This period is called the Guañape after a tiny fishing village near the mouth of the Virú River where burial sites of this era were excavated.

About 850 BC, a major new cultural influence began to leave its mark on the area. This was the cultist period, named after a feline-worshipping cult which had one of its main centres at Chavín de Huantár, on the eastern slopes of the Cordillera Blanca. The Chavín influence swept over the northern mountains and the northern and central coasts of Peru. At its most simple, the Chavín influence consisted of a highly stylised art form based especially on jaguar motifs. The Chavín Horizon could be called the first major culture in Peru as well as one of the most artistically developed. The various areas and groups it encompassed were typified by the rapid development of their ceramic ware and a common art form. In the Trujillo area, the

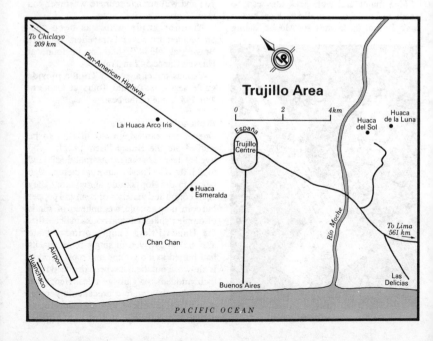

Chavín influence was represented by the Cupisnique culture. Examples of Cupisnique pottery can be seen in the museums of Lima and Trujillo, though there are no especially noteworthy ruins for the visitor to see.

Archaeologists identify several other geographically smaller and less important cultures of the Trujillo area which coincided with the later Cupisnique period. These include the Salinar, Vicus and Gallinazo.

So far, I've described a series of developments which have probably left you, the traveller, with little desire to head up to Trujillo to explore ancient sites and cities. This has just been by way of introduction.

With the decline of the Cupisnique period came the beginnings of the fascinating Moche period, a culture that has left impressive archaeological sites and some of the most outstanding pottery to be seen in Peru's museums.

The Moche culture is named after the river which flows into the ocean just south of Trujillo. The word Mochica has been used interchangeably with Moche and refers to a dialect spoken in the Trujillo area at the time of the conquest, though not necessarily spoken by the Moche people. Moche is now the preferred usage.

The Moche culture evolved from the Cupisnique at about the time of Christ. The Moche didn't conquer the Cupisnique; rather, there was a slow transition characterised by a number of developments. Ceramics, textiles and metalwork improved greatly, architectural skills allowed the construction of huge pyramids and other structures and there was enough leisure time for art and a highly organised religion.

As with the Nazca culture, which developed on the south coast at about the same time, the Moche period is especially known for its ceramics, considered the most artistically sensitive and technically developed of any found in Peru. The thousands of Moche pots preserved in museums are so realistically decorated with figures and scenes that they give us a very descriptive look at life during the Moche period. Pots were modelled into lifelike representations of people,

crops, domestic or wild animals, marine life and houses. Other pots were painted with scenes of both ceremonial and everyday life. From these pots, archaeologists know that Moche society was very class conscious. The most important people, especially the priests and warriors, were members of the urban classes and lived closest to the large ceremonial pyramids and other temples. They were surrounded by a middle class of artisans and then, in descending order, farmers and fishermen, servants, slaves and beggars.

The priests and warriors were both honoured and obeyed. They are the people most frequently shown in ceramics, which depict them being carried in litters wearing particularly fine jewellery or clothing. Their authority is evident from pots showing scenes of punishment, including the mutilation and death of those who dared to disobey. Other facets of Moche life illustrated on the pots include surgical procedures such as amputation and setting of broken limbs. Sex

Mochica pot

is realistically shown; one room in the Rafael Herrera Museum in Lima is entirely devoted to (mainly Moche) erotic pots depicting most sexual practices, some rather imaginative. Clothing, musical instruments, tools and jewellery are all frequent subjects for ceramics. As there was no written language, most of what we know about the Moche comes from this wealth of pottery.

The ceramics also show us that the Moche had well-developed weaving techniques but, because of rare rainstorms every few decades, most of their textiles have been destroyed. Metalwork, on the other hand, has survived. They used gold, silver and copper mainly for ornaments but some heavy copper implements have also been found.

The Moche did not live in towns as we know them. A more accurate description would be a high-density peasant population surrounding a central worship site such as a massive pyramid. Two of these survive, side by side, a few km south of Trujillo. They are known as the Huacas del Sol y de la Luna, or the 'Temples of the Sun and the Moon', and are easily visited. The Temple of the Sun is the largest pre-Columbian structure in South America and is described in more detail later in this section.

The Moche period declined around 700 AD and the next few centuries are somewhat confusing. The Wari culture, based in the Ayacucho area of the central Peruvian Andes, began to expand and its influence was felt as far north as the Chicama Valley.

The next important period in the Trujillo area, the Chimu, lasted from about 1000 AD to 1470 AD. The Chimu built a capital at Chan Chan, just north of Trujillo. Chan Chan is the largest pre-Columbian city in Peru, covering about 28 sq km, and is estimated to have housed about 50,000 people. The Chimu was a highly organised society – it must have been to have built and supported a city such as Chan Chan. Its artwork was less exciting than that of the Moche, tending more to functional mass production than artistic achievement. Gone, for the most part, is the technique of painting pots. Instead, they were fired by a simpler method than that

used by the Moche, producing the typical blackware seen in many Chimu pottery collections. Despite its poorer quality, this pottery still shows us life in the Chimu kingdom. Although the quality of the ceramics declined, metallurgy developed and various alloys, including bronze, were worked. The Chimu were also exceptionally fine goldsmiths.

It is as an urban society that the Chimu are best remembered. Their huge capital contained approximately 10,000 dwellings of varying quality and importance. Buildings were decorated with friezes, the designs moulded into the mud walls, and the more important areas were layered with precious metals. There were storage bins for food and other products from their empire, an empire which stretched along the coast from the Gulf of Guayaquil to Chancay. There were

Chimu god

huge walk-in wells, canals, workshops and temples. The royal dead were buried in mounds with a wealth of funerary offerings.

Chan Chan must have been a dazzling sight at one time. Today, only the mud walls and a few moulded decorations remain and the visitor is amazed by the huge expanse of the site as much as anything else. The Chimu were conquered by the Incas in about 1460 but the city was not looted until the arrival of the Spanish. Heavy rainfall has severely damaged the mud mouldings, though a few survive and others have been restored.

Huaqueros

This word is heard frequently, especially around Tru-jillo. A huaquero is literally a robber of huacas. The term huaca refers to any temple, shrine or burial area of special significance. Huacas are often characterised by their richness. Temples were decorated with sheets of precious metals and royalty was buried with a treasure trove. Huaqueros specialise in finding and opening these forgotten graves and removing the valuables within for sale to anybody prepared to pay for an archaeological artefact. Ever since the Spanish conquest, huaqueros have worked the ancient graves of Peru. To a certain extent, one can sympathise with a poor campesino grubbing around in the desert, hoping to strike it rich, but the huaquero is also one of the archaeologist's greatest enemies. So thorough has the huaqueros' ransacking been that an unplundered grave is almost never found by archaeologists – someone else has always been there first. Today's visitor to Trujillo and the surrounding sites is sometimes offered a 'genuine' archaeological arte-fact. These are not always genuine, and if they are, it is illegal to export them from Peru.

Chan Chan

Most visitors want to see Chan Chan, the huge ruined capital of the Chimu Empire. Built by the Chimu around 1300 AD, it is the largest pre-Columbian city in the Americas and the largest mud city in the world. At the height of the Chimu Empire, it housed an estimated 50,000 inhabitants and contained a vast wealth of gold, silver and ceramics. After Chan Chan's conquest by the Incas, the wealth remained more or less undisturbed. The Incas were interested in expanding their imperial control, not in amassing treasure. As soon as the Spaniards arrived, however, the looting began and within a few decades

there was little left of the treasures of Chan Chan. The remainder have been pillaged through the centuries by huaqueros, though remnants can be seen in museums.

The damage at Chan Chan has not been caused only by the huaqueros. Devastating floods and heavy rainfall have severely eroded the mud walls of the city. Several decades can go by with almost no rain but, occasionally, the climatic phenomenon of El Niño can cause rainstorms and floods in the coastal desert. The most recent occurred in 1983.

The Chimu capital consisted of nine major subcities, each built by a succeeding ruler. Hence the nine areas are often referred to as the Royal Compounds and have mainly been named after archaeologists and explorers. Each contains a royal burial mound where the ruler was buried with an appropriately vast quantity of funerary offerings, including dozens of sacrificed young women and chambers full of ceramics, weavings and jewellery. The partially restored Tschudi compound, named after a Swiss naturalist who visited Peru in the 1800s and published *Peruvian Antiquities* in Vienna in 1851, is open to visitors. You can spend hours wandering around these ruins.

Chan Chan is about 5 km west of Trujillo. To get there, take the white, yellow and orange 'B' colectivo which passes the corner of España and Mansiche every few minutes and costs about 10c. There is also a large yellow bus. Most of these buses continue on to Huanchaco, so ask the driver to let you off at Chan Chan. Tschudi lies to the left of the main road, a walk of about 500 metres along a dusty dirt road. As you walk, you'll see the crumbling ruins of the other compounds all around you. Stick to the footpath and do not be tempted to stroll off into the ruins on either side. Not only are these ruins in a very poor state of repair, but they are also the haunt of muggers who hope some unsuspecting, camera-toting tourist will enter alone. Stay on the path and go with a friend or guide if possible.

At the Tschudi complex you'll find an entrance booth, a snack/souvenir stand and a third booth where guides are available. There is usually a pair of tourist police on duty. Entry is from 9 am to 4 pm daily (except 1 January, 1 May and 25 December) and costs $1.70, plus a camera fee of a few cents. The ticket, which can also be bought at either the Huaca Esmeralda or Huaca Arco Iris ruins, is valid for all three sites but must be used within 2 days. You can hire a local guide for about $1.70 to make sure you don't miss anything and to be shown the original, not the restored, friezes and decorations. The complex is well marked by arrows, however, so you can see everything without a guide if you prefer.

Tschudi Complex Entry is through a thick defensive wall. Inside, you turn right and almost immediately enter the huge and largely restored Ceremonial Courtyard. All four interior walls are decorated with geometric designs, most of which are new. Just to the right of the massive doorway, as you enter, you'll see a few designs at ground level – the three or four nutria (furry aquatic mammals) closest to the door – which, I was told, are unrestored. They're slightly rougher looking than the modern work. The design is repeated all the way around the Ceremonial Plaza and is topped by a series of lines representing waves. A ramp joins the two levels at the far side of the plaza (stairways are not a frequent feature of the major Chimu structures). Note also the great restored height of the walls in this plaza. Though all the Chan Chan walls have crumbled with time, the highest of Tschudi's walls once stood over 10 metres high.

Follow the arrows out of the Ceremonial Courtyard through a door to the right and make a sharp left-hand turn to walk along the outside wall of the plaza. This is one of the most highly decorated and best restored of Tschudi's walls. The adobe friezes show waves of fish rippling along the entire length of the wall just above a line of seabirds. See if you can tell where the original mouldings end and the restored ones begin. As before, the rougher-looking fish are the originals. Despite their time-worn appearance, they

retain a fluidity and character somehow lacking in the modern version. Nevertheless, the modern work has been done with care and succeeds in restoring the entirety of the wall.

At the end of this wall, the arrowed path goes through a labyrinthine section known as the Sanctuaries. The function of these sanctuaries is not clear but their importance is evident in both the quantity and quality of the decorations. Though less restored than the waves-and-fish wall, they are the most interesting section of friezes in Tschudi. Their square and diamond-shaped geometric designs represent, quite simply, fishing nets. Being so close to the ocean, the Chimu based much of their diet on seafood and the importance of the sea reached venerable proportions. As we have seen, fish, waves, seabirds and sea mammals are represented throughout the city and here, in the Sanctuaries, you find all of them interspersed with the fishing nets. The moon was also very important and there are several series of full-moon symbols in the Sanctuaries. For the Chimu, the moon and the sea were of religious importance (unlike the Incas, who worshipped the sun and venerated the earth).

From the Sanctuaries, arrows lead the visitor into a second ceremonial plaza smaller in size than the major Ceremonial Plaza but similar in shape. It also has a ramp joining the two levels. From behind this plaza, you can see a huge rectangular depression resembling a drained swimming pool. In fact, it was once a water cistern which supplied the daily water needs of the Tschudi royal compound. The water level was reached by a series of ramps from the surface and each compound had its own cistern. The Tschudi cistern is the largest in Chan Chan and measures 130 by 45 metres.

To the left of the cistern is an area of several dozen small cells which have been called the military sector. Perhaps soldiers lived here, or the cells may have been used for storage. These constructions are not very well preserved. A straight path leads you from the military sector almost back to the main entrance, passing a series of storage bins. The final area visited is the Assembly Room. This large rectangular room has 24 seats set into niches in the walls and its acoustic properties are such that speakers sitting in any one of the niches can be clearly heard all over the room. Try it.

You are now back by the main entrance, free to wander around again to inspect more thoroughly those areas of particular interest to you.

Chan Chan has eight compounds similar to Tschudi. Unfortunately, as they are in much worse states of repair and there are no guards, visiting the others is neither as worthwhile nor as easy. It is possible to be robbed in these remote and dusty old ruins and it's recommended that those seriously interested in seeing less developed areas of Chan Chan do so in a group and with a guide who knows what he's doing. The path behind Tschudi leading down to and along the beach is particularly notorious for robberies and muggings. If you stay on the dirt road joining the main road with Tschudi, you shouldn't have any problems.

Detail from a Tschudi wall

La Huaca Esmeralda

This temple was built by the Chimu at about the same time as Chan Chan. The site is open daily from 9 am to 4 pm and entry costs $1.70, plus a few cents camera fee. The ticket is valid for Chan Chan and the Huaca Arco Iris on the same or the next day. Huaca Esmeralda lies at Mansiche, which is halfway between Trujillo and Chan Chan, so you can take the same bus as to Chan Chan or walk from either direction. If you're returning from Chan Chan to Trujillo, the huaca is to the right of the main road, about four blocks behind the Mansiche Church.

The site was buried by sand and was accidently discovered by a local landowner in 1923. He attempted to uncover the ruins but the El Niño of 1925 began the process of erosion which was exacerbated by the floods and rains of 1983. Little restoration work has been done on the adobe friezes but it is still possible to make out the characteristic designs of fish, seabirds, waves and fishing nets. The temple consists of two stepped platforms and an on-site guide will take you around for a tip.

La Huaca Arco Iris

This is the third Chimu site which can be visited at the same time and with the same ticket as Chan Chan and Huaca Esmeralda. Huaca Arco Iris, or the 'Rainbow Temple', is also known locally as the Huaca del Dragon. It is just to the left of the Pan-American Highway in the suburb of La Esperanza, about 4 km north-west of Trujillo. Red, blue and white minibuses or green-and-white buses for La Esperanza pass the corner of España and Mansiche; the driver can drop you right outside the ruin. The buses may have placards for 'Parque Industrial' or 'Milagro', a long way past the ruins, or for 'Directo' or 'Postes', closer to the ruins. Any one of them will drop you off at the huaca.

This is one of the best preserved of the Chimu temples simply because it was covered by sand until the 1960s. Its location was known to a handful of archaeologists and huaqueros but excavation did not begin until 1963. Unfortunately, the 1983 El Niño caused damage to the friezes.

The excavation of the temple took about 5 years and the upper parts were rebuilt. It used to be painted but now only faint traces of yellow paint can be seen. The temple consists of a defensive wall over 2 metres thick enclosing an area of about 3000 sq metres. Through the single entrance in this rectangular wall is one large structure, the temple itself. This building covers about 800 sq metres in two levels with a combined height of about 7½ metres. The walls are slightly pyramidal and covered with repeated rainbow designs, most of which have been restored. Ramps lead the visitor to the very top of the temple. From here, you can look down into a series of large storage bins. These almost surround the structure and have openings only at the top. There are also good views from the top level of the temple.

There is a tiny on-site museum and local guides, some speaking a little English, are available to show you around the ruin and museum. A tip is expected. You can buy inexpensive, well-made reproductions of Chimu ceramics from the souvenir stand near the entrance.

Las Huacas del Sol y de la Luna

The Temples of the Sun and the Moon were not built by the Chimu. They are about 700 years older than Chan Chan and are attributed to the Moche period. They are to be found on the south bank of the Río Moche, about 10 km south-east of Trujillo by rough road. To get there, take the blue-and-white minibus which leaves every 30 minutes or so from Calle Suarez. The 20-minute ride costs 15c. These vehicles are among the most dilapidated buses I've seen on the coast! The site is officially open from 8 am to 2 pm, but as there's no entrance booth, you can go in freely at any time. It's best to visit in the morning, however, because the wind tends to whip up the sand in the afternoon and buses run less frequently later in the day. There are usually a couple of tourist police near the site in the morning. In the afternoon and evening, there is a chance of being mugged because the site is a little out of the way. Single travellers, especially women, are advised to go with a friend or hire a guide.

The two huacas, both roughly pyramidal in shape, are usually visited together. The Huaca del Sol is the largest single pre-Columbian structure in Peru. Estimates of its size vary, depending on the points of reference used, but recent measurements give a maximum length of 342 metres, breadth of 159 metres and height of 45 metres. The structure was built using an estimated 140 million adobe bricks, many of them marked with symbols. These are not evidence of any kind of writing or hieroglyphics; they are merely the hallmarks of the workers who made them. Over 100 symbols have been identified and one theory holds that groups or communities of workers were taxed a certain number of adobe bricks and marked their contributions with distinctive hallmarks to keep track of how many bricks they had provided.

At one time, the pyramid consisted of several different levels connected by steep flights of stairs, huge ramps and walls sloping at 77° to the horizon. A millennium and a half have wrought their inevitable damage and today the pyramid looks like a giant pile of crude bricks partially covered with sand. Despite this, the brickwork remains very impressive from some angles. It appears that there are few graves or rooms within the structure and that it must have been primarily used as a huge ceremonial site. Certainly, its size alone makes the pyramid an awesome structure and the views from the top are excellent.

The smaller Huaca de la Luna is about 500 metres away across the open desert. Dozens of pottery shards lie around this open area. Although less impressive in size than the Huaca del Sol, the Huaca de la Luna has yielded many more artefacts. Unlike the almost solid Pyramid of the Sun, the Pyramid of the Moon is riddled with rooms which contained ceramics, precious metals and some of the beautiful polychrome paintings for which the Moche were famous. Unfortunately, the site is in an extremely bad state of repair and the murals are either badly damaged or covered with rubble. The rooms have been bricked up making entry impossible, but reproductions of some of the murals are displayed in the Archaeology Museum in Trujillo.

SUGAR ESTATES

Sugar cane is an important crop all along the northern Peruvian coast. Several sugar estates in the Trujillo area can be visited by those interested in sugar manufacturing. It is best to go in the morning when guided tours can be arranged. The Casa Grande and Hacienda Cartavio estates in the Chicama Valley, some 40 km north of Trujillo, can be reached by bus. Transport leaves from Avenida 29 de Diciembre, near España. The radio patrol office of the tourist police is nearby; ask there if you can't find the bus stop.

HUANCHACO

The fishing village of Huanchaco, a 15-km bus ride north- west of Trujillo, is developing a name as the best beach resort in the Trujillo area. You won't find expensive high-rise buildings, though. Huanchaco is still very low key and retains its fishing-village ambience.

Of particular interest are the tortora-reed boats. These look superficially like those found on Lake Titicaca in the southern highlands, but differ from the highland boats in that they are not hollow. Because the fishermen ride on them rather than in them, these high-ended, cigar-shaped boats are called *caballitos*, or 'little horses'. The caballitos are similar to the boats depicted on Moche ceramics 1500 years ago. The inhabitants of Huanchaco are among the few remaining people on the coast who still remember how to construct and use these precarious-looking craft and you can always see some stacked up at the north end of the beach. When the surf is good, the fishermen paddle the boats beyond the breakers to fish and then surf back to the beach with their catch. It's well worth seeing.

Apart from walking on the beach and

waiting for the caballitos to go into action, there's not much to do in Huanchaco and that's one of its attractions. It's a quiet, laid-back, relaxing sort of place. You can swim in the ocean but it's a little too cold for most of the year. When the El Niño current warms the water from January to March, Huanchaco gets a little busier. You can climb the tower of the massive church at the north end of the village for a good view of the surrounding area.

Warning

Although the beach of Huanchaco is no more dangerous than anywhere else, people have been mugged when walking a long way from the village. While it is possible to walk from Huanchaco to Chan Chan and on to the Trujillo beach at Buenos Aires, it is definitely not recommended unless you are in a large group. You'll be OK if you stay in Huanchaco and use the bus to get to Trujillo.

Places to Stay

Huanchaco is a small town and most people know where the hotels are; just ask. The *Hostal Bracamonte*, a few blocks back from the beach, is popular, friendly and secure. It has small bungalows in a walled compound and a cafeteria. The *Hotel Sol y Mar* is also set back from the beach but has some rooms with balconies and ocean views. Both hotels charge about $2 per person for clean rooms with bath (cold water) and are recommended.

Slightly cheaper are the *Hostal Huanchaco*, on Avenida Larco by the plaza, and the *Hostal Las Palmeras* on Calle Las Palmeras. Both have been recommended.

The *Caballitos de Tortora* is more expensive. It is on the beachfront road and has a swimming pool. Ask around for cheaper accommodation: for example, an unmarked house on the beach, opposite the Guardia Civil, has rooms for $1.50 per person. Other families also offer cheap rooms.

Places to Eat

Huanchaco has several seafood restaurants, especially near the tortora-reed boats stacked at the north end of the beach. None are luxurious but several are adequate – take your pick. Some places occasionally offer entertainment of sorts and they usually advertise this in the hotels a few days in advance.

The *Club Colonial* restaurant on the plaza has been recommended.

Getting There & Away

The orange, yellow and white bus from the corner of Mansiche and España in Trujillo goes past Chan Chan and on to Huanchaco two or three times an hour. The fare is 15c. The bus can drop you off near the hotel of your choice – ask the driver or you'll end up driving away from the hotels, through to the north end of the village. To return, just wait on the beachfront road for the bus as it returns from the north end, picking up passengers along the way. This service stops soon after sunset.

PUERTO CHICAMA

This small port is famous for its surf and has the longest left-handed wave in the world. Not being a surfer, I have no idea what that means but I guess it's pretty important.

Places to Stay

Puerto Chicama is a surfer's hangout. It has a couple of basic hotels and restaurants but no electricity at night. The 'best' hotel is the *Sony* at $1 per person. Two of its rooms face the ocean. Cheaper and really basic is *El Hombre*. I've also heard that you can camp.

Getting There & Away

To get to Puerto Chicama, wait for a bus near the Mansiche Stadium in Trujillo. There are a few direct buses but it may be easier to take a bus about 40 km north along the Pan-American Highway to Paiján and change there for a local bus to Puerto Chicama, a further 16 km away.

I once met an Australian surfer who was travelling from beach to beach along the Pacific coast. He had his board with him and seemed to have no problems transporting it on the buses.

PACASMAYO & PACATNAMÚ

The small port of Pacasmayo is 105 km north of Trujillo on the Pan-American Highway. The private Rodriguez Razzetto Museum here has a fine collection of textiles, pottery and jewellery of the Jequetepeque culture. Visits can be arranged by appointment.

The turn-off to Cajamarca is 15 km beyond Pacasmayo. A few km further along the Pan-American Highway, just before the village of Guadalupe, a track leads towards the ocean. The little-visited ruins of Pacatnamú lie several km along this track. The site has been inhabited by various cultures; the Gallinazo, Moche and Chimu have all left their mark.

Places to Stay

There are a couple of cheap, basic but clean hotels in Pacasmayo. These include the *Ferrocarril* and *Panamericano*. The *Hostal Pakatnamú*, on the boardwalk, charges $10 for a double with bath.

CHICLAYO

The next major coastal city north of Trujillo is Chiclayo, just over 200 km away on the Pan-American Highway. Chiclayo is not a historic city, and during the 1800s, it was no more than an outlying district of the older town of Lambayeque. Today, however, Lambayeque is small and almost forgotten while Chiclayo has become one of Peru's fastest growing modern cities. It is now an important commercial centre and the capital of the coastal desert Department of Lambayeque. With a population of about 350,000, it vies with Huancayo for the position of fourth largest city in Peru.

Because Chiclayo has little to see of historical or archaeological interest, I'd always thought of it as one of those cities to travel through as quickly as possible. One traveller I met, however, put it in a different perspective. He told me that he considered Chiclayo one of the most interesting cities in Peru because it is full of life and vitality. It isn't a colonial city using a faded past to attract tourists or a resort town with beaches or beautiful scenery, nor is it conveniently located near a set of superb pre-Columbian ruins; it's simply a thriving Peruvian city with no tourist pretensions and good opportunities to meet ordinary Peruvians. The next time I travelled north along the coast, I deliberately spent a couple of days in Chiclayo and found my informant's perspective surprisingly accurate. This is not such a boring place after all.

In 1987, there was dramatic news of the discovery of a royal Moche tomb at Sipán, about 30 km south-east of Chiclayo. This find proved to be extraordinary – it has been called the most important archaeological discovery in Peru in the last 50 years – and Peruvian archaeologists have recovered hundreds of dazzling and priceless artefacts from the site. Excavation continues at the site and it has not yet developed a tourist infrastructure, though it can be visited from Chiclayo. The spectacular finds are displayed in the Bruning Museum in Lambayeque, 11 km north of Chiclayo. The director of this museum, Walter Alva, wrote an exciting article about Sipán in the October 1988 issue of *National Geographic* magazine which is recommended reading.

Information

Tourist Information The tourist office (tel 227776) is north of the cathedral at San José 867. The office has moved several times in the last few years, and as there is no sign, it may be difficult to find. Try telephoning – the phone number tends to stay the same. At this time, opening hours are 9 am to 4 pm Monday to Friday and 9 am to 1 pm on Saturday. The staff are friendly, informative and helpful in finding bus companies for those wanting to travel to unusual destinations.

Money The Banco de Crédito and the Banco Nor Peru, on the 600 block of Balta by the Plaza de Armas, used to give the best exchange rates. (There are several other banks nearby.) Recently, the many moneychangers on the street outside the banks were giving much better rates than the banks, so check both.

Bookstalls Outdated *Time, Newsweek* and other magazines can sometimes be bought at one of the many of the bookstalls on the south side of the Plaza de Armas.

Market

If you're in Chiclayo, don't miss the huge market which, despite its modernity, is one of the most interesting in Peru. Wander around and see the herbalist and *brujo* (witch-doctor) stalls with their dried plants, bones, bits of animals and other healing charms. Other things to look for include heavy woven saddlebags called *alforjas*, an item typical of the area; they can be worn over the shoulder with a bag on your front and back or used as saddlebags. Woven straw items such as hats, baskets, mats and ornaments are also popular. And, of course, there is the usual cacophonous animal section and a food market.

Coastal Area

Three coastal villages can be conveniently visited from Chiclayo. These are, from north to south, Pimental, Santa Rosa and Puerto de Etén. All three can be reached quickly from Chiclayo by public transport, though the service to Puerto de Etén is relatively infrequent. It's suggested that you go to Pimental or Santa Rosa first and change there to local transport for Puerto de Etén.

Pimental is 14 km from Chiclayo and the closest of the three villages. The good sandy beach here gets very crowded on summer weekends (January to March) but is quiet during the off season. A few km south of Pimental is Santa Rosa, a busy fishing village where a few caballitos (tortora-reed boats described in the Huanchaco section) may still be seen. You can walk from Pimental to Santa Rosa in less than an hour or take a local bus. There is an inexpensive hotel in Santa Rosa and both villages have good seafood restaurants, though many are closed in the low season.

Colectivos operate from Santa Rosa to the small port of Puerto de Etén. Here, you can see a 19th century train engine in the (disused) train station. There are plans to

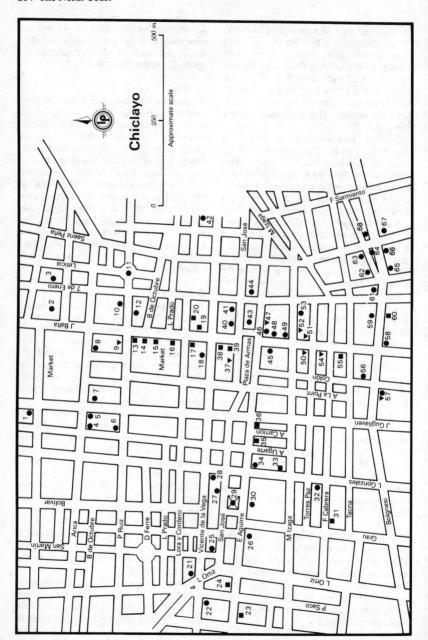

Chiclayo

Approximate scale

0   250   500 m

open a railway museum, but this doesn't look likely to happen in the near future. Alternatively, you can return to Chiclayo via the village of Monsefu, 15 km away from Chiclayo. Monsefu is known for its handicrafts. Several stores sell basketwork, embroidery and woodwork and a craft festival called Fexticum is held in the last week of July. The village has a few simple restaurants.

Colectivos to Pimental leave from the corner of Gonzalez and Vicente de la Vega in Chiclayo, continuing on from Pimental along the so-called 'beach circuit' through Santa Rosa, Etén and Monsefu before returning to Chiclayo the same day. Buses to Monsefu also leave from the market. Most beach-goers stay in Chiclayo.

Archaeological Sites

Sipán This site, also known as 'La Huaca Rayada' and described in the introduction to the Chiclayo section, can be visited even though the area is not officially open to tourism. Archaeologists continue to work at the site and photography is not allowed where the excavations are under way. The site is fascinating to those interested in seeing archaeology in action but is not particularly dramatic-looking to the untrained eye. The pyramids look like earthen hills with holes excavated in them. Most of the artefacts have been removed to museums for further study and some pieces can be seen at the Bruning Museum in Lambayeque. An on-site museum is planned but is unlikely to eventuate for some years. Walter Alva, director of the Bruning Museum, heads the project.

The site was first discovered by huaqueros (grave robbers) from the nearby village of Sipán. When local archaeologists became aware of a huge influx of beautiful objects onto the black market early in 1987, they realised that a wonderful burial site was being ransacked in the Chiclayo area. By the time they found out where it was, at least one major tomb had been pillaged by robbers. Fast protective action by local archaeologists and police stopped the huaqueros from plundering further and scientists were fortunate enough to discover other, even better, tombs that the grave robbers had missed. One huaquero was shot and killed by police in the early, tense days of struggle over the graves. The Sipán locals are obviously unhappy that this treasure trove has been made inaccessible to them and are not friendly to visitors.

It is not easy to reach Sipán on public transport, though it is possible. Most people go with a guide who will enable them to visit the ruins and minimise unfriendly interactions with the locals. Cheap public buses to Sipán leave from Avenida 7 de Enero, near the market, a few times a day at erratic hours. Go early in the morning if you want to return the same day.

Daily guided tours are available (according to demand) from Indiana Tours (tel 240833) at Izaga 774, which is run by an American/Peruvian couple. Tours cost between $6 and $16 per person, depending on the size of your group and whether other people are going. Indiana Tours also offer guided excursions to Túcume and other local sites of interest.

A local cab driver, José Olinden (tel 228133), knows some of the workers at the ruins and gives informative tours (in Spanish) to the area for about $20 (the cab takes up to four passengers). He lives at F Cabrera 845 and can also be contacted through Naylamp Tours.

Guided tours take about 3 hours.

Túcume This little-known site, about 38 km north of Chiclayo, covers an extensive area and consists of 28 pyramids. It may turn out to be bigger than Chan Chan. It is being actively excavated and the project is expected to last until the end of the century. The head archaeologist, the well-known Norwegian explorer Thor Heyerdahl, is assisted by the Peruvian archaeologist Hugo Navarro, who is overseeing excavation of the 'monumental sector', and the American Dan Sandweiss, who is working on the 'residential sector'. Visitors are asked to come in the afternoon, leaving the morning free for archaeological work.

You can get to Túcume on public transport. Take a bus to Lambayeque and ask at the Bruning Museum for further directions. The Túcume bus leaves from near the museum. You could also take one of the buses leaving from Ugarte and Arica, near the Chiclayo market.

Indiana Tours runs daily excursions (according to demand) for $8 to $20, depending on the number in the group. The tour can be combined with a visit to the Bruning Museum for a little extra cost.

Places to Stay – bottom end
Many of the cheaper hotels are along the main street of Avenida Balta, north of the Plaza de Armas. Some of them are very cheap but they are also extremely basic and have little to recommend them. The cheapest places charge as little as 60c per person in not particularly clean rooms with cold-water communal showers. These basic hostals include the *Ronald, Balta, Estrella, Adriatico* and *Chimu*. Of these, the Ronald has been recommended but the rest are pretty poor.

The *Hotel Royal*, on the Plaza de Armas, is a building full of character and one of the best cheapies. Singles/doubles with bath (cold water) cost $1.30/2 and there are some cheaper rooms without private showers. The *Hostal Madrid* is clean and similarly priced. For $2/2.70, you can get a reasonably clean room with cold-water bath at the *Hostal Venezuela*, *Hostal Lido* or *Hostal Americano*. The *Hostal Cruz de Galpon* costs about the same but is much worse. The *Hotel Europa*, at $2/3.25 for singles/doubles with bath, is quite good.

Places to Stay – middle

A good, clean, comfortable, reasonably priced mid-range hotel the *Hotel El Sol*, charges $3.30/4.70 for singles/doubles with bath and hot water. Rooms with bath at the more centrally located *Hostal Costa de Oro* cost $4/5.30. At about the same price, the *Hotel Obby* and *Hotel Inca* also have rooms with bath and hot water.

Places to Stay – top end

The *Garza* is a good, new hotel with efficient service, a decent restaurant and comfortable singles/doubles for $8.50/12. As usual, the government-run *Hotel de Turistas* is the best hotel in town. Make reservations at ENTURPeru (tel 721928) in Lima. The hotel has a restaurant and swimming pool and charges $15/20 for singles/doubles with bath. Some cheaper rooms with communal bath are also available. Prices include continental breakfast.

Places to Eat

The most expensive restaurant in the city centre is *Le Paris*, where a good meal with drinks will cost you about $5, but the service is poor. The *Restaurant Roma* has quite a wide and reasonably inexpensive variety of food and is popular with locals, though it has had mixed reviews. It is conveniently open from about 7 am until after midnight. The *Restaurant Imperial*, across the street, is cheaper but still quite good. *Mario's*, nearby, is a '24 hour' restaurant but is not open all night. One of my favourites is *Restaurant*

Cordano, on the Plaza de Armas. It's cheap and friendly and the food is good. The *Men Wha Chifa* has large portions and is inexpensive. The clean, modern *Galería Real* snack bar has inexpensive set lunches and a variety of sandwiches and cakes. The *Restaurant Ñusta*, by the TEPSA bus station, serves typical regional lunch dishes – it's cheap and far from fancy. You'll find more cheap but unremarkable restaurants on Avenida Balta, and there are a number of pollerías on the 800 and 900 blocks of Balta where you can get a quarter of a chicken for about 70c.

Entertainment

Chiclayo has several movie theatres, including two on the Plaza de Armas, as well as some peñas which have music late on Friday and Saturday nights. These include *La Brisa del Mar* at San José 125, *Hermanos Balcázar* at Lora y Cordero 1150 and *Peña Turistica Sachum* at Los Faiques in the Urbanizacion suburb of Santa Victoria (take a taxi to this peña).

Getting There & Away

Air AeroPeru and Faucett both have offices in Chiclayo. The airport is 2 km south-east of town. Between them, the airlines provide two or three flights a day from Lima ($68). Faucett's morning flights tend to be more punctual than AeroPeru's afternoon ones. Faucett also offers daily flights to Tumbes and one or two flights a week to Rioja and Tarapoto. AeroPeru has five flights a week to Trujillo and one flight a week to Chachapoyas. Schedules change frequently; check with the airlines.

Bus There is a large cluster of bus companies near the south end of town, at the corner of Saenz Peña and Bolognesi. This is often the best place to start looking for a long-distance bus, especially to Lima. Buses for local destinations tend to leave from other parts of town.

Empresa Chiclayo has the most frequent service to Piura with buses leaving hourly throughout the day. The 3-hour trip costs $2.50. Be warned that their buses rarely stay on schedule. Transportes Piura has two early morning buses to Piura. TRAMSA's old, slow buses leave frequently for Piura and Trujillo. TEPSA offers an expensive direct service to Tumbes (about $8, 10 hours) leaving daily at 2 pm, but it may be easier to go to Piura and change.

Most bus companies in the Saenz Peña/Bolognesi corner area have one or more buses a day to Lima, a journey taking about 11 hours and costing $7. These buses can drop you at intermediate towns such as Trujillo.

Travellers heading inland to Cajamarca ($3, 7 hours) can find transport with Empresa Diaz at noon but the buses are old. El Cumbe buses are newer and leave later. Empresa D Olano buses depart for Chachapoyas on Tuesday, Thursday, and Saturday (18 hours, $10). This is a rough journey because of the bad road. Transportes Chinchaysuyo used to operate two buses a week to Tarapoto but this service has been suspended because of poor road conditions and problems with drug traffickers and Sendero guerilla activitity on the trip's further reaches. The bus service may again resume when the situation returns to normal.

Buses for Chongoyape and other provincial towns often leave from the Parque Obrero area on Pedro Ruiz.

Getting Around

For destinations near Chiclayo, white Transportes San Pablo minibuses to Lambayeque leave from near the Plaza Aguirre every few minutes. They'll drop you right in front of the Bruning Museum for about 15c. A cheaper and more crowded service to Lambayeque is run by Empresa San Pedro, near the market. Comité 2 colectivo taxis also make the trip.

To get to Chiclayo's three coastal towns of Pimental, Santa Rosa, and Puerto de Etén, look for Comité 1 colectivos by the market or try the colectivos which leave from the corner of Gonzalez and V de la Vega.

The tourist office is very helpful with information about local bus departures.

LAMBAYEQUE

Lambayeque, 12 km north of Chiclayo, used to be the main town in the area. Today, it has a population of only 20,000 and has been completely overshadowed by Chiclayo. Some colonial architecture can be seen but the town's museum is its best feature.

Named after a local collector and businessman, the Bruning Museum was opened on its present site in the 1960s. The modern building houses a good collection of archaeological artefacts from the Chimu, Moche, Chavín and Vicus cultures and a new exhibit features finds from the newly discovered site of Sipán. Entry costs 50c and the museum is open from 8 am to 6.30 pm Monday to Friday and 9 am to 1 pm on weekends and holidays. (It may close for lunch on weekdays, though didn't the last time I was there.) Colectivos from Chiclayo will drop you outside the museum.

CHONGOYAPE

This old village is about 65 km east of Chiclayo in the foothills of the Andes. A good road links Chiclayo with Chongoyape; buses leave from near the corner of P Ruiz and 7 de Enero in Chiclayo and take about 1½ hours. About halfway to Chongoyape, a few km beyond Tumán, a minor road on your left leads to the ruins of Batan Grande 31 km away, where about 50 pyramids have been excavated. As there is almost no public transport, you will have to find a taxi to take you.

Chongoyape has a cheap and basic hotel. The Chavín Petroglyphs of Cerro Mulato are 3 km away and there are a few other minor archaeological sites. The irrigation complex of Tinajones forms a large reservoir just before Chongoyape.

A rough but scenic road climbs east from Chongoyape into the Andes until it reaches Chota at 2400 metres, a 170-km journey which takes about 8 hours. Two buses a day from Chiclayo go through Chongoyape and continue on to Chota, where there are basic hotels. From Chota, a daily bus makes the rough journey via Bambamarca and Hualgayoc to Cajamarca.

THE SECHURA DESERT

The coastal desert between Chiclayo and Piura is the widest in Peru. South of Chiclayo, the Andes almost reach the coast, leaving only a narrow strip of flat coastal desert. North of Chiclayo, this strip becomes over 150 km wide in places; this is the Sechura Desert.

Two roads run between Chiclayo and Piura. The shorter, less interesting one goes via Mórrope, while the longer Pan-American Highway goes via Motupe. The 1983 El Niño flooded and devastated the Sechura Desert. Before the floods, the bus ride between Chiclayo and Tumbes took as little as 8 hours, but for several months in 1983, the roads were washed away and impassable in places. One year after the floods, the journey was still taking twice as long as before, but the roads were improving. The longer Pan-American Highway is in better condition and is therefore used by buses. The shorter route may reopen soon.

The Pan-American Highway between Chiclayo and Piura, across the Sechura Desert, passes the archaeological site of Túcume (see Archaeological Sites in the Chiclayo section of this chapter). Also nearby is the little-visited site of El Purgatorio where there are pyramids from the Chimu period. Near Motupe, almost 80 km north of Chiclayo, are the pre-Inca irrigation canals of Apurlec. None of these places is much visited.

PIURA

Piura, with a population of nearly 300,000, is the sixth largest city in Peru and the capital of its department. Intense irrigation of the desert has made Piura a major agricultural centre with rice being the main crop. Cotton, corn and plantains (bananas) are also cultivated. The department's petroleum industry, based around the coastal oil fields near Talara, is as valuable as its agriculture.

Piura's economic development has been precarious, buffeted by extreme droughts and devastating floods. The department was among the hardest hit by the disastrous El Niño floods of 1983 which destroyed almost 90% of the rice, cotton and plantain crops as well as causing serious damage to roads, bridges, buildings and oil wells in the area. Piura was declared a disaster area – with crops destroyed and land flooded, the people had no food, no homes and no jobs. The area is now recovering, though signs of the flood damage can still be seen.

Piura is referred to as the oldest colonial town in Peru. Its original site on the north banks of the Chira River was called San Miguel de Piura and was founded by Pizarro in 1532, before he headed inland and began the conquest of the Incas. The settlement moved three times before construction at its present location began in 1588. Piura's cathedral dates from that year and the city centre still has a number of colonial buildings, though many were destroyed in the earthquake of 1912. Today, the centre of the city is the large, shady and pleasant Plaza de Armas.

The centre of the Vicus culture, which existed around the time of Christ, was roughly 30 km east of Piura. Although no buildings remain, tombs have yielded a great number of ceramics which can be seen in the museums of Piura and Lima.

Information

Tourist Information There are two tourist offices. FOPTUR tourist information (tel 333720) is in the municipalidad, on the plaza, at Ayacucho 377. There is another office around the corner at Libertad 945.

Money The best place to change cash and travellers' cheques is the Banco de Crédito, just off the Plaza de Armas.

Museums

The archaeological museum is on the top floor of the municipalidad, on the Plaza de Armas, and is open from 8 am to noon Monday to Friday. Admission is free. The museum has a good collection of Vicus ceramics, which are characterised by the stumpiness and disproportion of the arms, legs and heads. Artefacts from other Peruvian cultures are also displayed.

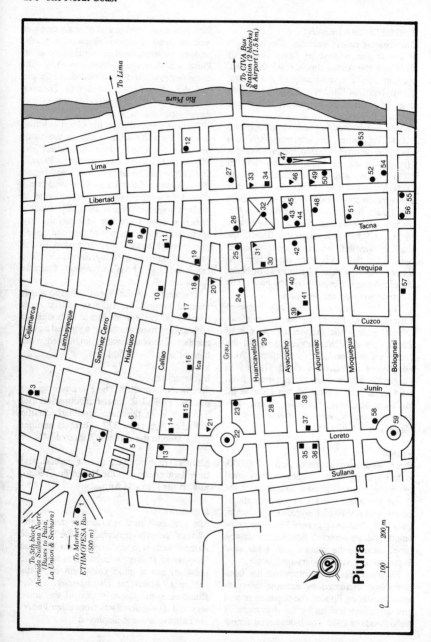

Piura

To 5th block
Avenida Suliana Norte
(Buses to Paita,
La Unión & Sechura)

To Market &
ETHMOPESA Bus
(500 m)

To Lima

Rio Piura

To CIVA Bus
Station (2 blocks)
& Airport (1.5 km)

0   100   200 m

Cajamarca
Lambayeque
Sanchez Cerro
Huánuco
Callao
Ica
Grau
Huancavelica
Ayacucho
Apurimac
Moquegua
Bolognesi

Lima
Libertad
Tacna
Arequipa
Cuzco
Junín
Loreto
Sullana

■ PLACES TO STAY

3	Hotel Esmeralda
5	Hostal Terraza
8	Hostal El Sol
10	Hotel Tambo
11	Hostal Oriental
14	Hostal Cristina
15	Hostal Ica
16	Hotel Hispano
19	Hostal Tangara
28	Hostal Lalo
30	Hotel Eden
34	Hotel de Turistas
35	Residencial Piura
36	Hostal San Jorge
37	Hostal Palmeras
38	Hostal Continental
41	Hostal Amauta
57	Residencial Bolognesi

▼ PLACES TO EAT

20	Restaurant Tres Estrellas
21	La Carreta Chicken Restaurant
29	Tacos Mexicanos Café
31	Heladería Chalan
33	Restaurant Orion
39	Café Concierto Coffee House
40	Las Tradiciónes Restaurant
46	El Gaucho Steak House
49	Heladería Venecia

● OTHER

1	Buses to Tumbes & Chiclayo
2	Empresa Petrolera (Bus)
3	ENTEL
4	ETHMOPESA Bus Office
6	EPPO (Bus)
7	Carmen Church
9	AeroPeru
12	San Francisco Church
13	Comité 2 to Sullana
17	Comité 24 to Lima
18	Choppería Munich
22	Grau Monument
23	Cine Variedades
24	Alex Chopp
25	Banco de Crédito
26	Cathedral
27	Faucett Airline
32	Plaza de Armas
42	Casa Grau
43	Archaeological Museum
44	Banco de la Nación
45	Art Museum
47	Plaza Pizarro
48	Las Redes Bar & Italian Restaurant
50	Transportes Piura & Colectivos to Catacaos
51	San Sebastian Church
52	Chinchaysuyo (Bus)
53	Expreso Sudamericano (Bus)
54	Roggero (Bus)
55	Comité 1 to Sechura
56	Cruz de Galpon (Bus)
58	TEPSA (Bus)
59	Bolognesi Monument

Next door to the municipalidad, in the Banco Central Hipotecario, is an art museum. It is open during banking hours.

The house where Admiral Miguel Grau was born, on 27 July 1834, has been turned into a naval museum. The house was almost completely destroyed by the 1912 earthquake and was later restored by the Peruvian navy. Admiral Grau was a hero of the War of the Pacific against Chile (1879-80) and captain of the British-built warship *Huascár*, a model of which can be seen in the museum.

For most of the year, the museum is open from 8 am to 1 pm and 3.30 to 6 pm on Monday, Wednesday, Friday and Saturday and from 8 am to noon on Sunday. From January to March, opening hours are 7.30 am to 1.30 pm daily (closed on Tuesday and Thursday).

Churches

The cathedral on the Plaza de Armas is the oldest church in Piura. Although parts of the cathedral date from 1588, the main altar was built in 1960. The side altar of the Virgin of Fatima, built in the first part of the 17th century, was once the main altar and is the oldest. The famed local artist Ignacio Merino painted the canvas of St Martin of Porres in the mid-19th century.

Other churches worth seeing are the Church of San Francisco, where Piura's independence was declared on 4 January 1821, and the 17th century Church of Carmen.

Jirón Lima
This street, a block south-east of the Plaza de Armas, has preserved its colonial character as much as any in Piura.

Catacaos
The village of Catacaos, 12 km south-west of Piura, is famous for its craft market and for its restaurants which are particularly recommended for lunch. You can get there by colectivo from the Plaza Pizarro in Piura.

The craft market sells a good variety of products including gold and silver filigree ornaments, wood carvings, leatherwork and panama hats.

There are dozens of little picanterías (local restaurants) serving maize beer (chicha) and typical dishes of the area. Most picanterías are only open 2 or 3 days a week, but as there are so many of them, you won't have any difficulty finding several open whichever day you visit. They open for lunch rather than dinner and live music is sometimes played. Typical norteño (northern) dishes include seco de chabelo (a thick plantain-and-beef-flavoured stew), seco de cabrito (goat stew), tamales verdes (green corn dumplings), caldo de siete carnes (a thick meat soup with seven types of meat), copus (made from dried goats' heads cured in vinegar and then stewed for several hours with vegetables such as turnips, sweet potatoes and plantains), carne aliñada (dried and fried ham slices, served with fried plantains) and many other dishes, including the familiar seafood cebiches of the Peruvian coast.

Catacaos is also famous for its Holy Week celebrations.

Places to Stay – bottom end
For some reason, I found Piura hotels slightly more expensive than those elsewhere along the coast. The best value hotels start at over $2 per person.

Budget travellers often stay at the Hostal Terraza. It charges $1.30 per person and is clean, but I found the staff bored and rude when I visited. Also in this price range is the Hostal Continental, which doesn't look too bad, and the basic, reasonably clean Hostal Lalo. The Hotel Hispano, Hotel Eden and Hostal Ica don't look particularly good. Old fashioned and interesting to look at, the Hostal Cristina is a little more expensive at $2/2.70 for singles/doubles with shared showers. Rooms with private bath cost an extra 30c.

If you can afford to pay a little more, I recommend the very clean and pleasant Hostal Palmeras. It charges $2.20 per person in rooms with a private shower, fan and hot water. If this hotel is full, try the similarly priced Hostal San Jorge across the street. It's clean, looks modern and offers rooms with private bath. The very clean Hostal Oriental costs about the same but has only cold water. The Residencial Bolognesi is a huge, ugly-looking building offering plenty of doubles with hot showers for $3.70. It has no singles. The Hostal Amauta charges the same and also has no singles.

Places to Stay – middle
All hotels in this section have rooms with private bath and hot water. The Residencial Piura is in a pleasant building and charges $3.30/5.30. A good choice is the clean Hotel Tambo at $4/6 for singles/doubles. The modern-looking Hotel Esmeralda has a cafeteria and charges $4.70/6.70. The Hostal El Sol is similarly priced and recommended. The Hostal Tangara costs $6/8.70 and has a cafeteria.

Places to Stay – top end
The best in town is the government run Hotel de Turistas in an attractive building on the Plaza de Armas. Singles/doubles cost $12/16, including a continental breakfast.

Places to Eat
Piura gets very hot and dusty, so there are several pleasant snack and beer bars. The Heladería Chalan, on the main plaza, has a good selection of juices, cakes and ice creams, as well as sandwiches and other

snacks. The *Heladería Venecia* also has an excellent variety of ice cream and sweets. If you prefer a beer, try Peruvian draught beer at one of the *Chopp* bars marked on the Piura map – personally, I can't tell the difference between draught and bottled Peruvian beer. *Las Redes* has a pleasant patio where you can relax, as well as a bar and an Italian restaurant. The *Café Concierto* is a coffee house offering occasional cultural entertainment.

As you walk along Avenida Grau, you'll find several cheap restaurants, including *La Carreta*, an inexpensive fried-chicken restaurant. The *Restaurant Orion*, on the Plaza de Armas, is good for light meals or, if you're looking for something unusual, try the *Tacos Mexicanos* café. The nearby village of Catacaos is recommended for a typical, inexpensive Peruvian lunch.

The better restaurants include the *Restaurant Tres Estrellas, Las Tradiciónes Restaurant* and *El Gaucho Steak House*. These tend to be open only in the evening.

Getting There & Away

Air The airport is on the south-west bank of the Río Piura and about 2 km from the centre. Both Faucett and AeroPeru have offices in Piura. There are daily flights to Lima ($82) in the evening with AeroPeru and in the morning with Faucett. Faucett flights may continue to Talara and Tumbes; check with the airline.

Bus & Colectivo People travelling to the nearby towns of Sullana, Paita and Sechura often take the faster, more expensive colectivo taxis. Comité 1 cars to Sechura leave from the intersection of Bolognesi and Libertad and cost $1.20 for the 1-hour drive. Comité 2 has cars to Sullana (45 minutes, 80c).

Buses, cars and trucks for various local destinations leave from the 5th block of Avenida Sullana Norte. Empresa Petrolera has five buses a day to Talara via Sullana and ETHMOPESA has several daily buses on the same route. As the ETHMOPESA office

downtown is usually closed, it's easiest to go direct to the departure point at the corner of Sanchez Cerro and the market, in front of the Goodyear tyre dealer. EPPO has three buses a day to Talara ($1.70, 2 hours) and more frequent departures for Sullana.

There are two routes into Ecuador. The one used most frequently is via Tumbes but there is also a rarely travelled route via La Tina. ETHMOPESA has a daily bus service to La Tina leaving from the Piura market at about 7.30 am (5 hours, $3). Transportes Roggero and Empresa Petrolera both operate a daily service to Tumbes. Empresa Chiclayo, Transportes El Dorado and Comité 1 all have their offices near the junction of Sullana and Sanchez Cerro. Between them, they provide frequent services to Tumbes ($4, 6 hours by bus and $8, 4½ hours by colectivo taxi). These companies also provide frequent transport to Chiclayo ($2.50, 3 hours).

If you're heading east into the mountains, try CIVA which has a daily 9 am bus to Huancabamba ($4.70, 8 hours). ETRANCH, half a block from CIVA, has buses to Chulucanas (90c, 1¼ hours) leaving several times a day. For Cajamarca and across the northern Andes, it's best to go to Chiclayo and change. Chinchaysuyo has a daily departure to Huaraz ($11.80).

Several companies offer services to Lima – the length of the journey, number of stops, crowding of the buses and comfort of the seats vary along with the prices. The cheapest is Cruz de Galpon (their recent special price to Lima was $6.70 and the trip was said to take 18 hours). Expreso Sudamericano buses are also cheap ($8.20) but usually slow. TEPSA is probably the best and charge $10.70 for the 16-hour trip. Other companies going to Lima include CIVA, Transportes Roggero, Transportes Piura and Chinchaysuyo. Most will sell you pro-rata tickets to intermediate destinations. As you can imagine, prices and schedules vary from month to month. If you're in a great hurry, take an overnight colectivo taxi with Comité 24. They charge $16.50 and claim to do the trip in 13 hours.

SECHURA

The fishing village of Sechura is on the estuary of the Río Piura, about 54 km by road south-west of Piura. It is famous for its 17th century cathedral and for its nearby beaches, which are crowded with Piurans on summer weekends (January to March). The most interesting beach is at San Pedro, 11 km along a dirt road which branches off the Piura to Sechura road to your right about 10 km before Sechura. Here, there is an excellent beach and a lagoon – the haunt of many seabirds, including flamingoes.

The beaches have few facilities. Sechura has a few simple restaurants and a basic hostal, which is usually full. Camping is possible but carry plenty of drinking water with you.

PAITA

Piura's main port is the historic town of Paita (population 50,000), 50 km due west by paved road. Paita's secluded location on a natural bay surrounded by cliffs did not protect it from the seafaring conquistadors; Pizarro landed here in 1527 on his second voyage to Peru. Since then, Paita has had an interesting history. It became a Spanish colonial port and was frequently sacked by pirates and buccaneers.

According to local historians:

In 1579, Paita was the victim of the savage aggression of the English filibuster, Francis Drake. Apparently, he heard that the Spanish galleon *Sacafuego* was in the area, laden with treasure destined for the Spanish crown. With shooting and violence, he attacked the port, reducing its temple, monastery and houses to ashes, and fleeing with his booty.

And to think I was taught that Sir Francis was a hero! Drake was not the only one making life miserable for the Spaniards. Numerous privateers arrived during the centuries that followed, with another notable episode occurring in the 18th century when the Protestant buccaneer George Anson tried to decapitate the wooden statue of Our Lady of Mercy. The statue, complete with slashed neck, can still be seen in the Church of La Merced. The feast of La Virgen de la Merced is held annually on 24 September.

Paita is also famous as the home of the influential mistress of Simón Bolívar, the liberator. She was an Ecuadorian, Manuelita Sáenz, who arrived here upon Bolívar's death in 1850 and, forgoing the fame and fortune left her by her lover, worked as a seamstress until her death over 20 years later. Her house still stands and in front of it is a Paitan landmark, La Figura, a wooden figurehead from a pirate ship.

The port has good beaches to the north and south which are popular with Piuran holidaymakers during the summer season. A few km to the north is the good beach of Colán. The church here is reputedly the oldest colonial church in Peru. The beach of Yasila, some 12 km to the south, is also popular.

Places to Stay

Despite Paita's beaches and historic interest, the town has only two hotels. The *Hotel Pacífico*, on the Plaza de Armas, is cheaper than the *Hostal Miramar*, which is housed in an attractively restored wooden colonial building at Avenida Jorge Chávez 418.

SULLANA

Sullana is a modern city 38 km north of Piura. It is an important agricultural centre and has a surprisingly large population of about 150,000. Despite its size and importance, most travellers find Sullana of little interest and prefer to visit nearby Piura. There is nothing much to see in Sullana except the hustle and bustle of a Peruvian market town.

The town has half a dozen cheap hotels and plenty of restaurants. One of the best hotels is the friendly and reasonably priced *Hostal San Miguel* at Avenida Farfán 208, near the Plaza Grau. There are several bus offices nearby.

HUANCABAMBA

The eastern side of the Department of Piura is mountainous, has few roads and is infrequently visited by travellers. Huancabamba,

210 km east of Piura by rough road, is one of the most important and interesting of the department's highland towns.

The western slopes of the Piuran Andes are an important fruit and coffee-growing area. As you travel east from Piura, first on the asphalt Pan-American Highway and then, after 64 km, along the dirt road to Huancabamba, you pass citrus groves, sugarcane fields and coffee plantations. You can break the journey at Canchaque, two-thirds of the way from Piura to Huancabamba, where there are a couple of simple hotels. Beyond Canchaque, the road climbs steeply over a 3000-metre pass before dropping to Huancabamba at 1957 metres. This last 70-km stretch is very rough and there may be long delays in the wet season (December to March).

Huancabamba is an attractive country town in a lovely setting – at the head of the long, very narrow Huancabamba River valley and surrounded by mountains. The Huancabamba River is the most westerly major tributary of the Amazon. Although

A brujería doll, used to bestow abundance

only 160 km from the Pacific Ocean, the waters of the Huancabamba empty into the Atlantic, some 3500 km away as the macaw flies. The banks of the Huancabamba are unstable and constantly eroding. The town itself is subject to frequent subsidence and slippage and so has earned itself the nickname la ciudad que camina, or 'the town which walks'.

Huancabamba has a long history. In Inca times, it was a minor settlement along the Inca Andean Highway between Ecuador and the important town of Cajamarca. Although the Inca town is lost, you can still see remnants of Inca paving along the Huancabamba River.

Huancabamba is not just geographically, geologically and historically interesting; it is also one of Peru's major centres of *brujería*, loosely translated as witchcraft or sorcery. The traditional brujería methods are used both to influence the client's future and to heal and cure. The use of local herbs or potions is combined with ritual ablutions in certain lakes said to contain waters with curative powers. People from all walks of life and from all over Peru (and other countries) visit the brujos (witch doctors) and *curanderos* or 'healers', paying sizeable sums in their attempts to find cures for ailments which have not responded to more conventional treatments or to remedy problems such as unrequited love, bad luck or infertility.

Although a few curanderos can be found in Huancabamba, those with the best reputation are to be found in the highlands north of the town in a lake region known as the Huaringas, almost 4000 metres above sea level. The main lake is Shumbe, about 35 km north of Huancabamba, though the nearby Laguna Negra is the one most frequently used by the curanderos. Trucks go as far as Sapalache, about 20 km north of Huancabamba, and you can hire mules from there. Many people visit the area, so finding information and guides is not difficult. However, the tradition is taken very seriously and gawkers or sceptics will get a hostile reception.

Places to Stay

The best of Huancabamba's three cheap and basic hotels is the clean, centrally located *Hotel El Dorado* at Medina 118. It also has a decent restaurant. The other hotels are the *Minerva* at Medina 208 and the *Andino* at Grau 310.

Getting There & Away

The daily CIVA bus from Piura takes 8 hours if the going is good, but in the wet season, the trip can easily take twice as long. The CIVA office in Huancabamba is on the Plaza de Armas.

AYABACA

Ayabaca (altitude 2715 metres) is a small highland town in the north-eastern part of the Department of Piura, close to the Ecuadorian border. It is in an isolated and rarely visited region but is attractive to the adventurous traveller.

There is an Inca ruin at Ayapata, several hours away on foot. The site contains walls, flights of stairs, ceremonial baths and a central plaza, but is overgrown. Other Inca sites can be found in the region, many unexplored, as well as a variety of pre-Inca ruins. There are also mysterious caves, lakes and mountains, some of which are said to be bewitched. Those with time could mount an expedition to find unexplored ruins; mules and guides are indispensable.

Visit the area in the dry season (late May to early September) when the trails are easily passable; the wet months, especially December to April, are to be avoided. You should not attempt to travel through this region alone as it's easy to become lost and there are drug smugglers in the area. Señor Celso Acuña Calle is recommended as a knowledgeable guide. He lives at Cáceres 161 and can provide you with mules and information.

The very colourful religious festival of El Señor Cautivo, held from 12 to 15 October, is rarely seen by tourists.

Places to Stay & Eat

There are three small, basic hotels. The *Hotel Señor Cautivo* is at Cáceres 109, the *San Martín* at Cáceres 192 and the *Alex* at Bolívar 112. They are not well marked.

Ayabaca has a few simple restaurants and shops, but if you plan on an expedition, bring what you will need with you as supplies in Ayabaca are limited and basic.

Getting There & Away

There is no regular bus service from Piura at this time and the best way to get to Ayabaca is on the morning ETHMOPESA bus to La Tina. Get off at the Ayabaca turn-off at Santa Ana de Quiroz, about 3 hours from Piura and 83 km from Ayabaca. From here, there is a dirt road to Ayabaca and, if you arrive in Santa Ana in the morning, you can usually find a truck to Ayabaca. Check at the Piura tourist office to see whether a better service is now available.

LA TINA

The small border post of La Tina is too small to qualify as a town. There are no hotels and it is suggested that you cross the Ecuadorian border to Macará, where there are better facilities. La Tina is reached by daily ETHMOPESA bus from Piura. Buses and colectivos also leave from Sullana early in the morning. This international route continues to the Ecuadorian mountain town of Loja and is much less frequently travelled but more scenic than the desert route via Tumbes and Huaquillas.

Crossing the Border

The border is open from 8 am to 6 pm daily with irregular lunch hours. Formalities are fairly relaxed as long as your documents are in order. There are no banks and few moneychangers. If you ask around, you'll find someone who will change cash but not travellers' cheques.

Travellers entering Ecuador are rarely asked to show onward tickets or money. Normally, only a valid passport is required. You are given a tourist card at the border which you must surrender when leaving the country. It is about an hour's walk from the border to the town of Macará and there are pick-up trucks and taxis doing the journey.

Macará has four hotels, the best of which is the *Parador Turistico* on the outskirts of town. Singles/doubles with bath are $3.50/6. There are cheaper hotels in the town centre. Also in the town centre is Transportes Loja, which has three buses a day to Loja (7 hours), and daily buses to Guayaquil (15 hours) and Quito (22 hours). See the Lonely Planet book *Ecuador & the Galápagos Islands – a travel survival kit* for further information.

Travellers entering Peru, especially those who require a visa, are occasionally asked for a ticket out of the country. If you don't need a visa, you probably won't be asked. If you are asked, and you don't have an airline ticket, you can usually satisfy the exit-ticket requirement by buying a round-trip bus ticket to Sullana or Piura. The unused portion is nonrefundable. Most nationalities, however, require only a tourist card, obtainable from the border authorities, and a valid passport. Australians and New Zealanders do require visas. There is a Peruvian consul in Macará. If you arrive at Macará in the afternoon, it is best to stay the night there. The ETHMOPESA bus from La Tina to Piura leaves early in the afternoon.

TALARA

Talara lies on the coast, in the centre of Peru's major coastal oil-producing region. On the 120-km desert drive along the Pan-American Highway from Piura, you'll see plenty of *lufkins*, the automatic pumps used in oil extraction. Although there are some good beaches near Talara, the town has little to interest the tourist, particularly since floods severely damaged the town, including its hotels, in 1983. Nevertheless, the authorities are promoting the beaches in an attempt to attract tourists, though the town's few hotels are often full of oil workers. One of the better beaches is the beach at Las Peñitas, 3 km to the north.

Forty years ago, Talara was a small fishing village. Today, it has a population of 45,000 and is the site of Peru's largest oil refinery, which produces between 60,000 and 100,000 barrels of petroleum a day. Talara is

a desert town, so everything, including water, must be imported.

Negritos, 11 km south of Talara by road, is on the Punta Pariñas, the most westerly point on the South American continent. The tar pits of La Brea, where Pizarro dug tar to caulk his ships, can be seen on the Pariñas Peninsula.

On the north side of Talara are the Pariñas Woods. According to a local tourist information booklet, the woods 'are perhaps the city's major tourist attraction, where one can encounter magnificent examples of wild rabbits and squirrels, etc as well as a diversity of little birds which belong to the fauna of the place'. Don't miss them.

Places to Stay

Talara's five or six hotels are often full and not very cheap. As I haven't stayed in any of them, I can't recommend one in particular. There are plenty of restaurants, cafeterias and bars.

Getting There & Away

Air Both AeroPeru and Faucett have flights to Talara as well as daily or twice-daily flights to and from Lima ($86). There are also AeroPeru flights to Tumbes and Faucett flights to Piura, but schedules and destinations change often.

Bus Plenty of buses go to Talara from Piura or Tumbes.

CABO BLANCO

From Talara, the Pan-American Highway heads north-east for 200 km to the Ecuadorian border. The road runs parallel to the ocean with frequent views of the beach.

About 30 km north of Talara is Cabo Blanco, famous for sport fishing. Ernest Hemingway fished here in the early 1950s. The largest fish ever landed on a rod, a 710-kg black marlin, was taken here in 1953 by Alfred Glassell Junior. The angling is still good, though it has declined somewhat. The fishing club can usually provide accommodation or you can camp nearby.

MÁNCORA

The small fishing village of Máncora, about 30 km further north, has the next well-known beach. This surfers' beach has recently become popular with Brazilian surfers. It's been described as 'quite a scene' and the surf is particularly good from November to March. Máncora has two or three medium-priced hotels.

TUMBES

Soon after leaving Máncora, you enter the Department of Tumbes, Peru's smallest department. This area of Peru's northern coast has tolerably warm water all year round, even in the cooler months of April to December when swimming is rare further south. En route to Tumbes, the Pan-American Highway passes several beaches including Punta Sal, Zorritos and Caleta Cruz. The latter two can be reached by local bus from Tumbes. You can also visit the nearby Cerros de Amotape National Park.

Tumbes was an Ecuadorian town until Peru's victory in the 1940-41 border war but is now about 30 km away from the border. A garrison town with a strong military presence and a population of about 50,000, it is also the capital of its department. Be careful taking photographs in the Tumbes area – it is illegal to photograph anything remotely concerning the military.

History

Most travellers pass through Tumbes without realising that the city has a long history. The small, dusty town library on the Plaza de Armas displays a few ceramics discovered by workers on the site of the Hotel de Turistas. These pottery vessels have been tentatively dated as being about 1500 years old.

At the time of the conquest, Tumbes was an Inca town on the coastal highway. It was first sighted by Pizarro in 1528 during his second voyage of exploration (the first voyage never reached Peru). Pizarro invited an Inca noble to dine aboard his ship and sent two of his men ashore to inspect the Inca city. They reported the presence of an obviously well-organised and fabulously rich civilisation. Pizarro returned a few years later and began his conquest of Peru.

Present-day Tumbes is about 5 km northeast of the Inca city marked on maps as San Pedro de los Incas. The Pan-American Highway passes through the site but there is little to see.

Information

Tourist Information The FOPTUR tourist office (tel 5054) is on Alfonso Ugarte, in the Edificio Majestad. The Ecuadorian Consulate is on the corner of Huascar and Piura and is open from 9 am to 12.30 pm and 4 to 6 pm Monday to Friday.

As the town's single cinema is not functioning, the only thing to do in the evening is hang out in one of the pavement cafés on the spacious Plaza de Armas. During the day you can walk along the Malecón for views of the Río Tumbes.

Telephone As in all Peruvian towns, long-distance and international phone calls can be made from the ENTEL office. It is normally open from 8 am to 10 pm daily.

Money There are exchange facilities in Tumbes and in Aguas Verdes, on the border. Generally, I've found better value at the border but you have to know the exchange rates and bargain with the moneychangers (recognisable by their black briefcases). If you don't bargain, especially in Ecuador, they'll cheerfully give you an exchange rate anywhere from 5% to 50% lower than it really is. Try to find out what the dollar is worth in both Ecuador and Peru from travellers going the other way. Also, beware of being short-changed and make sure you understand the rate (some changers will quote an exchange such as 4500 intis and give you only 4050, hoping you didn't clearly understand their quote).

There is a bank in Aguas Verdes which gives good rates, better than those offered by the banks in Tumbes. Banks are usually closed in the afternoon and are the only places to change travellers' cheques.

Moneychangers in Tumbes hang out on the Plaza de Armas and give fairly good rates if you bargain. Because you are close to the border and the exchange rate can change dramatically in a few days, moneychangers will sometimes hope to mislead you into accepting a low rate, thinking you may have just arrived from Ecuador and won't know any better. Ask around before changing large sums of money. It is best to change intis to dollars in Peru and then dollars to sucres in Ecuador (or vice versa) to get the best rates.

Beaches

The two popular beaches are at Caleta La Cruz and Zorritos, south-west of Tumbes, and are easy to reach on local transport. Colectivos to Zorritos (1 hour, 60c) leave from the market, as do cheaper, slower buses. The road passes banana plantations on the way to the sea at Caleta La Cruz, about 20 km from Tumbes. Caleta La Cruz has a couple of basic restaurants.

There are sandy beaches all the way along the coast from La Cruz to Zorritos and you'll see many surf fishermen catching shrimp larvae in red nylon hand nets. The larvae are transferred to commercial shrimp farms for rearing. Both villages also have picturesque fishing fleets. The water is fairly warm at around 18°C or 70°F all year round, though few Peruvians (except for the fishermen) venture into the sea outside the hottest months of January, February and March. Women are advised not to visit the beaches alone.

A further 10 km brings you to Zorritos. On the outskirts of town, about 4 km before the town centre, is the government-run *Hotel de Turistas*. It charges about $5/8 for singles/doubles with bath and has a restaurant. There are other more basic restaurants in the town. Both villages are interesting for their fishing activities and for their coastal bird life. You can see frigate birds, pelicans, egrets and many migratory birds.

Another side trip is to Puerto Pizarro, about 30 minutes north of Tumbes. Col-

ectivos leave from near the bus stations and charge 40c. Here, the character of the ocean front changes from the coastal desert which stretches over 2000 km north from central Chile to northern Peru. At Puerto Pizzaro begin the mangrove swamps which dominate much of the Ecuadorian and Colombian coastlines. This change of environment also signals a different variety of birdlife.

Although the water is a bit muddier, it is still pleasant enough for swimming and is less crowded with fishermen than the beach at Zorritos. If you don't want to stay at the cheap, basic *Hotel Venecia*, try the pleasant *Motel Pizarro* on the beach ($4.50/7 with bath). Its restaurant has good meals, though the service is desperately slow. If you have the time, money and inclination, the motel can arrange fishing boat and water-skiing trips (skis can be hired).

Many people stay in Tumbes and visit Puerto Pizaro on a day trip.

Cerros de Amotape National Park

This desert-dry tropical forest ecosystem has been protected by the creation of the 90,000 hectare national park in 1974. The flora and fauna are interesting and crocodiles, jaguars, condors and anteaters have been reported, though you are unlikely to see much in the way of wildlife without a guide.

Guides are available from the village of Rica Playa within the park. Two have been recommended: Manuel Porras Sanchez and Roberto Correo. The Mellizos Hidalgo family is a good source of local information.

During the dry season, a morning bus leaves for Rica Playa from the Tumbes market (about 2½ hours), though the road may be impassable during the wet months (January to April). Trucks also make the trip – one is Señor Esteban Hidalgo's truck *Flecha de Oro*. Señor Hidalgo can be contacted at San Ramon 101 in Tumbes.

Rica Playa is a small, friendly village. Although there are no hotels, you can camp and local families will cook meals for you. It's a good idea to bring some of your own food.

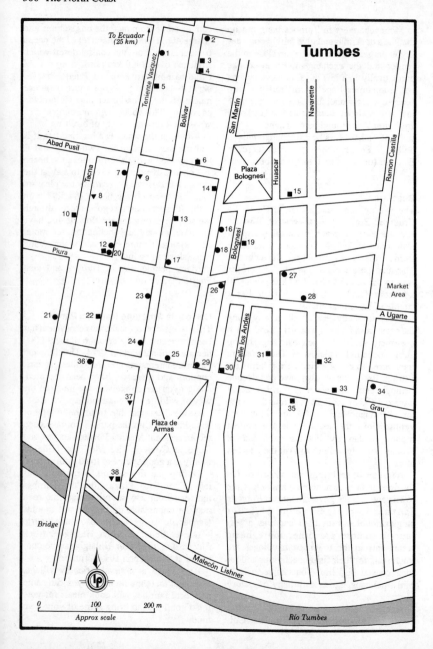

Tumbes

To Ecuador
(25 km)

Teniente Vasquez

Bolívar

San Martín

Navarette

Ramon Castilla

Abad Pusil

Tacna

Plaza
Bolognesi

Huascar

Piura

Bolognesi

Market
Area

A Ugarte

Calle los Andes

Grau

Plaza de
Armas

Bridge

Malecón Lishner

0   100   200 m
Approx scale

Río Tumbes

■ PLACES TO STAY

3	Hostal Kiko's
4	Hostal Toloa II
5	Hostal Toloa
6	Hostal Cordova
10	Hostal Elica
11	Hostal Amazonas
13	Hostal Jugdem
14	Hotel de Turistas
15	Residencial Internacional
19	Residencial Gandolfo
20	Hostal Los Once
22	Hostal Premier
30	Hostal Roma
31	Hostal César & Hostal Estoril
32	Hostal Lourdes
33	Hostal Italia
35	Hostal Tumbes
38	Hotel Bolívar

▼ PLACES TO EAT

8	Restaurant El Huerto de mi Amada
9	Restaurant Menova

37	Restaurant Latino
38	Restaurant Curich & Restaurant Europa

● OTHER

1	Expreso Sudamericano (Bus)
2	EMTRAFESA (Bus)
7	Empresa D Olano (Bus)
12	Travel Agent
16	ENTEL
17	Colectivos to Border
18	Post Office
20	Bus Terminal Corner
21	Faucett Airline
23	Banco de Crédito
24	Banco de la Nación
25	Cathedral
26	AeroPeru
27	Ecuadorian Consulate
28	Ministry of Tourism
29	Library
34	Colectivos to Zorritos & Caleta La Cruz
36	TEPSA (Bus)

Fiestas

Fiestas in Tumbes usually take the form of international trade fairs with Ecuador. The major ones are the International Integration Fair in the first week in August, the Festival of the Patroness of Perpetual Help in the first 10 days of September and the Regional Fair (8 December) in the first two weeks of December. A Tumbes Tourist Festival is also held sometime in August.

Places to Stay

The large amount of border traffic means that the hotels tend to be crowded, and during the major holidays and trade fairs, they are often full by early afternoon. During the rest of the year, it can be difficult to find single rooms by afternoon, though doubles are usually available. Most hotels have only cold water but that's no problem in the heat. All but the most basic hotels have fans – ask at the front desk. Air-conditioned rooms or fans are recommended during the hottest months (December to March). One reader reported

bad mosquitoes in June – a fan tends to discourage them from flying.

Places to Stay – bottom end

Hotels are a little more expensive here than in many other small Peruvian towns. The cheapest include the *Residencial Internacional*, where rooms with bath cost $1.25 per person, and the *Residencial Gandolfo*, which offers singles/doubles for $1.50/2.50 and rooms with bath for almost twice this price. The staff at the Gandolfo have been described as indifferent and the communal bathrooms are rather grotty. The basic *Hotel Bolívar* is also cheap and reasonably clean.

Slightly more expensive, but with friendly staff, are the *Hostal Elica* and *Hostal Italia*. They charge $2.50/3 for singles/doubles with bath and are both recommended. The similarly priced *Hostal Premier* is basic and friendly but has no singles. The *Hostal Amazonas*, which is reasonably clean and close to the bus terminals, has double rooms with bath for around $3, though the hotel staff have been criticised as surly.

Other hotels in the $1.25 to $2 per person price range include the *Hostal Florian* and the clean *Hostal Los Once*, which are near the bus terminals and so tend to be noisy, the quieter *Hostal Cordova* and the friendly *Hostal Estoril*. The Florian is not marked on the Tumbes map because it is a recent recommendation – it will be included in the next edition.

Places to Stay – middle

The *Hostal Tumbes, Jugdem* and *Kiko's* charge about $3.50/5.50 for singles/doubles with bath, but are not particularly special. The *Hostal Toloa* is in an ugly building but is clean and has plenty of singles/doubles at $4/6. For the same price, the *Hostal Toloa II* is better; its rooms have private baths.

The clean and friendly *Hostal Lourdes* also charges $4/6 for singles/doubles with bath and has been recommended as one of the best hotel deals in Tumbes. Also clean, friendly and good value is the *Hostal César* where singles/doubles cost $4.50/5.50. Rooms with bath are an extra $1.50. The new *Hostal Roma*, on the corner of the Plaza de Armas, is clean and comfortable but you pay a little more for the central location – about $7/9 with bath.

Places to Stay – top end

The best hotel in town is the government-run *Hotel de Turistas*. It has a good restaurant, a garden and singles/doubles with bath for $14/18, including continental breakfast.

Places to Eat

There are several bars and restaurants on the Plaza de Armas, many with shaded tables and chairs outside – a real boon in hot weather. It's a pleasant place to sit and watch the world go by as you drink a cold beer and wait for your bus. One Sunday lunch time I was doing just that when I noticed a big crowd gathering in the plaza. I asked what was going on and was told that a Peruvian Air Force paratrooper was going to land in the Plaza de Armas. The plaza had several tall trees, and worse still, a couple of very sharp-looking flag poles in the centre. The

thought of jumping onto one by accident was so unpleasant that I had to order another beer. An hour later the paratrooper made an appearance, his descent marked with smoke canisters. Despite the hazards of flag poles, trees and spectators, he made a perfect landing right in front of the restaurant where I was sitting.

The best restaurants on the plaza seem to be on the west side. The *Latino, Curich* and *Europa* are all reasonably priced and serve a variety of tasty dishes, including excellent local seafood. Travellers arriving from Ecuador should try the cebiche – this marinated raw-seafood dish is much spicier than the Ecuadorian version and goes down very well with a cold beer.

If you're in a hurry to catch a bus or are on a budget, the *Restaurant Menova* and the *Huerta de mi Amada*, both within a block of most bus terminals, sell good, cheap food.

It's unlikely that you will be in Tumbes very long but if you are, there are plenty of other inexpensive places to choose from.

Getting There & Away

Air Both AeroPeru and Faucett have offices in Tumbes. There are daily flights to Lima ($91), either via Talara with AeroPeru on Wednesday, Friday and Sunday or via Chiclayo with Faucett every day. Although these schedules and routes change frequently, you can rely on flights to Lima.

Bus Most bus company offices are on Avenida Teniente Vasquez, especially around the intersection with Avenida Piura. Services are improving since the devastating 1983 floods washed away parts of the Pan-American Highway, but the section to Piura is still rather slow. You can usually find a bus to Lima within 24 hours of your arrival in Tumbes but they're sometimes booked up a few days in advance. In that case, take a bus south to any major city and try again from there. Carry your passport with you – there are several passport control stops south of Tumbes.

Buses to Lima take 22 to 24 hours; fares vary but $10 is average. Most major companies have two departures a day and TEPSA (which is usually the fastest but also the most expensive) has four daily departures. TEPSA also has a nonstop 'presidential' service leaving daily at 2.30 pm. It takes 18 to 20 hours and costs more. Expreso Sudamericano buses are usually the slowest and cheapest.

Most companies will sell you tickets to intermediate cities at pro-rata prices. Transportes El Dorado and El Aguila have buses to Piura ($3, 7 hours) and colectivo taxis to Piura ($6, 5 hours) which leave from in front of their offices. EMTRAFESA runs night buses to Chiclayo ($4) and to Trujillo ($6, 15 hours).

Getting Around

Airport Transport The airport is north of town, about $1 by taxi. For about this price, the airlines will pick you up from your hotel if you reconfirm with them the day before your flight.

Local Transport If you're heading for Puerto Pizarro, use Comité 6 colectivos which leave from a stand on Avenida Piura, near the main bus stations. Colectivos to the beaches of Zorritos and Caleta La Cruz depart from near the market. The market area is also the place to find colectivo taxis, buses and trucks to most local destinations.

Colectivo cars for the border town of Aguas Verdes leave from the corner of avenidas Bolívar and Piura and cost about 70c for the 26-km journey. Ask around for the exact price as not all the drivers are honest. (One tried to charge me $2 for the trip, though he wasn't successful). If you're in a group, hire a car to take you to the border.

GOING TO ECUADOR

A few years ago, Peru built a new migraciónes (immigration) office in the middle of the desert about 2 km from the border at Aguas Verdes. This operated for a couple of years and made the border crossing a little more time consuming than before. Recently, this office stopped issuing entry and exit stamps for travellers and you can

now go directly from Tumbes to the border immigration office in Aguas Verdes itself, though the situation could change again if Peru decides to reopen the desert office. The colectivo service to Aguas Verdes stops by the immigration office.

Before leaving Peru, travellers must surrender their Peruvian tourist cards and obtain an exit stamp from the immigration office. Assuming your documents are in order, exit formalities are usually fairly quick. The immigration office is open daily from 8.30 am to noon and 2 to 6 pm.

Aguas Verdes is basically a long street full of stalls selling consumer products. It has a bank and a few simple restaurants but no hotels. The terminal for colectivo taxis between Aguas Verdes and Tumbes is on the main street, about 300 metres from the border.

An international bridge across the Río Zarumilla links Peru with Ecuador. The long market street of Aguas Verdes continues into the Ecuadorian border town of Huaquillas, which has similar stalls. The Ecuadorian immigration office is on the left-hand side of the street, about 200 metres beyond the international bridge, and is identified by the yellow, blue and red striped Ecuadorian flag. The office is open from 8 am to noon and 2 to 5 pm daily and all Ecuadorian exit and entrance formalities are carried out here.

Ecuadorian entrance formalities are usually straightforward. No tourist needs a visa but everyone needs a T3 tourist card, available free at the immigration office. You must surrender your T3 when you leave the country, so don't lose it. Exit tickets and sufficient funds ($20 per day) are legally required but very rarely asked for. Stays of up to 90 days are allowed but usually only 30 days are given. Extensions can be easily and freely obtained in Guayaquil or Quito. Note that you are allowed only 90 days per year in Ecuador. If you've already been in the country for 90 days and try to return, you will be refused entry. If you have an international flight from Ecuador, you can usually get a 72-hour transit visa to get you to the airport and out of the country.

There are some basic hotels on the main street of Huaquillas but most people make the 2-hour bus trip to the city of Machala, where there are much better facilities. See Lonely Planet's *Ecuador & the Galápagos Islands – a travel survival kit* for further information.

Plenty of people will offer their services as porters and guides. They can be very insistent and usually overcharge, so unless you really need help, they're more of a hassle than they're worth.

Travellers leaving Ecuador for Peru must surrender their Ecuadorian T3 card at the immigration office in Huaquillas and obtain an Ecuadorian exit stamp in their passports. Cross the international bridge (guards usually inspect but don't stamp your passport) and continue for about 300 metres to the colectivo taxi rank. You get your passport stamped at the immigration office nearby. Passports used to be stamped at the other immigration office, 1½ km further on. Check locally for the current location.

Most European nationals don't need a visa to visit Peru, nor do North Americans. Australians and New Zealanders do. Visas are not available in either Aguas Verdes or Huaquillas and you have to go back to the Peruvian Consul in Machala to get one. Other nationalities usually just need a tourist card, available at the Peruvian immigration office. Remember to look after your tourist card – you will need to surrender it when you leave Peru. Although an exit ticket out of Peru is officially required, gringo travellers are rarely asked for one unless they look thoroughly disreputable. As Latin American travellers are often asked for an exit ticket, be prepared for this eventuality if you're a non-Peruvian Latin American (or are travelling with one). The bus office in Aguas Verdes sells (nonrefundable) tickets out of Peru. The immigration official will tell you where it is – a *colaboración* may help here.

Once entrance formalities have been observed, you will find colectivo taxis leaving for Tumbes when they are full; there's one every 15 minutes or so. The buses are cheaper but less frequent.

Top: Alpaca at Machu Picchu (RR)
Left: Machu Picchu (RR)
Right: Machu Picchu, the traditional view (TW)

Top: Plaza de Armas, Ayacucho (RR)
Left: Huancavelica Cathedral (RR)
Right: Gourd seller, Huancayo Market (RR)

The Huaraz Area

Huaraz is the most important climbing, trekking, and backpacking centre in Peru, perhaps even in all of South America. The historic city of Huaraz has been demolished several times by massive earthquakes and is therefore not particularly attractive. The surrounding mountains, however, are exceptionally beautiful and many travellers come to Peru specifically to visit the Huaraz area.

The mountains offer a wide range of attractions. There are glacial lakes and hot springs. There are Inca and pre-Inca ruins, including the fascinating centre of the 3000-year-old Chavín feline-worship cult at Chavín de Huantar. There are friendly, interesting people living in remote villages, accessible only by mule or on foot. And there are fascinating flora and fauna, including the 10-metre-high *Puya raymondii*, the tallest flower spike and largest bromeliad in the world, and the magnificent Andean condor, one of the largest flying birds on earth.

The Andes Around Huaraz

Huaraz is 3091 metres above sea level and lies on the Santa River valley, flanked to the west by the Cordillera Negra and to the east by the Cordillera Blanca. The valley between these two mountain ranges is popularly referred to as 'El Callejón de Huaylas' after the district of Huaylas at the northern end of the valley. A road runs the length of this valley, linking the main towns and providing spectacular views of the mountains. The Callejón de Huaylas is roughly 300 km north of Lima, about 8 hours by bus.

The Cordillera Negra, though an attractive range in its own right, is snowless and completely eclipsed by the magnificent snowcapped mountains of the Cordillera Blanca. The lower range is sometimes visited by road from the coast en route to the Cordillera Blanca.

The Cordillera Blanca is about 20 km wide and 180 km long. In this fairly small area, there are more than 50 peaks of 5700 metres or higher. By contrast, North America has only three peaks in excess of 5700 metres (Orizaba in Mexico, Logan in Canada and Denali in Alaska) and Europe has none. Only in Asia can mountain ranges higher than the Andes be found. Mt Huascarán, at 6768 metres, is Peru's highest mountain and the highest peak in the tropics anywhere in the world. However, this string of statistics does not do the Cordillera Blanca justice. Its shining glaciers, sparkling streams, awesome vertical walls and lovely lakes must be seen to be appreciated.

South of the Cordillera Blanca is the smaller, more remote but no less spectacular Cordillera Huayhuash. It contains Peru's second highest peak, the 6634-metre-high Yerupaja, and is a more rugged and less frequently visited range. The main difference between the two ranges, for the hiker at least, is that you walk *through* the Cordillera Blanca surrounded by magnificent peaks and you walk *around* the smaller Huayhuash, one of the most spectacular mountain circuits in the world. Both ranges are highly recommended for climbers and hikers.

Note, however, that the Cordillera Huayhuash area has recently been raided by Sendero guerillas and travel here is inadvisable at present. The Cordillera Blanca and the Callejón de Huaylas are both safe at this time.

HUASCARÁN NATIONAL PARK

Protecting the beauty of the Cordillera Blanca was first suggested by the well-known Peruvian mountaineer César Morales Arnao in the early 1960s. The idea did not become reality until 1975 when the Huascarán National Park was established. The park encompasses not only the highest peak in Peru but also the entire area of the Cordillera Blanca above 4000 metres, except Champará in the extreme northern part of the range.

The objectives of the park are the protection and conservation of the Cordillera Blanca's flora, fauna, archaeological sites and scenic beauty, the promotion of scientific investigation of its natural resources, the publicising of the park's natural and historic attractions on regional, national and international levels, the stimulation and control of tourism in the park and the raising of living standards for the people living within the park boundaries.

Visitors to the park should register at the park office (see the Huaraz section) and pay a small park fee. This is about $2 but may change in the future. You can also register and pay your fee at one of the control stations on the main trails entering the park. The money from the fees is used to help maintain trails, pay park rangers (there are a few) and regulate user pressure in the area. Some oppose regulation; however, the number of visitors to the Cordillera Blanca, while still relatively small by Western standards, is increasing fast enough to warrant some sort of regulation if the inherent attraction of the mountains is not to be damaged. It seems to me that as foreign visitors are the ones who get the most joy out of the Cordillera Blanca and are among those causing the greatest change within the area, they should also contribute to the financing of the national park with their user fees.

Present park regulations are largely a matter of courtesy and common sense. 'Do not litter' is the most obvious one – obvious, that is, to almost all of us. There are always a few visitors who leave a trail of yellow film cartons, pink toilet paper, broken bottles and jagged tin cans to mark their path. This is thoughtless, rude and illegal. It is true that the locals are among the worst offenders, but 'When in Rome...' is not a sensible reason for imitating the offence. It is also true that people tend to litter more where litter already exists, so each candy wrapper contributes to the overall problem by beginning or continuing this chain reaction. Don't do it.

Other park regulations are: don't disturb, feed or remove the flora and fauna, don't cut down trees or live branches for fires or other use, don't destroy or alter park signs, no off-road vehicle use, no hunting, no fishing during the off season (May to September), no fishing with explosives or nets and no taking of fish below 25 cm in length.

Visiting the Mountains

Basically, there are two ways to visit the mountains. One is to stay in the towns of the Callejón de Huaylas and take day trips by bus or taxi. A casual glance at the map reveals that the summit of Peru's highest peak is a mere 14 km from the main valley road and spectacular views can certainly be obtained from public transport. For many people, that is enough. The more adventurous will want to take their backpacks and hike, trek, camp or climb in the mountains. This book gives details of public transport but does not pretend to be a trail guide.

When to Go

The best months for hiking, climbing and mountain views are the dry months of June, July and August. May and September are also usually quite good. For the rest of the year, the wet season makes hiking difficult, especially from December to March, because the trails are so boggy. Despite the wet weather, you may be lucky and see some

Huascarán – Peru's highest mountain

spectacular mountain views between the clouds.

Mountain Guide Services

Guiding services range from a single arriero (mule driver) with a couple of pack animals for your camping gear to a complete trekking expedition with arrieros, burros, cooks, guides, food and all equipment provided. You can also hire high-altitude porters and guides for mountaineering expeditions.

Several guide services are available. One of the best, though certainly not the cheapest, is Pyramid Adventures (office tel 722525, home tel 721864) run by the five Morales brothers (Marcelino, Pablo, Eleazar, Eudes and Néstor). They are knowledgeable, hardworking, honest and friendly and provide every level of service at fair prices. The brothers are accomplished mountaineers and have been involved in new ascents as well as mountain-rescue activities. They specialise in providing a full service to trekking and climbing groups but can also put you in contact with a couple of arrieros if that's all you want. Eudes Morales speaks English. Pyramid Adventures is at Luzuriaga 530 and can be contacted in advance by writing to Casilla 25, Huaraz, Ancash, Peru.

Mountaineers and trekkers should also check out the Casa de Guias, on a little square just north of the Plaza de Armas in Huaraz. They offer a good guide service, information and a café where you can meet other climbers and trekkers.

Some cheaper guide services are available if you shop around but try to get references from other travellers before contracting with them. The cheapest option is to hire arrieros directly, though this involves speaking Spanish and perhaps some bargaining. Again, get references first. The national park office has a list of arrieros and will tell you what the going rate is – usually around $5 per day for a driver and $2 per burro. Often, a tip is added for good service and you have to supply food for the arriero while he is working for you. It's difficult to hire a pack animal for yourself; the arrieros will not send out burros without experienced drivers.

Horses and mules for riding purposes are also available. Bear in mind that it is far easier to make arrangements in Huaraz than anywhere else in the area and that in some towns and villages, arrieros are difficult to find.

Of course, many experienced backpackers go camping in the mountains without any local help. Just remember that carrying a backpack full of gear over a 4800-metre pass requires a lot more effort than trekking at low altitudes.

Equipment Rental

The better guide services will be able to supply everything from tents to ice axes. There are also rental agencies in Huaraz which will rent equipment without your having to hire guides. You'll find plenty of rental agencies along Luzuriaga, so if the first one you try doesn't have what you want, don't give up. Prices are fairly similar but the quality of the equipment varies a good deal – check around before you rent.

If you bring your own equipment, remember that *kerex* (kerosene) can be purchased from gas stations but *bencina* (white gas) is more difficult to find, though hardware stores and pharmacies do carry it. Camping Gaz canisters are usually, but not always, available. Firewood is in short supply and what there is should not be burned indiscriminately; come prepared with a kerosene stove. As it often freezes at night, you'll need to bring a warm sleeping bag – a lightweight tropical one won't do. It can rain even in the dry season so rain gear and a waterproof tent are needed. Sun protection is also essential. Wear a brimmed hat and sunglasses and bring strong suntan lotion with you as it is difficult to find in Huaraz. The same applies to effective insect repellent.

Food is no problem. Expensive, lightweight, freeze-dried food is occasionally left over from mountaineering expeditions and can be bought at the trekking and rental agencies. You can easily make do with oatmeal, dried soups, fast-cooking noodles and the usual canned goods, all of which are readily available in Huaraz.

Trail Guidebooks

One book which is particularly recommended for those wanting to camp or hike in these mountains is Jim Bartle's *Trails of the Cordilleras Blanca & Huayhuash of Peru*. It details 18 different hikes in the Cordillera Blanca and the complete circuit of the Cordillera Huayhuash, provides a wealth of background information and has plenty of detailed maps and photographs. Unfortunately, it is now out of print but a new edition may become available in the 1990s. Ask at the South American Explorers Club.

Also recommended is *Backpacking & Trekking in Peru & Bolivia* (5th Ed, 1989) by Hilary Bradt. Four Cordillera Blanca hikes and the Cordillera Huayhuash circuit are included in this book, which also has plenty of background information, including a useful natural history section.

John Ricker's *Yuraq Janka* is recommended for mountaineers. This sensitively written and well-illustrated guidebook gives fascinating historical, geological, meteorological, linguistic and sociological information about the region and is therefore of interest to nonclimbers too. Prospective climbers should be aware that this book offers only very broad outlines rather than detailed descriptions of the routes. The latter can be found in *The Peruvian Andes* by Phillipe Beaud – a trilingual book in Spanish, English and French.

Caracara

HUARAZ

The Santa River valley, on which Huaraz lies, has long been a major Andean thoroughfare and the Incas' main Andean road passed through here. However, little remains of the valley's archaeological heritage because a series of devastating natural disasters has repeatedly destroyed the towns of the Callejón de Huaylas.

The major cause of these natural disasters has been the build up of water levels in high mountain lakes, causing them to breach and water to cascade down to the valley below. The high lakes are often held back by a relatively thin wall of glacial debris which can burst when the lake levels rise. This can occur suddenly, as when an avalanche falls from high above the lake, or more slowly with rain and snow melt. Earthquakes can also cause the lakes to breach. When this happens, a huge wall of water, often mixed with snow, ice, mud, rocks and other matter, flows down from the lakes, wiping out everything in its path. Such a mixture of avalanche, waterfall and landslide is referred to as an *alluvion*.

Records of alluvions date back almost 300 years and three recent ones have caused particularly devastating loss of life. The first of these occurred in 1941 when an avalanche in the Cojup Valley, west of Huaraz, caused the Laguna Palcacocha to break its banks and flow down onto Huaraz, killing about 5000 of its inhabitants and flattening the centre of the city. Then, in 1962, a huge avalanche from Huascarán roared down its western slopes and destroyed the town of Ranrahirca, killing about 4000 people. The worst disaster occurred on 31 May 1970 when a massive earthquake, measuring 7.8 on the Richter scale, devastated much of central Peru, killing an estimated 80,000 people. About half of the 30,000 inhabitants of Huaraz died and only 10% of the city was left standing. The town of Yungay was completely buried by an alluvion and almost its entire population of 18,000 was buried with the city. Evidence of the disaster can still be seen throughout the valley.

Since these disasters, a government

agency has been formed to control the lake levels by building dams and tunnels, thus minimising the chance of similar catastrophes. The agency concerned is the Instituto Geológico Minero y Metalúrgico, known by the acronym INGEMMET.

Most of Huaraz has been rebuilt and it is now a modern, not especially attractive city of over 50,000 and the capital of the Department of Ancash. Its renown as the centre for visiting the Cordillera Blanca has led to the development of a thriving tourist industry, with a multitude of hotels and other facilities.

Information

Tourist Information The tourist office (tel 721031) on the Plaza de Armas is open from 9 am to 1 pm and 4 to 7 pm on weekdays and from 9 am to noon on Saturday. The office is a good source of general information about the area.

The Huascarán National Park office is in the Ministry of Agriculture building at the east end of Avenida Raimondi. Working hours are 7 am to 2.15 pm Monday to Friday, but avoid arriving just before they close. Staff can help you with information about visiting the national park.

The INGEMMET office is useful for dyeline maps of the Cordillera Blanca which are among the most detailed available. Sometimes you have to give them 24 hours notice to print the maps you need. The Instituto Geográfico Nacional and the South American Explorers Club, both in Lima, are also good sources of maps and information.

Money There are several banks on the north side of the Plaza de Armas and on the 600 block of Luzuriaga. The Banco de Crédito used to give the best rates with the least hassle, but moneychangers on the street outside the banks also give good rates at this time. Many of the better hotels and tourist agencies will accept cash US dollars at reasonable rates. I suggest that you shop around because rates seem to vary more in Huaraz than in other cities.

Acclimatisation Huaraz's altitude of 3091 metres will make you feel a little breathless and may give you a headache during your first few days, so take it easy and don't overexert yourself. The surrounding mountains are high enough to ensure that you will definitely get altitude sickness if you venture into them without spending at least a couple of days acclimatising in Huaraz. See the introductory Health section in the Facts for the Visitor chapter for more information.

Hot Showers Some of the cheaper hotels have only cold water but you can get a good hot shower at the *Duchas Raimondi*. The hot showers are open to the public from 8 am to 6 pm daily and cost 20c for 20 minutes.

Museum

The Archaeology Museum on the Plaza de Armas is small but quite interesting. There are a few mummies, some trepanned skulls and a garden of stone monoliths from the Recuay culture (400 BC to 600 AD) and the Wari culture (800 to 1200 AD). The museum is open every day and entry is about 20c.

Trout Hatchery

You can make an unusual and interesting excursion to the trout hatchery on the eastern outskirts of town. The best way get there is to walk east on Raimondi to the end and then cross the Río Quilcay on a small bridge. The hatchery is a little beyond. It is open to visitors between 9 am and noon on Sunday and from 2 to 5 pm on Saturday and Sunday.

Ruinas Wilcahuaín

This small pre-Inca ruin about 8 km north of Huaraz is in quite a good state of preservation. It can be reached on foot or you can hire a taxi for a few dollars. To get there, head north out of town on Avenida Centenario. You'll find a signposted dirt road to your right, a few hundred metres past the Hotel de Turistas. From here, the dirt road climbs 6 or 7 km (passing through the small communities of Jinua and Paria) to the ruins. The road continues on for another 20 km to Laguna

Huaraz

Approx scale

0 100 200 m

■ PLACES TO STAY

5   Hostal Los Pinos del Puente
8   Hostal Colombo
9   Hostal Yanett
15 Hostal San Isidro
16 Hostal Alpamayo
17 Edward's Inn
18 Pensión Stela
19 Hostal Los Andes
22 Hotel Barcelona
23 Hotel Cataluña
27 Hostal Tabariz
28 Hostal Los Portales
30 Hostal Raimondi
35 Pensión Galaxia
36 Pensión Maguina
37 Alojamiento Quintana
38 Hostal Huaraz
41 Hostal Huaraz & Hotel Oscar
44 Hostal El Pacífico
46 Hostal Regalon
48 Hotel Landauro
55 Hostal Continental
57 Hotel El Tumi
58 Hostal Andino

▼ PLACES TO EAT

4   Pio Pio Chicken Restaurant
7   Recreo La Unión
23 Pepe's Place-International Restaurant
25 Creperie Patrick
29 Chifa Familiar & Other Restaurants
38 Las Puyas Restaurant
41 Restaurant Samuels
42 Tasco Bar
46 Pizzería Ticino
55 Pizzerías Mama Mia & Posada

58 Hostal Andino Restaurant

● OTHER

1   Cine Soraya
2   Peña La Pascana
3   INGEMMET
6   Pacccha'k Pub
10 Empresa 14 (Bus)
11 Empresa Huandoy (Buses to Monter-
    rey, Carhuaz, Yungay & Caraz)
12 Trout Hatchery
13 Transportes Moreno (Bus)
14 Comité 11
20 Petrol Station
21 Discotec Any & Empresa Norpacifico
    (Bus)
24 TROME & Transportes Huascarán
    (Buses)
25 Imantata Bar
26 Taxis 1, 2 & 3 (Local & to Caraz)
27 Expreso Ancash (Bus)
31 Hot Showers (Duchas Raimondi)
32 National Park Office
33 Transportes Rodriguez (Bus)
34 Transportes Cóndor de Chavín (Bus)
39 Chavín Tours
40 Pyramid Adventures
41 Pablo Tours
43 El Tambo Bar
45 ENTEL
46 Peña La Tremenda
47 Banks
49 Casa de Guías
50 Taberna Amadeus
51 Police Station
52 Post Office & FOPTUR Office
53 Archaeology Museum
54 Cine Radio

Llaca, where there are excellent mountain views. There is no regular transport.

The site dates to about 1000 AD and is an imitation of the temple at Chavín done in the Tiahuanaco style. The three-storey temple has a base of about 11 by 16 metres and each storey has seven rooms, most of which have been filled with rubble. The site can be visited daily for a 50c fee.

Places to Stay
The increase in tourism over the last decade has meant an increase in the number of hotels, especially of the cheaper variety. Often, they have only a few rooms and are family run and very friendly. Hotel staff may meet buses arriving at the main bus offices; the staff generally give straight answers to questions about price, availability of hot water or private showers and distance from the bus station. If you arrive after dark when you're tired, this is very useful.

Places to Stay – bottom end
Probably the cheapest place in town is the basic but adequate *Hostal Tabariz*, which

charges 70c per person and sometimes has hot water in the communal showers. Some small, family-run places include the *Alojamiento Quintana*, *Pensión Galaxia*, *Pensión Stela* and the last, at Nuevo Grande 519, has no sign. They charge about $1 per person, have hot water in communal showers, and though basic, are clean, friendly and recommended. Also charging about $1 per person is the friendly *Hostal Alpamayo*, which has hot water in the morning (but one reader claims it is unsafe for left luggage), and the *Pensión Maguina*, opposite the Rodriguez bus terminal (with a very small sign). The Maguina has hot water some of the time. A reader also recommends the cheap, new *Hotel Chimu* at Tarapaca 656. These prices may rise slightly at the height of the tourist season.

For about $1.50 per person, you can stay at the *Hostal Regalon*. It has spacious rooms, some with bath, but an erratic hot-water supply and no singles. The *Hostal San Isidro* is similarly priced but not as good. The *Hotel Barcelona* has balconies with great mountain views. Prices start at $1.50 per person, more in rooms with showers, but the hotel has only cold water.

Edward's Inn is slightly out of the way but is friendly and popular with international backpackers. The inn has hot water, laundry facilities and a cafeteria and is secure, quiet and recommended. Edward senior and junior are good sources of tourist information. Accommodation is simple but clean and costs $2 per person in dormitory rooms (sleeping up to four) and $6 per double room with shower. There are no singles but they might give you a double if the hotel isn't very full. Also friendly and with hot water and laundry facilities is the *Hostal Los Andes* at $2 per person.

The *Hostal Huaraz* is rather run down but does have hot water. Singles/doubles cost $1.70/3 and rooms with bath are $2.30/4.30. A second, newer *Hostal Huaraz* over Las Puyas restaurant is reportedly cleaner. The *Hotel Landauro* charges $2.70 for doubles with cold-water communal showers and also has more expensive rooms with private

shower. The *Hotel Cataluña* (Pepe's Place) has singles/doubles with bath for $2/3.30. The rooms are small but the beds are comfortable and hot water is available if you ask to have it turned on. There are excellent views from the balconies.

The clean, friendly *Hostal Yanett* has a small garden and is recommended. Double rooms with bath cost $3.70 and there is hot water morning and evening. The *El Tumi II* (a recent offshoot of the Hotel El Tumi) is good value at $3 for a double with bath; there are no singles. Also new are the *Hostal Continental*, which charges $2/3.50 for singles/doubles with bath and hot water, and the *Hotel Oscar*, which is in the same price range, though I haven't checked it. Another good, friendly, clean choice is the *Hostal El Pacífico*. It charges $2.30/4.30 for singles/doubles with bath and hot water, but try to avoid some of the viewless inside rooms. The long-established *Hostal Raimondi*, the last hotel in this price range, is clean with a pleasant courtyard. Singles/doubles with bath and hot water cost $3/4.40 and rooms with shared showers are about 30% less.

Places to Stay – middle

The *Hostal Los Pinos del Puente*, an interesting stone and wood building on the banks of the Río Quilcay, is clean, quiet and charges $5 for doubles with bath and hot water.

The *Hotel El Tumi* is clean, comfortable and quiet and many of its rooms have great mountain views. There is a good and inexpensive hotel restaurant. Singles/doubles with bath and hot water are officially $10/15, but when I was last there, they had a promotional tariff of $3.50/6 – this special price seems to be the norm rather than the exception and is good value. Closer to the centre is the *Hostal Los Portales*. It is bare and modern looking and has clean singles/doubles with bath and hot water for $4.30/7.

Places to Stay – top end

Hotels in the upper price bracket are often full during the busy season. The modern government-run *Hotel de Turistas* has clean, spacious singles/doubles with bath for $13/18, including breakfast. A little cheaper is the *Hostal Colombo*, which has comfortable bungalows set in a large pleasant garden. The best is the Swiss-run *Hostal Andino* with great views of the mountains and the best restaurant in Huaraz. Singles/doubles with bath and oodles of hot water cost $18/26.

Places to Eat

There are several restaurants near the town's major intersection (Raimondi and Luzuriaga), the best of which is the reasonably priced *Chifa Familiar*. Across the street, the *Restaurant Sandy* (which seems to change names every couple of years) is also quite good and may have music at night. Slightly away from the centre, the simple, inexpensive *Pio Pio* chicken restaurant has been recommended by travellers. For a cheap and typical local lunch, try the *Recreo La Unión*. It's not fancy but it is quite authentic. *Restaurant Samuels* is inexpensive, serves big helpings and is popular with both locals and gringos. *Las Puyas* has very large, inexpensive meals and is popular with budget travellers, probably for food quantity rather than quality.

For good Italian food, the place to go is the *Pizzería Ticino*. It's more expensive than most of the other restaurants but often has a line of people waiting outside in the evening. (They can't all be wrong!) Cheaper pizzerías include the *Mama Mía* and *Posada*, though the quality of their food is variable.

The *Tasco Bar* is a bar rather than a restaurant, but it does serve Mexican food which goes down well with a couple of beers. It is open in the evening and is popular with climbers and trekkers. Also popular with climbers and trekkers is the *Casa de Guias*, which serves great breakfasts (yoghurt and fruit as well as more traditional fare). It also has a cafeteria, which is open all day and is a relaxed place to write postcards.

The *Ebony 76* and *84* restaurants on the Plaza de Armas have been recommended, though I've never eaten there because they

often seem deserted. The *Creperíe Patrick* has been recommended for crepes but its opening hours are somewhat irregular – they sometimes put tables out on the sidewalk if the weather is good. The best and priciest restaurant in the town centre is the small and cosy *Pepe's Place – International Restaurant*. It has a limited menu but the food is good and the service attentive. For top quality, the *Hostal Andino* has a Swiss-run kitchen and delicious food – the best in Huaraz. It opens at meal times only and is primarily for guests of the hotel, but casual diners will also be served if there's room, particularly if you make a reservation.

Entertainment

Huaraz has two cinemas which sometimes screen English-language movies.

There are also several bars, discos and peñas. The *Tasco Bar*, at Lucar y Torre 560, is a popular hangout for climbers and trekkers and a good place to meet people. It has taped rock music, friendly management and Mexican snacks. For a more typically Peruvian evening, you might want to try *El Tambo Bar*, a couple of blocks away. This place is popular with gringos and Peruvians and usually has good live music and crowded dancing, though it doesn't get underway till about 10 pm. The *Imantata Bar*, a peculiarly low-roofed drinking and dancing establishment, also gets underway at about 10 pm – it used to be the best place to go for live music but has recently been eclipsed by El Tambo. Ask around to find out where the latest scene is. For dancing, try the inexpensive *Discotec Any*. The promisingly named *Pacccha'k Pub* looks good but is very quiet most nights and the *Taberna Amadeus* can be good on some evenings. Another possibility is the *Peña La Tremenda*. Bear in mind that there is much less entertainment outside the tourist season.

Things to Buy

An outdoor crafts market is held along Luzuriaga every evening during the tourist season. Inexpensive thick woollen sweaters, scarves, hats, socks, gloves, ponchos and blankets are available for travellers needing warm clothes for the mountains. Tooled leather goods are also popular souvenirs.

Getting There & Away

Air The Huaraz area airport is at Anta, about 23 km north of town. Scheduled air services from Lima were suspended in the early 1980s, and though there is occasional talk of resuming flights, I don't think this is likely to happen. The only aircraft normally seen here are the topiary ones decorating the perimeter of the terminal area.

Bus & Colectivo – local Buses and colectivo taxis heading north along the length of the Callejón de Huaylas leave from the corner of Fitzcarrald and Raimondi. Local transport goes as far as Caraz, 67 km north of Huaraz. The bus journey takes about 2 hours and costs 80c. Colectivo taxis take about 1¼ hours and charge $1.25. There are frequent departures throughout the day but none after nightfall, so plan to travel early.

Bus & Colectivo – long distance Several companies have departures for Lima ($3, 8 hours). These include Transportes Rodriguez with one day bus and two night buses, Empresa Ancash (the subsidiary of Ormeño) with two or three buses a day, Empresa Huaraz with three daily departures, Empresa 14 with one departure in the morning and one at night and TROME with a daily bus. Many of these buses start from or continue to Caraz, 67 km north of Huaraz.

There are three main bus routes to Chimbote ($3, 8 hours) on the north coast. One follows the Callejón de Huaylas and passes through the narrow, spectacular Cañón del Pato before descending to the coast at Chimbote. This is a scenic route but, unfortunately, most buses travel it by night. A route more frequently taken by day crosses the 4100-metre-high Punta Callán, 30 km west of Huaraz, and provides spectacular views of the Cordillera Blanca. This road comes out at Casma and continues north along the coastal Pan-American Highway to Chimbote. Finally, some buses take the road to Pativilca (the same route as Lima-bound

buses) and then head north on the highway. Of the three choices, the Punta Callán route is presently the best because the views are excellent, the journey can be done in daylight and those coming from Lima avoid retracing their steps. Transportes Moreno has both daily and nightly departures and Empresa Huaraz has night buses via Pativilca.

Cóndor de Chavín buses for Chavín de Huantar (5 hours, $2.20) continuing on to Huari (7 hours, $3) run every other day. Transportes Huascarán also provides this service.

To get to Chiquián by bus, it's best to go directly from Lima on TUBSA. There is no direct service from Huaraz, so if you want to reach Chiquián, you should head south along the Callejón de Huaylas on the earliest bus you can find. Get off at Conococha, a high, cold lake with a little huddle of buildings nearby, and wait for any transport to Chiquián, a further 32 km by dirt road.

Transportes Huascarán has two vehicles a week to La Unión, about 9 hours away to the east. From there, it is possible to find daily trucks to Huánuco.

Note, however, that the Huánuco area has recently been raided by Sendero guerillas and it is inadvisable to travel there at present.

Getting Around

The three most popular trips around Huaraz each take a full day. One visits the ruins at Chavín de Huantar, another passes through Yungay to the beautiful Lagunas Llanganuco, where there are spectacular views of Huascarán and other mountains, and the third takes you through Catac to see the giant *Puya raimondii* plant. These destinations are described in greater detail in the appropriate sections later in the chapter.

There are many tour agencies in Huaraz which will provide vehicles for local tours – you'll find several along Avenida Luzuriaga. Two companies which generally give good service are Pablo Tours and Chavín Tours, but these are by no means the only ones. Prices vary but are about $6 per person for a day trip, including transport (usually in minibuses) and a guide (who may or may not speak English). You should bring a packed lunch, warm clothes, drinking water and sun protection. There are tours almost daily during the high season, but at other times, departures depend on whether there are enough passengers.

NORTH OF HUARAZ

The Callejón de Huaylas road north of Huaraz follows the Santa River valley and is paved for the 67 km to Caraz. This road passes within 14 km of Peru's highest peak and links the departmental capital with the other main towns in the area. Buses for all towns mentioned in the following sections leave from the corner of Fitzcarrald and Raimondi.

MONTERREY

Just 5 km north of Huaraz is the small village of Monterrey, famous for its natural *baños termales* or 'hot springs'. The bus terminates right in front of the springs so you won't have any difficulty in finding them. The hot springs are divided into two sections; the lower pools are cheaper (10c) and more crowded than the upper pools (25c), which are within the grounds of the Hotel de Turistas. Tickets for pools on both levels are sold at the lower entrance.

Places to Stay

The government-run *Hotel de Turistas* is a pleasant building set in gardens right next to the hot springs. There is a good, simple restaurant with outdoor dining (overlooking the pool) and meals for under $2. Both the pool and restaurant are open to nonresidents of the hotel. Singles/doubles with bath are about $7/11 and reservations can be made in Lima through ENTURPeru (tel 721928). The similarly priced *El Patio* nearby is also good. There are no budget hotels.

Getting There & Away

Monterrey is reached by local buses from Huaraz, which pass the Plaza de Armas and continue north along avenidas Luzuriaga, Fitzcarrald and Centenario. Try to catch a bus early in the route as they soon fill up. The fare for the 15-minute ride is 10c.

CARHUAZ

Twenty-three km north of Huaraz, the road passes the rarely used Anta airport (look for the topiary airplanes around the terminal). A few km beyond is the small village of Marcará. From here, trucks and buses leave for the hot springs of Chancos, 3 km to the east, and occasionally continue a further 4 km to the ruins at Vicos. Beyond Vicos, the Quebrada Honda trail (for hikers only) continues across the Cordillera Blanca. The rather rustic Chancos hot springs are popular with locals at weekends, when they tend to be crowded. There are private cubicles and steam baths for 25c per person.

The small town of Carhuaz is 31 km north of Huaraz. It is not a particularly interesting place but trekkers heading into the Cordillera Blanca via the beautiful Quebrada Ulta may want to stay there. Vehicles from Carhuaz to Shilla and Llipta (in the Quebrada Ulta) are frequent on Sunday, which is market day, but there's usually only one truck in the morning on other days.

Carhuaz's annual La Virgen de La Merced fiesta is celebrated on and around 24 September with processions, fireworks, dancing, bullfights and plenty of drinking. This is the most interesting time to visit Carhuaz.

Places to Stay & Eat

There are several small, cheap hotels in Carhuaz but none of these have private bathrooms and few have hot water. Expect to pay between 60c and $1.30 per person.

The clean and friendly *Hotel La Merced*, on the Plaza de Armas, has hot water. The not so good *Hotel Peru* is on the corner of the plaza, on Avenida Progreso. Also on Progreso, a block away from the plaza, is the *Hotel Carhuaz*. It has a pleasant courtyard. At the north exit of town is the *Hostal Delicias*; this place advertises hot water, but don't expect too much. The *Hotel Victoria* is another option.

There are a few cheap and basic restaurants.

The *Palmeras* and the *Hotel Peru* restaurants on Avenida Progreso are OK.

YUNGAY

Continuing north from Carhuaz, the road takes you through the village of Mancos, from where there are excellent views of Huascarán. Shortly beyond Mancos is the newly rebuilt village of Ranrahirca (devastated in the 1962 earthquake), followed by the rubble-strewn area of old Yungay, site of the worst single natural disaster in the Andes. It was near here that the earthquake of 31 May 1970 loosened some 15 million cubic metres of granite and ice from the west wall of Huascarán Norte. The resulting alluvion picked up a speed of about 300 km/h as it dropped over 3 vertical km on its way to Yungay, 14 km away. The town and almost all of its 18,000 inhabitants were buried. The earthquake also killed about 60,000 people in other parts of central Peru. Today, the site is marked by a huge white statue of Christ on a knoll overlooking old Yungay. The path of the alluvion can plainly be seen from the road. (The November 1985 alluvion which swept through Armero, Colombia, had the unfortunate distinction of killing more people – 23,000 – than the Yungay alluvion, though the Yungay disaster was, in itself, just a small part of a greater catastrophe.)

New Yungay has been rebuilt just beyond the alluvion path and about 59 km north of Huaraz. A stark, hastily built town, it offers no attraction in itself but it is from here that you begin one of the most beautiful and popular excursions in the Cordillera Blanca.

Information

Almost everything of importance for tourists happens around the Plaza de Armas. There is a small tourist office here, though it may well be closed outside of the high season and hours are erratic at other times.

Places to Stay & Eat

Although there are several cheap places to stay in Yungay, there's little point in spending more than a night here en route to the mountains. One of the best hotels is the friendly *Hostal Gledel*, a block from the plaza, at about $1.50 per person. Hot water and meals are available. Also popular is the *Hostal Turistico Blanco*, a tiny rustic hotel about 10 minutes from the plaza, situated behind the maternity hospital in a quiet eucalypt grove. It is friendly but has only cold water.

Cheaper hotels include the *Yuly* and the *Yungay*, both on the plaza, and the *Confort* on the road south of town. Hotels may close in the off season and private homes often offer accommodation during the high season.

There are no particularly noteworthy restaurants but you'll find several cheap and simple *comedores* (dining rooms) in the market next to the plaza.

Getting There & Away

Frequent minibuses run from the Plaza de Armas to Caraz (20c, 15 minutes) and buses en route from Caraz will pick up passengers to Huaraz (70c, 1½ hours) from the southwest side of the plaza.

Empresa TROME has an office on the plaza for buses to Lima (7 and 11 am and 7 pm) and Empresa Moreno operates buses to Chimbote (day bus via Casma and night bus via Cañón del Pato). Other buses pass the plaza en route from Caraz to Lima.

LAGUNAS LLANGANUCO

A dirt road goes up the Llanganuco Valley to the two lovely lakes of the same name, about 28 km east of Yungay. There are great views of the giant mountains of Huascarán (6768 metres), Chopicalqui (6354 metres), Chacraraju (6112 metres), Huandoy (6395 metres) and others, particularly if you drive a few km beyond the lakes. The road continues over the pass beyond the lakes and down to Yanama on the other side of the Cordillera Blanca and there is often a morning truck between here and Yungay.

It is also from Yungay that the walker begins the Llanganuco to Santa Cruz loop, the most popular and spectacular trek of the Cordillera Blanca. This takes an average of 5 fairly leisurely days (though it can be done in 3 days) and is a good hike for everybody, especially beginners, because the trail is relatively well defined. The Llanganuco road is also the access route to the Pisco base camp, where the ascent of Nevado Pisco (5800 metres) begins. This is considered one of the most straightforward high-snow ascents in the range, though it is not to be taken lightly and requires snow and ice-climbing equipment and experience.

To get to the Llanganuco Lakes, you can go on a tour from Huaraz or take buses or taxis from Yungay. During June, July and August (the height of the dry season) minibuses carrying 10 or more passengers leave from the Yungay Plaza de Armas. The round trip costs about $2 and allows about 2 hours in the lake area. A national park admission fee of around $1 is also charged. Taxis carrying up to five passengers charge about $15 for the round trip. Go in the early morning for clear views; it's often cloudy in the afternoon. Outside the tourist season, it is more difficult to find minibuses (they don't want to go with less than 10 passengers), but you can find taxis to take you.

CARAZ

The pleasant little town of Caraz lies 67 km north of Huaraz and is the end of the road as far as regular and frequent transport is concerned. Caraz is one of the few places in the area which, while suffering some damage, has managed to avoid total destruction by earthquake or alluvion. The town has an attractive Plaza de Armas and several hotels and restaurants, and you can take pleasant walks in the surrounding hills. Caraz is both the end point of the popular Llanganuco to Santa Cruz trek and the point of departure for excursions by road to the beautiful Laguna Parón and to the Cañón del Pato.

Excursions to both places can be made from the Plaza de Armas. Pick-up truck drivers will charge about $20 (bargain) for either round trip and can easily fit half a dozen people in the back of the pick-up.

The bright blue Laguna Parón is 32 km east of Caraz and surrounded by spectacular snowcapped peaks, of which Pyramide

(5885 metres) at the end of the lake looks particularly magnificent. The road to the lake goes through a canyon with 1000-metre-high granite walls. Although this excursion takes you further from Huaraz than a visit to the Llanganuco Lakes and is therefore neither as popular nor as crowded, it is just as attractive as the Llanganuco tour.

The Cañón del Pato is at the far north of the Callejón de Huaylas and its narrowest point. Buses en route to Chimbote used to take this road every day but now go only at night, so if you want to see the canyon, you have to take a pick-up truck or taxi from Caraz. It is a spectacular canyon but the hydroelectric plant at Huallanca is now out of bounds to visitors and the area has become sensitive of late. Terrorist activities have threatened to close the trip to tourists, so ask locally about the situation. There is a cheap, clean hotel in Huallanca.

If you spend any time in Caraz, you might want to check out the town's two cinemas.

Places to Stay & Eat

You'll find two hotels half a block from the Plaza de Armas – the *Suizo Peruano* and the *Chavín*. Both charge about $1.50 per person, are reasonably clean and have hot water and some rooms with private showers. The *Hostal Morovi* has rooms at $1 per person and hot-water communal showers. There is also the *Residencial El Rosedal*, which is often full with local workers, and the *Pensión Caraz*, which seems the most basic of the lot.

There are several simple cafeterias on the Plaza de Armas, including the *Djuradjura, Paris* and *Jeny's Bar*, but they are nothing to write home about. My favourite restaurant in Caraz is *La Punta*, a short distance from the town centre and particularly good for lunch. They serve very cheap and typical highland dishes (including guinea pig) and there is a garden to eat in. If you don't feel like guinea pig, try a hearty bowl of soup.

Also good for typical lunches is the pleasant *Restaurant La Collampa*, about 1½ km west of town on the road to Cañón

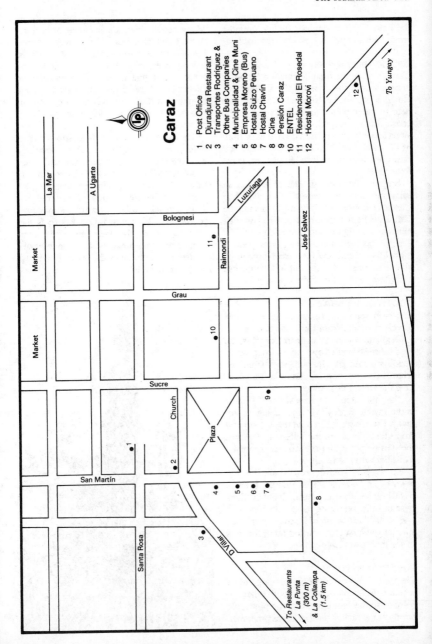

Caraz

1 Post Office
2 Djuradjura Restaurant
3 Transportes Rodriguez &
  Other Bus Companies
4 Municipalidad & Cine Muni
5 Empresa Moreno (Bus)
6 Hostal Suizo Peruano
7 Hostal Chavín
8 Cine
9 Pensión Caraz
10 ENTEL
11 Residencial El Rosedal
12 Hostal Morovi

To Yungay

La Mar

A Ugarte

Bolognesi

Luzuriaga

Raimondi

Market

Grau

Market

Sucre

Church

Plaza

San Martín

Santa Rosa

José Galvez

D Villar

To Restaurants
La Punta (300 m)
& La Collampa (1.5 km)

del Pato. It offers outdoor dining around a small lake and prices are very reasonable.

Getting There & Away

Caraz is often the final destination for buses heading from the coast to the Callejón de Huaylas and there is frequent transport from here to other points in the area and to the coast. Taxis and pick-ups for local excursions leave from the Plaza de Armas in front of the town hall. Minibuses to Yungay and buses or colectivo taxis to Huaraz also leave from here.

Empresa Moreno, on the plaza, has an early morning departure to Chimbote via Casma (8 hours, $4) and a night bus via the Cañón del Pato. Expreso Ancash has two day buses and a night bus to Lima (9 hours, $4), Transportes Rodriguez has a morning and a night bus to Lima and Empresa Norpacifico also has buses to the capital. Empresa Cribillera runs a slow old bus to Lima.

SOUTH OF HUARAZ

The road south of Huaraz is the one most travellers to and from Lima use to enter the Callejón de Huaylas but, apart from this, the road is little travelled by tourists. Local buses heading south of Huaraz leave from the frigorífico bus stop on Avenida Tarapaca, near the Hostal Los Andes.

The first place of interest south of Huaraz is the Puente Bedoya (bridge) about 18 km away. From here, a dirt road leads 2 km east from the highway to the village of Olleros, the starting point for the easy trek across the Cordillera Blanca to Chavín.

Recuay is 25 km from Huaraz and the only town of any size south of Huaraz. It has a basic hotel and a small museum but is otherwise of little interest to most travellers.

Catac, 10 km south of Recuay, is an even smaller town and the starting point for trips to see the *Puya raimondii*.

Puya Raimondii

The giant *Puya raimondii* is a strange plant which is frequently confused with others. It belongs to the bromeliads, or the pineapple family, of which it is the largest member.

Many people think it's an agave, or century plant, to which it has a certain resemblance but is not closely related; the century plants belong to the amaryllis family. One guidebook claims that the *Puya raimondii* is a cactus but there is no comparison – they belong to different classes and are about as closely related as a chicken and a flying squirrel!

The *Puya raimondii* is a huge spiky rosette of long, tough, waxy leaves. This rosette can be 2 metres or more in diameter and takes about 100 years to grow to full size. Then it flowers by producing a huge spike, often 10 metres in height, which is covered by approximately 20,000 flowers – a magnificent sight. This spiky inflorescence is the largest in the world and remains in flower for about 3 months, during which time it is pollinated by hummingbirds. After flowering once, the plant dies.

Obviously, with flowering occurring only once at the end of a century, most of the plants you'll see won't be flowering. When they do flower, they tend to do so in groups and this occurs about every 3 or 4 years; it is not known why this happens, nor is it clear when the best time for flowering is. Some guides claim the end of the wet season (May) is best. Others say the beginning of the wet season (October and November) is the time to go. You should make local inquiries if you hope to see the *Puya raimondii* in flower, though even when not flowering, it is a fascinating sight. The spiky rosette offers protection to a variety of birds and you may find several nests within the leaves of one plant.

The giant bromeliad is also considered to be one of the most ancient plant species in the world and has been called a living fossil. It is rare and found only in a few isolated areas of the Peruvian and Bolivian Andes. The sites in the Cordillera Blanca are two of the best known and receive protection as part of the Huascarán National Park.

Getting There & Away

There are two ways to visit the *Puya raimondii* sites. One site is on the southern slopes of the upper Quebrada Queshque, about 20 km south-east of Catac. You can hike on a trail from Catac, as described in Bartle's book.

The other site is at the intersection of the Quebrada Raria with the Río Pachacoto and can be reached by road. Drive 10 km south of Catac on the main road and turn left at the Río Pachacoto (there is a national park sign which reads Sector Carpa). Follow the dirt road for about 18 km to the Quebrada Raria where the puyas are to be seen. These areas are also the best place in the Cordillera Blanca to watch for the beautiful vicuña, an infrequently seen wild relative of the alpaca and llama. Camping is possible in both areas.

Tour companies in Huaraz make trips to the second site and charge about $6 per person. If travelling by public transport, take any early morning Lima-bound bus to the Sector Carpa turn-off (60c) and wait for a truck going along the Río Pachacoto road (there are usually several a day). Start heading back by early afternoon if you don't want to spend the night. These trucks act as buses for the locals and you are expected to pay a bus fare, which shouldn't be more than about 50c.

The road continues as far as La Unión, a town several hours away. In La Unión you can find basic hotels and transport on to Huánuco.

CHIQUIÁN

This small town is the centre for visiting the small but spectacular Cordillera Huayhuash, the next mountain range south of the Blanca. It has basic hotels and restaurants, but hikers should bring what they will need with them because few supplies are available.

Chiquián is at 3400 metres and there are good views of the Cordillera Huayhuash as you drive to the village. The highest mountain in the range is Yerupajá which, at 6634 metres, is also the second-highest mountain in Peru. Hiking in the Huayhuash usually involves making a circuit of the entire range – this is fairly strenuous and takes almost 2 weeks. Bartle's book describes the trail in detail.

In May 1989, Sendero activity put the Huayhuash off limits to trekkers. A group of hikers was stopped by a large armed Sendero patrol and told, in no uncertain terms, that the area was in Sendero hands, that tourists were not welcome and that they should return and tell others. Trekkers did not enter the area after that warning (it remained off limits during 1990). Ask locally whether the situation has changed.

Places to Stay & Eat

The best hotel in Chiquián is the *Hostal San Miguel* at Comercio 211. It is basic but clean and charges a little over $1 per person per night. If the San Miguel is full, there are a couple of other even more basic places, and people have slept in the church when all else failed.

The town has a couple of simple restaurants.

Getting There & Away

There is no regular direct bus service from Huaraz to Chiquián, though trucks do make the journey two or three times a week. Despite this, it is not too difficult to get here from Huaraz. Simply take any early morning Lima-bound bus to Laguna Conococha, about 80 km south of Huaraz. At the lake, there is a small huddle of houses and the turn-off to Chiquián, which is a further 32 km away. Several vehicles a day travel this road, so if you get to Conococha in the morning, you should have no difficulty continuing to Chiquián.

TUBSA and Landauro bus companies have a daily service to Lima ($4.50, 10 hours). Their offices are on the Plaza de Armas in Chiquián. In Lima, TUBSA is at Leticia 633 and Landauro at Ayacucho 1040, near the Parque Universitario.

CAJATAMBO

This is the only other village on the Cordillera Huayhuash trek which is accessible by road. Empresa Espadín runs an old, slow bus between Lima and Cajatambo on a daily basis. In Lima, the company is found opposite the Ormeño bus station. There are two basic hotels in Cajatambo.

CHAVÍN DE HUÁNTAR

This small village is of little interest in itself, but the ruins of Chavín on the southern edge of the village are well worth a visit.

Archaeology

The Chavín culture is named after its type site at Chavín de Huántar and is the oldest major culture in Peru. It existed from about 1300 to 400 BC, predating the Incas by about 2000 years. The major period of influence was from about 800 to 400 BC, and the Chavín certainly was an influential culture. Its people didn't conquer by warfare – they simply influenced the artistic and cultural development of all of northern Peru. Archaeologists refer to this cultural expansion as the Chavín Horizon. Signs of Chavín influence are evident in ruins ranging from the present-day Ecuadorian border to as far south as Ica

and Ayacucho. None of these sites are as well preserved or as frequently visited as Chavín de Huántar.

The principal Chavín deity was feline (a jaguar or puma) and lesser condor, snake and human deities also existed. Highly stylised representations of these deities are carved in Chavín sites. The experienced eye can see similarities in the precise yet fluid lines of these carvings, while the non-expert can tell that any culture capable of such fine work 3000 years ago must indeed have been well advanced.

The artistic work of Chavín is much more stylised and cultist than the naturalistic art of the later Moche and Nazca cultures. Because of this, archaeologists lack an accurate picture of life in Chavín times. However, excavations of middens (garbage dumps) indicate that corn became a staple food and agriculture improved with the introduction of squash, avocados, yucca and other crops. Better agriculture meant less reliance on hunting, fishing and gathering, and more importantly, allowed leisure time. Thus, art and religion could develop and so the Chavín horizon, linking art and religion in its feline-worship cults, was able to influence a large part of Peru.

Visiting the Ruins

At first glance, the site at Chavín de Huántar is not particularly prepossessing. There are two reasons for this: most of the site's more interesting parts were built underground and the area was covered by a huge landslide in 1945. To visit the site properly and to get the most from your visit, you should enter the underground chambers. Although these are supposedly lit, the lighting system is rarely functioning and you are advised to bring your own torch (flashlight). It is also worth hiring a guide to show you around.

The site contains a huge central square, slightly sunken below ground level, with an intricate and well-engineered system of channels for drainage. From the square, a broad staircase leads up to the single entrance of the largest and most important building in Chavín de Huántar, the Castillo. With an area of about 75 sq metres and height of up to 13 metres, the Castillo was built on three different levels, each of dry stone masonry. At one time the walls were embellished with 'key' stones consisting of large projecting blocks carved into a stylised human head. Only one of these remains in its original place; the others have been moved inside the Castillo in the underground chambers.

Tello Obelisk

The underground tunnels are an exceptional feat of 3000-year-old engineering; they are so well ventilated that the air is not musty, yet the main entrance is the only external window or doorway. In the heart of the underground complex is an exquisitely carved rock known as the Lanzón de Chavín. It is a thrilling and distinctly mysterious experience to come upon this 4-metre-high, dagger-like rock stuck into the ground at the intersection of four narrow passageways, deep within the Castillo.

Travellers interested in the Chavín Horizon are advised to visit the Museum of Anthropology & Archaeology in Lima. Two carved rocks, the Raimondi Stela and the Tello Obelisk, smaller but similar to the Lanzón de Chavín, may be seen in the museum. The museum also has several of the large, carved 'key' stones which once decorated the Castillo. All of these exhibits are originally from the Chavín de Huántar site.

The site is open daily from 8 am to noon and 2 to 4 pm. Entry is about 60c, with an extra fee for photography. A small tip will probably ensure entrance to the site during the lunch break. Spanish-speaking local guides are available to show you around and charge about $1 for this service. There is a soft drink and snack stand.

Places to Stay & Eat

Hotels in the village of Chavín de Huántar are found on or near the Plaza de Armas and are very cheap and basic. The best of a not particularly good lot is the *Montecarlo*. Other choices are the *Inca* and *Gantu*.

The *Albergue de Turistas Chavín*, which charges about $5/8 for singles/doubles with bath and hot water, is reportedly pleasant but I've never been there. It is about 2 km north of the town and reservations can be made in Lima by phoning 270323.

There are some basic comedores in town but they have a reputation for closing around sunset. Camping is reportedly possible at the hot springs about 3 km south of town.

Getting There & Away

Tour buses make day trips from Huaraz to

Chavín for about $6 per passenger. Daily public transport from Huaraz ($2.20, 5 hours) is provided by Transportes Cóndor de Chavín or Transportes Huascarán. Cóndor de Chavín runs buses to and from Lima ($6, 11 hours) every day. Their Lima office is at Montevideo 1039 near Nicolas de Pierola.

The drive across the Cordillera Blanca from Catac is a scenic one. The road passes the Laguna Querococha at 3980 metres; from here, there are good views of the peaks of Pucaraju (5322 metres) and Yanamarey (5237 metres). The road deteriorates somewhat as it continues climbing to the Cahuish tunnel at 4178 metres above sea level. The tunnel cuts through the Cahuish Pass, which is over 300 metres higher, before the road descends to Chavín at about 3145 metres.

Hikers can walk to Chavín from Olleros in about 3 days (see Bartle's or Bradt's book) but should be wary of staying in town halls or other public buildings in mountain villages.

A British hiker was killed in Olleros in 1989. He was sleeping in the municipalidad (town hall) when the town was raided by Senderistas. It is unclear whether the Senderistas thought that the hiker was polit-ically affiliated with the town, but hikers are urged not to stay in the town hall (or similar) in any village. Camping is much safer.

HUARI

Many of the buses bound for Chavín continue to Huari, a small town about 40 km and 2 hours to the north and the end of the road as far as regular daily bus services are concerned. Huari has a couple of small hotels.

NORTH OF HUARI

The road north of Huari goes through the villages of San Luis, Piscobamba, Pomabamba and Sihuas. The further north you go, the more difficult transport becomes and it may stop altogether during the wet season. Basic accommodation is available in these towns, which may be the end of various cross-cordilleran hikes. From Sihuas, it is possible to continue on to Huallanca via Tres Cruces and thus return to the Callejón de Huaylas. This round trip is scenic, remote and rarely made by travellers. It shouldn't be too difficult to find transport during the dry season if you really want to get off the beaten track.

Across the Northern Highlands

The traveller heading into the mountains north of the Cordillera Blanca is unable to do so conveniently without returning to the coast. You must then travel north along the coast before returning inland and into the mountains again. The first major city north of Huaraz is Cajamarca, reached by three roads from the coast. The dirt roads from Trujillo and Chiclayo are both rough and difficult but the road which leaves the Pan-American Highway between these two cities is paved all the way to Cajamarca. All three routes are described in this chapter.

From Cajamarca, a very poor road continues north-east across the Andes to Chachapoyas, capital of the Department of Amazonas. A better road to Chachapoyas via Bagua leaves the Pan-American Highway north of Chiclayo. Beyond Chachapoyas, this road continues down the eastern slopes

Indian mountain village

of the Andes to the jungles of the Department of San Martín. However, travel in this region is inadvisable at present. The Department of San Martín is split by the Río Huallaga valley, Peru's major coca and marijuana-growing area, and the Sendero Luminoso and the drug cartels of the region have formed a strange alliance, making the area unsafe to visit.

Although Cajamarca remains one of the most charming and safest towns in Peru, continuing across the northern highlands to the Department of San Martín is currently inadvisable. Most descriptions in the latter part of this chapter are based on trips I made there in the mid-1980s, when things were relatively peaceful and safe. Make local inquiries before venturing into this fascinating region.

Note that moneychanging facilities throughout the area are limited; it is suggested that you change enough money on the coast to cover your inland trip.

CAJAMARCA

Cajamarca, 2650 metres above sea level, is 5 hours east by paved road from Pacasmayo on the coast. This traditional and tranquil colonial city is the capital of its department and has a friendly population of about 70,000. The surrounding countryside is green and attractive.

Cajamarca and its environs are steeped in history and prehistory. Once a major Inca city, Cajamarca played a crucial role in the Spanish conquest of the Incas. It was in Cajamarca that Pizarro tricked, captured, imprisoned for ransom and finally assassinated the Inca Atahualpa. The city remains important today as the major city in Peru's northern Andes. It has impressive colonial architecture, excellent Andean food and interesting people and customs. Despite this, it is not a major international tourist centre because it lies some way inland from the 'gringo trail'. Perhaps this makes it even

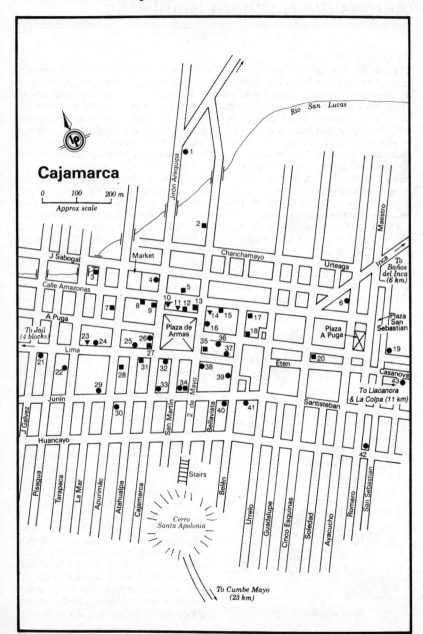

Cajamarca

0   100   200 m
Approx scale

■ PLACES TO STAY

2	Hostal Turismo
3	Hostal Chota
5	Hostal Yusovi
7	Hotel Delfort
8	Hotel Amazonas
9	Hotel Becerra
12	Hotel Plaza
13	Hostal 2 de Mayo
15	Hotel Continental
17	Hotel San Francisco
18	Hostal Sucre
20	New Hotel
27	Hotel de Turistas
28	Hostal Bolívar
31	Hostal Atahualpa
34	Hotel Cajamarca
35	Hotel Casa Blanca

▼ PLACES TO EAT

10	Chifa Zarco
11	Restaurant Salas & Hostal Peru
14	La Taberna Restaurant
15	El Cajamarques Restaurant
23	Helados Capri
43	To Restaurant La Namorina (800 m)

● OTHER

1	Local Buses to Airport & Otuzco
4	Archaeological Museum
6	Empresa Diaz (Bus)
16	San Francisco Church & Religious Art Museum
19	Recoleta Church
21	Post Office
22	Banco de la Nación
24	Banco de Crédito
25	AeroPeru
26	Cathedral
29	Cine San Martín
30	Teatro Cajamarca
32	ENTEL
33	Cine los Andes
34	Cajamarca Tours
36	El Cuarto del Rescate
37	PIP Police
38	Cine Ollanta
39	The Belén Complex (Church, Hospital, Art & Archaeology Museums)
40	Ethnography Museum
41	FOPTUR Tourist Office
42	Peña El Imperio
43	To Empresa Cajamarca (200 m), TEPSA, El Cumbe, Atahualpa & Empresa Fortaleza (Buses)

more attractive. I consider Cajamarca the most interesting Peruvian Andean city after Cuzco.

History

Little is known about the various pre-Inca sites discovered in the Cajamarca area, though they are generally attributed to the Chavín-influenced Cajamarca culture.

In about 1460, the Incas conquered the Cajamarca people and Cajamarca became a major Inca city on the Inca Andean highway linking Cuzco with Quito.

After the death of the Inca Huayna Capac in 1525, the Inca Empire, by then stretching from southern Colombia to central Chile, was divided between the half-brothers Atahualpa and Huascar. Atahualpa ruled the north and Huascar ruled the south. Civil war soon broke out and Atahualpa, who had the support of the army, gained the upper hand. In 1532 he and his victorious troops marched southward towards Cuzco to take complete control of the Inca Empire. During this march south, Atahualpa and his army stopped at Cajamarca to rest for a few days. The Inca emperor was camped at the natural thermal springs, known today as Los Baños del Inca, when he heard the news that the Spanish were nearby.

By 1532, Atahualpa was certainly aware of the existence of the strange, bearded white men. In 1528, during his second voyage, Francisco Pizarro had invited an Inca noble from Tumbes to dine aboard his ship and word of this would undoubtedly have been passed on to Atahualpa. Atahualpa, supported by his army and flushed with his victory in the civil war, would not have considered the small, ragged Spanish force a threat, let alone a fully-fledged invasion.

Pizarro and his force of about 160 Spaniards arrived in Cajamarca on 15 November 1532. They found a temple of the sun, the Inca fortress, some well-made build-ings housing the Inca's chosen women and a central square surrounded by assembly halls called *kallankas*. The city was almost deserted; most of its 2000 inhabitants were with the Atahualpa at his encampment by the hot springs, 6 km away. Pizarro sent a force of about 35 cavalry and a native interpreter to Atahualpa's camp to ask the Inca emperor where the Spaniards were to stay. They were told to lodge in the kallankas surrounding the plaza and that the Inca would join them the next day.

The small force of Spaniards spent an anxious night, fully aware that they were severely outnumbered by the Inca troops, estimated at 40,000 to 80,000. The Spaniards plotted throughout the night, deciding to try and entice Atahualpa into the plaza and, at a prearranged signal, capture the Inca emperor should the opportunity present itself. If this did not occur, they were to maintain a 'friendly' relationship and hope for another chance to capture Atahualpa. The next morning Pizarro stationed his troops in the kallankas, which were perfect for his plan. The kallankas surrounded three sides of the plaza and each had about 20 doorways so that a large number of the Spaniards could emerge and attack at the same time.

Atahualpa kept the Spanish waiting all day, much to their consternation. He didn't break camp until the afternoon and reached Cajamarca early in the evening, accompanied by his vast army. Upon arriv-ing at the outskirts of the city, the Inca emperor ordered the majority of his troops to stay outside while he entered the plaza with a retinue of nobles and about 6000 men armed with slings and hand axes. He was met by the Spanish friar, Vicente de Valverde. The friar, bible in hand, attempted to explain his position as a man of God and presented the Inca with the Bible. Atahualpa angrily threw the book to the ground and Valverde saw this action as an insult to Christianity. This provided the excuse he needed to absolve the Spaniards in advance for an attack upon the Inca. He rushed back to the kallankas and prevailed upon Pizarro to

order the firing of his cannon into the group of Indians. This was the prearranged signal to attack.

The cannon were fired and the Spanish cavalry attacked with much trumpeting and yelling. The Indians, who had never seen cannon or horses before, were terrified and completely bewildered by the fearsome onslaught. Their small hand axes and slings were no match for the well-armoured Spaniards swinging razor-sharp swords from the advantageous height of horseback. The Indians tried to flee but the entrance to the plaza was too narrow to allow escape. By sheer weight of numbers, they knocked down a section of wall 2 metres thick and swarmed out of the plaza in total disarray. Pizarro's horsemen charged after them, hacking down as many Indians as they could. Meanwhile, Pizarro himself led a small con-tingent and succeeded in capturing Atahualpa. As the sun set over Cajamarca on the evening of 16 November, the course of Latin American history was changed forever. With an estimated 7000 Indians dead and Atahualpa captured, the small band of Spaniards had succeeded beyond their wildest hopes. Now they literally were con-quistadors.

Almost immediately after his capture, Atahualpa became aware of one of the weaknesses of the Spaniards – namely, a lust for gold. Accordingly, he offered to fill a large room once with gold and twice with silver in return for his freedom. Astounded by their good fortune, the conquistadors quickly agreed to the offer and led Atahualpa to believe that they would not only release him after the ransom was paid, but would also return him to his northern lands around Quito.

This was a wily move on the part of Pizarro. By promising Atahualpa's return to Quito, he effectively controlled the northern part of the Inca Empire. And by holding Atahualpa captive, Pizarro also maintained control of the southern half of the empire because the inhabitants of this region, having just been beaten by Atahualpa in a civil war, considered him an enemy and looked upon

Pizarro as a liberator rather than an invader. Playing off one Inca faction against the other in this way was Pizarro's strongest weapon. If the Inca Empire had been united when the Spanish arrived, the story of the conquest would have been entirely different.

The gold and silver slowly began to arrive at Cajamarca. Pizarro sent some of his men to Cuzco to ensure the collection of the ransom. Meanwhile, Atahualpa was held as a royal prisoner with the servants and comfort to which he was accustomed. The Spanish were in no great hurry to collect the ransom; they were also waiting for reinforcements. On 14 April 1533, Diego de Almagro arrived from the coast with 150 soldiers, almost doubling the Spanish force at Cajamarca. Atahualpa began to suspect that the Spaniards were lying to him and that he

wouldn't be released and allowed to return to Quito on payment of the ransom.

Finally, in mid-June of 1533, the ransom was complete and Pizarro ordered the melting down and distribution of the treasure. Careful records were kept of these procedures and it is known that about 6000 kg of gold and 12,000 kg of silver were melted down into gold and silver bullion. At today's prices, this is worth roughly $75 million but the artistic value of the ornaments and implements which were melted down is impossible to estimate or recover. The gold and silver was distributed among the conquistadors in strictly controlled quotas.

Atahualpa, still a prisoner, now knew he was not going to be released. He sent desperate messages to his followers in Quito to come to Cajamarca and rescue him. The Spaniards heard of the rescue attempt and became panic-stricken. Although Pizarro was not anxious to kill the Inca emperor, intending instead to further his own aims by continuing to hold Atahualpa hostage and using him as a puppet ruler, the other leading Spaniards insisted on the Inca's death. Despite the lack of a formal trial, Atahualpa was sentenced to death for attempting to arrange his own rescue. On 26 July 1533, Atahualpa was led out to the centre of the Cajamarca plaza to be burnt at the stake. At the last hour, Atahualpa accepted baptism and his sentence was changed to a more humane death by strangulation.

Immediately after Atahualpa's death, the Spaniards crowned Tupac Huallpa, a younger brother of Huascar, as the Inca emperor. With this puppet ruler, the Spaniards were free to march into Cuzco as liberators. During the march, the new Inca emperor died of an unknown illness and the Spanish arrived in Cuzco on 15 November without an Inca ruler.

Today, little remains of Inca Cajamarca. Most of the great stone buildings were torn down to be used in the construction of Spanish homes and churches. The great plaza where Atahualpa was captured and later killed was in roughly the same location as today's Plaza de Armas though, in

~ᗽ𝕌erdadera relacion de la conquista del Peru.
y prouincia del Cir: co llamada lanucua Castilla: Conquistada por el magnifico y esforçado cauallero Francisco piçarro hijo del capitan Conçalo piçarro caua llero de la ciudad de Trugillo: como capitan general de la cesarea y catholica magestad el emperador y rey nio señor. Embiada a su magestad por Francisco de Xerec: natural de la muy noble y muy leal ciudad de Seuilla secretario del sobredicho señor en todas las prouincias y conquista de la nueua Castilla y vno de los primeros conquistadores della. ✠✠✠✠✠✠✠✠✠✠✠✠
✠ fue vista y examinada esta obra por mandado de los señores inquisidores del arçobispado de Seuilla: e impressa en casa de Bartholome perez en el mes de Julio. Año del parto virginal mil e quinientos y treynta y quatro.✠✠
✠ ✠ ✠

The conquest of Peru showing the scene in the Plaza at Cajamarca – Pizarro, the priest Valverde and Atahualpa in his litter.

Atahualpa's time, it was a much larger plaza. The ransom chamber, which Atahualpa had filled once with gold and twice with silver, is the only building still standing.

For a much more detailed description of the momentous events which took place in Cajamarca in 1532 and 1533, see John Hemming's excellent *The Conquest of the Incas*.

Information

Tourist Information The FOPTUR tourist office (tel 922228) is at Santisteban 144. It provides information about Cajamarca and the surrounding area.

Various tourist agencies around the Plaza de Armas provide tourist information and guided tours of the city and surroundings. Cajamarca Tours, next to the Hotel Cajamarca, is the most expensive and claims to have English-speaking guides, though most of their guides don't speak English.

Tuesday is a bad day to tour the town as the museums are usually closed. Friday and Saturday nights are peña nights.

Post & Telecommunications The post office at the corner of Lima and Galvez is open from 8 am to 8 pm daily, except Sunday when it's open from 8 am to noon. You can make long-distance telephone calls every day from 8 am to 10 pm at ENTEL on the Plaza de Armas.

Money The Banco de la Nación and other nearby banks will change money, though it's a slow process and rates are not good. For better rates and service, change money in Trujillo or Chiclayo. Moneychangers are sometimes active outside Cajamarca's banks and were recently giving the best rates with the least hassle.

The Ransom Chamber

El Cuarto del Rescate, as the Ransom Chamber is known in Spanish, is the only Inca building still standing in Cajamarca. Although called the Ransom Chamber, the room shown to visitors is where Atahualpa was imprisoned and not where the ransom

was stored. The small room has three trapezoidal doorways and a few trapezoidal niches in the inner walls – a typical sign of Inca construction. Although well constructed, it does not compare with the Inca buildings to be seen in the Cuzco area.

In the entrance, there are a couple of modern paintings depicting Atahualpa's capture and imprisonment. The site is open from 9 am to noon on weekends and 8 am to noon and 2 to 5 pm on weekdays (closed on Tuesday). Entrance is $1 for nonresidents and 15c for residents; the ticket can be used to visit the church and hospital of Belén and the Ethnography Museum.

The Belén Complex

Construction of the church and hospital of Belén began in the latter part of the 17th century. The hospital (which is being restored) was run by nuns. Inside the hospital, 31 tiny, cell-like bedrooms line the walls of the T-shaped building. In what used to be the women's hospital there is a small Archaeology Museum. The kitchen and dispensary of the hospital now houses an Art Museum.

The church next door has a fine cupola and a well-carved and painted pulpit. There are several interesting wood carvings, including an extremely tired-looking Christ sitting cross-legged on his throne, propping up his chin with a double-jointed wrist and looking as though he could do with a pisco sour after a hard day's miracle working.

The outside walls of the church are lavishly decorated. Local guides tell you that the church facade has strange carvings of women with four breasts, but I couldn't find them.

Opening hours and admission are the same as for the Ransom Chamber and the admission fee includes both these sites as well as the Ethnography Museum.

Ethnography Museum

This small, attractively housed museum is just a few metres from the Belén Complex and has the same opening hours and admission fee. Here, you can examine local costumes and clothing, domestic and agricultural implements, musical instruments and craftwork in wood, bone, leather and stone, as well as other examples of Cajamarcan culture.

Plaza de Armas

The plaza is pleasant and has a well-kept topiary garden. The fine central fountain dates to 1692 and commemorates the 200th anniversary of Columbus's landing in the Americas. The town's inhabitants congregate in the plaza every evening. Strolling and discussing the day's events are traditionally popular activities, more so in this area of northern Peru than anywhere else in the country.

Two churches face onto the Plaza de Armas: the cathedral and the Church of San Francisco. Both are often illuminated in the evening, especially at weekends. The cathedral is a squat building which was begun in the late 1600s and has only recently been finished. Like most of Cajamarca's churches, the cathedral has no belfry. This is because the Spanish crown levied a tax on finished churches and so the belfries were not built, leaving the church unfinished and thereby avoiding taxes. The Church of San Francisco's belfries were finished this century – too late for the Spanish crown to collect its tax!

San Francisco

The Church of San Francisco and its religious art museum are open from 2 to 5 pm on weekdays. Admission is about 7c. The intricately sculpted Chapel of La Dolorosa (to the right of the church) is considered one of the finest chapels in the city.

Archaeological Museum

This small but well-stocked museum (not related to the even smaller one in the Belén Complex) is well worth a visit. Its remarkably varied collection of ceramics includes a few examples of Cajamarca pots and an unusual collection of ceramic ceremonial spears also from the same culture. The Cajamarca culture, which existed in the area before the Inca Empire, is little studied and

not very well known. The museum also has black-and-white photographs of various historic and prehistoric sites in the Cajamarca area; it's director is knowledgeable and willing to talk about the exhibits.

The museum is run by the University of Cajamarca and charges a token admission (6c when I was last there). Opening hours vary and you often have to knock on the door to get in. The museum is open from 8 to 11.30 am on weekends and is closed on Tuesdays. During the rest of the week, it is open from 8 am to 12.15 pm and 3 to 5.45 pm, except from January to March when it is open only in the mornings.

Cajamarca plate

Cerro Santa Apolonia

This hill overlooks the city from the southwest and is a prominent Cajamarca landmark. It is easily reached by climbing the stairs at the end of Jirón 2 de Mayo. The pre-Hispanic carved rocks at the summit are mainly Inca but are thought to originally date back to the Chavín period. One of the rocks, known as the Seat of the Inca, is carved into the shape of a seat. The Inca is said to have reviewed his troops from here.

Fiestas

Like most Peruvian Andean towns, Cajamarca is famous for its carnival – this one is a particularly wet affair and its water fights are worse (or better, depending on your point of view) than usual. The Corpus Christi processions are also very colourful. Both are Catholic feast days and the dates vary each year, depending on the dates for Easter. Carnival is the week before Lent (which, in itself, is 40 days before Easter). Corpus Christi is the Thursday after Trinity Sunday, which is the Sunday after Whitsunday, which is the seventh Sunday after Easter. Confused fiesta-goers would do well to buy a Catholic calendar for the year they plan on being in Peru.

Cajamarca's Tourist Festival is around the second week in August. The various cultural events include art shows, folk music and dancing competitions, beauty pageants and processions.

Places to Stay – bottom end

There are several cold-water places which cost less than $1 per night. The *Hotel Plaza*, an old building on the Plaza de Armas, has some rooms with balconies and plaza views. Singles/doubles cost $1/1.60. Similarly priced are the more modern *Hotel Amazonas* and *Hostal Peru*, both of which have rooms with cold-water showers. A few cents cheaper is the *Hostal Sucre*, where rooms have a sink and toilet. There is no sign, so it is a bit difficult to find. Cheapest of all is the otherwise unrecommended *Hostal Bolívar*.

At about $1.50/2.50 for singles/doubles, a little more in rooms with bath, try the *Hotel Becerra*. The following hotels only have hot water in the morning. The *Hostal Yusovi* is clean but the water pressure leaves something to be desired. Singles/doubles are $1.80/2.80 with bath. The *Hostal 2 de Mayo* charges $1.25/2.10 for singles/doubles with toilets and communal showers and the *Hotel Delfort*, $2.25/3.75 for singles/doubles with bath.

The clean *Hostal Atahualpa*, on a pleasant, pedestrians-only street, is a good choice. Singles/doubles with cold-water bath are $1.75/3. The *Hotel San Francisco* is clean and costs $1/1.70 for singles/doubles with cold-water bath. Doubles with bath and hot water cost $5. The bare-looking *Hostal Turismo* charges about $2.50/3.75 for singles/doubles. All rooms are clean, carpeted and have comfortable beds and hot showers.

Places to Stay – middle

A good choice is the *Hotel Casa Blanca*, a thick-walled, creaky-floored, interesting old building on the Plaza de Armas. It has an excellent 24-hour hot-water supply and charges $3/5 for singles/doubles with bath. All rooms are very spacious and some have up to five beds. These work out more cheaply if you are travelling with a group. The hotel cafeteria opens at 8.30 am.

The clean, pleasant *Hotel Cajamarca* is in a colonial house and is recommended for reasonable comfort. It has a good restaurant and charges $6/8.50 for singles/doubles with bath and hot water. This hotel often has promotional discounts of up to 40%.

The *Hotel Continental* is over a modern shopping mall, which makes some rooms noisy but means that shops, a café and a bar are conveniently close. Good, clean singles/doubles with bath and hot water are $6/10 and the hotel has been recommended.

A new hotel is under construction at the corner of A Puga and Cinco Esquinas. It will be in the middle price range and will probably be open by the time you read this.

Places to Stay – top end

The government-run *Hotel de Turistas*, right on the Plaza de Armas, is the most comfortable hotel in town. Nonresidents are charged $12/16 for singles/doubles with bath (residents pay substantially less).

If you want quiet country comfort, go to the Baños del Inca, 6 km away. Here, the excellent *Hostal Lago Seco* will charge you $12/18 for pleasant rooms with bath. They also have four-bed bungalows for $36. The hotel has a warm swimming pool and the hot water in all rooms is fed by the natural thermal springs nearby. There is a pleasant garden and a good restaurant.

Places to Eat

My favourite restaurant is the *Salas*, a big barn of a place on the Plaza de Armas. It's popular with the locals and serves various local dishes such as cuy (guinea pig), delicious ·corn tamales and sesos (cow brains), which I must admit I've never tried.

You can eat well here for about $1. Similar to the Salas but a little cheaper, the *Chifa Zarco* serves Chinese food as well as local Peruvian dishes. Both are recommended.

La Taberna, on the corner of the plaza, is more modern and serves good 'international' food at prices that are a little higher than the other places. *El Arlequin*, also on the plaza, is not expensive and has music on weekend evenings. The restaurant in the *Hotel Cajamarca* also has a nice ambience and although it's a little pricier, like most restaurants in Cajamarca, it cannot really be called 'expensive'. Also good is *El Cajamarques*, next to the Hotel Continental. Try *Helados Capri* for good ice cream.

For a typical local lunch, try *La Namorina*, about 1½ km from the town centre on the road to the Baños del Inca. Cuy is the main attraction at this inexpensive and authentic highland restaurant. It is a fly-blown, hole-in-the-wall place but the cuy is good and the restaurant is close to most of the bus stations.

Entertainment

Cajamarca has four cinemas and there's usually a reasonably good English-language film screening at one of them. A few bars have live music on Friday and Saturday nights; these include the *Peña El Imperio*, which is a big barn of a place in the southeastern part of town – it doesn't get underway until about 10.30 pm. Earlier in the evening, music can be heard at *El Arlequin* and *El Cajamarques* restaurants, but don't expect anything much before 9 pm. Also recommended is the peña at the *Hotel Cajamarca* which often starts earlier in the evening.

Things to Buy

The market on Calle Amazonas is lively and interesting. Local products to look for include alforjas (heavy wool or cotton saddle bags) which can be worn over the shoulder or used on horseback. Woven baskets and leatherwork are also local crafts; the latter can be bought cheaply from prisoners in the jail, which is just past the arch on Jirón Lima. They are open from 8 to 11.30 am and 2 to 4.30 pm. The local eucalyptus honey sold at the market is worth trying.

Getting There & Away

Although it is possible to fly, most travellers arrive by bus from the coast.

Air AeroPeru is the only airline with an office or air service in Cajamarca. Local buses for Otuzco pass by the airport. There are two flights a week to and from Lima ($59).

Bus Cajamarca is at an ancient crossroads dating back many centuries before the Incas. Today, daily buses leave Cajamarca on roads heading for all four points of the compass.

The most important road is the westbound one, which is paved all the way to the Pan-American Highway near Pacasmayo on the coast. From here, you can head north to Chiclayo or south to Trujillo and Lima. The best bus services to Trujillo ($3, 7 hours) and Lima ($8, 15 hours) are with TEPSA, which has a daily departure at 6 pm, except Sunday when the bus leaves at 4 pm. The TEPSA terminal is about 1 km south-east of town on the road to the Baños del Inca. To save yourself the walk, buy tickets from the travel agent under the Hotel Plaza on the Plaza de Armas. Cheaper, slower buses are operated by Empresa Fortaleza, a block from the TEPSA terminal. Their buses to Trujillo tend to arrive at the inconvenient hour of 1 am. Transportes Atahualpa, also near the TEPSA terminal, has older buses for Trujillo and Lima leaving at 2 pm, while Empresa Diaz has the oldest buses of all – they leave at 1 and 9 pm daily and go only as far as Trujillo. Empresa El Cumbe runs daily buses to Chiclayo ($2.50, 6 hours), with departures at 11 am and 3 pm. Empresa Diaz has a Chiclayo departure at 2 pm. Empresa Cajamarca runs two or three buses a week to Trujillo and Lima.

The southbound road is the old route to Trujillo via Cajabamba and Huamachuco. The trip to Trujillo takes three times as long on this rough dirt road than it does along the newer paved road via Pacasmayo, although the old route is only 60 km longer. The scenery is supposedly prettier on the longer route but most buses beyond Cajabamba travel at night so you can't see a thing. Transportes Atahualpa has a noon bus to Cajabamba ($2.50, 7 hours) and an Empresa Diaz bus leaves at 11 am on the same route. The Diaz buses are older and more likely to break down, but the better Atahualpa buses are already half full with passengers from Lima and Trujillo when they reach Cajamarca and the best seats are taken.

The rough northbound road passes through wild and attractive countryside via the towns of Hualgayoc ($2.20) and Bambamarca ($2.50) to Chota ($2.90, 9 hours). Hualgayoc is a mining village in a beautiful setting. Bambamarca has a colourful Sunday morning market. There is a basic hotel in Bambamarca and more hotels in Chota. Buses run from Chota to Chiclayo along a very rough road. Daily Empresa Diaz buses to Chota leave Cajamarca at 7 am.

The eastbound road heads to Celendín, then across the Andes, past Chachapoyas and down into the Amazon lowlands. The road between Celendín and Chachapoyas is very bad and transport is unreliable; if you're going to Chachapoyas, you are advised to travel from Chiclayo via Bagua, unless you have plenty of time and patience. Daily buses to Celendín ($2.30, 5½ hours) leave Cajamarca at noon with Empresa Diaz and 1 pm with Transportes Atahualpa.

Getting Around

It is easy to find transport to the Baños del Inca. Colectivo taxis leave frequently from in front of the Church of San Francisco. The fare is 15c. For about 10c, you can take a Comité 3M bus, which travels along Jirón Lima and through the Plaza de Armas.

Buses for the Ventanillas de Otuzco leave frequently from the end of Jirón Arequipa, about 500 metres from the Plaza de Armas and two blocks past the bridge. The fare is 10c. The buses go past the airport and on to Otuzco, leaving you within 500 metres of the archaeological site.

Bus routes and departure points change occasionally, so ask at the tourist office for the latest details. Other local places are not served by public bus, though it is worth checking with the tourist office to see if this has changed. Walk, hitchhike, take a taxi or join a tour.

AROUND CAJAMARCA

There are several places of interest around Cajamarca. Some can be reached on public transport while others must be visited on foot, by taxi or with a guided tour. There are several tour agencies around the Plaza de Armas and they normally pool their clients to form a tour group for any trip. Cajamarca Tours will arrange more expensive individual outings.

Baños del Inca

These natural hot springs are 6 km from Cajamarca. The water is channelled into many private cubicles, some large enough for up to six people at a time. These are available for a few cents an hour. There is no public pool.

Atahualpa was camped by these hot springs when Pizarro arrived in the area, but there is nothing to see today except for the springs themselves.

Cumbe Mayo

According to the locals, the name of this site is derived from the Quechua term *kumpi mayo*, or 'well-made water channel'. The site, about 23 km from Cajamarca by road, has some extraordinarily well-engineered pre-Inca channels running for several km across the bleak mountain tops. Nearby are some caves containing petroglyphs. The countryside is high, windswept and slightly eerie. Locals tell superstitious stories about the area's eroded rock formations, which look like groups of shrouded figures climbing the mountain.

The site can be reached on foot via a signposted road from the Cerro Santa Apolonia. The walk takes about 4 hours if you take the obvious short cuts and ask every passer-by for directions. Tours are offered in Cajamarca for about $5 per person.

Ventanillas de Otuzco

This pre-Inca necropolis (graveyard) consists of hundreds of funerary niches built into the hillside, hence the name *ventanillas*, or 'windows'. The site is in beautiful countryside and it is possible to walk here from either Cajamarca or the Baños del Inca. There are also local buses. Further away are the larger Ventanillas de Combayo, but these are rarely visited because the road is in bad shape.

Llacanora & Hacienda La Colpa

The picturesque little village of Llacanora is 13 km from Cajamarca. Some of the inhabitants still play the traditional 3-metre-long bamboo trumpets, called *claríns*. A few km away is the Hacienda La Colpa, which is usually visited on a tour combined with Llacanora (about $3 per person). The hacienda is a working cattle ranch, and in the afternoons the cattle are herded into their stalls one by one, the ranch-hands calling each animal by name. This is a locally famous tourist attraction.

The Road from the Coast

The highway from the coast to Cajamarca is paved all the way, passing through Trembladera 46 km from the Pan-American junction. Interestingly enough, Trembladera is named not after the tremors of earthquakes but after the trembling and shivering of malaria victims. The disease was once common in this rice-growing area. A further 41 km brings you to the mining village of Chilete and a basic hotel.

On a side road 34 km north of Chilete is the village of San Pablo. It has a basic hotel and two or three buses a day to Chilete. An hour's walk from San Pablo is the Chavín site of Kuntur Wasi with its stone monoliths. You can also walk from San Pablo to Cumbe Mayo and on to Cajamarca; the walk takes about 3 days and is described (in reverse) in Bradt's book *Backpacking & Trekking in Peru & Bolivia*.

CAJABAMBA

The old route from Cajamarca to Trujillo takes 22 hours along 360 km of dirt road via

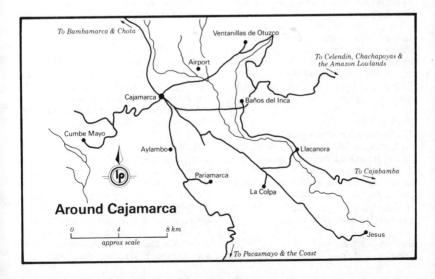

Around Cajamarca

Cajabamba and Huamachuco. Although this route passes through more interesting scenery and towns than the new road, the Huamachuco to Trujillo section is presently unrewarding because buses travel at night in both directions. From Cajamarca via Cajabamba to Huamachuco, however, daytime travel is possible. Check with the bus companies in case they've changed their schedules for daylight hours all the way.

Cajabamba is a very quiet, pleasant small town with a 19th century atmosphere. You'll see more mules than motorcars in the streets and the whitewashed houses and red-tiled roofs give the place a colonial air. There is a cinema on the pretty Plaza de Armas. The feast of the Virgin of the Rosary is celebrated around the second week of October with bullfights, processions, dances and general bucolic carousing. Hotels tend to be full at this time.

Places to Stay
All hotels suffer from periodic water shortages and dim light bulbs. The best place to stay is the *Hostal Flores* on the Plaza de Armas, next to the Banco de Crédito – there is a very small sign on the door. They charge $1 per person. Ask for a room with a balcony onto the plaza.

On the street behind the Flores, at José Sabogal 692, is a basic hotel without a sign (knock on the door) and charges 60c per person. At Grau 624 is the *Hotel Ramal* (75c per person) and the similarly priced *Hostal Bolívar* is at Ugarte 603. Both are within a block of the plaza.

Places to Eat
The *Restaurant La Peña* is half a block from the Banco de Crédito, just off the Plaza de Armas. It has loud music and passable food. *El Cid*, just beyond, has the brightest lights for reading and writing and serves a limited but tasty menu. A meal and a drink at either of these places costs under $1. There are other, still cheaper, places.

Getting There & Away
Travel to and from Cajabamba is by road only. Empresa Diaz, at Balta 132 on the outskirts of town, has a daily 5 am bus to Cajamarca. Transportes Atahualpa, one block from the Plaza de Armas at Alfonso Ugarte 601, has better-maintained buses leaving at 5.30 am daily for Cajamarca and continuing on to Trujillo and Lima. The fare for the 6-hour trip to Cajamarca is $2.50.

On the corner of Lloza and Caceres, by the main market, is Empresa Antisuyo. They have a daily 5 pm bus to Huamachuco ($1.25, 2½ hours) and Trujillo. If you want to travel to Huamachuco by day, there is usually a truck leaving from the market in the morning.

HUAMACHUCO
The village of Huamachuco is about 50 km beyond Cajabamba and 190 km from Trujillo. It has two or three places to stay and an impressive Plaza de Armas.

During the dry season, you can find transport east to Pataz. From Pataz, expeditions can be mounted to the little-explored ruins of various jungle cities, including the recently discovered Gran Pajaten. This is an undertaking for explorers and archaeologists only. One ruin, the pre-Inca hilltop fort of Marcahuamachuco, lies within reach of Huamachuco itself, 2 to 3 hours away on foot.

Places to Stay & Eat
There are three or four cheap hotels in Huamachuco, the best of which is the *Hostal San Francisco* at Sánchez Carrión 380. It boasts hot water – the others don't.

Most restaurants are either along Sánchez Carrión or on the Plaza de Armas.

CELENDÍN
This pleasant village is 118 km away from Cajamarca and at approximately the same altitude. However, the bus journey takes about 5 hours because the road is so rough and hilly. There's not much to do in Celendín and most travellers just pass through en route to Chachapoyas. There is one cinema which, when I was there in October, was unseasonably showing a film about the resurrection.

Top: Cathedral, Trujillo (TW)
Bottom: Plaza de Armas, Trujillo (TW)

Top: Reed canoes at Huanchaco, near Trujillo (TW)
Left: Carving of warrior, Sechín ruins (RR)
Right: Carvings at Huaca Arco Iris, near Trujillo (RR)

Market day is Sunday. The annual fiesta, held from 29 July to 3 August, coincides with the Fiestas Patrias and features bullfighting with matadors from Mexico and Spain.

Places to Stay & Eat

There are three basic hotels on the 300 block of 2 de Mayo, the cheapest of which is the *Maxmar* at 70c per person. It's just acceptable and some rooms even have private, if smelly, bathrooms with cold showers. A few cents more expensive and slightly better are the *Hotel José Galvez* and the *Amazonas*. Best of all is the *Hostal Celendín* on the Plaza de Armas. It charges $1.25/2 for singles/doubles with a toilet and sink. Hot water is available in the communal shower. There are a couple of other basic hotels.

The best restaurant (though nothing to get excited about) is the *Jalisco* on the Plaza de Armas.

Getting There & Away

Although both roads into Celendín are terrible, the road from Cajamarca is better than the one from Chachapoyas. Transport from Celendín to Chachapoyas consists of infrequent trucks because most buses are unable to negotiate the very demanding but beautiful 228-km road, which may be impassable during the wet season. Road improvements are planned and bus connections may improve – ask in Cajamarca. The road drops steeply from Celendín at 2625 metres to the River Marañon at Balsas, only 46 km away but 1600 metres lower than Celendín. From Balsas, the road climbs through spectacular rain and cloud forest to emerge at the 3678-metre-high point of the drive, the aptly named Abra de Barro Negro, or 'Black Mud Pass', which gives you an idea of the road conditions. From here, the road drops to Leimebamba (2280 metres) at the head of the Utcubamba River valley and follows the river as it descends past Tingo (near the Kuelap ruins) and on to Chachapoyas at 1834 metres above sea level.

When trucks do leave on this journey, they often travel in convoy, so you can be stuck in Celendín for several days waiting for the next departure. One trucking company which does the 12 to 20-hour trip is Transportes Gueverra, at 2 de Mayo 211 (a private house). They usually know when the next truck is leaving. The route from the coast at Chiclayo to Chachapoyas via Bagua is much more frequently travelled, though not as spectacular as the Celendín route. Trucks for Chachapoyas and Cajamarca also leave from the blue monument on the street parallel to 2 de Mayo.

Both Empresa Diaz, on the Plaza de Armas, and Transportes Atahualpa, at 2 de Mayo 630 (one block from the plaza), have daily 6.30 am departures to Cajamarca ($2.30, 5 hours). The latter company connects with and sells tickets for their 2 pm bus from Cajamarca to Trujillo and Lima.

CHACHAPOYAS

This quiet, pleasant little town of 18,000 inhabitants stands on the eastern slopes of the Andes at an altitude of 1834 metres. It is the capital of the Department of Amazonas which, despite its name, is a mainly Andean department. The department receives its name from the River Marañon, which is one of Peru's two major tributaries of the Amazon and the one which reaches furthest west into the Andes. The Marañon bisects the department and forms most of its western border with the Department of Cajamarca.

The Department of Amazonas has long been difficult to reach, and even today, it remains one of the least visited areas of Peru. Along with the neighbouring Department of San Martín, it contains vast tracts of the little-explored cloud forest of the Andes' eastern slopes. Within these highland forests are some of Peru's most fascinating and least known archaeological ruins. Although the ravages of weather and time and the more recent attentions of grave robbers and treasure seekers have caused damage to many of the ruins, some have survived remarkably well and can be visited by the adventurous traveller. The best known and one of the most accessible is the magnificent ruin of Kuelap, described later in this section. Chachapoyas provides an excellent base for visiting ruins

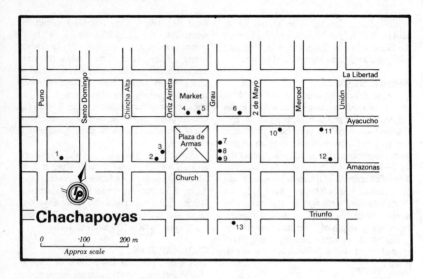

1 PIP Police
2 Tourist Office
3 Instituto Nacional de Cultura
4 Cine Central
5 AeroPeru
6 Kuelap Restaurant
7 Chacha Restaurant
8 Olano Buses to Chiclayo
9 Hotel Amazonas
10 Hostal Johumaji
11 Hostal Marañon
12 Post Office
13 ENTEL

and has been called 'the archaeological capital of Peru'.

Information

Chachapoyas is a military zone and foreign travellers should register with the PIP (see the Chachapoyas map). They simply check that your passport and tourist card are valid – it only takes a minute.

There is a small museum at the Instituto Naciónal de Cultura. At the tourist office around the corner, you can obtain the useful booklet (in Spanish only) *Guia Arqueológica del Departamento de Amazonas* by Victor M Zubiate Zabarburu (Chachapoyas, 1984). If you are seriously interested in visiting the remoter ruins, talk to the director of the Cultural Institute, Dr Carlos Torres Mas. General information on visiting the more accessible ruins is available at the tourist office. Practical information, such as maps and letters of introduction to people living in remote regions, can be obtained from Padre Pedro Rodríguez Arista, Calle Santo Domingo 643.

Another useful book about the region is *Antisuyo – the Search for the Lost Cities of the Amazon* by Gene Savoy (New York, 1970). The British edition is entitled *Vilcabamba – the Lost City of the Incas* (London, 1971). This book is Savoy's account of explorations in the region during the 1960s. Most professional archaeologists pooh-pooh his rather unscientific style but it makes entertaining and informative reading. A more textbook approach is taken in the well-illustrated *The Peoples & Cultures of Ancient Peru* by L G Lumbreras, translated by B J Meggers (Smithsonian Institution Press, 1974).

A visit to the ruins of Kuelap is definitely the most rewarding and representative of the available trips to ruins in the area. Travellers or archaeologists who want to visit one of the scores of other sites in the Chachapoyas area should seek further information in Chachapoyas. Most trips will require at least sleeping bags and sometimes tents and food as well. One good centre for exploration is Levanto, a small village about 3-hours walk away.

It is not easy to change money in Chachapoyas, so you should change as much as you need before getting there. The town has a reasonably well-stocked market and several general stores and most basic supplies can be obtained here. Items such as specialised foods, camera gear and film, suntan lotion and so on are best brought with you.

Chachapoyas is a quiet, friendly town. The traditional evening pastime of strolling around the Plaza de Armas socialising is a favourite way of relaxing. There is also one cinema.

Places to Stay & Eat

Chachapoyas suffers from water shortages and none of its hotels had water when I was last there, though buckets of water were available for washing. The *Hostal Johumaji* costs about $1 per person in small rooms with good light and bath (but no water!). Also good is the similarly priced but older *Hostal Marañon* – it has cheaper rooms without bath as well. Another cheap option is the *Hotel Amazonas* on the main square. Some of its rooms have a view over the plaza. *El Dorado*, at Ayacucho 1062, has been recommended as has the *Hostal Kuelap* at Chincha Alta 631. Both have hot water.

My favourite restaurant is the *Kuelap*. It is cheap, friendly and has a fairly good selection of dishes, but arrive before 8 pm – they start running out of food by then. For a change, try the *Chacha*; it is more expensive though hardly any better. Near the post office on Amazonas, you'll find the *Chifa El Turista* and the *Pio Pio* chicken restaurant. There are other places.

Getting There & Away

There are two routes from the coast. The one through Cajamarca and Celendín is more difficult but also more spectacular – it is described in the Celendín section earlier in this chapter. The more frequently travelled route from Chiclayo via Bagua takes 20 or more hours. This is described below.

The route follows the Pan-American Highway north for 100 km to Olmos. From here, a rough unpaved road heads east into the Andes and climbs over the Porculla Pass which, at 2145 metres, is the lowest pass across the Peruvian Andes. The road then drops to the Marañon River valley. About 190 km from the Pan-American Highway turn-off, you reach Jaén where there are a couple of basic hotels and restaurants. The town is a few km off the main road and not all buses go there. From Jaén, a northbound road heads to San Ignacio near the Ecuadorian border, about 100 km away. Because of the 1942 border dispute, it is not possible to enter Ecuador and there is no transport.

About 50 km beyond the Jaén turn-off is the village of Bagua. The bus usually goes through Bagua Grande at 522 metres. Bagua, in the Marañon valley and Peru's most westerly jungle town, is on the main road and offers basic accommodation. From Bagua, a long and difficult trip can be made by road and river to Iquitos (see the Amazon Basin chapter). Buses and pick-up trucks make the journey from Bagua to Moyobamba. The road follows the Utcubamba River valley upwards for about 70 km to the crossroads town of Pedro Ruiz, which is not marked on most maps. From here, a southbound road branches down to Chachapoyas, 54 km away.

Air A new airport has been built and Aero-Peru flights started in 1985. The AeroPeru office is on the Plaza de Armas. There is a weekly flight to Lima (via Chiclayo) on Monday but this may well change. The fare is $39 – very cheap because Chachapoyas is so far off the normal tourist route.

Bus The main bus company, Olano, has daily (except Sunday) departures for Chiclayo via Bagua at 10 am (20 hours, $8).

Small minibuses and pick-up trucks leave the Plaza de Armas for various destinations. About three a day go to Tingo ($1, 1½ hours) and on to Leimebamba (3 hours, $1.50). They usually leave between 8 am and 1 pm. This is also the service for Kuelap. A couple of times a week, trucks depart for Leimebamba and travel on to Celendín – ask around.

To continue further down the eastern slopes of the Andes into the Amazon Basin, you must first take a bus to the crossroads at Pedro Ruiz ($1, 1½ hours). The first departure of the day is usually the Olano bus to Chiclayo; they'll drop you off at Pedro Ruiz if they aren't full of passengers travelling further. After the Olano bus leaves, there are usually two or three minibuses which will make the journey. No direct buses run from Chachapoyas to Moyobamba at this time, so you have to wait in Pedro Ruiz to continue eastwards.

Other local destinations are serviced by pick-up trucks, which leave from the Plaza de Armas or from the market. It's a matter of asking around. The tourist office can also help.

TINGO

From the village of Tingo, you can visit the important ruin of Kuelap. Tingo has a couple of very basic hotels, the *Viajero* and the *Tingo*, and some simple restaurants. The *Hacienda Chillo*, about 5 km south of Tingo, has been recommended as a good place to stay, to get information about local ruins and to arrange mule hire.

KUELAP

This immense ruined city in the mountains south-east of Chachapoyas is, for most travellers, the main reason to spend time in the region. Kuelap is the best preserved and most accessible of the major ruins in the area – note that by 'most accessible' I do not mean 'easily accessible'. Reaching the ruins takes several hours of hard climbing on foot from

the village of Tingo, so it is remote enough to discourage casual tourists. The site averages about one visitor or small group of visitors per day during the dry season. Climbing up into the mountains to finally emerge at Kuelap, which is not easy to see until you are almost in front of the ruins, is an exhilarating experience.

In common with the other sites in the area, Kuelap is referred to as a pre-Inca city, though little is known about the people who built it. The Chachapoyas area was the centre of a highland people, known variously as the Chachapoyans or the Sachupoyans, who were incorporated into the Inca Empire by the Inca Huayna Capac in the late 1400s. They left massive walled cities and fortresses on many of the area's mountain tops. The stonework of these sites is somewhat rougher looking than Inca stonework but is embellished with patterns and designs missing from the Inca work.

Kuelap is about 3100 metres above sea level on a ridge high above the left bank of the River Utcubamba. It is an oval-shaped city about 600 metres long and entirely surrounded by a massive defensive wall 6 to 8 metres high. Three entrances pierce this wall. The principal entrance, and the one used today to gain access to the site, leads into an impressive, bottle-shaped, high-walled passageway. This is a highly defensible entrance; it would have been well-nigh impossible for attackers to scale these high walls without being repulsed by raining projectiles from the defenders perched high on the walls. Once inside the site, the visitor will find dozens of mainly round buildings – over 300 have been counted. One has a mysterious underground chamber and another forms a lookout tower. The views are excellent.

Information

There are two guardians at Kuelap who are very friendly and helpful. At least one of them is almost always on hand to show visitors around and answer questions. When I was there, I was helped by Don José Gabriel Portocarrero Chávez. He gave me a guided tour of the ruins and his wife cooked me a simple meal. He and Domingo, the other guardian, are good sources of information on other ruins in the area. The small hostal on the site has only two beds but, if there are more of you, sleeping on the floor is no problem (bring sleeping bags). The two beds have blankets. If you have a tent, camping is also possible. You should carry or purify water, though soft drinks are sometimes for sale. Only very basic food is available – bringing your own is a good idea.

Entry to the site is about $1 and use of the hostal costs about 50c. A small tip or present for the guardians is appreciated – flashlight batteries, a magazine or newspaper, chocolate or canned food are good gifts.

Getting There & Away

Several vehicles a day travel from Chachapoyas to Tingo. There is a Guardia Civil post at the entrance to Tingo and they will be happy to point out the path to you. There are a couple of very basic hotels and restaurants. You can hire mules to take you or your gear up to the ruins, but most people walk.

The trail climbs from the south end of Tingo at 1900 metres to the ruins about 1200 metres above. There are some signposts on the way and the trail is not very difficult to follow; the main problem is the steepness of the climb. It takes about 5 hours to climb to Kuelap, so it's best to spend the night there. If you leave Chachapoyas in the morning, you can easily reach the ruins by midafternoon. Remember to bring water because there is little available at Kuelap and none on the trail. During the rainy season (October to April), especially the latter half, the trail can become very muddy and travel difficult.

PEDRO RUIZ

This is the small village at the junction of the Chachapoyas road and the Bagua to Moyobamba road. If travelling from Chachapoyas, you have to wait here for vehicles to Rioja and Moyobamba. The earliest vehicle to Pedro Ruiz does not leave Chachapoyas until 10 am, so it's almost noon before you reach the junction. It's a good idea to spend the night at Pedro Ruiz before continuing the rough journey eastward. The cheap, basic but adequate *Hostal & Restaurant El Marginal* is within a few metres of the junction.

Very crowded and uncomfortable pick-up trucks travel from Pedro Ruiz to Rioja every 1 or 2 hours throughout the day. These vehicles come from Bagua and are often full to overflowing when they arrive (I counted 33 people in the back of the Datsun pick-up I rode on). They claim that the journey takes 6 hours but it often takes more like 9 hours, longer in the wet season when landslides can close the road. The fare is about $3. Large trucks do the journey in about 15 hours. If you're very lucky, you might get onto one of the daily buses plying this route from the coast, but these are often full. Ask the locals what time the buses are expected to come through.

The journey east from Pedro Ruiz is spectacular – the road climbs over two major passes and drops into fantastic high jungle vegetation in between. It's definitely worth travelling this section in daylight, though the very rough road and uncomfortable, overcrowded conditions sometimes make appreciating the beauty of the landscape a bit difficult.

About 2 hours east of Pedro Ruiz is Laguna Pomacocha. A government-run *Hotel de Turistas* opened here in the mid-1980s, but I don't know if it's still operating. Singles/doubles cost about $6/10. This is the only place with facilities to break the journey until Nueva Cajamarca, at least 5 hours beyond Pedro Ruiz.

Nueva Cajamarca is a brand-new town built in the 1970s and inhabited by colonists from the highlands. It has two basic hotels, the *Peru* and the *Carrazon*, both charging less than $1 per person. From Nueva Cajamarca, pick-up trucks and minibuses leave frequently along the improved road to Rioja. The fare for the 1-hour trip is about 50c.

RIOJA

Rioja is the first town of importance on the road heading inland across the Andes from the Pan-American Highway. It is a small but busy and friendly town. The nearby airport serves both Rioja and nearby Moyobamba, the capital of the Department of San Martín. Both towns were severely damaged by earthquake on 29 May 1990. Reportedly, few buildings survived. Make inquiries before travelling to this area. The following information is based on the situation before the earthquake.

Places to Stay

There are two or three basic hotels along Avenida Grau. Of these, the *Hostal San Martín* at Grau 540, about a block from the Plaza de Armas, is reasonable at about $1 per person.

Getting There & Away

Air AeroPeru and Faucett have one or two flights per week to and from Lima ($74) via Chiclayo. Other destinations are occasionally served; Faucett recently had a weekly connection to Tarapoto. Taxis to the airport leave from the Plaza de Armas.

Bus Pick-up trucks leave for Pedro Ruiz and Bagua from the corner of the Plaza de Armas. Both pick-up trucks and plenty of minibuses leave from the plaza for Moyobamba (50c, 45 minutes) and Tarapoto ($4, 4 to 6 hours).

MOYOBAMBA

A good road links Rioja at 1400 metres with the small town of Moyobamba at 860 metres. Moyobamba is the capital of the Department of San Martín and was the first town to be founded in the Peruvian eastern lowlands, soon after the conquest. There isn't a great deal to see but it is a quiet and pleasant town nonetheless. Despite its departmental capital status, Moyobamba does not have proper foreign-exchange facilities and travellers are advised to change money on the coast before getting there.

Museum

The Instituto Nacional de Cultura has a small office with an even smaller display of local stuffed animals, including many frogs in little costumes. Photographs are allowed.

Hot Springs

The local hot springs or baños termales are near Alto Mayo, about an hour's walk from town. A taxi will cost about $1. Alto Mayo is out along the Rioja road – almost anyone can give you directions. There are both hot and cold swimming pools.

Places to Stay & Eat

There are several cheap, basic places to stay in Moyobamba. Try the *Hostal Monterrey*, on the main plaza, which charges 70c per person and has a few rooms with bath. The basic *Hostal Mesia, Hostal Los Andes* and *Pensión Weninger* cost 60c and have cold water in the communal showers.

A bit more expensive, but good value, is the clean *Hostal Cobos*, which charges $1.25/2.25 for singles/doubles with bath (cold shower) – less with communal bath. The hotel staff will help arrange transport to the nearby hot springs. The *Hostal Inca* is a clean and relatively modern central hotel, while the *Albricias*, a few blocks from the town centre, has a garden. Both are good and charge $2/3.50 for singles/doubles with bath and cold water.

The best hotel in Moyobamba is the government-run *Hotel de Turistas*. Make reservations in Lima through ENTURPeru (tel 721928). The hotel is about 2 km out of town on Calle Sucre (take a taxi) and rates are about $6/9, including continental breakfast.

The town has plenty of restaurants, all inexpensive. My recommendation is the *Restaurant Moscu*.

Entertainment

Nightlife is limited to the *La Tapala* bar, which occasionally has music, and a couple of cinemas.

Getting There & Away

Air Both Faucett and AeroPeru have offices in Moyobamba but all flights leave from or arrive in Rioja. There are direct taxis from Moyobamba to Rioja Airport.

Bus & Colectivo Colectivos to Rioja (60c, 45 minutes) and Tarapoto ($4.30, 3½ hours) leave from the taxi rank on Canga as soon as they have five passengers. Slightly cheaper minibuses leave from the bus stop on J R Guerra. They take a long time to fill up and normally only go to Rioja, unless a bunch of passengers want to go elsewhere. For cheaper transport to Tarapoto, stand by the taxi rank until a minibus or pick-up truck comes by with the driver yelling 'Tarapoto'.

TARAPOTO

From Moyobamba, the road drops still further down the Mayo River valley to Tarapoto, 356 metres above sea level, on the very edge of the eastern Andean foothills. It is a 116-km journey but the road is one of the

1 Hostal Albricias
2 Bus Stop
3 Cine Verde
4 ENTEL
5 Faucett Airline
6 Instituto Nacional de Cultura
7 Restaurant Moscu
8 Banco de la Nación
9 Hostal Inca
10 Colectivos to Rioja & Tarapoto
11 Hostal Los Andes
12 Hostal Mesia
13 AeroPeru
14 Hostal Cobos
15 Pensión Weninger
16 La Tapala Bar
17 Hostal Monterrey
18 Cine Viena

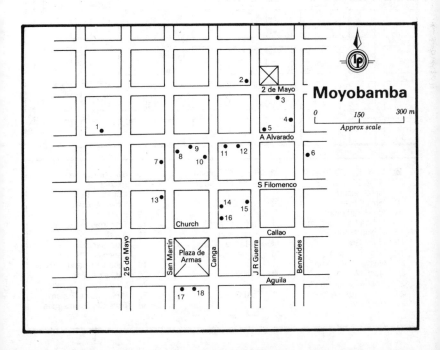

best in the Department of San Martín. Tarapoto is the largest and busiest town in the department and the centre for the northern lowlands' expanding agricultural colonisation. The town has the region's best accommodation and air services but is also the most expensive. Some of the agricultural expansion has come from the coca growing in the Huallaga River valley and there have been reports of drug-related problems in the Moyobamba-Tarapoto region. Check before travelling in the area.

Information

Although rates are not very favourable, Moyobamba is one of the few towns in the region where money exchange is usually possible. It is said that this is because Tarapoto is on the fringe of the major drug-growing and smuggling industry to the south along the Huallaga River valley. Be that as it may, you can try both the Banco de Crédito and the Sanchez Money Exchange for changing cash dollars (travellers' cheques

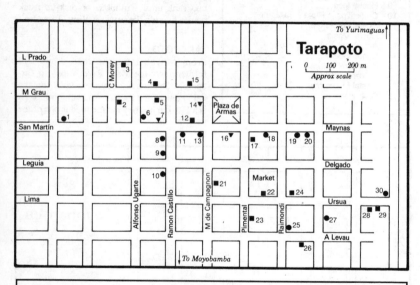

■ PLACES TO STAY			
	28	Hostal El Dorado	
2	Hotel Acosta	29	Hostal Melendez
3	Hostal Misti		
4	Hotel Tarapoto	▼ PLACES TO EAT	
5	Hostal Las Palmeras		
12	Hostal America	7	La Cajamarquina Restaurant
15	Hotel Gran	14	La Terraza Café
17	Hotel Edinson	16	La Mesón Restaurant
21	Hostal San Martín		
22	Hostal Miami	● OTHER	
23	Hostal Pasquelandia		
24	Hostal Juan Alfonso	1	Post Office
26	Hostal Viluz		

6	Sanchez Money Exchange
8	Comité 1 to Moyobamba
9	ENTEL
10	Transport to Lamas
11	AeroPeru
13	Cine Central
18	Banco de Crédito
19	León de Huánuco (Bus)
20	Faucett Airline
25	Minibuses to Juanjui
27	Ministerio de Turismo
30	Trucks to Yurimaguas

with persuasion), but expect to receive almost 20% less than in Lima or Iquitos.

Things to Do

There is not much to do in Tarapoto itself apart from hanging out in the Plaza de Armas, swimming at the Hotel de Turistas pool or going to the cinema.

Nearby Lamas is worth a day trip. This interesting Indian village is well off the normal tourist circuit and has an early morning market, a small museum and a reasonable restaurant, but no hotels.

Places to Stay – bottom end

The best of the cheap hotels, the *Hostal Juan Alfonso*, charges $1.30/2 for basic singles/doubles with communal cold showers and an extra 30c for rooms with private showers. Other basic hotels charging the same for rooms with communal showers are the acceptable *El Dorado*, *Melendez*, *Las Palmeras* and *Gran*. Cheapest of all is the very basic *Hostal Pasquelandia*. Many of the cheaper hotels have water available at only certain times of the day, so ask about this if you're desperate for a shower.

The *Hostal Viluz* is new and clean and charges $2/3.50 for singles/doubles with showers. The older, centrally located *Hostal America* is similarly priced and provides towels, toilet paper, soap and a fan in all rooms – very civilised. The *Hotel Tarapoto* is a little more expensive but also good.

Several hotels charge $2.75/4.75 for singles/doubles with bath. Of these, the *Hostal Miami* is good and clean and the *Hotel Edinson* is also recommended. The *Hostal San Martín* has similar rates but will give you a discount if you stay for a few days. The *Hostal Misti* charges the same but doesn't look as good.

Places to Stay – middle

The best hotel near the town centre is the *Hotel Acosta*, which has comfortable rooms for $4.75/6. Most expensive is the government-run *Hotel de Turistas* where singles/doubles cost $9/14, including continental breakfast. Reservations can be made in Lima through ENTURPeru (tel 721928) or in Tarapoto (tel 2225). The hotel is almost 2 km out of town on Jirón Pablo Cruz. It has a swimming pool which is free for hotel residents and open to others for a small fee. The recently opened *Hostal Lily* at Pimental 405 is also in this price range.

Places to Eat

The best of the cheaper restaurants is *La Cajamarquina*. Good, but slightly more expensive, is *La Mesón* on the Plaza de Armas. *La Terraza*, also on the plaza, is a pleasant place for a snack or cold drink. There are plenty of other places to choose from.

Getting There & Away

Air The busy Tarapoto airport is 2 or 3 km out of town. There are no buses; a taxi will cost about $1. Both AeroPeru and Faucett have flights but they are often booked out well in advance. Both airlines have offices in central Moyobamba. In addition, smaller airlines have offices at the airport and offer frequent light-aircraft flights to several jungle destinations.

Between them, AeroPeru and Faucett provide one or two flights a day to Lima ($57). There are also flights to Chiclayo, Trujillo, Rioja, Yurimaguas and Iquitos with these airlines.

AeroTaxi Iberico has an office at the airport and flies light aircraft to Yurimaguas ($17), Juanjui ($19) and Tocache ($28). These are good alternatives to the difficult journeys by road, but remember that there isn't much room for baggage and you may have to pay for an extra seat if you're lugging a huge backpack around. AeroTaxi Iberico doesn't take reservations – just go to the airport in the morning. Flights leave as soon as the plane is full. Most have five passenger seats, so it doesn't take long for them to fill up. Departures start around 9 am and continue all day – it's a great way to see some of the jungle from the air. When I flew from Tarapoto to Tocache, the pilot pointed out what he claimed were clandestine airstrips used by drug runners. In this respect, the area is becoming increasingly dangerous – make local inquiries.

You can charter a flight to other jungle destinations – you have to pay for all five passenger seats but that's no problem if you can get a group together.

If you have to spend a few hours at the airport, an inexpensive snack bar sells sandwiches and ice-cold beer.

Bus Tarapoto is an important junction. From here, roads head west to Moyobamba, south to Juanjui and north to Yurimaguas and the Amazon Basin, in descending order of road quality.

The 145-km southbound journey via Bellavista to Juanjui is not recommended because of Sendero and drug-running problems. The trip takes 5 to 8 hours in colectivo taxis ($5.50) and minibuses ($5). Vehicles leave from the corner of Raimondi and Levau and supposedly depart throughout the day as soon as they are full, but it's advisable to go in the morning. León de Huánuco buses leave at 9 am on Tuesday and Friday for Juanjui ($4), continuing on to Tocache ($12.75) and Tingo María ($13.25), where there are connections to Pucallpa and Huánuco. The 485-km journey to Tingo María takes about 2 days, mainly because the section between Juanjui and Tocache is very bad. The journey may be broken at Juanjui and Tocache (described later). Tingo María, an important town on the road from Lima to the jungle at Pucallpa, is described in the Central Peru chapter.

Heading west from Tarapoto to Moyobamba takes about 3 to 4 hours in Comité 1 colectivo taxis. They leave from the first block of Ramon Castillo and charge $4.30 per person. Cheaper, slower minibuses also make the trip but leave less frequently. A block away is the taxi and pick-up truck stand for Lamas (75c, 1½ hours).

THE ROAD TO YURIMAGUAS

This 130-km road climbs over the final foothills of the Andes, and emerges on the Amazonian plains before continuing on to Yurimaguas. It is one of the most beautiful and one of the worst roads in the area and is almost impassable during the rainy season. There is no regular bus but pick-up trucks and other vehicles leave almost every morning (if the road is open) from the end of Jirón Ursua. The journey costs about $5, takes from 7 to 14 hours (sometimes at an average speed of less than 10 km per hour) and is usually very crowded and uncomfortable. There are no set departure times and vehicles usually leave anywhere between 4 and 10 am. If you're lucky, you might get the front seat of a jeep; if not, it might be standing room only in the back of a truck.

I had a memorable trip from Tarapoto to Yurimaguas. I was waiting at the usual departure point when a man offered me a ride to Yurimaguas. I couldn't see any trucks or jeeps, but he told me he was ready to go right away and pointed to a new VW Beetle standing a few metres away. I looked at it in disbelief – how was a little VW Beetle going to negotiate a road which buses didn't dare attempt? Nevertheless, the thought of riding in comfort soon overcame my worries and I climbed in.

The road was absolutely terrible. The driver couldn't get out of first gear and, when he tried using second, the car would invariably stall. While we moved along at walking pace, the driver told me the story of his trip. The car was new – he had bought it in Lima and was driving it to Yurimaguas, a distance of well over 2000 km. He was planning to ship it from Yurimaguas to Iquitos, where it would be sold as new at the Iquitos VW dealership. I was amazed by the story and asked why he didn't just air freight it from Lima to Iquitos. I was told that driving it over 2000 km of bad road plus several days on the river was cheaper.

At last, we managed to get over the final pass and were on the flat 60-km stretch to Yurimaguas. The driver became very confident and even managed to get into third gear. While we splashed through the few puddles in the road, the driver happily began telling me that the worst part was over and we were as good as there. Unfortunately, one of the puddles turned out to be extremely deep and, just as the driver was blithely telling me how close we were to Yurimaguas, the vehicle sank almost up to its windows and the engine stopped. Despondently, the driver opened the door to see how bad the situation was and a 30-cm wall of water gushed into the car. So much for delivering a new car to the Iquitos dealership!

We tried pushing it out, but to no avail – the car was well and truly stuck. After about 2 hours, a large truck came along (which gives you an idea of the frequency of traffic on this road) and pulled the car out. Another 2 hours were spent drying the starter and engine. Finally, we managed to get the car started and limped into Yurimaguas. Here, the driver dried out and cleaned up the car as best he could before arranging river transport to Iquitos. I guess the moral of that story is 'Don't buy a new car in Iquitos'.

For more information about Yurimaguas and river travel into the jungle, see the Amazon Basin chapter.

TOCACHE

The Tocache area is one of the most expensive in Peru and the story circulates that everything is priced in dollars. It is near here that much of Peru's clandestine coca and marijuana crops are produced. For this reason, the area is not recommended at this time. Tocache is a new but growing town on the verdant, fertile Huallaga River. From here, there is a fairly good road south to Tingo María and a terrible road north to Juanjui and Tarapoto. Unless you actually like gruelling bus trips, you might want to fly if you're heading to or from Tarapoto.

Places to Stay

There are four basic hotels, the patriotic-sounding *Bolívar, Sucre* and *San Martín* and the *Comercio*, none of which is up to much. The showers don't always work, but despite this, the hotels are often full. Try to get into town early or you'll end up sleeping on the floor in one of the hotel lobbies. The hotels all charge about $2 per person.

Getting There & Away

Air The airport is about a km from town. AeroTaxi Iberico has an office at the airport and daily flights to and from Juanjui or Tarapoto; just show up and wait for a plane. If you can't get to Tarapoto, there are basic hotels in Juanjui and frequent minibuses from there to Tarapoto, about 5 to 8 hours away.

Bus & Colectivo Comité 1, on the main plaza, has buses and cars to Tingo María ($6.30, 5 hours). There are also a couple of buses a week to Tarapoto with León de Huánuco. These take almost 2 days and are often full with passengers from Tingo María – it is better to fly.

The Amazon Basin

About half of Peru is in the Amazon Basin, yet it merits only one chapter in this book. Why is this? The answer is inaccessibility. Few roads penetrate the rainforest of the Amazon Basin and, therefore, few towns of any size have been built. Those that exist started as river ports and were connected with towns further downstream, usually in Brazil or perhaps Bolivia. Only a few decades ago, the traveller from Peru's major jungle port of Iquitos had to travel thousands of km down the Amazon River to the Atlantic and then go either south around Cape Horn or north through the Panama Canal to reach Lima – a journey taking several months. With the advent of roads and airports, these jungle areas have slowly become a more important part of Peru. Nevertheless, they still contain only about 5% of the nation's population.

Five main jungle areas are accessible to the traveller. Starting in the south-east, near the Bolivian border, the first of these is Puerto Maldonado, which lies at the junction of the Tambopata and Madre de Dios rivers. Puerto Maldonado is most easily reached by air (there are daily flights from Cuzco) or by an atrociously bad dirt road (an uncomfortable 2 or 3 day journey by truck).

In central Peru, almost due east of Lima, is the area known as Chanchamayo. It consists of the two small towns of San Ramón and La Merced, both easily accessible by road from Lima, and several nearby villages.

A new jungle road has almost been completed from La Merced north to Pucallpa, the capital of the Department of Ucayali and the third region described in this section. Because Pucallpa is a major road connected with Lima by daily flights or a 24-hour bus journey, this region used to be one of the easiest to reach for the traveller wanting a quick glimpse of the Peruvian jungle. Unfortunately, however, in recent years, the road to Pucallpa (and to a certain extent Pucallpa itself) have fallen under the control of the

Sendero Luminoso. At this time, the road trip is dangerous and buses are frequently stopped by Senderistas, who shoot politicians, police, and military personnel, then ask for a 'voluntary contribution' from the surviving passengers.

Further north is the small port of Yurimaguas, reached by road (the difficult journey is described in the Across the Northern Highlands chapter) or by air from Lima. Though not as risky as the road to Pucallpa, the route is not recommended at this time.

Finally, travellers can reach Peru's major jungle port, Iquitos, by river boat from Pucallpa and Yurimaguas or by air from several cities, including Lima. It is impossible to reach Iquitos by road.

PUERTO MALDONADO

Founded at the turn of the century, Puerto Maldonado has been important as a rubber boom town, a logging centre, and more recently, as a centre for gold and oil prospectors. It is also important for jungle crops such as Brazil nuts and coffee. Because of the logging industry, the jungle around Puerto Maldonado has been almost totally cleared. There is also some ranching.

The various commercial enterprises centred on Puerto Maldonado have made it the most important port and capital of the Department of Madre de Dios. It is an unlovely fast-growing town with a busy frontier feel. It is interesting to experience this boom-town atmosphere, but otherwise, there isn't much to see. Puerto Maldonado can be used as a starting point for trips into the jungle. The best of these are to the nearby jungle lodges. It is also possible to continue into the Brazilian or Bolivian jungle or to Manu National Park, but these trips are not straightforward.

Information

Immigration If you're leaving Peru via Iñapari (for Brazil) or Puerto Heath (for

To Iberia
(Approx 220 km)

Río Madre de Dios

Stairs

Billinghurst

Loreto

Plaza de Armas

Carrion

Cuzco

2 de Mayo

To Laberinto

G Prada

Market

J Troncoso

Market

Tacna

Ica

Moquegua

Puno

Velarde

Fitzcarrald

To Airport (4 km)

To Hotel
de Turistas
(4 blocks)

26 de Diciembre

Arequipa

Río Tambopata

Puerto Maldonado

0   100   200 m

■	PLACES TO STAY	●	OTHER
2	Hostal Moderno	1	River Boat Hire
7	Hotel Oriental	3	Money Exchange
11	Hotel Chavez	5	Cine Grau
12	Hotel Rey Port	6	LASA Airline
14	Hotel Tambo de Oro	8	Cine Madre de Dios
16	Hotel Mary	10	Banco de Crédito &
17	Hotel Wilson		Banco de la Nación
19	Hotel Central	13	Faucett Airline
		15	ENTEL
▼	PLACES TO EAT	17	AeroPeru
4	Juanito's Bar	20	Post Office
9	El Café Danubio Azul	21	Motorcycle Hire
18	Rulman's Restaurant	22	Emilio's Store
23	Café Don Pancito	24	Peña El Cajamarquino
		25	Explorer's Inn Office

Bolivia), check first with immigration officials in Puerto Maldonado or Cuzco – recently, exit stamps were not obtainable at the borders. In Puerto Maldonado, the migraciónes office is found in the riverside complex opposite the Hotel Moderno. If you're flying from Cuzco to Iñapari, check with migraciónes in Cuzco. There is no Brazilian consul in Puerto Maldonado but a Bolivian consul has reportedly opened on Jirón Cuzco.

Money The Banco de Crédito will change cash dollars at the unfavourable official rate; 20% more can be obtained in Cuzco at the favourable financial rate. There are no casas de cambio but the lawyer at Velarde 140 will sometimes give you a better rate for cash dollars if he has intis available. You might be able to get rid of Brazilian cruzeiros in the Banco de Crédito but changing any travellers' cheques or Bolivian pesos is difficult.

Motorcycle Hire You can rent motorcycles if you want to see some of the surrounding countryside; go in pairs in case of breakdowns. The motorcycle rental place marked on the Puerto Maldonado map charges about $2 per hour and has mainly small 100cc bikes. Bargain for all-day discounts. (Rental motorcycles have recently become difficult to find; ask around and don't rely on finding an available bike.)

Madre de Dios Ferry A cheap way of seeing a little of this major Peruvian jungle river is to cross it. Even the most impecunious traveller can afford this trip – it costs about 15c each way. The crossing takes about 5 minutes and peki-pekis leave from the dock several times an hour. The Madre de Dios is about 500 metres wide at this point and, on the other side, you can continue by motorcycle or on foot.

Other The town's two cinemas screen films irregularly. One Saturday night when I was there, neither had a film playing, but you might get lucky. There are many pool halls

but not much else to do. Personal items such as film, soap and batteries are expensive, so buy them before you arrive.

Places to Stay – bottom end
Puerto Maldonado has about 10 hotels but they tend to start filling up by late morning and single rooms, especially in the cheaper hotels, may be hard to find. Several inexpensive hotels provide your basic four walls, a bed and a cold communal shower for about $1.50 per person. One of these is the *Hotel Oriental*, a typical, basic Amazonian hotel with a tin roof and rough wooden walls painted an unappealing green. Despite its unprepossessing appearance, it's OK at a pinch. Other cheapies to try are the *Hotel Tambo de Oro* and the *Hotel Central*, which aren't bad, or the *Hotel Mary* and *Hotel Chavez*, neither of which is up to much.

For a better room with a cold shower and fan, the *Hostal Moderno* is a good choice at $2.50/3.50 for singles/doubles; it is quiet, clean and has many rooms. Similarly priced and also good is the *Hotel Rey Port*. The *Hotel Wilson* has long had a reputation for being the best run hotel in the town centre. It has clean rooms with communal showers for $2 per person, singles/doubles with private cold shower and fan for $3/4.50 and a basic cafeteria and pool room on the premises.

Places to Stay – top end
About 1 km south-west of the town centre on Jirón Velarde and pleasantly located above the banks of the Río Tambopata, is the government-run *Hotel de Turistas*. It charges $7.50/11.50 for clean singles/doubles with cold shower and fan and has a restaurant which opens on demand. Rooms at the hotel can be booked through ENTURPeru (tel 721928) but it costs more to do it this way. The hotel is rarely full.

Outside Puerto Maldonado are three jungle lodges, described more fully later in this section.

Places to Eat
There are no fancy restaurants in Puerto Maldonado and most are fairly basic. My

favourite, *Rulman's*, is clean and has fruit juices and a good selection of food for no more than $1 per plate. It's the most reliable restaurant in Puerto Maldonado – others are often out of everything, except chicken, or serve only beer. Another good place is *El Café Danubio Azul* on the plaza. The friendly staff help travellers with local information and can put you in touch with guides or almost anybody else in town. *Juanito's*, also on the plaza, is good for cold drinks and ice cream.

Some of the early pioneers of Puerto Maldonado were Japanese (see the pagoda-like clock tower on the Plaza de Armas). *Café Don Pancito* is run by the Fukomoto family, descendants of Japanese pioneers. This basic but clean and friendly restaurant occasionally serves jungle food and will sometimes change US dollars. Also worth checking out is *Emilio's* store in the market for excellent home-made hot chocolate and other jungle staples such as fariña, a muesli-like yucca concoction eaten fried or mixed in lemonade(!) Also in the market, look out for children selling hot, fresh pan de arroz in the early morning (7 to 8 am). This bread is made from rice flour, yucca and butter and takes 3 days to prepare.

A little way from the town centre (20 minutes walk), by the pioneer cemetery (itself a tourist attraction) on Piura near Cuzco, is the local restaurant *Califas*; taxi drivers know it. This place is only open for lunch and usually serves regional dishes. Get there early for the best selection of food.

Regional specialities include juanes (fish or chicken steamed in a banana leaf with rice or yucca), chocana (a broth of fish chunks flavoured with the native cilantro herb) and parillada de la selva (a barbecue of marinated meat in a Brazil-nut sauce). The banana-like plantain (platano) is served boiled or fried as a side dish to many meals.

Getting There & Away

Most people fly from Cuzco; this is cheap and convenient. The road or river trips are only for adventurous travellers who are pre-

pared to put up with both discomfort and delay.

Air The airport is about 4 km out of town. Colectivos leave from the airport after plane arrivals and from near the AeroPeru or Faucett offices before departures and charge about 70c. Taxis cost about $2.

There are daily scheduled flights every morning to and from Lima via Cuzco with either AeroPeru or Faucett but these may be cancelled because of rain (the wet season is December to April, but cancellations are possible at other times), so allow some flexibility in your schedule. Flights to Lima cost about $97 and there is a $7 departure tax for nonresidents.

Grupo 8 (the military airline) has one flight a week to Iberia on Thursday and occasionally flies to Iñapari. (It is a 7-km walk from the Iñapari airstrip to the village.) Flights are subject to delay, cancellation or overbooking. Grupo 8 can be contacted at the Cuzco and Puerto Maldonado airports. If you want to fly, get to the airport early on the day of the flight and be persistent. The flight to Iberia costs about $15. Grupo 8 also has a flight to Lima most weeks which is cheaper than the commercial flight but very difficult to get on.

LASA has an office in Puerto Maldonado; you can charter a light aircraft to anywhere as long as you pay for five seats and the return trip. The office is often closed but you can try at the airport in the mornings.

Truck During the dry season, trucks to Cuzco leave from outside the Hotel Wilson (where the drivers sometimes stay). Although it's only about 500 km, the trip takes 3 days, depending on road and weather conditions, which indicates how rough the road is. A Peruvian road engineer I met in Chiclayo told me that this was undoubtedly Peru's worst road between two major towns. The journey costs roughly $10, though for a few dollars more, you can talk the driver into letting you ride in the cab if you don't want to stand up in the back. (See the Road to

Puerto Maldonado section in the Cuzco chapter.)

River Boat You can hire boats at the Madre de Dios ferry dock for local excursions or to take you downriver to the Bolivian border. It is difficult to find boats up the Madre de Dios (against the current) to Manu and, although it is possible to fly to Boca Manu on chartered light aircraft, this is more frequently done from Cuzco. Cuzco is a better place than Puerto Maldonado from which to reach Manu, so the national park is described near the end of the Cuzco chapter.

Occasionally, people reach Puerto Maldonado by boat from Manu (with the current) or from the Bolivian border, but transport is infrequent and irregular. Be prepared for long waits of several days or more.

AROUND PUERTO MALDONADO
Tours & Guides

A pleasant jungle lake, Lago Sandoval, is about 1½ hours away down the Madre de Dios. Half the trip is done by boat and the other half on foot. Bring your own food and water. For about $20 (several people can travel for this price), a boat will drop you at the beginning of the trail and pick you up later. The boatman will also guide you to the lake if you wish. If you're lucky, you may see caiman, turtles, exotic birds and perhaps other wildlife.

About 20 minutes before Lago Sandoval there is a cacao plantation, Fondo Concepción, which can be visited. In the nearby jungle, there is an abandoned steamship. Local guides will tell you that this is the boat of the rubber baron, Fitzcarraldo (the story is told in Werner Herzog's movie *Fitzcarraldo*). In fact, this boat has nothing to do with Fitzcarraldo, but it makes too good a story for guides to resist.

Various overnight trips can be undertaken. One is to Lago Valencia, just off the Madre de Dios about 60 km away, near the Bolivian border. At least 2 days are needed, though 3 or 4 days are suggested. This lake reportedly offers the region's best fishing as well as good bird watching and nature observation

(bring binoculars). There are trails into the jungle around the lake.

Between the Madre de Dios and Heath rivers (the latter forming the border between Peru and Bolivia), a 100,000-hectare reserve has been established – the Río Heath Pampas Sanctuary, known locally as Las Pampas. This is another good place for nature study.

Apart from fishing and nature trips, visits to beaches, Indian communities, and gold-panning areas can be made in the Lago Valencia/Las Pampas area. Most excursions involve camping or staying in simple thatched shelters, so bring a sleeping bag and hammock if you have them. Be prepared for muddy trails – two pairs of shoes are recommended, a dry pair for camp use and a pair which can get thoroughly wet and covered with mud. Insect repellent, sun protection and a means of purifying water are essential.

Various guides have been recommended. Señor Alberto Gombringer lives on Loreto, just off the Plaza de Armas towards the river. He has a huge, two-story hacienda near a lake, several hours down the Madre de Dios from where he organises excursions. Ask for him at El Danubio Azul Café on the Plaza de Armas, where you can also ask for other guides.

Señora Barbara Fearis is an American naturalist and photographer who has lived in the area since the 1970s. She spends about half the year here and knows the region very well. She will guide groups and can be contacted at El Danubio Azul or the Hotel de Turistas. Barbara, in turn, recommends the *motorista* (boatman) Victor Yarikawa, who lives out of town on Velarde. Go south-west on Velarde, past the Hotel de Turistas, over a bridge and past a brick kiln; his yellow, tin-roofed house is on your left. He is a good fisherman and his tours emphasise jungle foods.

Other recommended guides are Alberto Amachi, Arturo Balarezo (who lives near the Plaza de Armas), Benigno Diaz, Arturo Revilla and Victorio Suárez.

For trips to Lago Valencia or Las Pampas, it may be necessary to register with the *capitanía* or 'harbour master' in Puerto Maldonado; ask your motorista. There are control points near the Bolivian border, so carry your passport. It is normal to negotiate trip costs beforehand and to bargain hard. Roughly $30 to $40 per day seems to be the going rate. It is cheapest to go as a group because most boats will accommodate eight or more people with ease.

Jungle Canopy Trips

Until recently, biologists working in the rainforest made their observations and collected specimens from the forest floor and along the rivers, unaware that many plant and animal species spent their entire lives in the canopy. When scientists began to venture into the tree tops, they discovered so many new species that the canopy has become known as the new frontier of tropical biology. It is very difficult to visit the canopy unless you are a researcher, but it is possible for interested and adventurous travellers to climb to the top of the rainforest.

Ornithologist Paul Donahue has recently been involved in constructing platforms in the rainforest canopy, 100 metres above the ground These platforms are available to researchers, photographers and travellers. By making the canopy more accessible, it is hoped to draw attention to the value of the tropical rainforest habitat. It has been estimated that two-thirds of rainforest species live in the canopy – literally millions of species, most unknown to science. One way to slow the destruction of the rainforest is to make it a valuable cash resource as it stands. With access to the canopy, the rainforest will attract more tourist dollars and encourage countries with rainforests to preserve more of them.

Spending the day in the topmost branches of a giant tree gives a fascinating glimpse of the little-known canopy ecosystem. Reaching the platforms is strenuous, requires training in mountaineering-style techniques of rope ascent and is not for those afraid of heights. The platforms are simply a metal girder on which you sit, attached by a safety rope. Paul Donahue organises canopy trips, including training, for those with the stamina and interest. He spends half the year in the

USA and can be contacted at PO Box 554, Machias, Maine 04654, USA, (tel (207) 255 6542). His mail is forwarded to Peru when he is down there. In the past, he has constructed platforms at the Explorer's Inn and he is currently working with the Cuzco Amazonico Lodge and the Manu Lodge. He charges $25 per day of canopy sitting and supplies all necessary equipment. (The fee covers the cost of building the platforms and providing mountaineering equipment, which is expensive. You also have to pay the normal fees for use of the lodges.)

Places to Stay – jungle lodges

The area's three jungle lodges can only be reached by boat. Reservations should be made in Cuzco or Lima as it is difficult to contact the offices in Puerto Maldonado. Although 2-day and 1-night packages are available, I recommend a minimum stay of 3 days and 2 nights because the first and last day are geared to plane connections from Cuzco. This means that the last day usually involves departing after breakfast to catch the late-morning flight to Cuzco. Prices given here are per person for 3-day and 2-night packages in double-occupancy rooms. All prices should include transfers to and from Puerto Maldonado airport by vehicle to the river and by boat to the lodge, as well as meals, accommodation and some local tours. If it's the low season (December to April) or you are travelling as a group (usually five or more) or planning on a long stay, discounts can normally be arranged.

The closest lodge to Puerto Maldonado is the *Tambo Lodge*, 10 km downstream on the Madre de Dios River. It is the cheapest of the jungle lodges; 3 days and 2 nights cost $90 and extra days are $25. Being so close to Puerto Maldonado means that you won't see virgin jungle around the lodge; nevertheless, nearby walks and tours to Lake Sandoval or to gold-panning areas give the visitor a good look at jungle life. Reservations can be made in Cuzco (tel 222332), on the Plaza de Armas at Portal de Panes 109. In Puerto Maldonado, ask at El Danubio Azul.

Further down the Madre de Dios, about 15

km away from Puerto Maldonado, the more comfortable *Cuzco Amazonico Lodge* also offers local tours and perhaps a better look at the jungle. They charge $143 for 3 days and 2 nights but will offer discounts of up to 20% if you arrive at their Cuzco office and space is available (usually no problem). Reservations for the Cuzco Amazonico Lodge can be made at Andalucia 174, Lima (tel 462793) and at Procuradores 48, Cuzco (tel 232161).

My favourite lodge is the *Explorer's Inn*, 58 km from Puerto Maldonado on the Tambopata River. It takes 3 to 4 hours of river travel to reach the lodge, which is located in the protected 5500-hectare Tambopata Forest Reserve. The best chances of observing wildlife are here. The Tambopata Reserve holds the world record for bird species sighted in one area (over 540 species) and other similar records for plants and animals, including over 1100 butterflies. The 38 km of trails around the lodge can be explored by yourself or with guides. Naturalists are on hand to identify and explain the wildlife; most are field biologists involved in some kind of research and they can teach visitors a lot about jungle biology. Normally, several speak English.

Accommodation is in simple but comfortable bungalows with private (cold) showers – there is no electricity because the noise of the generators tends to frighten away wildlife. Trips lasting 3 days and 2 nights cost $150 (additional nights are $45) and stays of 7 days and 6 nights are good value at $270. There is a 10% discount in the low season and discounts for groups, biology students and members of the South American Explorers Club can be arranged. Reservations for the Explorer's Inn can be made at Garcilazo de la Vega 1334, Lima 1, Peru (tel 316330, 313047, telex 20416 PE SAFARI) and at Plaza San Francisco 122, Cuzco (tel 235342). The inn's Puerto Maldonado office is at Fitzcarrald 136.

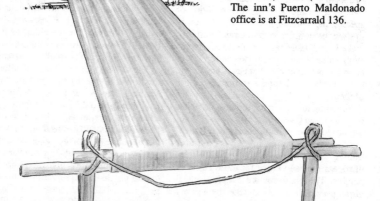

GOING TO BOLIVIA

You can hire a boat at the Madre de Dios dock to go to the Bolivian border at Puerto Pardo. The trip takes half a day and costs about $80 – the boat will carry several people. With time and luck, you may be able to find a cargo boat that's going there anyway and will take passengers more cheaply. It is possible to continue down the river on the Bolivian side, known as Puerto Heath, but this can take several days to arrange and is not cheap. It's best to travel in a group and share costs. Basic food and accommodation (bring a hammock or sleeping pad) can be found. Travellers should have their passports checked at the migraciónes office in Puerto Maldonado before leaving. I have received a report that the Bolivian border officials are unfriendly and demand bribes. From Puerto Heath, you can continue down the Madre de Dios as far as Riberalto in northern Bolivia, where road and air connections can be made.

GOING TO BRAZIL

A track to Iñapari, on the Brazilian border, is open but in very bad shape and I don't know of any vehicles taking this route. It is possible to get through on a motorcycle. You can reach the Iñapari road by crossing the Madre de Dios by ferry. Along the road, there are a few small settlements of people involved in the Brazil-nut industry. The road is merely bad for the first 100 km and absolutely terrible after that. After some 200 km, you reach Iberia, where there is a basic hotel. People in Puerto Maldonado told me that you can get to Iberia by motorcycle in 1 long day and I've read newspaper reports that a vehicle reached the town in 1982.

To go on to Iñapari, it's another 70 km by motorcycle or on foot. Few, if any, vehicles have done this section. The story here is 'Watch for snakes', which is a typical response to any question you have about travelling off the beaten track anywhere in the Amazon Basin.

From Iñapari, it is possible to cross the Río Acre to Assis in Brazil, but I've heard that the river must be waded. At Assis, you'll find a basic hotel and a dry season road to Brasiléia and Río Branco, but there is no regular transport. Travel along the Río Acre is possible. There is no immigration office in Iñapari; see the police instead. (More information on Brazilian visa and entry requirements is provided in the Iquitos section.) Let me know if you travel this way – it'll be worth a free LP book. And good luck!

You can also fly to Iberia or Iñapari with Grupo 8 and almost everyone heading to Brazil travels by air. The Iñapari airport is about 7 km from the village. Whatever you do, make sure you visit the migraciónes office in Puerto Maldonado before you leave.

LABERINTO

There is a bus service from Puerto Maldonado to the nearby gold-rush town of Laberinto ($1.30, 1½ hours). Buses leave several times during the morning from in front of the Hotel Wilson, supposedly at fixed times but usually not until they are full. Faster colectivo pick-ups also leave from here ($2, 1 hour). This is the only local bus journey you can take to see the countryside around Puerto Maldonado. You can leave in the morning and return in the afternoon, but don't miss the last bus as the one hotel in Laberinto is a real dive and usually full of drunk miners.

Laberinto itself is just a shanty town. However, you can take trips up and down the Madre de Dios River to various nearby communities, some of which are involved in gold panning. The miners come into Laberinto to sell their gold at the Banco de Minero. You may see buyers blow torching the gold to melt and purify it. If the bank runs out of money, the miners may barter their gold in exchange for gas, food and other supplies.

CHANCHAMAYO (La Merced, San Ramón)

The jungle region east of Lima which is most accessible from the capital is known as Chanchamayo and comprises the towns of La Merced and San Ramón. These towns are entry points for further excursions into the

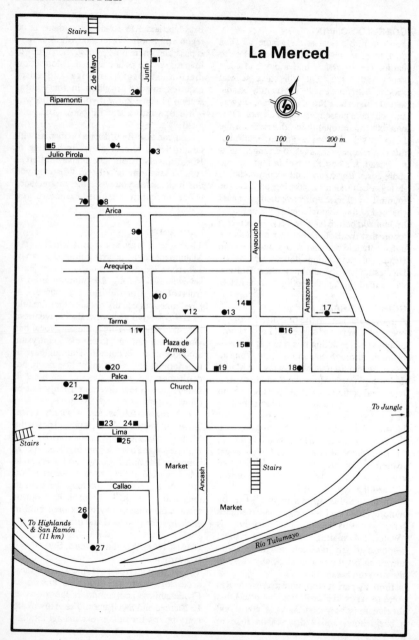

La Merced

jungle. San Ramón is about 300 km east of Lima and La Merced a further 11 km.

All buses to the region terminate in La Merced, the centre for ground transport in the region and the more important town. It has a population of over 10,000 and is a major coffee-marketing centre. La Merced has a greater choice of hotels and restaurants, though the region's best hotel is in the smaller and quieter San Ramón. Although less important, San Ramón boasts the regional airport nearby. The two towns are linked by frequent colectivos and locals consider them to be one unit.

La Merced is the centre for vehicles north to Oxapampa and Pozuzo, north-east to Puerto Bermudez and south-east to Satipo.

Information

Moneychanging is difficult in Chanchamayo, though you can try the Banco de Crédito. It is best to change money in Huancayo or Lima.

There is a colourful daily market in La Merced and the weekend market at San Luis de Shuaro, 22 km beyond La Merced, is interesting – local Indians visit it. You'll find a basic hotel here. Campa Indians occasionally come into La Merced to sell handicrafts.

Avenida Dos de Mayo is good for views of La Merced; the stairs at the north end afford a good view of the town, and from the balcony at the south end, there is a wonderful view of the river'– excellent for photography.

An interesting botanical garden is in the grounds of El Refugio Hotel in San Ramón.

Places to Stay

La Merced This is the most convenient place to stay if you are continuing on by road rather than by air. The town has several cheap, very basic hotels charging about $1 per person. They are not particularly clean and most have an erratic water supply, though you can always bathe in the river as the locals do. The cheapest places are the *Hostal Roca, Hostal TB Palermo, Hostal Básico Chuncho* and the *Hostal Básico San Felípe*. The last of these, at $1.40/2.25 for singles/doubles, is the most expensive of the cheap hotels, but none are very good.

Similar in price to the San Felípe but marginally better looking are the *Hostal Santa Rosa, Hostal Lima* and the *Gran Hotel*.

If you want something a little better than basic, try the *Hotel Cristina* at $2/3.20 for singles/doubles with bath. The *Hostal Mercedes* next door is similar and costs a few cents more. Unfortunately, both hotels are quite small and tend to be full.

The larger *Hotel Cosmos* charges $2.80/4.50 for clean singles/doubles with bath. The best hotel in La Merced is the *Hostal El Rey*, which provides towels, soap and toilet paper, though you must still put up with cold showers. There are telephones in the rooms and a top floor cafeteria serves good breakfasts. Climb onto the roof for a good view of the town. Rooms are $3.60/5.50.

San Ramón Most of San Ramón's hotels are clustered within a block of the intersection of Avenida Paucartambo and the main street, Avenida Progreso. The cheapest are the *Hotel Progreso* and *Hotel Colón*. The *Hotel Chanchamayo* is good value at about $1.75 per person in rooms with bath. More expensive but no better, the *Hostal de la Selva* charges $2.20/3.50 for singles/doubles. The *Hotel Conquistador* is a good hotel and worth the $4/6 for singles/doubles.

The best hotel in the Chanchamayo region is *El Refugio* (also known as the *Albergue de la Selva*), which is about a 10-minute walk from the town centre. The hotel grounds are also a small but well-laid out botanical garden. I was impressed by the owner's enthusiasm and pride in the garden – the various exotic plants are labelled and tend to attract butterflies and birds. Accommodation is in comfortable bungalows which even boast hot showers; rates are about $20 a double. There is a restaurant.

Places to Eat

The 'best' place in San Ramón is the *Tumi*, below the Hotel Chanchamayo. There are a few other chifas and cafeterias along the main street, none of which is especially noteworthy. Guests at *El Refugio* will do best to eat at the hotel.

La Merced has many more restaurants. The best is definitely the *Restaurant Shambari Campa*, down a little alley just off the main plaza, where meals are good and not very expensive. It serves both Chinese and Peruvian dishes. There is an outdoor area where you can dine under thatched roofs. You will also find several chicken restaurants and chifas; *Chifa Roberto Sui* on the plaza is OK.

Getting There & Away

Air The Chanchamayo airstrip is about 30-minutes walk from San Ramón. Colectivo taxis leave irregularly from the plaza but are not reliable. You can hire your own taxi for about $1.

The local airline, SASA, operates daily flights into the jungle. AeroPeru and Faucett do not fly into this airstrip. Although SASA has an office in San Ramón, it is rarely open and you are better off just turning up at the airport early (before 9 am) and waiting for a flight. Planes carry between five and nine passengers and leave as soon as they are full. There are flights to Puerto Bermudez ($15) on most days. There are also flights to other jungle villages on a less regular basis – staff at the airport can tell you when a plane may be leaving. The most frequent destinations are Atalaya, Satipo and Puerto Inca. If you are travelling in a group, you can charter your own plane to almost anywhere in the region (you can charter a plane by yourself, too, but you have to pay for the empty seats).

There is a simple cafeteria serving snacks and cold drinks, including beer.

Bus It is possible to find direct buses from Lima to Chanchamayo, but most travellers find it more convenient to break the journey at Tarma. The 70-km stretch from Tarma to San Ramón (at 850 metres above sea level) drops 2200 metres - it is worth trying to travel on this section in daylight hours for the views.

All buses to Lima via Tarma and La Oroya leave from La Merced. Companies which make the 10 to 12-hour journey are Expreso Lobato, Transportes Arellano, Transportes Los Andes and Transportes Chanchamayo. Fares vary from $5 to $7.

Expreso Lobato and ETUCSA charge about $2 for the 5-hour journey to Huancayo. Colectivo cars from Avenida Tarma at Amazonas are faster and charge about $3.

Transportes Andahuaylas run three buses a week on the long and gruelling route to Andahuaylas, though I haven't the faintest idea why anybody would want to go direct from La Merced to Andahuaylas.

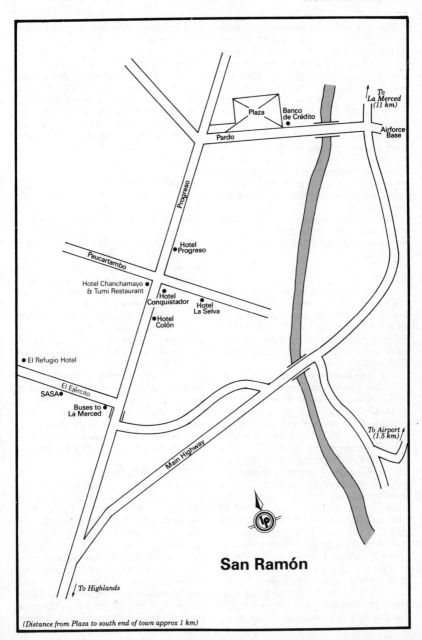

Plaza

Banco
de Crédito

To
La Merced
(11 km)

Pardo

Airforce
Base

Progreso

Hotel
Progreso

Paucartambo

Hotel Chanchamayo ●
& Tumi Restaurant

Hotel
Conquistador

Hotel
La Selva

Hotel
Colón

● El Refugio Hotel

El Ejército

SASA ●

Buses to
La Merced

Main Highway

To Airport
(1.5 km)

San Ramón

To Highlands

(Distance from Plaza to south end of town approx 1 km)

If you are looking for transport further into the jungle, go to the east end of Avenida Tarma where you'll find all kinds of trucks, cars, minibuses and jeeps. Larger buses don't travel on the narrow jungle roads. Minibuses will take you to Satipo ($4, 6 hours), Oxapampa ($3, 4 hours) and Puerto Bermudez ($5, 8 hours), as well as to intermediate towns such as San Luis de Shuaro en route to Oxapampa. Colectivo taxis are more expensive. Schedules are haphazard – go down there as early as you can and ask around. Sometimes, you can buy tickets the night before, but as things are generally disorganised, you may have to rely on luck and persuasiveness.

Turismo Chanchamayo (not Transportes Chanchamayo) has frequent minibuses between La Merced and San Ramón; fares are about 15c.

SATIPO

This small jungle town lies about 130 km by road south-east of La Merced. Satipo is the centre of a small fruit-producing region but its main claim to fame at this time is as the southernmost town on the Carretera Marginal de la Selva (the Marginal Jungle Highway).

This huge road project was devised by the Peruvian architect and president for two terms, Señor Fernando Belaúnde Terry. Belaúnde's dream was to open up the Amazon Basin, not by a road cutting across it but by a road encircling the entire western boundary of the Amazon Basin. The scheme called for a road beginning in Asunción, the capital of Paraguay, and going through the jungle lowlands of Bolivia, Peru, Ecuador and Colombia before terminating at the Caribbean near Caracas, the capital of Venezuela. Only relatively small sections of this highway have been built and it is unlikely that the project will ever be completed. The section from Satipo to La Merced is fairly well established but further north, there are long breaks in the highway.

Satipo is also linked by road to the highlands of Huancayo and a round trip is possible by public transport. Although the scenery is spectacular, the trip is rarely made by foreigners.

Places to Stay

For such an isolated little town, Satipo has a surprising number of hotels. The best is the Hotel Majestic, at Plaza Principal 408, where a double room with bath costs $6. For about half that price, you can get a room with bath at the Hostal Palermo at Manuel Prado 228. There are several other cheap and basic hotels.

OXAPAMPA

About 75 km north of La Merced is the ranching and coffee centre of Oxapampa. It used to be important for logging but most of the trees have now been cut down. Look around at your fellow passengers on the bus north from La Merced – you'll see some blonde heads and blue eyes. This is because several hundred German settlers arrived in the area in the mid-1800s. Their descendants live in Oxapampa or in Pozuzo, about 4 hours north of Oxapampa by daily minibus, and have preserved many Germanic customs; buildings have a Tyrolean look to them, Austrian-German food is prepared and an old-fashioned form of German is still spoken by some families. Although the area has been settled for over 100 years, it is still remote and rarely visited. The people are friendly and interested in talking with tourists. Both towns have simple hotels; the Bolívar is the best in Oxapampa and the Tirol the best in Pozuzo. It's an interesting trip.

PUERTO BERMUDEZ

Puerto Bermudez is a sleepy port on the Río Piches about 9 hours north-east of La Merced by bus. Looking at the huddle of dugout canoes tied up to the mud bank of the small river flowing past the town, it is difficult to imagine that one could embark here on a river journey which would eventually lead down the Amazon to the Atlantic. Until recently, this was the only way to continue past Puerto Bermudez but, in the mid-1980s, the new Carretera Marginal de la Selva was opened as far as Pucallpa. I thought it would be interesting to travel this new section of road and see how Peru is opening up its frontier.

Places to Stay & Eat

Two basic hotels right by the river, the *Hotel Tania* and the *Hotel Prusia*, provide a bed, four walls and a river view. Both charge about 70c per person and you get what you pay for. At least the river view is pretty, especially at dawn and dusk. If these places are full, there are a couple of other even more basic hotels a few streets away from the river. The town has one main street, on which you'll find places to eat.

CIUDAD CONSTITUCIÓN

Constitution City is a recently conceived major town which is to be built in the middle of the jungle along a particularly unpopulated stretch of the new highway. Schools, a hospital, a cathedral, political offices and many blocks of streets with shops and housing have all been mapped out and an area of the jungle has been cleared. That's about as far as the project had gone when President Belaúnde's second term of office came to a close. Now, with a new president and different political priorities, it is entirely possible that Ciudad Constitución will remain a forgotten and fly-blown huddle of huts on the Río Palcazu with the new road passing by 1 km away.

Although the road has been pushed as far as Ciudad Constitución, only heavy trucks and road-building equipment were able to get through when I did the trip. (I have heard that pick-up trucks are doing it now.) At Puerto Bermudez, I found someone heading down the Río Piches to Constitución who gave me a ride in his peki-peki. The journey cost $5, took 7 hours and was much more pleasant than grinding over the newly churned mud of the highway. If you're lucky, you might be able to find a boat with an outboard motor which will do the trip in about 4 hours. From the point where the boat drops you off to the huts which comprise the 'town' is a walk of 2 or 3 km.

The only place to stay is a hut with mud floors and no locks on room doors. There is a small store where cold drinks and a simple meal are available.

THE NEW ROAD TO PUCALLPA

On most days, there is one vehicle from Pucallpa which gets to Constitución late in the morning and turns around after a quick lunch stop. The return trip takes about 7 hours and costs $5. This section of the new highway is, for the most part, gravelled and in reasonable shape. You'll pass occasional small communities and the closer you get to Pucallpa, the more open the country becomes, a sign of the logging followed by ranching which is typical of the opening up of the Peruvian rainforest.

About 1½ hours beyond Ciudad Constitución, where a small river is crossed by raft, is the village of Zungaro. Here, you'll find a basic hotel and restaurant. From Zungaro, there are both road and river communications with Puerto Inca on the Río Pachitea, about 10 km away. During the wet season, the road is often closed and, during the dry season, the river between Zungaro and Puerto Inca is too low, so ask around for the best way to go. At Puerto Inca, ask for Don José, an old Czech gentleman who has lived in the area for many years and who is a great source of local information. He is something of a local identity and owns a simple hostal pleasantly situated on the river.

Beyond Zungaro, the scenery is all forest for about an hour, but this soon gives way to ranch land and small homesteads. Alternatively, you can travel to Pucallpa by boat from Puerto Inca.

PUCALLPA

With a population approaching 100,000, Pucallpa is Peru's fastest growing jungle town and the biggest to be linked directly with Lima by road. Until 1980, it played second fiddle to Iquitos, capital of the huge Department of Loreto. Since 1980, a new department has been formed and Pucallpa is now experiencing political and economic growth as the capital of the new Department of Ucayali.

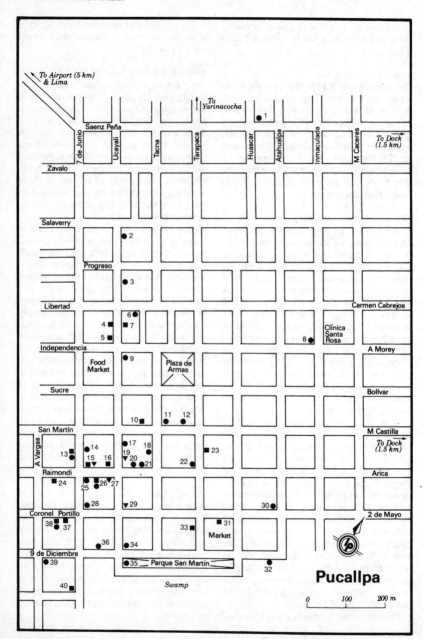

To Airport (5 km)
& Lima

To Yarinacocha

Saenz Peña

7 de Junio
Ucayali
Tacna
Tarapaca
Huascar
Atahualpa
Inmaculada
M Caceres

To Dock
(1.5 km)

● 1

Zavalo

Salaverry

● 2

Progreso

● 3

Libertad

Carmen Cabrejos

● 6
4 ■   ● 7
5 ■

Clínica
Santa
Rosa

8 ●

Independencia

A Morey

Food
Market

● 9

Plaza de
Armas

Sucre

Bolívar

10 ■

11 ●   12 ●

San Martín

M Castilla

To Dock
(1.5 km)

A Vargas

13 ●

● 14
15 ■   16 ■

17 ●   18 ●
19 ●
▼ 20
21 ●

22 ●

■ 23

Raimondi

Arica

■ 24

25 ●   ● 26 ▼ 27

28 ●

▼ 29

30 ●

2 de Mayo

Coronel   Portillo

38 ■   ● 37

36 ●

34 ●

33 ■

■ 31
Market

9 de Diciembre

● 39

● 35 — Parque San Martín

32 ●

Pucallpa

40 ■

Swamp

0   100   200 m

■ PLACES TO STAY

4	Hotel Komby
5	Hostal Sun
7	Hostal Donita
10	Hotel de Turistas
13	Hostal Excelsior
15	Hostal Residencial Barbtur
16	Hotel Mercedes
23	New Hotel
24	Hostal Toriri & Hospedaje Mori
26	Hostal Peru
31	Hostal Alex & Hotel America
33	Hostal TB Ucayali
37	Hostal Amazonia
38	Hostal Confort
40	Hostal Europa

▼ PLACES TO EAT

15	Chifa Hong Kong & Restaurant Raymondi
19	Don José 1 Restaurant
27	Don José 2 Restaurant & Pizza Restaurant
29	Cafeteria Restaurant Roma

● OTHER

1	FOPTUR Tourist Office
2	ENTEL
3	Empresa Sol de Oriente (Bus)
6	Cine Ucayali
8	Grupo 8 Airline
9	PIP Police
11	Banco de la Nación
12	Post Office
13	Transportes Ucayali (Bus)
14	Faucett Airline
17	Cine Rex
18	Transportes Arellano (Bus)
20	AeroPeru
21	ETPOSA (Bus)
22	Banco de Crédito
25	TEPSA (Bus)
26	Motorcycle Hire
28	Shop & Money Exchange
30	Comité 6 to Yarinacocha
32	La Capitanía
34	Guardia Civil
35	Clock Tower
36	SASA Airline
38	Various Travel Agencies
39	León de Huánuco (Bus)

Despite a few pleasant modern buildings, such as the Hotel de Turistas, Pucallpa is not a particularly attractive city. Many of its buildings have been hastily constructed in concrete with tin roofs. Its roads are slowly being paved but many of those away from the centre are still red-mud quagmires in the wet season and choking dust in the dry. The huge flocks of vultures lazily circling over the markets, plazas and dock areas are one of Pucallpa's most startling sights. The roofs of the buildings around the food market are often crowded with scores of the huge black birds silently waiting for scraps to be thrown out.

Pucallpa has a palpable feeling of civic pride, progress and growth. This is more than just another sleepy jungle port; this is Peruvians working to make Peru work. Nevertheless, after feeling the pulse of the city and watching the languid flapping of the vultures, the visitor is not left with much to do.

Those leaving town have two good choices. One is to take the short bus trip to nearby Yarinacocha, a lovely oxbow lake where you can go canoeing, observe wildlife, visit Indian communities and purchase their handicrafts and stay in pleasantly rustic, lakeside jungle lodges. Yarinacocha is the tourist area of Pucallpa, yet it is far from touristy – hotel, restaurant and boat services are provided in a casual, easy-going atmosphere. It's worth spending a couple of days here. (There is a full description after the Pucallpa section.) When you are ready to move on, go down to the Pucallpa docks to find a river boat heading down to Iquitos; while you're looking, you can experience at first hand the rough-and-tumble atmosphere of a busy, hard-working river port.

Information
Warning
The Sendero made its presence strongly felt in Pucallpa during 1989. The mayor and many farmers were killed in a shoot-out with police. A few gringos, including a tourist,

have reportedly been shot and tourism in the Pucallpa area has declined drastically. There have been Sendero patrols in the town streets during daylight. The overland bus trip from Lima is definitely not recommended and the jungle trip from La Merced, as described earlier in this chapter, may be dangerous – ask locally before attempting it. It is safest to visit Pucallpa by air, but if you want to continue to Iquitos or elsewhere by river, make sure you aren't on a drug-running boat. The Sendero and drug-trafficking situation is a changeable one, so stay informed.

This section is based mainly on information gathered prior to the 1989 problems.

Tourist Information The FOPTUR tourist office (tel 5008) is at Sáenz Peña 298.

Money Cash dollars and travellers' cheques can be changed at the Banco de Crédito for a 1% commission. Recent reports indicate that the Banco Continental gives better rates but I haven't been able to verify this. Some stores also change money; one is marked on the Pucallpa map. The better hotels and the airlines normally change money for their clients; make sure they give you the favourable financial rate and not the unfavourable official rate.

Pronunciation Just as you've become used to remembering that 'll' is always pronounced 'y' in Spanish, you come to one of the very few exceptions to this rule. Pucallpa is pronounced 'pukalpa'.

Medical The Clínica Santa Rosa on A Morey is quite good for stool, urine or blood tests if you get sick.

Travel Agencies & Guides There are several travel agencies on Portillo near 7 de Junio but for jungle-trip guides, go to Yarinacocha - there are fewer middlemen. By trying different travel agencies, you may be able to get the lower (resident) air fare out of Pucallpa.

Of the guides in Pucallpa, Marco Antonio Menendez is knowledgeable and honest.

You can find him by asking at the Hotel Mercedes or by writing to Apartado 83, Pucallpa, Ucayali. Also recommended is the English-speaking botanist Francesco Montes Shuna, who runs a small but well-labelled botanical garden just off Yarinacocha. He lives at Sanchez Cerro 465 (head north-west on the Yarinacocha road until you reach Sanchez Cerro, about the 7th block on your right; the last few blocks cannot be reached by car). You can also contact him c/o Lenin Mera Rengifo at Elmo Tours (tel 6798), 7 de Junio 767.

Motorcycle Hire A couple of places (including one at Raimondi 654, near the Hostal Peru) hire motorcycles for about $2 per hour – bargain for a discount if you are renting for several hours.

Other The Plaza de Armas isn't up to much – the intersection of Raimondi and Ucayali is considered to be the town centre. There are a couple of cinemas which occasionally show English-language films.

Places to Stay

Hotels are often full by early afternoon, so start looking as soon as you arrive. Many travellers prefer to stay at Yarinacocha, though it has fewer hotels.

Places to Stay – bottom end

The cheapest hotel in town, though often full, is the *Hostal Donita*. It charges 75c/$1 for singles/doubles but it's not very clean and cannot be recommended.

Several hotels charge $1/1.70 for singles/doubles. The *Hostal Europa* used to be popular with budget travellers but is now dirty, run down and unsafe. Other cheapies in ascending order of appearance are the *Hostal Alex, Hostal TB Ucayali, Hostal Excelsior* and *Hospedaje Mori*, none of which are particularly recommended. The best of the cheap hotels are the small, friendly *Hostal Residencial Barbtur* and the basic *Hostal Peru*. The Peru also has some triples and rooms with bath for an extra 50c, and as it has more rooms than the other hotels, you stand a better chance of getting a bed here if you arrive late. Otherwise, it's not particularly recommended and the water supply is erratic.

Places to Stay – middle

The *Hostal Sun* is clean and charges $2.30/3.70 for singles/doubles with bath. Similarly priced are the *Hostal Confort* and *Hostal Amazonia*, which are both OK. The *Hotel America* charges about $3 per person and is quite good, while the *Hostal Toriri* charges $4/6.50 for singles/doubles with bath and has a reasonable restaurant. A new hotel was opening when I was last in town – it's marked on the Pucallpa map and looks as though it will be in this price range.

Two hotels, both recommended, charge $6/10 for singles/doubles with bath. Both boast a swimming pool. The central *Hotel Mercedes* was Pucallpa's first good hotel and has a certain dated charm and character. A few blocks away is the *Hotel Komby*.

Places to Stay – top end

The modern, government-run *Hotel de Turistas* (tel 6381) in the city centre, has a swimming pool, bar, restaurant and rooms with telephones. Singles/doubles with bath cost $12/15, including continental breakfast. Reservations can be made through ENTURPeru in Lima (tel 721928). The *Hotel Inambu* is good; it is similarly priced and has air-conditioning.

Places to Eat

As Pucallpa is usually hot, places to drink are as important as places to eat. For a huge variety of cold, freshly squeezed fruit juices, *Don José's* is the best place in town. There are two locations, called simply *Don José 1 & 2* (1 is marginally cheaper). As well as their excellent juices, they serve a wide variety of good, reasonably priced meals. The heat in the middle of the day means that restaurants tend to open early (by 7 am) for breakfast. If you want a change, you'll find several slightly cheaper restaurants marked on the Pucallpa map, but I always ended up eating at Don José's. The *Chifa Hong Kong*

is quite good and not expensive. The better hotels have decent, if not particularly cheap, restaurants.

The local beer, San Juan, has the distinction of being the only beer brewed in the Amazon – whether that is the entire Amazon or just the Peruvian Amazon is open to discussion. At any rate, because it is brewed locally, it is cheaper than the coastal beers and, for a light bottled beer, it is good and refreshing.

If you want to splash out a little, go to *El Establo* steak house; it's out of town on the road to the airport (take a taxi) and serves the best steaks in town.

Getting There & Away

Air Pucallpa's airport is small but busy. Faucett and AeroPeru both have offices in the city centre and at the airport, and between them, provide a daily service to Iquitos and Lima ($50 one way). Services to jungle towns other than Iquitos are provided but schedules change frequently.

SASA has an office in Pucallpa but it is frequently closed and you're better off asking about their services at the airport. They have fairly frequent flights to Atalaya and services to places like San Ramón less often – you'll have to ask. They also have irregular flights to Cruzeiro do Sul in Brazil but this service is not very reliable.

Grupo 8 (also called TANS) is the military airline and provides occasional services to Lima and Iquitos. However, as their city office is often closed and flights are not much cheaper than the commercial airlines, it's generally not worth the hassle. TANS and Alas del Oriente also have a float-plane service from Puerto Callao in Yarinacocha. It usually leaves on Saturday mornings and goes down the Ucayali to Iquitos, stopping off at various river ports along the way. This service is always full and preference is given to locals. However, if you get down to the float plane dock very early on a Saturday morning and sign onto the waiting list, you might (with a good deal of luck and persistence) get a seat. It would be an interesting trip.

Bus The easiest way to get to Pucallpa is on one of the daily flights from Lima or Iquitos but it is much more interesting to travel overland. Unfortunately, the overland journey is dangerous because of guerilla and drug-trafficking activity and is not recommended at this time. The following description was written before the current problems and is being retained in the hope that the situation will improve.

A direct bus from Lima takes about 24 hours but you can break the journey in several places; Huánuco and Tingo María are the best of these. A journey from coastal Lima takes you up the steep western slopes of the Andes to a breathless 4843 metres above sea level, continues along the Andes at an average of over 4000 metres for several hours, then begins the dizzying descent down the cloud-forested slopes of the eastern Andes to Pucallpa at a mere 154 metres. This incredible change of scenery and altitude gives the traveller an exceptional look at Peru in cross section and is one of the continent's most exciting and demanding 24-hour intercity bus journeys.

The journey as far as Tingo María is described in the Central Peru chapter. From Tingo, the road climbs over a final pass in the eastern Andes before descending to Pucallpa in the Amazon Basin proper. There is an interesting story connected with building the road over this pass. Until the 1930s,

the road reached only as far as Huánuco and engineers were carrying out surveys to assess the easiest route for the road on to Pucallpa. They were unable to find an obvious pass over the last range of the Andes and were preparing for an expensive road-building project. One of the engineers had been studying historical documents and maps of the region, some of which had been made as long ago as the 1700s by Franciscan missionaries exploring the area. One document, recounting a 1757 expedition by Father Abad, led to the rediscovery of an extremely narrow, steep-walled gorge through the final mountain barrier. The road was built through this pass, saving much time and money, and reached Pucallpa in 1941. The pass is now named after Padre Abad.

Driving through the pass is spectacular and should be done in daylight. Exotic vegetation clings to waterfall-covered vertical walls and there are several natural pools where it is possible to swim. The bird life is prolific and the careful observer may see troops of monkeys scurrying along the cliff ledges.

Unfortunately, public transport only takes you through the pass; it's not a destination. Ideally, you could take a Tingo to Pucallpa bus and get off at the pass, walk through it (it's about a 4-km walk along the road) and flag down a later bus. Otherwise, you'll have

to be content with tantalising glimpses through the bus windows.

Although the bus trip between Pucallpa and Lima is supposed to take 24 hours, it can take 2 or 3 days during the rainy months (especially January to April) if the road has been closed by mud slides. During the rest of the year, TEPSA usually provides the best service and has been known to do the trip in 20 hours. They charge just under $10 and leave two or three times a day. Other companies are cheaper but slower; these include ETPOSA and León de Huánuco. The last mentioned also operates three buses a week on the gruelling 2-day route to Tarapoto ($11). Intermediate towns are also serviced by these companies. Empresa Sol de Oriente only goes as far as Tingo María, while Transportes Ucayali has a daily bus to Huancayo ($8).

Some maps show roads continuing east of Pucallpa to Cruzeiro do Sul in Brazil. This is wishful thinking in the extreme because there is not even a jeep track part of the way there. Absolutely nothing. Japanese lumber importers are making an effort to get this road built so they can import Amazonian timber from Brazil more cheaply. Environmentalists are concerned that this will contribute drastically to the felling of the Amazon rainforest, which is already out of control.

River Boat Pucallpa's port, called La Hoyada, is about 2½ km north-east of the town centre along unpaved roads. You can get river boats along the Río Ucayali from here to Iquitos, (5 days, $30). It's much easier to get a passage when the river is high - towards the end of the dry season (July to November), the river is too low for many of the boats. Finding a boat to the ports of Contamana and Requena is not difficult. However, accommodation is hard to find in Contamana (though you can stay with local families) and onward passage is no more frequent than from Pucallpa. Requena, on the other hand, has a couple of very basic hotels and boats to Iquitos leave on most days, taking about 12 hours. Locals in the small villages along the river are often helpful and friendly.

Because air fares are not much more expensive than river boats fares, there are fewer passenger boats than there used to be and travel conditions are rough. Food is provided but it is very basic and travellers often get sick – bring some of your own food. Hammocks and mosquito repellent are essential but not provided. The capitanía should be able to provide you with a list of boats and their destinations, though their information is rarely reliable until after the boat has gone! Passengers from Pucallpa to Iquitos normally need to have their passport inspected by both the PIP and the Capitanía before beginning the trip. If you are heading on to Brazil, it is more convenient to fly as far as Iquitos and then begin your river journey from there.

Jungle 'guides' approaching you on the Pucallpa waterfront are usually unreliable and sometimes dishonest. There isn't much to do in the way of jungle trips from the dock anyway. If you want to make an excursion into the jungle, you should look for a reliable service in Yarinacocha. For a river-boat passage, ask on any likely looking boat but don't hand over any money until you and your luggage are actually aboard the boat of your choice. Then pay the captain and no one else.

Don't wander around the docks with your luggage looking for a boat; arrange a trip, then return with your luggage. Boats are sometimes delayed for some days before the cargo is loaded but captains will often let you sling your hammock and stay aboard at no extra cost while you wait for departure. Be aware of the danger of theft in the La Hoyada dock area and the fact that drug-running boats leave from here, too.

Getting Around

Comité 6 (green) leaves for Yarinacocha from the corner of Atahualpa and Dos de Mayo. There are several buses an hour and the fare is 10c for the 30-minute trip. Comité 1 goes north-west along Ucayali to the airport (10c, 20 minutes). Taxis will take you to the airport for about $1 and to Yarinacocha for about $2 but you'll probably have to bargain.

YARINACOCHA
Yarinacocha lies about 10 km north-east of Pucallpa. This attractive oxbow lake, once part of the Ucayali River, is now entirely landlocked, though a small canal links the two bodies of water during the rainy season. The road from Pucallpa goes to the small port of Puerto Callao, which is the main population centre on the lake. Here, there are two cheap hotels, a more expensive jungle lodge, plenty of bars and restaurants and boats for trips around the lake. You can visit Shipibo Indian villages and buy handicrafts or watch for wildlife in and around the lake. My wife and I have seen freshwater dolphins in the lake, a sloth and a metre-long green iguana in the trees around the lake and plenty of exotic birds, ranging from the curiously long-toed wattled jacana, which walks on lily pads and other floating vegetation, to the metallic green flash of the Amazon kingfisher.

Information
Warning The political and drug-trafficking problems mentioned earlier have spread to Yarinacocha, causing the closure of tourist lodges and a decline in tourism. Make local inquiries about the current situation.

Money With persistence, you can change money here but don't expect favourable rates. Take the short bus ride into Pucallpa for much better facilities.

The Shipibo Indians
The Shipibo Indians live along the Ucayali and its tributaries in small villages of simple, thatched platform houses. They are a matriarchal society. San Francisco, at the

Left: Children at Jankapampa, below Nevado Taulliraju (5830 m), Cordillera Blanca (RR)
Right: Laguna Cullicocha (4625 m) below Nevado Santa Cruz (6259 m), Cordillera Blanca (RR)
Bottom: Unknown ruins below Nevado Alpamayo (5947 m), Cordillera Blanca (RR)

Top: Author trekking by Huascarán (6768 m), Cordillera Blanca (RR)
Bottom: Keystone head at Chavín (RR)

north-west end of the lake, is one village which is often visited.

The Shipibo women make fine ceramics and textiles decorated with highly distinctive, geometric designs. Some of the women come into Pucallpa to sell their pottery and material but it is easy enough to buy direct from their villages. The Shipibo are also involved in a very fine cooperative craft store which collects work from about 40 villages. The store, called Maroti Shobo, is on the main plaza of Puerto Callao. Here, there are literally thousands of ceramics to choose from, and because each piece is hand made, it can be considered unique. Lengths of decorated cloth and other handicrafts are also available but it is the ceramics which make the place really worth while. The pieces range from small pots and animal figurines to huge urns. The friendly, helpful staff will arrange international shipping if you buy a large piece. Prices are fixed (no bargaining) but I found them very fair. I was also impressed by the easy-going noncommercial ambience of the place. Although it is a well-run business, no one breathes down your neck and it is a delight to just browse. I have a really soft spot for Maroti Shobo – I bought my favourite South American handicraft here and every time I look at my sensitively moulded, two-headed, ceremonial drinking pot, I am reminded of Peru.

Tours

Whether your interest lies in bird watching, photography, visiting Indian villages or just relaxing on a boat ride around the lake, you'll find plenty of peki-peki boat owners ready to oblige. Take your time in choosing; there's no point in going with the first offer unless you are sure you like your boatman. Ask around and be aware that some boatmen are dishonest and may be involved in drug trafficking. A boatman for the trip to San Francisco and back might charge less than $10, while a guide who goes with you and shows you around will charge twice as much. It is always worth bargaining over the price but the best way to do it is to set a price for the boat and then ask the boatman if you can

bring a couple of friends. As long as there are only two or three of you, they don't normally complain and you can split the cost. Guides are also available for walking trips into the surrounding forest, including some overnight trips. Recommended guides include Daniel Saavedra, Thierry Giles and the García family.

A good afternoon trip is up the north-east arm of the lake (to your right as you look at the lake from Puerto Callao). Ask the boatman to float slowly along and look for bird life at the water's edge or sloths (*perezoso*) in the trees. Sunset is a good time to be on the lake. A day trip up the north-western arm is a good way to visit San Francisco and perhaps another Shipibo village. Fishing trips can also be organised.

The Mission

There is a large, modern American missionary base on the outskirts of Puerto Callao which is affiliated to the SIL (Summer Institute of Linguistics). The missionaries have made contact with various Amazonian tribes and work to translate the Indian languages into English and Spanish. By making a workable alphabet for these previously unwritten languages, the missionaries hope to translate the New Testament into the area's many different Indian languages.

I realise that to the unsympathetic ear this work sounds like proselytising and may represent unacceptable meddling in traditional societies. Many people think that whether you are a missionary, oil prospector, tourist or logger, the end result for the Indians tends to be disease, starvation, misunderstanding and lack of care. This is not always true, however, and I feel that the Summer Institute of Linguistics does have a genuine concern for the people they work with and are involved in meeting physical needs, such as improved living conditions and basic medical and schooling facilities, as well as with facilitating the acceptance of the Indians into the Peruvian system. It may be unrealistic to hope that in today's world, the Indian tribes can be totally left alone to continue traditional ways of life unchanged. I believe that missions like the SIL, though far from ideal, do more good than harm for the Indians in the long run and their approach certainly seems more practical than any other proposed solution to the 'Indian problem'.

Isolation is an ideal solution but the modern world is incapable of allowing it. Asking a poor Third World country to leave its oil-rich areas undisturbed so that the Indians can continue their traditional way of life creates difficulties – the other citizens of the country want to improve their lot too. Idealism cannot work while slum dwellers starve in cities which could be improved by revenue from the jungle development of oil and other resources. The traditional approach has been (and in some remote areas apparently continues to be) a policy of wiping out the Indian tribes standing in the way of progress. This cannot be condoned. The only viable alternative seems to be a gradual integration and the Summer Institute of Linguistics seems closer than others to achieving this.

Places to Stay – bottom end

Travellers arriving on Comité 6 from Pucallpa can choose from two hotels within a block of the terminus. The *Hotel El Pescador*, at $1.50/2.50 for singles/doubles, is the cheapest place to stay. Its main attraction is its waterfront location; otherwise it's a pretty basic hotel with an erratic water supply in bathrooms which are none too clean.

If you turn left from the bus terminus, a short dirt road leads to the *Hostal El Delfin*, which is not visible until you reach it. Rooms here are better and only a little more expensive than those at El Pescador. Some have a private bath, though they're not up to much. El Delfin is full more often than the El Pescador. By asking around, you can sometimes find a room in a private home.

Places to Stay – top end

There used to be several jungle lodges around the lake but terrorist problems have closed all but the Swiss-run *La Cabaña*, a 15-minute peki-peki ride across the lake

from Puerto Callao. The owner also runs the *Mercedes* in Pucallpa, so you can make inquiries there. The lodge is good, quiet, has a restaurant and charges $16/26/32 for singles/doubles/triples with bath.

Places to Eat

Several inexpensive restaurants and lively bars line the Puerto Callao waterfront – just wander around until you find one that seems OK.

YURIMAGUAS

Locals call Yurimaguas 'the pearl of the Huallaga'. It is the major port on the Río Huallaga and boats to Iquitos can be found here. Reaching Yurimaguas can involve a long, adventurous road trip of several days (see Across the Northern Highlands) or a simple flight from Lima. With a population of about 25,000, Yurimaguas is a quiet, pleasant little town, quite different from the bustling boom-town atmosphere of Pucallpa. There are signs of the rubber-boom days, such as the expensive imported tiles which decorate the walls of the buildings at the end of Avenida Arica, but generally, it is a sleepy port where you may have to wait a week or more for a river boat to Iquitos. Bring a couple of good books.

Again, however, guerilla activity has been reported. Make local inquiries before visiting the town.

Information

The Consejo Regional on the Plaza de Armas can give tourist information. The Banco Amazonico used to be the best place to change cash dollars and travellers' cheques but, recently, only the Interbanc was changing money and that at poor rates. There are a couple of cinemas where English-language films are sometimes shown.

Places to Stay

My favourite is the *Cheraton Hotel*. (The hotel has recently been renamed *Leo's Palace*, but locals still call it the Cheraton.) It has a few simple but spacious rooms with bath and a balcony overlooking the Plaza de

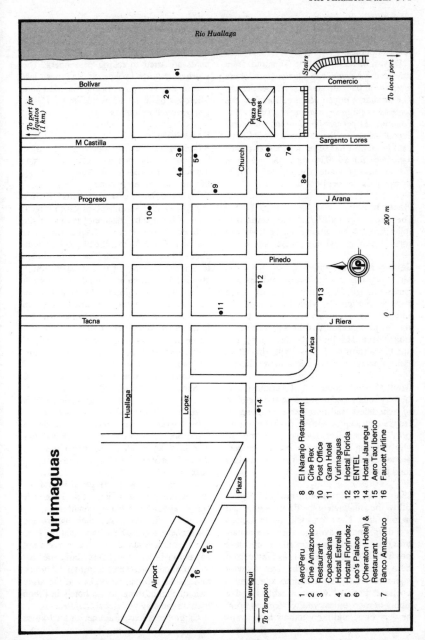

Yurimaguas

1 AeroPeru
2 Cine Amazonico
3 Restaurant Copacabana
4 Hostal Estrella
5 Hostal Florindez
6 Leo's Palace (Cheraton Hotel) & Restaurant
7 Banco Amazonico
8 El Naranjo Restaurant
9 Cine Rex
10 Post Office
11 Gran Hotel
12 Hostal Florida
13 ENTEL
14 Hostal Jauregui
15 Aero Taxi Iberico
16 Faucett Airline

Armas, though not all the rooms are this good. The hotel charges about $2/3 for singles/doubles.

Drivers heading back to Tarapoto often stay at the *Gran Hotel Yurimaguas* where rooms with bath are about $1.75 per person. The similarly priced *Hostal Florindez* has some air-conditioned rooms for an extra 50c. For about $1 per person in rooms with communal baths, try the recommended *Hostal Estrella*; it now has some new double rooms with bath for $4. The basic but adequate *Hostal Jauregui* and the *Hostal Florida* charge about $1 per person.

Places to Eat
The *Copacabana, El Naranjo Restaurant* and *Cheraton* are among the best, though none of them is anything special.

Getting There & Away
Air Faucett and AeroPeru schedules and routes change frequently. Recently, there were three flights a week to Lima ($77). Some flights to Lima go via Tarapoto, others via Trujillo and still others continue to Iquitos. Aero Taxi Iberico has an office opposite the airport and flies light aircraft to various nearby towns – ask at their office.

Truck The only route out of Yurimaguas is the very rough road to Tarapoto and there are no scheduled transport services along it. Trucks and jeeps do leave for Tarapoto on most days, however, and you can find out who is going by asking in hotels and restaurants. The Gran Hotel Yurimaguas is a good place to start.

River Boat Cargo boats from Yurimaguas follow the Huallaga to the Río Marañón and on to Iquitos. The trip usually takes about 3 to 5 days, and on average, there are departures once a week. Passages should cost less than $20. Boat information is available from the Agencia Fluviales, by the river. As with other river trips, bring a hammock, mosquito repellent, purified water or tablets and a supply of food, unless you're prepared to eat the very basic and monotonous food avail-

able on board. Because Yurimaguas has fewer air and road services than Pucallpa, the river link is more important and the cargo boats are used to taking passengers. The journey can be broken at Lagunas, just before the Huallaga meets the Marañón. There is a basic hotel here and onward boats can be found to Iquitos.

SARAMERIZA
Sarameriza is a tiny port on the upper Marañón and the most westerly point to start a river journey down the Amazon, though this trip is very rarely done.

To get to Sarameriza (or Puerto Delfus, a few km away), you must first get to Bagua, on the Chiclayo to Chachapoyas route in the northern Andes. Beyond Bagua, the going gets rough. Trucks travel daily to Nazareth, about 80 km to the north-east, and continue to Imazita (where there is a basic hotel), about 30 km further on. Your documents will be checked at a police checkpoint about halfway between the two towns. Bear in mind that, as you are close to the disputed Ecuadorian border here, police may be sensitive to anyone wearing a 'Galápagos' T-shirt or even to the presence of an Ecuadorian stamp in a passport.

From the checkpoint, a road branches off to Sarameriza, about 150 km to the north-east. This road is in very bad shape and you have to hitch a ride (expect to pay) on any vehicle which comes along. Vehicles do the trip about two or three times a week and may take days, depending on the state of the road. Be self-sufficient with food and sleeping gear.

Alternatively, you can get a boat from Imazita along the Marañón to Santa María de Nieve (about $6, 8 hours, departures every few days). The river is relatively narrow and the scenery good. The village is at the confluence of the Marañón and Nieve rivers and has a basic hotel. From Santa María, the boat trip to Sarameriza takes a further 12 hours, though the trip can be broken at the army base of Pingo; there are no hotels in Pingo but you can stay with local families.

Cargo boats leave Sarameriza for Iquitos

every 10 or 15 days, so be prepared to wait. The river journey takes about 5 days. Obviously, this is a trip for the self-sufficient traveller with a spirit of adventure, plenty of common sense and a lot of spare time. Good luck!

IQUITOS

With a population of over 200,000 (one local guide book claims 350,000 but I am unable to substantiate this), Iquitos is Peru's largest jungle city and the capital of the huge Department of Loreto, largest of Peru's 24 departments. Iquitos is linked with the outside world by air and the Amazon River – it is the largest city in the Amazon Basin without outside roads.

Iquitos has a varied and interesting history. It was founded in the 1750s as a Jesuit mission, fending off attacks from Indian tribes who didn't want to be missionised. The tiny settlement survived and grew very slowly until, by the 1870s, it had some 1500 inhabitants. Then came the great rubber boom and the population increased about 16-fold by the 1880s. For the next 30 years, Iquitos was the scene of ostentatious wealth and abject poverty. The rubber barons became fabulously rich and the rubber tappers, mainly local Indians and poor mestizos, suffered virtual enslavement and sometimes death from disease or harsh treatment. Signs of the opulence of those days can still be seen in some of the mansions and tiled walls of Iquitos.

The bottom fell out of the rubber boom as suddenly as it had begun. A British entrepreneur smuggled some rubber-tree seeds out of Brazil and plantations were seeded in Malaya. It was much cheaper and easier to collect the rubber from the orderly rows of rubber trees in the plantations than from the wild trees scattered in the Amazon Basin and, by WW I, Peru's rubber industry was at an end.

Iquitos suffered a period of severe economic decline during the ensuing decades, supporting itself as best it could by a combination of logging, agriculture (Brazil nuts, tobacco, bananas and barbasco – a poisonous vine used by the Indians to hunt fish and now exported for use in insecticides) and the export of wild animals to zoos. Then, in the 1960s, a second gold boom revitalised the area. This time, the 'black gold' was oil and it's discovery made Iquitos a prosperous modern town. In recent years, tourism has also played an important part in the economy of the area.

Information

Tourist Information The FOPTUR tourist office (tel 238523) is on the Plaza de Armas and is open from 8 am to noon on weekdays. They can give you maps of the area as well as up-to-date information.

Various commercial jungle guides and jungle lodges give tourist information. This is obviously biased towards selling their services, which is fine if you are looking for guides, tours or jungle lodges.

Money Exchange rates for cash dollars and travellers' cheques vary from place to place, so it is worth checking two or three before changing a large sum. There are several banks on Raimondi, within a block or two of the Plaza de Armas. I found that the Banco de Crédito gave the best rate, though the nearby Banco Amazonico was also quite good. Alternatively, you can try the casas de cambio; there are a couple on Fitzcarrald and elsewhere. Their rates may be lower than bank rates but they are open longer hours.

Motorcycle Hire You can find someone to rent you a motorcycle if you are persistent enough – there is a place on the 5th block of Brasil and another on the 2nd block of Raimondi. Costs are about $2 an hour. The tourist office can help to find motorcycles for rent.

Immigration Before leaving Peru for Brazil or Colombia, you should check at the migraciónes office at Arica 477.

Things to See

Although most travellers use Iquitos as a base for excursions into the jungle or as a place to wait for river boats along the Amazon, there are several interesting places to see in and around the city itself.

The Iron House Every guidebook tells of the 'majestic' Iron House designed by Eiffel (of Eiffel Tower fame). It was imported, piece by piece, into Iquitos during the opulent days of the rubber boom to beautify the city. Unfortunately, no one knows exactly which building it is – during my research, I have read of three different buildings which are supposedly the famous Iron House. Even the people at the tourist office were vague when I questioned them. To me, the most likely building seems to be the one on the north-east corner of Putumayo and Raimondi, on the Plaza de Armas. It looks like a bunch of scrap-metal sheets bolted together and is certainly nothing to get excited about. I can't help wondering whether the famous Iron House is a myth perpetrated by generations of guides.

Azulejos Some impressive remnants of those boom days remain, however. The best are the *azulejos*, hand-made tiles imported from Portugal to decorate the mansions of the rubber barons. Many buildings along Raimondi and the Malecón (literally, dike or seawall) are lavishly decorated with azulejos. Some of the best are Cohen's Cafeteria and various government buildings along the Malecón.

Belén A walk down Raimondi (which turns into Prospero) and back along the Malecón is interesting, not only to see some of the tile-faced buildings but also to visit the Belén market area at the south-east end of town. Belén itself is a floating shanty town with a certain charm to it (the locals call it an Amazonian Venice but others would call it a slum). It consists of scores of huts built on rafts, which rise and fall with the river. During the dry months, these rafts sit on the river mud and are dirty and unhealthy but, for most of the year, they float on the river – a colourful and exotic sight. Several thousand people live here and canoes float from hut to hut selling and trading jungle produce. If you speak a few words of Spanish, you can find someone to paddle you around for a fee. Ask at the end of 9 de Diciembre. Although it is a very poor area, it seems reasonably safe, at least in daylight hours.

The city market, within the city blocks in front of Belén, is the usual raucous, crowded affair common to most Peruvian towns. All kinds of strange and exotic products are sold here among the mundane bags of rice, sugar, flour and cheap plastic

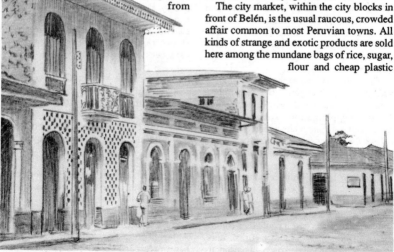

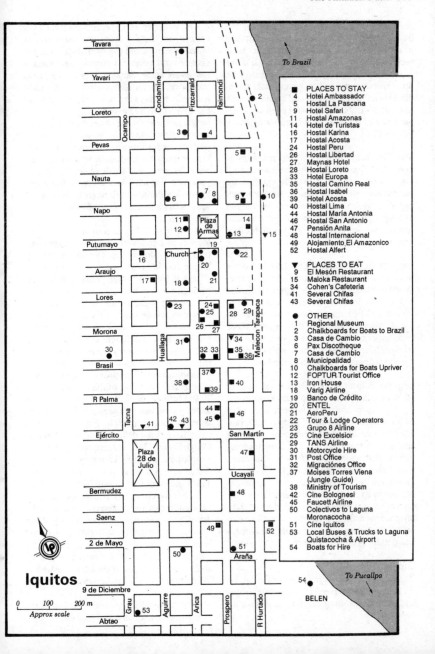

Iquitos

0   100   200 m
Approx scale

PLACES TO STAY
4   Hotel Ambassador
5   Hostal La Pascana
9   Hotel Safari
11   Hostal Amazonas
14   Hotel de Turistas
16   Hostal Karina
17   Hostal Acosta
24   Hostal Peru
26   Hostal Libertad
27   Maynas Hotel
28   Hostal Loreto
33   Hotel Europa
35   Hostal Camino Real
36   Hostal Isabel
39   Hotel Acosta
40   Hostal Lima
44   Hostal María Antonia
46   Hostal San Antonio
47   Pensión Anita
48   Hostal Internacional
49   Alojamiento El Amazonico
52   Hostal Alfert

PLACES TO EAT
9   El Mesón Restaurant
15   Maloka Restaurant
34   Cohen's Cafeteria
41   Several Chifas
43   Several Chifas

OTHER
1   Regional Museum
2   Chalkboards for Boats to Brazil
3   Casa de Cambio
6   Pax Discotheque
7   Casa de Cambio
8   Municipalidad
10   Chalkboards for Boats Upriver
12   FOPTUR Tourist Office
13   Iron House
18   Varig Airline
19   Banco de Crédito
20   ENTEL
21   AeroPeru
22   Tour & Lodge Operators
23   Grupo 8 Airline
25   Cine Excelsior
29   TANS Airline
30   Motorcycle Hire
31   Post Office
32   Migraciónes Office
37   Moises Torres Viena
     (Jungle Guide)
38   Ministry of Tourism
42   Cine Bolognesi
45   Faucett Airline
50   Colectivos to Laguna
     Moronacocha
51   Cine Iquitos
53   Local Buses & Trucks to Laguna
     Quistacocha & Airport
54   Boats for Hire

To Brazil

To Pucallpa

BELEN

and metal household goods. Look for the bark of the Chuchuhuasi tree which is soaked in rum for weeks and used as a tonic drink (served in many of the local bars). All kinds of other medicinal and culinary offerings are on sale: piles of dried frogs and fish, armadillo shells, piranha teeth and a great variety of tropical fruits. It makes for exciting shopping or sightseeing but remember to watch your wallet.

The Regional Museum The museum is open daily, except Sunday, from 8 am to 7 pm and entry is 10c. The main exhibits are stuffed animals of the region. As one might expect in the heat and humidity, they are not in a very good state of repair, but if you're interested in Amazonian wildlife, the museum is worth a look.

Laguna Moronacocha This lake forms the western boundary of the town. To get there, take the colectivo which departs from Dos de Mayo and leaves the city centre along Ejército. The 15-minute ride costs 10c. There really isn't much to see but it's a good place to relax with a cold beer and watch the sun set over Moronacocha. There are a couple of very basic bars with views of the lake.

Laguna Quistacocha This lake lies roughly 15 km south of Iquitos and makes a pleasant day trip. Buses and trucks leave several times an hour from the corner of Abtao near Grau. There is a small zoo of local fauna and a fish hatchery where you can see 2-metre-long paiche fish swimming around. This huge river fish is one of the tastiest I've eaten but its popularity has apparently caused a severe decline in its numbers. An attempt to rectify the situation is being made with the breeding programme at the fish hatchery. People swim in the lake (though it looks rather unsavoury) and paddle boats are for hire.

Jungle Trips
Basically, excursions into the jungle can be divided into two types: visits to jungle lodges and more demanding camping and walking trips.

The majority of the operators have their offices on Calle Putumayo, between the Plaza de Armas and the river, so it is easy to visit several before choosing. Because the lodges are some distance from Iquitos, river transport is included in the price and a short trip of 2 or 3 days can be expensive. Most of the area within 50 km of the city is not virgin jungle and the chance of seeing big game is remote. Any Indians will be acculturated and performing for tourism. Nevertheless, much can be seen of the jungle way of life and birds, insects, and small mammals can be observed. For wildlife, I think the Manu and Puerto Maldonado regions are better, though Iquitos has a better choice of more comfortable lodges.

A typical 2-day trip involves a river journey of 2 or 3 hours to a jungle lodge with reasonable comforts and meals, a 'typical jungle lunch', a guided visit to an Indian village to buy crafts and, perhaps, see dances (though tourists often outnumber Indians), an evening meal at the lodge, maybe an after-dark canoe trip to look for caimans by searchlight and a walk in the jungle the following day to see jungle vegetation and, if you are lucky, monkeys or other wildlife. A trip like this will set you back $20 to $100, depending on the operator, the distance travelled and the comfort of the lodge.

The further your lodge is from Iquitos, the better your chance of seeing wildlife. Operators in Iquitos include Explorama Tours (who have three different lodges), Amazon Lodge Safaris, Jungle Amazon Inn, Amazon Sinchicuy Lodge, Tamshiyacu Lodge, Amazonia Expeditions, Amazon Selva Tours and Amazon Camp Tourist Service (which is the cheapest). All these companies have built up reasonable reputations and will detail what you get for your money. Most operators are fairly straightforward and honest; they are required to list their prices with the Ministry of Tourism (Arica 566) and, if you feel you have been cheated or overcharged, you should check with the ministry.

English-speaking Freddie Valles Wing runs Amazona Adventure Tours (tel 237306)

Top: Passing the Chicha & playing the Clarín, Llacanora (RR)
Bottom: Aerial view, eastern slopes of Andes near Tarapoto (RR)

Left: Dusk over Iquitos, Amazon Basin (RR)
Right: Trekker below Nevado Alpamayo (5947 m), Cordillera Blanca (RR)
Bottom: Ucayali area from the air (RR)

at Lores 220, where he teaches jungle survival courses. His 6-day introductory course for five people costs $180 per person. You bring suitable jungle clothing and he provides the rest. It's a tough trip and involves a lot of walking through the jungle without trails. Sleeping shelters are built in a different place every night and food is fished or hunted. If you do OK in the introductory course, he'll take you on a 15-day trip for five people at $350 per person. There are also cheaper, shorter, easier trips.

The jungle expeditions led by Moises Torres Viena, at Soledad 718 (which crosses Bermudez about six blocks north-west of Grau), are cheaper and somewhat less demanding than Freddie's tours, though they also include long walks in the jungle and catching your own food. Some river travel is involved and overnights are in Indian villages rather than 'in the wild'. Moises doesn't speak English. I have heard good reports about all these operations.

Places to Stay

There are plenty of hotels to choose from but the nicest and cheapest tend to fill up early so, for the best choice, look as soon as you arrive. Most of the budget places are near the Belén area and the majority have an erratic or nonexistent water supply. Even some of the mid-range hotels suffer from a water shortage and it is important to look at your room and check the water supply before paying. Almost all the hotels, even if they have water problems, provide private bathrooms, though this can be a hindrance if you can't flush the toilet. Mosquitoes are rarely a serious problem and mosquito netting is not provided, though there should always be a fan. If there isn't one in your room, ask the management for one.

Places to Stay – bottom end

The basic Hostal Alfert is friendly, which is why it's popular with travellers on a tight budget. Singles/doubles with bath and fan cost $1/1.50 but, unfortunately, all water for washing and toilet flushing must be hauled by bucket. Other similarly priced basic hotels with erratic water supplies include the Hostal Internacional, Pensión Anita and Hostal San Antonio. Also cheap and good value is the quiet, clean Hostal Económico, at Moore 1164 (one block south-west of Grau in the south-west part of town – away from the centre).

The Maynas Hotel is very good value at $1.90/3.30 for clean singles/doubles with bath and fan. It's often full. A similarly priced alternative is the Hostal Lima, which is a bit more basic but clean, and the Alojamiento El Amazonico, which is also clean but tends to have water only at night. The Hostal Camino Real and the friendly Hostal Karina are in the same price range.

For $2.70/3.30, you can stay in good, clean singles/doubles with bath and fan at the Hostal Isabel, which is popular with travellers. For a few cents more, you get similar facilities at the Hostal Peru or at the quiet Hostal La Pascana. Further out of the way, at Portillo 687 (Portillo is the continuation of Fitzcarrald at the north end), is the friendly Residencial Wagner. The last two are popular with gringos.

Places to Stay – middle

The Hostal Loreto is quite good at $3/4.50 for air-conditioned singles/doubles with bath; there are some cheaper rooms without air-conditioning. The Hostal Libertad also has air-conditioned rooms with bath for $3.70/5. The Hostal María Antonia, once quite a good hotel, is getting rather run down but is still probably worth the $4/5.50 for air-conditioned singles/doubles with bath. Cheaper rooms with fans are also available.

The Hostal Amazonas charges $5.30/6.70 for air-con singles/doubles with bath. Also offering air-conditioned rooms with bath are the quite good Hotel Safari and Hotel Europa; both charge $6/8.

Places to Stay – top end

The government-run Hotel de Turistas charges $11/15 for clean, air-conditioned singles/doubles. Many of its rooms look out over the Amazon and the price includes a continental breakfast; cheaper rooms with fans are available.

Also in this price range is the Hotel Ambassador which is air-conditioned and has been recommended.

The fanciest place in town, the *Hotel Acosta* (R Palma 252) provides all modern conveniences, including a mini refrigerator in rooms for $21/28 singles/doubles. The owners also run the *Hostal Acosta* (on Huallaga at Araujo) which, though much cheaper at $7.50/10.50, is also very good.

There are two 1st class hotels a little way out of town (take a taxi). The *Amazon Bungalows* are out by the Río Nanay, about 4 km west of town. Air-conditioned bungalows cost about $20 a double and there is a restaurant and swimming pool. About halfway to the airport is the *Amazonas Hotel* (formerly the Holiday Inn), which charges about $60 a double and has the amenities you'd expect at a Holiday Inn.

Places to Eat

Those wishing to economise can eat at small restaurants and stalls in the market area, but this is not recommended if your stomach is unaccustomed to Peruvian food. There are several chifas on and near the Plaza 28 de Julio, varying in price from fairly cheap to moderately expensive.

You'll find several good restaurants between the Plaza de Armas and the waterfront. *El Mesón* is a favourite lunch-time haunt for locals; the set lunch is quite cheap and the other meals are good and reasonably priced. My favourite place is the *Maloka*, a floating restaurant on the Amazon. Considering its pleasing location, the prices are very reasonable and the food is good. If you are on a strict budget, you can always come here for a beer and watch the river flow by. After all, you're not on the Amazon very often!

Along Raimondi, the main drag, there are several cafeterias serving juices, ice cream and other snacks. The most attractive of these, and the highest in price, is *Cohen's* with its ornate, tiled exterior. Several others along the same street serve similar food at lower prices.

Entertainment

For a large and busy international port, Iquitos has surprisingly little nightlife. There are several cinemas, three of which are in the central city area (marked on the Iquitos map). You'll find a few discotheques, along the northern end of the Malecón and around Putumayo but these are usually short-lived affairs which close down every few months. Wander around the area near the Plaza de Armas and you'll find bars blaring out music. There isn't much in the way of typically Peruvian music.

Getting There & Away

Plane or river boat are your only choices – all roads into the jungle stop within 20 km or so.

Air Iquitos has Peru's most important airport after Lima. There are international flights to Miami and Brazil, as well as local flights.

Both AeroPeru and Faucett have offices in town, and between them, operate about three flights a day to Lima ($73). Flights to other cities are available, usually Pucallpa, Tarapoto, Yurimaguas and Trujillo, but schedules and services change frequently.

Grupo 8 operates military flights to Lima and TANS has military flights to Requena, Contamana and Pucallpa, as well as to Islandia, by the border with Brazil. Military flights to Lima and Pucallpa cost about 20% less than commercial flights but leave only once a week, are often full and are subject to cancellation or postponement. The flight to the border, if you are lucky enough to get on it, is the best value because it costs only about $16. Schedules, destinations and fares change frequently (check locally) but there are usually departures every week.

Varig charges $77 to Tabatinga (on the Brazilian side of the border) and $208 on to Manaus. There are two flights a week. Faucett has an expensive weekly flight to Miami ($775 to $1010 for the round trip, depending on advance purchase etc). Airport departure tax is $15 for international flights and $6 for domestic flights. Other international flights are sometimes possible from

Iquitos and you can connect to many points from Manaus.

River Boat Iquitos is Peru's largest and best organised river port and is quite capable of accepting ocean-going vessels as it did in the rubber-boom days. Most boats today, however, ply only Peruvian waters and voyagers must change boats at the border.

The Iquitos docks have a chalkboard system to tell you which boats are leaving when, for where and whether they are accepting passengers. There are two different chalkboard locations marked on the Iquitos map – one for upriver boats and the other for downriver.

Upriver passages to Pucallpa or Yurimaguas take 6 and 10 days respectively and cost about $20 to $30 per person. Boats leave about once a week, less often if the river is low, but there are more frequent departures for the closer intermediate ports. Downriver boats to Islandia or Ramón Castilla, on the Peruvian side of the border with Brazil and Colombia, leave about twice a week and take 2 days. Fares are $15 to $20 per person. Read the River Boat section in the Getting Around chapter for more detailed descriptions of these journeys. If you need a hammock, Iquitos is a good place to buy one.

Expensive luxury boats, charging several hundred dollars, also do the trip. Ask around the travel agencies.

Getting Around

A distinctive local taxi is the two-passenger motorcycle rickshaw. These strange-looking contraptions cost a little less than a taxi and are fun to ride.

Most buses and trucks for nearby destinations, including the airport, leave from the area between Grau and Aguirre, at the south end of town.

Taxis tend to be more expensive than in other Peruvian cities and a taxi ride to the airport costs about $3 or $4. A motorcycle rickshaw charges $2 to $3 for the 10-km ride.

CROSSING THE BORDER

Before leaving Peru, you need to get an exit stamp in your passport and you can't get an exit stamp if your entry stamp has expired. However, don't think that just because you are in the middle of the Amazon jungle, nobody will bother to check. On the contrary, border officials have very little to do other than refuse you passage if your documents are not in order, so make sure you have enough days left on your visa or tourist card before attempting the trip.

Exit formalities change frequently. When I last left Peru for Brazil, I received my exit stamp at a Peruvian guard post just before the border (the boat stopped there long enough for travellers to do this, though make sure that the captain agrees to this before you leave Iquitos). It's worth checking at the migraciónes office in Iquitos (at Arica 477) to make sure that an exit stamp will be available near the border. The office is open from 9 am to 1 pm on weekdays.

There are different entry requirements for travellers of different nationalities when crossing into Brazil or Colombia; again, formalities change, so it is worth checking with the Brazilian or Colombian embassy at home or in Lima before you go. In Iquitos, there is a Brazilian consul at Morona 283 and a Colombian consul at Malecón Tarapaca 260.

The most recent Brazilian regulations require consular visas for citizens of the USA, France, Canada, Australia and New Zealand, while most other citizens of Europe and Latin America need only their passport to obtain a tourist card (valid for 90 days) at the border.

Colombian regulations require that New Zealand, Australian, French, Canadian and US nationals, as well as citizens of some other countries, have visas. Citizens of the UK, Ireland and almost all Western European countries, as well as most Latin American countries, do not require visas and can get a tourist card on presentation of a valid passport at the border.

There are several ports at the three-way border which are several km apart and connected by public ferries. The biggest town, Leticia in Colombia, boasts the best hotels and a hospital. From Leticia, you can take one of the infrequent boats to Puerto Asis on the Río Putumayo – the trip can take almost 2 weeks. From Puerto Asis, you can catch a bus into Colombia. Alternatively, you can fly from Leticia to Bogotá on almost daily commercial flights. If you are looking for a boat up or down the Amazon, it is better to stay in Brazil or Peru, though accommodation is poorer.

There are two small ports in the Brazilian section: Tabatinga and Benjamin Constant. Both have basic hotels and moneychangers who will convert your intis or cash dollars at unfavourable rates, so cash only enough to get to Manaus. Tabatinga has an airport with flights to Manaus and Iquitos. Benjamin Constant is the better place to find boats for Manaus.

In the Peruvian section are the small ports of Ramón Castilla and Islandia. Most boats from Iquitos will drop you at Islandia, from where a motor canoe can take you to Benjamin Constant, literally a stone's throw away (well, maybe two throws). This is the best place to look for boats to Manaus. Ask at the

port, the hotel, the restaurants, the moneychangers or the stores. Everyone will have an opinion and you can soon figure out which boat is going where and when. If you are heading for Colombia or Brazil, Lonely Planet travel survival kits are available for both countries.

If you are arriving from Colombia or Brazil, again, Benjamin Constant is a good place to stay while looking for a boat from Islandia to Iquitos. There are no hotels in Islandia.

Bear in mind that the border hotels and restaurants are fairly basic and slightly more expensive than other parts of Peru. Also remember that, however disorganised things may appear, you can always get meals, beds, money changed, boats and other services simply by asking around. The locals are used to the different way of doing things on the river, so ask them. As my Polish mother used to tell me, 'Koniec języka za przewodnika' – which, perhaps, is an appropriate way to finish this book. Roughly translated, it means 'Use your tongue as your guide'.

Glossary

Aduana – customs
Agave – century plant
Agua potable – tap water
Aguardiente – sugar cane alcohol
Alcalde – mayor
Alforjas – heavy woven saddlebags
Alluvion – avalanche/waterfall/landslide caused by a burst highland lake
Ambulantes – street vendors
Antaras – panpipes
Apartado – post office box
Apartamento – apartment
Arpilleras – handicraft hangings, often showing scenes made from little cloth dolls
Arriero – muleteer
Autovagon – fast train for tourists
Azulejos – hand-made Portuguese tiles

Bahía – bay
Baja – down
Baños termales – hot springs
Bencina – white gas
Bodegas – wineries
Brujería – witchcraft/sorcery
Brujo – witch doctor

Caballitos – tortora-reed fishing boats
Caballos de paso – pacing horses
Caja – box
Cama matrimonial – double bed
Campesinos – peasants
Canchas – Inca village blocks
Capitanía – harbour master's office
Cárcel – prison
Casas de cambio – currency exchange
Casilla – post office box
Cédula – identification card
Centro – centre
Cine – cinema
Ciudad – town
Clarins – long bamboo trumpets
Comedore – dining room in market stall, cheap restaurant or simple hotel
Comités – bus or taxi companies
Cuevas – caves
Curanderos – healers

Chasquis – Inca messengers (runners)
Chicha – local corn beer
Chichería – Andean chicha tavern
Chifas – Chinese restaurants
Chullpas – funerary towers

Duchas – showers

El menú – set menu
Empresa – company
Esquina – corner

Ferretería – hardware store
Fiches RIN – telephone tokens
Folklórico – folkloric (referring to music, fiesta or handicrafts)
Futbol – soccer

Garua – coastal mist
Gaseosas – soft drinks
Grifo – petrol (gas) station
Guinda – cherry brandy

Heladerías – ice-cream parlours
Hospedaje – cheap hotel
Huacas – burial sites

Iglesia – church
Incunables – books dating from before 1550
Inglés – English
Inti – currency unit

Jirón – avenue/boulevard
Jugos – juice

Kallankas – Inca assembly halls
Kerex – kerosene

Lago – lake
Laguna – lagoon
Lavandería – laundry
Librería – library
Limeño – inhabitant of Lima
Lufkins – automatic oil pumps

Malecón – jetty/pier/dike/sea wall
Mañana – morning
Marinera – coastal Peruvian dance
Mercado – market
Mestizos – people of mixed Indian/Spanish
Migraciónes – immigration office
Mirador – observation tower/platform
Mixtos – half truck/half bus
Motorista – boatman
Municipalidad – town hall
Museo – museum

Norteño – northerner
Nuevo – new

Paquetes pequeños – small package mail service
Paseo – parade/avenue
Peki-pekis – motorised river boats
Pensión – boarding house/guest house
Peñas – music halls
Perezoso – sloth
Picanterías – restaurants serving spicy foods
Piruru – flute
Platano – plantain
Prefectura – mayoral offices
Pueblos jovenes – shanty towns
Puna – Andean highlands
Puro – pure

Quebrada – ravine/gorge
Quenas – bamboo penny whistle
Quintas – country inns

Quipus – knotted strings used by Incas as mnemonic devices

Residencial – cheap hotel

Salvo conductos – safe conduct passes often issued at borders
Sapo – game played in Andean restaurants
Sendero Luminoso – Maoist guerilla group
Serrano – mountain dweller
Sikus – panpipes
Sillar – light-coloured volcanic rock
Sol – sun; also currency unit before 1986

Tallarines – noodles
Tambo – resting place used by the Inca *chasquis* or 'runners' who carried messages from one part of the Inca empire to another
Té – tea
Torre – tower
Tortora – reed used for construction and weaving, especially by the Lake Titicaca Indians

Usnu – five-tiered pyramid

Vacacional – holiday (adj)
Ventanillas – windows
Via de evitamiento – route to be avoided

Wankaras – large drums

Zampoñas – panpipes

Index

MAPS

TEXT

ARCHAEOLOGICAL SITES

PLANET TALK
Lonely Planet's FREE quarterly newsletter

We love hearing from you and think you'd like to hear from us.

When...is the right time to see reindeer in Finland?
Where...can you hear the best palm-wine music in Ghana?
How...do you get from Asunción to Areguá by steam train?
What...is the best way to see India?

For the answer to these and many other questions read PLANET TALK.

Every issue is packed with up-to-date travel news and advice including:

- *a letter from Lonely Planet founders Tony and Maureen Wheeler*
- *travel diary from a Lonely Planet author - find out what it's really like out on the road*
- *feature article on an important and topical travel issue*
- *a selection of recent letters from our readers*
- *the latest travel news from all over the world*
- *details on Lonely Planet's new and forthcoming releases*

To join our mailing list contact any Lonely Planet office (address below).

LONELY PLANET PUBLICATIONS
Australia: PO Box 617, Hawthorn 3122, Victoria (tel: 03-9819 1877)
USA: Embarcadero West, 155 Filbert St, Suite 251, Oakland, CA 94607 (tel: 510-893 8555)
TOLL FREE: (800) 275-8555
UK: 10 Barley Mow Passage, Chiswick, London W4 4PH (tel: 0181-742 3161)
France: 71 bis rue du Cardinal Lemoine – 75005 Paris (tel: 1-46 34 00 58)

Also available: Lonely Planet T-shirts. 100% heavyweight cotton (S, M, L, XL)

Guides to the Americas

Alaska – a travel survival kit
Jim DuFresne has travelled extensively through Alaska by foot, road, rail, barge and kayak, and tells how to make the most of one of the world's great wilderness areas.

Argentina, Uruguay & Paraguay – a travel survival kit
This guide gives independent travellers all the essential information on three of South America's lesser-known countries. Discover some of South America's most spectacular natural attractions in Argentina; friendly people and beautiful handicrafts in Paraguay; and Uruguay's wonderful beaches.

Backpacking in Alaska
This practical guide to hiking in Alaska has everything you need to know to safely experience the Alaskan wilderness on foot. It covers the most outstanding trails from Ketchikan in the Southeast to Fairbanks near the Arctic Circle – including half-day hikes, and challenging week-long treks.

Baja California – a travel survival kit
For centuries, Mexico's Baja peninsula – with its beautiful coastline, raucous border towns and crumbling Spanish missions – has been a land of escapes and escapades. This book describes how and where to escape in Baja.

Bolivia – a travel survival kit
From lonely villages in the Andes to ancient ruined cities and the spectacular city of La Paz, Bolivia is a magnificent blend of everything that inspires travellers. Discover safe and intriguing travel options in this comprehensive guide.

Brazil – a travel survival kit
From the mad passion of Carnival to the Amazon – home of the richest ecosystem on earth – Brazil is a country of mythical proportions. This guide has all the essential travel information.

Canada – a travel survival kit
This comprehensive guidebook has all the facts on the USA's huge neighbour – the Rocky Mountains, Niagara Falls, ultramodern Toronto, remote villages in Nova Scotia, and much more.

Central America on a shoestring
Practical information on travel in Belize, Guatemala, Costa Rica, Honduras, El Salvador, Nicaragua and Panama. A team of experienced Lonely Planet authors reveals the secrets of this culturally rich, geographically diverse and breathtakingly beautiful region.

Chile & Easter Island – a travel survival kit
Travel in Chile is easy and safe, with possibilities as varied as the countryside. This guide also gives detailed coverage of Chile's Pacific outpost, mysterious Easter Island.

Colombia – a travel survival kit
Colombia is a land of myths – from the ancient legends of El Dorado to the modern tales of Gabriel Garcia Marquez. The reality is beauty and violence, wealth and poverty, tradition and change. This guide shows how to travel independently and safely in this exotic country.

Costa Rica – a travel survival kit
Sun-drenched beaches, steamy jungles, smoking volcanoes, rugged mountains and dazzling birds and animals – Costa Rica has it all.

Eastern Caribbean – a travel survival kit
Powdery white sands, clear turquoise waters, lush jungle rainforest, balmy weather and a laid back pace, make the islands of the Eastern Caibbean an ideal destination for divers, hikers and sun-lovers. This

guide will help you to decide which islands to visit to suit your interests and includes details on inter-island travel.

Ecuador & the Galápagos Islands – a travel survival kit
Ecuador offers a wide variety of travel experiences, from the high cordilleras to the Amazon plains – and 600 miles west, the fascinating Galápagos Islands. Everything you need to know about travelling around this enchanting country.

Guatemala, Belize & Yucatán: La Ruta Maya – a travel survival kit
Climb a volcano, explore the colourful highland villages or laze your time away on coral islands and Caribbean beaches. The lands of the Maya offer a fascinating journey into the past which will enhance appreciation of their dynamic contemporary cultures. An award winning guide to this exotic fregion.

Hawaii – a travel survival kit
Share in the delights of this island paradise – and avoid its high prices – both on and off the beaten track. Full details on Hawaii's best-known attractions, plus plenty of uncrowded sights and activities.

Honolulu – a travel survival kit
Honolulu offers an intriguing variety of attractions and experiences. Whatever your interests, this comprehensive guidebook is packed with insider tips and practical information.

Mexico – a travel survival kit
A unique blend of Indian and Spanish culture, fascinating history, and hospitable people, make Mexico a travellers' paradise.

South America on a shoestring
This practical guide provides concise information for budget travellers and covers South America from the Darien Gap to Tierra del Fuego.

Trekking in the Patagonian Andes
The first detailed guide to this region gives complete information on 28 walks, and lists a number of other possibilities extending from the Araucanía and Lake District regions of Argentina and Chile to the remote icy tip of South America in Tierra del Fuego.

Venezuela – a travel survival kit
Venezuela is a curious hybrid of a Western-style civilisation and a very traditional world contained within a beautiful natural setting. From the beaches along the Caribbean coast and the snow-capped peaks of the Andes to the capital, Caracas, there is much for travellers to explore. This comprehensive guide is packed with 'first-hand' tips for travel in this fascinating destination.

Also available:
Brazilian phrasebook, **Latin American Spanish** phrasebook and **Quechua** phrasebook.

Lonely Planet Guidebooks

Lonely Planet guidebooks cover every accessible part of Asia as well as Australia, the Pacific, South America, Africa, the Middle East, Europe and parts of North America. There are five series: *travel survival kits*, covering a country for a range of budgets; *shoestring guides* with compact information for low-budget travel in a major region; *walking guides*; *city guides* and *phrasebooks*.

Australia & the Pacific
Australia
Australian phrasebook
Bushwalking in Australia
Islands of Australia's Great Barrier Reef
Outback Australia
Fiji
Fijian phrasebook
Melbourne city guide
Micronesia
New Caledonia
New South Wales
New Zealand
Tramping in New Zealand
Papua New Guinea
Bushwalking in Papua New Guinea
Papua New Guinea phrasebook
Rarotonga & the Cook Islands
Samoa
Solomon Islands
Sydney city guide
Tahiti & French Polynesia
Tonga
Vanuatu
Victoria
Western Australia

North-East Asia
Beijing city guide
China
Cantonese phrasebook
Mandarin Chinese phrasebook
Hong Kong, Macau & Canton
Japan
Japanese phrasebook
Korea
Korean phrasebook
Mongolia
North-East Asia on a shoestring
Seoul city guide
Taiwan
Tibet
Tibet phrasebook
Tokyo city guide

Middle East
Arab Gulf States
Egypt & the Sudan
Arabic (Egyptian) phrasebook
Iran
Israel
Jordan & Syria
Middle East
Turkey
Turkish phrasebook
Trekking in Turkey
Yemen

South-East Asia
Bali & Lombok
Bangkok city guide
Cambodia
Indonesia
Indonesian phrasebook
Jakarta city guide
Laos
Malaysia, Singapore & Brunei
Myanmar (Burma)
Burmese phrasebook
Philippines
Pilipino phrasebook
Singapore city guide
South-East Asia on a shoestring
Thailand
Thai phrasebook
Thai Hill Tribes phrasebook
Vietnam
Vietnamese phrasebook

Indian Ocean
Madagascar & Comoros
Maldives & Islands of the East Indian Ocean
Mauritius, Réunion & Seychelles

Mail Order

Lonely Planet guidebooks are distributed worldwide. They are also available by mail order from Lonely Planet, so if you have difficulty finding a title please write to us. US and Canadian residents should write to Embarcadero West, 155 Filbert St, Suite 251, Oakland CA 94607, USA; European residents should write to 10 Barley Mow Passage, Chiswick, London W4 4PH; and residents of other countries to PO Box 617, Hawthorn, Victoria 3122, Australia.

Indian Subcontinent
Bangladesh
India
Hindi/Urdu phrasebook
Trekking in the Indian Himalaya
Karakoram Highway
Kashmir, Ladakh & Zanskar
Nepal
Trekking in the Nepal Himalaya
Nepali phrasebook
Pakistan
Sri Lanka
Sri Lanka phrasebook

Africa
Africa on a shoestring
Central Africa
East Africa
Trekking in East Africa
Kenya
Swahili phrasebook
Morocco
Arabic (Moroccan) phrasebook
North Africa
South Africa, Lesotho & Swaziland
Zimbabwe, Botswana & Namibia
West Africa

Europe
Baltic States & Kaliningrad
Britain
Central Europe on a shoestring
Central Europe phrasebook
Czech & Slovak Republics
Dublin city guide
Eastern Europe on a shoestring
Eastern Europe phrasebook
Finland
France
Greece
Greek phrasebook
Hungary
Iceland, Greenland & the Faroe Islands
Ireland
Italy
Mediterranean Europe on a shoestring
Mediterranean Europe phrasebook
Poland
Prague city guide
Scandinavian & Baltic Europe on a shoestring
Scandinavian Europe phrasebook
Switzerland
Trekking in Spain
Trekking in Greece
USSR
Russian phrasebook
Vienna city guide
Western Europe on a shoestring
Western Europe phrasebook

Central America & the Caribbean
Baja California
Central America on a shoestring
Costa Rica
Eastern Caribbean
Guatemala, Belize & Yucatán: La Ruta Maya
Mexico

North America
Alaska
Backpacking in Alaska
Canada
Hawaii
Honolulu city guide
USA phrasebook

South America
Argentina, Uruguay & Paraguay
Bolivia
Brazil
Brazilian phrasebook
Chile & Easter Island
Colombia
Ecuador & the Galápagos Islands
Latin American Spanish phrasebook
Peru
Quechua phrasebook
South America on a shoestring
Trekking in the Patagonian Andes
Venezuela

The Lonely Planet Story

Lonely Planet published its first book in 1973 in response to the numerous 'How did you do it?' questions Maureen and Tony Wheeler were asked after driving, bussing, hitching, sailing and railing their way from England to Australia.

Written at a kitchen table and hand collated, trimmed and stapled, *Across Asia on the Cheap* became an instant local bestseller, inspiring thoughts of another book.

Eighteen months in South-East Asia resulted in their second guide, *South-East Asia on a shoestring*, which they put together in a backstreet Chinese hotel in Singapore in 1975. The 'yellow bible' as it quickly became known to backpackers around the world, soon became *the* guide to the region. It has sold well over half a million copies and is now in its 8th edition, still retaining its familiar yellow cover.

Today there are over 140 Lonely Planet titles in print – books that have that same adventurous approach to travel as those early guides; books that 'assume you know how to get your luggage off the carousel' as one reviewer put it.

Although Lonely Planet initially specialised in guides to Asia, they now cover most regions of the world, including the Pacific, South America, Africa, the Middle East and Europe. The list of *walking guides* and *phrasebooks* (for 'unusual' languages such as Quechua, Swahili, Nepali and Egyptian Arabic) is also growing rapidly.

The emphasis continues to be on travel for independent travellers. Tony and Maureen still travel for several months of each year and play an active part in the writing, updating and quality control of Lonely Planet's guides.

They have been joined by over 50 authors, 110 staff – mainly editors, cartographers & designers – at our office in Melbourne, Australia, at our US office in Oakland, California and at our European office in Paris; another five at our office in London handle sales for Britain, Europe and Africa. Travellers themselves also make a valuable contribution to the guides through the feedback we receive in thousands of letters each year.

The people at Lonely Planet strongly believe that travellers can make a positive contribution to the countries they visit, both through their appreciation of the countries' culture, wildlife and natural features, and through the money they spend. In addition, the company makes a direct contribution to the countries and regions it covers. Since 1986 a percentage of the income from each book has been donated to ventures such as famine relief in Africa; aid projects in India; agricultural projects in Central America; Greenpeace's efforts to halt French nuclear testing in the Pacific; and Amnesty International.

Lonely Planet's basic travel philosophy is summed up in Tony Wheeler's comment, 'Don't worry about whether your trip will work out. Just go!'.